GUESTHOUSES FARMHOUSES & INNS IN BRITAIN

WARNING

VAT: The majority of prices quoted include VAT at the rate in operation prior to the Budget of 12 June 1979 and are liable to adjustment

Editor: Joan Fensome

Designer: Richard Brown Associates

Gazetteer compiled by the Publications Research Unit

Maps by Cartographic Department

Advertising: Peter Whitworth

Tel Basingstoke 20123

ABBREVIATIONS		**ABRÉVIATIONS**	
(A . . .)	Annexe. The number indicates number of rooms	(A . . .)	Annexe. Le chiffre indique le nombre de chambres
alc	à la carte	alc	à la carte
B&b	Bed and breakfast per person per night	B&b	Chambre et petit déjeuner par personne et par nuit
Bdi	Inclusive dinner, bed and breakfast. When B&b prices not shown, rate always charged whether dinner taken or not	Bdi	Diner, chambre petit déjeuner compris. Si des prix B&b ne sont pas indiqués, le tarif est toujours facturé, que l'on prenne le diner ou non
CTV	Colour television	CTV	TV en couleurs
D	Dinner/evening meal (last order taken, not when meal served) and price (only inns show prices)	D	Diner/repas du soir (dernière commande prise, pas lorsque le repas est servi) et prix (seules les auberges indiquent les prix)
Etr	Easter	Etr	Pâques
fr	From	fr	à partir de
GH	Guesthouse	GH	Pension
. . .hc	Number of bedrooms with hot and cold water	. . .hc	Nombre de chambres avec eau chaude et froide
lake/sea/ river	Some bedrooms overlooking lake/sea/river	lake/sea/ river	Certains chambres donnent sur le lac/la mer/la rivière
L	Lunch price (only inns show prices)	L	Prix du déjeuner (seules les auberges indiquent les prix)
Lic	Licensed	Lic	Licence de boissons alcooliques
Ł	No lunches included in weekly price	Ł	Le tarif hebdomadaire ne comprend pas le déjeuner
Ӎ	No main meals included in weekly price	Ӎ	Le tarif hebdomadaire de comprend pas de repas principaux
nc	No children eg nc. . .no children under . . . years of age	nc	Pas d'enfants, par ex nc. . . pas d'enfants au-dessous de . . . ans
P	Parking for cars	P	Stationnment pour voitures
rm	Total rooms in main building where 100% hot and cold water not provided	rm	Total des chambres dans l'établissement principal ou de l'eau chaude et froide à 100% n'est pas fournie
rs	Restricted service	rs	Service limité
S%	Service levied and included in price	S%	Service compris
sn	Snacks available	sn	Casse-croûte disponible
Tem	Temperance	Tem	Tempérance
TV	Black & white television	TV	TV noir et blanc
W	Weekly terms	W	Tarif à la semaine

SYMBOLS		**SYMBOLES**	
⊢⊣	Bed and breakfast for less than £6	⊢⊣	Chambre et petit déjeuner pour moins de £6
☎	Telephone number	☎	Numéro de téléphone
🛁	Private bath/shower & wc	🛁	Salle de bain/douche particulière avec W.C.
🎛	Full central heating	🎛	Chauffage central integral
🚌	Coach parties not accepted	🚌	Groupes en autocars pas reçus
🏠	Garage accommodation for . . . cars	🏠	Garage pour . . . voitures
♧	Special facilities for children	♧	Facilités spéciales pour enfants
🐕	No dogs	🐕	Pas de chiens
*	1979 prices	*	Détails pour 1979
♿	Facilities for the disabled	♿	Facilités pour invalides

Town Plan Symbols		**Symboles du Plan de la Ville**	
═══	Recommended route	═══	Itinéraire recommandé
═ ═	Other roads	═ ═	Autres routes
= = = =	Restricted roads (Access only – buses only)	= = = =	Routes restreintes (Accès seulement – autobus seulement)
♜	Castle	♜	Château
⚓	Cathedral	⚓	Cathédrale
🇮	Tourist information centre	🇮	Syndicat d'initiative
✉	Post office	✉	Bureau de poste
Ⓐ	AA service centre	Ⓐ	Centre service AA
Ⓟ	Official car park free (open air)	Ⓟ	Stationnement de voitures officiel gratuit (à ciel ouvert)
🅿	Multi-storey car park	🅿	Garage à plusieurs étages
⬦Ρ	Parking available on payment (open air)	⬦Ρ	Stationnement disponible contre palement (à ciel ouvert)
→	One-way street	→	Sens unique
❹	Guesthouses, inns, etc	❹	Pensions, auberges, etc
3 ½m	Distances to guesthouse etc from edge of plan	3 ½m	Distances aux pensions, etc du bord du plan
KESWICK 12m	Mileages to towns from edge of plan	**KESWICK 12m**	Nombre de milles vers la ville du bord du plan

AFKORTINGEN	**ABKÜRZUNGEN**
(A. . .) Bijgebouw. Het cijfer geeft het aantal kamers aan	(A. . .) Nebengebäude. Die Anzahl bezeichnet die Zimmerranzahl
alc à la carte	alc à la carte
B&b Kamer met ontbijt per persoon per nacht	B&b Übernachtung mit Frühstück pro person
Bdi Kamer met ontbijt en avondmaaltijd inbegrepen. Wanneer er geen prijs voor kamer met ontbijt aangegeven is, wordt de prijs voor halfpension berekend onafhankelijk of avondmaattijd wordt genuttigd of niet	Bdi Übernachtung einschl. Frühstück und Abendessen. Wenn Preis für Zimmer & Frühstück nicht angegeben, weden die Halbepensionspreise immer in Rechung gestellt, ob eingenommen oder nicht
CTV Kleurentelevisie	CTV Farbfernsehen
D Avondmaaltijd (lastste bestellingstijd niet wanneer de maaltijd wordt geserveerd) en prijs (alleen herbergen geven prijzen aan)	D Abendessen (letzte Bestellungszeit, nicht wenn das Essen serviert wird) und Preis (nur Gasthäuser geben Preise an)
Etr Pasen	Etr Ostern
fr Van	fr Von
GH Pension	GH Pension
. . .hc Aantal kamers met warm en koud water	. . .hc Zimmer mit Warm-und Kaltwasser
lake/sea/ river Sommige kamers kijken uit op meer/zee/rivier	lake/sea/ river Einige Zimmer mit einem Blick auf den See/das Meer/den Fluss
L Lunch prijzen (alleen hotels geven prijzen aan)	L Mittagessenpreis (nur Gasthäuser geben Preise an)
Lic Tapvergunning	Lic Ausschank alkoholischer Getränke
Ł Middagmaaltijd niet bij weekprijs inbegrepen	Ł Mittagessenspreis nicht im Wochenpreis eingeschlossen
M Hoofdmaaltijd niet bij weekprijs inbegrepen	M Keine Hauptessen im Wochenpreis eingeschlossen
nc Geen kinderen bijv nc. . . geen kinderen onder . . . jaar	nc Kinder nicht gestattet zB nc. . . Kinder unter . . . Jahren nicht gestattet
P Parkeergelegenheid voor auto's	P Parken für Wagen
rm Totaal aantal kamers in hoofdgebouw waar geen warm en koud water aanwezig is	rm Gesamtzimmeranzahl im Hauptgebäude, wo Vollwarm-und Kaltwasser nicht vorhanden ist
rs Beperkte service	rs Beschränkte Dienstleistungen
S% Bedieningsgeid geheven en bij prijs inbegrepen	S% Bedienungsgeld aufgehoben und Preise sind einschl. Bedienungsgeid
sn Snacks beschikbaar	sn Imbisse vorhanden
Tem Geen alcoholgebruik	Tem Alkoholverbot
TV Zwart/wit televisie	TV Schwarzweissfernsehen
W Weekprijs	W Wochenpreis

TEKENS	**ZEICHEN**
⋈ Kamers met ontbijt voor minder dan £6	⋈ Bett mit Frühstück für unter £6
☎ Telefoonnummer	☎ Telefonnummer
Eigen bad/douche & W.C.	Privatbad/dusche + W.C.
Volledige centrale verwarming	Vollfernheizung
Geen busgezelschappen	Busgesellschaften nicht angenommen
Garage voor . . . auto's	Garagen für . . . Autos
Speciale voorzieningen voor kinderen	Sonderdienstleistungen für Kinder
Geen honden	Hundeverbot
* 1979 details	* 1979 Angaben
♿ Geschikt voor invaliden	♿ Für Köperbehinderte geeignet

Stadsplattegrond tekens	**Stadplanzeichen**
Aanbevolen route	Empfohlene Strasse
Andere wegen	Andere Strassen
Wegen met beperkte toegang (alleen toegang – alleen bussen)	Strassen mit bestimmten Beschränkungen (nur Zufahrt – nur Buss)
Kasteel/slot/burg	Burg/Schloss
Kathedraal/dom	Dom
ℹ VVV-kantoor	ℹ Auskunftsstelle
✉ Postkantoor	✉ Postamt
AA service post	AA Dienststelle
P Officiële parkeerplaats (openlucht)	P Kostenloser amtilcher Parkplatz (im Freien)
Torengarage	Parkhochhaus
Parkeergelegenheid na betaling	Gebührenpflichtiges Parken (im Freien)
Eénrichtingsverkeer	Einbahnstrasse
➍ Pensions, herbergen, enz	➍ Pension, Gasthäus usw
3 ½m Afstand tot pension, enz vanaf rand van plattegrond	3 ½m Entfernung vom Stadtplanrand zur Pension usw
KESWICK 12m Afstand in mijlen vanaf rand van plattegrond tot steden	**KESWICK 12m** Entfernung in Meilen vom Stadtplanrand zu Städten

CONTENTS

The contents of this book are believed correct at the time of printing. Nevertheless, the AA can accept no responsibility for errors or omissions, or for changes in the details given.

Produced by the Publications Division of the Automobile Association, Fanum House, Basing View, Basingstoke, Hampshire RG21 2EA.

Photographic sources: AA Photo Library, J Henderson, J Palmer, J Price-Jones, H Reid, P Smart

Town plans in this book are based on the Ordnance Survey Map with the sanction of the Controller, HMSO.

Photo-typeset by Petty & Sons Ltd, Leeds
Printed by William Clowes & Sons Ltd, London, Beccles & Colchester.
Colour printing by Camgate Litho Ltd, London

ISBN 0 86145 005 1

THE AA AND THAT SPECIAL SOMETHING

The AA Guesthouse of the Year –
Under Rock, Bonchurch, Isle of Wight

Over the years the AA has done its bit to encourage an improvement in accommodation and catering in this country. By setting minimum requirements for equipment, hygiene, facilities, service, etc., we can ensure that establishments listed by the AA offer good value within their category and price range, and many proprietors have thought it worthwhile to spend money and effort on bringing their standards up to an acceptable level, or improving their facilities so that they fit into a different category. However, within each group there are always a number which cannot be regarded because size or other factors limit the facilities offered, and yet are so much better than other places of the same type that we feel they should be given a special accolade.

The 'Inn of the Year' competition highlighted in the 1979 edition of this book was so popular that we have followed it up with a 'Guesthouse of the Year'. In choosing the winner we have looked for the intangible qualities of hospitality and a relaxed atmosphere as well as assessing attributes such as cleanliness, comfort and cuisine. Our regional inspectors put forward candidates for the award and a senior member of head office staff and your editor stayed overnight (incognito) in each one, awarding marks for various aspects – from environment to bathroom appointments, from friendliness to food – independently of one-another. When, at the end of our journeying, we compared notes, it was surprising how nearly alike our assessments proved to be.

We were in no doubt that the winner should be Under Rock, Bonchurch, near Ventnor in the Isle of Wight, and are particularly pleased at this outcome as the owners, Mr and Mrs Denis Kelleway, have had a guest house in the locality for many years – they have been at Under Rock since 1967 – and not only achieve high standards in comfort, hospitality and food but obviously enjoy their life and take pleasure in looking after their guests. This is not to say that we found Under Rock – or any other of the places we visited – perfect in every respect. That would be too much to expect even of a 5-star hotel!

Of the finalists visited, only the Prospect Hill Hotel in Kirkoswald offered a choice of main dish for dinner, but everywhere the standard of cooking was high and few expensive restaurants match the excellence in quality and preparation of vegetables which we found in all our guesthouses. Most offered alternative starters and sweets, and an abundance of breakfast permutations. Portions were generous and meals were served hot and freshly-cooked. Furnishings, too, were of a very high standard, and those houses which lacked a little on the visual side made up for this by their home-like comfort.

Where proprietors slipped up was on points which were quite minor but yet brought one up with a start. In a house which had the most beautiful table settings a boiled egg was brought in a plastic cup with a matching plastic spoon. In another place an after-dinner cup of tea was served with a teabag still swimming in the cup (the milk was in a separate jug) and yet at breakfast tea arrived in a teapot (and tasted much better as a result). An over-businesslike greeting – 'Fill in this form, sign the book' – marred our immediate impression of what was otherwise a friendly establishment. At others, a failure to point out bathrooms and WCs could have proved embarrassing, especially where the doors were not labelled, and in one or two the lighting of landings and stairs at night was inadequate.

Everywhere we went beds were comfortable and most had white or light-coloured sheets. I advise all who let rooms to avoid the use of dark-coloured sheets as guests like to be able to *see* that bed linen is perfectly fresh and clean.

Running a guesthouse is extremely hard work and it must be almost impossible to keep a cheerful face in spite of personal troubles, VAT and the various crises which beset us all. That all our hosts and hostesses achieved a high degree of amiability as well as running their establishments with commendable efficiency is remarkable in itself. We enjoyed our visits, and hope that the features on page 33 will encourage others to strive to reach the standard of excellence which we found in our six regional winners.

EDITOR

Here are the regional winners and runners-up in our Guesthouse of the Year Competition:

SOUTH-EAST ENGLAND
Winner and GUESTHOUSE OF THE YEAR: Under Rock, Bonchurch, Ventnor, IOW (see entry under Ventnor)
Runner-up: Dunselma, Bexhill, East Sussex

SOUTH-WEST ENGLAND
Winner: The Old Rectory, Nettlecombe, Somerset (see entry under Williton)
Runner-up: Villa Magdala, Henrietta Road, Bath, Avon

MIDLANDS
Winner: Broad Marston Manor, Broad Marston, Herefs & Worcs
Runner-up: Lower House Country Lodge, Hopton Castle, Salop

NORTHERN ENGLAND
Winner: Prospect Hill Hotel, Kirkoswald, Cumbria
Runner-up: Foxholm Hotel, Ebberston, N. Yorks

WALES
Winner: Guidfa House, Crossgates, Powys
Runner-up: Maesteilo Mansion, Capel Isaac, Llandeilo, Dyfed (see entry under Capel Isaac)

SCOTLAND
Winner: Moorside, Braemar Rd, Ballater, Grampian
Runner-up: Dalrachney Lodge, Carrbridge, Highland

Now turn to page 33 for colour pictures and descriptions of Britain's Top Six guesthouses.

In The Country-

Kill nothing but time

Take nothing but photographs

Leave nothing but footprints

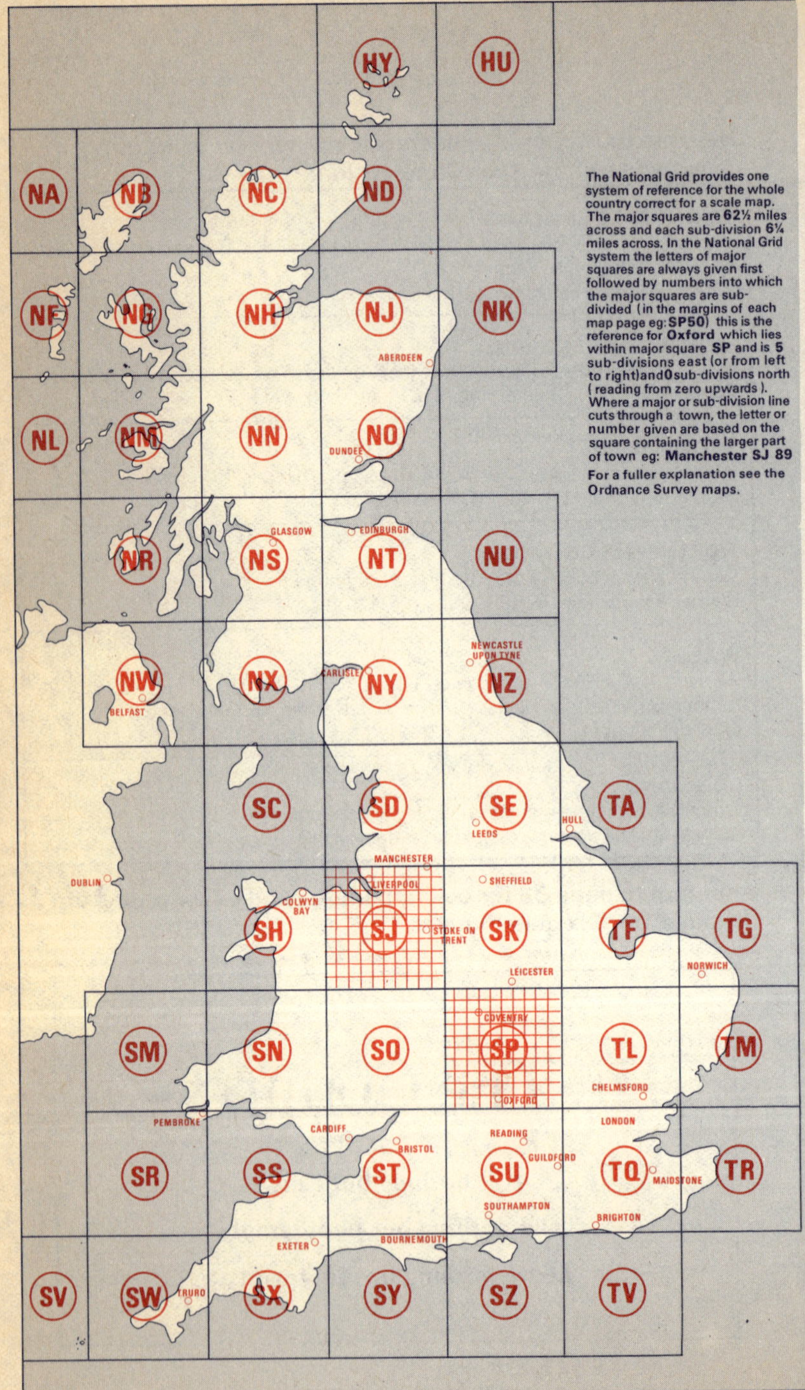

The National Grid

The National Grid provides one system of reference for the whole country correct for a scale map. The major squares are **62½ miles** across and each sub-division **6¼ miles** across. In the National Grid system the letters of major squares are always given first followed by numbers into which the major squares are sub-divided (in the margins of each map page eg: **SP50**) this is the reference for **Oxford** which lies within major square **SP** and is **5** sub-divisions east (or from left to right) and **0** sub-divisions north (reading from zero upwards). Where a major or sub-division line cuts through a town, the letter or number given are based on the square containing the larger part of town eg: **Manchester SJ 89**

For a fuller explanation see the Ordnance Survey maps.

Key to Atlas

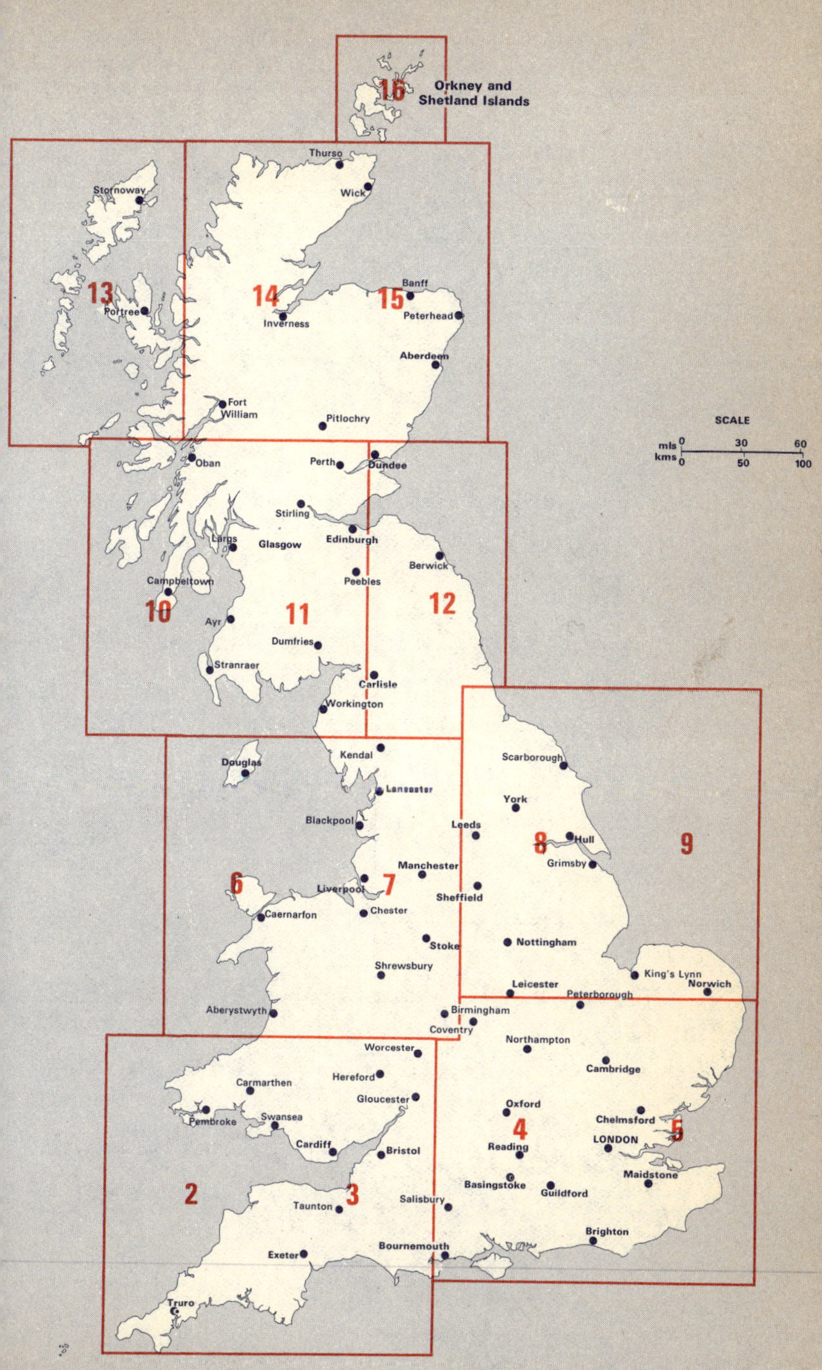

This atlas is for location purposes Only:
see Member's Handbook for current road
and AA road services information

Maps produced by
The AA Cartographic Department
(Publications Division), Fanum House,
Basingstoke, Hampshire RG21 2EA

Based on the Ordnance Survey Map with
the Sanction of the Controller H.M.S.O.

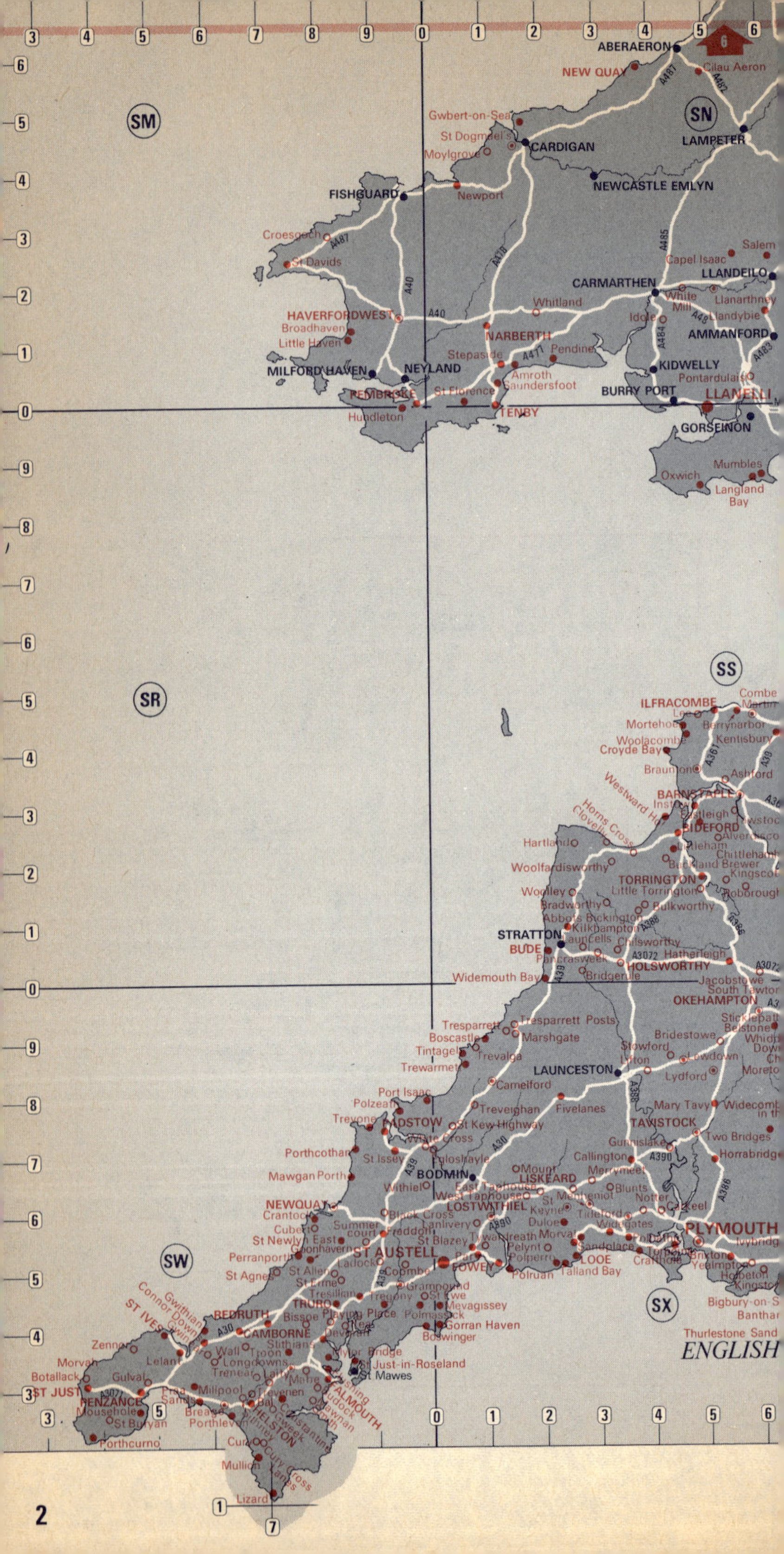

SM
SN
SR
SS
SW
SX
ABERAERON
NEW QUAY
Cilau Aeron
Gwbert-on-Sea
St Dogmael
Moylgrove
CARDIGAN
LAMPETER
NEWCASTLE EMLYN
FISHGUARD
Newport
Croesgoch
St Davids
Salem
Capel Isaac
LLANDEILO
CARMARTHEN
Llanarthney
White Mill
Llandybie
AMMANFORD
Whitland
Idole
HAVERFORDWEST
Broadhaven
Little Haven
NARBERTH
Stepaside
Pendine
Pontardulais
KIDWELLY
MILFORD HAVEN
NEYLAND
Amroth
Saundersfoot
BURRY PORT
LLANELLI
PEMBROKE
St Florence
GORSEINON
Hundleton
TENBY
Oxwich
Mumbles
Langland Bay
ILFRACOMBE
Combe Martin
Lee
Berrynarbor
Mortehoe
Kentisbury
Woolacombe
Croyde Bay
Braunton
Ashford
Westward Ho
BARNSTAPLE
Instow
Bideleigh
Tawstock
BIDEFORD
Horns Cross
Clovelly
Alverdiscott
Hartland
Weare Giffard
Chittlehampton
Buckland Brewer
Kingscott
Woolfardisworthy
TORRINGTON
Little Torrington
Roborough
Woolley
Bradworthy
Bulkworthy
Abbots Bickington
Kilkhampton
Chilsworthy
STRATTON
Launcells
BUDE
Pancrasweek
Hatherleigh
Bridgerule
HOLSWORTHY
Jacobstowe
Widemouth Bay
South Tawton
OKEHAMPTON
Sticklepath
Belstone
Tresparrett
Tresparrett Posts
Boscastle
Marshgate
Bridestowe
Stowford
Whiddon Down
Tintagel
Trevalga
Lifton
Lewdown
Trewarmet
Moreton
LAUNCESTON
Lydford
Camelford
Mary Tavy
Widecombe in the
Port Isaac
Trevighan
Fivelanes
Polzeath
TAVISTOCK
Trevone
PADSTOW
St Kew Highway
Gunnislake
White Cross
Two Bridges
St Issey
Egloshayle
Callington
Horrabridge
Porthcothan
BODMIN
Merrymeet
Withiel
Mount
LISKEARD
Mawgan Porth
East Taphouse
St Mellenion
Blunts
NEWQUAY
West Taphouse
LOSTWITHIEL
Tideford
Notter
Keel
Crantock
Black Cross
St Keyne
Cubert
Summercourt
Freddon
Duloe
St Newlyn East
Tregondean
St Blazey
Tiverath
Morval
Ivybridge
Perranporth
Goonhavern
ST AUSTELL
Pelynt
Polperro
LOOE
Yeelmpton
St Agnes
St Allen
Ladock
Copmba
FOWEY
Polruan
Talland Bay
Brixton
St Erme
Tresillian
Tregony
Grampound
Holbeton
Connor Down
Gwithian
TRURO
Playing Place
St Ewe
Mevagissey
Bigbury-on-Sea
ST IVES
Gwinear
REDRUTH
Bissoe
Polmassick
Gorran Haven
Banthar
Zennor
CAMBORNE
Devoran
Creed
Boswinger
Thurlestone Sand
Morvah
Stithians
Longdowns
Ruan
Tyler Bridge
Botallack
Gulval
Lelant
Treneale
Long
Maine
St Just-in-Roseland
ST JUST
Penna
Millpool
St Mawes
PENZANCE
Samsa
Constantine
Mousehole
Breage
Penryn
Mawnan
St Buryan
Porthleven
Gweek
HELSTON
Porthcurno
Cury Cross
Mullion
Cadgwith
Lizard
A487
A478
A40
A485
A40
A484
A40
A477
A40
A48
A483
A487
A30
A39
A361
A39
A30
A386
A3072
A3072
A3
A388
A390
A389
A30
A3074
A3071
A3083
A394
A3078
ENGLISH

REDDITCH
Wychbold
DROITWICH
Oddingley
Norton
WORCESTER
BROMYARD
GREAT MALVERN
EVESHAM
Malvern Wells
LEOMINSTER
KINGTON
Hundred House
Bryngwyn
Aberedw
Whitney on-Wye
Clyro
HAY-ON-WYE
HEREFORD
LEDBURY
TEWKESBURY
Bishops Cleeve
CHELTENHAM
GLOUCESTER
STROUD
CIRENCESTER
Minchinhampton
NAILSWORTH
Uley
MALMESBURY
Chipping Sodbury
CHIPPENHAM
CALNE
Shaw
MELKSHAM
BATH
DEVIZES
TROWBRIDGE
BRADFORD-ON-AVON
WESTBURY
Chapmanslade
WARMINSTER
FROME
SHEPTON MALLET
Chicklade
SHAFTESBURY
Marnhull
Stalbridge
Fiddleford
SHERBORNE
BLANDFORD FORUM
Cerne Abbas
WIMBORNE MINSTER
POOLE
DORCHESTER
WAREHAM
Winfrith Newburgh
WEYMOUTH
Lulworth
SWANAGE
FORTUNESWELL
LLANDRINDOD WELLS
Cross Gates
Penybont
PRESTEIGNE
Bircher
Middleton on the Hill
Kimbolton
Hatfield
Howey
Tregaron
Rhandirmwyn
LLANWRTYD WELLS
BUILTH WELLS
BRECON
Tretower
Crickhowell
Pantygelli
Llangattock
ABERGAVENNY
Govilon
BRYNMAWR
MONMOUTH
Llanarth
GLANAMAN
EBBW VALE
TREDEGAR
BLAENAVON
BLAINA
Raglan
MERTHYR TYDFIL
RHYMNEY
ABERTILLERY
ABERSYCHAN
USK
Llandogo
Clearwell
NEATH
ABERDARE
MOUNTAIN ASH
BARGOED
GELLIGAER
PONTYPOOL
CWMBRAN
CHEPSTOW
Stone
Falfield
Cromhall
Hillesley
SWANSEA
RHONDDA
ABERCARN
BEDWAS
RISCA
CAERLEON
Almondsbury
PORT TALBOT
MAESTEG
PONTYPRIDD
CAERPHILLY
NEWPORT
PORTHCAWL
BRIDGEND
COWBRIDGE
PENARTH
CARDIFF
PORTISHEAD
CLEVEDON
BRISTOL
MANGOTSFIELD
Marshfield
Tormarton
KINGSWOOD
KEYNSHAM
Tickenham
Flax Bourton
WESTON-SUPER-MARE
Congresbury
Churchill
Burrington
Farrington Gurney
RADSTOCK
Ston Easton
Beckington
BURNHAM-ON-SEA
Axbridge
Cheddar
WELLS
Wookey
MINEHEAD
West Huntspill
Mark
Causeway
Bleadney
North Wootton
West Pennard
GLASTONBURY
STREET
Bruton
WILLITON
Spaxton
Stawell
BRIDGWATER
Burrow Bridge
Othery
North Cadbury
Templecombe
SOUTH MOLTON
Wiveliscombe
Rumwell
TAUNTON
Langport
Curry Rivel
Queen Camel
Henstridge
Millborne
SHAFTESBURY
Bampton
WELLINGTON
Hatch
Martock
Nether Compton
Staple Fitzpaine
YEOVIL
SHERBORNE
TIVERTON
Sampford Peverell
ILMINSTER
CREWKERNE
Holnest
Cullompton
CHARD
Yarcombe
Seaborough
Halstock
BLANDFORD FORUM
Bradninch
Monkton
Drimpton
CREDITON
Thorncombe
Pilsdon
WHITCHURCH
EXETER
Axminster
Canonicorum
BRIDPORT
Frampton
DORCHESTER
OTTERY ST MARY
Musbury
LYME REGIS
Chideock
Winterbourne Abbas
EXMOUTH
SEATON
Beer
SIDMOUTH
Branscombe
BUDLEIGH SALTERTON
DAWLISH
TEIGNMOUTH
NEWTON ABBOT
Stokeinteignhead
Kingskerswell
BUCKFASTLEIGH
TORQUAY
PAIGNTON
TOTNES
BRIXHAM
Kingswear
DARTMOUTH
KINGSBRIDGE
Strete
SALCOMBE
SO
ST
SY
BRISTOL CHANNEL
CHANNEL
Scale
0   10   20 miles
0   10   20   30 kilometres
Town with guesthouse or inn
Town with guesthouse or inn and farmhouse
Town with farmhouse only
Other Towns for Location only

3

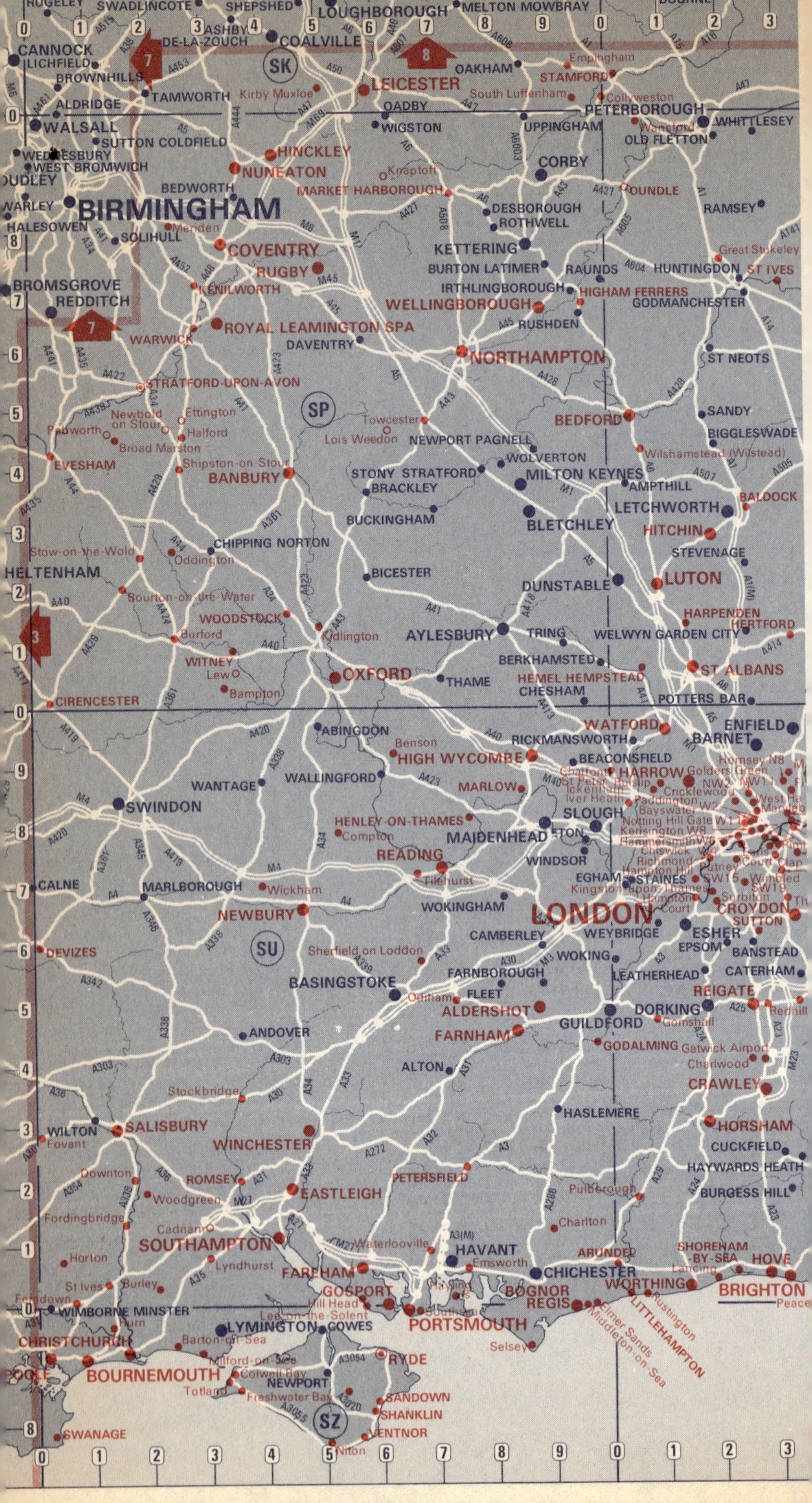

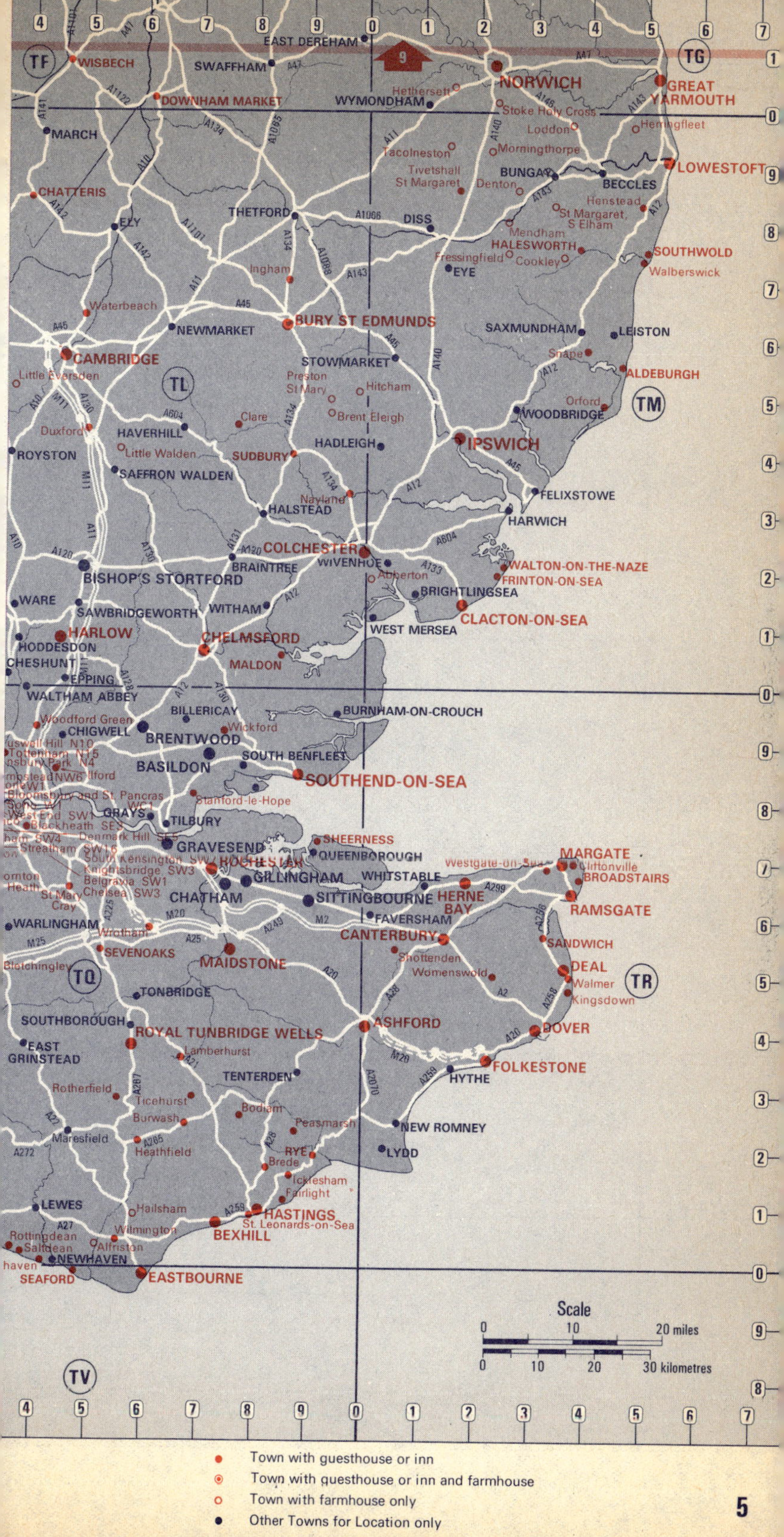

Town with guesthouse or inn
Town with guesthouse or inn and farmhouse
Town with farmhouse only
Other Towns for Location only
Scale
10
20 miles
0
10
20
30 kilometres
5

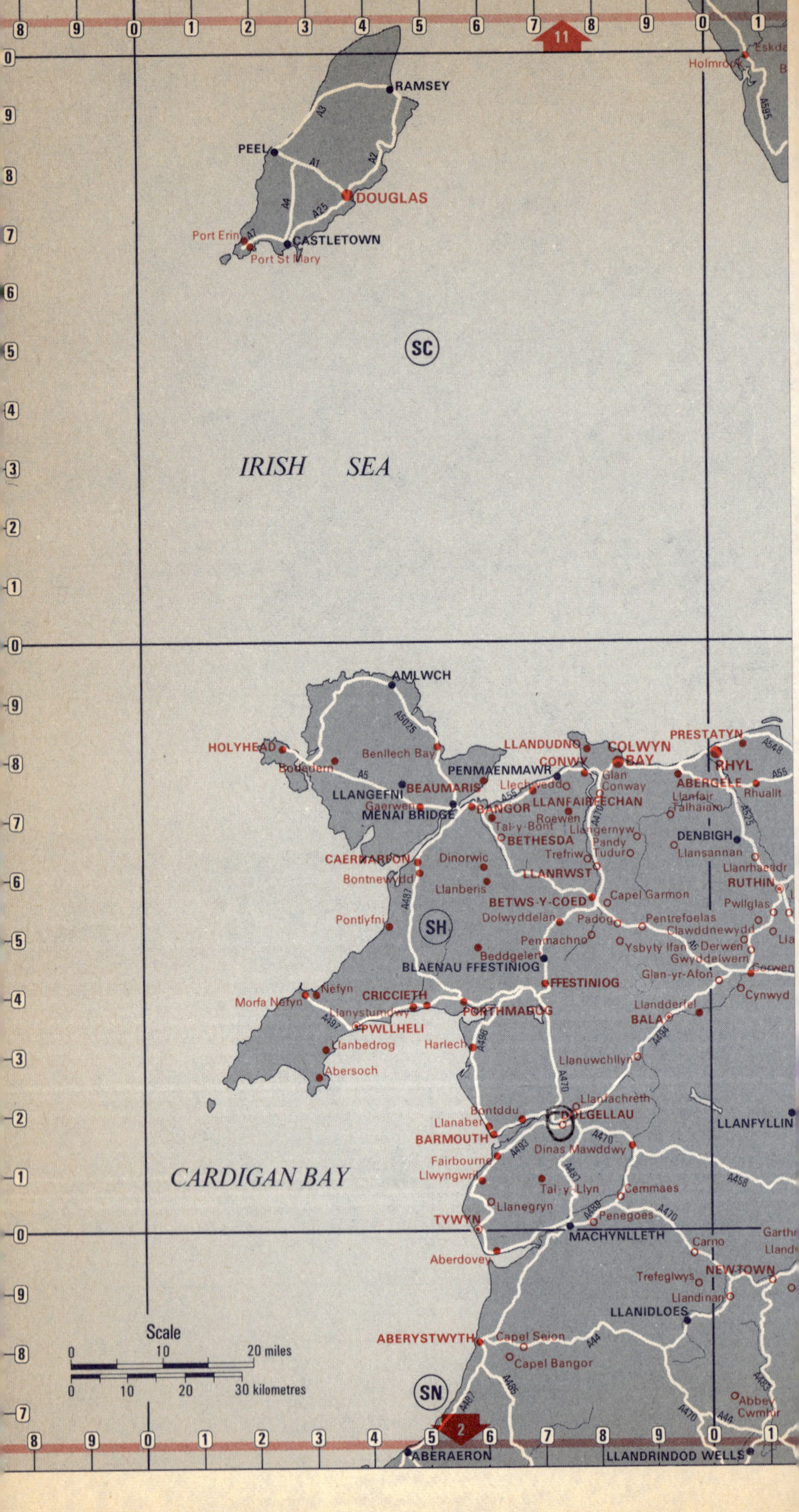

11
IRISH SEA
SC
RAMSEY
PEEL
A3
A2
A1
A4
A25
DOUGLAS
Port Erin
A7
CASTLETOWN
Port St Mary
Eskda
Holmrock
A595
AMLWCH
A5025
HOLYHEAD
Bodedern
Benllech Bay
A5
LLANDUDNO
CONWY
COLWYN BAY
PRESTATYN
A548
RHYL
PENMAENMAWR
Llechwedd
Glan Conway
ABERGELE
A55
LLANGEFNI
BEAUMARIS
A55
Llanfair Talhaiarn
Rhuallt
A525
Gaerwen
BANGOR
LLANFAIRFECHAN
MENAI BRIDGE
Roewen
Llangernyw
DENBIGH
Tal-y-Bont
BETHESDA
Pandy Tudur
Llansannan
CAERNARFON
Dinorwic
Trefriw
Llanrhaeadr
Bontnewydd
LLANRWST
RUTHIN
Llanberis
Capel Garmon
Pwllglas
A487
BETWS-Y-COED
Pontlyfni
SH
Dolwyddelan
Pentrefoelas
Lla
Padog
Clawddnewydd
Pennachno
Ysbyty Ifan
Derwen
Beddgelert
Gwyddelwern
BLAENAU FFESTINIOG
Glan-yr-Afon
Cerwen
Nefyn
FFESTINIOG
Cynwyd
Morfa Nefyn
CRICCIETH
Llanddertel
Llanystumdwy
PORTHMADOG
BALA
A497
PWLLHELI
A496
A494
Llanbedrog
Harlech
Llanuwchllyn
Abersoch
A470
Llanfachreth
Bontddu
DOLGELLAU
LLANFYLLIN
Llanaber
BARMOUTH
A493
Dinas Mawddwy
CARDIGAN BAY
Fairbourne
A470
A458
Llwyngwril
A487
A489
Tal-y-Llyn
Cemmaes
Llanegryn
Penegoes
A470
TYWYN
MACHYNLLETH
Carno
Garthm
Lland
Aberdovey
NEWTOWN
Trefeglwys
Llandinam
LLANIDLOES
Scale
0   10   20 miles
0   10   20   30 kilometres
ABERYSTWYTH
Capel Seion
A44
Capel Bangor
A485
A483
SN
Abbey
Cwmhir
A470
A44
2
ABERAERON
LLANDRINDOD WELLS
A487

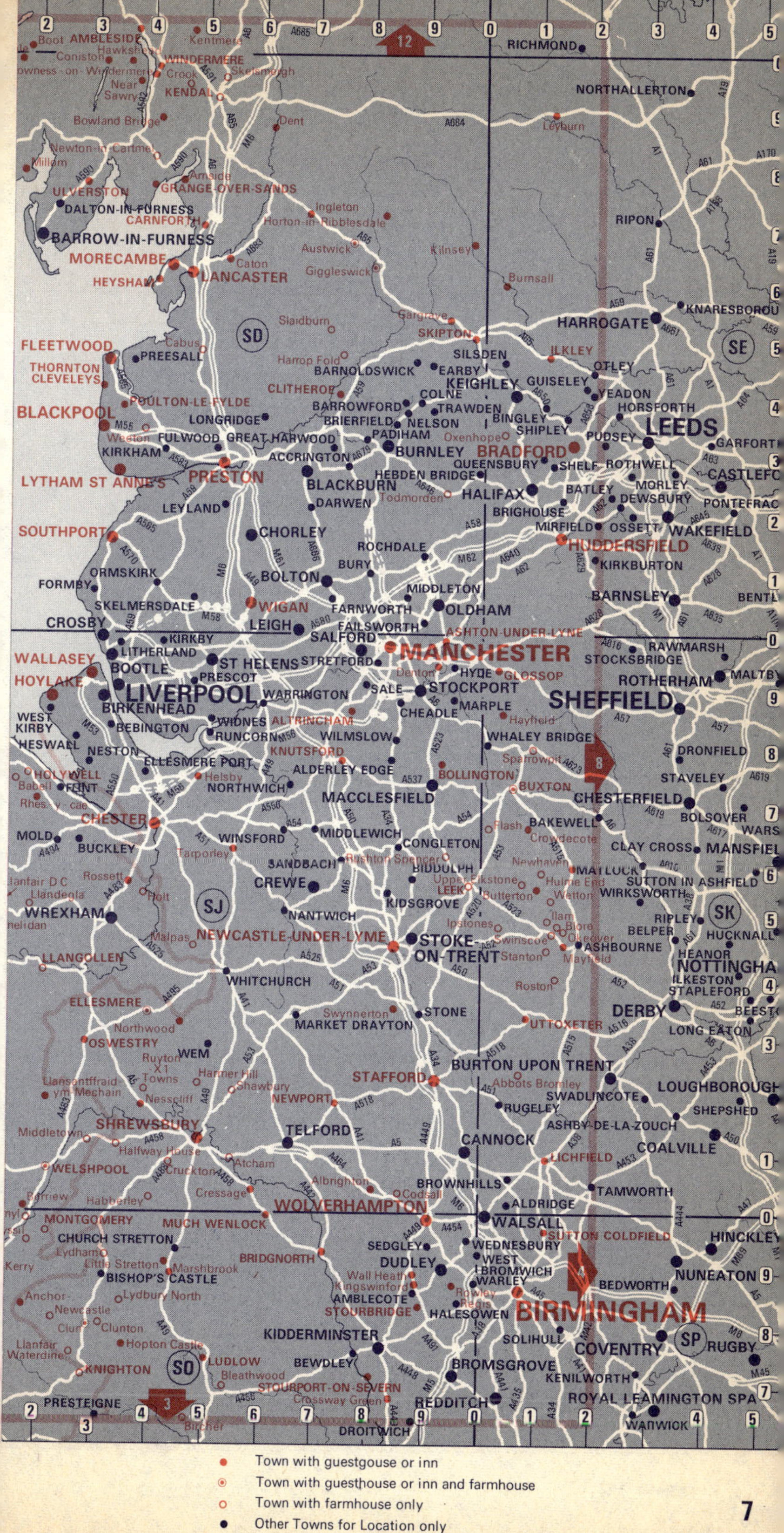

Town with guestgouse or inn
Town with guesthouse or inn and farmhouse
Town with farmhouse only
Other Towns for Location only

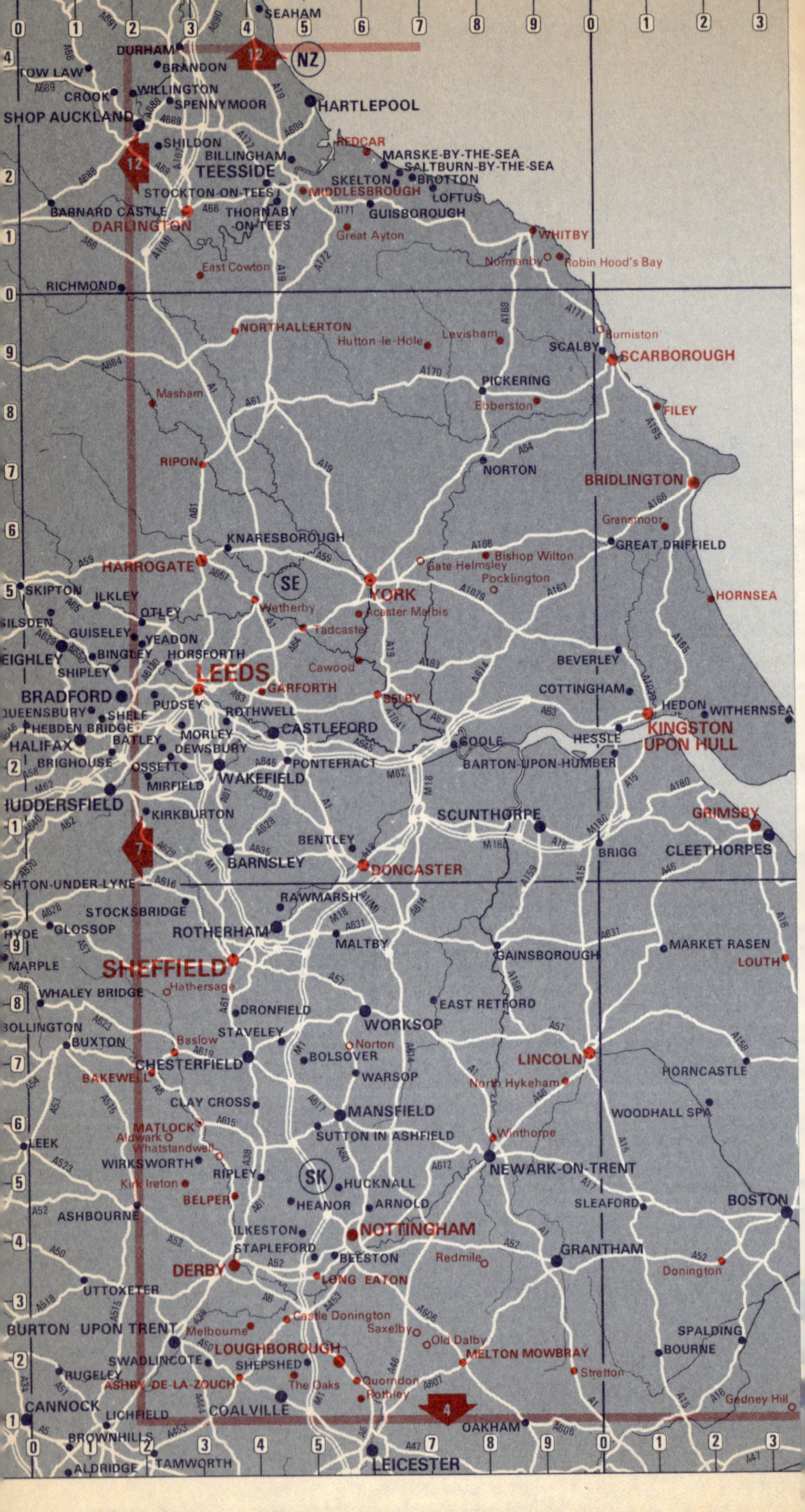

SEAHAM
NZ
12
DURHAM
BRANDON
TOW LAW
WILLINGTON
CROOK
SPENNYMOOR
HARTLEPOOL
SHOP AUCKLAND
SHILDON
BILLINGHAM
REDCAR
MARSKE-BY-THE-SEA
SALTBURN-BY-THE-SEA
TEESSIDE
SKELTON
BROTTON
STOCKTON-ON-TEES
MIDDLESBROUGH
LOFTUS
12
BARNARD CASTLE
THORNABY
GUISBOROUGH
DARLINGTON
-ON-TEES
WHITBY
East Cowton
Great Ayton
Normanby
Robin Hood's Bay
RICHMOND
NORTHALLERTON
Burniston
Hutton-le-Hole
Levisham
SCALBY
SCARBOROUGH
A170
PICKERING
Masham
Ebberston
FILEY
RIPON
NORTON
BRIDLINGTON
Gransmoor
GREAT DRIFFIELD
KNARESBOROUGH
HARROGATE
SE
Bishop Wilton
HORNSEA
SKIPTON
ILKLEY
Wetherby
Gate Helmsley
Pocklington
SILSDEN
OTLEY
YORK
BEVERLEY
GUISELEY
YEADON
Acaster Malbis
COTTINGHAM
KEIGHLEY
BINGLEY
HORSFORTH
Tadcaster
HEDON
WITHERNSEA
SHIPLEY
Cawood
LEEDS
GARFORTH
SELBY
KINGSTON
BRADFORD
PUDSEY
UPON HULL
QUEENSBURY
SHELF
ROTHWELL
HESSLE
HEBDEN BRIDGE
BATLEY
CASTLEFORD
GOOLE
BARTON-UPON-HUMBER
HALIFAX
MORLEY
BRIGHOUSE
DEWSBURY
PONTEFRACT
OSSETT
GRIMSBY
HUDDERSFIELD
MIRFIELD
WAKEFIELD
SCUNTHORPE
KIRKBURTON
BENTLEY
BRIGG
CLEETHORPES
7
BARNSLEY
DONCASTER
ASHTON-UNDER-LYNE
RAWMARSH
STOCKSBRIDGE
MARKET RASEN
HYDE
GLOSSOP
ROTHERHAM
GAINSBOROUGH
LOUTH
MARPLE
MALTBY
SHEFFIELD
EAST RETFORD
WHALEY BRIDGE
Hathersage
BOLLINGTON
DRONFIELD
WORKSOP
BUXTON
STAVELEY
Norton
LINCOLN
HORNCASTLE
CHESTERFIELD
BOLSOVER
BAKEWELL
WARSOP
North Hykeham
WOODHALL SPA
CLAY CROSS
LEEK
MANSFIELD
MATLOCK
SUTTON IN ASHFIELD
Winthorpe
Aldwark
Whatstandwell
WIRKSWORTH
RIPLEY
SK
NEWARK-ON-TRENT
Kirk Ireton
HUCKNALL
BELPER
HEANOR
Arnold
SLEAFORD
BOSTON
ASHBOURNE
ILKESTON
NOTTINGHAM
GRANTHAM
STAPLEFORD
BEESTON
Redmile
DERBY
LONG EATON
UTTOXETER
Donington
Castle Donington
A606
BURTON UPON TRENT
Melbourne
Saxelby
Old Dalby
SPALDING
LOUGHBOROUGH
BOURNE
SWADLINCOTE
SHEPSHED
MELTON MOWBRAY
RUGELEY
Stretton
ASHBY-DE-LA-ZOUCH
The Oaks
Quorndon
CANNOCK
Rothley
Gedney Hill
LICHFIELD
COALVILLE
OAKHAM
BROWNHILLS
ALDRIDGE
TAMWORTH
LEICESTER

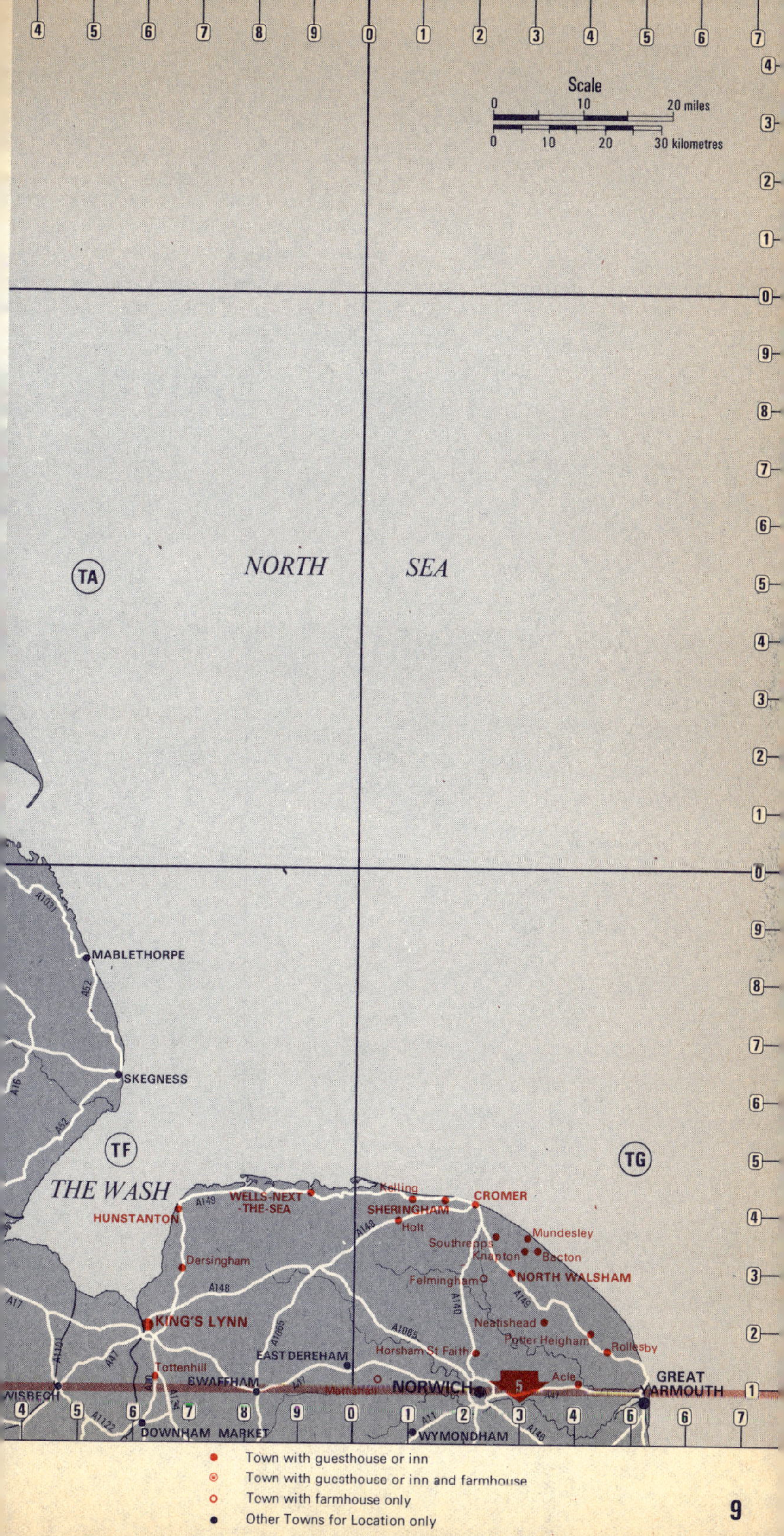
Scale
0
10
20 miles
0
10
20
30 kilometres
TA
NORTH
SEA
MABLETHORPE
SKEGNESS
TF
THE WASH
TG
HUNSTANTON
Wells-Next-The-Sea
Kelling
SHERINGHAM
CROMER
Holt
Mundesley
Southrepps
Bacton
Knapton
Dersingham
Felmingham
NORTH WALSHAM
Neatishead
KING'S LYNN
Potter Heigham
Rollesby
Tottenhill
EAST DEREHAM
Horsham St Faith
GREAT
Mattishall
Acle
YARMOUTH
WISBECH
SWAFFHAM
NORWICH
DOWNHAM MARKET
WYMONDHAM
Town with guesthouse or inn
Town with guesthouse or inn and farmhouse
Town with farmhouse only
Other Towns for Location only

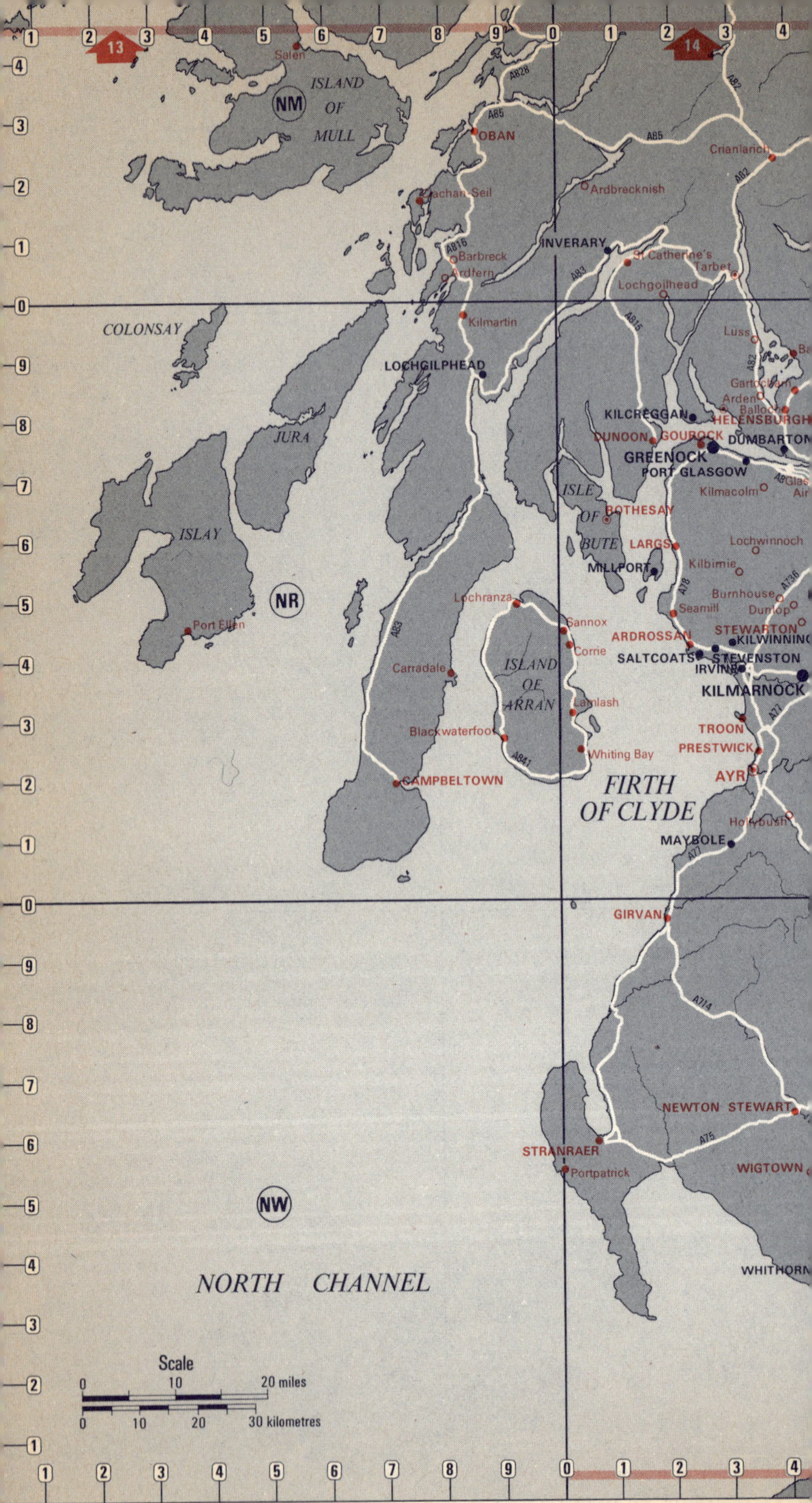
13
14
Salen
ISLAND OF MULL
NM
OBAN
A828
A85
Crianlarich
A82
Clachan-Seil
Ardbrecknish
INVERARY
A816
Barbreck
Ardfern
St Catherine's
Tarbet
A83
Lochgoilhead
Kilmartin
A815
Luss
COLONSAY
A82
Ba
LOCHGILPHEAD
Gartocha
Arden
Balloch
KILCREGGAN
HELENSBURGH
JURA
DUNOON
GOUROCK
DUMBARTON
GREENOCK
PORT GLASGOW
Kilmacolm
A8 Glas
Air
ISLE
BOTHESAY
OF
Lochwinnoch
BUTE
LARGS
ISLAY
MILLPORT
Kilbimie
A78
NR
Lochranza
Burnhouse
A736
Seamill
Dunlop
Gannox
STEWARTON
Port Ellen
ARDROSSAN
KILWINNING
Corrie
SALTCOATS
STEVENSON
Carradale
ISLAND
OF
IRVINE
ARRAN
KILMARNOCK
A83
Lamlash
Blackwaterfoot
TROON
A841
PRESTWICK
A77
Whiting Bay
AYR
CAMPBELTOWN
FIRTH
OF CLYDE
Hollybush
MAYBOLE
A77
GIRVAN
A714
NORTH CHANNEL
NEWTON STEWART
A75
STRANRAER
WIGTOWN
Portpatrick
NW
WHITHORN
Scale
0
10
20 miles
0
10
20
30 kilometres

NN
NO
NT
NX
NY
15
12
7
ABERFELDY
RATTRAY
ALYTH
FORFAR
BLAIRGOWRIE
ARBROATH
Lawers
A827
COUPAR ANGUS
A929
CARNOUSTIE
A92
Moneydie
Guidtown
DUNDEE
MONIFIETH
A9
A85
NEWPORT-ON-TAY
TAYPORT
A90
PERTH
Comrie
A914
Strathyre
CRIEFF
NEWBURGH
A91
ST ANDREWS
A84
AUCHTERARDER
AUCHTERMUCHTY
CUPAR
A915
A917
CRAIL
Port of
CALLANDER
LADYBANK
KILRENNY
Menteith
KINROSS
FALKLAND
PITTENWEEM
ANSTRUTHER
DOUNE
DUNBLANE
KINROSS
MARKINCH
LEVEN
ELIE
ST MONANS
Gartmore
Ruskie
LESLIE
METHIL
EARLSFERRY
Buchlyvie
ALVA
DOLLAR
A977
GLENROTHES
maha
Kippen
BRIDGE OF ALLAN
TILLICOULTRY
METHIL
A811
Balfron Station
Fintry
ALLOA
LOCHGELLY
BUCKHAVEN
Carronbridge
STIRLING
Kincardine-on-Forth
COWDENBEATH
KIRKCALDY
NORTH BERWICK
DUNIPACE
DUNFERMLINE
A985
KINGHORN
DENNY
A901
KILSYTH
FALKIRK
GRANGEMOUTH
BURNTISLAND
EAST LINTON
DUNBAR
MILNGAVIE
CUMBERNAULD
BO'NESS
INVERKEITHING
COCKENZIE
CLYDE
LINLITHGOW
QUEENSFERRY
A1
BANK
Moodiesburn
M9
LEITH
PRESTONPANS
HADDINGTON
GLASGOW
BATHGATE
EDINBURGH
TRANENT
PAISLEY
Glenmavis
ARMADALE
Newbridge
MUSSELBURGH
JOHNSTONE
COATBRIDGE
AIRDRIE
M8
LIVINGSTON
Straiton
Chapelhall
A8
A68
BARRHEAD
RUTHERGLEN
WHITBURN
A7
PENICUIK
DUNS
HAMILTON
MOTHERWELL
A702
A721
A703
NT
EAST KILBRIDE
WISHAW
West Linton
A701
LAUDER
A697
Chapelton
A726
Dunsyre
Strathaven
LANARK
A7
A73
Boghead
Symington
BIGGAR
INNERLEITHEN
PEEBLES
GALASHIELS
COLDSTREAM
NEWMILNS
DARVEL
A72
A698
MELROSE
KELSO
GALSTON
A701
SELKIRK
A699
A708
Abington
JEDBURGH
CUMNOCK
Ettrick
HAWICK
A76
Kirkconnel
A68
New Cumnock
A74
A702
SANQUHAR
MOFFAT
Thornhill
A701
Wamphray
A713
A702
LANGHOLM
A7
NEW GALLOWAY
LOCKERBIE
A712
Shawhead
Eaglesfield
Canonbie
A75
DUMFRIES
Carrutherstown
Gretna Green
CASTLE DOUGLAS
Clarencefield
A75
Beeswing
Cummertrees
ANNAN
Gretna
A6071
A69
Haugh of Urr
DALBEATTIE
A689
Creetown
GATEHOUSE OF FLEET
Kirkbean
CARLISLE
Auchencairn
Newton Arlosh
NY
KIRKCUDBRIGHT
A595
A686
A596
Sebergham
A595
Aspatria
Caldbeck
A6
MARYPORT
Bassenthwaite
Mosedale
COCKERMOUTH
PENRITH
WORKINGTON
A66
Mungrisdale
A66
A66
Thornthwaite
A66
A5086
St John's in the Vale
KESWICK
WHITEHAVEN
Newlands
Glenridding
Grange in Borrowdale
A592
A595
A66
A6
A591
Rydal
A595
Grasmere
AMBLESIDE
A685
A5091
A6
A689

Town with guesthouse or inn
Town with guesthouse or inn and farmhouse
Town with farmhouse only
Other Towns for Location only

11

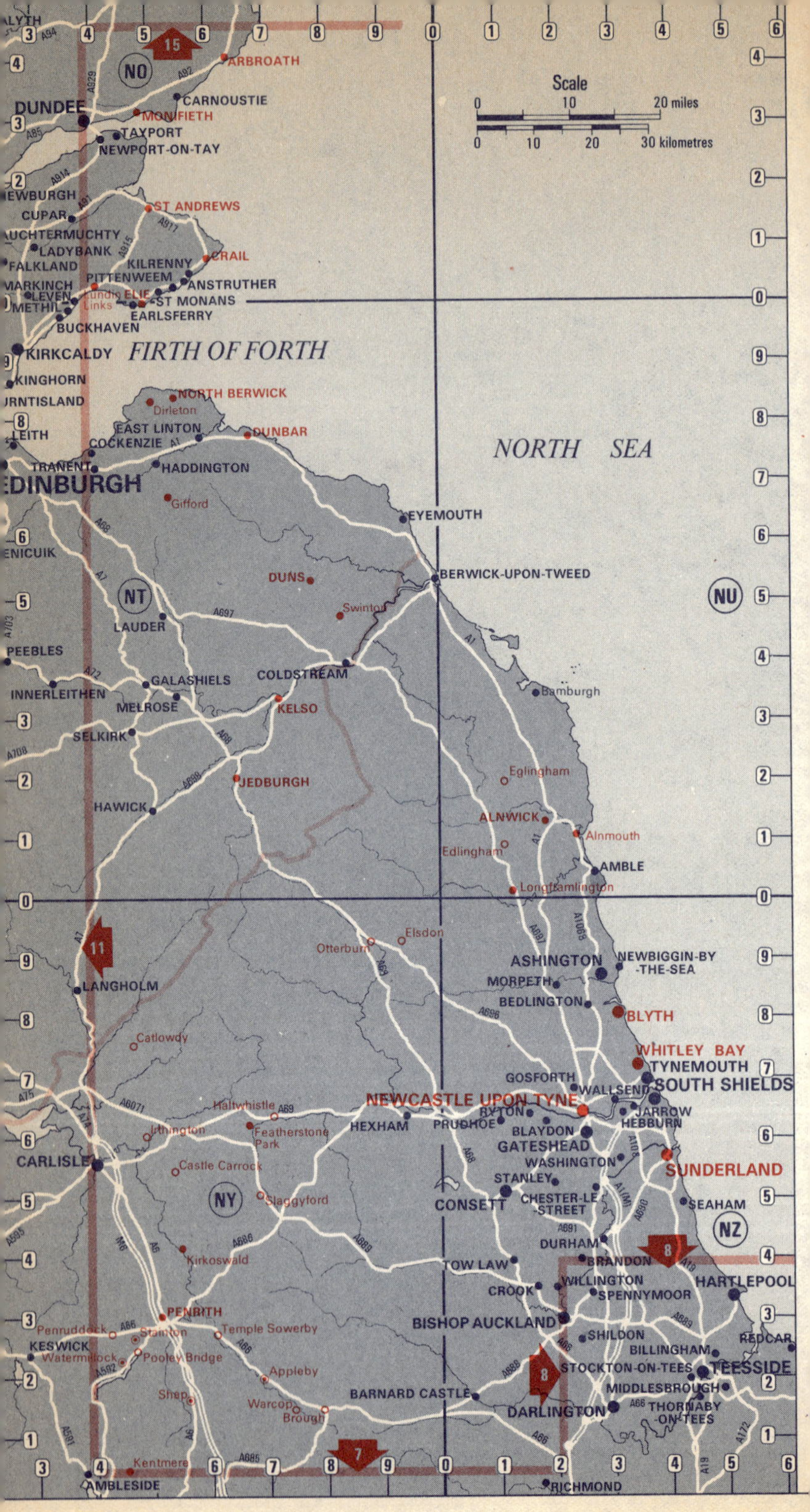

BLYTH
A94
15
NO
ARBROATH
A97
CARNOUSTIE
DUNDEE
MONIFIETH
A85
TAYPORT
NEWPORT-ON-TAY
A914
A919
NEWBURGH
CUPAR
ST ANDREWS
A911
AUCHTERMUCHTY
A915
LADYBANK
CRAIL
FALKLAND
KILRENNY
MARKINCH
PITTENWEEM
LEVEN
ELIE
ANSTRUTHER
METHIL
Lundin
ST MONANS
Links
EARLSFERRY
BUCKHAVEN
FIRTH OF FORTH
KIRKCALDY
KINGHORN
BURNTISLAND
NORTH BERWICK
LEITH
Dirleton
EAST LINTON
DUNBAR
TRANENT
COCKENZIE
NORTH SEA
EDINBURGH
HADDINGTON
Gifford
A68
EYEMOUTH
PENICUIK
A7
NT
NU
BERWICK-UPON-TWEED
A703
DUNS
A697
LAUDER
Swinton
A1
PEEBLES
A72
GALASHIELS
A698
COLDSTREAM
Bamburgh
INNERLEITHEN
MELROSE
KELSO
A708
SELKIRK
A698
A698
Eglingham
JEDBURGH
HAWICK
ALNWICK
Alnmouth
Edlingham
AMBLE
Longframlington
A697
A1068
A7
Elsdon
A697
11
Otterburn
ASHINGTON
NEWBIGGIN-BY
-THE-SEA
LANGHOLM
MORPETH
A68
BEDLINGTON
A698
BLYTH
Catlowdy
WHITLEY BAY
GOSFORTH
TYNEMOUTH
A75
WALLSEND
SOUTH SHIELDS
A7
NEWCASTLE UPON TYNE
A6071
Haltwhistle
A69
RYTON
JARROW
Irthington
Featherstone
HEXHAM
PRUDHOE
HEBBURN
Park
BLAYDON
CARLISLE
GATESHEAD
WASHINGTON
SUNDERLAND
Castle Carrock
STANLEY
NY
Slaggyford
CONSETT
CHESTER-LE
SEAHAM
-STREET
NZ
A6
A686
DURHAM
A689
Kirkoswald
8
A19
TOW LAW
BRANDON
HARTLEPOOL
A689
WILLINGTON
PENRITH
CROOK
SPENNYMOOR
Penruddock
A66
Temple Sowerby
BISHOP AUCKLAND
SHILDON
REDCAR
KESWICK
Stainton
BILLINGHAM
Watermillock
Pooley Bridge
A66
8
STOCKTON-ON-TEES
TEESSIDE
A592
Appleby
MIDDLESBROUGH
Shap
BARNARD CASTLE
THORNABY
Warcop
DARLINGTON
-ON-TEES
Brough
A66
A685
7
A591
Kentmere
A685
A66
A19
A172
AMBLESIDE
RICHMOND
Scale
0   10   20 miles
0   10   20   30 kilometres

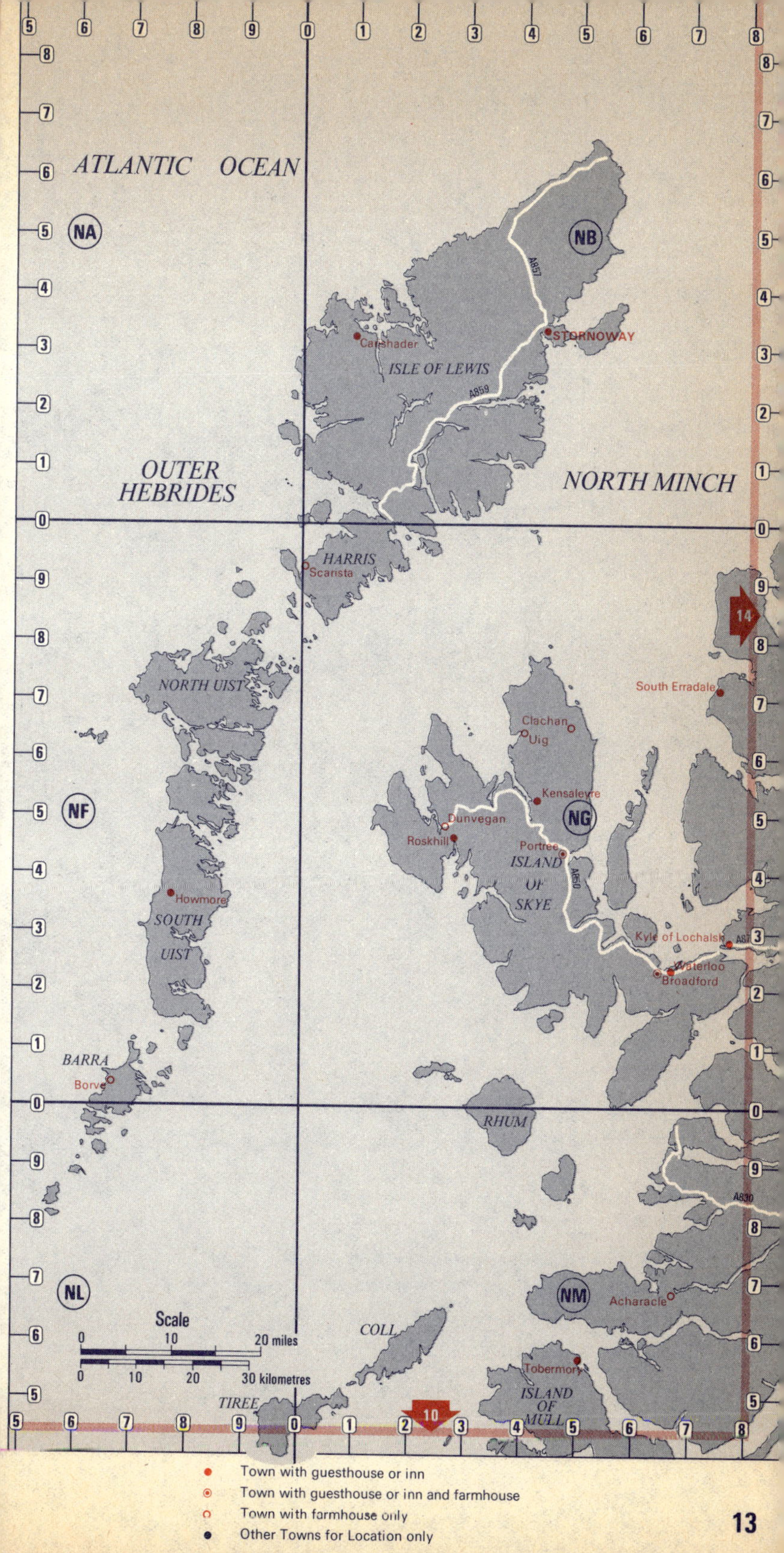

Town with guesthouse or inn
Town with guesthouse or inn and farmhouse
Town with farmhouse only
Other Towns for Location only

13

NB
NC
NG
NH
NM
NN
MORA
Durness
Lochinver
Lairg
Rogart
Ullapool
Croick
Bonar Bridge
DORNOCH
Gairloch
TAIN
INVERGORDON
CROMARTY
FORRES
13
Strathpeffer
DINGWALL
NAIRN
FORTROSE
Ardersier
Cawdor
Beauly
Kirkhill
INVERNESS
Culloden Moor
Kiltarlity
Daviot
Scaniport
Plockton
Dornie
Drumnadrochit
Moy
GRANTOWN-ON-SPEY
Carrbridge
Invermoriston
Foyers
Aviemore
Tomdoun
Fort Augustus
Invergarry
KINGUSSIE
Newtonmore
South Laggan
Banavie
Spean Bridge
FORT WILLIAM
Blair Atholl
Ardgour
Onich
Killiecrankie
Glencoe
PITLOCHRY
Balnaguard
ABERFELDY
Dalg
10
11
A838
A836
A897
A835
A837
A9
A832
A836
A835
A9
A832
A835
A96
A832
A890
A87
A850
A82
A887
A87
A82
A86
A830
A82
A828
A82
A9
A9
A827

14

East Mey
Huna
A836
THURSO
A9
A882
A895
A9
WICK
ND
Latheron
NORTH SEA
Y FIRTH
LOSSIEMOUTH
PORTKNOCKIE
BURGHEAD
FINDOCHTY
CULLEN
ROSEHEARTY
FRASERBURGH
BUCKIE
BANFF
MACDUFF
ELGIN
PORTSOY
A98
A95
A852
Longmorn
Fochabers
King Edward
A92
A941
Strichen
ROTHES
KEITH
ABERCHIRDER
NJ
NK
CHARLESTOWN
TURRIFF
PETERHEAD
OF ABERLOUR
DUFFTOWN
HUNTLY
A947
Fyvie
A96
Colpy
ELLON
OLDMELDRUM
A92
INVERURIE
A939
KINTORE
Strathdon
Cushnie
Kingswells
ABERDEEN
A93
Durris
BALLATER
(Kirkton)
Braemar
BANCHORY
A957
A92
STONEHAVEN
A93
LAURENCEKIRK
INVERBERVIE
A94
A92
BRECHIN
Scale
MONTROSE
0   10   20 miles
KIRRIEMUIR
FORFAR
Leysmill
0   10   20   30 kilometres
ise
ALYTH
NO
A94
RATTRAY
BLAIRGOWRIE
A926
12
COUPAR ANGUS
ARBROATH
Town with guesthouse or inn
Town with guesthouse or inn and farmhouse
Town with farmhouse only
Other Towns for Location only

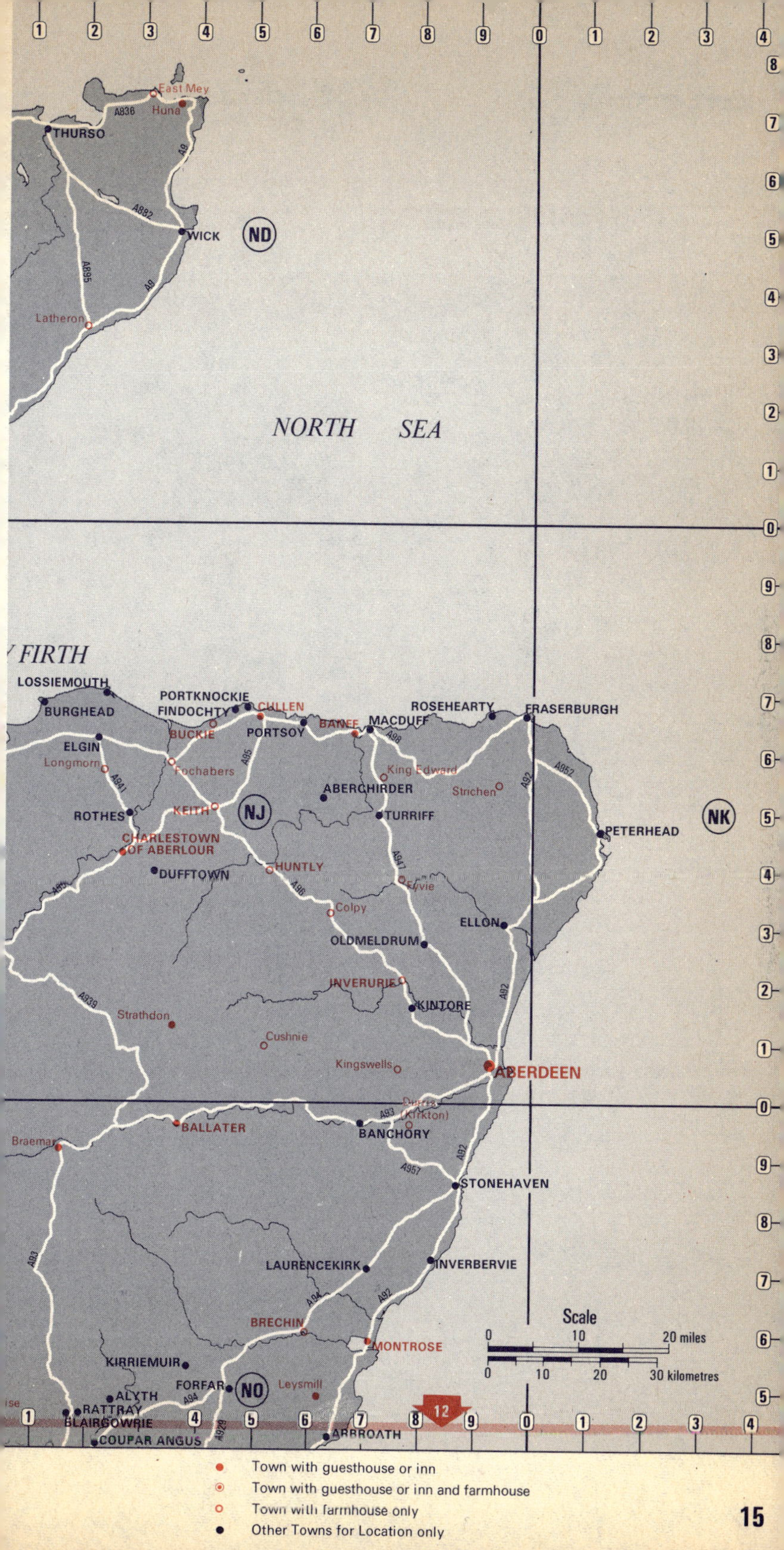

15

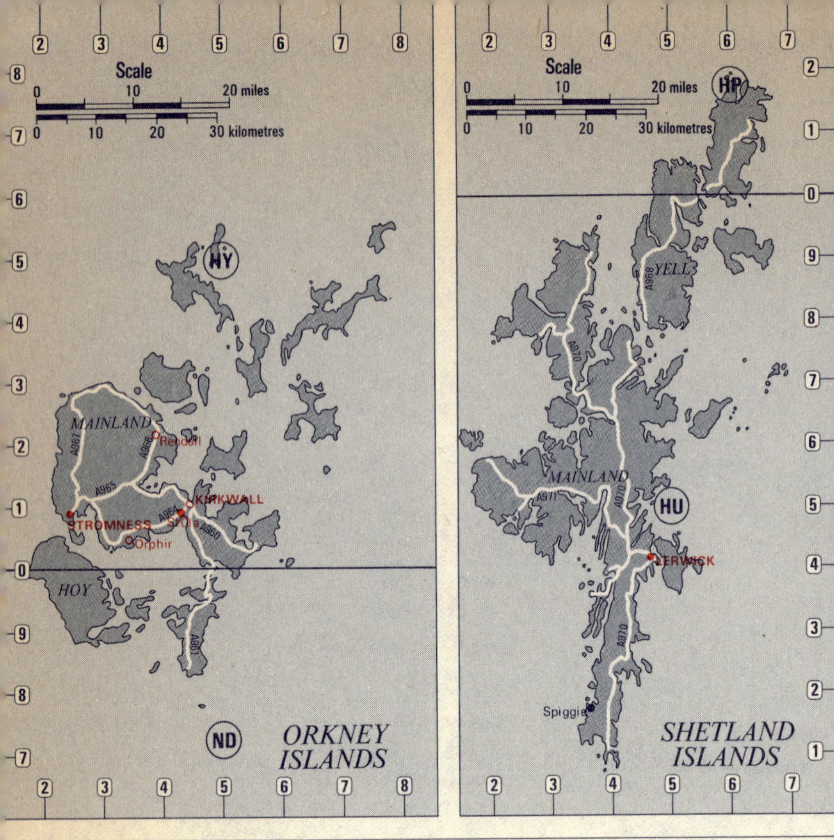

Town with guesthouse or inn
Town with guesthouse or inn and farmhouse
Town with farmhouse only
Other Towns for Location only

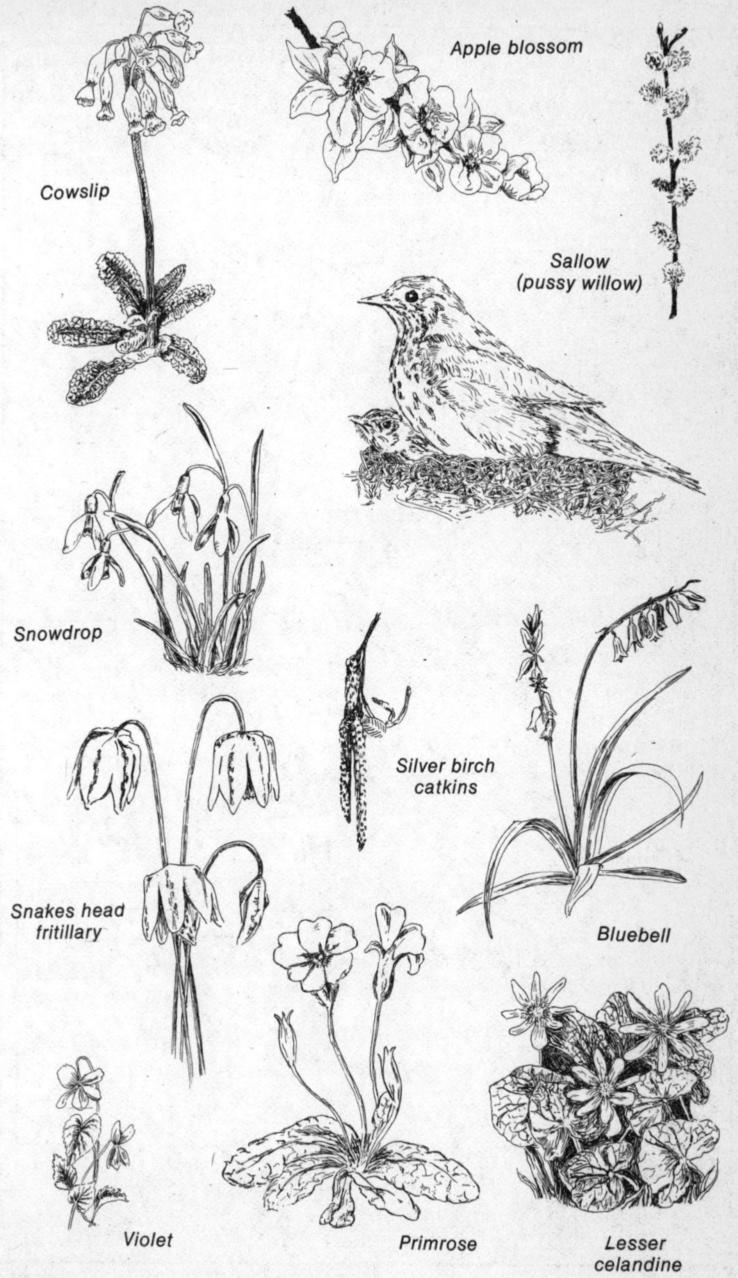

Treat yourself to a holiday in
SPRING

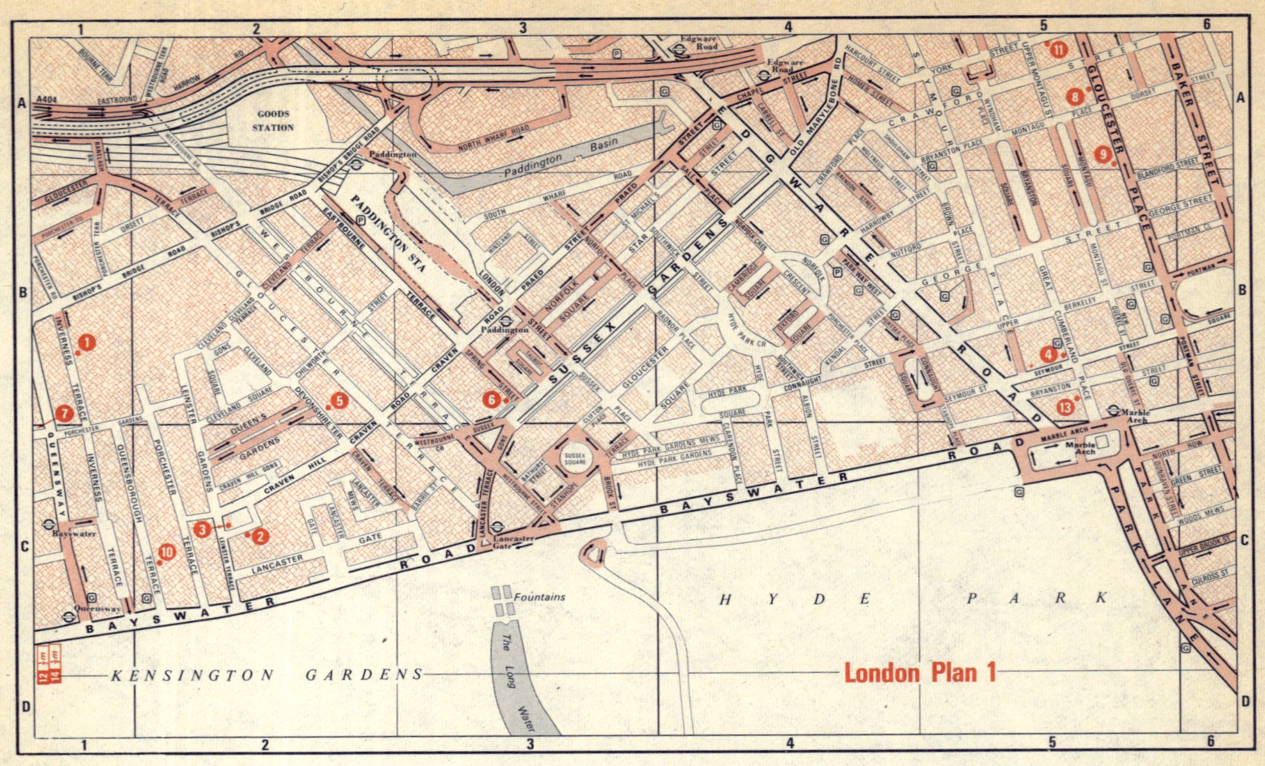

London Plan 1
GOODS STATION
PADDINGTON STA
Paddington Basin
NORTH WHARF ROAD
BISHOP'S BRIDGE ROAD
Paddington
HYDE PARK
KENSINGTON GARDENS
The Long Water
Fountains
BAYSWATER ROAD
BAKER STREET
GLOUCESTER PLACE
UPPER MONTAGU ST
MONTAGU SQUARE
BRYANSTON SQUARE
GREAT CUMBERLAND PLACE
SEYMOUR STREET
GEORGE STREET
BLANDFORD STREET
PORTMAN SQUARE
HARCOURT STREET
HOMER STREET
CRAWFORD STREET
YORK STREET
WYNDHAM PLACE
BRYANSTON PLACE
NUTFORD PLACE
MOLYNEUX STREET
OLD MARYLEBONE RD
CHAPEL STREET
CAPEL ST
EDGWARE ROAD
Edgware Road
Marble Arch
PARK LANE
NORTH ROW
GREEN STREET
WOODS MEWS
DUNRAVEN STREET
UPPER BROOK ST
CULROSS ST
PORTMAN STREET
BERKELEY
UPPER BERKELEY ST
SEYMOUR PL
BRYANSTON PLACE
CONNAUGHT SQUARE
CONNAUGHT STREET
ALBION STREET
HYDE PARK STREET
CLARENDON PLACE
STANHOPE PLACE
HYDE PARK SQUARE
SUSSEX GARDENS
SUSSEX SQUARE
NORFOLK SQUARE
HYDE PARK CR
GLOUCESTER SQUARE
CAMBRIDGE SQUARE
HYDE PARK GARDENS
HYDE PARK GARDENS MEWS
BATHURST STREET
WESTBOURNE ST
BROOK ST
PRAED STREET
LONDON STREET
SOUTH WHARF ROAD
ST MICHAEL'S STREET
STAR STREET
SOUTHWICK STREET
SPRING STREET
CRAVEN ROAD
CRAVEN TERRACE
WESTBOURNE TERRACE
GLOUCESTER TERRACE
BISHOP'S BRIDGE ROAD
CLEVELAND SQUARE
CLEVELAND GARDENS
CLEVELAND TERRACE
LEINSTER GARDENS
LEINSTER TERRACE
PORCHESTER TERRACE
PORCHESTER GARDENS
QUEEN'S GARDENS
DEVONSHIRE TER
CHILWORTH STREET
CRAVEN HILL
CRAVEN HILL GARDENS
LANCASTER GATE
LANCASTER MEWS
LANCASTER TERRACE
LANCASTER GATE
INVERNESS TERRACE
QUEENSBOROUGH TERRACE
QUEENSWAY
Bayswater
Queensway
INVERNESS TERRACE
GLOUCESTER TERRACE
ORSETT TERRACE
PORCHESTER SQ
GLOUCESTER TERRACE
EASTBOURNE TERRACE
WESTBOURNE TERRACE
HARROW RD
A404
EASTBOUND
BOURNE TERR
RANELAGH BR
WESTBOURNE TERR
A
B
C
D
1
2
3
4
5
6

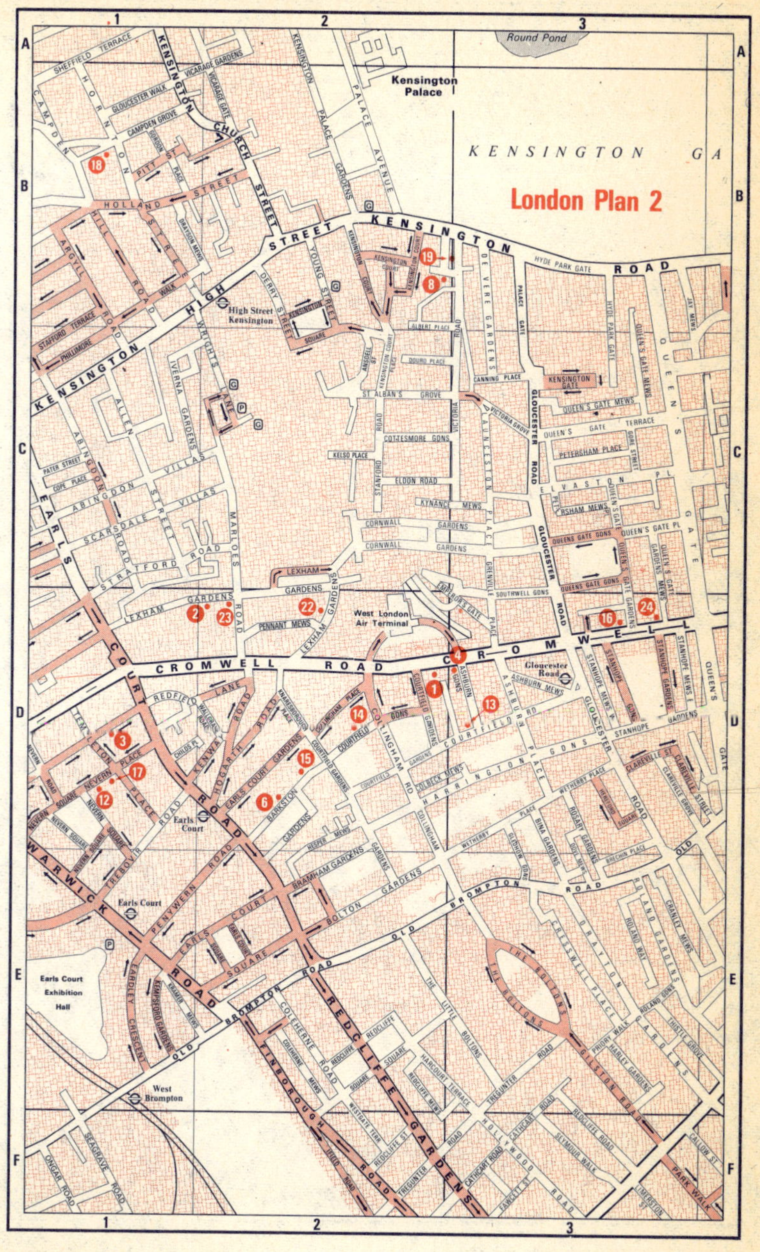

London Plan 2
Round Pond
Kensington Palace
KENSINGTON GA
KENSINGTON ROAD
Hyde Park Gate
High Street Kensington
Kensington Gate
Queen's Gate Mews
Queen's Gate Terrace
Petersham Place
Elvaston Pl
Harsham Mews
Queens Gate Gdns
Queen's Gate Pl
Sheffield Terrace
Vicarage Gardens
Campden Grove
Gloucester Walk
Pitt St Place
Holland Street
Stafford Terrace
Phillimore
Kensington Palace Gardens
Palace Avenue
Kensington Church Street
Young Street
Kensington Square
Derry Street
Kensington Court
Albert Place
De Vere Gardens
Canning Place
Douro Place
St Alban's Grove
Cottesmore Gdns
Kelso Place
Eldon Road
Kynance Mews
Stanford Road
Victoria Grove
Victoria Road
Gloucester Road
Cornwall Gardens
Cornwall Gardens
Grenville Place
Southwell Gdns
Lexham Gardens
Pennant Mews
Lexham Gardens
Marloes Road
Pater Street
Cope Place
Abingdon Villas
Scarsdale Villas
Stratford Road
Allen Street
Iverna Gardens
Abingdon Road
Earls Court Road
Kensington High Street
Argyll Road
Campden Hill Road
Hornton Street
Church Street
West London Air Terminal
Lexham Gardens
Emperor's Gate
CROMWELL ROAD
Gloucester Road
Ashburn Gardens
Ashburn Place
Ashburn Mews
Stanhope Gardens
Queen's Gate Gdns
Queen's Gate Mews
Stanhope Mews
Cromwell Road
Redfield Lane
Childs Place
Kenway Road
Hogarth Road
Earls Court Gardens
Courtfield Gardens
Courtfield Road
Collingham Place
Collingham Gardens
Collingham Road
Colbeck Mews
Harrington Road
Wetherby Place
Wetherby Gardens
Rosary Gardens
Stanhope Place
Clareville St
Clareville Street
Old Brompton Road
Nevern Place
Nevern Square
Trebovir Road
Penywern Road
Earls Court
Bramham Gardens
Bolton Gardens
Knaresborough
Barkston Gardens
Kempsford Gardens
Warwick Road
Earls Court Road
Earls Court Square
Philbeach Gardens
Earls Court Exhibition Hall
West Brompton
Old Brompton Road
Bolton Gardens
The Little Boltons
The Boltons
Gilston Road
Priory Walk
Roland Gardens
Hereford Square
Drayton Gardens
Rosary Gardens
Brechin Place
Bina Gardens
Old Brompton Road
Seagrave Road
Ongar Road
Lillie Road
Finborough Road
Redcliffe Gardens
Redcliffe Square
Redcliffe Road
Harcourt Terrace
Coleherne Road
Hollywood Road
Cathcart Road
Tregunter Road
Fawcett St
Seymour Walk
Limerston St
Park Walk
Callow St
Redcliffe Gardens
Ifield Road

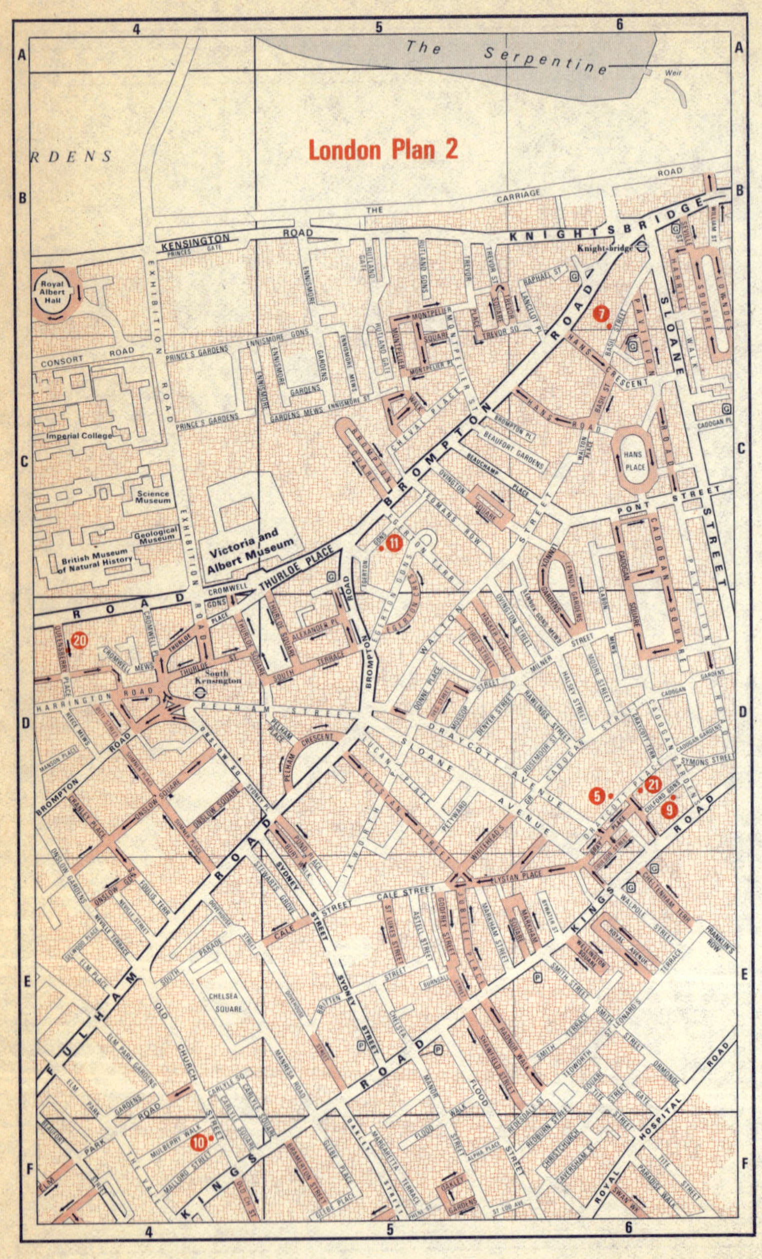
The Serpentine
Weir
London Plan 2
ROAD
CARRIAGE
THE
KENSINGTON
ROAD
KNIGHTSBRIDGE
Knight-bridge
PRINCES GATE
WILLIAM ST
Royal
Albert
Hall
EXHIBITION
MONTPELIER
RUTLAND GDNS
TREVOR ST
RAPHAEL ST
BASIL STREET
PAVILION
SLOANE
HARRIET WALK
SLOANE SQUARE
LOWND
PRINCE'S GARDENS
ENNISMORE GONS
RUTLAND GATE
MONTPELIER
MONTPELIER SQUARE
LANCELOT PL
TREVOR SQ
BASIL ST
ROAD
CONSORT
ROAD
ENNISMORE
GARDENS
MONTPELIER PL
HANS CRESCENT
CADOGAN PL
Imperial College
PRINCE'S GARDENS
GARDENS MEWS
ENNISMORE ST
BROMPTON PL
BEAUFORT GARDENS
HANS ROAD
HANS
PLACE
Science
Museum
RANELAGH PLACE
OVINGTON
BEAUCHAMP
PLACE
WALTON
PONT STREET
CADOGAN SQUARE
PAVILION
STREET
Geological
Museum
EXHIBITION ROAD
OVINGTON SQUARE
LENNOX GARDENS
British Museum
of Natural History
Victoria and
Albert Museum
EGERTON
GDNS
THURLOE PLACE
WALTON STREET
CADOGAN GARDENS
CROMWELL
GDNS
PLACE
CROMWELL
ROAD
ALEXANDER PL
CADOGAN GARDENS
ROAD
QUEENSBERRY
CROMWELL MEWS
THURLOE
SOUTH
TERRACE
MILNER STREET
HALSEY STREET
SYMONS STREET
ROAD
South
Kensington
HARRINGTON ROAD
PELHAM STREET
DRAYCOTT AVENUE
MANSION PLACE
REECE MEWS
PELHAM CRESCENT
SLOANE
AVENUE
CADOGAN
ONSLOW SQUARE
LUCAN PLACE
DRAYCOTT PLACE
BROMPTON
PELHAM
PELHAM PLACE
ONSLOW SQUARE
CADOGAN
BRADFORD
BLACKLANDS
CALE STREET
KINGS
ROAD
ONSLOW GARDENS
ELM PLACE
SOUTH PARADE
SYDNEY STREET
CALE
STREET
ST LUKES STREET
FLOOD STREET
WALPOLE STREET
ROYAL AVENUE
SMITH STREET
FRANKLIN'S ROW
CHELSEA
SQUARE
SYDNEY STREET
BRITTEN STREET
OAKLEY STREET
HOSPITAL ROAD
FULHAM
ELM PARK GARDENS
PARK
ROAD
CHURCH STREET
MULBERRY WALK
MALLORD STREET
KINGS
ROAD
GLEBE PLACE
OAKLEY STREET
ROYAL
SWAN WK
CARLYLE

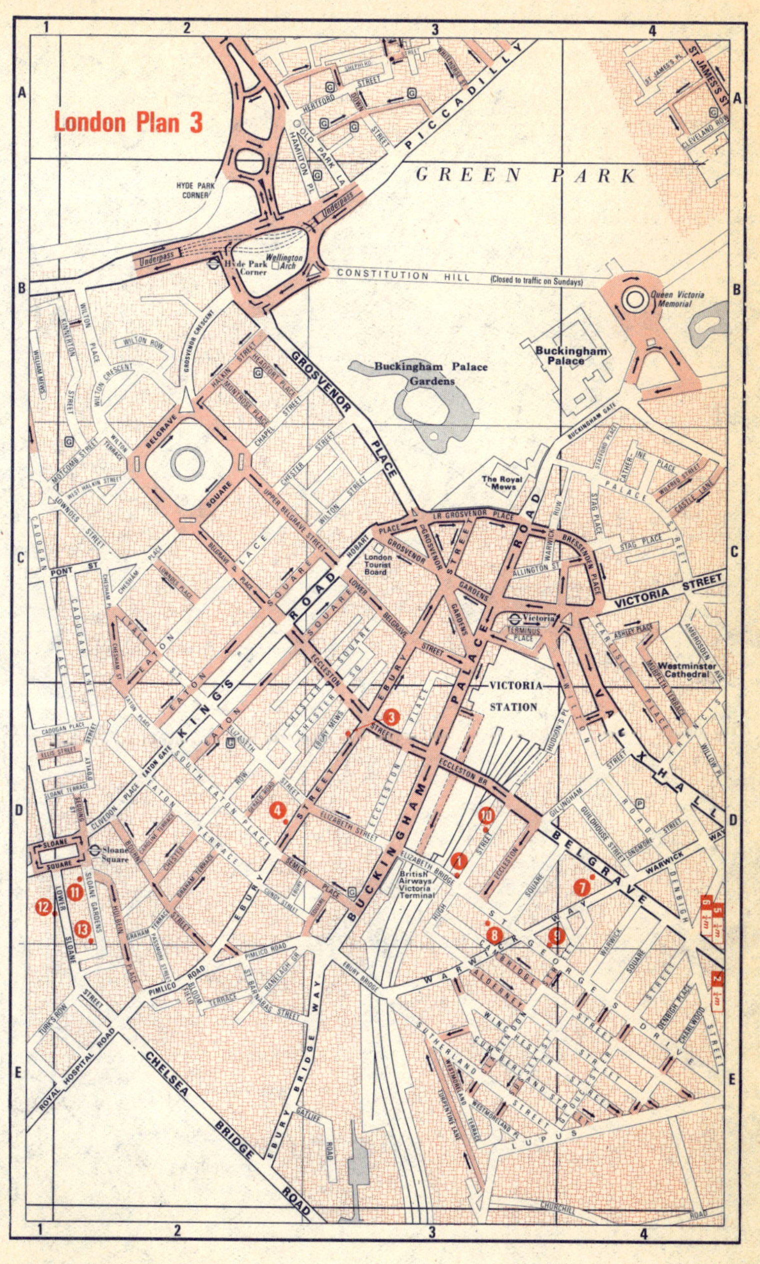

London Plan 3
PICCADILLY
GREEN PARK
HYDE PARK CORNER
Underpass
Hyde Park Corner
Wellington Arch
CONSTITUTION HILL (Closed to traffic on Sundays)
Queen Victoria Memorial
Buckingham Palace
Buckingham Palace Gardens
The Royal Mews
GROSVENOR PLACE
BELGRAVE SQUARE
VICTORIA STREET
London Tourist Board
LR GROSVENOR PLACE
VICTORIA STATION
Victoria TERMINUS PLACE
Westminster Cathedral
KING'S ROAD
PONT ST
VAUXHALL
SLOANE SQUARE
Sloane Square
British Airways Victoria Terminal
BELGRAVE WAY
CHELSEA BRIDGE ROAD
WARWICK WAY
PIMLICO ROAD
EBURY BRIDGE ROAD
LUPUS STREET
½ km
¼ km
¼ m

London Postal Districts and ways in & out of London

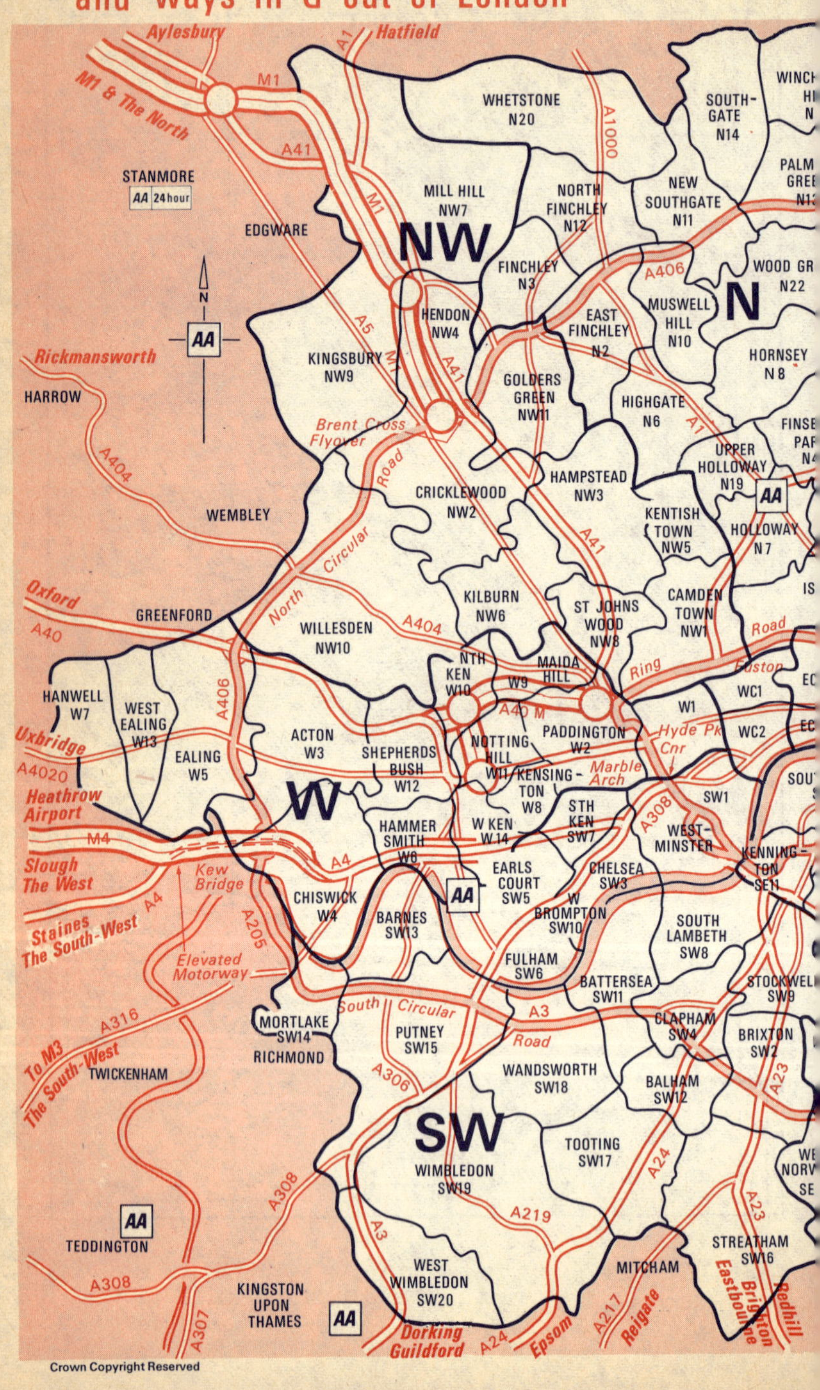

Crown Copyright Reserved

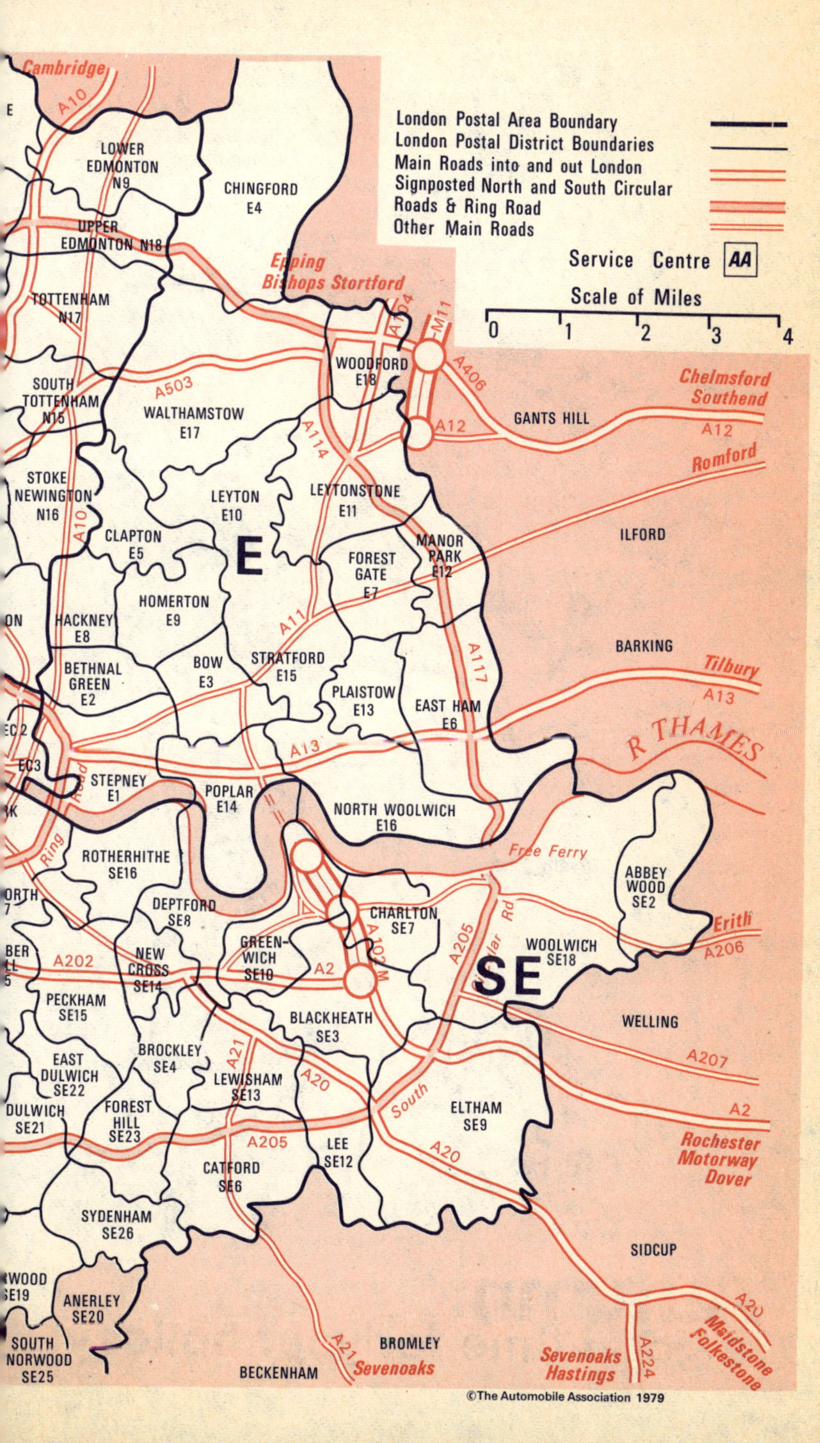

London Postal Area Boundary
London Postal District Boundaries
Main Roads into and out London
Signposted North and South Circular
Roads & Ring Road
Other Main Roads
Service Centre AA
Scale of Miles
0 1 2 3 4
Cambridge
A10
LOWER EDMONTON N9
CHINGFORD E4
UPPER EDMONTON N18
TOTTENHAM N17
Epping
Bishops Stortford
A104
M11
WOODFORD E18
A406
Chelmsford
Southend
SOUTH TOTTENHAM N15
A503
WALTHAMSTOW E17
GANTS HILL
A12
A12
Romford
A114
STOKE NEWINGTON N16
A10
CLAPTON E5
LEYTON E10
LEYTONSTONE E11
E
ILFORD
FOREST GATE E7
MANOR PARK E12
HACKNEY E8
HOMERTON E9
BARKING
BETHNAL GREEN E2
BOW E3
STRATFORD E15
A11
A117
Tilbury
A13
PLAISTOW E13
EAST HAM E6
EC2
A13
R THAMES
EC3
STEPNEY E1
POPLAR E14
NORTH WOOLWICH E16
Ring Road
ROTHERHITHE SE16
Free Ferry
ABBEY WOOD SE2
DEPTFORD SE8
CHARLTON SE7
WOOLWICH SE18
Erith
A206
A202
NEW CROSS SE14
GREEN-WICH SE10
A2
A102M
A205
SE
PECKHAM SE15
BLACKHEATH SE3
WELLING
EAST DULWICH SE22
BROCKLEY SE4
A21
LEWISHAM SE13
A20
A207
DULWICH SE21
FOREST HILL SE23
South
ELTHAM SE9
A2
A205
LEE SE12
A20
Rochester
Motorway
Dover
CATFORD SE6
SYDENHAM SE26
SIDCUP
WOOD SE19
ANERLEY SE20
A20
Maidstone
Folkestone
SOUTH NORWOOD SE25
A21
BROMLEY
Sevenoaks
BECKENHAM
Sevenoaks
Hastings
A224
©The Automobile Association 1979

Season of mists and mellow fruitfulness

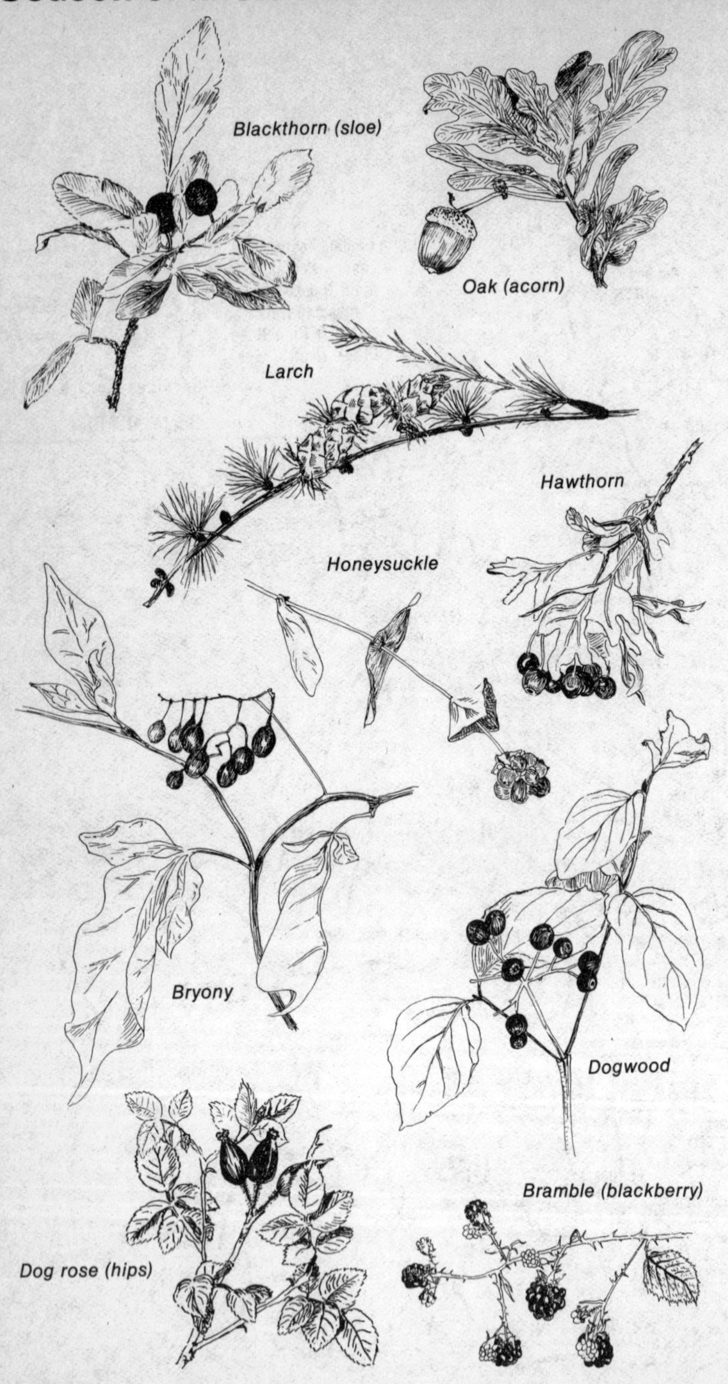

Autumn
a good time for your holiday

Peace and seclusion go hand in hand with comfort and friendliness at Under Rock, but the house is not isolated. Even without a car the whole of the Isle of Wight is within reach by bus (about 10 minutes' walk away), coach (from Ventnor) and train (from Shanklin). Yet many of Denis and Mollie Kelleway's guests don't stray far from the house and garden.

Bonchurch village is tucked between St Boniface Down and the sea; the hills shelter it from the west, north, and north-east, and this corner of the island has one of the best sunshine records in Britain. It is therefore an ideal place for a holiday, especially in the spring or autumn.

Denis and Mollie bought Under Rock in 1967, after 14 years running a guesthouse in nearby Shanklin. The house dates from the end of the 18th century and has the elegance associated with that period combined with architectural inventiveness. Built against the rocky hillside, the house is angled to catch all the daylight possible. The bedrooms overlook the delightful gardens, created by Denis over the past 12 years; quiet lawns, rock gardens, shrubs and trees (including palms, camellias,

Denis and Mollie Kelleway

azaleas and other tender subjects which flourish in the sub-tropical climate) cover upwards of an acre of ground; a tree-lined drive leads to Shore Road which descends gently to the promenade just a short walk away.

This area has always been beloved of artists and writers so it comes as no surprise that Under Rock was once the home of a poet, Edmund Peel (whose work is not generally remembered now but was popular with his contemporaries) and his brother Sir Laurence Peel; they were nephews of Sir Robert Peel, one-time Home Secretary, after whom 'Peelers' or 'Bobbies' were named. Several writers are regular guests now, finding there the quiet comfort in which their blossoming ideas can come to fruition.

What does Under Rock offer for the average holiday-maker? To start with a very friendly, but not garrulous, welcome which makes one feel immediately at home, and enjoyable food. (Molly and Denis both like cooking but Mollie is in charge of the kitchen.) Bedrooms are comfortably furnished, with plenty of storage space and cosy beds. There is not the clinical perfection that one finds in some newly-equipped places, but sanitary arrangements meet the AA's stringent standards. The comfortable lounge overlooks the garden and although the dining room, with its windows onto the rocky hillside and its dark wood furniture, may seem dim after the sun-filled rooms on the other side of the house, it is pleasantly cool on a hot day and quite romantic when candlelit for dinner on the darker evenings. Amongst attractive pictures throughout the house are a number of tapestries (worked by Denis) and two pictures of the house executed by guests — one in oils, the other entirely in coloured sands from Alum Bay.

The sheltered terrace of Under Rock

The pleasure which the Kelleways derive from looking after their guests is reflected in the whole atmosphere of Under Rock. They do not wish to develop their business to the stage where they can no longer care personally for their guests; neither do they want to spoil the character of the house by extensions or radical alterations internally. They carefully pace themselves and their resources so as to offer the same good service and relaxed atmosphere at the end of the season as at the beginning. Both born and bred in the Isle of Wight, they are knowledgeable about the less-frequented parts of the island, and are always ready to advise and inform guests about places worth visiting, entertainments available, and sports facilities in the vicinity including horse-riding or pony-trekking on the downs.

Under Rock is particularly suitable for those content with peaceful, relaxed comfort, and to preserve its calm orderliness the Kelleways find it best not to take small children or pets. But it is not the sort of house where one feels constrained to talk in whispers or to sit on the edge of one's chair. Denis puts the shyest guests at ease without being brash or obtrusive.

Under Rock will be remembered for the beauty of its gardens and the flower arrangements and plants which adorn the house, for its quiet charm and good food, and the unruffled good humour of its owners. With twenty-six years' experience, Denis and Mollie Kelleway have proved that they can stay the course and it is with great pleasure that we choose their lovely home as Guesthouse of the Year.

The Old Rectory, Nettlecombe, Williton, Taunton, Somerset

The Old Rectory, Nettlecombe

Staying at The Old Rectory is like visiting a gracious, tastefully-furnished, home.

The house, on a bank well above the level of B3188 about a mile north-west of Monksilver, was built in 1901 for a relative of the family who own nearby Nettlecombe Court, and is designed somewhat in the style of the older residence, with massive stone walls, mullioned windows, and interestingly-varied roof angles. It became a rectory when a descendant married the incumbent of the 13th-century Nettlecombe Church but later reverted to private ownership.

It had been used as a guesthouse for a while before it was purchased, in 1975, by Jim Price-Jones, an engineer who had been transferred to the area. He and his wife bought The Old Rectory as a home, redecorating it in pleasantly light colours and furnishing it with treasures collected over a number of years. They were rather taken by surprise when tourists who knew the house before it changed hands came to the door asking for accommodation. This happened so often that eventually they asked themselves 'why not?' Since then the business has grown of its own volition.

One look at the visitors' book shows how The Old Rectory's fame has spread. Australia, New Zealand, Canada, the United States, Germany, Switzerland — all are well represented. And when these visitors go home they tell their friends about the

Jim and Eileen Price-Jones

beautiful house with its antiques, objects d'art, and paintings, and the friendly welcome they received from Jim and Eileen Price-Jones.

Well-appointed bedrooms and nicely-presented meals are a pre-requisite of a recommended guesthouse; but in these respects The Old Rectory offers that little extra, too. Eileen, who is an expert cook and once owned a restaurant, uses locally-produced meat and vegetables as far as possible. Meals are imaginative, visually artistic, and appetising. And the bedrooms? A box of boudoir tissues on the vanity unit, a single rose on the dressing table, these are the little things which make one feel like an honoured guest.

Of course, The Old Rectory is not the place for a jolly family holiday. But if you are looking for quietly helpful service, beautiful surroundings, enjoyable food, and peace, in a good touring area near to the Somerset and North Devon coasts and Exmoor, with plenty of waymarked walking country nearby too, you will like The Old Rectory.

WINNER, ENGLISH MIDLANDS

Broad Marston Manor, Broad Marston, Pebworth, Herefs & Worcs

Broad Marston Manor

We felt Broad Marston Manor had to be included amongst our finalists although breakfast is the only meal provided, as it is a pleasant place in which to stay and the house and grounds are of particular interest. It is a medieval manor, dating back to the 12th-century, built of honey-coloured Cotswold stone with mullioned windows and a wealth of exposed timbers inside.

For 400 years it belonged to the Bushell family until, in the reign of Henry VIII, it changed hands. Shakespeare was a frequent visitor for a time, his sister-in-law having married into the family which then occupied the house. In 1797 it was purchased by William Bonner Shekell and it stayed in his family until 1922 when it was sold to an Irishman, Horace Rochfort. The last-named ran it as a farm and his son, Alexander, who now owns the property, continued in his father's footsteps until a disability forced him to give up most of his farming activities. Alex and his wife, Emily, then turned their attention to catering for visitors, had modern sanitation installed, and furnished the seven letting rooms comfortably and attractively.

Broad Marston stables

Many of the pieces with which the house is furnished are family heirlooms, a carved court-cupboard being of particular interest, and there is a huge open hearth which the Rochforts discovered after removing four other fireplaces which had been installed within the original stone structure. In spite of its many beams — records show that some were installed during the reign of James I at the beginning of the 17th century — the rooms are high-ceilinged.

Outside, the moat which surrounded the house has been filled in as modern drainage schemes had interfered with the natural water supply. Now sweeping lawns and beds bright with flowers make a perfect foil for the building. The outbuildings are worth looking at, too. The stable block has an air of tranquillity not to be found in modern buildings, while the ancient dovecote with its row upon row of nesting boxes formed from stone shingles is a fascinating rarity.

The great attraction of the area is, of course, Stratford-upon-Avon, but this is delightful countryside in its own right and riding, fishing, boating and golf can all be found in the near vicinity. For those who like formal entertainment there are theatres at Stratford and Birmingham, while special events take place frequently at Sudeley Castle in Winchcombe. The delightful villages of the Cotswolds lie to the south, the fertile Vale of Evesham to the west, and Stately Homes within easy reach include Blenheim Palace, Compton Wynyates and Ragley Hall.

Full of character, with an aura of past romance and surroundings of present beauty, Broad Marston Manor offers visitors an experience as well as a comfortable sojourn.

WINNER, NORTHERN ENGLAND

Prospect Hill Hotel, Kirkoswald, nr Penrith, Cumbria

A recent photograph of Prospect Hill Hotel

If hard work results in achievement, Isa and John Henderson will make a go of their enterprise. They were both in television — he a designer, she a production assistant — and had successfully tackled two conversions for private occupation when they decided to look for a building which might be transformed into a hotel. Isa comes from nearby Kirkby Thore and they both worked at Border Television in Carlisle, so the beautiful Eden Valley was a natural choice for their project. They were lucky to find Prospect Hill — an 18th-century farmhouse and outbuildings on the Staffield Hall Estate about 1 mile north of Kirkoswald on the Armathwaite road. It had previously been occupied by tenant farmers but they were able to buy the freehold of the buildings and four acres of land.

They then set about renovating and modernising the house, converting the byre to a bar, and the barn to a function room with bedrooms over. Sensibly, they consulted with planning, building, and fire officers so that they could incorporate all these authorities' requirements into their plans.

It was three years before they could open to the public and they are continuing to develop and improve the building and its surroundings as they go along. John went on working in television for a while, but has now joined Isa in running the business. He had long been an avid collector of bygones, particularly old farm implements (tractor seats make surprisingly comfortable bar stools!) and of antique furniture. By the time the hotel had

opened he had collected brass bedsteads for all seven bed-rooms. They are fitted to modern bases and are both comfort-able and attractive. The dining room – where meals are served to non-residents as well as people staying overnight – contains antique chairs and tables, and the small residents' lounge, formerly the farm kitchen, is furnished with leather-upholstered armchairs and chesterfield.

Because it has a restaurant, Prospect Hill Hotel is able to offer a wider choice of dishes than the other guesthouses visited, and some flexibility in meal times. Much of the food is delightfully different – a paté of apple, mushroom and cognac made a light and delicious starter, while a syllabub was out of this world. Service, by pleasant local girls, is quick and efficient. John, who looks after the bar in the evening, is a mine of information; he has prepared a booklet describing walks in the immediate area and has also written a history of the locality.

The Hendersons have some ambitious plans and Prospect Hill may not stay in the 'guesthouse' category much longer. While it does, it offers extremely good value for money in a characterful building situated in a delightful part of the country within easy reach of Lakeland, Hadrian's Wall, the coast, the northern Pennines and the Border Country.

Isa Henderson

WINNER, WALES
Guidfa House, Cross Gates, nr Llandrindod Wells, Powys

Guidfa House, Cross Gates

Geraldine MacKenzie runs Guidfa House with the help of her mother and an assortment of children, while husband Grant looks after his travel agency across the border in England. That she enjoys the challenge is obvious from her energy and cheerfulness. She taught domestic science for five years so perhaps it is not so surprising that the house is run efficiently, the food is good, and visitors are made to feel really at home, even to being cheered by an open fire on a June evening which was not really cold enough to make heating necessary.

Guidfa House is situated conveniently, though perhaps not ideally, by a roundabout at the junction of the A44 and the A483, three miles north of Llandrindod Wells. Traffic is audible from the house but quietens down at night and would not worry any but the most noise-conscious people. The house was built about 1830 in Colonial style, well-proportioned and with a canopied verandah on two sides. It is approached from the road via neat and attractive gardens.

The large lounge is provided with plenty of comfortable chairs and, sensibly, with tables suitable for laying out maps or playing games. A large map of the area, mounted on board, is kept handy, and Grant has worked out some tours and walks centred on Cross Gates. These are described in a sheaf of papers available on a side table which also holds quite a good selection of magazines and books. The bedrooms, two of which have private shower and wc, concentrate on comfort.

Geraldine MacKenzie

There's no doubt that Geraldine is a good cook; home-made mushroom soup was full of flavour, and rhubarb tart served with cream drew praise from all the guests.

Externally the house could do with some refurbishing; the Hendersons know this but haven't quite made up their minds what to do about the metal canopy, sections of which had been removed by a previous occupant to let more light into the downstairs rooms. But don't let this put you off; the inside decorations and appointments are of a good standard and the house merits high marks for comfort. This is a happy place and staying in it is an enjoyable experience.

A list of regional winners and runners-up is given on page 7, and fuller details can be found in the gazetteer entries. Our introduction on page 5 explains how we chose our winner and comments on the things we liked — and a few we didn't like — about the guesthouses we visited.

WINNER, SCOTLAND

Moorside, Braemar Rd, Ballater, Grampian

Moorside, Ballater

Ian Hewitt was working for Tate & Lyle in Barbados when he met his wife, Ann, who had lived in that tropic island all her life. When he brought her home to England they both found city life intolerable and decided to start a guesthouse – the best way, they thought, to make a living in a quiet rural area. They liked Royal Deeside between Balmoral and Aberdeen and when they found Moorside it seemed ideal for their purpose.

The house was built as a manse about 90 years ago but was later turned into a private house. When the Hewitts bought it in 1976 it was badly in need of repair but offered scope for extension and modernisation. It is built of pink granite and is typically Scottish, uncompromisingly solid with bay windows on the ground floor and dormer windows in the steeply-pitched roof. A house to withstand the elements and keep its occupants cosily safe.

Ian and Ann set about their task in a radical way, equipping the house with modern sanitary fittings, laying good-quality carpet

Ian and Ann Hewitt

throughout, and providing practical modern furniture in all the rooms, as well as meeting the requirements of planning and fire authorities. Everything is sparklingly clean and bright, beds are warm and comfortable, and more-than-adequate drawer and wardrobe space is provided; in fact very few hotels, even the most expensive, keep to such a high standard.

The lounge, though comfortable, is barely large enough when the house is full. Ian and Ann are aware of this and plans have been approved for a new lounge to be built over the garage, when the present lounge can be devoted to television. They hope to extend the dining room, too, which is a little cramped though not uncomfortably so.

Food is served piping hot and is prepared from good fresh materials. No choice is offered at dinner but the breakfast menu caters for the ravenous as well as the diet-conscious (ie a good range between porridge followed by egg, bacon and sausage with lots of toast, butter and marmalade and a big pot of tea or coffee, to fruit juice and a boiled egg).

Ann supervises the housekeeping and acts as cook while Ian serves at table and is a correct and considerate host, willing to help when help is requested but not in any way pushing.

Anyone who looks for bright modernity and absolute cleanliness at very reasonable cost, in quiet surroundings yet within reach of the coast and tourist attractions, will find Moorside much to their liking.

THE PICTURE CHANGES

Imagination is needed to visualise some buildings as comfortable guesthouses or inns. We pick a courthouse, a railway station, a boathouse and a windmill, all of which now offer accommodation for guests and prove just what can be done by someone with the right sort of vision and the courage to put their ideas into practice.

Avon Causeway Hotel, Hurn, nr Christchurch, Dorset

For exactly a hundred years the Avon Causeway was used as a railway station. The line was disused from 1962 and seven years later Mr and Mrs Joseph Palmer bought the station buildings and converted them into an inn. Railway enthusiasts will like the bar, with its Pullman seats (complete with luggage racks) and other relics of the great days of steam. A complete Pullman coach, formerly used on the Kings Cross-Newcastle route, now stands beside the platform, as can be seen in the colour photograph.

Hennlys Private Hotel, Betws-y-Coed, Gwynedd

Pete and Joan Smart converted their premises from a former Court-house and Police Station.

Externally the building is not much changed, though attractive gardens have softened its outlines. Inside, the ten bedrooms include double rooms with names such as the Interrogation Room and the Judge's Chambers, and single rooms converted from cells – the Convicted Felon's Room is one. The Courtroom is now a lounge, and you can dine on an elevated platform where the judge used to sit.

This cell has been turned into a comfortable bedroom, much in demand by visitors.

Tea gardens make the rear of the building a pleasant place though the building is not much altered from its erstwhile forbidding aspect.

Fiddler's Yard, Woodbush Brae, Dunbar, E Lothian

Fiddler's Yard was not much more than a ruin in 1975 when Helen and Bob Reid took it over and rebuilt it into a comfortable guesthouse. Situated almost on the beach, this two-hundred-year-old building was originally a boat house,

Ye Olde Mill House, Redmile, Nottinghamshire

There was a windmill at Redmile from the 13th century. This, the last mill, was still in use in the 1920s but, alas, it exists no longer.

Sketches by Joan Fensome

The house where the miller and his family lived is some 250 years old, and has a peaceful country cottage atmosphere. Present owners, Murray and Annette Barton, have taken care to preserve its character while bringing its amenities up to present-day standards.

HOW TO USE THE GUIDE

The gazetteer
This forms the body of the book and is divided into three main sections – England, Wales and Scotland. The Channel Islands and Isle of Man follow England. Each section is split into two categories of establishments which are generally more modest in the way of facilities than the AA hotels classified by stars.

1 Guesthouses, small hotels and inns
2 Farmhouses

There is also a section on countryside facilities. Near the front of the book is a 16-page atlas showing the location of establishments.

Reading a map reference
In the gazetteer section of this guide, the main place name is given a two-figure map reference to key with the location atlas. However, in each of the Farmhouse sections and in the Picnic Sites sections, six-figure references have also been given. These can be used in conjunction with a larger scale Ordnance Survey map to pinpoint the exact position.

Example: Two-Figure Reference
Map 3ST76: This is the map reference for Bath in the county of Avon. Turn to Map 3 in the atlas, refer to the group of squares ST as indicated in the diagram opposite. Find sub-division 7 from *left* to *right* and sub-division 6 from *bottom* to *top*. While every effort has been made to ensure the correct gazetteering of establishments, in some cases the information received by us has been insufficient. In these instances the establishments have been marked at the nearest town..

Town Plans
A number of town plans have been included in the text to show the positions of establishments in some of the larger towns or cities. Included on these maps are the following: one-way streets, car parks, post offices, information centres, cathedrals, castles. As the gazetteer information is continually being updated, some of the establishments shown on the town plans may have been deleted from the text; conversely some more recent gazetteer entries do not appear on the relevant town plans. The mileages at road exits are calculated from the border of the plan. A list of town plan symbols appears on pages 4 and 5.

To find a guesthouse, farmhouse or inn
Look at the area you wish to visit in the atlas. *Towns with guesthouses or inns* are marked with a solid dot ●

Towns with guesthouses, farmhouses or inns are marked with a dot in an open circle ⊙
Towns with farmhouses only are marked with an open circle ○

Remember that farmhouses are listed under the nearest identifiable town or village and may in fact be a few miles away. See also paragraph above, 'Reading a map reference'.

Gazetteer notes
A key to abbreviations and symbols in gazetteer entries and on the town plans appears on pages 4 and 5.

Accommodation for under £6
Not all guesthouses or inns shown in this publication provide bed and breakfast accommodation for under £6 per person per night. Where they *do*, they carry the appropriate symbol (⋈). This applies to 1980 prices only.

Annexes
The number of bedrooms in an annexe is indicated by the abbreviation A followed by the number, both bracketed (*eg* A6). It should be noted that annexes often used only during the season may lack some of the facilities available in the main building. It is advisable, therefore, that the exact nature of the accommodation and the charges should be checked before reservations are confirmed.

Bathrooms
New for 1980, the gazetteer entry will indicate the number of rooms with bath or shower and wcs where applicable.

Central Heating
Some establishments which are noted as having central heating (▥) may not have it operating — especially in bedrooms — during cold weather outside the normally recognised winter months. Central heating is indicated only where establishments have **full** central heating.

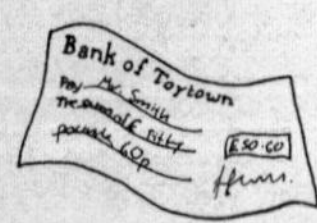

Cheques
Most establishments will accept cheques in payment of accounts only if notice is given and some form of identification (preferably a banker's card) is produced.

Children
Guesthouses and farmhouses usually accommodate children of all ages unless a minimum age is given (*eg* nc8 — no children under eight), but it does not necessarily follow that they are able to provide special facilities. If you have very young children, enquire about the arrangements that can be made and the provision of any special amenities such as cots and high-chairs. In the guesthouse gazetteer, establishments which do have special facilities for children are indicated by the

symbol . All the following amenities will be found at these establishments: baby-sitting service or baby intercom system, playroom or playground, laundry facilities, drying and ironing facilities, cots and high-chairs, and special meals. Before reserving accommodation it is advisable to ask about facilities and whether reductions are made for children.

Complaints
If you have any complaints you should inform the proprietor immediately so that the trouble can be dealt with promptly. If a personal approach fails, inform the AA using the report form at the back of the book, as soon as possible – within at least a week – so that we can make an investigation. State whether or not you want your name disclosed to the proprietor, and whether you took up the complaint with him/her at the time.

County Names & Postal Addresses
After the place name, the name of the administrative county is shown; it is not necessarily the correct postal address. For places in Scotland the region is given followed by the old county name in *italics*.

Deposits
Some establishments require a deposit before accepting a booking.

Disabled Persons
If the wheelchair symbol & is shown in an establishment's entry it means that the disabled can be accommodated. This information has been supplied to the AA by the proprietor but it is advisable to check before making reservations. Details more relevant to disabled persons may be obtained from *The AA Guide for the Disabled* available from AA offices, free to members. Members with any form of disability should notify proprietors so that appropriate arrangements can be made to minimise difficulties, particularly in the event of an emergency.

Dogs
Establishments which do not accept dogs are indicated by the symbol. There may be restrictions on dogs of certain sizes or the rooms into which they may be taken. The conditions under which pets are accepted should be confirmed with the management when making reservations.

Farms
Incorporated into each gazetteer entry is the six-figure reference number to be used in conjunction with Ordnance Survey maps. This number follows the establishment name and is in *italics*.

The acreage of each establishment is shown in the body of each entry (*eg* 55 acres) followed by the type of farming

that predominates in the relevant farm (*eg* dairy, arable etc).

Fire Precautions

So far as can be ascertained at the time of going to press, every unit of accommodation listed in this publication, provided it is subject to the requirements of the Act, has applied for and not been refused a fire certificate. The Fire Precautions Act 1971 does not apply to the Channel Islands or the Isle of Man, both of which exercise their own rules with regard to fire precautions for accommodation units.

Gazetteer Entry

Establishment names shown in *italics* indicate that particulars have not been comfirmed by the management in time for this 1980 edition.

Licences

An indication is given in each entry where a guesthouse or farmhouse is licensed. Most places in the guesthouse and farmhouse category do not hold a full licence but all inns do. Licensed premises are not obliged to remain open throughout the permitted hours and may do so only when they expect reasonable trade. Note that at establishments which have registered clubs, club membership cannot take place — nor can a drink be bought — until 48 hours after joining. For further information refer to leaflet HH20 'The Law about Licensing Hours and Children/Young Persons on Licensed Premises' available from AA offices.

London

It is common knowledge that in London prices tend to be higher than in the provinces. For hotels, we have tried to select establishments where the accommodation is inexpensive and where a bed and breakfast is normally provided. We have also included a few which provide a full meal service and whose charges are consequently higher.

Meals

In some parts of the country, high tea is generally served in guesthouses although dinner is often also available on request. The latest time that the evening meal can be **ordered** is indicated in the text. On Sundays, many establishments serve their main meal at midday and will charge accordingly. This may mean that only cold supper is available in the evening.

Prices

Prices are liable to fluctuation and it is advisable to check when you book. Also, make sure you know exactly what facilities are being offered when you are verifying charges, because there are variations in what an establishment may provide within inclusive terms. Weekly terms, for

instance, vary from full board to bed and breakfast only.
This is shown in the text by the symbol Ł (no lunches) and
Ṁ (no main meals). Some establishments provide packed
lunches, snacks or salads at extra cost — inns providing
snacks are identified in entries by the abbreviation sn.
All prices quoted normally include VAT and service, where
applicable.

*1979 Prices
When proprietors have been unable to furnish us with
1980 prices, those for 1979 are quoted, prefixed by an
asterisk (*).

Requests for Information
If you are writing to an establishment requesting
information it is important to enclose a stamped,
addressed envelope. Please quote this publication in any
enquiry.

Reservations
Please book as early as you possibly can or you may be
disappointed. If you are delayed or have to change your
plans, let the proprietor know at once. You may be held
legally responsible if the room you booked cannot be
re-let. Some establishments, especially those in short-
season holiday centres, do not accept bookings for bed
and breakfast only. Additionally, some guesthouses —
particularly in seaside resorts — do not take bookings from
midweek to midweek, and a number will not accept
period bookings other than at full board rate, *ie* not at
nightly bed and breakfast rate plus individual meals.

It is regretted that the AA cannot undertake to make any
reservations.

Restricted Service
Some establishments operate a restricted service during
the less busy months. This is indicated by the prefix rs.
For example, rs Nov–Mar indicates that a restricted
service is operated from November to March. This may be
a reduction in meals served and/or accommodation
available.

Seasonal Openings
Unless otherwise stated sites are open all year. Where
dates are shown these are inclusive; eg *Apr–Oct*
indicates that the establishment is open from the
beginning of April to the end of October.

Telephone Numbers
In some areas telephone numbers are likely to be
changed by the Post Office during the currency of this
publication. If any difficulty is found when making a
reservation it is advisable to check with the operator. It is
most important that the following note on telephone
numbers is read and understood. Much confusion has
arisen in the past by members not reading it and

consequently misinterpreting numbers in the gazetteer
entries.

**IMPORTANT – Unless otherwise stated, the
exchange is that of the place under which the entry
is listed.**

For instance, if an establishment is listed under Whitby
and the telephone number is given as (☎12345), the
exchange to dial is Whitby. In a case such as the Traddock
Guest House, however, which is listed under Austwick,
the number is given as (☎Clapham 224), and the
exchange to dial is Clapham. For details of dialling codes,
see Post Office *Telephone Dialling Codes*.

Television
If the gazetteer entry shows 'CTV' or 'TV', either colour or
monochrome television is available in lounge.

VAT and Service Charge
In the United Kingdom and the Isle of Man, Value Added
Tax is payable on both basic prices and any service. The
symbol S% in the gazetteer indicates that the inclusive
prices shown reflect any separate accounting for service
made by the establishment. VAT does not apply in the
Channel Islands. With this exception, prices quoted in the
gazetteer are inclusive of VAT at 8% (see note on page 1).

Explanation of a gazetteer entry

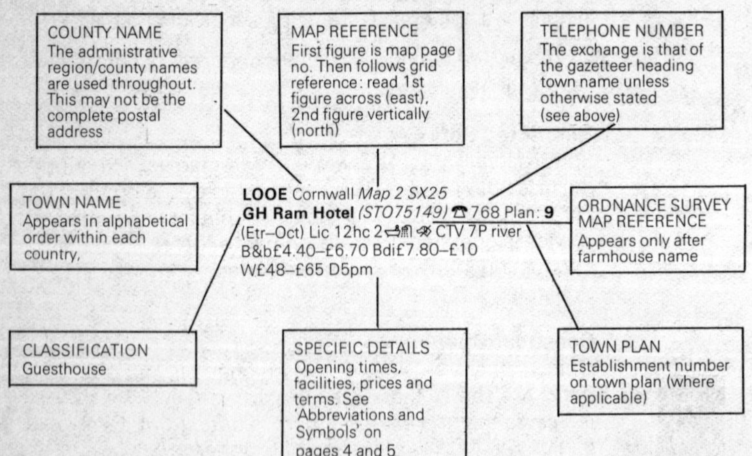

ACASTER MALBIS N Yorks *Map 8 SE54*
⊢⊣**INN Ship** ☎ York 703888 Closed Xmas
Lic 5hc 27P 🍴 river S% B&b£4.75–£7.50
Bdi£9.25–£12 Bar lunch 45p–£1.50
D9.30pm£3.50–£5.25

ACLE Norfolk *Map 9 TG41*
GH *Fishley Manor Hotel & Country Club*
South Walsham Rd ☎ Great Yarmouth
750377 Lic 12hc nc6 CTV 40P D9.30pm

ALBRIGHTON *(Nr Wolverhampton)* Salop
Map 7 SJ80
INN *Crown Hotel* High St ☎2204 Lic
3hc ⊗ 80P 🍴

ALDEBURGH Suffolk *Map 5 TM45*
GH *Granville Hotel* 243–247 High St
☎2708 Closed 22–30Dec Lic 9hc ⊗ CTV
1🏠 🍴 D8.30pm

ALDERSHOT Hants *Map 4 SU85*
GH Glencoe Hotel 4 Eggars Hill ☎20801
11hc ⊗ nc7 CTV 12P 🍴 S% B&b fr£7
Bdi fr£10 D10am

ALMONDSBURY Avon *Map 3 ST58*
GH *Hill Farm* 6 Gloucester Rd ☎613206
11rm 10hc ⊗ ♨ CTV 10P D6.30pm

ALNMOUTH Northumb *Map 12 NU21*
GH Marine House Private Hotel
1 Marine Dr ☎349 Lic 8hc ♨ CTV 10P 🍴
sea S% Bdi£7–£8 W£66–£78 ⌡

ALNWICK Northumb *Map 12 NU11*
During the currency of this publication
Alnwick telephone numbers are liable to
change.
⊢⊣**GH Eradell** 1 Beaconsfield Ter, Upper
Hawick St ☎2619 8hc nc5 TV 8P 🍴 S%
B&b£4.86–£5.94 Bdi£7.83–£8.91
W£52.92–£54.81 ⌡ D6pm
⊢⊣**GH Hope Rise** The Dunterns ☎2930
Lic 7hc ⊗ CTV 14P 🍴 S% B&b£5.50–£6.50
Bdi£8–£10 W£52–£65 ⌡ D4pm
⊢⊣**GH Surrey House** Prudhoe St ☎2265
Closed Xmas to New Year 5hc ⊗ nc3 CTV
5P 🍴 B&b£5–£5.50 Bdi£7.50–£8.50
W£51–£58 ⌡ D5.30pm

ALTRINCHAM Gt Manchester
Map 7 SJ78
GH *Bollin Hotel* 58 Manchester Rd
☎061-928 2390 10hc CTV 12P

AMBLESIDE Cumbria *Map 7 NY30*
GH *Compston House* ☎2305 Closed
Nov & Xmas 9hc ⊗ nc5 CTV D5pm

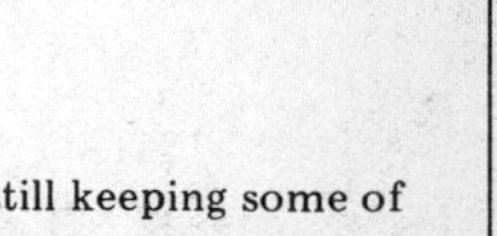

⊢⊣**GH Gables** Church Walk (Compston Rd) ☎3272 Mar–end Oct Lic 14hc CTV 7P B&b£5.25–£6 Bdi£7.50–£8.50 W£52.50–£59.50 Ł D7pm

⊢⊣**GH Hillsdale Private Hotel** Church St ☎3174 Lic 7hc ⊗ CTV 卌 S% B&b£5–£6 Bdi£8–£9 W£54.75–£60 Ł D6pm

⊢⊣**GH Horseshoe** Rothay Rd ☎2000 Mar–Dec 6hc CTV 10P 卌 S% B&bfr£5.50 Wfr£36.75 M

⊢⊣**GH Norwood House** Church St ☎3349 8hc ⊗ CTV S% B&b£4.50–£5 Bdi£6.75–£7.25 W£45–£49 Ł D7pm

⊢⊣**GH Oaklands Country House Hotel** Millans Pk ☎2170 Mar–Nov Lic 6hc ⊗ CTV 8P 卌 B&b£5.94–£6.53 Bdi£10.09–£10.69 W£64.15–£70.10 Ł D5pm

GH Riverside Hotel Gilbert Scar ☎2395 Mar–Nov Lic 10hc 2🛁 ⊗ nc10 CTV 10P 卌 river S% Bdi£11–£12.75 W£75–£85 Ł D7pm

GH Rothay Garth Hotel Rothay Rd ☎2217 15hc 1🛁 CTV 13P 卌 S% B&b£7.56–£9.18 Bdi£9.99–£12.15 W£62.37–£77.49 Ł D6pm

GH *Smallwood Hotel* Compton Rd ☎2330 Mar–Nov 12hc CTV 10P D6pm

ANCHOR Salop *Map 7 SO18*
INN Anchor ☎ Kerry 250 Lic 6hc 4🛁 ⌂ CTV 50P 4🏠 卌 B&b£6–£7.50 sn L£3 alc D9.30pm £3.25alc

APPLEBY Cumbria *Map 12 NY62*
⊢⊣**GH Bongate House** ☎51245 7hc CTV 6P 2🏠 卌 S% B&b£4.50 Bdi£6 W£36 Ł D6pm

⊢⊣**GH Howgill House** ☎51574 6hc ⊗ CTV 6P S% B&bfr£4.50 D6pm

ARNSIDE Cumbria *Map 7 SD47*
GH Grosvenor Private Hotel The Promenade ☎761666 Mar–Oct Lic 13hc CTV 10P 卌 S% *B&b£4.80–£5.50 Bdi£7.50–£8.50 Wfr£50 Ł D5pm

ARRETON Isle of Wight *Map 4 SZ58*
GH Stickworth Hall ☎233 May–Sep Lic 25hc ⊗ nc5 CTV 40P *B&b£7.50–£8.50 W£65.50–£72.50 Ł D7pm

ARUNDEL W Sussex *Map 4 TQ00*
⊢⊣**GH Bridge House** 18 Queen St ☎882142 Closed Xmas wk 5hc CTV 卌 river S% B&b£4–£7 W£21–£40 M

ASHBURTON Devon *Map 3 SX76*
GH Tugela House 68–70 East St ☎52206 Lic 10hc nc7 CTV 3P 卌 S% B&b£6–£8 Bdi£10–£12 W£60–£72 Ł D6pm

ASHBY-DE-LA-ZOUCH Leics *Map 8 SK31*
GH Fernleigh 37 Tamworth Rd ☎4755 6hc CTV 8P 卌 S% B&b£9 Bdi£13 D6.30pm

ASHFORD Kent *Map 5 TR04*
GH Croft Hotel Canterbury Rd, Kennington ☎22140 Lic 15hc 1🛁 ⊗ CTV 24P 卌 B&b£8.50–£13.50 Bdi£11–£16 W only 30Oct–Mar D8pm

GH Downsview Hotel Willesborough Rd, Kennington ☎21953 Closed Xmas Lic

16hc 6⇨🛁 CTV 20P 🍴 B&b£8.22–£8.95
Wfr£40.45 📶 D9pm

ASHTON-UNDER-LYNE Gt Manchester
Map 7 SJ99
⊷**GH Lancaster Hotel** 17 Richmond St
☎061-330 1350 rs Sun (no meals) Lic
6hc 5⇨🛁 CTV 8P 🍴 B&bfr£5.50
D9.30pm

AUSTWICK N Yorks *Map 7 SD76*
GH Traddock ☎ Clapham (N Yorks) 224
Lic 11hc 4⇨🛁 nc5 CTV 12P 🍴 S%
B&b£7–£9 Bdi£11–£13 W£75–£79
Ⳑ D4.30pm

AYTON, GREAT N Yorks *Map 8 NZ51*
INN Royal Oak Hotel High Green ☎2361
Lic 5hc 1⇨🛁 CTV S% ✳B&b£8.55 Bdi£14
D9.15pm

BACTON Norfolk *Map 9 TG33*
GH Keswick Hotel Walcott Rd
☎ Walcott 468 Lic 6hc 3⇨🛁 ⊗ nc12
CTV 30P 🍴 sea S% B&b£8.25–£11.50
D10pm

BAKEWELL Derbys *Map 8 SK26*
GH Holmdale The Avenue ☎2427
Apr–Nov 8hc ⊗ nc8 TV 8P 🍴 S%
B&b£6–£7 Bdi£9–£10 W£48–£50 Ⳑ
D7pm

GH Poplars Ashford Ln, Monsal Head
☎ Great Longstone 475 Closed 3–30Jan
Lic 6hc 1⇨🛁 CTV 6P 🍴 B&b£7–£8
Bdi£10.50–£11.50 W£65–£72 Ⳑ
D7.15pm

BALDOCK Herts *Map 4 TL23*
GH Butterfield House Hitchin St

☎892701 Lic 11hc 8⇨🛁 ⊗ 12P 🍴
S% B&b£8.10 Bdi£12.10 D8.45

BAMPTON Oxon *Map 4 SP30*
GH Bampton House Bushey Row
☎ Bampton Castle 850135 Closed Xmas
Lic 6rm 2hc 3⇨🛁 CTV 15P S%
B&b£6.25–£8 Bdi£11.25–£13
W£74–£86 Ⳑ D7pm

BANBURY Oxon *Map 4 SP44*
GH Lismore 61 Oxford Rd ☎2105
Closed Xmas wk 8hc ⊗ CTV 4P 2🏠 🍴
S% B&b£7.50

⊷**GH Tredis** 15 Broughton Rd ☎4632
5hc CTV 🍴 S% B&b£5–£5.50

BANTHAM Devon *Map 3 SX64*
INN Sloop ☎ Thurlestone 489 Lic 6hc
1⇨🛁 nc14 30P 🚘 river & sea S%
✳B&b£6.75 Bar lunch 55p–£2.75&alc
D10pm£3.25&alc

BARNSTAPLE Devon *Map 2 SS53*
⊷**GH Cresta** Sticklepath Hill ☎4022
Closed Xmas 5hc (A1hc 1⇨🛁) ⊗ nc5
CTV 7P 🍴 S% B&b£4.50–£5.50
Bdi£7–£8.50 W£45.50–£56 Ⳑ D2pm

GH Northcliff 8 Rhododendron Av
(Off A39) ☎2524 9hc ⊗ CTV 9P 2🏠
D2pm

⊷**GH Yeo Dale Hotel** Pilton Bridge
☎2954 10hc CTV 5P B&b£5.50 Bdi£8.25
W£53 Ⳑ Dnoon

BARTON-ON-SEA Hants *Map 4 SZ29*
⊷**GH Barton Court Hotel** 31 Marine
Drive East ☎ New Milton 613030 Etr–Oct
Lic 12hc 2⇨🛁 ⊗ CTV 20P 🍴
B&b£5.50–£6.95 Bdi£8.50–£9.95
W£55.65–£61.95 D6.30pm

𝕿he 𝕮roft Hotel

**Kennington, Ashford, Kent
Tel: Ashford 22140 (0233)**

The Croft Hotel is approximately 2 miles
from Ashford town centre on the A28
Canterbury Road.
The hotel stands in an acre of garden
with large car parking area.
There is a pleasant dining room,
comfortable lounge with colour television
and a cosy bar with congenial company.
The bedrooms are comfortable with
spring interior mattresses and hot and
cold water.

DOWNSVIEW HOTEL

Ashford, Kent   Licensed

An ideal base for touring the 'Garden of England' and for
cross-Channel travellers.
Peacefully situated on the B2164 but with easy access to
the A20 and A28 — the Weald of Kent, Canterbury, and
the coast are all within easy reach.
Downsview stands in an acre of mature grounds, adjoining
orchards and has fine views across the Stour Valley to the
North Downs.

**Willesborough Road,
Kennington
Tel: Ashford 21953**

An ideal base for holidaymakers and businessmen

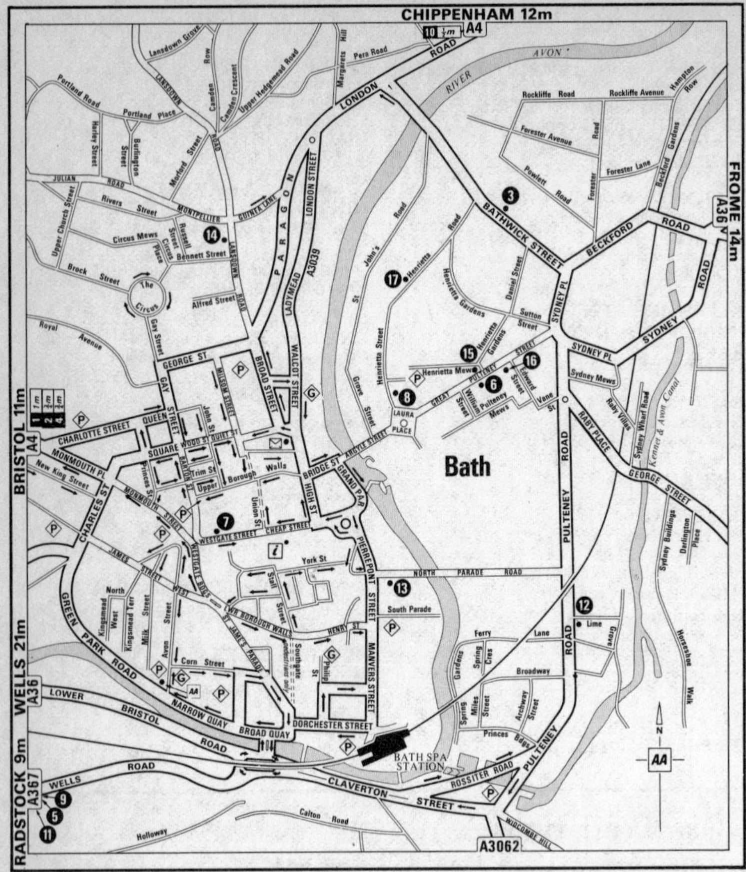

1 Apsley Garden House Hotel	**6** Edgar Hotel	**11** Kingsley House Private Hotel	**15** Richmond Hotel
2 Ashley Villa Hotel	**7** Edwardian Hotel *(Inn)*	**12** Lynwood	**16** St Monica's Hotel
3 Avon Hotel	**8** Georgian	**13** North Parade Hotel	**17** Villa Magdala Private Hotel
4 Dorset Villa	**9** Glenbeigh Hotel	**14** Oxford Private Hotel	
5 Eastfield House	**10** Grove Lodge		

GH Binley Hotel Beach Ave ☎ New Milton 610460 Mar–Oct rs Nov–Mar Lic 9hc CTV 9P ⑭ S% B&bf7.75–£9 Bdif11–£12 Wf72–£78.75 ⊾ D7pm

GH Dome Hotel Barton Court Av ☎ New Milton 616164 Lic 10hc 2⇨🖩 CTV 18P 1🏠 ⑭ sea S% ✳B&bf7.80–£8.40 Bdif10.70–£11.30 Wf48–£58 ⊾ D7.30pm

GH Old Coastguard Hotel 53 Marine Drive East ☎ New Milton 612987 Lic 8hc ⊗ nc12 CTV 7P sea S% B&bf6.48–£7.02 Bdif8.64–£9.72 Wf56.16–£64.80 ⊾ D7pm

BASINGSTOKE Hants see **Sherfield-on-Loddon**

BASLOW Derbys *Map 8 SK27* **INN Wheatsheaf Hotel** ☎2240 Mar–Nov Lic 4hc TV 80P

BASSENTHWAITE Cumbria *Map 11 NY23* **GH Bassenfell Manor Hotel** ☎ Bassenthwaite Lake 366 Mar–Dec Lic 19hc 6⇨🖩 ⊗ CTV 20P ⑭ lake

B&bf6.70–£7.50 Bdif11–£11.50 Wf80.50–£91 ⊾ D8.30pm

BATH Avon *Map 3 ST76* **See Plan** **GH Apsley Garden House Hotel** Newbridge Hill ☎21368 Plan:**1** Lic 9hc CTV 10P S% B&bf8–£8.50 Bdif12–£13 Wf75–£80.50 ⊾ D7pm

GH Ashley Villa Hotel 26 Newbridge Rd ☎21683 Plan:**2** Lic 18hc 6⇨🖩 ⋒ CTV 10P ⑭ ⟁ B&b fr£9 D9.30pm

GH Avon Hotel Bathwick St ☎22226 Plan:**3** Lic 15hc 7⇨🖩 18P 2🏠 ⑭ S% B&bf7.50–£12.50 Bdif14.20–£15.50 D10pm

⋈GH Dorset Villa 14 Newbridge Rd ☎25975 Plan:**4** Mar–Oct 6hc ⊗ nc12 CTV 6P ⑭ ⟁ S% B&bf5–£5.50

GH Eastfield House 57 Upper Oldfield Park ☎314990 Plan:**5** Mar–Nov rs Dec–Feb Lic 10hc 1⇨🖩 ⊗ CTV 6P ✳B&b fr£7.50

GH Edgar Hotel 64 Great Pulteney St ☎20619 Plan:**6** Lic 11hc 4⇨🖩 ⊗ CTV ⑭ S% B&bf7.50–£10 Bdif11–£13.50

GH Georgian 34 Henrietta St
☎24103 Plan:**8** 8hc CTV 2🏠 S%
✳B&b£5.50

GH Glenbeigh Hotel 1 Upper Oldfield
Park ☎26336 Plan:**9** Closed Xmas wk Lic
8hc CTV 10P 3🏠 🍴 B&b£5.50–£6.50
Bdi£9–£10 W£81 ⱡ D9am

GH *Grove Lodge* 11 Lambridge, London
Rd ☎310860 Plan:**10** Closed Xmas Lic
8hc ⌀ TV 🍴 D8.30pm

GH Kingsley House Private Hotel
53 Upper Oldfield Park ☎25749 Plan:**11**
Feb–Dec Lic 6hc 4⇨🍴 ⌀ nc 6P 🍴
B&b£8

GH Lynwood 6 Pulteney Gdns ☎26410
Plan:**12** Closed Xmas 6hc nc2 CTV
B&b£5.50–£6

GH North Parade Hotel North Pde
☎60007 Plan:**13** Feb–Nov Lic 17hc CTV
🍴 river S% B&bfr£7.50

GH Oxford Private Hotel 5 Oxford Row,
Lansdown Rd ☎314039 Plan:**14** 7hc ⌀
nc10 CTV S% B&b£6–£9

GH *Richmond Hotel* 11 Gt Pulteney St
☎25560 Plan:**15** Closed Xmas Lic 31hc
CTV 🍴 D10am

GH *St Monica's Hotel* Gt Pulteney St
☎62092 Plan:**16** Lic 23hc ⚘ CTV 2🏠 🍴
D7.50pm

GH Villa Magdala Private Hotel
Henrietta Rd ☎25836 Plan:**17** Closed
Xmas 8hc 6⇨🍴 ⌀ ⚘ 20P 3🏠 🍴 B&b£10

INN Edwardian Hotel 38 Westgate St
☎61642 Plan:**7** Closed Xmas Day
(evening) Lic 26hc 15⇨🍴 🍴 S% ✳B&b£10
W£70 sn L£2.90alc D11.15pm£4.20alc

BEDFORD Beds *Map 4 TL04*
GH Kimbolton Hotel 78 Clapham Rd
☎54854 Closed Xmas wk Lic 18hc CTV
24P 🍴 S% B&b£7.02–£7.56 Bdifr£9.45
D6.30pm

BEER Devon *Map 3 SY28*
GH *Bay View* Fore St ☎ Seaton (Devon)
20489 Etr–Oct 6hc nc5 CTV

BELPER Derbys *Map 8 SK34*
INN *Lyon Hotel* Bridge St ☎2388 Lic 6hc
TV 100P 20🏠 D8pm

BENSON Oxon *Map 4 SU69*
INN White Hart Hotel ☎ Wallingford
35244 Lic 10hc TV 60P B&bfr£9 sn
Bar lunch 32p–£1.65&alc
D9pm 32p–£1.65&alc

BERRYNARBOR Devon *Map 2 SS54*
GH Seacliffe Country Hotel ☎ Combe
Martin 3273 10hc ⌀ CTV 10P 🍴 sea S%
✳B&b£6.32–£6.90 Bdi£9.20–£10.35
W£45–£54 ⱡ D5pm

BEXHILL-ON-SEA E Sussex *Map 5 TQ76*
GH Alexandra Hotel 2 Middlesex Rd
☎210202 Closed Nov & Xmas rs Jan–Mar
Lic 9hc ⌀ CTV 1P 🍴 S% B&b£5.25–£7.25
Bdi£8–£9.50 W£50–£60 ⱡ D4pm

GH Dunselma Hotel 25 Marina ☎212988
Etr–4Oct 11hc 2⇨🍴 nc5 sea
B&b£6.90–£9.20 Bdi£9.20–£11.58
W£56.35–£65.55 ⱡ D7.30pm

The Wessex House Hotel

Sherfield-on-Loddon,
Basingstoke

Turgis Green 243 (025-684-243)

The hotel is an extension of an attractive
old house and stands in an acre of land
with ample parking space. Rooms have
private bathroom, TV, tea/coffee-making
facilities, comfortable lounge with colour
TV. Full breakfast with home-baked
bread, farm produce, home-made
marmalade etc. Personal attention of
resident owners.

THE TORS, BELSTONE

BELSTONE is a picturesque village on the High Moor
near Okehampton. It is reached by turning off the main
A30 highway at Tongue End, where there is a signpost
advertising The Tors. Distance one mile.
The village itself dates back to Saxon times and is quiet,
being well away from the noise and disturbance of traffic.
Some of the most beautiful and wild parts of Dartmoor are
within easy walking distance. Riding and pony trekking
centres are in the village itself, and fishing can be had close
by. Golf at Okehampton (18 holes).
THE TORS is a small, and intimate, family run hotel which
also serves as the village inn with traditional atmosphere.
The emphasis is on comfort, good food and value for money.
The attractive Long Bar is a well known rendezvous for all
users of the Dartmoor National Park in which the Hotel
stands. The restaurant is renowned for many miles around
for its standard of food and service.
The well furnished bedrooms have either double or single
beds, and hot & cold water in each. A family room for up
to 4 persons is also available. There is a comfortable
residents' lounge separate from the public rooms in the
hotel. Colour and black & white TV is available in the
lounge. Centrally heated throughout. "Cleanliness &
friendliness" is paramount in this hotel.
Proprietor: Robt. H Callaghan

**Enquiries to the Tors Hotel, Belstone, Nr. Okehampton,
Devon. EX20 1 QZ. Tel. Sticklepath 397 STD Code 083 784.**

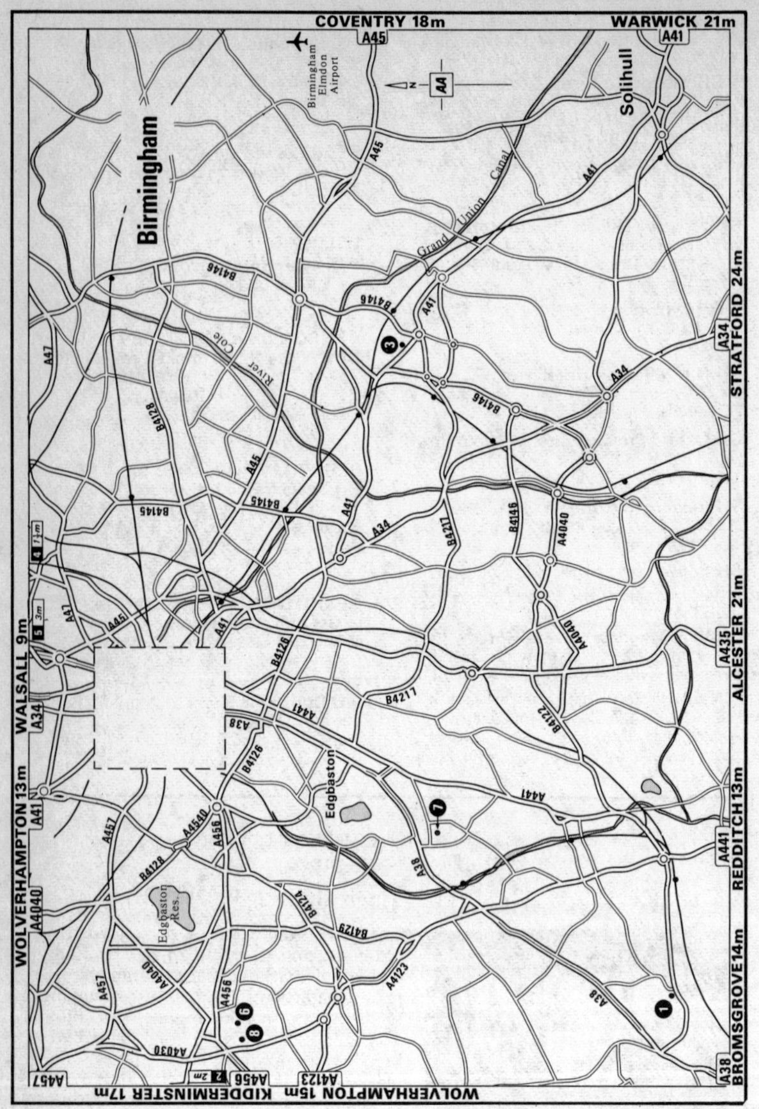

1 Alexander	**3** Kerry House Hotel	**6** Wellesley House	**8** Wentworth Hotel
2 Highfield House *(see under Rowley Regis)*	**4** Lyndhurst Hotel	**7** Wentsbury Hotel	
	5 Stanbridge Hotel *(see under Sutton Coldfield)*		

GH Victoria House 1 Middlesex Rd
☎210382 Closed Dec rs Nov, Jan & Feb
Lic 11hc CTV 6P S% B&bf7–£7.50
Bdif8.50–£9.50 Wfrf40 ⊁ D6.30pm

BICKINGTON *(Nr Newton Abbot)* Devon
Map 3 SX77

GH *Privet Cottage* ☎319 8hc CTV P
D6.30pm

BICKLEIGH *(Nr Tiverton)* Devon
Map 3 SS90

GH Bickleigh Cottage ☎230 May–Sep
rs Apr (except Etr & Oct; B&b only)
11rm 9hc 2⇨▥ ⊗ TV 10P river B&bf6–£8
Bdif10–£12 Wf70–£84 ⊁ D5pm

BIDEFORD Devon *Map 2 SS42*

⊶**GH Edelweiss** 2 Buttgarden St ☎2676
Mar–Oct rs Nov–Feb Lic 10hc CTV river
S% B&bf5.50–£6 Bdif8.25–£8.75
Wf43–£48.50 ⊁ D9pm

⊶**GH Mount Private Hotel** Northdown Rd
☎3748 Mid Jan–mid Dec Lic 7hc 1⇨▥
⊗ TV 1🏠 ♨ S% B&bf5.50–£6.50
Bdif8.50–£9.50 Wf59.50–£66.50 ⊁
D8.30pm

⊶**GH Sonnenheim** Heywood Rd, Northam
☎4989 Lic 7hc CTV 10P ⅃ S%
B&bf4.50–£6.50 Bdif7.50–£9.50
Wf42–£49 ⊁ D7pm

BIGBURY-ON-SEA Devon *Map 3 SX64*
GH Easton House Private Hotel ☎296
Mar–Oct & Xmas Lic 15hc 7⇄🛏 ⚓ CTV
15P 🕭 S% B&b£6.90–£9.20
Bdi£9.20–£12.10 W£64.40–£78.20
↳ W only Jul & Aug D7pm

BILBROOK Somerset *Map 3 ST04*
GH Bilbrook Lawns Hotel ☎ Washford
331 Etr–Oct Lic 6hc (A 6hc 1⇄🛏) nc5
CTV 12P 🕭 & ✳B&b£6.48 Bdi£10.80
W£56.35 ↳ D7.45pm

GH Bilbrook Lodge Hotel ☎ Washford
561 Feb–Oct rs Nov–Jan 7hc ⊗ nc8 10P
🕭 S% B&b£6.50–£7 Bdi£7.50–£8.50
W£50–£55 ↳ W only Jul & Aug D6.30pm

BIRMINGHAM W Midlands *Map 7 SP08*
See Plan
GH Alexander 44 Bunbury Rd,

Northfield ☎021-475 4341 Plan:**1** 12hc
CTV 12P 🕭 S% ✳B&b£5.40 Bdi£8.64
Dnoon

GH Kerry House Hotel 946 Warwick Rd,
Acocks Green ☎021-707 0316 Plan:**3**
Lic 22hc 2⇄🛏 CTV 25P 🕭 S%
B&b£7.56–£9.18 Bdi£11.06–£12.68
D7pm

GH Lyndhurst Hotel 135 Kingsbury Rd,
Erdington ☎021-373 5695 Plan:**4**
Closed Xmas 18hc ⊗ nc3 CTV 15P 🕭
✳B&b fr£5.50 Bdi fr£7.50 D6.30pm

GH Wellesley House 57 Wentworth Rd
☎021-427 1577 Plan:**6** Closed Xmas
8hc ⊗ TV 7P 🕭 S% B&b£6.60

GH Wentsbury Hotel 21 Serpentine Rd,
Selly Park ☎021-472 1258 Plan:**7**
Closed Xmas 8rm 7hc CTV 10P 🕭
B&b£6 Bdi fr£9.25 D6pm

Bilbrook Lawns Hotel

BILBROOK, Nr. MINEHEAD

'Far from the Madding Crowd' twixt moorland and the sea

A delightfully modernised Georgian country
house offering first class accommodation and
service in a friendly relaxing atmosphere.
Much recommended for its excellent cuisine and
reasonably priced table wines.
Full central heating, some private bathrooms.
Ground and first floor bedrooms. Family and
party suites. Separate colour TV lounge.
Ample parking within pleasant gardens.

Write **R. S. Murlis** or phone **Washford 331**
for brochure.

The Alexandra Hotel

2 Middlesex Road, Bexhill-on-Sea
East Sussex TN40 1LP
Res. Prop: Philip J Offord   Tel: (0424) 210202

Where tourists and business visitors to East Sussex are
discovering that really good accommodation needn't cost the
earth . . . . it's the proprietor's ' Know-how' from USA,
Canada, France and London that counts.

Ample, quiet street parking; Attractive 'winter-break' terms

Standbridge Hotel

Sutton Coldfield

Private hotel of character with a quiet and relaxed atmosphere, in 1/3 acre
of grounds with most bedrooms overlooking the rear gardens. Situated 3
miles from Spaghetti Junction for M5 and M6 Motorways, 11 miles from
National Exhibition Centre and within easy reach of most commercial
areas of Northern Birmingham. Personal attention by resident Directors:
Tonia and Howard Watts.

138 Birmingham Road, Sutton Coldfield, B72 1LY. Tel: 021 354 3007

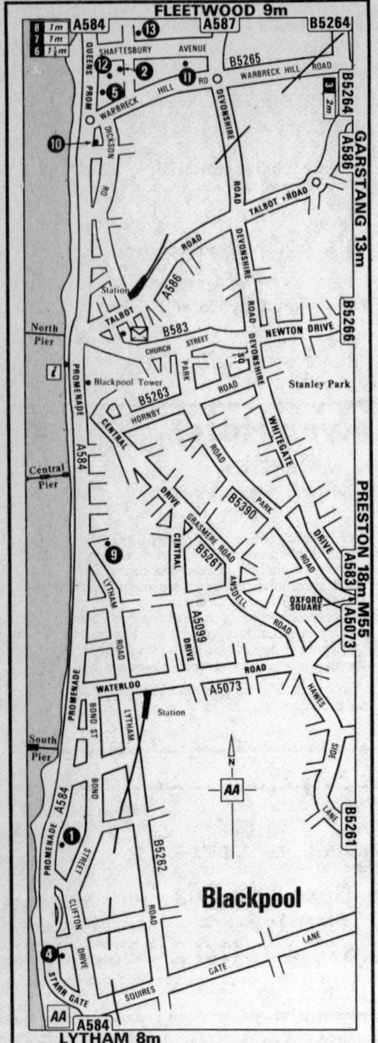

☎52555 Not on plan Etr–Oct & Xmas Lic 16hc CTV 5P D5pm

GH *Beaucliffe Private Hotel* 22 Holmfield Rd, North Shore ☎51663 Plan:**2** Etr–1Nov 12hc ✻ CTV 10P 🕮

GH *Channings* 557 New South Prom ☎41380 Plan:**4** Lic 20hc CTV 14P sea

GH *Deneley Private Hotel* 15 King Edward Av ☎52757 Plan:**5** 8hc ✻ CTV 5P 🕮 D4.30pm

⊯**GH** *Garville Hotel* 3 Beaufort Av, Bispham (2m N) ☎51004 Plan:**6** Etr–Nov Lic 7hc 2⇘ CTV 6P 🕮 S% B&b£4–£6 Bdi£5–£7 D5.15pm

GH *Manxonia Hotel* 248 Queen's Prom, Bispham (1m N A584) ☎51118 Plan:**7** Mid May–Oct Lic 20hc CTV 10P 🕮 sea D11am

GH *Mavern Private Hotel* 238 Queen's Prom, Bispham (1m N A584) ☎51409 Plan:**8** Etr–Oct & Xmas Lic 22hc ✻ nc5 CTV 14P 1🏠 🕮 sea D4.30pm

GH *Motel Mimosa* 24A Lonsdale Rd ☎41906 Plan:**9** Closed 24–28 Dec 15hc ✻ nc11 CTV 12P 1🏠 🕮

GH *Sunnycliff* 98 Queen's Prom ☎51155 Plan:**10** Etr–Oct 12hc CTV 12P D5pm

GH *Sunray Private Hotel* 42 Knowle Av, Queen's Prom ☎51937 Plan:**11** May–Oct 7hc CTV 6P 🕮 D2pm

⊯**GH Surrey House Hotel** 9 Northumberland Av ☎51743 Plan:**12** Apr–Oct rs Nov & Mar 12hc 4⇘ CTV 7P 1🏠 🕮 S% B&b£4.25–£6.25 Bdi£5.50– £8 W£38–£55 ⱔ D5pm

GH *Ventnor Private Hotel* 57 Holmfield Rd ☎51314 Plan:**13** Closed Xmas 8hc ✻ CTV 🕮 S% ✳B&b fr£4.75 Bdi fr£5.75 W£38–£40 ⱔ D3pm

BLANDFORD FORUM Dorset *Map 3 ST80*
GH *Portman Lodge Hotel* Whitecliff, Mill St ☎2842 Jan–23 Dec Lic 8hc ✻ nc6 CTV 10P 🕮 D1pm

BLEADNEY Somerset *Map 3 ST44*
⊯**GH Threeway Country House Hotel & Restaurant** ☎Wells 78870 Closed Xmas & New Year Lic 10hc ✻ CTV 40P 3🏠 🕮 river B&b£5.40–£6.20 Bdi£7.50–£9 D9.30pm

BLETCHINGLEY Surrey *Map 4 TQ35*
INN Whyte Harte ☎ Godstone 843231 Lic 9hc 4⇘ ✻ CTV 100P 🐾 B&b£8.50–£10 sn Lfr£3.50&alc D10pm£7alc

BLUE ANCHOR Somerset *Map 3 ST04*
⊯**GH Camelot** ☎ Dunster 348 Feb–Nov 8hc nc10 CTV 7P 🕮 sea S% B%b£4.50–£5.50 Bdi£7–£8 W£43–£48 ⱔ D5pm

⊯**GH Newlands** ☎ Dunster 354 Lic 5hc CTV 5P 🕮 sea S% B&b£4.50–£5.50 Bdi£7–£8.50 W£42–£51 ⱔ D6pm

⊯**GH Wentworth Hotel** 103 Wentworth Rd, Harborne ☎021-427 2839 Plan:**8** Closed Xmas wk 23hc 4⇘ CTV 14P 2🏠 🕮 B&b£5.50–£8 Bdi£8–£10.50 D7pm

BISHOP'S CLEEVE Glos *Map 3 SO92*
⊯**GH Old Manor House** 43 Station Rd ☎4127 6hc CTV 7P S% B&b£4.50–£5.50 Bdi£7.50–£9 D9.30am

BISHOP WILTON Humberside *Map 8 SE75*
⊯**INN Fleece** ☎251 Lic 4hc ✻ CTV P 🕮 B&b£5–£6 Bdi£11 Bar lunch 50p–£3 D9pm£5

BLACKPOOL Lancs *Map 27 SD33*
See Plan
GH Arandora Star Private Hotel 559 New South Prom ☎41528 Plan:**1** Closed Nov–Xmas Lic 18hc CTV 12P 4🏠 sea ✳B&b fr£5.50 Bdi fr£6.75 D3pm

GH *Arosa Hotel* 18 -20 Empress Dr

Arandora Star
Private Hotel

559 New South Promenade.
Blackpool, Lancs. FY4 1NF.
Tel 0253 41528.

Licensed to Residents.
FREE PARKING GARAGE.
Res Prop Mr and Mrs A E Trow.

Offers you the finest position overlooking the beach and promenade. Bathing from hotel. Lounges with television. Hot and cold services in all rooms. All bedrooms fitted with divans and spring-interior beds. Bedhead lighting. Room keys. Shaving points and electric fires. Twin beds available if desired. Central heating in most rooms. Christmas festivities. Fire certificate obtained. Modern bathrooms and separate shower room available. Cocktail bar. Established 32 years ago. Finest English cuisine and personal service.

Denely Private Hotel

15 King Edward Avenue, Blackpool, FY2 9TA

Tel: Blackpool 52757 (STD 0253)

The Denely Private Hotel is ideally situated close to the Promenade, cliffs and Gynn Square.
Easy access to town centre and station. Car park. The Hotel offers you every modern convenience including full central heating. H&C and shaving points in all rooms, and some with private shower. Visitors' lounge with colour television. Spacious dining room. Excellent cuisine. Open all year.
Resident proprietress: Mrs Pauline Davis

Sunray
Private Hotel

One of the very few guesthouses in England so far awarded a special commendation by the British Tourist Authority for the outstanding quality of service offered to visitors. Quiet residential area, off Queens Promenade by North Shore Golf Club. All bedrooms first floor. Full central heating. Electric blankets. Good food and service. Free car park. Mrs. Jean A. Dodgson.

42 Knowle Avenue, North Shore, Blackpool, FY2 9TQ Tel: 51937.

Sunny Cliff Hotel
Blackpool

A small hotel overlooking the sea on the north shore cliffs, 12 bedrooms with heating, razor points etc . . . TV lounge and sun lounge. Lovely 'home style' cooking and helpful personal service by owner Mr Starr and his family. Ample private parking. Established 30 years.

98 Queen's Promenade, North Shore, Blackpool, FY2 9NS
Tel: 51155

Arosa Hotel

18/20 Empress Drive, Blackpool FT2 9SB
Reception: 52555 Visitors: 53476 (STD 0253)

The Arosa Hotel is situated adjacent to Queens Promenade in an area noted for good hotels. Near to many of the main attractions of this world famous resort. Nearby you will find boating, golf, Gynn Gardens and Derby Baths, with the Tower, and the centre of town. Entertainments quickly reached. Table d'hôte service, cocktail bar, central heating in all public rooms, modern sun lounge, car parking, all bedrooms with heaters — razor points — fitted carpets. Snacks served in bar lunch times.

Beaucliffe Hotel

22 Holmfield Road, North Shore, Blackpool
Tel: 51663

Adjacent to Gynn Square and Queens Promenade. Large lounge with colour TV. Separate dining room. Private car park. Part central heating. Keys to all bedrooms. Divan beds. Hot and cold water. Shaver sockets. Bed lights. Electric heaters in all bedrooms. Open all year. Conference delegates welcome. Special fare and tariff during Christmas period.

There are electric blankets.

Under the personal supervision of the proprietors:
Mr and Mrs C Jamieson.

The Channings Hotel

557 New South Promenade
BLACKPOOL·FY4 1NF
Tel: (0253) 41380

Small family-owned hotel, commanding one of the finest positions on the promenade, overlooking the Irish Sea.
The hotel has 20 well appointed bedrooms with electric fires and shaving sockets. Ample bath and shower facilities. Centrally heated and tastefully decorated in a modern style. Licensed bar, colour TV/sun lounge.
Free car parking. Open during the year.
Enquiries to Maureen Spalding.

Manxonia Hotel

248 Queens Promenade, Bispham, Blackpool,
Lancs FY2 9HA

The Manxonia is a small private hotel catering for good tastes and offering a first-class cuisine prepared and dispensed under the personal supervision of the proprietors. Our facilities include a large cocktail bar, sun lounge and sun terraces with open views of the Irish Sea. Children are catered for at reduced rates and baby listening can be arranged. The hotel has all the modern amentities and satisfies the most discerning clientele.
Book early to avoid disappointment.
Proprietors: Ron and Miriam Garnett
Tel (0253) 51118

"*Motel Mimosa*"

24A LONSDALE ROAD, BLACKPOOL, FY1 6EE
Tel: (STD 0253) 41906
Proprietor: Mr F A Smith

Enjoy complete privacy and freedom in a modern, tastefully furnished suite comprising private bathroom (some combined bath/shower) with separate toilet. Colour TV, tea/coffee facilities and ingredients provided. Full central heating and double glazing. Breakfast served in own suite 7.30 - 9.30am. Ideal for conference and business representatives. Drive-in car park at rear.
OPEN ALL YEAR ROUND.

The comfortable friendly small hotel with the reputation for good food — and plenty of it.

VENTNOR PRIVATE HOTEL

57 HOLMFIELD ROAD; NORTH SHORE
Tel: (0253) 51314

Shower room, bathroom, H & C all bedrooms. Colour TV. Free access to rooms at all times. Quiet area — 2 minutes from promenade. Short or long term stays. Bed & breakfast. Bed, Breakfast and evening dinner. Our attractive tariff includes early morning tea and evening hot drink with biscuits. Write or phone for details. Open most of the year.

Props. MARGARET & JOHN GREER
Associate Members — North West Tourist Board

BLYTH Northumb *Map 12 NZ38*
INN Kitty Brewster 549 Cowper Rd
☎2732 Lic 7hc ≉ CTV 20P 🍴 S%
B&b£7.50–£8.25 Bdi£10.50–£11.40
W£72–£81 sn L£1–£5&alc
D9.30pm£2.50–£6&alc

BODIAM E Sussex *Map 5 TQ72*
GH Justins Hotel ☎ Staplecross 372
Closed Nov Lic 9hc ≉ ♨ CTV 20P 🍴 S%
B&b£8.64–£9 Bdi£12.64–£13.20
W£80–£85 ⅄ D7.45pm

BOGNOR REGIS W Sussex *Map 4 SZ99*
⊶GH Homestead Private Hotel
90 Aldwick Rd ☎23443 6hc (A2⇆🚿)
CTV 10P S% B&b£4–£4.70 Bdi£6–£6.60
W£40–£44.20 ⅄ D8.30pm

⊶**GH Landsdowne Hotel** 55–57 West St
☎5552 Closed Xmas Lic 10hc CTV 6P 🍴
sea S% B&b£4.50–£8 Bdi£7.50–£10.50
W£48–£68 ⅄ D5pm

BOLLINGTON Cheshire *Map 7 SJ97*
INN Turners Arms Hotel 1 Ingersley Rd
☎73864 Lic 5rm 4hc TV 🍴 S% B&b£8
sn Lfr£2&alc D10pm£5&alc

BOOT Cumbria *Map 7 NY10*
GH Brook House ☎ Eskdale 288
Closed Dec–Feb Lic 6hc 7P B&b£7.56
Bdi£10.25 W£60 ⅄ W only 25Jul–10Sep
Dnoon

BOSCASTLE Cornwall *Map 2 SX09*
⊶**GH St Christopher's Country House
Hotel** High St ☎412 Mar–Nov Lic 6hc
1⇆🚿 CTV 6P 🍴 sea S% B&b£5–£6.50
Bdi£8.50–£10 W£56–£70 ⅄ D7.30pm

GH Tolcarne Private Hotel ☎252 Lic
9hc (A5hc) ♨ CTV 30P 🍴 B&b£7–£8
Bdi£9–£9.50 W£58–£63 ⅄ D7.30pm

BOSWINGER Cornwall *Map 2 SW94*
GH Van Ruan House ☎ Mevagissey 2425
Mar–Oct Lic 8rm 7hc ≉ nc7 CTV 9P 🍴
sea S% B&b£6–£7 Bdi£9.50–£10.50
W£60–£65 ⅄ W only Jul&Aug D6.30pm

BOURNEMOUTH AND BOSCOMBE
Telephone Exchange 'Bournemouth'
Dorset *Map 4 SZ09* **See Central &
District Plans.** For additional guesthouses
see **Poole** and **Christchurch**
⊶**GH Alcombe Private Hotel** 37 Sea Rd,
Boscombe ☎36206 Central plan:**1** 12hc
CTV 6P S% B&b£4.10–£5.50
Bdi£6.25–£8.50 W£42–£58 D4.30pm

⊶**GH Alum Bay Hotel** 19 Burnaby Rd
☎761034 District plan:**2** Lic 13hc CTV
10P 🍴 S% B&b£5.50–£7.50 Bdi£7–£9
W£38–£58 ⅄ D6.30pm

GH Alumcliff Hotel 121 Alumhurst Road,
Westbourne ☎764777 District plan:**3**
Lic 17hc 10⇆🚿 ≉ nc7 CTV 14P 🍴 sea
S% B&b£9–£10.50 Bdi£11.50–£12.50
W£78–£82 ⅄ W only Jun–mid Sep

⊶**GH Alum Court Hotel** 10 Studland Rd
☎761069 District plan:**4** Lic 12hc 1⇆🚿
CTV 9P 1🏠 🍴 sea S% B&b£5.50–£6.50
Bdi£8.50–£9.50 W£50–£60 ⅄ D10pm

GH Alum Grange Hotel 1 Burnaby Rd,
Alum Chine ☎761195 District plan:**5**
Mar–Oct&Xmas Lic 14hc 2⇆🚿 ≉ nc3
CTV 11P S% B&b£7–£8.50 Bdi£9.50–£11
W£67–£75 ⅄ W only Jul&Aug D4pm

GH Arundale Hotel 38 Christchurch Rd
☎28088 Central plan:**6** 43hc 1⇆📶 nc5
CTV 26P 1🛏 📺 S% B&bfr£7.35
Bdifr£10.50 W£78 ⚡ D6pm

⤞**GH Balmer Lodge Hotel** 23 Irving Rd,
Southbourne ☎424879 District plan:**8**
Closed Xmas 8hc ⊗ CTV 5P S%
B&Bf£4–£6 Bdif£6–£8 W£40–£48 ⚡
W only Jul&Aug D4pm

⤞**GH Blinkbonnie Heights Hotel**
26 Clifton Rd, Southbourne ☎426512
District plan:**10** 12hc 1⇆📶 🚿 CTV 10P
📺 B&bf£5.75 Bdif£7.50–£9 W£49–£60
⚡ D6pm

GH Bracken Lodge Private Hotel
5 Bracken Rd, Southbourne ☎428777
District plan:**12** Etr–Oct 12hc ⊗ CTV 12P
📺 D6.30pm

GH Britannia Hotel 40 Christchurch Rd
☎26700 Central plan:**13** Closed Xmas

28hc ⊗ nc3 CTV 30P 📺 D6pm

GH Bursledon Hotel Gervis Rd ☎24622
Central plan:**15** 23hc 5⇆📶 nc3 CTV 12P
5🛏 📺 S% B&bf£7.50–£9 Bdif£9–£11.50
W£55–£88 ⚡ W only Jul&Aug D6.30pm

GH Carisbrooke Hotel 42 Tregonwell Rd
☎20432 Central plan:**16** 24May–mid Oct
25hc nc4 CTV 19P S% B&bf£8.05–£9.20
Bdif£9.20–£11.50 D6pm

⤞**GH Carysfort Lodge Private Hotel**
19 Carysfort Rd, Boscombe ☎36751
Central plan:**17** 12hc 1⇆📶 ⊗ nc3 CTV
13P S% B&bf£4.50–£5 Bdif£7–£7.50
Wfr£42 ⚡ D6pm

⤞**GH Hotel Cavendish** 20 Chine Cres,
West Cliff ☎20489 Central Plan:**18**
Etr–Oct 18hc ⊗ CTV 15P S%
B&bf£5.94–£7.56 Bdif£7.56–£9.75
W£46.44–£65.88 ⚡ W only last wk Jun–
first wk Sep D6.30pm

ARUNDALE HOTEL

38 Christchurch Road, Bournemouth, Dorset Tel: 28088

Excellent food. Cocktail bar and Nite Bite at popular prices. Car park. Dancing regularly to resident disco. Radio and intercom. Colour TV. Washing/drying facilities. Weekly film show throughout the season.

Resident proprietor: E R Fitzjohn
REMEMBER — THERE'S ALWAYS A WELCOME AT THE ARUNDALE WHERE HAPPY HOLIDAYS BEGIN — YOUR LEISURE IS OUR PLEASURE

Britannia Hotel

40 CHRISTCHURCH ROAD, BOURNEMOUTH

Tel: 0202 26700

Completely new and modernised hotel facing south. A few minutes walk from the beach and town centre. Pleasant dining room, separate tables. TV lounge and sun lounge. Ground floor bedrooms available and also rooms with private bathroom. Full central heating. The resident proprietors offer the utmost comfort and best food available. Children sharing parents room at reduced terms. Large free car park. No restrictions, and access to rooms at all times. Open throughout the year. Mid week bookings accepted.

Cintra Hotel

10-12 Florence Road, Boscombe, Bournemouth, BH5 1HF
Telephone (0202) 36103

Well established comfortable Hotel * Residential Licence * Few minutes' Boscombe Pier and Shops * 2 Lounges, TV and Games Room * Children welcome * Intercom in all Bedrooms * Some rooms with Private Bath/Toilet * Bargain weekends early and late Season.

Terms: B.B.E.M. from £49 Plus VAT.
Full Board from £63 Plus VAT.
according to Season.   No Service Charge.
Resident Proprietors: Mr & Mrs A Filer & Family.

1 Alcombe Private Hotel
6 Arundale
13 Britannia Hotel
15 Bursledon Hotel
16 Carisbrooke Hotel
17 Carysfort Lodge Private Hotel
18 Hotel Cavendish
19 Charles Taylor Hotel
20 Chilterns Hotel
22 Cintra
23 Cliffside Hotel
24 Clock House Hotel
30 Derwent House
33 East Cliff Cottage Private Hotel
34 Eglan Court Hotel
35 Fallowfield Hotel
36 Farlow Private Hotel
38 Freshfields Touring Hotel
39 Gervis Court Hotel
41 Hamilton Hall Private Hotel
42 Hawaiian
44 Hollyhurst Hotel
48 Kings Barton
51 Linwood House Hotel
53 Mae-Mar Private Hotel
62 Penmone Hotel
64 Pine Beach
70 Sandelheath
71 Seastrole Private Hotel
72 Sea View Court Hotel
77 Hotel Sorrento
78 Southlea Hotel
80 Sylvania Hotel
81 Tower House Hotel
82 Tudor Grange Hotel
85 Wenmaur House
86 West Bay Hotel
88 Whitley Court Hotel
89 Windsor Court Hotel
92 Wood Lodge Hotel

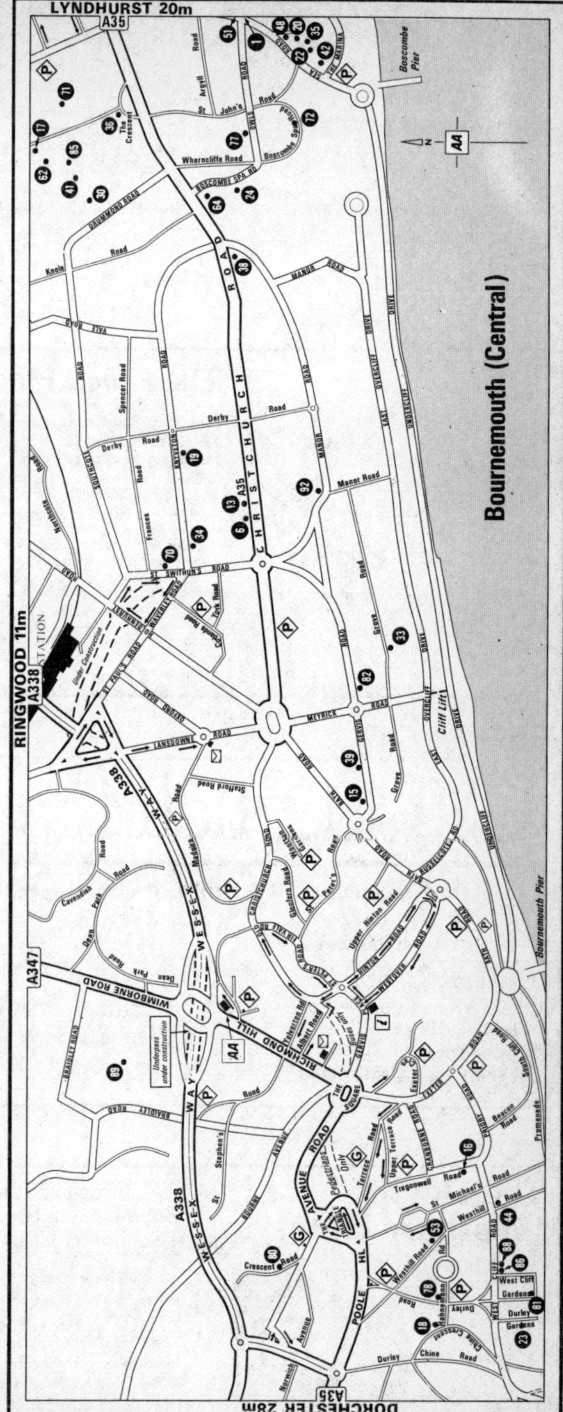

GH Charles Taylor Hotel 40/44 Frances Rd, Knyveton Gdns ☎22695 Central plan:**19** Etr–Nov Lic 27hc 11⇊🈑 nc3 CTV 12P 🍲 B&b£6.60–£8.60 Bdi£9.20–£12 W£55–£72 ⚡ W only mid Jul–first wk Sep D7pm

⊢⊣**GH Chilterns Hotel** 44 Westby Rd ☎36539 Central plan:**20** Apr–Nov Lic 19hc CTV 17P 2🏠 S% B&b£4.75–£7.25 Bdi£7–£9.50 W£45–£65 ⚡ D5pm

⊢⊣**GH Chine Cote Private Hotel** 25 Studland Rd, Alum Chine ☎764108 District plan:**21** Etr–Oct 9hc CTV 4P S% B&b£5–£5.50 Bdi£7–£7.50 W£51.75–£58.65 ⚡ D6pm

⊢⊣**GH Cintra Hotel** 10–12 Florence Rd, Boscombe ☎36103 Central plan:**22** 15Mar–18Oct Lic 39hc 5⇊🈑 CTV 16P 2🏠 B&b£5–£6.50 Bdi£7.75–£9.50 W£65–£70 D6pm

GH *Cliffside Hotel* 7 Durley Gdns, West Cliff ☎27833 Central Plan:**23** Closed Nov Lic 21hc nc3 CTV D7pm

⊢⊣**GH Clock House Hotel** 13 Boscombe Spa Rd ☎36988 Central plan:**24** Mar–Nov Lic 20hc CTV 11P 🍲 sea S% B&b£5.50–£7 Bdi£7–£8.50 W£45.50–£56 ⚡ D7pm

The Clock House Hotel

Boscombe Spa Road, Bournemouth, BH5 1AW
Tel. & Telegrams:
Management B'm'th (0202) 36988
Guests   33132

The Clock House Hotel is a 20-bedroomed, licenced hotel conveniently situated and within three minutes' walking distance of the sea through Boscombe Chine Gardens, into which we have our own entrance. These gardens give direct access to Boscombe Pier, the Promenade and beach between Boscombe and Bournemouth. The shops and all entertainments are close by. You have access all day to your room, in which there is a gas fire (with no meter), radio and washbasin with hot and cold water. There are five newly fitted bathrooms and shower rooms. There is colour television in the lounge.

Cliffside Hotel

**0202
27833**

7 Durley Gardens, West Cliff, Bournemouth, BH2 5HT

* **Licensed cocktail bar**
* **Colour TV**
* **Full Fire certificate**
* **Superb position — close to beach and centre**
* **Good food**
* **Family rooms with colour TV**

Terms:
B, B & E M from
£35 + VAT per week
or £6 + VAT per day

The Dorset Westbury Hotel

62 Lansdowne Road
Bournemouth BH1 1RS
Telephone (0202) 21811

Looking for a comfortable, friendly hotel? We're open all the year, central position, ample free parking, full central heating, licensed, colour television, ground floor bedrooms, children and dogs welcome, landscaped gardens, access all day, beautifully cooked fresh food, extensive snacks to midnight, low off-peak rates, reductions for children sharing, no service charge, bargain mini breaks. You're welcome — Bournemouth (0202) 21811.

2 Alum Bay Hotel
3 Alumcliff Hotel
4 Alum Court Hotel
5 Alum Grange Hotel
7 Avalon Private Hotel *(see under Poole)*
8 Balmer Lodge
9 Belvedere Hotel *(see under Christchurch)*
10 Blinkbonnie Heights
11 Blue Shutters *(see under Poole)*
12 Bracken Lodge Private Hotel
14 Broomway Hotel *(see under Christchurch)*
21 Chine Cote Private Hotel
25 Collindale Lodge
26 Coniston *(see under Poole)*
27 Crossroads
28 Curzon House
29 Dene Hotel *(see under Poole)*
31 Dorchester Hotel
32 Dorset Westbury Hotel
37 Ferndale *(see under Christchurch)*
40 Grassmere
43 Heathcote Hotel
45 Holmcroft Hotel
46 Holme Lacy Hotel
47 Hurley Lodge
49 Laurels *(see under Christchurch)*
50 Lewina *(see under Poole)*
52 Loddington Grange
54 Mariner's
55 Moorings
56 Mount Lodge
57 Naseby-Nye
58 Northover Private Hotel
59 Oak Hall Private Hotel
60 Ormonde House *(see under Poole)*
61 Park House *(see under Christchurch)*
65 Pines *(see under Christchurch)*
66 Redcroft Private Hotel *(see under Poole)*
67 St Albans Hotel *(see under Christchurch)*
68 St Wilfred's Private Hotel
69 Sandbourne *(see under Poole)*
73 Sea Witch Hotel *(see under Christchurch)*
74 Sheldon Lodge *(see under Poole)*
75 Shortwood House *(see under Christchurch)*
76 Silver Trees Hotel
79 Stratford Hotel
83 Twin Cedars Hotel *(see under Poole)*
84 Valberg
87 West Dene Private Hotel
90 Westminister Cottage Hotel *(see under Poole)*
91 Woodford Court Hotel

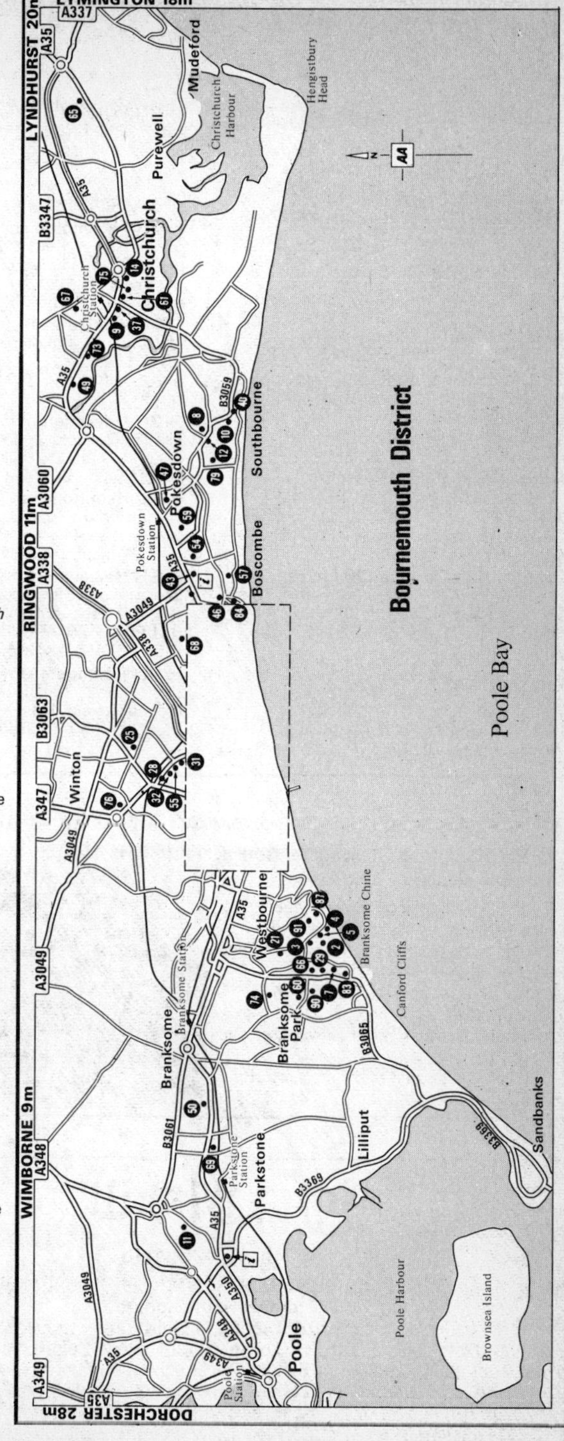

⊶**GH Collindale Lodge** 145 Richmond Park Rd ☎514528 District plan:**25** Lic 10hc 8⇆🛁 ⊘ nc8 CTV 12P S% B&bf£5.90–£8.25 Bdif£8.85–£11.20 W£53.60–£74.25 ⚡ D4pm

⊶**GH Crossroads Hotel** 88 Belle Vue Rd, Southbourne ☎426307 District plan:**27** 10hc ⊘ nc5 CTV 10P S% B&bf£4.60–£6.90 Bdif£6.32–£9.77 W£40.25–£63.25 ⚡ D4.30pm

⊶**GH Curzon House Hotel** 46 Lansdowne Rd ☎27152 District plan:**28** Jan–Oct 11hc 2⇆🛁 nc7 CTV 10P 🍴 S% B&bf£4.89–£5.75 Bdif£7.39–£8.65 W£46–£57.50 ⚡ D4.30pm

⊶**GH Derwent House** 36 Hamilton Rd, Boscombe ☎39102 Central plan:**30** 10hc ⊘ CTV 10P 🍴 S% B&bf£5–£5.50 Bdif£6.50–£7.50 W£38.50–£52 ⚡ D6pm

GH Dorchester Hotel 64 Lansdowne Rd North ☎21271 District plan:**31** Lic 16rm 15hc 15⇆🛁 ♨ CTV 15P 🍴 S% B&bf£6.05–£9.72 Bdif£14.58 W£36.72–£79.23 ⚡ D7pm

⊶**GH Dorset Westbury Hotel** 62 Lansdowne Rd ☎21811 District plan:**32** Lic 20hc 1⇆🛁 nc6 CTV 20P 🍴 S% B&bf£4.75–£6.50 Bdif£7–£8.75 W£45–£59 ⚡ D6.30pm

GH East Cliff Cottage Private Hotel 57 Grove Rd ☎22788 Central plan:**33** Apr–Oct 10hc 4⇆🛁 nc5 CTV 9P S% B&b £8.05–£10.95 Bdif£12–£14.95 W£65–£87.20 ⚡ D6pm

GH Eglan Court Hotel 7 Knyveton Rd ☎20093 Central plan:**34** Etr–Oct Lic 15hc 3⇆🛁 ⊘ nc5 CTV 12P 🍴 S% B&bf£6.33 Bdif£9.20 W£44–£54 ⚡ W only Jun–Oct D6pm

GH Fallowfield Hotel 25 Florence Rd, Boscombe ☎37094 Central plan:**35** Jan–10Nov Lic 12hc CTV 12P 1🏠 B&bf£6.50–£9.05 Bdif£8.10–£10.65 W£48.60–£63.75 ⚡ W only Jul&Aug D6pm

⊶**GH Farlow Private Hotel** 13 Walpole Rd, Boscombe ☎35865 Central plan:**36** Closed 1wk in Spring & 2wks in Oct 13hc ⊘ nc4 CTV 14P S% B&bf£4.70–£5.50 Bdif£7.42–£8.25 W£46.20–£54 ⚡ W only Jul&Aug D4pm

⊶**GH Freshfields Touring Hotel** 55 Christchurch Rd ☎34023 Central plan:**38** Lic 12hc nc5 CTV 12P 1🏠 🍴 S% B&bf£5.50–£7.50 Bdif£8–£10 W£47.50–£59.50 ⚡ D2pm

GH Gervis Court Hotel 38 Gervis Rd ☎26871 Central plan:**39** Etr–Oct Lic 18hc ⊘ ♨ CTV 20P 1🏠 S% B&bf£9–£11 Bdif£11.50–£13.50 W£63.18–£85.86 ⚡ D7pm

⊶**GH Grassmere** 5 Pine Av, Southbourne ☎428660 District plan:**40** Etr–Oct 10hc ⊘ nc3 CTV 8P S% B&bf£5–£6 Bdif£7–£8.50 W£44–£50 ⚡ D4.30pm

⊶**GH Hamilton Hall Private Hotel** 1 Carysfort Rd, Boscombe ☎35758 Central plan:**41** 12hc 8⇆🛁 ⊘ nc5 CTV 10P S% B&bf£3.78–£5.40

⊶**GH Hawaiian Hotel** 4 Glen Rd, Boscombe ☎33234 Central plan:**42** Apr–Oct 12hc 2⇆🛁 ⊘ nc5 CTV 9P S% B&bf£5.40–£6.48 Bdif£7.02–£8.10 W£45.36–£54 ⚡ D6pm

⊶**GH Heathcote Hotel** 2 Heathcote Rd, Boscombe ☎36185 District plan:**43** Closed Nov Lic 16hc 4⇆🛁 ⊘ CTV 14P S% B&bf£5.52–£7 Bdif£8.05–£10.35 W£46–£69 D6.15pm

Fallowfield Hotel

25 Florence Road, Boscombe, Bournemouth BH5 1HJ
Tel: Bournemouth 37094 (0202)

A friendly family hotel run with the comfort of their guests in mind, with special attention to the excellent food and good old fashioned service.
Cocktail bar lounge. Car parking. A la carte menu available. Residential and restaurant licence. Central between sea and shops.
Resident proprietors: Max and Marjorie Smith.

Farlow

PRIVATE HOTEL

WALPOLE ROAD, BOSCOMBE, BOURNEMOUTH

Telephone: Bournemouth 35865

Small, detached private hotel of 14 bedrooms with colour TV lounge and car park. First class cuisine. Four course English breakfast and four course and coffee dinner. We are noted for comfort, consideration and courtesy. Own keys to come and go as you please. Personal attention at all times. Near sea and shops.

Terms: B&B from £32.20 per week.
BB&EM from £48.50 to £57.50 (VAT inclusive)
No service charge.   SAE for brochure please.

Collindale Lodge

154 Richmond Park Road, Bournemouth, Dorset,
BH8 8TW
Telephone: Bournemouth 514528 & 524627

A warm welcome awaits your arrival at Collindale Lodge where you are assured of comfort, service, and excellent cuisine in a warm friendly atmosphere.

The Lodge is situated close to shops, churches, swimming baths, tennis courts, also Queens Park Golf Course. We have ample car parking facilities, and bus stops for the town centre, Boscombe and Poole, are only a few yards away.

The well appointed accommodation includes, spacious Lounge with ample easy chairs and colour TV, and a separate well-stocked residents bar to relax in over your favourite drink.

Well furnished bedrooms, all with hot and cold water most with showers, and some with toilets. Pleasant well-equipped dining room with separate tables where we provide a full English breakfast and a high quality 4-course evening dinner. Light refreshments are served in the evening on request.

There is relaxation for those who want to get away from it all . . . and there is action for the active. It's a beautiful town: clean and sparkling, with a warm welcome for visitors. The sea is clean and fresh too! Bournemouth's beaches are among the best in Britian. Miles of sunny sands are flanked by a promenade which is free of traffic all summer long. You can walk right from the heart of the shopping centre on to the beach and never cross a road. There are breathtaking panoramic views across the bay to the Purbecks and the Isle of Wight from the Overcliff drives on the West Cliff and East Cliff.

⊢⊣**GH Hollyhurst Hotel** West Hill Rd
☎27137 Central plan:**44** Etr–Oct Lic
23hc 4⇔🍴 CTV 16P sea B&b£5–£7
Bdi£7–£9 W£58–£68 ⠗ W only mid
Jun–Aug D6pm

⊢⊣**GH Holmcroft Hotel** 5 Earle Rd,
Alum Chine ☎761289 District plan:**45**
Apr–Oct 22hc nc4 CTV 17P S%
B&b£5.20–£7.50 Bdi£7.45–£10
W£48–£65 ⠗ D6.45pm

⊢⊣**GH Holme Lacy Hotel** Florence Rd
☎36933 District plan:**46** Etr & mid May
to early Oct 27hc nc3 CTV 16P S%
B&b£5.50–£6.50 Bdi£7.75–£8.95
W£49–£59 ⠗ W only late Jul to mid Aug
D5.30pm

⊢⊣**GH Hurley Lodge** 20 Castlemain Av,
Southbourne ☎427046 District plan:**47**
6hc ⊛ nc5 CTV 6P 🍴 S% B&b£4.50–£6
Bdi£6.50–£8 W£36–£44 ⠗ W only
Jul & Aug D4pm

⊢⊣**GH Kings Barton** 22 Hawkwood Rd,
Boscombe ☎37794 Central plan:**48** Lic
17hc 1⇔🍴 CTV 17P 🍴 S%
B&b£5.75–£7.48 Bdi£7.48–£9.78
D4.30pm

⊢⊣**GH Linwood House Hotel**
11 Wilfred Rd ☎37818 Central plan:**51**
Lic 10hc nc3 CTV 6P 🍴 S%
B&b£5.94–£7.56 Bdi£8.64–£10.06
W£60.48–£66 ⠗ W only Jul & Aug D4pm

⊢⊣**GH Loddington Grange Hotel**
13 Knowle Rd ☎36117 District Plan:**52**
10hc ⊛ CTV 8P S% B&b£4.32–£5.94
Bdi£6.48–£8.64 W£38.88–£52.92 ⠗
W only Jun–Aug

GH *Mae-Mar Private Hotel* 91–93
Westhill Rd, West Cliff ☎23167 Central
plan:**53** Lic 28hc ⊛ CTV 4P lift 🍴

⊢⊣**GH Mariner's Hotel** 22 Clifton Rd,
Southbourne ☎420851 District plan:**54**
Etr–Sep 15hc CTV 20P 🍴 sea S%
B&b£5.50–£6.50 Bdi£7.50–£8
W£45.50–£56 ⠗ D6.30pm

GH Moorings Hotel 66 Lansdowne Rd
North ☎22705 District plan:**55** Lic 18hc
nc10 CTV 18P 🍴 B&bfr£6.90
Bdifr£10.05 Wfr£56.70 ⠗ D7pm

GH Mount Lodge Hotel 19 Beaulieu Rd,
Westbourne ☎761173 District plan:**56**
Closed Jan & Feb Lic 11hc CTV 6P 🍴
S% B&b£6.50–£8 Bdi£9.50–£11
W£64–£68 D6.15pm

GH Naseby-Nye Hotel Byron Rd,
Boscombe ☎34079 District plan:**57** Lic
13hc 3⇔🍴 nc4 CTV 10P 🍴 sea
✳B&b£6.50–£9 Bdi£9.50–£12.50
W£44–£57 ⠗ D6.30pm

GH Northover Private Hotel 10 Earle
Rd, Alum Chine ☎767349 District plan:**58**
Etr–Oct 11hc 2⇔🍴 nc2 CTV 10P S%
✳B&bfr£5.50 Bdifr£7.50 W£49–£56 ⠗
D5pm

⊢⊣**GH Oak Hall Private Hotel** 9 Wilfred
Rd, Boscombe ☎35062 District plan:**59**
Mar–Nov Lic 12hc 1⇔🍴 nc5 CTV 8P 🍴
S% B&b£5–£8 Bdi£7–£8 W£45–£55 ⠗
D6pm

⊢⊣**GH Penmone Hotel** 17 Carysfort Rd,
Boscombe ☎35903 Central plan:**62** Lic
9hc CTV 10P 🍴 S% B&b£5–£6
Bdi£7.50–£8.50 W£44–£48 ⠗ D6pm

GH *Perran Court Hotel* 58 Lansdowne Rd
☎27881 Not on plan 14hc ⊛ nc7 CTV
12P D8pm

⊢⊣**GH Pine Beach Hotel** 31 Boscombe
Spa Rd ☎35902 Central plan:**64** Etr–Oct

Lic 20hc ❄ nc8 CTV 17P sea S%
B&b£5–£5.50 Bdi£7.50–£8
W£42–£47.50 ⅃ D6.30pm

GH St Wilfreds Private Hotel 15 Walpole
Rd, Boscombe ☎36189 District plan:**68**
8hc ❄ nc5 CTV 4P S% ✱B&b£5.69–£6.48
Bdi£8.10–£8.64 W£49.45–£51.75 ⅃
D6.15pm

⋈GH Sandelheath Hotel 1 Knyveton Rd,
East Cliff ☎25428 Central plan:**70**
Closed two wks in Nov Lic 15hc 3⊐🇲 ❄
nc8 CTV 9P 🍴 S% B&b£4.50–£6.50
Bdi£7.50–£9 W£48.60–£59.40 ⅃ D4pm

GH Seastrole Private Hotel 12 Campbell
Rd, Boscombe ☎36996 Central plan:**71**
Lic 9hc ❄ CTV 6P S% ✱B&b£3.75–£6
Bdi£5.50–£7.75 W£34–£50 ⅃ D6pm

⋈GH Sea View Court Hotel
14 Boscombe Spa Rd ☎37197 Central

plan:**72** Mar–Oct Lic 14hc 2⊐🇲 nc5
CTV 16P S% B&b£5–£10 Bdi£7.50–£12
W£45–£65 ⅃ Dnoon

⋈GH Silver Trees Hotel 57 Wimborne Rd
☎26040 District plan:**76** 10hc ❄ nc5
CTV 12P S% B&b£4.86–£6.75 Bdi£8–£10
W£48.60–£60.50 ⅃ D5pm

GH Hotel Sorrento 16 Owls Rd,
Boscombe ☎34019 Central plan:**77**
Apr–Oct Lic 19hc 3⊐🇲 ❄ nc5 CTV 19P
B&b£6.33–£7.48 Bdi£8.63–£10.35
W£46–£69 ⅃ D6pm

GH Hotel Sorrento 8 Studland Rd,
Alum Chine Westbourne ☎762116
Not on plan Lic 19hc 6⊐🇲 nc5 CTV 10P
sea S% B&b£7.50–£8.50 Bdi
£9.50–£10.50 W£54–£61 ⅃ D6.30pm

Hotel Cavendish

Chine Crescent,

Bournemouth BH2 5LF

Tel: 0202 20489

Pleasant family hotel, situated in own grounds and only 5 mins to
sea, sand and all town amenities ● colour TV, Radio-intercom
baby listening service ● Children welcome ● Excellent cuisine ●
Free car parking ● Access to hotel at all times ● Ground floor
bedrooms ● Packed lunches & evening refreshments available ●
No service charge.

KINGS BARTON HOTEL

Hawkwood Road, Boscombe, Bournemouth.
Tel: Bournmouth (0202) 37794

Ample car parking, Residents' licenced bar,
Colour T.V. lounge, Varied adequate menu,
separate dining tables. Hotel is conveniently
situated close to sea, shops and public
transport and is open all year.
The resident proprietors assure you of a
warm homely welcome.

Naseby-Nye Hotel

Byron Road, Boscombe
Overcliffe, Bournemouth
Telephone: Bournemouth 34079

Situated overlooking cliff top, a small hotel of
character and charm standing in its own
delightful grounds, and offering an excep-
tionally high standard of comfort. Central
heating. Sea views. Restaurant and residential licence. Ample parking facilities.

GH Southlea Hotel Durley Rd, West Cliff
☎26075 Central plan:**78** Apr–Oct 18hc
nc3 CTV 14P B&bf6.90–£7.20
Bdif9.20–£11.50 W£64.40–£75.90 ⚸
D6.30pm

GH *Stratford Hotel* 20 Grand Av,
Southbourne ☎424726 District plan:**79**
Closed 24Dec–1Jan Lic 11hc ⊘ CTV 11P
🍴 D4pm

GH Sylvania Hotel 6 Crescent Rd,
The Triangle ☎23959 Central plan:**80**
Lic 12hc ⊘ nc5 CTV 10P 🍴 S%
B&bf6–£8.25 Bdif8.75–£11 W£55–£70
⚸ W only mid Jun–mid Sep D6pm

⋈**GH Tower House Hotel** West Cliff Gdns
☎20742 Central plan:**81** Mar–Oct Lic
34hc 12⇱🛁 CTV 18P lift sea S%
B&bf5.50–£8.50 Bdif7.50–£10.50
W£49–£79 W only mid Jul–Aug D7pm

GH Tudor Grange Hotel 31 Gervis Rd
☎291472 Central plan:**82** Mar–1Nov
Lic 12hc 1⇱🛁 CTV 8P 🍴 S%
B&bf7.25–£10.50 Bdif10–£13.25
W£67–£90 ⚸ D7.30pm

⋈**GH Valberg Hotel** 1A Wollstonecraft
Rd, Boscombe ☎34644 District plan:**84**
10hc 7⇱🛁 ⊘ nc5 CTV 8P 🍴 S%
B&bf4.50–£9.50 Wfr£28 Ⓜ
W only Jul & Aug

⋈**GH Wenmaur House** 14 Carysfort Rd,
Boscombe ☎35081 Central plan:**85** Lic
12hc ⊘ CTV 10P 🍴 S% B&bf5.18–£5.75
Bdif8.05–£9.20 Wfr£46 ⚸
W only Jul & Aug D11.30pm

GH West Bay Hotel West Cliff Gdns
☎22261 Central plan:**86**
Etr & 17May–4Oct 13hc CTV 6P
B&bf6.25–£8.75 Bdif8.25–£10.75
W£49.50–£65 ⚸ W only 14Jun–13Sep
D6.30pm

⋈**GH West Dene Private Hotel**
117 Alumhurst Rd, Westbourne ☎764843
District plan:**87** Apr–Oct Lic 15hc 5⇱🛁
⊗ CTV 15P sea S% B&bf5.50–£8
Bdif7.50–£10 W£53–£66 ⚸
W only mid Jul & Aug D6.15pm

⋈**GH Whitley Court Hotel** West Cliff
Gdns ☎21302 Central plan:**88** Closed Jan
16hc nc3 CTV 10P 🍴 sea S%
B&bf4.86–£7.56 Bdif7.56–£10.80
W£43.20–£70.20 ⚸ D5pm

GH Windsor Court Hotel 34 Bodorgan Rd
☎24637 Central plan:**89** Lic 35hc
16⇱🛁 ⚖ CTV 20P S% B&bf6.40–£9.70
Bdif8.60–£16.30 W£41.40–£96.80 ⚸
D8.15pm

⋈**GH Woodford Court Hotel**
19–21 Studland Rd, Alum Chine
☎764907 District plan:**91** Etr–1Nov
12hc 4⇱🛁 (A 10hc 4⇱🛁) nc2 CTV 14P sea
S% B&bf5–£6.50 Bdif7.50–£8.50
W£46–£56 ⚸ D6.15pm

GH Wood Lodge Hotel 10 Manor Rd,
East Cliff ☎20891 Central plan:**92**
Etr–mid Oct Lic 15hc 8⇱🛁 CTV 12P 🍴
S% B&bf7.50–£11.50 Bdif10.25–£14.25
W£61.50–£85.70 ⚸ W only mid Jun–Aug
D6pm

BOURTON-ON-THE-WATER Glos
Map 4 SP12
INN Mousetrap ☎20579 Lic 3hc nc14
16P 🍴 ⇲ S% B&bf8.25 Bdif10.25–
£12.25 Bar lunch £1.50alc D9.30pm£4alc

BOVEY TRACEY Devon *Map 3 SX87*
⋈**GH Kestor** Challabrook Ln ☎832277
6hc ⚖ CTV 6P 🍴 S% B&bfr£4.50 Bdifr£7
Wfr£42 D7pm

WEST BAY HOTEL

West Cliff Gardens, Bournemouth BH2 5HL

Tel: Management — 22261, Visitors — 26949 (STD Code 0202)

Excellent position — 250 yards from the cliffs and 350 yards from the beach. The pier, town centre and leading entertainments are within a few minutes easy walking distance of the hotel.

* Free hotel car park
* Well equipped bedrooms
* Excellent varied cuisine
* Evening refreshments available
* Colour television
* Ground floor bedrooms
* Separate tables
* Access to hotel at all times
* Reduced rates for children sharing room with two adults

Write or telephone for illustrated brochure "C".

Stratford Hotel

Grand Avenue,
Southbourne,
Bournemouth
Telephone: (0202) 424726

*Close to the seafront
*Colour television
*Central heating throughout
*Morning tea, evening refreshments and packed lunches available
*Residents' car park
*Residents' bar
*No service charges
*Open all year
*Off-peak rates
*Hosts Barbara and Peter Bennett

West Dene HOTEL LICENSED

117, Alumhurst Road, Alum Chine,
BOURNEMOUTH BH4 8HS
Telephone: 0202 764843
Guests: 0202 767007

Delightfully situated overlooking sea at the foot of Alum Chine with uninterrupted views of Bournemouth Bay. Lounge, cocktail bar, dining room and most bedrooms having sea views. Some bedrooms with bathroom en-suite. Ample car parking. Excellent varied menus. Open most of the year including Christmas. Personal attention is given to all guests by the Proprietors Barbara and Geoff Ramsden.

Bowness-on-Windermere   Fairfield Hotel

FAIRFIELD is a country house situated in half an acre of secluded gardens. It is close to the lake and village, yet peaceful. The hotel is centrally heated throughout and tea and coffee making equipment is in every bedroom.

Guests are welcome in our elegant cocktail bar and residents' lounge.

The hotel is personally supervised by the owners Joan Glaister and Beryl Bush.

There is amply parking space.

A fire safety certificate is held.

**Brantfell Rd., Bowness-on-Windermere, Cumbria.
Tel: Windermere 3772.**

BOWLAND BRIDGE Cumbria
Map 7 SD48
INN Hare & Hounds ☎ Crosthwaite 333
Lic 4hc (A 4hc 4⇔🖭) 70P 2🏠 S%
✱B&bf6.50–£8.50 Bdif10.50–£13.50
Wf73.50–£90 ⏘ sn Lf1.75–£2.50
D8pmf4.50–£5

BOWNESS-ON-WINDERMERE Cumbria
Map 7 SD49 **Guesthouses are listed
under Windermere**

BRADFORD W Yorks *Map 7 SE13*
GH Belvedere Hotel 19 North Park Rd,
Manningham ☎492559 Closed Xmas,
rs weekends Lic 13hc CTV 10P 🖭
✱B&bf8.32 Bdif11.29 D6.45pm
⊱GH Maple Hill** 3 Park Dr, Heaton
☎44061 10hc ⊗ CTV 10P 4🏠 🖭 S%
B&bf4.80–£5.20

GH Midway 218 Keighley Rd, Frizinghall
☎42667 rs Fri, Sat & Sun (no dinner)
6hc CTV 🖭 S%✱B&bf4.95 Bdif7.30
D previous day

BRAUNTON Devon *Map 2 SS43*
⊱GH Brookdale Hotel** 62 South St
☎812075 Lic 10hc 1⇔🖭 ⊗ ♨ CTV 10P
1🏠 🖭 S% B&bf4.50–£4.75
Bdif7–£7.25 Wf45–£47 ⏘ D5pm

BREAGE Cornwall *Map 2 SW62*
⊱GH Hillsdale Hotel** Polladras
☎ Germoe 3334 Lic 9hc ♨ CTV 9P 🖭
S% B&bf5.75–£6.90 Bdif9.77–£10.93
Wf51.75–£63.25 ⏘ D7pm

BREDE E Sussex *Map 5 TQ81*
GH Roselands Private Hotel ☎882338
Closed 15Dec–15Jan 16hc CTV 20P 🖭

S% B&bf7.75–£8.75 Bdif11.65–£12.65
D6pm

BRENT KNOLL Somerset *Map 3 ST35*
GH Battleborough Grange Hotel ☎208
Feb–Oct, rs Nov–Jan Lic 12hc CTV 60P
🖭 ✱B&bf6.12 Bdif8.52 Wfrf55.90 ⏘
D7pm
GH *Woodlands* Hill Ln ☎232 Lic 10hc TV

BRIDFORD Devon *Map 3 SX88*
⊱GH Bridford** ☎ Christow 52563 6hc
⊗ TV 6P 🖭 S% B&bf5.25–£6
Bdif7.25–£8.50 Wf47–£56 ⏘ D4.30pm

BRIDGNORTH Salop *Map 7 SO79*
INN Ball Hotel East Castle St ☎2478
Lic 5hc ⊗ 11P 🚗 S% B&bf7
Bar lunch 75p–£2.75

BRIDLINGTON Humberside *Map 8 TA16*
GH *Shirley Private Hotel* 47 & 48 South
Marine Dr ☎72539 Apr–Oct & Xmas Lic
33hc CTV 11P lift D6pm
⊱GH Southdowne Hotel** South Marine
Dr ☎73270 Mar–mid Oct Lic 10hc CTV
8P 🖭 sea S% B&bf5.50 Bdif7.50 Wf52
W only July & Aug D6pm

BRIDPORT Dorset *Map 3 SY49*
GH Britmead House 154 West Bay Rd
☎22941 Lic 8hc 2⇔🖭 CTV 10P 🖭 S%
B&bf6.20–£7 Bdif9.50–£10.50
Wf58–£63 ⏘ D6.30pm

GH Roundham House Hotel West Bay Rd
☎22753 mid Jan–Nov Lic 8hc CTV 8P 🖭
sea B&bf7.50–£8 Bdif11.50–£12
Wf77–£80 ⏘ D7pm

⊢⊣INN **Railway Terminus** 114 St Andrews Rd ☎22911 Lic 4hc ⊗ 12P 2🏠 S% B&b£5 Bdi£8 sn Lfr70p D10pm fr£2

BRIGHTON E Sussex *Map 4 TQ30*
⊢⊣**GH Downlands Private Hotel**
19 Charlotte St ☎601203 Lic 10hc CTV P 🍴 S% B&b£4.80–£6.80 Bdi£6.80–£8.80 W£33–£43 ⓚ D10am

⊢⊣**GH Ellesmere** 8 New Steine ☎607812 Feb–Oct 12hc 1⇆🍴 nc4 CTV S% B&b£5–£7.50 Bdi£8–£10.50 W£45–£62.70 ⓚ Dnoon

⊢⊣**GH Marina** 8 Charlotte St ☎605349 Closed Xmas Lic 11hc ⊗ CTV 🍴 S% B&b£4–£5 Bdi£5.50–£6.50 W£38–£45 ⓚ D9.30am

GH Melford Hall Hotel 41 Marine Pde ☎681435 Mar–24Dec Lic 12hc ⊗ CTV 6P sea B&b£7–£9

GH Regency Hotel 28 Regency Sq ☎202690 Closed Jan Lic 13hc 5⇆🍴 CTV 🍴 S% B&b£10–£14.50 Bdi£18–£22.50 D10.30pm

⊢⊣**GH Rowland House** 21 St George's Ter, Kemp Town ☎603639 Lic 10hc CTV 1P 🍴 B&b£5.50–£6.50 Bdi£8–£9.50 W£50–£57 ⓚ D5pm

⊢⊣**GH Trouville** 11 New Steine, Marine Pde ☎697384 9hc ⊗ nc14 CTV S% B&b£5–£6.50 W£35–£45.50 Ⓜ

⊢⊣**GH Twenty Three** 23 New Steine ☎684212 9hc CTV S% B&b£3.25–£4 Wfr£22.75 Ⓜ

BRISTOL Avon *Map 3 ST57* **See Plan**
GH *Birkdale Hotel* 11 Ashgrove Rd, Redland ☎33635 Plan:**1** Closed Xmas Lic 19hc (A 16hc) CTV 14P 🍴 D7.30pm

GH *Burlington* 19 Henleaze Rd, Henleaze ☎622078 Plan:**2** 5hc CTV 🍴

GH Cambridge Hotel Redland Rd ☎36020 Plan:**3** 12hc ⊗ nc5 CTV 🍴 S% B&b fr£6.15 Bdi fr£8.90 D10am

⊢⊣**GH Cavendish House Hotel** 18 Cavendish Rd, Henleaze ☎621017 Plan:**4** 6hc CTV 5P 🍴 B&b£5.40–£5.94 Wfr£37.80

GH Chesterfield Hotel 3 Westbourne Pl, Clifton ☎34606 Plan:**5** 2Jan–24Dec 12hc CTV S% ✱B&b fr£5.98

GH Hotel Clifton St Paul's Rd, Clifton ☎36882 Plan:**6** 63hc 25⇆🍴 CTV 12P lift S% B&b fr£6.07

GH Glenroy Hotel 30 Victoria Sq, Clifton ☎39058 Plan:**7** Closed Xmas wk Lic 32hc 4⇆🍴 CTV 16P 🍴 B&b£6.50 W£45.50 Ⓜ

GH Oakdene Hotel 45 Oakfield Rd ☎35900 Plan:**8** Closed Xmas 10hc 🍴 S% B&b£7.59 W£48.30 Ⓜ

GH Oakfield Hotel 52–54 Oakfield Rd ☎35556 Plan:**9** Closed Xmas 27hc CTV 6P 2🏠 🍴 B&b fr£6 Bdi fr£8.50 D6.45pm

GH Pembroke Hotel 13 Arlington Villas ☎35550 Plan:**10** Closed Xmas wk 13hc CTV 🍴 S% B&b£6.07

GH Rodney Hotel 4 Rodney Pl, Clifton Down Rd ☎35422 Plan:**11** Closed Xmas 30hc ⊗ CTV 🍴 ♿ B&b£7.48

GH *Seeley's Hotel* 19–27 St Paul's Rd, Clifton ☎38544 Plan:**12** Lic 40hc (A 20hc) CTV 8P 18🏠 🍴 D11pm

GH Washington Hotel 11–15 St Paul's Rd, Clifton ☎33980 Plan:**13** 32hc CTV 13P S% B&b£6.20

Roundham House Hotel

West Bay Road, Bridport, Dorset.
Tel: Bridport 22753 (STD 0308)

Special commendation recommended by British Tourist Authority.

A fine old, mellowed stone house in lovely surroundings with every comfort and convenience, Standing in its own grounds of three quarters of an acre, overlooking Eype Down, cliffs and sea.

Full choice of interesting and varied menus daily with fresh homegrown vegetables.

Hot, cold and shaving points in all rooms, colour television, library and bar.

Restaurant and residential licence.

Guests warmly welcomed with personal attention.

Inclusive terms: dinner, bed & breakfast — £12.00 daily and £80.00 weekly inclusive of Value Added Tax.

Telephone or write for brochure, tariff and sample menus.

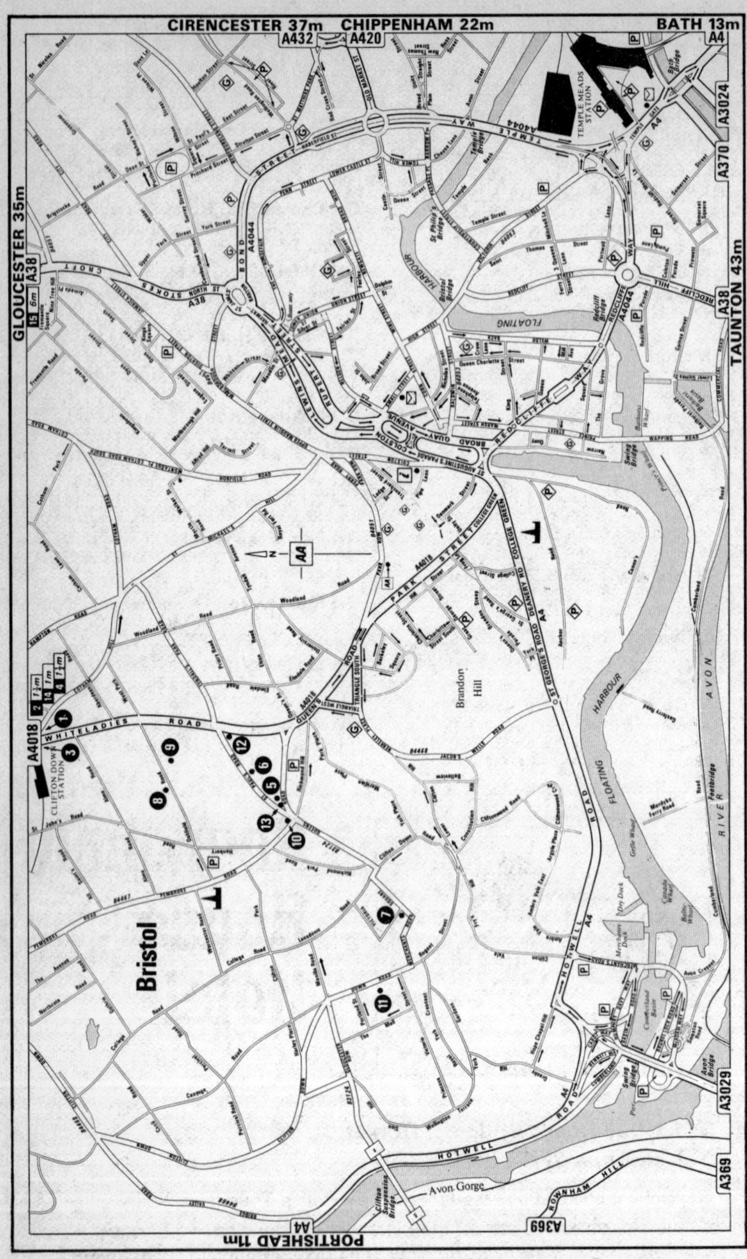

1	Birkdale Hotel	5	Chesterfield Hotel	10	Pembroke Hotel	15	Willow
2	Burlington	6	Hotel Clifton	11	Rodney Hotel		
3	Cambridge Hotel	7	Glenroy Hotel	12	Seeley's Hotel		
4	Cavendish House Hotel	8	Oakdene Hotel	13	Washington Hotel		
		9	Oakfield Hotel	14	Westbury Park Hotel		

GH Westbury Park Hotel 37 Westbury Rd ☎620465 Plan:**14** Closed Xmas & New Year Lic 9hc ✠ 5P ⬛ S% B&b£6.28 Bdi£9.12 D7.30pm

GH Willow 209 Gloucester Rd, Patchway ☎ Almondsbury 612276 Plan:**15** Lic 6hc CTV 14P ⬛ S% B&b£5 Bdi£6.50 D4pm

BRIXHAM Devon *Map 3 SX95* **See Plan**
GH Beverley Court Private Hotel
Upton Manor Rd ☎3149 Plan:**1** May–Sep Lic 11hc CTV 18P ⬛ S%✳B&b£6.37–£8.12 Bdi£9.61–£11.36 W£52.92–£62.64 ⅃ D6.30pm

GH *Brioc Private Hotel* 11 Prospect Rd
☎3540 Plan:**2** Mar–Oct 10hc CTV sea
D6.30pm

⋈**GH Cottage Hotel** Mount Pleasant Rd
☎2123 Plan:**3** mid May–Sep Lic 10hc nc3
CTV 5P sea S% B&b£5–£6 Bdi£7–£8
W£42–£52 ⅃ W only 22Jun–23Aug D6pm

⋈**GH Harbour View Hotel** King St
☎3052 Plan:**4** 9hc CTV 1P sea S%
B&b£5.35–£8.62 Bdi£8.51–£11.78
D6.30pm

GH *Holwell Villa* 119 New Rd ☎3496
Plan:**5** Closed late Oct 7hc nc4 CTV 10P

⋈**GH Orchard House** St Mary's Rd
☎3590 Plan:**6** Lic 7hc ⊗ CTV 14P S%
B&b£3.95–£4.95 Bdi£6–£8.50
W£42–£58 ⅃ D6.30

GH Parkway House Private Hotel
2 Greenswood Rd ☎2730 Plan:**7**
Closed Xmas 7hc ⊗ CTV 6P 1⌂ S%
✳B&b£5 Bdi£6.75 W£47⅃D5pm

⋈**GH Pola** 63–65 Berry Head Rd
☎2019 Plan:**8** Closed 22–30Dec 12hc
CTV sea S% B&b£4–£5 Bdi£7–£8.50
W£77–£94 D10am

GH Raddicombe Lodge Kingswear Rd
☎2125 Plan:**9** 10hc ⊗ nc1 CTV 10P sea
S% B&b£6.25 Bdi£9.50 W£66.50 ⅃
D4.30pm

BRIXTON Devon *Map 2 SX55*
⋈**GH Rosemount** ☎ Plymouth 880770
Lic 7hc ⊗ CTV 12P ⊞ S% B&b£5 W£35
M

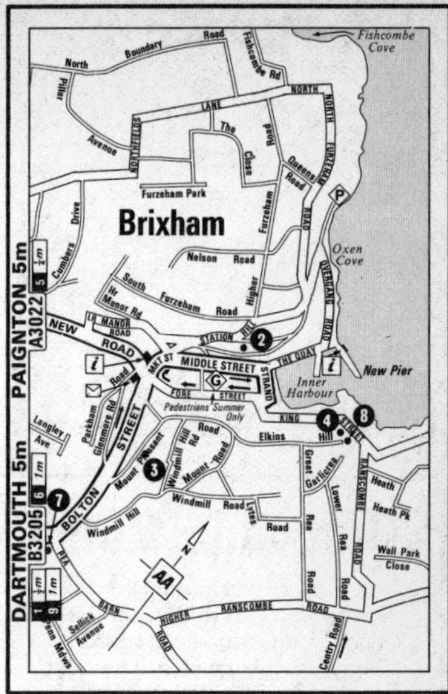

1	Beverley Court Private Hotel	6	Orchard House
2	Brioc Private Hotel	7	Parkway House Private Hotel
3	Cottage Hotel	8	Pola
4	Harbour View	9	Raddicombe Lodge
5	Holwell Villa		

Oakfield Hotel

Oakfield Road, Clifton, BRISTOL
Tel: Bristol 35556

Near   University
       Shopping Centre
       Zoo
       Clifton Suspension Bridge
       Clifton College

Facilities   Parking
             TV Lounge
             Shaving Units
             Central Heating

Dunridge Hotel

The Hotel overlooks the golf course yet is only 2 mins from Crocklets famous surfing beach. The proprietors offer the best of home cooking with spotless accommodation. Flats also available. Brochure on request or telephone Bude 2589.

Dunridge House,
30 Downs View, Bude,
N. Cornwall.

BROADHEMPSTON Devon *Map 3 SX86*
GH Downe Manor ☎ Ipplepen 812239
Apr–Oct 6hc CTV 7P 1🏠 S%
✳B&b£3.50–£3.75 Bdi£6.25 W£40 ⅃
D6.30pm

BROAD MARSTON Heref & Worcs
Map 4 SP14
GH Broad Marston Manor
☎ Stratford-upon-Avon 720252 Mar–Nov
7hc 2⊐🚿 ❀ TV 30P 🍴 S% B&b£6–£6.50

BROADSTAIRS Kent *Map 5 TR36*
GH Bay Tree Hotel 12 Eastern Esp
☎ Thanet 62502 Lic 9hc ❀ nc3 CTV 8P
🍴 sea S% ✳B&bfr£6.50 Bdifr£9.50
Wfr£41.25 ⅃ D4.30pm

↦GH Corner Ways 49–51 West Cliff Rd
☎ Thanet 61612 Closed Dec Lic 12hc
CTV 13P S% B&b£5.94–£6.75
Bdi£7.02–£7.83 W£45.36–£50.76 ⅃
D6.30pm

GH Denmead Hotel 13 Granville Rd
☎ Thanet 62580 Lic 8hc 3P 🍴 B&b£6.50
Bdi£10 W£47–£54 ⅃ D10pm

GH Dutch House Hotel 30 North
Foreland Rd ☎ Thanet 62824 Lic 10hc
❀ CTV 6P 🍴 S% B&b£6.50–£8.50
Bdi£8.50–£10.50 W£53.50–£58.50 ⅃
D7pm

GH Keston Court Hotel 14 Ramsgate Rd
☎ Thanet 62401 Lic 9hc ❀ nc1 CTV 6P
🍴 S% B&b£6–£6.50 Bdi£8.50–£9
W£45–£51 ⅃ D8pm

GH Kingsmead Hotel Eastern Esp
☎ Thanet 61694 Lic 12hc CTV 12P 🍴
B&b£6–£7 Bdi£8–£9 W£45–£49 ⅃
D6pm

GH St Augustines Private Hotel
19 Granville Rd ☎ Thanet 65017
May–Oct & Xmas rs Nov, Dec & Feb–Apr
Lic 15hc 1⊐🚿 CTV 🍴 B&b£6.32–£7.18
Bdi£9.79–£10.21 W£55.20–£71.30 ⅃
W only Aug D7.15pm

↦GH Seapoint Private Hotel 76 West
Cliff Rd ☎ Thanet 62269 Mar–Oct
rs Jan & Feb (B&b only) Lic 10hc CTV
9P 🍴 sea S% B&b£5.50–£6 Bdi£6.50–£7
W£45–£47 ⅃ D6pm

BUCKFASTLEIGH Devon *Map 3 SX76*
↦GH Black Rock Buckfast Rd, Dart
Bridge (At Buckfast 1m N) ☎2343 Lic
10hc CTV 20P 🍴 river S% B&b£5–£6
Bdi£7.50–£8.50 W£50–£57 ⅃ D8pm

GH *Furzeleigh Mill* ☎2245 Closed Xmas
& New Year Lic 16hc TV 20P

BUDE Cornwall *Map 2 SS20* **See Plan**
GH *Bude Haven Hotel* Creathorne Rd
(off Flexbury Av) ☎2305 Plan:**1** Lic 10hc
CTV 6P 🍴 sea D5pm

↦GH Dunridge 30 Downs View ☎2589
Plan:**2** Etr–Oct 10hc CTV 9P S%
B&b£5.52–£7.25 Bdi£8.60–£10.06
W£48.30–£54.50 ⅃ D6pm

↦GH Kisauni 4 Downs View ☎2653
Plan:**3** Etr–Sep 6hc CTV 5P S% B&b£4–£5
Bdi£5.75–£6.75 W£35–£40 ⅃ D5pm

↦GH Links View 13 Morwenna Ter
☎2561 Plan:**4** Closed Xmas Lic 7hc
CTV 🍴 sea S% B&b£5–£6 Bdi£7–£8
W£42–£48 ⅃ D6pm

↦GH Pencarrol 21 Downs View ☎2478
Plan:**5** Mar–Oct 7hc 1🏠 S%
B&b£3.75–£4.90 Bdi£6.05–£7.50
W£36.80–£45 ⅃ D5pm

↦GH Sandiways 35 Downs View
☎2073 Plan:**6** Lic 11hc ❀ CTV 8P S%
B&b£4.50–£5.50 Bdi£6.75–£7.50
W£42–£50 ⅃ D8pm

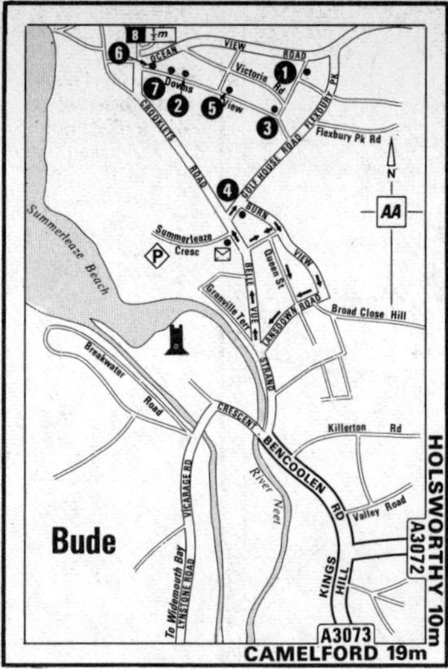

1 Bude Haven Hotel
2 Duridge
3 Kinsauni
4 Links View
5 Pencarrol
6 Sandiways
7 Surf Haven
8 Surf Motel

☎**GH Surf Haven** 31 Downs View
☎2998 Plan:**7** Apr–Oct Lic 6hc ⚓ CTV
6P sea S% B&b£4.89–£5.75
Bdi£7.19–£8.05 W£43.70–£52.90
↳ D5pm

GH *Surf Motel* Maer Down, Crooklets
☎3584 Plan:**8** Jun–Sep rs Mar–May &
Oct–7Nov 15hc (A 18hc) TV 70P sea

BUDLEIGH SALTERTON Devon
Map 3 SY08
GH Park House Hotel 7 Park Ln, Little
Knowle ☎3303 Etr–Oct Lic 10hc ⚓ CTV
12P sea S% ✱B&b£6–£8 Bdi£9–£11
W£54–£66 ↳ D5pm

☎**GH Willowmead** 12 Little Knowle
☎3115 5hc CTV 7P S% B&b£5.50–£6.50
Bdi£7.95–£9 W£48.50–£55 ↳ D8pm

BURFORD Oxon *Map 4 SP21*
GH Corner House Hotel High St ☎3151
mid Feb–mid Dec Lic 10hc 1⌂▥ CTV ▥
S% B&b£7.50–£8 Bdi£10.80–£11.30
D8pm

BURLEY Hants *Map 4 SU20*
GH Highcroft Hotel Highcroft Woods
☎2525 Closed 2 wks Xmas Lic 11hc
CTV 12P ▥ S% B&b£9.25–£16
Bdi fr£13.75 D4pm

GH *Tree House* New Forest ☎3448 Lic
8hc ✗ nc5 CTV 12P ▥

BURNSALL N Yorks *Map 7 SE06*
GH Manor House ☎231 Lic 8hc nc5
CTV 6P B&b£6.65 Bdi£10 W£65 ↳ D5pm

BURROW BRIDGE Somerset *Map 3 ST33*
GH *Old Bakery* ☎234 Closed Xmas 6hc
TV 12P 2⌂ D9.30pm

BURWASH E Sussex *Map 5 TQ62*
INN Admiral Vernon ☎882230 Lic 5hc
1⌂▥ nc10 CTV 30P 1⌂ S% B&b£8–£9
Bdi£10.50–£12 sn L£3–£3.50&alc
D9.15pm£3.50–£4.50&alc

INN Bell High St ☎882304 rs Xmas
(no accommodation & restaurant closed)
Lic 5hc 15P ▥ ⇄ ✱B&b£4.50–£5.50
W£28–£35 ⓜ sn L£3&alc D9.30pm£3alc

BURY ST EDMUNDS Suffolk *Map 5 TL86*
GH *Swan* 11 Northgate St ☎2678
Closed 24–31Dec 6hc CTV

BUTTERTON Staffs *Map 7 SK05*
INN *Black Lion* ☎ Onecote 232 Lic 4hc
✗ nc12 TV 14P ▥ D9pm

BUXTON Derbys *Map 7 SK07*
☎**GH Fairhaven** 1 Dale Ter ☎4481
7hc CTV ▥ S% B&b£5–£6 Bdi£7–£7.50
W£45–£47.50 Dnoon

☎**GH Griff** 2 Compton Rd ☎3628
Closed Dec 6hc CTV 5P ▥
B&b£4.50–£5.50 W£28–£33.50 ⓜ

☎**GH Hawthorn Farm** Fairfield Rd
☎3230 Closed Xmas rs Oct–Etr 6hc
(A 8hc) TV 14P 2⌂ B&b fr£5.75
Bdi fr£9.20 Wfr£50.60 ↳ W only May–Sep
Dnoon

☎**GH Kingscroft** 10 Green Ln ☎2757
Lic 7hc CTV 9P 2⌂ ▥ S% B&b£5–£5.50
Bdi£7–£7.50 W£45–£47 ↳ D5pm

☎**GH Roseleigh** 19 Broadwalk ☎4904
Closed Xmas & New Year rs Nov–Mar
(B&b only) Lic 14hc nc7 CTV 12P
B&b fr£5.94 Bdi fr£9.18 Wfr£61.56 ↳
D4.30pm

GH Thorn Heyes Private Hotel
137 London Rd ☎3539 Lic 7hc nc2 CTV
7P ▥ S% B&b£6.53–£7.50
Bdi£10.58–£12.17 W£67.53–£77.68
↳ D6.30pm

GH Westminster Hotel 21 Broadwalk
☎3929 Closed Xmas Lic 14rm CTV 11P
S% B&b£6.32–£6.90 Bdi£9.20–£10.06
W£60.95–£66.70 ↳ D5pm

CALLINGTON Cornwall *Map 2 SX36*
GH *Chantry* Liskeard Rd ☎3215 Lic 9hc
CTV 5P D6.30pm

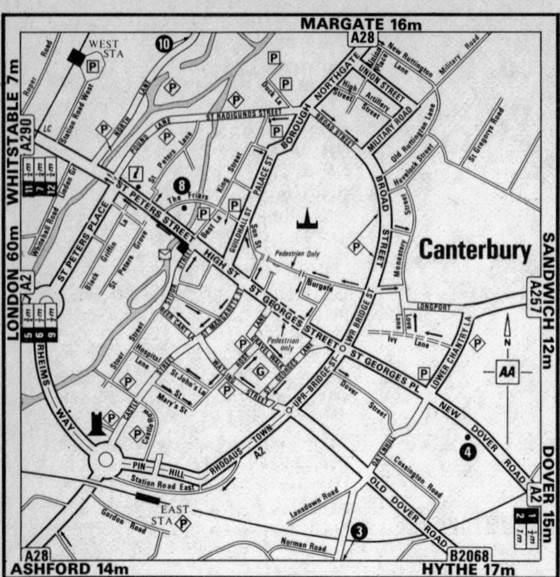

CALNE Wilts *Map 3 ST97*
INN White Hart Hotel 2 London Rd
☎812413 Lic 8hc 1⇔🍴 ⚘ CTV 10P 🎪
S% B&bfr£6.50 Bdi£9.90 sn Lfr£2
D8pm fr£3

CAMBORNE Cornwall *Map 2 SW64*
GH Pendarves Lodge ☎712691 Closed
Oct Lic 8hc ⚘ ♨ CTV 8P S% B&b£6
Bdi£9 W£60 ⚡ D7pm

GH Regal Hotel Church Ln ☎713131
Closed Xmas Lic 13hc 2⇔🍴 CTV 12P 🎪
S% B&b£6 Bdi£9.50 D8pm

GH St Clair Hotel Basset Rd ☎713289
Lic 12hc ⚘ CTV 20P 4🏠 🎪 S%
B&b£7.06–£7.56 Bdi£10–£13 W£92
D10pm

CAMBRIDGE Cambs *Map 5 TL45*
During the currency of this publication
some Cambridge telephone numbers are
liable to change.
⋈**GH Belle Vue** 33 Chesterton Rd
☎51859 8hc 6P river S% B&b£5–£6

GH *Guest House Hotel* 139 Huntingdon
Rd ☎52833 Closed 1 wk Xmas 13hc ♨
13P 🎪 D7.15pm

GH *Helen's Hotel* 167–169 Hills Rd
☎46465 5Jan–5Dec Lic 19hc (A 6hc)
CTV 20P 🎪

GH Suffolk House 69 Milton Rd ☎352016
6hc ⚘ TV 7P 🎪 S% B&b£6.35–£7.95
Bdi£9.10–£10.70 D10pm

CAMELFORD Cornwall *Map 2 SX18*
GH Sunnyside Hotel ☎2250 Mar–Sep
rs Oct–Feb (reservations only) Lic 10hc ♨
CTV 16P 🎪 S% B&b£7.50–£9
Bdi£11–£13.25 W£61.75–£74 ⚡D6pm

GH *Tor Crag* Valley Truckle ☎2369
May–Sep 6hc nc10 CTV 6P D6.30pm

GH Warmington House 32 Market Pl
☎3380 Lic 7hc 2⇔🍴 ♨ CTV 2P 3🏠 🎪
S% B&b£6–£7 Bdi£9.50–£11 Wfr£63
⚡ D9.30pm

CANTERBURY Kent *Map 5 TR15*
See Plan
GH Barcroft 56 New Dover Rd ☎69177
Plan:**1** 14hc CTV 16P 🎪 S% B&bfr£7

GH Canterbury Hotel 71 New Dover Rd
☎68750 Plan:**2** Lic 16rm 8hc 8⇔🍴
CTV 20P 🎪 S% ✳B&b£9.20–£12.65

⋈**GH Carlton** 40 Nunneryfields ☎65900
Plan:**3** 10hc 6P 🎪 B&b£5–£7

Enjoy a stay at Cambridge's premier
Guest House. Situated in its own
grounds with private car park. All
rooms are fully carpeted with central
heating, H & C, razor sockets,
radio etc. Bath and shower facilities.
Comfortable lounge with TV.
Conveniently situated for colleges
and city.

Member of EATB.

Suffolk House

69 Milton Road, Cambridge. Tel; 52016 STD (0223)

LICENSED

Woodpeckers Country Hotel

LTD.
Womenswold nr. Canterbury, Kent
Barham 319 (STD 022 782)

The ideal hotel for visiting south east Kent

WOODPECKERS COUNTRY HOTEL was built over 100 years ago as a rectory and has been an hotel for over fifteen years. *PAT AND TED MILLARD* continue to provide the friendly, informal and relaxing atmosphere for which the hotel has become known and trusted. The proprietors will by arrangement take guests on short tours in their 1936 taxi.

Everything is provided for families, including cots, high chairs, baby listening and simple washing, ironing and airing facilities. Each of the 13 bedrooms is fitted with a wash basin having hot and cold running water, tea and coffee-making facilities. The house is centrally-heated throughout.

The Hotel has acquired a reputation for serving well-cooked, traditional English meals and is a member of "A Taste of England". Highly recommended for country home baking. Packed lunches. The staff are ready and willing to help in every way to ensure the satisfaction of the guests. The two comfortable lounges provide adequate opportunity for indoor relaxation: one of the lounges being equipped with television and a selection of children's games.

Ample car parking space is available in the grounds of over two acres, which have a plentiful variety of trees, shrubs, flowers and extensive lawns. There is a swing, sandpit, "pets corner" and <u>a heated swimming pool with diving board and water slide.</u>

The hotel is ideally situated for those wishing to travel to and from the Continent via Dover, Folkestone or the Ramsgate Hoverport. Over eighty miles of beautiful and varied coastline is within easy reach by road and the wealth of historical interest in towns and villages throughout East Kent is but a few minutes away by car or bus.

Bed and full breakfast from £7.50. Dinner, bed and breakfast £11.00. Reduced rates for off-season, three day breaks. All prices inclusive of VAT, service and tea or coffee.

GH Ersham Lodge 12 New Dover Rd
☎63174 Plan:**4** Lic 14hc 5⇱▥ ✗ CTV
17P 2🏠 ▥ S% B&b£7–£10

⋈**GH Harbledown Court** 17 Summerhill,
Harbledown ☎60659 Plan:**5** 7hc 1⇱▥
CTV 8P ▥ S% B&b£5.75–£6.50

GH Highfield Hotel Summer Hill,
Harbledown ☎62772 Plan:**6** Closed Xmas
Lic 11hc 1⇱▥ nc3 CTV 12P ▥
B&b£6–£8.50

⋈**GH Magnolia House** 36 St Dunstan's
Ter ☎65121 Plan:**7** Closed Xmas wk 6hc
✗ TV 6P S% B&b£4.50–£5.50

GH Pilgrims 18 The Friars ☎64531
Plan:**8** Closed 4 days Xmas 14hc CTV
8P ▥

GH Red House Hotel London Rd
☎63578 Plan:**9** Closed Xmas & New
Year Lic 19hc 8⇱▥ ♨ CTV 18P ▥ S%
B&b£7.50–£9.75 Bdi£11–£14
W£45.50–£65 Ⓜ D8pm

⋈**GH St Stephens** 100 St Stephen's Rd
☎62167 Plan:**10** Lic 9hc 1⇱▥ ✗ CTV
8P ▥ S% B&b£5.40–£7.56 W£36–£50 Ⓜ

GH Victoria Court 61 London Rd
☎65447 Plan:**11** Lic 25hc 12⇱▥ CTV
25P ▥ B&b£8.25–£8.75 D9pm

GH Wesley Manse 71 Whitstable Rd
☎55164 Plan:**12** 8hc ✗ ♨ CTV 3P ▥

CAREY Heref & Worcs Map 3 SO53
INN Cottage of Content ☎242
Closed Xmas Day Lic 3hc ✗ nc14 CTV
20P ▥ 🚃 B&b£7.50–£8.50
Bdi£15–£17.50 sn L£6alc D8.30pm£8alc

CARLISLE Cumbria Map 11 NY35
GH Angus Hotel 14 Scotland Rd ☎23546
Closed Xmas–New Year Lic 8hc CTV ▥
D6pm

⋈**GH Claremont Private Hotel**
30 London Rd ☎24691 9hc CTV 5P S%
B&b£4–£5.50

GH Cumbria Park Hotel 32 Scotland Rd
☎22887 Closed Xmas Lic 19hc 8⇱▥
(A 9hc 2⇱▥) ✗ CTV 28P 1🏠 ▥ S%
B&b£7.50–£9.50 Bdi£11.50–£14
D7.45pm

GH East View 110 Warwick Rd ☎22112
Closed Dec 8hc ✗ nc5 TV P

⋈**GH Kenilworth Hotel** 24 Lazonby Ter
☎26179 5hc CTV 5P ▥ S% B&bfr£4
Wfr£26.25 Ⓜ

CARNFORTH Lancs Map 7 SD47
GH Holmere Hall Yealand Conyers

(2m N A6) ☎2931 Lic 7hc CTV 16P 4🏠
▥ D8pm

CASTLE DONINGTON Leics Map 8 SK42
GH Delven 12 Delven Ln ☎810153 Lic
7hc nc16 CTV 6P ▥ D£3pm

CATON Lancs Map 7 SD56
INN Ship Hotel Lancaster Rd ☎770265
Lic 3hc ✗ nc TV 20P 3🏠 ▥ 🚃 S%
B&b£6–£6.50 Bar lunch £2&alc

CAWOOD N Yorks Map 8 SE53
GH Compton Court Hotel ☎315 Lic 7hc
3⇱▥ (A 3hc 1⇱▥) CTV 8P ▥ S%
B&b£9.25–£10.25 Bdi£15–£16.50
D8pm

CHAGFORD Devon Map 3 SX78
GH Glendaragh ☎3270 Lic 8hc CTV 9P
▥ S% B&b£7–£7.50 Bdi£11.50–£12
W£78–£81 Ⓛ D7.30pm

CHALFONT ST PETER Bucks
Map 4 TQ09
INN Greyhound High St ☎ Gerrards
Cross 83404 rs Sun evening & Mon
(no a la carte restaurant) Lic 11hc ✗ 30P
▥ 🚃 B&b£6.75–£8.25 sn L£1.60–£4.86
D10pm£1.35&alc

CHANNEL ISLANDS
Details will be found between the England
and Wales section.

CHARD Somerset Map 3 ST30
⋈**GH Watermead** 83 High St ☎2834
Lic 7hc ♨ CTV 8P ▥ S% B&b£5.50 Bdi£7
W£35 Ⓜ D10pm

CHARLTON W Sussex Map 4 SU81
GH Woodstock House Hotel
☎ Singleton 666 Closed Jan rs Nov,
Dec & Feb (weekend breaks only) Lic 12hc
3⇱▥ ✗ nc8 CTV 12P ▥ S% B&b£8–£10
Bdi£12–£14 W£72–£85 Ⓛ D7.30pm

CHARLWOOD Surrey Map 4 TQ74
For accommodation details see under
Gatwick Airport

CHARMOUTH Dorset Map 3 SY39
⋈**GH Cottage** High St ☎60407
Closed Xmas 6hc (A 1hc) TV 30P S%
B&b£5–£5.50 Bdi£8–£8.50 D7.30pm

⋈**GH Newlands House** Stonebarrow Ln
☎60212 Apr–Oct Lic 8hc 7⇱▥ ✗ nc3
CTV 12P ▥ S% B&b£5.50–£6
Bdi£8.10–£8.60 W£51.20–£54.20 Ⓛ
D5pm

Brookside Hotel
2 Grange Road, Brook Lane, Chester CH2 2AN
(off Liverpool Road)
Tel: Reception (STD 0244) 27279. Guests (STD 0244) 49603

* Large private car park
* 21 bedrooms (4 with private
  shower) all hot and cold
* On main bus route
* Lounge with colour TV
* Licensed
* Near city centre
* Central heating
* Electric fires in bedrooms

GH White House 2 Hillside ☎60411 Apr–Oct Lic 8hc 1⇆🛁 ⊗ nc4 CTV 12P 🍴 ✱B&b£4–£5.50 Bdi£6.50–£7.95 W£41–£50.50 ⅃ D6pm

CHATTERIS Cambs *Map 5 TL38*
INN *George Hotel* High St ☎2208 Lic 5hc D9pm

CHEDDAR Somerset *Map 3 ST45*
↦**GH Arundel House Hotel** The Cross ☎742264 Lic 6hc CTV 6P 🍴 S% B&b£4.75 Bdi£8.50 W£31.50 M D7.30pm

GH *Gordons Hotel* Cliff St ☎742497 Closed Dec Lic 14hc CTV 10P

INN *Bath Arms Hotel* Bath St ☎742425 Lic 8hc TV 30P 2🏠 🍴 D10pm

CHELMSFORD Essex *Map 5 TL70*
GH Beechcroft Private Hotel 211 New London Rd ☎352462 Closed Xmas 26hc CTV 15P 🍴 B&b£8.20–£8.93

GH Tanunda Hotel 219 New London Rd ☎354295 Closed Xmas 20hc 8⇆🛁 nc5 CTV 20P 🍴 B&b£7–£10

CHELTENHAM Glos *Map 3 SO92*
GH Bowler Hat Hotel 130 London Rd ☎23614 Lic 6hc 1⇆🛁 ⊗ CTV 8P 🍴 S% B&bfr£6

↦**GH Brennan** 21 St Lukes Rd ☎25904 5hc CTV S% B&b£4.50

GH *Cotswold Grange Hotel* Pittville Circus Rd ☎55119 Lic 18hc CTV 18P 🍴 D6.30pm

GH Hollington House Hotel 115 Hales Rd ☎519718 Lic 7hc CTV 9P 🍴 S% B&b£6.90–£7.94 Bdi£10.35–£11.91 W£65.20–£75 ⅃ Dnoon

GH *Ivy Dene* 145 Hewlett Rd ☎21726 7hc CTV 5P 1🏠 🍴

↦**GH Micklinton Hotel** 12 Montpellier Dr ☎20000 6hc TV 5P 🍴 B&b£4.50 Bdi£7 W£49 ⅃ Dam

GH North Hall Hotel Pittville Circus Rd ☎20589 Lic 21hc CTV 20P 🍴 B&bfr£6.50 Bdifr£9 Wfr£60.50 ⅃ D6.45pm

CHESTER Cheshire *Map 7 SJ46*
↦**GH Brookside Private Hotel** 12 Brook Ln ☎27279 Lic 21hc 4⇆🛁 CTV 13P 1🏠 🍴 S% B&b£5.50–£6

GH Chester Court Hotel 48 Hoole Rd ☎20779 Closed Xmas wk Lic 8hc 3⇆🛁 (A 7hc 7⇆🛁) CTV 15P 🍴 S% B&b£7–£9 Bdi£10.50–£12.50 D7pm

↦**GH Eversley Private Hotel** 9 Eversley Pk ☎25620 7hc ⊗ nc3 CTV 10P 🍴 S% ✱B&b£5.50

GH Green Bough Hotel 60 Hoole Rd ☎26241 Closed Xmas & New Year Lic 11hc 5⇆🛁 CTV 11P 🍴 S% B&b£6–£8.50 Bdi£9–£11.50 W£63–£77 ⅃ D6.30pm

GH Hamilton 5–7 Hamilton St ☎45387 Lic 10hc CTV 3🏠 🍴 S% B&b£6–£8 Bdi£7.50–£11 W£49 ⅃ D5pm

GH *Malvern* 21 Victoria Rd ☎41922 Closed Xmas & New Year 7hc ⊗ nc2 CTV 3P

GH *Riverside Private Hotel* 22 City Walls, off Lower Bridge St ☎26580 Closed 2 wks Xmas Lic 20hc CTV 20P river D7.30pm

GH Weston Hotel 82 Hoole Rd ☎26735 Lic 15hc 4⇆🛁 ⊗ CTV 40P 🍴 S% B&b£8–£10.50 D9pm

CHICKLADE Wilts *Map 3 ST93*
↦**GH Old Rectory** ☎ Hindon 226

Green Bough Hotel

60 Hall Road, Chester CH2 3NL Tel: Chester 26241 (STD 0244)

A personally-run small private hotel offering you comfort and cleanliness. The Green Bough provides first-class cuisine prepared and served under the personal supervision of the hotel-trained proprietors. Other facilities include:—

Hot and cold water and shaver points in all rooms. Rooms available with private shower/toilet. Full central heating. Comfortable lounge with colour TV.

Car park, evening meals, table licence. Fire certificate. On a bus route.

The hotel is situated on the A56 north of the city. North West Tourist Board recommended.

The Old Rectory

CHICKLADE

On A303 road, in beautiful rural scenery. Ideal Wessex touring centre. Charming old house, every modern comfort. Home cooking and personal service by the hosts. Overnight and holiday guests welcome. Open all year.

D & R Head, The Old Rectory, Chicklade, Hindon, Salisbury, Wilts. SP3 5SU Tel: 074 789 226.

Closed 1–11May, 1–17Oct & 24–31Dec
8hc TV 9P 1🔒 🍽 S% B&bf£5.92–£6.66
Bdi£8.86–£9.95 W£48.88–£56.93 ⚸
D2pm

CHIDEOCK Dorset *Map 3 SY49*
GH Thatch Cottage ☎473 Apr–Oct Lic
5hc ⊗ nc10 CTV 3P 2🔒 🍽 S% ✳B&bf£6
Bdi£11 W£70 ⚸ D8.30pm

CHILLINGTON Devon *Map 3 SX74*
GH Fairfield ☎ Torcross 388 Lic 12hc
1🔊 ◓ TV 30P 3🔒 🍽 S%
B&bf£6.90–£8.05 Bdi£9.77–£10.92.
W£64.40–£72.45 ⚸ D7pm

CHIPPING SODBURY Avon *Map 3 ST78*
GH Moda Hotel 1 High St ☎312135
Closed Xmas Lic 7hc (A 3hc) ⊗ nc2 TV
🍽 S% B&bf£7–£7.50 Bdi£10.50 D5pm
INN *Portcullis* ☎312004 Lic 5hc ⊗ TV
3P D9pm

CHITTLEHAMHOLT Devon *Map 3 SS62*
GH Beares Farm ☎523 Closed Xmas
& New Year Lic 6hc 12P 🍽 ✳B&bf£5.75
Bdi£10.35 D9pm

CHRISTCHURCH Dorset *Map 4 SZ19*
For locations and additional guesthouses
see **Bournemouth**
⊷GH **Belvedere Hotel** 59 Barrack Rd
☎485978 Bournemouth district plan:**9**
Lic 10hc TV 12P 🍽 S% B&bf£4.50–£5
Bdi£7.50–£8 W£50–£55 ⚸ D6.30pm

GH Broomway Hotel 46 Barrack Rd
☎483405 Bournemouth district plan:**14**
Closed Xmas Lic 10hc ⊗ nc3 CTV 10P S%
B&bf£6.90–£8.63 Bdi£10.93–£12.65
W£51.75–£69 ⚸ D6.30pm

⊷**GH Burton Grange** Burton Gn (2m N
on B3347) ☎485018 Not on plan
Closed Dec 6hc TV 10P S% B&bf£4–£4.50
W£28–£31.50 Ⓜ
GH Ferndale 41 Stour Rd ☎482616
Bournemouth district plan:**37** rs B/B only
Oct–May 6hc ⊗ CTV 6P 🍽 S% W only
Jul–Sep D6pm

⊷**GH Laurels** 195 Barrack Rd ☎485530
Bournemouth district plan:**49** Closed
Xmas Lic 14hc 3🔊 CTV 12P 2🔒 🍽 S%
B&bf£4.75–£6.50 Bdi£7.25–£9 W£35–£55
⚸ D5.30pm

GH Park House Hotel 48 Barrack Rd
☎482124 Bournemouth district plan:**61**
Lic 10hc 1🔊 CTV 12P 🍽 S% B&bf£8
Bdi£13 W£91 ⚸ D2pm

⊷**GH Pines** 39 Mudeford Rd ☎482393
Bournemouth district plan:**65** Mar–Dec
11hc 2🔊 CTV 12P 🍽 S% B&bf£5–£6
Bdi£7–£8 D6pm

⊷**GH St Albans Hotel** 8 Avenue Rd
☎481096 Bournemouth district plan:**67**
Apr–Oct & Xmas Lic 9hc 1🔊 CTV 12P
S% B&bf£5.50–£6.50 Bdi£8–£9
W£53–£60 ⚸ D2pm

⊷**GH Sea Witch Hotel** 153/5 Barrack
Rd ☎482846 Bournemouth district plan:
73 Lic 9hc ⊗ CTV 22P 🍽 S% B&bf£5–£7
Bdi£6.50–£9 W£40–£60 ⚸ D5pm

GH *Shortwood House* Magdalen Ln
☎485223 Bournemouth district plan:**75**
6hc CTV 6P

CHULMLEIGH Devon *Map 3 SS61*
INN *Red Lion Hotel* East St ☎384 Lic
4hc CTV 10P D8.30pm

CINDERFORD Glos *Map 3 SO61*

INN White Hart Hotel St Whites Rd,
Ruspidge (B4227) ☎23139 rs Xmas Day
Lic 6hc 80P B&b£6–£9 W£40–£60 sn
L£1.25–£2.50&alc
D9.45pm£1.25–£2.50&alc

CIRENCESTER Glos *Map 4 SP00*
GH *Arkenside* 44 Lewis Ln ☎3072 Lic
10hc TV 10P D6.30pm

⊢⊣GH Raydon 3 The Avenue ☎3485
Closed Xmas & New Year 10rm 8hc CTV
6P S% B&b£4.86–£5.13

⊢⊣GH Rivercourt Beeches Rd ☎3998
Closed Xmas 6hc (A 4hc) ⚡ TV 12P 10🛏
🍴 S% B&b£4.50–£5.50

GH La Ronde 52–54 Ashcroft Rd ☎4611
Lic 10hc CTV 🍴 B&b£6.25–£8.50
Bdi£10.75–£13.50 D7.30pm

⊢⊣GH Wimborne Victoria Rd ☎3890
1Jan–23Dec 6hc ⚡ nc5 CTV 6P S%
B&b£5–£6 Bdi£8.50–£10 Dnoon

CLACTON-ON-SEA Essex *Map 5 TM11*
GH Argyll Private Hotel 8 Colne Rd
☎23227 Closed Jan, Feb & Mar Lic 24hc
1🛏 (A 4rm 2🛏) ⚡ nc2 CTV 6P S%
B&b£7.50–£9.50 Bdi£10.50–£12.50
W£54–£60 D6pm

GH Sandrock Hotel 1 Penfold Rd
☎28215 Feb–Dec Lic 6hc ⚡ CTV TV 6P
🍴 sea S% B&b£7.50

GH York House 19 York Rd, Holland-on-
Sea (2m NE B1032) ☎814333 Closed Nov
rs Xmas, Dec–Mar (B&b only) Lic 6hc 🌣
CTV 12P 2🛏 🍴 S% B&b£6–£7 Bdi£9–£10
W£55–£61 ⚡ Dnoon

CLARE Suffolk *Map 5 TL74*
GH Old Bear & Crown Hotel 20 Market
Hill ☎440 Lic 6hc TV 6P 2🛏 B&b£8–£9
Bdi£13–£16.50 W£90 ⚡ D8pm

CLEARWELL Glos *Map 3 SO50*
INN Wyndham Arms ☎ Coleford 3666
Closed Mon Lic 3hc 30P 1🛏 🍴 🚆 S%
B&b£6.50 sn L£2.25&alc D10pm£8alc

CLITHEROE Lancs *Map 7 SD74*
GH *Fairway House* 48 King St ☎22025
rs late Dec–early Jan (B&b only) Lic 10hc
⚡ CTV D5pm

CLUN Salop *Map 7 SO38*
INN Sun ☎277 Lic 4hc ⚡ nc3 TV 4P 🍴
S% B&b fr£6 D9.30pm

COCKERMOUTH Cumbria *Map 11 NY13*

GH Hundith Hill Hotel Lorton Valley
(2m SE B5292) ☎822092 Mar–Nov Lic
14hc 7🛏 (A 6hc 1🛏) CTV 30P 🍴
B&b£7.50–£9.50 Bdi£11–£13.50
W£70–£87.50 ⚡ D7pm

COLCHESTER Essex *Map 5 TM02*
GH Cloisters 94 Maldon Rd ☎73756
Closed Jan & Dec Lic 11hc ⚡ nc5 CTV
10P 🍴 S% B&b£6.50–£7

COLESTOCKS Devon *Map 3 ST00*
GH Colestocks House ☎ Honiton 850633
Closed Jan & Feb Lic 6rm 5hc 2🛏 ⚡ nc
CTV 6P S% B&b£7–£8 Bdi£9.50–£10.50
W£60–£67 ⚡ D8pm

COLLYWESTON Northants *Map 4 TF00*
INN Cavalier Main St ☎ Duddington 288
Lic 6hc 60P 🍴 ✳B&b£8.05 Bar lunch
60p–£1.40 D9.30pm£2.50–£5

COLYFORD Devon *Map 3 SY29*
GH *Elmwood Hotel* Swanhill Rd
☎ Colyton 52750 Lic 9hc (A 3hc) ⚡ CTV
12P 1🛏 🍴 D7pm

⊢⊣GH St Edmunds ☎ Colyton 52431
Mid May–Sep & Etr 9rm 8hc CTV 10P 🍴
S% B&b£5.83 Bdi£9.78 W£60.30 ⚡
D7pm

COLYTON Devon *Map 3 SY29*
GH Old Bakehouse ☎52518 Mar–Oct
Lic 7hc 1🛏 ⚡ 10P 🍴 S% B&b£9–£10
Bdi£15–£17 W£105–£115 ⚡
D8.30pm

COMBE MARTIN Devon *Map 2 SS54*
GH Britannia Private Hotel Moorey
Meadow ☎2294 Lic 10hc ⚡
CTV 14P 2🛏 🍴 sea S% B&b£7.70–£9.35
Bdi£9.90–£11.55 W£77–£88 D6.30pm

GH *Coulsworthy House Hotel* ☎2463
Lic 12hc 🌣 CTV 25P 🍴

⊢⊣GH Firs Woodlands ☎3404 Closed
Xmas Lic 9hc ⚡ 🌣 CTV 10P 🍴 sea S%
B&b fr£5.18 Bdi fr£8.05 W£40.25–£43.70
⚡ (W only Jul & Aug)

⊢⊣GH Miramar Victoria St ☎3558
Etr–Oct 11hc 🌣 CTV 9P S% B&b£5.75
Bdi£7.48 W£46 ⚡ D6.30pm

⊢⊣GH Newberry Lodge Hotel Newberry
Rd ☎3316 mid Mar–Oct Lic 15hc 3🛏
nc3 CTV 12P sea B&b£5.75–£8.05
Bdi£8.05–£10.95 W£49.45–£65.55 ⚡
D7pm

COMPTON Berks *Map 4 SU57*
INN Swan Hotel ☎269 Lic 4hc TV 40P

White Hart Inn

Cinderford 23139

Proprietors: Sue and James Newman

Situated close to centre of Forest of Dean, with views of the Forest from the front rooms. All rooms have H & C. TV if required. B & B accommodation from £6. Restaurant available for dinner. Traditional Sunday lunches. Cold buffet daily throughout the summer.

Facing park   Residential area

Croft Hotel
STOKE GREEN   (off Binley Road)
COVENTRY

10 minutes from city centre and Cathedral

20 minutes from the National Exhibition Centre.

Car parking   Licensed

S% B&b£7–£7.50 Bdi£10.50–£12.50 W£75 ⊬ sn L£2.50–£3.75&alc D9pm£4–£6&alc

CONGRESBURY Avon *Map 3 ST46*
GH *Lyndhurst* ☎ Yatton 832279 6hc ⊗ CTV 2P 3🏠 D1pm

CONISTON Cumbria *Map 7 SD39*
GH Low Bank Ground Country House Hotel ☎525 Mar–7Nov Lic 4🛏🏠 10P 🍴 Bdi£16.50–£18.50 W£115.50–£129.50 ⊬ D7.30pm

CONNOR DOWNS Cornwall *Map 2 SW53*
⋈**GH Pine Trees** ☎ Hayle 753249 Closed Nov rs Jan–Etr B&b only Lic 6hc ⊗ CTV 15P S% B&b£5–£6.50 Bdi£7–£9 W£45–£58 ⊬ D4pm

CONSTANTINE Cornwall *Map 2 SW72*
GH *High Cross* ☎373 Closed Xmas 5hc ⊗ CTV 6P D4pm

COVENTRY W Midlands *Map 4 SP37*
⋈**GH Ciska & Rikki** 7–9 Coundon Rd ☎25998 12rm 10hc CTV 🍴 S% B&b£5.50
GH Croft Hotel 23 Stoke Green (off Binley Rd) ☎457846 Lic 13hc CTV 14P 🍴 S% B&bfr£7 Bdifr£10.20 D7pm
⋈**GH Fairlight** 14 Regent St ☎24215 12hc CTV 8P 🍴 S% B&b£4.50–£5 Wfr£24.50 Ⓜ
⋈**GH Northanger House** 35 Westminster Rd ☎26780 7hc ⊗ CTV 🍴 S% B&b£5.50

CRAFTHOLE Cornwall *Map 2 SX35*
INN *Finnygook* ☎ St Germans (Cornwall) 338 Lic 7hc ⊗ nc CTV sea sn D10.30pm

CRANTOCK Cornwall *Map 2 SW76*
GH Crantock Cottage Private Hotel West Pentire Rd ☎232 mid May–late Sep Lic 11hc ⊗ nc7 CTV sea S% B&b£7.50 Bdi£9.50 W£57–£67 ⊬ D5pm

CRAWLEY W Sussex *Map 4 TQ23*
For accommodation details see under Gatwick Airport

CRESSAGE Salop *Map 7 SJ50*
⋈**INN Cound Lodge** ☎322 Lic 7hc ⊗ CTV 45P 🍴 S% B&b£5.50–£6.50 D9.30£4alc

CROMER Norfolk *Map 9 TG24*
⋈**GH Chellow Dene** 23 Macdonald Rd ☎513251 7hc nc3 CTV 6P 🍴 S% B&b£4.50–£5 Bdi£7.25–£7.75 W£40–£45 ⊬ D6pm
⋈**GH Coolhurst** 25 Macdonald Rd ☎512073 7hc CTV 3P S% B&b£4.25–£4.75 Bdi£6.30–£6.80 W£42–£45 ⊬ D9pm
⋈**GH Home Farm** ☎511600 Closed Xmas Lic 8hc ♨ CTV 10P 🍴 S% B&bfr£5.27 Bdifr£7.37 W£51.59–£59.84 ⊬ D7pm
GH Westgate Lodge 10 Macdonald Rd ☎512840 Lic 12hc ⊗ nc3 CTV 14P 🍴 S% B&bfr£6.04 Bdifr£8.05 Wfr£46 ⊬ D6.30pm

CROSSWAY GREEN Heref & Worcs *Map 7 SO86*
INN Mitre Oak ☎ Hartlebury 352 Lic 8hc ⊗ CTV 90P 3🏠 S% B&b£6.80 sn L£2.50 D9.15pm£6.50alc

CROWDECOTE Derbys *Map 7 SK06*
INN *Pack Horse* ☎ Longnor 210 Lic 3hc
nc10 TV 20P river B&b£4 sn D9pm£4alc

CROYDE BAY Devon *Map 2 SS43*
GH Seabirds Hotel Baggy Point
☎890224 Apr–Oct Lic 6hc ⊗ nc5 CTV
23P 🍽 sea ✳B&b£6.21–£8.37
W£41.04–£56.16 🅜 D9pm

CROYDON Gt London *Map 4 TQ36*
GH Friends 50 Friends Rd
☎01-688 6215 8hc 5P S%
✳B&b£5.50–£7.50

GH Oakwood Hotel 69 Outram Rd
☎01-654 2835 Lic 9hc 2⇄🚿 CTV 5P
3🏠 🍽 S% B&b£8.50 Bdi£12 D6.30pm

DARLINGTON Co Durham *Map 8 NZ21*
GH Raydale Hotel Stanhope Rd South
☎58993 Lic 10hc ⊗ CTV 12P 🍽 S%
✳B&bfr£8.05 Bdifr£11.44 Wfr£80.08
↳ D6pm

DARTMOUTH Devon *Map 3 SX84*
◄GH Orleans** 24 South Town ☎2967
5hc ⊗ 🍽 river sea S% B&b£5.50–£6.50

DAWLISH Devon *Map 3 SX97*
◄GH Barton Grange Private Hotel**
5 Barton Villas ☎863365 Etr–Nov 9hc
CTV 6P S% B&b£5.15–£6.30
Bdi£7.45–£8.50 D4.30pm

GH Brockington 139 Exeter Rd
☎863588 9hc ⊗ nc5 CTV 7P 🍽

◄GH Broxmore Private Hotel**
20 Plantation Ter ☎863602 Feb–Dec
8hc ⊗ CTV 🍽 S% B&b£4.50–£5
Bdi£7–£8.50 D6pm

GH *Coval House Hotel* West Cliff
☎862437 rs Nov–Feb (party bookings
only) Lic 9hc CTV 8P 🍽 sea

GH *Fairfield House* Ashcombe Rd
☎862173 Closed Nov Lic 15hc CTV
20P 3🏠 D7pm

◄GH Lamorna Private Hotel** 2 Barton
Ter ☎862242 Closed Dec & Jan Lic 10hc
⊗ nc5 CTV 4P S% B&b£5–£6.25
Bdi£7.50–£8.50 W£35–£42 🅜 Dnoon

◄GH Lynbridge Private Hotel** Barton
Villas ☎862352 Apr–Oct 9hc ⊗ nc2
CTV 6P 🍽 S% B&b£5–£6 Bdi£7–£8
W£48–£55 ↳ D5pm

◄GH Marldon House Hotel** 6 Barton
Villas ☎862721 8hc nc4 CTV 6P 🍽 S%
B&b£4.45–£5.10 Bdi£7.20–£7.80
W£46.90–£51.25 ↳ Dnoon

◄GH Mimosa** 11 Barton Ter ☎863283
Mar–Sep 9hc ⊗ nc5 CTV S% B&b£5–£6
Bdi£6.50–£7.50 W£36–£42 ↳ D3pm

◄GH Portland House** 14 Marine Pde
☎864040 Etr–Oct 7hc ⊗ CTV 6P sea
B&b£5–£7 Bdi£7.50–£9.50
W£45–£60 ↳ D4pm

GH Radfords Dawlish Water ☎863322
Mar–Nov Lic 19⇄🚿 (A 3hc 2⇄🚿) ⌂ CTV
50P ✳B&b£6.48–£8.64 W£64.80–£77.76
↳ D6pm

DEAL Kent *Map 5 TR35*
GH Pension Castle Lea 2 Gladstone Rd
☎2718 Closed Xmas 3⇄🚿 ⊗ nc2 CTV 🍽
sea S% ✳B&b£6.50 Bdi£10 W£70 ↳
D6.30pm

GH *Winthorpe Private Hotel* Kingsdown
Rd, Walmer ☎5788 Etr–Oct Lic 7hc ⊗
nc14 CTV 7P 🍽 sea D6.30pm

DENT Cumbria *Map 7 SO78*
INN George & Dragon ☎256 Lic 9hc
TV 14P 🍽 ⇔ S% B&b£7.30 W£49 M
Bar lunch 65p–£1.60 D10pm£2.40alc

DENTON Gt Manchester *Map 7 SJ99*
GH Elsinore 121 Town Ln ☎061-320
7606 Lic 12⇱🛏 CTV 18P 🍽 S%
B&b£12.50 Bdi£15.50 D8pm

DERBY Derbys *Map 8 SK33*
GH Ascot Hotel 724 Osmaston Rd
☎41916 rs Weekends Lic 17hc CTV 15P
🍽 S% B&b£7.60 Bdi£11 D6.15pm
GH Georgian House Hotel 34 Ashbourne
Rd ☎49806 16hc 2⇱🛏 ⊗ CTV 17P 🍽
✷B&bfr£5.50 Bdifr£7.75 D9am
GH *Rouz Hotel* 686–688 Osmaston Rd
☎41026 11hc TV 5P 3🏠 🍽 D6pm

DERSINGHAM Norfolk *Map 9 TF63*
⋈**GH Westdene House Hotel**
60 Hunstanton Rd ☎40395 Lic 5hc ⊗
CTV 15P 🍽 S% B&bfr£5 D9pm

DEVIZES Wilts *Map 4 SU06*
INN *Castle Hotel* New Park St ☎2046
Lic 13hc CTV 8🏠 🍽 D9pm

DEVORAN Cornwall *Map 2 SW73*
GH *Driffold* 8 Devoran Ln ☎863314 Lic
7hc ⊗ CTV 6P 🍽 Dnoon

DODDISCOMBSLEIGH Devon
Map 3 SX88
INN Nobody Inn ☎ Christow 52394
Closed Xmas Day pm, rs Suns & Mons
(restaurant closed) Lic 4hc 1⇱🛏 ⊗ nc14
50P ⇔ ✷B&b£5.50–£7.50 Bar lunch
£1.50alc D9.15pm£4.50alc

DONCASTER S Yorks *Map 8 SE50*
GH Regent Hotel Regent Sq ☎64180
Closed 26Dec–1Jan rs Suns no dinner
Lic 19hc ⊗ CTV 20P 🍽 S% B&b£10–£14
Bdi£13.50–£17.50 D10pm

DONINGTON Lincs *Map 8 TF23*
INN *Red Cow* ☎298 Lic 7hc TV 30P sn

DORCHESTER Dorset *Map 3 SY69*
⋈**INN White Hart Hotel** High East St
☎3545 Closed Xmas Day Lic 6hc TV
12P 6🏠 🍽 S% B&b£5.18–£5.75 sn
L£2.25alc D9.30pm£2.25alc

DOVER Kent *Map 5 TR34*
⋈**GH Allwyn Cottage** 337 Folkestone Rd
☎201126 Closed 22Dec–30Dec 6hc ⊗
CTV 10P 1🏠 🍽 S% B&b£4.25–£5

GH Beulah House 94 Crabble Hill,
London Rd ☎ Kearsney 4615 7hc 1⇱🛏 ⊗
⚿ 10P 2🏠 🍽 river S% ✷B&b£5–£7
GH Dover Stop 45 London Rd, River
(2m NW A256) ☎ Kearsney 2751 Lic 5hc
(A 5hc) CTV 15P 🍽 river S% B&b£7–£8.80
Bdi£10.50–£12.80
GH Gordon House Hotel 31–32 East
Cliff ☎204459 Closed Dec Lic 18hc CTV
🍽 S% B&b£6.75 D8.30pm
GH *St Brelade's* 82 Buckland Av
☎206126 Lic 8hc ⊗ TV 6P 1🏠 🍽
GH Whitfield Hotel 107 Sandwich Rd
☎820236 Lic 9hc nc5 CTV 12P 🍽 S%
B&b£6 Bdi£9.50 D9pm
⋈**INN Railway Bell Hotel** London Rd
☎ Kearsney 2016 Apr–Sep rs Oct–Mar
(no dinners) Lic 6hc ⊗ nc14 20P 🍽 ⇔
S% B&b£5.50 Bdi£7–£8 L£1.50
D7.30pm£2.50–£3

DOWNHAM MARKET Norfolk
Map 5 TF60
INN Castle Hotel High St ☎2157 Lic
13hc 1⇱🛏 CTV 30P 3🏠 🍽 ⇔ S%
B&b£9 Bdi£13 Wfr£77 ⚿ sn L£1.50–£2.50
D10pm£4&alc

DOWNTON Wilts *Map 4 SU12*
⋈**GH Warren** High St ☎20263 7hc
1⇱🛏 ⊗ CTV 8P 🍽 B&b£5.75–£6.50

DREWSTEIGNTON Devon *Map 3 SX79*
GH Old Inn The Square ☎276 Closed Feb
Lic 4hc ⊗ CTV B&bfr£7 Bdifr£10 Wfr£40
M D10pm

DULOE Cornwall *Map 2 SX25*
GH Duloe Manor Hotel ☎ Looe 2795
Etr–Oct Lic 11hc 8⇱🛏 CTV 20P 🍽 S%
B&b£13–£16.75 Bdi£17.75–£21.20
W£124–£148.50 ⚿ D7.30pm

DUNSFORD Devon *Map 3 SX88*
INN Royal Oak Inn ☎ Christow 52256
Closed Xmas Lic 3hc ⊗ nc10 TV 10P
2🏠 S% B&b£9.20 Bar lunch £1.30alc
D9.30pm£2.50alc

DUXFORD Cambs *Map 5 TL44*
GH Highfield House 55 St Peter's St
☎ Cambridge 833160 8hc 3⇱🛏 ⚿ CTV
11P 🍽 S% B&b£6.90–£10.35

EASTBOURNE E Sussex *Map 5 TV69*
See Plan
⋈**GH Aberfoyle Hotel** 83 Royal Pde
☎22161 Plan:**1** Lic 8hc nc5 CTV 2P 🍽
sea S% B&b£5.50–£8 Bdi£7.50–£9
W£44–£49.50 ⚿ D6pm

MAY WE WELCOME YOU TO

HOTEL MARINA

86/87 Royal Parade, Eastbourne, Sussex
Telephone: (STD 0323) 20297

HOTEL MARINA is a seafront detached hotel run by experienced hoteliers.
Sea views from most rooms. Ten minutes' walk to the pier and town amenities.
Car parking within 80 yards. Tea/coffee making facilities. Central heating. Good
English breakfast and four course evening dinner with coffee — varied menu.
Some rooms en suite. No restrictions — no service charge — own keys. Resident
proprietors: George and Margaret Bennett.

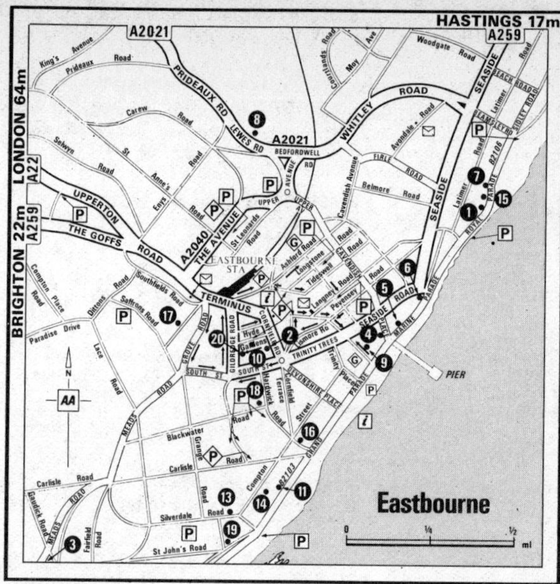

1 Aberfoyle Hotel
2 Alfriston Hotel
3 Beachy Rise
4 Cavendish House
5 Le Chalet
6 Chesleigh Hotel
7 Courtlands Hotel
8 Downlands Private Hotel
9 Edelweiss
10 Edmar
11 Elmscroft Private Hotel
13 Little Crookham
14 Lynwood Hotel
15 Marina
16 Mowbray
17 Orchard House
18 Somerville Private Hotel
19 South Cliff
20 Traquair Private Hotel

GH *Alfriston Hotel* Lushington Rd ☎25640 Plan:**2** Closed Xmas & 1st 3 wks Nov rs last wk Nov–Mar Lic 10hc ⊗ nc5 CTV 1🏠 D10am

GH Beachy Rise Beachy Head Rd ☎639171 Plan:**3** Closed Dec 6hc nc8 CTV 🍴 B&b£5–£5.50 Bdi£7–£7.50 W£47.50–£52 ⚿ D4.30pm

GH Cavendish 1 Cavendish Pl ☎24284 Plan:**4** Feb–Oct 11hc nc3 TV sea S% B&b£5.75–£7.50 Bdi£8.62–£10.35 W£51.75–£57.50 ⚿ D4pm

GH *Le Chalet* 7 Marine Pde ☎20029 Plan:**5** 8hc ⊗ nc8 CTV 🍴 sea D6pm

GH Chesleigh Hotel 4 Marine Pde ☎20722 Plan:**6** mid Apr–mid Oct 7hc 2🛁🚿 nc7 CTV sea S% B&b£6

GH Courtlands Hotel 68 Royal Pde ☎21068 Plan:**7** Lic 7hc 1🛁🚿 ⊗ CTV 1P 2🏠 sea S% B&b£8 Bdi£10 W£65 ⚿ D5pm

GH Downland Private Hotel 37 Lewes Rd ☎32689 Plan:**8** Lic 14hc 10🛁🚿 ⊗ nc3 CTV 14P 🍴 S% B&b£8–£10.50 Bdi£10.50–£14 W£65–£80 ⚿ D6.30pm

GH Edelweiss 10 Elms Av ☎32071 Plan:**9** Spring Bank Hol–Sep 6hc ⊗ CTV 🍴 B&b£7 W£38.50 Ⓜ

GH *Edmar* 30 Hyde Gdns ☎33024 Plan:**10** Etr–mid Oct 9hc 1🛁🚿 ⊗ nc5 CTV 🍴 S% B&b£4.75–£5.75 Bdi£7.25–£8.25 W£37.31–£59.29 ⚿ D6pm

GH *Elmscroft Private Hotel* 53 Jevington Gdns ☎21263 Plan:**11** 12hc ⊗ CTV D5pm

GH *Little Crookham* 16 Southcliffe Av ☎34160 Plan:**13** Apr–Oct 8hc CTV 🍴 S% ✱B&b£5.50 Bdi£8.50 Wfr£56 D5pm

GH Lynwood Hotel Jevington Gdns ☎23982 Plan:**14** Lic 78hc 13🛁🚿 CTV 6P 6🏠 lift sea S% B&b£8.05–£14.38 Bdi£10.35–£17.25 W£78.20–£124.78 D7.45pm

GH Hotel Marina 86–87 Royal Pde ☎20297 Plan:**15** 18hc 1🛁🚿 nc5 CTV 🍴 sea S% B&b£5.40–£8.64 Bdi£8.64–£11.88 W£48.60–£64.80 ⚿ W only Jun–Aug D4.30pm

GH Mowbray Hotel Lascelles Ter ☎20012 Plan:**16** Etr–Oct 16hc 4🛁🚿 nc7 CTV lift ✱B&b£7.93 W£47.43 Ⓜ

GH Orchard House 10 Old Orchard Rd ☎23682 Plan:**17** 8hc 2🛁🚿 CTV 🍴 S% B&b£5.50–£7.50 Bdi£8–£10 W£49–£60 ⚿ D6.15pm

GH Somerville Private Hotel
6 Blackwater Rd ☎29342 Plan:**18**
Etr–21Sep 11hc CTV B&b£6.33 Bdi£8.63
W£48.30–£54.05 D4pm

GH South Cliff House 19 South Cliff Av
☎21019 Plan:**19** rs Xmas (B&b only) Lic
6hc CTV ⑩ S% B&b£6–£8
Bdi£8.50–£10.50 W£50–£67.50 ⚲ D6pm

GH Traquair Private Hotel 25 Hyde
Gdns ☎25198 Plan:**20** Lic 10hc 5⇨🛁
CTV B&b£7.50–£8.75 Bdi£12.40–£13.60
W£75–£86 ⚲ D6pm

EAST COWTON N Yorks *Map 8 NZ30*
INN *Beeswing* ☎ North Cowton 349 Lic
3hc ⊛ P ⑩ D10pm

EASTLEIGH Devon *Map 2 SS42*
GH Pines Farmhouse Hotel
(2½m NE of Bideford off A39) ☎ Instow
860561 Etr–mid Oct 7hc ⊛ nc4 CTV 12P
⑩ S% B&b£6.50 Bdi£9 W£50.40–£56
⚲ D5pm

EASTLEIGH Hants *Map 4 SU41*
GH *Lynden* 28 Romsey Rd ☎613054
9hc ⊛ CTV 10P ⑩

EBBERSTON N Yorks *Map 8 SE88*
GH Foxholm Hotel (on B1258)
☎ Scarborough 85550 Mar–Oct Lic 10hc
6⇨🛁 CTV 12P 2🏠 ⑩ B&b£7–£9
Bdi£11–£14 W£70–£90 ⚲ D7pm

ELLESMERE Salop *Map 7 SJ33*
GH Grange Grange Rd ☎2735
Closed 24–31Dec Lic 11hc 4⇨🛁 CTV 20P
B&b£6.95–£8.20 Bdi£10.30–£11.50
W£66.50–£79.20 ⚲ D6.30pm

ELY Cambs *Map 5 TL58*
GH Nyton 7 Barton Rd ☎2459 Lic 8hc
1⇨🛁 TV 10P ⑩ S% B&b£6–£8
W£38.50–£52.50 Ⓜ

EMPINGHAM Leics *Map 4 SK90*
INN White Horse ☎221 Lic 3hc ⊛ CTV
50P 6🏠 S% B&b£7 Bdi£12 W£80 ⚲ sn
L£3–£5 D9.30pm£3.50–£5.50&alc

EMSWORTH Hants *Map 4 SU70*
⊷**GH Jingles** 77 Hordean Rd ☎3755
8hc CTV 7P ⑩ S% B&b£5–£6
Bdi£6.50–£7.50 W£43–£51 ⚲ D8pm

GH Merry Hall 73 Horndean Rd ☎2424
Lic 6hc ⊛ 10P 2🏠 ⑩ S% B&b£8.05
Bdi£11.21

ESKDALE Cumbria *Map 7 SD19*
INN Bower House ☎244 Closed Xmas
Lic 5hc (A 7⇨🛁) 100P 6🏠 ⑩ ⇨ S%
✳B&b£9.75–£11.50 Bdi£16.15–£17.90
W£108.50–£120.75 Bar lunch 45p–£2.50
D8.30pm£6.40

EVESHAM Heref & Worcs *Map 4 SP04*
GH Waterside Family Hotel
56/59 Waterside ☎2420 Lic 10hc
7⇨🛁 (A 3hc 1⇨🛁) ⚱ CTV 14P ⑩ river S%
B&b£6–£6.80 Bdi£9–£9.75 W£61–£64.75
⚲ D7.30pm

EXETER Devon *Map 3 SC99* **See Plan**
⊷**GH Hotel Gledhills** 32 Alphington Rd
☎71439 Plan:**1** Closed Xmas 12hc ⊛
nc2 CTV 12P ⑩ S% B&b£5.75 Bdi£8.34
W£46 ⚲ D5pm

⊷**GH The Guest House** 27 New North
Rd ☎74932 Plan:**2** 7hc CTV S%
B&b£5.25–£5.75

⋈**GH Park View Hotel** 8 Howell Rd
☎71772 Plan:**3** 9hc (A 4hc) ⚘ CTV 6P ▥
S% B&b£5.40–£6.48 W£34 Ⓜ

⋈**GH Radnor Hotel** 79 St David's Hill
☎72004 Plan:**4** Closed Xmas 9hc CTV
7P ▥ S% B&b£5.75 Bdi£8.75 D4.30pm

GH Regents Park Hotel Polsloe Rd
☎59749 Plan:**5** Closed Xmas 11hc CTV
16P S% B&bfr£7.48 Bdifr£11.51
Wfr£80.57 ⚖ D noon

GH *Telstar Hotel* 77 St David's Hill
☎72466 Plan:**6** 9hc TV 6P D am

⋈**GH Trees Mini Hotel** 2 Queen's Cres,
York Rd ☎59531 Plan:**7** Closed Xmas
12hc ✿ CTV 2P 3🏠 ▥ S% B&b£5.75–£6
Bdi£9.20–£9.50 D6.30pm

⋈**GH Trenance House Hotel** 1 Queen's
Cres, York Rd ☎73277 Plan:**8** Closed Xmas
Lic 9hc 1⇱🛏 CTV 6P ▥ S% B&bfr£5.40
Bdifr£8.64 D noon

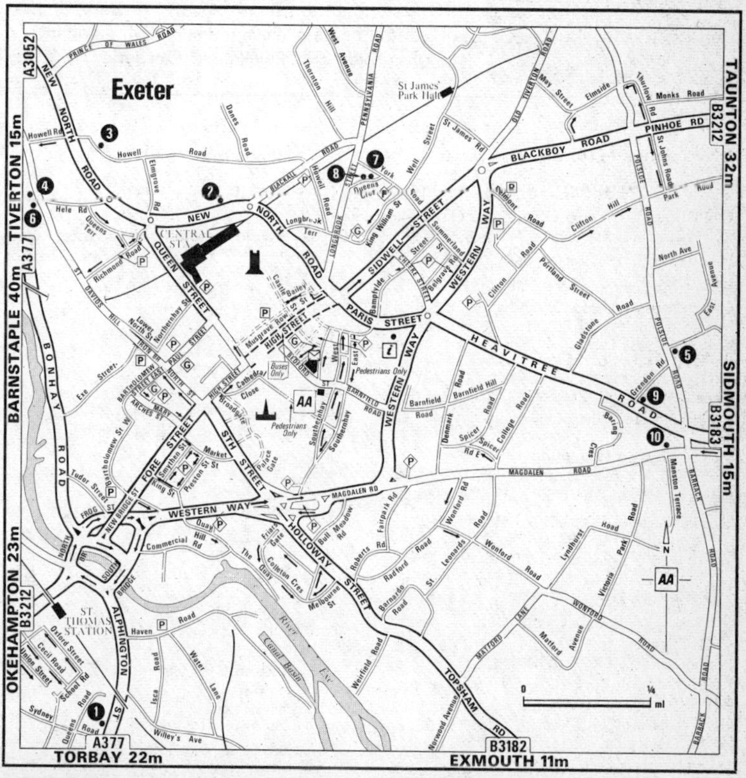

1 Hotel Gledhills	**5** Regent's Park Hotel	**8** Trenance House Hotel
2 The Guest House	**6** Telstar House	**9** Westholme Hotel
3 Park View Hotel	**7** Trees Mini Hotel	**10** Willowdene Hotel
4 Radnor Hotel		

GH Westholme Hotel 85 Heavitree Rd ☎71878 Plan:**9** Closed Xmas 7hc nc2 CTV 10P S% B&bf6.70 Bdif9.70 D11am

GH Willowdene Hotel 161 Magdalen Rd ☎71925 Plan:**10** Closed Xmas 7hc ✍ CTV S% B&bfrf6

EXFORD Somerset *Map 3 SS83*
GH *Exmoor House* ☎304 Mar–Oct 5hc (A 12hc) TV 18P 🏴 D6pm

EXMOUTH Devon *Map 3 SY08*
⊢⊣**GH Anchoria** 176 Exeter Rd ☎72368 Closed Xmas 8hc 2🛏 ✍ CTV 8P 1🏠 S% B&bfrf5.40 Bdifrf8.50 Wfrf51.30 ⅃ D4pm

⊢⊣**GH Clinton House** 41 Morton Rd ☎71969 Apr–Sep 8hc nc5 CTV S% B&bf4.50 Bdif6 Wfrf38.50 ⅃ D6pm

⊢⊣**GH Dawson's** 8 Morton Rd ☎72321 Closed Xmas 7hc ✍ CTV 2P 2🏠 S% B&bfrf4.60 Bdifrf6.90 Wf46–f51.75 ⅃ D6pm

GH *Dolphin House* 4 Morton Rd ☎3832 25hc CTV 8P 1🏠 ⅃ D7pm

⊢⊣**GH Farthings** 81 Salterton Rd ☎72161 Lic 6hc 1🛏 ✍ CTV 10P 🏴 S% B&bf5.50–f6 Bdif8.50–f9 Wf54–f59 ⅃ D6pm

GH *Morton Villa* 37 Morton Rd ☎73164 Closed Xmas Lic 6hc ✍ CTV 4P 🏴

FALMOUTH Cornwall *Map 2 SW83* See Plan
GH Bedruthan 49 Castle Dr ☎311028 Plan:**1** Lic 6hc ✍ CTV 4P 🏴 sea S% B&bf6.50–f7.50 Bdif9.25–f10.50 Wf57–f62 ⅃ D3pm

GH Collingbourne Hotel Melvill Rd ☎311259 Plan:**2** Apr–Oct Lic 10hc ✍ CTV 12P S% B&bf7–f8.60 Bdif8.60–f10.20 D6.30pm

GH Cotswold House Private Hotel 49 Melvill Rd ☎312077 Plan:**3** Lic 11hc 2🛏 ✍ nc13 CTV 13P sea S% B&bf6.50–f7.75 Bdif8.50–f10 Wf48–f65 ⅃ D5.30pm

GH Hotel Dracaena Dracaena Av ☎314470 Plan:**4** Lic 10hc CTV 20P S% B&bf6–f7 Bdif7.50–f9.50 Wf38.50–f58.50 ⅃ D6.30pm

⊢⊣**GH Evendale Private Hotel** 51 Melvill Rd ☎314164 Plan:**5** May–Oct 10hc 3🛏 nc3 CTV TV 10P sea S% B&bf5.50–f7.50 Bdif7.50–f10 Wf52–f70 ⅃ D6.30pm

GH *Florence* 6 Florence Pl ☎313494 Plan:**6** 6hc ✍ CTV 6🏠 🏴 river sea D6.30pm

GH Gyllyngvase House Hotel Gyllyngvase Rd ☎312956 Plan:**7** Mar–Oct Lic 16hc 5🛏 ✍ CTV 16P B&bfrf8.05 Bdifrf10.35 Wfrf69 ⅃ D7.15pm

⊢⊣**GH Homelea** 31 Melvill Rd ☎313489 Plan:**8** 10May–27Sep 7hc ✍ nc12 TV 4P B&bf5.50–f6.50 Bdif8–f9 Wf50.40–f56.40 ⅃ D5pm

GH *Kelbrook* 8 Florence Pl ☎312961 Plan:**9** Closed Nov 9hc TV 5P sea D6.30pm

⊢⊣**GH Langton Leigh** 11 Florence Pl ☎313684 Plan:**10** Apr–Oct 8hc CTV 6P 1🏠 🏴 sea S% B&bf4.50–f5.50 Bdif6.25–f7.50 Wf42–f49.50 ⅃ D6.30pm

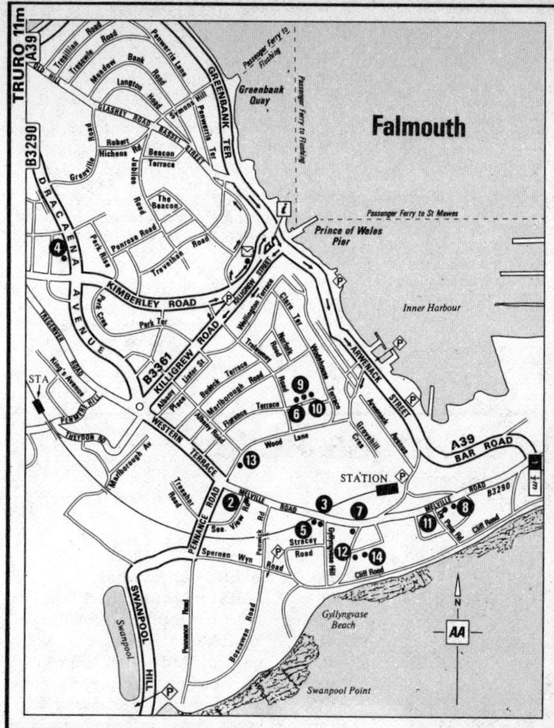

GH *Milton House* 33 Melvill Rd ☎314390 Plan:**11** rs Oct–Apr (booking only) 7hc ⊘ nc5 CTV 6P sea

GH Rosemary Hotel 22 Gyllyngvase Ter ☎314669 Plan:**12** Mar–mid Oct Lic 11hc 1⇆▥ ⊘ CTV 3P sea S% ✳B&b£5.94–£7.56 Bdi£7.02–£8.64 W£45.36–£58.32 ⚹ D6.30pm

GH Trevone Hotel 33 Wood Ln ☎313123 Plan:**13** Apr–Oct Lic 16hc 2⇆▥ CTV 12P S% ✳B&b£6.21–£7.02 Bdi£9.99–£11.34 W£59.94–£64.80 ⚹ D5pm

⋈**GH Wickham** 21 Gyllyngvase Ter ☎311140 Plan:**14** Mar–Oct 11hc ⊘ nc3 CTV 3P sea B&b£5–£6 Bdi£6.50–£8 W£45–£52 ⚹ D5pm

FAREHAM Hants *Map 4 SU50*
GH Carrick House 11–13 East St ☎234678 Lic 10hc CTV ▥ B&b£6

GH Maylings Manor Hotel 11A Highlands Rd ☎286451 rs no Sun Dinner and Mon Lunch Lic 10hc 60p ▥ S% B&b£8

FARNHAM Surrey *Map 4 SU84*
GH Eldon Hotel 43 Frensham Rd, Lower Bourne ☎ Frensham 2745 Lic 5hc 9⇆▥ 50P ▥ S% ✳B&b£7–£14

GH Trevena House Hotel Alton Rd ☎716908 Lic 19hc nc5 CTV TV 40P ▥ S% B&b£9–£10 Bdi£12–£13 W£84–£91 ⚹ D7.30pm

FEATHERSTONE PARK Northumb *Map 12 NY66*
INN *Wallace Arms Hotel* ☎ Haltwhistle 20375 Lic 3hc CTV 30P 2🛏 ▥ D9pm

Crellow Country House Hotel
STITHIANS, NR TRURO, CORNWALL
Tel: Stithians 860523

Crellow Country House Hotel is a fine Georgian house listed as a building of historic and architectural interest. The hotel is noted for a high standard of food and there is an extensive wine list. Here you can relax in a quiet country atmosphere with the modern amenities close at hand.

FERNDOWN Dorset *Map 4 SU00*
GH Broadlands Hotel West Moors Rd
☎877884 Lic 12hc 1⇦🛁 CTV 15P S%
B&b£6.50–£7.50 Bdi£9.50–£10.50
W£63–£70 ⸖ D6.30pm

FIDDLEFORD Dorset *Map 3 ST81*
INN Fiddleford ☎ Sturminster Newton
72489 Closed Xmas rs Sun–Tue
Restaurant closed Lic 3rm 2hc 1⇦🛁 ⊘
nc14 30P 🍺 ⇦ S% B&b£8–£11
Bdi£15–£18 Bar lunch £1.50alc
D9.45pm£7alc

FILEY N Yorks *Map 8 TA18*
⋈**GH Beach Hotel** The Beach
☎ Scarborough 513178 Apr–Oct Lic
23hc CTV sea S% B&b£5 Bdi£6–£7.50
W£42–£52.50 ⸖ D6pm

GH Downcliffe Hotel The Beach
☎ Scarborough 513310 Etr–Sep 16hc

2⇦🛁 ⊘ CTV 9P 1🏠 sea ✳B&b£5.67–£5.94
Bdi£6.16–£7.46 D6pm

FIVE LANES Cornwall *Map 2 SX28*
INN Kings Head Hotel ☎ Pipers Pool
241 Lic 5hc 24P 🍺 S% ✳B&b£5.50 sn

FLAX BOURTON Avon *Map 3 ST56*
INN Jubilee Farleigh Rd ☎2741 Lic 4hc
nc14 S% B&b£6.90 D9.30pm

FLEETWOOD Lancs *Map 7 SD34*
GH *Southbrook Private Hotel* Esplanade
☎3944 rs Xmas wk Lic 11rm 10hc ⊘ nc3
CTV 3P D8pm

FLUSHING Cornwall *Map 2 SW83*
GH Nankersey Hotel St Peters Rd
☎ Penryn 74471 Mar–Oct Lic 7hc ⊘
CTV P 🍺 sea S% B&b£6–£8
Bdi£9.50–£11.50 D7pm

GYLLYNGVASE HOUSE HOTEL

Gyllyngvase Road, Falmouth, Cornwall
Tel: (0326) 312956

A well appointed hotel standing in own grounds with car parking facilities. Comfortably furnished quiet lounge & colour TV lounge. Ideally situated for beaches, town, parks, Biergarten, pavilion etc. Ideal touring centre. Coast & country atmosphere. Bus stop at hotel entrance, railway station 200 yards. Residential Licence.

Penmere Guesthouse

Falmouth Tel: Penryn 74470

A six-bedroomed, family run guesthouse with a homely atmosphere and personal attention. Overlooking Creek of the River Fal. Superb views from front bedrooms. H&C in all rooms. Some family rooms. Children very welcome; Reduced rates for sharing. Separate tables in dining room, home cooking. Colour TV in lounge. Convenient for Falmouth and Mylor Yatch Harbour. Central for touring both coasts.
Bed and breakfast daily: £5.00. Dinner optional: £2.75. Weekly: £44.00.

Built in 1820 in Georgian style, this is a very comfortable hotel of 16 bedrooms. Situated in a lovely part of Falmouth and facing south, we have several rooms overlooking the bay and our own large secluded walled garden where we have lawns, subtropical shrubs and a pleasant sun terrace ideal for relaxing and enjoying a peaceful drink. We also grow a lot of our produce and our home cooking has earned us a regular clientelle.
The hotel is located between the beaches and shopping centre which are within easy walking distance and the bus stops are within a few yards from the main entrance. The Falmouth Golf Club is within a mile, the Tennis & Squash Club just a few minutes' walk and the harbour is also within easy reach for boating and making fishing arrangements.
We invite you to spend a holiday where you can be assured of comfort, hospitality and relaxed friendly atmosphere.

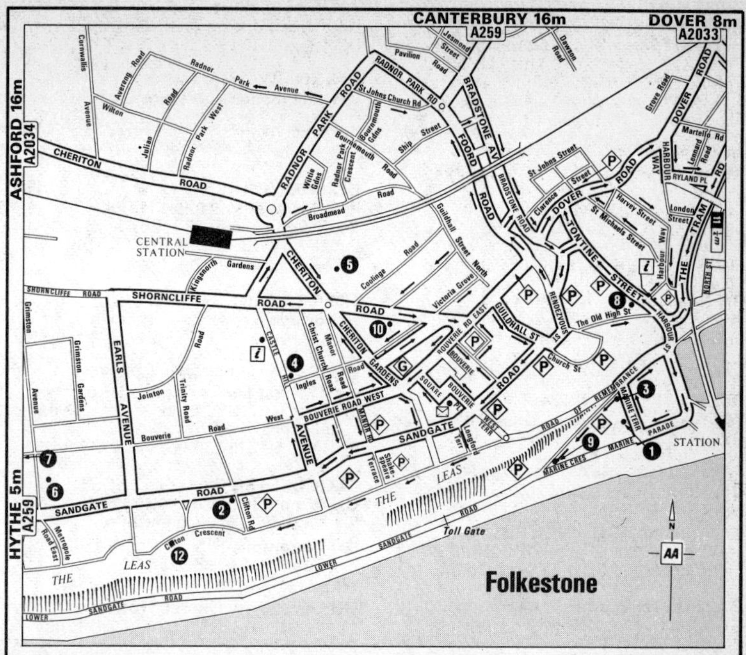

1 Argos Private Hotel
2 Arundel Hotel
3 Beaumont Private Hotel
4 Belmonte Private Hotel
5 Claremont Private Hotel
6 Horseshoe Private Hotel
7 Kasfaret
8 Michael's
9 Pier Hotel
10 Shannon Private Hotel
11 Wearbay
12 Westward Ho! Private Hotel

FOLKESTONE Kent *Map 5 TR23*
See Plan
GH Argos Private Hotel 6 Marine Ter
☎54309 Plan:**1** 9hc ✷ nc3 CTV P S%
B&b£6.90–£7.59 Bdi£9.20–£11.04
W£57.96–£66.24 ⚡

⊷**GH Arundel Hotel** 3 Clifton Rd
☎52442 Plan:**2** Lic 13hc ✷ CTV S%
B&b£4.50–£5.50 Bdi£6–£7 W£38–£40
⚡ D6.30pm

⊷**GH Beaumont Private Hotel**
5 Marine Ter ☎52740 Plan:**3** Lic 9hc
1⇴🍽 ✷ CTV P B&b£4.50–£6
Bdi£7.50–£9 D am

⊷**GH Belmonte Private Hotel** 30 Castle
Hill Av ☎54470 Plan:**4** 10hc (A 4hc)
✷ nc5 CTV 8P S% B&b£5.75–£6.30
Bdi£8–£8.40 W£49–£50.60 ⚡ D6pm

GH Claremont Private Hotel
20–22 Claremont Rd ☎54897 Plan:**5**
Apr–Oct 14hc nc10 CTV 7P S%
B&bfr£6.33 Bdifr£8.62 W£40.25–£46 ⚡

GH Horseshoe Private Hotel
29 Westbourne Gdns ☎52184 Plan:**6**
Apr–Sep 10hc 1⇴🍽 ✷ nc6 CTV 15P 🍴
S% B&b£6–£6.50 Bdi£8–£8.50
W£44–£48 ⚡

⊷**GH Kasfaret** 91 Bouverie Rd West
☎53705 Plan:**7** Apr–Sep 9hc ✷ CTV 10P
🍴 S% B&bfr£5.18 Bdifr£7.50 W£42.55
⚡ D4pm

GH *Michael's* 35 Tontine St ☎55961
Plan:**8** Feb–mid Dec Lic 12hc CTV 1🏠 🍴
D10.30pm

GH *Pier Hotel* 1 Marine Cres ☎54444
Plan:**9** Lic 30hc CTV 3P sea D5pm

GH Shannon Private Hotel
59–61 Cheriton Rd ☎52138 Plan:**10**

Apr–Sep Lic 24hc 2⇴🍽 CTV 11P 🍴
B&b£6–£7.50 Bdi£9–£10.50 W£55 ⚡
D7.15pm

⊷**GH Wearbay Hotel** 25 Wearbay Cres
☎52586 Plan:**11** Lic 7hc CTV 1P 1🏠 sea
S% B&b£5.48–£8.30 Bdi£7.92–£12.87
W£56.71–£81.82 ⚡ D11pm

GH *Westward Ho! Private Hotel*
13 Clifton Cres ☎52663 Plan:**12** Lic 12hc
✷ CTV 10P D6.30pm

FORDINGBRIDGE Hants *Map 4 SU11*
GH *Ivy* High St ☎52358 Closed Xmas
4hc (A 2hc) nc10 TV 6P

GH Oakfield Lodge 1 Park Rd ☎52789
Jan–Oct 10hc ✷ CTV 10P ✳B&bfr£5
Wfr£35 Ⓜ

GH St Ives & Seven Wives High St
☎52006 Restaurant closed Tue & Sun Lic
8hc B&b£6.32

FOVANT Wilts *Map 4 SU02*
INN Cross Keys Hotel ☎284 Closed
Wed, 2 wks Oct & Xmas Lic 4hc ✷ nc8
TV 14P 🍴 ⇷ ✳B&bfr£6.60 sn Lfr£3.60
D9pmfr£5.60

FOWEY Cornwall *Map 2 SX15*
GH Ashley House Hotel 14 Esplanade
☎2310 Mar–Nov Lic 6hc S%
B&b£6.50–£7 Bdi£9.75–£11 W£60–£70
⚡ D7pm

GH Carnethic House Lambs Barn
☎3336 Mar–Oct & Dec–Feb Lic 7hc
2⇴🍽 nc8 20P 🍴 S% B&b£6.20–£8.60
Bdi£9.98–£12.38 D6.45pm

⊷**GH Polmear** 62 Esplanade ☎3464
6hc ✷ nc12 TV B&b£4.50–£6
Bdi£8.50–£10.50 W£49–£63 ⚡ D6pm

FRADDON Cornwall *Map 2 SW95*
⊢⊣**GH St Margaret's Private Hotel**
☎860375 Closed 2wks Xmas Lic 12hc
CTV 12P 🍴 S% B&bf£4.86–£5.40
Bdif£7.02–£7.56 Wf£42.12–£50.48 ᵏ
W only Jul & Aug D8pm

FRAMPTON Dorset *Map 3 SY69*
GH Wessex Barn ☎ Maiden Newton 282
Closed Oct–Apr & Aug Lic 4hc ⊗ nc 4P
1🏠 🍴 S% B&bf£6 Bdif£10 Wf£65 ᵏ
D9.30pm

FRESHWATER BAY Isle of Wight
Map 4 SZ38
GH Blenheim House Gate Ln
☎ Freshwater 2858 May–Oct 9hc nc5
CTV 6P 4🏠 🍴 sea D7pm

⊢⊣**GH Saunders Hotel** Coastguard Ln
☎ Freshwater 2322 Apr–Oct Lic 13hc
CTV 10P sea B&bf£5.18–£5.75
Bdif£8.63–£9.50 Wf£56.35–£60.38 ᵏ
D5.30pm

FRINTON-ON-SEA Essex *Map 5 TM21*
GH Forde Queen's Rd ☎4758 6hc ⊗
nc5 TV 1P 🍴

GH Uplands 41 Hadleigh Rd ☎4889
Mar–Oct Lic 7hc CTV 8P S% B&bf£6.90
Bdif£8.60 Wf£51.20–£52.60 ᵏ D6.30pm

GARFORTH W Yorks *Map 8 SE43*
GH Coach House Hotel 58 Lidgett Ln
☎ Leeds 862303 Closed Xmas–New Year
6hc (A 4hc) ⊗ CTV 8P 3🏠 🍴 S% B&bf£6.50

GARGRAVE N Yorks *Map 7 SD95*
⊢⊣**GH Kirke Syke** 19 High St ☎356
Lic 6hc 1🛏🍳 CTV 10P 🍴 S% B&bf£5.50
Bdif£9.25 Wf£63–£65.25 ᵏ D5pm

GATWICK AIRPORT, LONDON
W Sussex *Map 4 TQ24*
GH Barfield Farm Stanhill, Charlwood
☎ Norwood Hill 862545 Closed Xmas 5hc
⊗ nc4 CTV 10P 🍴 S% B&bf£8–£10

GH Barnwood Hotel Balcombe Rd,
Crawley ☎ Crawley 882709 Lic 28hc
25🛏🍳 ⊗ CTV 35P 🍴 ⟨ S% B&bf£9.50
D8.45pm

GH Gainsborough Lodge Massetts Rd,
Horley (2m NE A23) ☎ Horley 3982
Closed Mar 6hc 1🛏🍳⊗ TV 10P 🍴 S%
B&bf£8.05 Bdif£10.35

GH Skylodge Motel Country Oak,
Crawley (2m S of airport on A23)
☎ Crawley 514341 Lic 21hc 21🛏🍳 ⊗
CTV 45P 🍴 S% B&bf£9.77
GH Trumbles Hotel & Restaurant
Stanhill, Charlwood ☎ Crawley 862212

Lic 5hc 5🛏🍳 ⊗ nc9 22P 🍴 B&bf£9
D9.15pm

GIGGLESWICK N Yorks *Map 7 SD86*
GH Woodlands The Mains ☎ Settle 2576
Closed Xmas & New Year Lic 6hc ⊗ nc3
6P 🍴 S% B&bf£7.25 Bdif£11.50 Wf£77.50
ᵏ D noon

GLASTONBURY Somerset *Map 3 ST53*
⊢⊣**GH Hawthorn House Hotel**
8–10 Northload St ☎31255 Lic 12hc
2🛏🍳 ⊗ TV 20P 2🏠 🍴 B&bf£5.75–£6.90
Wf£37.95–£45.30 M D7.45pm

GLENRIDDING Cumbria *Map 11 NY31*
GH Bridge House ☎236 Mar–Nov 6rm
5hc 7P 🍴

GLOSSOP Derbys *Map 7 SK09*
⊢⊣**GH Hurst Lee** Derbyshire Level,
Sheffield Rd ☎3354 Closed Xmas–New
Year Lic 6hc 1🛏🍳 CTV 8P 🍴 S%
B&bfr£5.50 Bdifr£8 Wfr£51 ᵏ D4pm

GLOUCESTER Glos *Map 3 SO81*
GH Alma 49 Kingsholm Rd ☎20940
8hc ⊗ TV 6P 1🏠 🍴 S% B&bf£6

GH Claremont 135 Stroud Rd ☎29540
6hc TV 6P 🍴 S% ✳B&bf£4.75–£5.50
Wf£32.00–£35 M

GH Hucclecote Garden Hotel
164 Hucclecote Rd ☎67374 Lic 12hc
2🛏🍳 ⊗ CTV 20P 🍴 S% B&bf£7.25
Wf£49.50 M D10.30pm

GH Monteith 127 Stroud Rd ☎25369
8hc CTV 8P 🍴 S% ✳B&bf£4.50–£5

⊢⊣**GH New Bridge Hotel** West End Ter
☎34792 Lic 10hc CTV 10P S%
B&bf£5.50–£6.50 Bdif£7–£8 Wf£42–£46
ᵏ D10pm

GH Stanley House Hotel 87 London Rd
☎20140 Lic 7hc (A 6hc) ♨ CTV 30P 1🏠
🍴 S% B&bf£6.23–£6.46 Bdif£9.22–£9.45
Wf£74.85–£80.25 W only in winter D7pm

GODALMING Surrey *Map 4 SU94*
INN King's Arms Royal Hotel ☎21545
Lic 17hc ⊗ CTV 50P D8.45pm

GOMSHALL Surrey *Map 4 TQ04*
INN Black Horse ☎ Shere 2242 Lic
6hc ⊗ nc12 CTV 60P ⊞ B&bf£9.18
Bdif£15.18 sn Lf£3 D9.30pmf£6

GOONHAVERN Cornwall *Map 2 SW75*
⊢⊣**GH Reen Cross Farm** ☎ Perranporth
3362 Closed Xmas & New Year Lic 6hc
CTV 10P S% B&bf£3.50–£4.50 Bdif£6–£8
D8pm

Hurst Lee Guest House

Prop: Mrs B D Porter
Derbyshire Level, Glossop
Telephone: Glossop 3354

One mile from town centre, off A57, Sheffield
Road, overlooking Glossop Golf course.
Full central heating. Hot and cold in all
bedrooms. Residential licence. Fire certificate.
TV lounge and every comfort. Magnificent views
from all rooms. Some four-poster beds.
Adjacent to Peak District National Park.
Bed/breakfast with optional evening meal.
Good home cooking. Convenient — M1, M6,
M62, M56. Car park. Nearby — Dinting
Railway centre, angling, riding, Pennine Way.

GORRAN HAVEN Cornwall *Map 2 SX04*
GH Perhaver ☎ Mevagissey 2471
Apr–mid Oct Lic 5hc ✳ nc18 CTV 5P sea
S% B&b£6.75 Bdi£9.25 W£56.50 ⚓ D5pm

GOSPORT Hants *Map 4 SZ69*
GH Bridgemary Manor Hotel Brewers Ln
☎ Fareham 232946 Lic 16hc CTV 15P
S% B&b£7.50 Bdi£11 D5.30pm

GRAMPOUND Cornwall *Map 2 SW94*
GH *Tregoose* Grampound Rd
☎ Grampound Road 882460 Apr–Sep
rs Oct–Mar Lic 7rm 6hc ✳ TV 12P

GRANGE *(in Borrowdale)* Cumbria
Map 11 NY21
GH Grange ☎ Borrowdale 251 Etr–Oct.
6hc 1⊷🛁 7P 卿 S% B&b£6 Bdi£9.50
W£65 ⚓ D5pm

GRANGE-OVER-SANDS Cumbria
Map 7 SD47
⋈**GH Elton Private Hotel** Windermere Rd
☎2838 Closed Xmas & last two wks Oct
9hc CTV 3P S% B&b£5–£6 Bdi£7.50–£8
W fr£50 ⚓

GH Thornfield House Kents Bank Rd
☎2512 Etr–mid Oct 6hc ✳ nc5 CTV 6P 卿
sea S% ✳B&b£4.60 Bdi£6.90 W£44.75
⚓ W only Jun–Aug D2pm

GRANSMOOR Humberside *Map 8 TA15*
GH Gransmoor Lodge Country House
☎ Burton Agnes 340 Lic 6hc ✳ TV 20P
S% B&b fr£6.50 Bdi fr£9 D9pm

GRASMERE Cumbria *Map 11 NY30*
GH Bridge House Hotel Stock Ln ☎425
Mar–Oct Lic 12hc 4⊷🛁 20P
Bdi£14–£15.50 W£90–£100 ⚓ D7pm

⋈**GH Chestnut Villa Private Hotel**
Keswick Rd ☎218 Closed Nov 7hc 10P
卿 S% B&b£5.25–£5.75 W£36.75–£40.25
M

⋈**GH Dunmail** Keswick Rd ☎256 5hc
CTV 6P S% B&b£4.95 Bdi£7.50 W£52
⚓ D5pm

⋈**GH 'Titteringdales'** Pye Ln ☎439
Mar–Oct Lic 6hc TV 8P 卿 S% B&b£5–£6
Bdi£8–£9.25 W54–£63 ⚓ D4pm

GREAT
Placenames incorporating the word 'Great',
such as Gt Malvern and Gt Yarmouth, will
be found under the actual placename,
ie Malvern, Yarmouth

GRIMSBY Humberside *Map 8 TA20*
INN *Wheatsheaf Hotel* Bargate ☎54729
Closed Xmas Lic 4hc ✳ nc10 TV 60P 卿

GWITHIAN Cornwall *Map 2 SW54*
GH *Glencoe House Hotel* 23 Churchtown
Rd ☎ Hayle 752216 Lic 12hc CTV 12P 卿
sea D9pm

HALESWORTH Suffolk *Map 5 TM37*
INN Angel Hotel The Thoroughfare
☎3365 Lic 8hc 2⊷🛁 CTV 100P 6🏠
B&b£9.25–£10.25 Bdi£15.25–£16.25
W£100 ⚓ sn L£6alc D9pm£6alc

HALFORD Warwicks *Map 4 SP24*
INN Bell ☎ Stratford-on-Avon 740382
Lic 8hc CTV 50P 2🏠 S% B&b£6.50–£8.50
sn L£4alc D9pm£4alc

HALWELL Devon *Map 3 SX75*
GH *Stanborough Hundred Hotel*
☎ East Allington 236 Etr–mid Nov 6hc TV
10P 卿 D5pm

HAMPTON COURT Gt London
Map 4 TQ16
INN Cardinal Wolsey The Green
☎01-941 3781 Lic 19hc ✳ 30P 卿 S%
B&b£10.92 sn L£3.50 D9pm£3.50

HAMPTON HILL Gt London *Map 4 TQ17*
GH Jasmin House 88–94 High St
☎01-977 2117 9hc 4⊷🛁 (A 7hc) 6P 卿
S% ✳B&b£9.02–£11.32 W£63.19–£79.29
M

HAREWOOD END Heref & Worcs
Map 3 SO52
⋈**INN The Inn** ☎637 Lic 5hc nc8 TV
30P S% B&b£5.75 Bdi£7.75

HARLOW Essex *Map 5 TL41*
INN *Green Man Hotel* Mulberry Gn
☎21342 rs Bank Hols (no restaurant) Lic
7hc TV 60P D9.30pm

HARPENDEN Herts *Map 4 TL11*
GH Milton Private Hotel 25 Milton Rd
☎2331 Lic 9hc CTV 9P S%
B&b£8.64–£9.72 Bdi£11.35–£12
W£65–£70 ⚓ D8pm

HARROGATE N Yorks *Map 8 SE35*
GH Boston Private Hotel 3–7 Swan Rd
☎502918 Lic 19hc CTV 10P 卿 S%
B&b£7–£8 Bdi£10.50–£11.50
W£70–£75 ⚓ D7pm

⋈**GH Franklin Private Hotel** 25 Franklin
Rd ☎69028 Lic 6hc CTV 4P S% B&b£5

⋈**GH Gillmore** 98 King's Rd ☎503699 .
Lic 18hc CTV 15P 卿 S% B&b£5.35–£5.75
Bdi£7.60–£8

⋈**GH Hartington** Franklin Mount ☎69534
12hc CTV 1🏠 S% B&b£5–£5.50
Bdi£7.32–£8.06 W£48.73–£51.17 ⚓
D4.30pm

GH Manor Hotel 3 Clarence Dr ☎503916
Lic 15hc ♨ CTV 6P 🍴 S% B&b£7.78–£8.40
Bdi£11.02–£12 W£87.10–£96 D8.15pm

GH Norman Hotel 41 Valley Dr ☎58416
Lic 18hc 4⇔🛏 CTV 🍴 S% B&b£7.50–£8.75
Bdi£11.25–£12.50 W£75–£82 ⅃ D8.30pm

⋈GH Oakbrae 3 Springfield Av ☎67682
Closed Xmas 6hc 1⇔🛏 CTV 6P 🍴 S%
B&b£4.50–£5 Bdi£6.50–£7 Wfr£45 ⅃
D5pm

⋈GH Roan 90 King's Rd ☎503087
Closed Xmas 6hc ❀ CTV 🍴 B&b£5
Bdi£7.50

GH Shelbourne 78 King's Rd ☎504390
Closed Xmas wk Lic 7hc nc3 CTV 2P 🍴
✳B&b£6.90 Bdi£9.50 D7pm

GH Springfield 80 King's Rd ☎67166
rs Xmas & New Year 6hc ❀ CTV 5P
🍴 B&b£6.60–£6.93 W£44–£46.20 M

⋈GH Strayend 56 Dragon View, Skipton
Rd ☎61700 6hc CTV 6P 🍴 S%
B&b£5.50–£6.50 Bdi£7.50–£8.50
D4pm

GH Wessex Hotel 23 Harlow Moor Dr
☎65890 Lic 15hc 8⇔🛏 CTV
B&b£7.20–£8.20 Bdi£11–£12
W£72–£75.60 ⅃ D7pm

GH Youngs Private Hotel 15 York Rd
☎67336 Lic 8hc 3⇔🛏 CTV 8P 2🏠 🍴 S%
B&b£7 Bdi£11 W£70 ⅃ D6.30pm

HARROW Gt London *Map 4 TQ18*
GH Harrow Hotel 12–18 Pinner Rd
☎01-427 3435 rs Xmas (B&b only) Lic
70hc 31⇔🛏 (A 11hc 11⇔🛏) CTV 44P 🍴
S% B&b£9.50–£18 Bdi£14–£22.50
D8.45pm

HASTINGS & ST LEONARDS E Sussex
Map 5 TQ80
GH Burlington Hotel 2 Robertson Ter
☎429656 Lic 15hc CTV sea S%
B&b£7–£8.50 Bdi£10.25–£11.75
W£78–£95.50 D5.30pm

GH Chimes Hotel 1 St Mathews Gdns
☎434041 Closed 29Oct–16Nov Lic 11hc
2⇔🛏 CTV 🍴 S% B&b£6.50–£9
Bdi£10.50–£13.50 W£62–£80 ⅃
D5.30pm

⋈GH Harbour Lights 20 Cambridge
Gdns ☎423424 8hc ❀ CTV 🍴 S%
B&b fr£5 Bdi fr£7 D am

HATHERLEIGH Devon *Map 2 SS50*
INN *Bridge* Bridge St ☎357 rs Dec–Feb
(no accommodation) Lic 3hc ❀ CTV 20P
D9.30pm

HAWKSHEAD Cumbria *Map 7 SD39*
GH Highfield House Hawkshead Hill
☎344 Feb–Nov Lic 11hc nc2 12P 🍴
B&b£7 Bdi£10.50 W£68.50 ⅃ D7pm

⋈GH Ivy House ☎204 Mar–Nov Lic
6hc (A 5hc) CTV 12P 🍴 S%
B&b£5.80–£6.80 Bdi£8.50–£10
W£55–£68 ⅃ W only mid May–Sep
D5pm

⋈GH Rough Close Country House
☎370 Apr–Oct 6hc ❀ CTV 12P 🍴 lake
S% B&b£4.50–£5.50

INN Kings Arms Hotel ☎372 Lic 6hc
CTV 🍴 S% B&b£6.50 W£40 M sn L£2alc
D10pm£2alc

HAYFIELD Derbys *Map 7 SK08*
GH Hazel 1–2 Valley Rd ☎ Chinley 43671
8hc 1⇔🛏 CTV 8P 🍴 S% ✳B&b£5.50
W£35 M

𝕭urlington 𝕳otel (𝕳astings)

0424 429656 (Management)
Robertson Terrace TN34 1JE

Everything you could wish for is in easy reach of this splendid, town centre, sea front hotel.

All rooms have:— TV, radio. Tea and coffee preparing facilities, 24 hour residents' drinks service.

Exceptional out of season tariff, for weekend or weekly bookings that will astound you. Example:— £36.95 for one week's dinner, bed and breakfast, per person, exc. VAT.

Write or phone for brochure and tariff. All major credit cards accepted.

Sawrey House Private Hotel

is a small, family-run hotel in the village of Near Sawrey, made famous by Beatrix Potter, of Peter Rabbit fame.

Standing in its own grounds, the hotel gives friendly, comfortable service. H & C in all rooms. Colour TV, excellent home cooking, residents' licence. Magnificent views over Esthwaite Lake and Langdale Pikes. Brochure on request with SAE to M C Lambert, Sawrey House Private Hotel, Near Sawrey, Ambleside LA22 0LF. Phone: Hawkshead 387 & 310.

HAYLING ISLAND Hants *Map 4 SU70*
⊢⊣**GH Avenue** 5 Wheatlands Av ☎3121
7hc ⊗ CTV 10P 🍽 sea S% B&b£5 £5.60
Bdi£7.50–£8 W£46–£50 ⌀ D noon

⊢⊣**GH Dolphin Court Hotel**
37 St Leonard's Av ☎2910 8hc TV 6P
🍽 S% B&b£5–£5.50 Bdi£7.25–£7.75
W£43.75–£46.50 ⌀ D6.30pm

HEASLEY MILL Devon *Map 3 SS73*
⊢⊣**GH Heasley House** ☎ North Molton 213
Mar–mid Oct rs Jan–Feb Lic 7hc 1⇌🚿
(A 4hc) CTV 12P 🍽 river B&b£5 Bdi£7.50
W£50 ⌀ D7pm

HEATHFIELD E Sussex *Map 5 TQ52*
⊢⊣**GH Broadhurst** Swife Ln, Broad Oak
(3½m NE A265) ☎ West Burwash 461
5hc 1⇌🚿 TV 15P 🍽 S% B&b£5.50–£6.50

HEDDONS MOUTH Devon *Map 3 SS64*
INN *Hunters'* ☎ Parracombe 230
Etr–end Oct Lic 11hc nc6 CTV 200P
D9pm

HELSBY Cheshire *Map 7 SJ47*
GH *Poplars Private Hotel* 130 Chester Rd
☎3433 Closed 25–31Dec 6hc ⊗ nc4
CTV 10P D4.30pm

HELSTON Cornwall *Map 2 SW62*
GH *Bona Vista* 22 Meneage Rd ☎2579
Lic 6hc TV 10P D6pm

⊢⊣**GH Hillside** Godolphin Rd ☎4788
7hc ⊗ CTV 6P S% B&b£4 Bdi£6.50
Wfr£45 ⌀ D5pm

HEMEL HEMPSTEAD Herts *Map 4 TL00*
GH Eversleigh 40 Alexandra Rd ☎51366
6hc ⊗ nc3 CTV 🍽 S% B&b£5.50–£6

GH South Lea Private Hotel 8 Charles St
☎3061 11hc ⊗ CTV 8P 1🏠 🍽 S%
✱B&b fr£6

GH Southville Private Hotel 9 Charles St
☎51387 12hc ⊗ CTV 9P 🍽 S%
✱B&b£5.50–£6

HENLEY-ON-THAMES Oxon
Map 4 SU78
GH Sydney House Hotel Northfield Rd
☎3412 Lic 10hc 3⇌🚿 ⊗ nc10 CTV 6P 🍽
S% B&b£8.60

GH Thamesmead Remenham Ln
☎4745 7hc ⊗ nc6 7P 🍽 B&b£6.80

HENSTEAD Suffolk *Map 5 TM48*
GH Henstead Hall Country Hotel
☎ Lowestoft 740345 Lic 14hc nc5 CTV
14P S% ✱B&b£6.32–£7.75
Bdi£10.35–£11.78 W£65.20–£74.26
⌀ D6pm

HEREFORD Heref & Worcs *Map 3 SO54*
GH Ferncroft Hotel 144 Ledbury Rd
☎65538 Closed last 2wks Dec Lic 10hc
⊗ CTV 7P 🍽 S% B&b£6–£7.50
Bdi£9–£10.50 W£60–£65 ⌀ D7pm

⊢⊣**GH Munstone House** Munstone
(2m N unclass off A49) ☎67122
Closed Dec 6hc ⊗ TV 20P S% B&b£5

HERNE BAY Kent *Map 5 TR16*
⊢⊣**GH Beauvalle** 92 Central Pde ☎5330
Apr–Dec 8hc 1⇌🚿 CTV 🍽 sea S%
B&b£4–£5.50 Bdi£7.50

GH Northdown Hotel 14 Cecil Park
☎2051 Lic 5hc CTV 4P 🍽 S% B&b£7
Bdi£10 W£70 ⌀ D9pm

HERTFORD Herts *Map 4 TL31*
GH Tower House Private Hotel
2 Warren Park Rd, Bengeo ☎53247
6hc 1⇥🛏 TV 5P 🍽 S% ✳B&b£5

HEWISH Avon *Map 3 ST46*
⊷GH Kara ☎Yatton 834442 Closed Xmas
7hc ⊗ TV 7P 🍽 S% B&b£3.50–£4.50
Bdi£5–£6 W£32–£36 ⚹ D7pm

HEYSHAM Lancs *Map 7 SD46*
⊷GH Carr Garth Bailey Ln ☎51175
Spring Bank Hol–Sep rs Etr–Spring Bank
Hol & 1st 2 wks Oct 10hc CTV 7P
B&bfr£4.14 Bdifr£5.40 Wfr£44.56
W only Spring Bank Hol–Sep

HIGHAM FERRERS Northants
Map 4 SP96
INN Green Dragon Hotel 4 College St
☎Rushden 2088 Lic 6hc TV 30P S%
B&b£8 Bdi£12.50 sn L£4–£5
D9pm£5–£6&alc

HIGH WYCOMBE Bucks *Map 4 SU89*
GH Clifton Lodge Private Hotel
210–212 West Wycombe Rd ☎29062
rs Fri–Sun no main meals 12hc (A 3hc)
⊗ nc5 TV 15P 🍽 S% B&b£6 Bdi£8.50
D7pm

HILLESLEY Avon *Map 3 ST78*
⊷INN Fleece ☎Wotton-under-Edge
3189 Lic 3hc TV 20P ⊞ S% B&b£5–£5.50
sn L50p–£3.50 D9.30pm50p–£3.50

HILL HEAD Hants *Map 4 SU50*
⊷GH Seven Sevens Private Hotel
Hill Head Rd ☎Stubbington 2408
8hc CTV 10P 🍽 sea S% B&b£5.75
Bdi£8.75 W£40.25 M D4pm

HINCKLEY Leics *Map 4 SP49*
GH Cecilia's Private Hotel 13–19 Mount
Rd ☎37193 Closed Xmas 8hc CTV 8P 🍽
S% B&b£8

HINDON Wilts *Map 3 ST93*
INN Grosvenor Arms ☎253 Closed Xmas
Lic 3hc CTV 10P S% B&b£7 Bdi£10.50
Bar lunch £3alc D9.30pm£6alc

HITCHIN Herts *Map 4 TL12*
GH *Redcoats Farmhouse Hotel* Little
Wymondley ☎ Stevenage 3500 Closed
Xmas Lic 7hc (A 1hc) CTV 25P D9pm

HOLMROOK Cumbria *Map 6 SD09*
GH Carleton Green ☎608 Apr–Oct
6hc 1⇥🛏 ⊗ nc8 TV 6P 🍽 S% B&b£6.90
Bdi£10.35 W£64.40 ⚹ D10pm

HOLNE Devon *Map 3 SX76*
INN Church House ☎ Poundsgate 208
Lic 5hc nc14 TV 7P 🍽 ⊞ B&b£8.50
Bdi£13 W£50 M sn L£6alc
D10pm£4.75&alc

HOLNEST Dorset *Map 3 ST61*
GH Manor Farm Country House
Holnest Park ☎474 Mar–Oct Lic 10hc
CTV 20P 🍽 B&b£6–£7 Bdi£9–£10.50
W£60–£70 ⚹ D7.30pm

HOLT Norfolk *Map 9 TG03*
⊷GH Lawns Private Hotel Station Rd
☎3390 Lic 9hc 2⇥🛏 nc7 CTV 9P 🍽 S%
B&b£5.50–£6.50 Bdi£9–£10 W£60–£65
⚹ D6pm

HOPE COVE Devon *Map 3 SX63*
⊷GH Fern Lodge ☎Galmpton 326
Mar–Oct 5hc 1⇥🛏 (A 2hc) ⊗ TV 4P 3🏠

Croft Hotel

**24 PALMEIRA AVENUE,
HOVE, SUSSEX**
Tel: Brighton 732860

Proprietors: Kay and Ron Freeman

This charming, small well-appointed hotel is pleasantly situated
only a few minutes from Palmeira Gardens, sea, shopping centre
and county cricket ground. Good food, personal supervision. Dining
room with separate tables. Access to rooms at all times. Free street
parking.

Henstead Hall Country Hotel

Henstead Hall is a Georgian mansion
standing in spacious grounds and woodlands lying well back from the road and
situated three miles from the sea and six
from the Broads.
We are approximately equidistant from
Lowestoft, Beccles, and Southwold (six
miles).
Pets very welcome.
Write for brochure. Henstead Hall Country
Hotel, Nr Beccles, Tel: Lowestoft
740345. Proprietress Mrs D K Farmiloe.

📞 B&bf4.25–£5 Bdif£7.25–£8.25
W£49.95–£54.95 ⊬ D7.30pm
GH Lantern Lodge Hotel ☎ Galmpton
280 Etr–Oct Lic 15⇔🚿 nc CTV 20P 2🏠
📞 sea S% B&bf8–£15 Bdif£14–£21
W£98–£147 ⊬ D7pm
GH Sand Pebbles Hotel ☎ Galmpton 673
Apr–Oct Lic 6hc 2⇔🚿 CTV 13P S%
B&bf8–£9 Bdif£10–£12 W£70–£84
⊬ D7pm

HOPTON CASTLE Salop *Map 7 SO37*
GH Lower House Country Lodge
☎ Bucknell 352 Closed Jan Lic 4hc nc14
CTV 10P 2🏠 S% B&bf11.25 Bdif£18.25
W£125 ⊬ D6pm

HORNSEA Humberside *Map 8 TA24*
⨝**GH Promenade Hotel** Marine Dr
☎2944 Closed Oct & Xmas 12hc 🚿
CTV 17P 📞 sea B&bfr£5 Bdifr£8 Wfr£52
⊬ D6pm
⨝**GH Hotel Seaforth** Esplanade ☎2616
7hc CTV 5P 📞 sea S% B&bf5
Bdifr£7.75 Wfr£50 ⊬ D4.30pm

HORRABRIDGE Devon *Map 2 SX56*
⨝**GH Overcombe** ☎ Yelverton 3501
Lic 7hc 1⇔🚿 CTV 7P 1🏠 📞 S%
B&bf5.75–£6.75 Bdif£9–£10.50
W£56.70–£67.20 ⊬ D7.15pm

HORSHAM W Sussex *Map 4 TQ13*
GH Wimblehurst Private Hotel
6 Wimblehurst Rd ☎62319 13hc 4⇔🚿
🚿 CTV 14P 📞 S% B&bf7.99–£14.99
Bdif£11.99–£18.99 D7pm

HORSHAM ST FAITH Norfolk
Map 9 TG21

GH Elm Farm Chalet Norwich Rd
☎ Norwich 898366 Closed 25 & 26Dec
12hc 4⇔🚿 CTV P 📞 S% B&bf7–£9.50
Bdif£10.75–£13.25 W£71.75–£89.25
⊬ D8pm

HORTON Dorset *Map 4 SU00*
INN Horton ☎ Witchampton 252 Lic 7hc
3⇔🚿 CTV 75P 📞 ⇄ S% ✳B&bf14–£22
Bdif£18–£26 sn L£2.35–£3&alc
D10pmf£4.50–£6

HORTON-IN-RIBBLESDALE N Yorks
Map 7 SD87
INN Crown ☎209 Lic 9hc CTV 20P 📞
⇄ B&bf6.32–£7.26 Bdif£10.35–£11.88
W£76.03 ⊬

HOVE Sussex *Map 4 TQ20*
GH Bigwood Lodge Hotel 40 Old
Shoreham Rd ☎ Brighton 737430 Lic
16hc 4⇔🚿 CTV 4P 4🏠 📞
B&bf7.50–£8.50 Bdif£10–£11.50
D4pm
GH Croft 24 Palmeira Av ☎ Brighton
732860 Apr–10 Jan 12hc CTV 📞 S%
✳B&bf5.50–£6
GH *Polonia Hotel* 36–38 St Aubyns
☎ Bighton 733640 Lic 51hc 🚿 🔥 CTV 28P
lift 📞 sea D8pm
⨝**GH Tatler Hotel** 26 Holland Rd
☎ Brighton 736698 Lic 12hc CTV S%
B&bf5.50–£6.50 Bdif8–£9 W£50–£58
D noon

HOYLAKE Merseyside *Map 7 SJ28*
GH Sandtoft Hotel 70 Alderley Rd
☎051-632 2204 Lic 9hc CTV 10P 3🏠
📞 S% ✳B&bf8.50 Bdif£12.75 D6pm

Overcombe Hotel

Horrabridge, Yelverton, Devon

A friendly, family-run hotel on
west Dartmoor between Plymouth and
Tavistock. A comfortable base for exploring
Devon and Cornwall. Conveniently placed
for walking, riding, golf, sea and river
fishing. Children and dogs welcome.
Open all the year. Good home cooking.
Bed and Breakfast. Dinner. Licensed.
Pam & Richard Kitchin.

Tel: Yelverton (082 285) 3501.

THE CRANBROOK HOTEL

24 COVENTRY ROAD, ILFORD, ESSEX

Telephone 01-554 6544 or 554 4765

AA Listed

Bed & Breakfast. Group Bookings.
Rooms with bathrooms, telephones and TVs.
Centrally heated.
Near main station & Valentines Park.
20 mins. by train to London.

HUDDERSFIELD W Yorks *Map 7 SE11*
GH Dryclough House Hotel Dryclough
Rd, Crossland Moor ☎651731
Closed Xmas Lic 10hc 1⇨訓 CTV 12P
3🏠 🎮 S% B&b fr£6.33 Bdi fr£9.43
D2pm

HULL Humberside *Map 8 TA02*
⊷**GH Ashford** 125 Park Av ☎492849
Closed Xmas wk 6hc ⊗ CTV 6P 🎮 S%
B&b£5.40 Bdi£8.80 D4pm

INN Good Fellowship Cottingham Rd
☎42858 rs Sun (no meals) Lic 8hc CTV
120P 🎮 B&b£8 Bdi£10.50 sn
L75p–£3.50 D8pm£2.50–£5&alc

HUNSTANTON Norfolk *Map 9 TF64*
GH Dolphin Private Hotel 15 Cliff Ter
☎2583 Lic 10hc CTV sea S% B&b£6.50
Bdi£10 W£60 ⊬ D8pm

GH Lincoln Lodge Private Hotel Cliff Pde
☎2948 Apr–Oct Lic 14hc nc2 CTV 6P sea
B&b£7.50–£8 Bdi£11–£11.50
W£73.50–£76.50 ⊬ D6.30pm

GH Norfolk Private Hotel 32 King's Lynn
Rd ☎2383 Lic 11rm 10hc ♨ CTV 13P
4🏠 🎮 S% B&b£6.50–£7.50 Bdi£9–£10
W£58–£64 ⊬ D8.30pm

GH Sutton House Hotel 24 Northgate
☎2552 Lic 10hc CTV 6P 🎮 S%
✳B&b£6.50 Bdi£9 W£58 ⊬ D9pm

GH Tolcarne Private Hotel 3 Boston Sq
☎2359 Etr–Dec Lic 11hc nc2 CTV 9P 🎮
S% B&b£6–£7.50 Bdi£8.50–£10.50
W£55–£66 ⊬ D5.30pm

HURN Dorset *Map 4 SZ19*
INN Avon Causeway Hotel
☎ Christchurch 482714 Lic 9hc TV 50P

HUTTON-LE-HOLE N Yorks *Map 8 SE79*
GH Barn Tea Shop & Craft Centre
☎Lastingham 311 Mar–Nov 10rm 9hc
TV 15P 🎮

ICKENHAM Gt London *Map 4 TQ08*
GH Woodlands 84 Long Ln ☎Ruislip
34830 Closed Xmas 9hc ⊗ nc5 CTV 9P 🎮

ICKLESHAM E Sussex *Map 5 TQ81*
⊷**GH Snailham House** Broad St ☎556
Mar–Nov Lic 7hc ⊗ CTV 7P 🎮 S%
B&b£5.50–£7 Bdi£8–£9.50
W£49–£59.50 ⊬ D6.30pm

ILFORD Gt London *Map 5 TQ48*
GH Blenheim House Hotel 2 Blenheim
Av, Gants Hill ☎01-554 4138 Lic 8hc ⊗
nc5 CTV 4P 1🏠 🎮 S% B&b£9.50
Bdi£12.75

GH Cranbrook Hotel 24 Coventry Rd
☎01-554 6544 Closed Xmas Lic 16hc
8⇨訓 CTV 13P 2🏠 🎮 S% ✳B&b fr£6.75
D9pm

GH Empress Hotel 448 Green Ln,
Seven Kings ☎01-590 3616 Lic 18hc
CTV 12P 🎮 S% B&b£6.50

GH Park Hotel 327 Cranbrook Rd
☎01-554 9616 Lic 21hc 1⇨訓 CTV 25P
🎮 S% B&b£8.63 Bdi£12.75 D8.30pm

ILFRACOMBE Devon *Map 2 SS54*
See Plan
GH Avenue Private Hotel Greenclose Rd
☎63767 Plan:**1** Apr–Oct Lic 24hc ⊗
CTV 12P B&b£7.70–£8 Bdi£10.12–£11.37
W£58–£66.70 ⊬ D7pm

⊷**GH Bickleighscombe House** 41 St
Brannocks Rd ☎63899 Plan:**2** Apr–Oct
Lic 13hc CTV 14P S% B&b fr£5.40
Bdi fr£8.10 Wfr£55.08 ⊬ D6pm

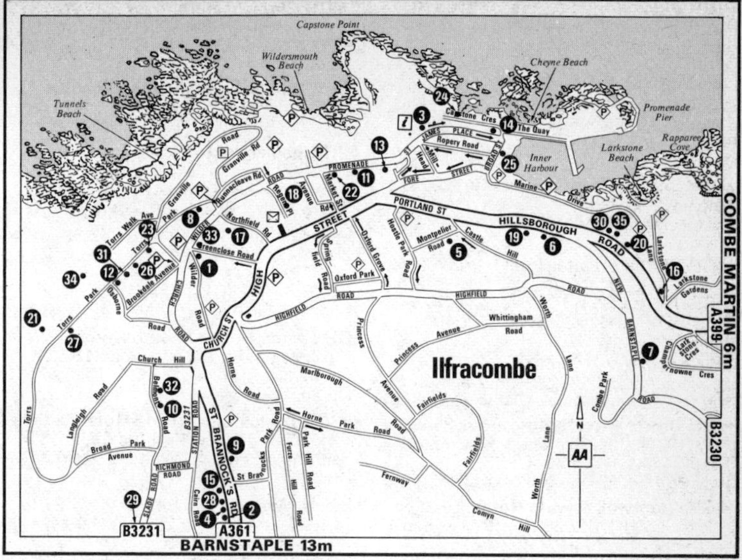

1 Avenue Private Hotel	**10** Darnley Private Hotel	**19** Merrydene Private Hotel	**28** Strathmore Private Hotel
2 Bickleighscombe House	**11** Dèdés Hotel	**20** New Cavendish Hotel	**29** Sunny Hill
3 Blenheim	**12** Elmfield Hotel	**21** Norbury	**30** Tamaris
4 Carbis	**13** Glendower	**22** Queen's Court Hotel	**31** Torrsvale Private Hotel
5 Cheddar	**14** Headlands Hotel	**23** Riversdale Hotel	**32** Wentworth House Private Hotel
6 Clutha Private Hotel	**15** Lantern House Hotel	**24** Rockcliffe Hotel	**33** Westbourne Private Hotel
7 Craigmillar	**16** Laston House Private Hotel	**25** Royal Britannia *(Inn)*	**34** Westwell Hall Private Hotel
8 Cresta Private Hotel	**17** Lympstone Private Hotel	**26** Southcliffe	**35** Wilson
9 Cromwell Private Hotel	**18** Marlyn	**27** South Tor Hotel	

𝕭𝖎𝖈𝖐𝖑𝖊𝖎𝖌𝖍𝖘𝖈𝖔𝖒𝖇𝖊 𝕳𝖔𝖚𝖘𝖊

A comfortable and spacious private hotel situated in its own grounds with splendid views and overlooking Bicklescombe Park. The hotel is in a quiet position yet only about ten minutes' from the town centre. There is a large comfortable lounge with TV, sun lounge, licensed bar, and a large car park. Family rooms are available for up to six persons. Baby listening service. Mid-week bookings accepted.

**41 St Brannock's Road, Ilfracombe, Devon.
Telephone. 0271 63899**

March to October

The Blenheim

**5 St James's Place
Ilfracombe, North Devon**
Telephone: Ilfracombe (0271) 63787
**Your hosts and personal supervisors:
Mr and Mrs H G Spooner**
Fire safety certificate

The Blenheim is ideally situated for your holiday, being only a hundred yards from the nearest beach or the start of a pleasant stroll around perfectly safe cliffs which overlook delightful sea views.

Comfortably furnished lounge for you to relax and enjoy resting, reading and watching the colour television.

The bedrooms are also comfortably furnished and have H & C, shaver points and tea/coffee-making facilities at no extra cost.

⊶GH **Blenheim** 5 St James Pl ☎63787 Plan:**3** Etr–Sep 11hc ⊗ CTV S% B&b£4–£6 Bdi£6–£8 W£39–£45 ⊮ D4pm

⊶GH **Carbis** 50 St Brannocks Rd ☎62943 Plan:**4** Closed Xmas wk 12hc CTV 12P B&b£4.32–£5.40 Bdi£6.48–£7.56 W£43.20–£48.60 ⊮ D4pm

⊶GH **Cheddar** 2 Montpelier Ter ☎63322 Plan:**5** Apr–Oct 6hc ⊗ CTV sea S% B&b£4–£4.50 Bdi£5–£5.50 W£35–£40 ⊮ D7pm

⊶GH **Clutha Private Hotel** Hillsborough Ter ☎62798 Plan:**6** Apr–mid Oct Lic 11hc ⊗ CTV 4P sea S% B&b£5.75–£8.63 Bdi£9.20–£12.08 W£55.20–£72.48 ⊮ D6.30pm

GH *Craigmillar* 22 Crofts Lea Pk (New Barnstaple Rd) ☎62822 Plan:**7** Spr Bank Hol–end Sep 8hc ⊗ nc1 CTV 5P sea D4pm

⊶GH **Cresta Private Hotel** Torrs Park ☎63742 Plan:**8** May–Oct rs Etr Lic 26hc CTV 30P S% B&b£5.75–£6.33 Bdi£8–£9.50 W£56–£66.50 ⊮ D6.30pm

⊶GH **Cromwell Private Hotel** 20–21 St Brannocks Rd ☎63829 Plan:**9** May–Sep Lic 15hc 2⇆🍴 ⊗ CTV 24P 2🏛 S% B&b£4.50–£6 Bdi£6.50–£8 W£39–£48 ⊮ D5.30pm

GH *Darnley Private Hotel* Belmont Rd ☎63955 Plan:**10** May–Sep 17hc nc5 CTV 15P 4🏛 D5pm

⊶GH **Dèdés Hotel** 1–2 The Promenade ☎62545 Plan:**11** Etr–mid Oct Lic 18hc 6⇆🍴 (A 5hc) CTV sea S% B&b£4.25–£7.30 Bdi£7.30–£10.25 W£51–£71.75 ⊮ D10pm

⊶GH **Elmfield Hotel** Torrs Park ☎63377 Plan:**12** Apr–Oct 6hc ⊗ CTV 12P S% B&b£3.50–£4.50 Bdi£5–£7 W£35–£49 ⊮ D4.30pm

GH **Glendower** Sea Front, Wilder Rd ☎62121 Plan:**13** Lic 12hc CTV 22P 🍴 sea S% B&b£8–£10 Bdi£12.65 D7.30pm

GH **Headlands Hotel** Capstone Cres ☎62887 Plan:**14** Lic 22hc CTV 12🏛 sea B&b£7.65–£8.50 Bdi£10–£11 W£63–£70 ⊮ W only Jul & Aug

⊶GH **Lantern House Hotel** 62 St Brannocks Rd ☎64401 Plan:**15** Lic 10hc nc3 CTV 10P 🍴 S% B&b£5.95–£6.95 Bdi£8.70–£9.70 W£52.50–£55 ⊮ W only Jul & Aug D5.45pm

GH *Laston House Private Hotel* Hillsborough Rd ☎62627 Plan:**16** Etr–mid Oct 11hc ⊗ nc4 CTV 12P sea D5pm

⊶GH **Lympstone Private Hotel** 14 Cross Park ☎63038 Plan:**17** 17hc CTV 5P S% B&b£5.75 Bdi£8.62 W£46–£50.60 ⊮ D5pm

⊶GH **Marlyn** 7 & 8 Regent Pl ☎63785 Plan:**18** Etr–Oct Lic 12hc CTV 4🏛 🍴 S% B&b£5–£5.50 Bdi£7–£7.50 W£45–£52 ⊮ D5pm

⊶GH **Merrydene Private Hotel** 10 Hillsborough Ter ☎62141 Plan:**19** May–Oct 12hc nc5 CTV 4P 4🏛 sea S% B&b£5–£6 Bdi£8–£8.50 W£50–£55 ⊮

GH **New Cavendish Hotel** 9–10 Larkstone Ter ☎63994 Plan:**20** Etr–Oct & Xmas Lic 22hc 1⇆🍴 ⊗ ⚓ CTV 20P sea S% ✳B&b£4.50–£6.50 Bdi£7.50–£9.50 W£48–£56 ⊮ W only Jul & Aug D5pm

New Cavendish Hotel

Larkstone Terrace, Ilfracombe, North Devon
Tel: 0271-63994

Commanding the finest view in Ilfracombe, with breathtaking views of harbour, Bristol Channel, etc., which can be seen not only from all our public rooms, but also from the majority of our tastefully furnished bedrooms. All bedrooms with H&C, shaver points, and continental quilts. 17 bedrooms with private shower units, plus two double, and two single bedrooms without showers, but with a bathroom on every floor. Separate colour TV lounge, bar lounge and games room which includes pool, table tennis and darts. Thursday is Fancy Dress night. Enjoy the party atmosphere! Music and dancing. Licensed. Excellent home cooking. Children welcome. Open for the Christmas festivities. Private car parking available.

Please write for coloured brochure (SAE) to the resident owners,
Ron and Marie Mourton.

Darnley Hotel
Telephone 63955 (STD 0271)

BELMONT ROAD, ILFRACOMBE, DEVON EX34 8DR

A friendly welcome awaits you at The Darnley. Homely atmosphere, personal service. Secluded but only a few minutes' walk from town & beaches, private nature walk to High Street. Pleasant grounds, quiet lounge, colour TV lounge, central heating, ample parking space. No restrictions — in fact everything to make your holiday perfect. LICENCE PENDING.

Dédés
Licensed

1-3 The Promenade, Ilfracombe, EX34 9BD
Tel: 0271 62545

Overlooking the sea!

*Situated in superb, level position on sea front, overlooking Bristol Channel. *Good varied food a speciality, all cooked under the owning family's supervision. *Colour TV lounge with balcony.

A special feature is the unusual times of meals. Breakfast 8-10 am, Dinner 6-10 pm, with a choice of menu. This gives you complete freedom to enjoy you days out. Reduced terms early and late season. Number of rooms with private bathroom & WC.

Illustrated coloured brochure from the proprietors: Mr and Mrs A B Napper.

HEADLANDS HOTEL

What do you look for in a Holiday? Is it . . .

* A garden set above a breathtaking seascape
* Good food & friendly service
* A relaxed holiday for all ages
* C/H public rooms with colour TV
* Individually heated bedrooms
* Private garage available

Then it must be the **HEADLANDS**
Write for free colour brochure (stamp please) to: DEPT AA
CAPSTONE CRESCENT
ILFRACOMBE, DEVON
TEL: (STD 0271) 62887

Queens Court Hotel

Wilder Road, Ilfracombe, N. Devon.
0271-63789

Open all year round. Small licensed hotel overlooking sea. Large free car park. Fresh, home-cooked food. No petty restrictions. Children and pets welcome. For your convenience we are always pleased to offer lunch and evening bar snacks. Full English breakfast always served. 4 course dinner optional. Fire certificate granted. Stamp for brochure please to

Jill and Gerry Hoskinson.
Queens Court Hotel
Sea Front, Ilfracombe.
Tel(0271) 63789.

THE ROCKCLIFFE HOTEL

and SALTY DOG FREE HOUSE
Open All Year.

The Rockcliffe stands at the foot of Capstone Hill on the water's edge. Private car park. A few minutes' walk to the harbour, amusements and town centre. All bedrooms have H & C, electric shaving points and self-controlled heating, some with private bathrooms. All double and family rooms with private TV.
Resident proprietors:
A & R Howell, Ref. AA
Capstone Parade, Ilfracombe, Devon.
Tel: 62267

The Royal Britannia Hotel

The Harbour, Ilfracombe, North Devon
Tel: (STD 0271) Management — 62939
**　　　　　　Visitors — 62129**

Situated right on the harbour's edge, this is a small family hotel with the amenities and welcome of a typical *English Country Inn*.

* Good Devon Fare
* Well appointed accommodation with showers
* Open all the year round
* Parking within 100 yards
* Special arrangements made for angling clubs, and parties for fishing weekends
* Attractive reduced terms for off-season weekend breaks
* Weddings and functions catered for

Bed and breakfast or Dinner, bed and breakfast at reasonable terms.

Write for free illustrated brochure.

⊨⊣GH Norbury Torrs Park ☎63888
Plan:**21** Apr–Oct Lic 8hc TV 8P sea S%
B&b£5–£6 Bdi£7.50–£8.50
W£52.50–£59.50 ⊭ D5pm
⊨⊣GH Queen's Court Hotel Sea Front
☎63789 Plan:**22** Mar–Oct Lic 17hc CTV
17P sea B&bfr£5.61 Bdifr£8.07
Wfr£55.80 ⊭ W only Jul & Aug D6.30pm
GH *Riversdale Hotel* Torrs Park ☎62535
Plan:**23** Apr–Sep rs Oct–Mar Lic 12hc ⊗
CTV 18P D4pm
GH *Rockcliffe Hotel* Capstone Pde
☎62267 Plan:**24** Lic 16hc nc4 CTV 12P
sea D10.30pm
⊨⊣GH Southcliffe Hotel Torrs Park
☎62958 Plan:**26** May–Oct Lic 20hc ⌂
CTV 12P S% B&b£5.50–£8 Bdi£6.50–£10
W£49.75–£59.75 ⊭ W only Aug D6.30pm
⊨⊣GH South Tor Hotel Torrs Park
☎63750 Plan:**27** Etr, May–Sep & Xmas
Lic 15hc 3⇨⋒ nc4 CTV 12P 2⌂ S%
B&b£5.50–£7.50 Bdi£8.50–£11
W£52–£64 ⊭ W only end Jul & Aug
D5.30pm
⊨⊣GH Strathmore Private Hotel
57 St Brannocks Rd ☎62248 Plan:**28**
Lic 9hc 2⇨⋒ ⌂ CTV 8P sea S%
B&b£4.25–£5 Bdi£6.50–£7.25
W£38–£48.85 D6pm
GH Sunny Hill Lincombe, Lee ☎62953
Plan:**29** Lic 8hc 2⇨⋒ nc5 CTV 6P ⊞ sea
S% B&b£6.50–£8.50 Bdi£9.50–£12
W£62.50–£77.50 ⊭ D8pm
⊨⊣GH Tamaris 17 Larkstone Ter ☎62223
Plan:**30** Lic 10hc CTV sea S% B&b£5–£6
Bdi£7.30–£8.30 W£51–£58 ⊭ D5pm
⊨⊣GH Torrsvale Private Hotel Torrs Park
☎63012 Plan:**31** Lic 9hc ⊗ CTV 15P S%
B&b£4.25–£5.40 Bdi£6–£7 W£40–£48
⊭ W only Jun–Aug D5pm

⊨⊣GH Wentworth House Private Hotel
Belmont Rd ☎63048 Plan:**32** Mar–Oct
10hc 1⇨⋒ CTV 10P S% B&b£4.90–£5.75
Bdi£6.90–£7.95 W£45–£53.50 ⊭
D5.30pm
⊨⊣GH Westbourne Private Hotel
Wilder Rd ☎62120 Plan:**33** mid Feb–Nov
Lic 51hc CTV lift S% B&b£5.50–£7
Bdi£6.50–£8 W£44–£54 D6.30pm
⊨⊣GH Westwell Hall Private Hotel
Torrs Park ☎62792 Plan:**34** Apr–Sep
Lic 14hc nc3 CTV 14P S%
B&b£5.50–£6.50 Bdi£7.50–£8.50
W£47–£54 D4pm
⊨⊣GH Wilson 16 Larkstone Ter ☎63921
Plan:**35** Mar–Oct Lic 9hc ⌂ CTV sea S%
B&b£4.50–£5.50 Bdi£6.50–£7.50
D6.30pm
INN *Royal Britannia* The Quay ☎62939
Plan:**25** Lic 12hc CTV sea D8pm

ILKLEY W Yorks *Map 7 SE14*
GH Greystones Private Hotel
Ben Rhydding Rd ☎607408 Lic 10hc
8⇨⋒ ⌂ CTV 15P S% B&b£10–£15
Bdi£17–£22 W£112–£147 ⊭ D8pm

INGHAM Suffolk *Map 5 TL87*
INN *Cadogan Arms* ☎ Culford 226 Lic
5rm 4hc ⊗ nc2 TV

INGLETON N Yorks *Map 7 SD67*
⊨⊣GH Springfield Private Hotel Main St
☎41280 Closed 3wks late Oct–early Nov
6hc CTV 12P river S% B&b£5.13–£5.67
Bdi£7.83–£8.37 W£48.60–£52.38 ⊭
D4.30pm

INSTOW Devon *Map 2 SS43*
GH *Anchorage Hotel* The Quay ☎860655
Mar–Oct rs Jan & Feb Lic 9hc ♨ CTV 9P
sea D6.30pm

⊶**GH Sandlea Hotel** The Quay ☎860475
Etr–Oct Lic 8hc ♨ CTV 9P sea S%
B&b£5.50–£7.50 Bdi£9–£11
W£52.50–£61 Ł D6pm

IPSWICH Suffolk *Map 5 TM14*
GH Gables Hotel 17 Park Rd ☎54252
Lic 12hc CTV 10P ⠿ S% B&b£6.90
Bdi£9.24 D6pm

ISLE OF MAN *Map 6* Details will be
found between the England & Wales
sections.

ISLE OF WIGHT *Map 4*
Places with AA listed accommodation are
indicated on the location map on page 4
of atlas section. Full details will be found
under individual place names within the
appropriate gazetteer sections.

ISLES OF SCILLY
See Scilly, Isles of

IVER HEATH Bucks *Map 4 TQ08*
⊶**GH Bridgettine Convent** Fulmer
Common Rd ☎ Fulmer 2645 19hc ⊗
nc3 TV 15P ⠿ S% B&b£4–£5
Bdi£5.50–£6.75 Wfr£48 D2pm

IVYBRIDGE Devon *Map 2 SX65*
⊶**GH Sunnyside** Western Rd ☎2561
Lic 8hc CTV 1P B&b£5.17–£6.90
Bdi£8.05–£10.35

KELLING Norfolk *Map 9 TG04*
INN Applehill Hotel ☎ Weybourne 382
Lic 6hc 2⇱☖ CTV 30P ⠿ B&b fr£8 sn
D9pm

KENILWORTH Warwicks *Map 4 SP27*
⊶**GH Enderley** 20 Queens Rd
☎55388 2Jan–Nov Lic 6rm 5hc CTV 2P
⠿ S% B&b£5–£6 Bdi£8–£9 D noon

GH *Ferndale* 45 Priory Rd ☎53214
10Jan–20Dec 6hc TV 8P ⠿

⊶**GH Hollyhurst** 47 Priory Rd ☎53882
9rm 8hc CTV 10P ⠿ S% B&b£4.25–£4.75

⊶**GH Nite Lite** 95 Warwick Rd ☎53594
Lic 12hc CTV ⠿ S% B&b£5.18–£5.75
Bdi£7.48–£8.05 D8.30pm

KENTISBURY Devon *Map 2 SS64*
⊶**GH Homeside** Kentisburyford
☎ Combe Martin 3506 Etr–Oct 6hc ⊗
nc8 CTV 6P S% B&b£4–£5
Bdi£7.50–£8.50 W£50–£55

KENTMERE Cumbria *Map 12 NY40*
GH *Grove* ☎ Staveley (Cumbria) 821548
Mar–Sep rs New Year Lic 7hc CTV ⠿
river D noon

KESWICK Cumbria *Map 11 NY22*
See Plan
⊶**GH Acorn House Private Hotel**
Ambleside Rd ☎72553 Plan:**1** Etr–Nov
8hc CTV 8P ⠿ S% B&b£5–£5.75
Bdi£8–£8.75 W£53.20–£58.20 Ł
D2.30pm

GH Bay Tree 1 Wordsworth St ☎73313
Plan:**2** Lic 6hc ⊗ CTV ⠿ river
B&b£4.95 Bdi£7.50–£7.95
W£49.50–£55 Ł

GH Burleigh Mead Private Hotel
The Heads ☎72750 Plan:**3**

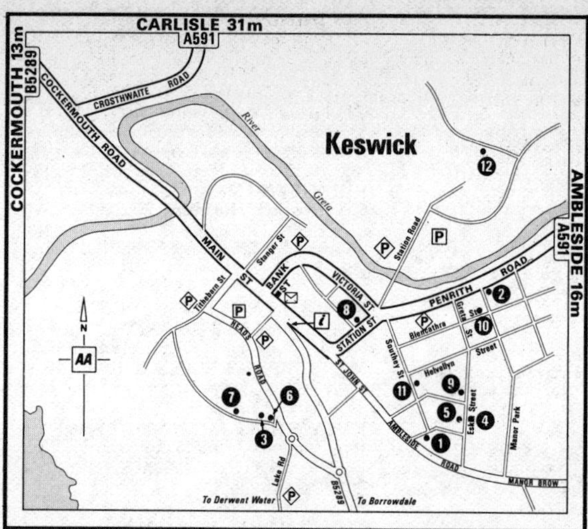

10Mar–10Nov Lic 8hc (A 6hc) CTV 6P B&b£6.80–£8 Bdi£8.70–£9.70 D5pm

⊷GH **Clarence House** 14 Eskin St ☎73186 Plan:**4** 8hc CTV ⑭ S% B&b£4.40–£4.70 Bdi£7.15–£7.45 D2pm

⊷GH **Foye House** 23 Eskin St ☎73288 Plan:**5** 6hc ⊘ nc5 TV ⑭ S% B&b£4.50 Bdi£7.25

GH **Hazeldene Hotel** The Heads ☎72106 Plan:**6** 10Mar–10Nov Lic 15hc CTV 12P ⑭ B&b£6.80–£8.00 Bdi£8.70–£9.70

⊷GH **Highfields** The Heads ☎72508 Plan:**7** Etr–Oct Lic 10hc nc5 CTV ⑭ lake B&b£5.32–£5.86 Bdi£8.52–£9.05 W£59.64–£63.35 ⱖ D5pm

⊷GH **Ravensworth Hotel** Station St ☎72476 Plan:**8** Etr–Sep rs Oct–Nov (reservations & wknds only) 9hc nc CTV 4P ⑭ S% B&b£4.80

⊷GH **Richmond House** 39 Eskin St ☎73965 Plan:**9** 6hc CTV ⑭ S% B&b£3.50–£4.25 Bdi£6.25–£7 W£50–£58 D7pm

⊷GH **Silverdale Hotel** Blencathra St ☎72294 Plan:**10** Mar–Oct & Xmas Lic 12hc ⊘ CTV 8P ⑭ S% B&b£5.50–£5.75 Bdi£7.85–£8.50 W£53–£58 D5pm

GH **Sunnyside** 25 Southey St ☎72446 Plan:**11** Mar–Nov 8hc ⊘ nc12 CTV 9P S% ✱B&b£4.60 Bdi£6.90 D5.30pm

GH **Woodlands** Brundholme Rd ☎72399 Plan:**12** Mar–Oct 7hc ⊘ nc6 CTV 10P ⑭ W only Mar–May (excluding Bank Hols) D6.45pm

KEYNSHAM Avon *Map 3 ST66*
⊷GH **Uplands Farmhouse** The Wellsway ☎5764 9hc CTV 20P ⑭ B&b£5–£6.50 Bdi£8.50–£10 W£51–£60 ⱖ D4pm

KIDLINGTON Oxon *Map 4 SP41*
GH **Bowood House** 238 Oxford Rd ☎2839 Closed Xmas wk 6hc 2⇱⋔ ⊘ CTV 10P ⑭ S% B&b£7–£9

KILKHAMPTON Cornwall *Map 2 SS21*
⊷INN **London** ☎343 Lic 3rm nc CTV 8P 4🏠 ⇞ B&b£5.85 Bdi£8.20 W£54 ⱖ Bar lunch 45p–£2.50 D8.30pm fr£3

KILNSEY N Yorks *Map 7 SD96*
GH **Chapel House** ☎ Grassington 752654 Mar–Nov Lic 12hc 6⇱⋔ TV 20P ⑭ river S% Bdi fr£11.50 W fr£68.43 ⱖ

KILVE Somerset *Map 3 SS14*
⊷INN **Hood Arms** ☎ Holford 210 Lic 5hc nc7 CTV 12P ⇞ B&b£5.50 W£33 M Bar lunch £1.80alc D9.30pm£4.50alc

KINGSBRIDGE Devon *Map 3 SX74*
GH Hotel Kildare Balkwill Rd ☎2451
Closed Xmas & New Year Lic 11hc (A 3hc)
♣ CTV 6P S% B&b£7.02 Bdi£10.80
W£64.53–£69.66 Ł D7.15pm

KINGSDOWN Kent *Map 5 TR34*
GH Blencathra Country Kingsdown Hill
☎ Deal 3725, Etr–Oct Lic 5hc nc3 CTV 7P
🏤 sea S% B&b£7 Bdi£10.50 W£63
Ł D6.30pm

KINGSKERSWELL Devon *Map 3 SX86*
⊷**GH Harewood** Torquay Rd ☎2228
Apr–Nov 6hc CTV 12P 🏤 S% B&b£4–£5
W£27.50–£31.50 M

KING'S LYNN Norfolk *Map 9 TF62*
GH Runcton House Hotel 53 Goodwins
Rd ☎3098 Lic 7hc ✗ CTV 14P 🏤 S%
B&b£8–£9

KINGSTON Devon *Map 2 SX64*
⊷**GH Trebles Cottage** ☎ Bigbury-on-Sea
268 Feb–Nov Lic 5hc 1⊷🏠 CTV 6P 🏤 S%
B&b£5–£7 Bdi£8.75–£10.75
W£54.50–£65 Ł D9am

KINGSTON UPON THAMES Gt London
Map 4 TQ16
GH Hotel Antoinette 26 Beaufort Rd
☎01-546 1185 Lic 50hc 50⊷🏠 (A 55hc
55⊷🏠) nc10 CTV 70P 🏤 S% B&b£8.05–
£12.65 Bdi£12.65–£17.25 D8.30pm
GH Lingfield House Hotel 29 Beaufort Rd
☎01-546 1988 7hc 7⊷🏠 ✗ nc5 CTV
6P 1🏠 🏤 S% B&b£6.25–£7 D9pm

KINGSWINFORD W Midlands
Map 7 SO88

INN Swan Hotel Stream Rd ☎3720 Lic
4hc ✗ nc5 TV 50P 🏤 🚗 S% B&b£7 sn
L£1.20–£2.50

KIRBY MUXLOE Leics *Map 4 SK50*
GH Forest Lodge Hotel Desford Rd
☎ Leicester 393125 Lic 35hc 3⊷🏠 CTV
60P 🏤 B&bfr£8.05 D9pm

KIRKOSWALD Cumbria *Map 11 NY54*
GH Prospect Hill Hotel ☎ Lazonby 500
Closed Feb Lic 9hc 2⊷🏠 ✗ ♣ CTV 24P
🏤 B&b£6.50 Bdi£10.15 W£39.81 M
D8.15pm

KNAPTON Norfolk *Map 9 TG33*
GH Knapton Hall Hotel ☎Mundesley
720405 Mar–Oct Lic 10hc 1⊷🏠 (A 4hc)
✗ CTV 14P S% ✳B&b£5.18 Bdi£7.48
W£48.30 Ł D7pm

KNOWSTONE Devon *Map 3 SS82*
INN Masons Arms ☎ Anstey Mills 231
Lic 3hc nc13 CTV 8P 🏤 🚗 S% B&b£7–£9
D9.30pm£5 alc

KNUTSFORD Cheshire *Map 7 SJ77*
GH *Longview Private Hotel*
55 Manchester Rd ☎2119 Closed Xmas
& New Year Lic 10hc CTV 6P 🏤 D9pm

LAMBERHURST Kent *Map 5 TQ63*
INN George & Dragon School Hill ☎277
Closed New Years Day Lic 4hc 1⊷🏠
70P 🏤 ✳B&b£7.30–£9.50 sn L£4.45–
£5.50&alc D10pm fr£3.50 alc

LANCASTER Lancs *Map 7 SD46*
⊷**GH Belle Vue** 1 Belle Vue Ter, Greaves
☎67751 6hc CTV 6P S% B&b£4.50–£5
W£28–£32 M

LANCING W Sussex *Map 4 TQ10*
⊷**GH Beech House** 81 Brighton Rd
☎3368 Closed mid Dec–mid Jan 6hc
CTV 6P 🍴 sea S% B&b£4.50–£7
W£29–£45 M

GH *Seaways* 83 Brighton Rd ☎2338
8rm 7hc CTV 6P 🍴 sea

LANGPORT Somerset *Map 3 ST42*
GH *Ashley* The Avenue ☎250386
Closed 2wks Oct Lic 9hc ⌦ TV 12P
D7.30pm

LEAMINGTON SPA Warwicks
Map 4 SP36 **See Plan**
GH Beech Lodge Hotel 28 Warwick
New Rd ☎22227 Plan:**1** Lic 12hc 9⇆🛏
CTV 8P 1🏠 🍴 S% B&b£8.05 Bdi£12.65
D6.30pm

⊷**GH Buckland Lodge Hotel** 35 Avenue
Rd ☎23843 Not on plan
rs wknds (no evening meals) 8hc CTV
12P 🍴 S% B&b£5.50–£6.50
Bdi£8–£9 D4pm

⊷**GH Glendower** 8 Warwick Pl
☎22784 Plan·**4** 9hc CTV 8P 2🏠 🍴 S%
B&b£5.50–£6.25

GH Veleta Hotel 42 Warwick New Rd
☎21380 Plan:**5** Lic 12hc 4⇆🛏 15P 🍴
S% ✳B&bfr£5.50 D8.30pm

⊷**GH Westella Hotel** 26 Leam Ter
☎22710 Plan:**6** Closed Xmas 10hc CTV
12P 🍴 S% B&b£5–£6 Bdi£7.50–£8.50
W£47.50–£53.50 ⌦ D4pm

⊷**GH White House** 22 Avenue Rd
☎21516 Plan:**7** Lic 7hc ⌦ TV 12P 🍴
S% B&b£5.50 Bdi£8.50 D9pm

GH *York* 9 York Rd ☎24195 Plan:**8** 8hc
CTV 3P river

VELETA HOTEL
42 Warwick New Road, Leamington Spa

Private car park. Spacious dining room.
Visitors' lounge with TV. Hot and cold
water, shaver points and heaters
in all rooms.
The Veleta Hotel is under the
personal supervision of the resident
proprietors, ensuring of cleanliness,
comfort and good food. A friendly
welcome is extended to all guests.
For your reservation telephone:
Leamington Spa 21380.

LEEDS W Yorks *Map 8 SE33*
GH Anrosa House Hotel 47 Cliff Rd, Hyde Park Corner ☎758856 Closed Xmas Lic 17hc nc2 CTV 8P ⋒ S% B&b£7.20 D8pm
⊷**GH Aragon Hotel** 250 Stainbeck Ln, Chapel Allerton ☎759306 Lic 10hc CTV 7P 2⋒ ⋒ S% B&b£5.75 Bdi£8.85 D7.30pm
GH Ash Mount Hotel 22 Wetherby Rd, Roundhay ☎658164 Closed Xmas 14hc ⊗ CTV 12P ⋒ S% ✱B&b£6
⊷**GH Clock Hotel** 317 Roundhay Rd, Gipton Wood ☎621259 Closed 25 & 26Dec Lic 23hc ⊗ CTV 12P S% B&b£4–£6.50 Bdi£6.50–£9.50 D7.30pm
GH Highfield Hotel 79 Cardigan Rd, Headingley ☎752193 10hc ⊗ CTV 7P ⋒ S% B&b£7
GH Oak Villa Hotel 57 Cardigan Rd, Headingley ☎758439 Closed Xmas 10hc CTV 8P ⋒ B&b£6.48–£7.02 W£38.88–£42.12 M

LEE-ON-THE-SOLENT Hants *Map 4 SU50*
⊷**GH Ash House Private Hotel** 35 Marine Parade West ☎550240 6hc CTV 6P ⋒ S% B&b£4–£5

LEICESTER Leics *Map 4 SK50*
GH Alexandra Hotel 342 London Rd ☎703056 Lic 25hc CTV 25P ⋒ S% ✱B&b£6.96 Bdi£10.58 W£74.06 ⋉ D4.30pm

GH Daval Hotel 292 London Rd ☎708234 Closed Xmas Lic 13hc nc2 CTV 20P ⋒ S% B&b£7.99 Bdi£11.50 D7pm

⊷**GH Old Rectory** Main St, Glenfield (3m W A50) ☎312214 12hc nc3 CTV 14P ⋒ S% B&b£5.25–£5.75 Bdi£8–£8.50 W£50–£53 ⋉ D6pm
⊷**GH Wyvernhoe Hotel** 2 Grace Rd, Aylestone ☎833508 8hc ⊗ TV 8P 2⋒ ⋒ S% B&b£4.75–£5.50 Bdi£7.50–£8.25 D3pm

LELANT Cornwall *Map 2 SW53*
⊷**GH Ar-Lyn Private Hotel** Vicarage Ln ☎ Hayle 753330 Lic 11hc CTV 10P ⋒ sea S% B&b£4.50–£5.50 Bdi£7–£8 W£49–£56 ⋉ D6.30pm

LEVISHAM N Yorks *Map 8 SE89*
⊷**GH Moorlands** ☎ Pickering 60247 Etr–Oct 5hc CTV 6P 1⋒ S% B&b£5 Bdi£8 W£55 ⋉ D6.30pm

LEWDOWN Devon *Map 2 SX48*
⊷**INN Blue Lion** ☎238 Lic 3hc CTV 25P ⋒ S% ✱B&b£5.40 Bar lunch 50p–£1.30

LEYBURN N Yorks *Map 7 SE19*
GH Eastfield Lodge St Matthews Ter ☎ Wensleydale 23196 Lic 8hc CTV 12P ⋒ S% ✱B&b£6–£8 Bdi£10–£12 D8pm

LICHFIELD Staffs *Map 7 SK10*
⊷**GH Oakleigh** 25 St Chads Rd ☎22688 4hc (A 2hc) CTV 18P ⋒ ⅋ B&b£4.86–£6.48 Bdi£7.56–£9.18 D6.30pm
INN Old Crown Hotel Bore St ☎22879 Lic 7hc 10P 2⋒ ⅋ S% B&b£7.50 Bar lunch 80p

𝕸𝖞𝖓𝖉 𝕳𝖔𝖚𝖘𝖊 𝕻𝖗𝖎𝖛𝖆𝖙𝖊 𝕳𝖔𝖙𝖊𝖑

**LITTLE STRETTON, CHURCH STRETTON
SHROPSHIRE SY6 6RB
RESIDENTIAL AND RESTAURANT LICENCE
TEL: (STD 06942) 2212**

Mynd House is a comfortably furnished Private Hotel standing in its own grounds which include terraced gardens, lawn and large private car park. Within the fully centrally-heated Hotel there is a comfortable lounge with coloured television, cocktail bar and a sun lounge adjoining the spacious dining room.
There are fine views from the Hotel which is situated near the base of the Long Mynd (on B4370) midway between Shrewsbury and Ludlow (A49) in an area renowned as a walking and motoring centre. Facilities for riding, pony trekking, tennis, golf, fishing and gliding are also available nearby.

Brochure on request.

CHARNWOOD HOTEL

(JUST OFF THE MOTORWAY)
Exit 21 (M1 Motorway & M69 link-up)
5 minutes along B4114 to Narborough Village.
48 Leicester Road, Narborough.

TEL. LEICESTER 862218 (STD CODE 0533)

★ 21 centrally heated bedrooms many with private bath
★ Restaurant á-la-carte & table d'hôte
★ Licensed bar. Colour television
★ National Exhibition Centre 30 minutes
★ Sensible prices

ONE STAR AA APPROVED

LINCOLN Lincs *Map 8 SK97*
GH Brierley House 54 South Park
☎26945 Lic 7hc CTV P 🍳 S%
B&b£6.90–£8.05 Bdi£10.35–£11.50
D5pm

LISKEARD Cornwall *Map 2 SX26*
GH Hotel Nebula 27 Higher Lux St
☎43989 Lic 10hc CTV 20P S% ✳B&bfr£5
Bdifr£7 Wfr£44 ⊬ D5pm

LITTLEHAM Devon *Map 2 SS42*
⊷**INN Crealock Arms** Shutta Farm
☎ Bideford 2791 Apr–Oct Lic 3hc ❀
CTV 30P S% B&bfr£5 Bdifr£7.50

LITTLEHAMPTON W Sussex
Map 4 TQ00
GH Arun Hotel 42–44 New Rd ☎21206

Lic 7hc ❀ CTV 6P 2🏠 🍳 S% B&b£7.50
Bdi£11.50 W£78 ⊬

GH *Braemar Private Hotel* Sea Front
☎5487 8hc CTV river

GH Burbridge Hotel 93 South Ter
☎21606 Lic 6hc ❀ CTV 🍳 S% B&b£6–£8
W£36–£50 M

GH *Harley House Hotel* St Catherines Rd
☎5851 Lic 7hc ❀ CTV 4P D6pm

GH *Regency Hotel* 85 South Ter ☎7707
Closed Xmas Lic 7hc CTV 🍳 sea S%
B&bf6.50 Bdif9.50 Wf54 ⊬ D6pm

LITTLE STRETTON Salop *Map 7 SO49*
⊷**GH Mynd House Private Hotel**
Ludlow Rd ☎ Church Stretton 2212
Closed Jan Lic 12hc CTV 14P 🍳 S%

B&b£5.35–£7.20 Bdi£7–£10.26
W£49–£64.80 *k* D5pm

LIZARD Cornwall *Map 2 SW71*
GH *Kynance Bay Hotel* ☎498 9hc CTV
9P sea D6.30pm

GH Parc Brawse House ☎466 Mar–Oct
Lic 6hc nc8 TV 6P S% ✱B&b£5
Bdi£7.15–£8.30 D7pm

GH *Penmenner House Hotel* Penmenner
Rd ☎370 Apr–Oct Lic 8hc ⊘ ♨ CTV 10P
sea D5pm

LONDON *Maps 4 & 5* **Also see Plans
pages 29–32
A map of the London postal area
appears on page 26 & 27**
Places within the London postal area are
listed below in postal district order
commencing North, then South and West,
with a brief indication of the area covered.
Other places within the county of London
are listed under their respective place
names.

N4 Finsbury Park
Redland Hotel 418 Seven Sisters Rd
☎01-800 1826 Not on plan 24rm 23hc
⊘ nc2 CTV 10P 🍴 B&bfr£8

N8 Hornsey
⊶**Aber Hotel** 89 Crouch Hill ☎01-340
2847 Not on plan 8hc ⊘ TV 🍴 S%
B&b£5–£6

Highgate Lodge Hotel 9 Waverly Rd
☎01-340 1590 Not on plan 19hc 1⇌🍴
CTV 5P S% B&b£6.50 W£38 M

N10 Muswell Hill
⊶**Princes Hotel** 36–38 Princes Av,
Muswell Hill ☎01-883 5676 Not on plan
12hc (A 8hc) ⊘ TV 4P 🍴 S%
B&b£4.86–£5.40 W£30.24–£34.02 M

N15 Tottenham
Granham House 97 Philip Ln
☎01-801 2244 Not on plan Lic 14hc
CTV 12P 🍴 S% B&b£8.63 D10.30pm

NW2 Cricklewood
⊶**Clearview House** 161 Fordwych Rd
☎01-452 9773 Not on plan Closed Aug
7hc nc5 CTV 🍴 S% B&b£4.50

Garth Hotel 72–76 Hendon Way,
Cricklewood ☎01-455 4742 Not on plan
Lic 36hc 23⇌🍴 ⊘ CTV 30P 🍴 S%
B&b£11.95–£14.95 D9pm

NW3 Hampstead and Swiss Cottage
Langorf Hotel 20 Frognal ☎01-794
4483 Not on plan 32hc CTV 🍴 S%
B&b£9–£10

Willow Hotel 32 Willow Rd, Hampstead
☎01-435 2205 Not on plan Lic 6hc ⊘
CTV 3P 🍴 S% B&b£8.50–£10
W£53.50–£63 M

NW6 Kilburn
⊶**Dawson House Hotel** 72 Canfield Gdns
☎01-624 0079 Not on plan 15hc ⊘ nc6
CTV 🍴 S% B&b£5.50–£7 W£35 M

Hazlewood House Hotel 109 Broadhurst
Gdns ☎01-624 8443 Not on plan 12hc
TV 🍴 S% B&b£6–£7 W£31.50 M
W only Nov–Mar

Mulroy 4–6 Burton Rd ☎01-624 0727
Not on plan 13hc ✿ CTV 7P ▥

NW11 Golders Green
Central 35 Hoop Ln ☎01-458 5636
Not on plan 18hc 3⇨⊓ (A 18hc 15⇨⊓)
✿ CTV 8P ▥ S% B&b£10–£12
Bdi£13–£15 D6.30pm
Croft Court Hotel 44 Ravenscroft Av
☎01-458 3331 Not on plan 20hc 5⇨⊓
CTV 4P ▥ S% B&b£10–£11 Bdi£13–£14
W£106–£113 D6pm
Ridgeway House Hotel 59 The Ridgeway
☎01-458 4146 Not on plan 6hc ✿ nc6
CTV P ▥ S% ✱B&b£6

SE3 Blackheath
Stonehall House Hotel 37 Westcombe
Park Rd ☎01-858 8706 Not on plan
23hc CTV ▥ S% B&bfr£6.50 Wfr£39 M
D7pm

SE19 Norwood
Crystal Palace Tower Hotel 114 Church
Rd ☎01-653 0176 Not on plan 13hc ✿
CTV 12P ▥ S% B&b£6.50–£7.50

SE25 South Norwood
Toscana 19 South Norwood Hill
☎01-653 3962 Not on plan Lic 8hc ✿
CTV 10P ▥ S% B&b£6.50–£7

SW1 West End–Westminster;
St James's Park, Victoria Station
Arden House 12 St Georges Dr
☎01-834 2988 Plan3:**1** 34hc 3⇨⊓
(A 14hc) ✿ CTV ▥ S% B&b£7.50–£9
Beverley Towers Hotel
106–108 Belgrave Rd ☎01-828 6767
Plan3:**2** Lic 53hc CTV ▥ D9.30pm

Chesham House 64–66 Ebury St,
Belgravia ☎01-730 8513 Plan3:**3** 23hc
✿ ▥ S% ✱B&b£8–£9 W only in winter
Chester House Hotel 134 Ebury St,
Belgravia ☎01-730 3632 Plan3:**4**
12hc 8⇨⊓ ✿ CTV ▥ S% B&b£6–£10.80
Corbigoe Hotel 101 Belgrave Rd,
Victoria ☎01-828 6873 Plan3:**5** 17hc
1⇨⊓ ✿ CTV ▥ S% B&b£6–£8
Corona Hotel 87–89 Belgrave Rd,
Victoria ☎01-828 9279 Plan3:**6**
Closed Xmas Lic 32hc 21⇨⊓ ✿ nc CTV
▥ S% B&bfr£6.48
Easton Hotel 36–40 Belgrave Rd, Victoria
☎01-834 5938 Plan3:**7** Lic 41hc
(A 13hc) ✿ CTV ▥ S% B&b£7.50–£8
Elizabeth Hotel 37 Eccleston Sq, Victoria
☎01-828 6812 Plan3:**8** 24hc 3⇨⊓
CTV ▥ S% B&b£7.50–£14
Hanover Hotel 30–32 St Georges Dr
☎01-834 0134 Plan3:**9** 34hc 10⇨⊓
CTV ▥ S% B&b£7–£14 W£40–£55 M
W only Oct–Mar
Holly House 20 Hugh St ☎01-834 5671
Plan3:**10** 9hc ✿ ▥
Sloane Hall Hotel 6 Sloane Gdns,
Sloane Sq ☎01-730 9206 Plan3:**11**
26hc 8⇨⊓ CTV ▥ B&b£9–£11
Sloane Rooms 30 Lower Sloane St
☎01-730 3217 Plan3:**12** Closed Xmas
12hc ✿ nc10 CTV ▥
Willet Hotel 32 Sloane Gdns, Sloane Sq
☎01-730 0634 Plan3:**13** 17hc 15⇨⊓ ✿
▥ S% ✱B&b£9–£14

SW3 Chelsea
Blair House Hotel 34 Draycott Pl
☎01-581 2323 Plan2:**5** 20hc TV ▥

Campden Court 28 Basil St ☎01-589 6286 Plan2:**7** 17hc 8⇔🛏 ⚹ 🍴 lift ✱B&b£16

Culford Hall Hotel 7 Culford Gdns ☎01-581 2211 Plan2:**9** 29hc 12⇔🛏 TV 🍴 S% B&b£8.50–£9.60 W only Nov–Mar

Eden House Hotel 111 Old Church St ☎01-352 3403 Plan2:**10** 15hc 6⇔🛏 CTV 🍴 S% B&b£6–£11.50 D9.30pm

Garden House Hotel 44–46 Egerton Gdns ☎01-584 2990 Plan2:**11** 30hc 12⇔🛏 🍴 B&b£6.50–£9.50

Rutland Court Hotel 21–23 Draycott Pl ☎01-589 9691 Plan2:**21** 30hc 11⇔🛏 ⚹ nc8 CTV 🍴 lift S% B&bfr£20.19

SW4 Clapham
⊷**Edwards** 91 Abbeville Rd, Clapham Common ☎01-622 6347 Not on plan 9hc ⚹ nc5 S% B&b£4–£6.50 W£26–£40 M

Regency Lodge Hotel 5 Crescent Gv, South Side, Clapham Common ☎01-622 2684 Not on plan Lic 30hc nc4 CTV 6P 🍴 D7.30pm

SW5 Earls Court
Arlanda Hotel 17 Longridge Rd ☎01-370 5220 Plan2:**3** 15hc 2⇔🛏 ⚹ nc16 CTV 🍴 S% B&b£7–£8.64 W£42–£49 M

Burns Hotel 18–24 Barkston Gdns ☎01-373 3151 Plan2:**6** Lic 104hc (A 20hc) CTV lift 🍴 D9.45pm

Kensington Court Hotel 33–35 Nevern Pl ☎01-370 5151 Plan2:**12** Lic 35hc 35⇔🛏 ⚹ 10P 2🚪 🍴 lift S% ✱B&bfr£15

Manor Court Hotel 35 Courtfield Gdns ☎01-373 8585 Plan2:**14** 60hc 25⇔🛏

CTV 🍴 lift S% ✱B&b£8.25–£10.25 Wfr£44.50 M W only 15Oct–Mar

⊷**Merlyn Court Hotel** 2 Barkston Gdns ☎01-370 1640 Plan2:**15** 18hc ⚹ CTV 🍴 S% B&b£5–£7 W only Oct–Apr

Nevern Hotel 29–31 Nevern Pl ☎01-370 4827 Plan2:**17** Lic 32hc 9⇔🛏 ⚹ CTV 🍴 lift S% B&b£6.90–£9.60

SW6 Fulham
Seagrave Lodge Hotel 21–27 Seagrave Rd ☎01-385 7771 Not on plan 30hc ⚹ CTV 10🚪 🍴

SW7 South Kensington
Adelphi Hotel 127–129 Cromwell Rd ☎01-373 7177 Plan2:**1** Lic 59hc ⚹ CTV lift 🍴

Ashburn Hotel 111 Cromwell Rd ☎01-370 3321 Plan2:**4** Lic 44rm 40⇔🛏 ⚹ CTV 50🚪 🍴 lift S% B&b£7.90–£10.90 W£35 M

Hotel Lindsay 12 Ashburn Gdns ☎01-370 5294 Plan2:**13** 22hc ⚹ CTV 🍴 S% B&b£6.75–£7.50

Milton Court Hotel 68–74 Cromwell Rd ☎01-584 7851 Plan2:**16** 105hc 17⇔🛏 CTV 🍴 lift S% B&b£8–£10.60

Queensberry Court Hotel 7–11 Queensberry Pl ☎01-589 3693 Plan2:**20** Lic 42hc 21⇔🛏 CTV 🍴 lift S% B&bfr£12

Tudor Court Hotel 58–66 Cromwell Rd ☎01-584 8273 Plan2:**24** 88hc 41⇔🛏 CTV 🍴 lift S% B&b£8–£10.60

SW13 Barnes
Arundel Hotel Arundel Ter ☎01-748 8005 Not on plan Closed Xmas 23hc ⚹ CTV 🍴

SW15 Putney
Lodge Hotel 52 Upper Richmond Rd
☎01-874 1598 Not on plan Lic 35hc
18⇔🛏🏕 CTV 16P 🍴 S% B&b£11–£14
Bdi£14–£17 W£79–£90 㔾 D7.30pm
⋈**Wilton House Hotel** 2 Ravenna Rd,
Putney ☎01-789 3768 Not on plan
10hc nc6 CTV 2P 🍴 S% B&b£4–£7

SW19 Wimbledon
Hatherley Hotel 87 Worple Rd,
☎01-946 5917 Not on plan 9hc ⊗ CTV
9P 🍴 S% B&b£7.25–£9.50
Trochee 21 Malcolm Rd,
☎01-946 1579 Not on plan 17hc CTV
6P 🍴 S% B&b£7.50–£10.50 (W only
Nov–Mar)
Wimbledon Hotel 78 Worple Rd
☎01-946 9265 Not on plan 9hc ⊗
CTV 9P 🍴 S% B&b£7.25–£9.50
Worcester House 38 Alwyne Rd
☎01-946 1300 Not on plan 7hc 4⇔🛏
⊗ 🍴 S% B&b£9–£18 W only Nov, Jan
& Feb

W1 West End, Piccadilly Circus,
St Marylebone and Mayfair
Concorde Hotel 50 Gt Cumberland Pl
☎01-402 6169 Plan1:**4** Lic 28hc CTV lift
🍴

Eros Hotel 67 Shaftesbury Av ☎01-734
8781 Not on plan 58hc 23⇔🛏 🍴 lift S%
B&b£12.45–£15.30
Georgian House Hotel 87 Gloucester Pl,
Baker St ☎01-486 3151 Plan1:**8** Lic 19hc
19⇔🛏 ⊗ nc4 CTV 🍴 lift S%
✳B&b£10.35–£17.25 W only Nov–Mar
Hart House Hotel 51 Gloucester Pl,
Portman Sq ☎01-935 2288 Plan1:**9**
15hc 9⇔🛏 ⊗ 🍴 S% B&b£8.50–£11.50
Milford House 31 York St ☎01-935
1935 Plan 1:**11** 8hc 2⇔🛏 ⊗ CTV 🍴 S%
B&b£6–£8 W only Nov–Mar
Rose Court Hotel 35 Gt Cumberland Pl
☎01-262 7241 Plan1:**13** Lic 60hc CTV
lift 🍴

W2 Bayswater, Paddington
Britannia Court Hotel 80 Inverness Ter
☎01-727 5918 Plan1:**1** 12hc 3⇔🛏 ⊗
CTV 🍴 S% B&b£9–£10 W only Nov–Mar
Caring Hotel 24 Craven Hill Gdns, Leinster
Ter, Hyde Pk ☎01-262 8708 Plan1:**2**
24hc ⊗ CTV 🍴
Century Hotel 18–19 Craven Hill Gdns
☎01-262 6644 Plan1:**3** Lic 60hc 60⇔🛏
⊗ CTV 2P 🍴 lift S% B&b£12.50–£18.08

Dylan Hotel 14 Devonshire Ter
☎01-723 3280 Plan1:**5** 15hc CTV
Edward Hotel 1A Spring St ☎01-262
2671 Plan1:**6** Lic 59hc CTV 12P 🍴 lift
S% B&b£9.40–£15.40 Bdi£13.40–£19.40
D9.30pm
Garden Court Hotel 30–31 Kensington
Gdns Sq ☎01-229 2553 Plan 1:**7** Lic
37hc 10⇔🛏 ⊗ CTV 🍴 S% B&b£9–£9.50
King's Hotel 60–62 Queensborough Ter
☎01-229 7055 Plan1:**10** 29hc CTV 🍴
Pembridge Court Hotel 34 Pembridge
Gdns ☎01-229 9977 Plan1:**12** Lic 28hc
21⇔🛏 CTV 2🏠 🍴 S% B&b£11–£13
Bdi£15–£18 D11pm
Slavia Hotel 2 Pembridge Sq
☎01-727 1316 Plan1:**14** Lic 30rm 28hc
⊗ CTV 2P 🍴

W5 Ealing
Grange Lodge 50 Grange Rd
☎01-567 1049 Not on plan Lic 10hc
CTV 2P 🍴 D9pm

W8 Kensington
Alexa Hotel 71–75 Lexham Gdns
☎01-373 7272 Plan2:**2** 49hc 6⇔🛏 ⊗
nc3 CTV 🍴 lift S% B&b£7.50–£10
Clearlake Hotel 18–19 Prince of Wales
Ter ☎01-937 3274 Plan2:**8** Lic 15⇔🛏
CTV 🍴 lift S% B&b£10.80–£12.96
Observatory House Hotel Observatory
Gdns ☎01-937 1577 Plan2:**18** 23hc ⊗
nc5 CTV 🍴 S% B&b£8.05–£10.92
W only Oct–Mar
Prince's Lodge 6–8 Prince of Wales Ter
☎01-937 6306 Plan2:**19** Lic 36hc ⊗ CTV
lift 🍴
Silver Star Hotel 13 Lexham Gdns
☎01-373 9426 Plan2:**22** 20hc 20⇔🛏
⊗ CTV 🍴 S% B&b£7–£15 W only Oct–Mar
Suncourt Hotel 57–67 Lexham Gdns
☎01-373 7242 Plan2:**23** 111hc CTV
lift 🍴

WC1 Bloomsbury, Holborn
Mentone Hotel 54–55 Cartwright Gdns
☎01-387 3927 Not on plan 23hc ⊗ TV 🍴
Mount Pleasant Hotel 53 Calthorpe St
☎01-837 9781 Not on plan Lic 402hc
36⇔🛏 CTV 🍴 lift S% B&b£8.50 Bdi£12
D8.45pm

LONGDOWN Devon *Map 3 SX89*
INN *Lamb* ☎226 Lic 3rm 2hc ⊗ nc10
CTV 25P sn D9.30pm

The Granby Inn

LONGFRAMLINGTON, MORPETH, NE65 8DP
Tel: Longframlington 228
Proprietors: Mr and Mrs G Hall

The Inn is centrally placed in the country on the A697, north of Morpeth, and within reach of the beautiful North Northumbrian coast, the Cheviot Hills and the ancient town of Alnwick. Holy Island, Farne Islands, Craster and Seahouses are just some of the places of interest. AA Listed. Fully Licensed. Lounge Bar. Good Food and Wine. Attractive Dining Room. Centrally Heated Throughout. Ample Car Parking. All rooms with H and C and TV. Formerly a coaching stop, the Inn is about 200 years old and has retained its oak beams. The Inn can cater for up to 24 diners, with a Wine List available, and for a lighter repast, Bar Lunches, Snacks and Sandwiches are always available.

COMMONWOOD MANOR HOTEL

EAST LOOE, CORNWALL, PL13 1LP
Tel: Looe 2929 (STD 05036)

The hotel stands in three acres of garden on the side of a wooded valley overlooking the East and West Looe rivers. There are superb views across the tidal waters and surrounding hills and the flower and rose gardens, rockeries and terraces offer a secluded setting for sunbathing.

This is a family-run hotel and the whole atmosphere is informal, friendly and relaxing. We try to ensure that your holiday here will be one to remember with pleasure.

There is a well-stocked bar, colour TV, solarium and ample parking space in the hotel grounds.

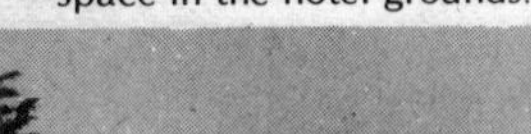

LONGDOWNS Cornwall *Map 2 SW73*
⋈**GH Marrack House** ☎ Stithians 860231
6rm 5hc ⚹ CTV 6P S% B&b£5 Bdi£7.50
W£42 ⚷ D6.30pm

LONG EATON Derbys *Map 8 SK43*
GH Camden Hotel 85 Nottingham Rd
☎62901 Lic 7hc 1⇱🍴 (A 6hc) nc3 CTV
16P 🍴 S% ✻B&b£6.90–£8.05 D6pm

LONGFRAMLINGTON Northumb
Map 46 NU10
INN Granby ☎228 Lic 3hc ⚹ nc12
30P 🍴 S% B&b£8.50 Bdi£12.50
Bar lunch £2.50alc D8.30pm£6alc

LOOE Cornwall *Map 2 SX25* **See Plan**
GH Annaclone Hotel Marine Dr,
Hannafore ☎2177 Plan:**1** Apr–Oct rs
Nov–Mar Lic 9hc 2⇱🍴 ⚹ CTV 2P 🍴 sea
S% B&b fr£6 Bdi fr£9 Wfr£40 ⚷ D7.30pm
GH Commonwood Hotel St Martin's Rd
☎2929 Plan:**2** Mar–Oct Lic 17hc 1⇱🍴
⚘ CTV 20P 🍴 river B&b£8–£9.50
Bdi£11.50–£13 W£80.50–£89 ⚷ D8.30pm
GH Deganwy Hotel Station Rd ☎2984
Plan:**3** Mar–Sep Lic 9hc ⚹ nc3 CTV 6P
river S% B&b fr£6.32 Bdi fr£9.80 Wfr£48
⚷ D5pm
GH Fieldhead Hotel Portruan Rd,
Hannafore ☎2689 Plan:**4** Jun–Aug
rs Mar–May & Sep–Oct (no swimming pool)
Lic 18hc 12⇱🍴 ⚹ nc5 CTV 7P 7🏠 🍴 sea
S% B&b£7–£12 Bdi£11.20–£16.20
W£72–£108 ⚷ D7pm
GH Hillingdon Portruan Rd, Hannafore
☎2906 Plan:**5** Mar–Oct 8hc ⚹ CTV 2🏠
🍴 sea B&b£6.33–£9.20 Bdi£8.92–£11.79
W£48.88–£58.08 ⚷ D5pm

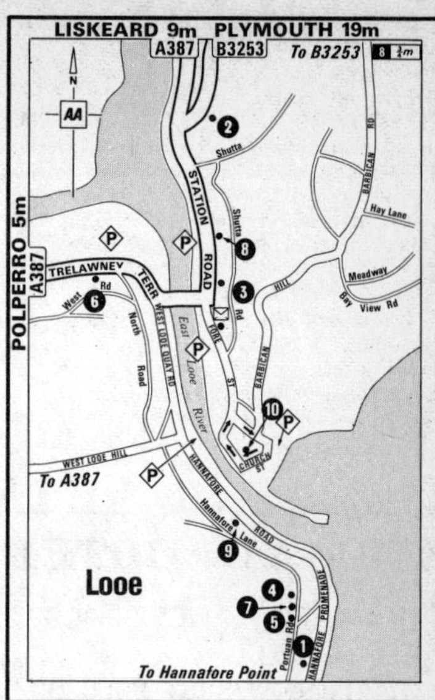

1	Annaclone Hotel	**6**	Kantara
2	Commonwood Hotel	**7**	Lemain Hotel
3	Deganwy Hotel	**8**	Riverside Hotel
4	Fieldhead Hotel	**9**	Rockwell Hotel
5	Hillingdon	**10**	Smuggler's House Hotel

Fieldhead Hotel

Looe Cornwall

Tel: (Management) Looe (STD 05036) 2689
Licensed
Overlooking the sea

Large free car park in own grounds.

Heated outdoor swimming pool with sunbathing patio. Children's play area and snack bar open throughout each day.

Attractive gardens for your leisure.

Private showers in most rooms. Two rooms with en suite bath & wc.

Baby listening, radios, shaving points and fire detectors in all rooms. Fire certificate issued.

Fieldhead is a family run hotel, and families are especially welcome. Many of the rooms will accommodate 4 or 5 and there are special terms for children sharing. Brochure and tariff by return of post.

Special off-season rates — March, April, May-Sept. and Oct.

⋈GH 'Kantara' 7 Trelawney Ter ☎2093 Plan:**6** Mar–Oct 6hc ⌘ TV river S% B&bf4–£5.50

GH Lemain Hotel Hannafore Ln, Hannafore ☎2073 Plan:**7** Etr–Sep Lic 9hc CTV 14P sea S% B&bf6.46–£7.37 Bdif9.36–£10.90 Wf58.50–£69.50 Ł D4pm

⋈GH Riverside Hotel Station Rd ☎2100 Plan:**8** Etr–mid Oct Lic 13hc ⌘ CTV 6P river B&bf5.40–£6.48 Bdif8.64–£9.72 Wf45.36–£64.80 Ł D3pm

GH *Rockwell Hotel* Hannafore Rd, Hannafore ☎2123 Plan:**9** Mar–Nov & Xmas Lic 12hc CTV 9P river sea

GH *Smugglers House Hotel* Middle Market St ☎2397 Plan:**10** Feb–Dec Lic 7hc TV D6.45pm

LOSTWITHIEL Cornwall *Map 2 SX15*
GH Trevone Hotel ☎872528 Feb–Nov Lic 8hc CTV 20P lift ✳B&bf7–£8 Bdif8.65–£10 Wf60–£70 Ł D7pm

LOUGHBOROUGH Leics *Map 8 SK51*
GH De Montfort Hotel 88 Leicester Rd ☎216061 Lic 9hc CTV ⑩ S% B&bf6.50 Bdif9.50 Wf57.50 Ł D4pm

⋈GH Sunnyside Hotel The Coneries ☎216217 11hc ⌘ CTV 8P 3🏠 ⑩ S% B&bf4.50–£5 Bdif6.50–£7 D6pm

LOUTH Lincs *Map 8 TF38*
INN Kings Head ☎602965 Closed Xmas Lic 17hc 1⇱🛏 ⌘ CTV 30P 10🏠 ⑩ S% ✳B&bf9.20 Bdif13.80 sn Lf2.30–£2.88&alc D10pmf3.45–£4&alc

---

LEMAIN HOTEL

HANNAFORE, WEST LOOE, CORNWALL.

Tel: Looe 2073 (STD 05036)

Offers high standard at budget rates. Situated in an elevated position overlooking the beautiful bay. Near sea. All rooms have sea view. Usual facilities all bedrooms. Colourful sun patio, colour television lounge, sun lounge, friendly bar lounge. Good food. Inexpensive wines. Personal service. Free car park on premises at road level. No service charge.

POLRAEN
COUNTRY HOUSE HOTEL

Licensed
SANDPLACE, LOOE, PL13 1PJ
Telephone: Looe 3956 (STD 050 36)
Resident Proprietors: **Harry and Eileen Haggan**
Built in early 1700s of Cornish stone. Ideally situated in quiet position in lovely Looe Valley, yet only two miles from Looe.
The spacious south-facing garden is available for you to relax and enjoy our mild climate and peaceful surroundings, while a wealth of home cooked food will satisfy the most discerning guest. Seven bedrooms are available; single, double or family size.
Terms: dinner, bed and breakfast from £58.00 per week, plus VAT, according to season.
Why not try Cornwall in spring or autumn? Special weekend terms on request.

Bishop's Cottage Licensed Hotel

Telephone: West Lulworth 261

Prop: Mrs P Rudd
Small private hotel, large garden overlooking famous Lulworth Cove. Good centre for touring historic Dorset and Thomas Hardy Country, also ideal walking including cliff walks along Dorset's beautiful coastline.
H & C all rooms, baby listening and radio facilities, colour TV, sun lounge, residents' large dining room — reputation for good food.
Restaurant open all day.
Specialities — local crab, lobster and cream teas.

INN Lincolnshire Poacher 211 Eastgate
☎603657 Lic 5hc ✗ CTV 25P ⅏ S%
B&b£6.90 W£47.40 M Bar Lunch75p–£1

LOWESTOFT Suffolk *Map 5 TM59*
GH Amity 396 London Road South
☎2586 6hc ✗ CTV 3P S% ✱B&b£4
Bdi£5.50 W£35 ⱡ D2pm
GH Cleveland House 9 Cleveland Rd
☎62827 6hc CTV 1P ⅏ S% ✱B&b£4.25–
£4.50 Bdi£6–£6.25 D10am
⤛GH Kingsleigh** 44 Marine Pde ☎2513
Closed Xmas 6hc nc5 CTV 6P S%
B&b£5–£8
GH Westview House Hotel Lyndhurst Rd
☎65774 Lic 13hc CTV 10P ⅏ S%
✱B&b£6.48 Bdi£9.18 W£51.84–£59.40
ⱡ Dnoon

LUCKWELL BRIDGE Somerset
Map 3 SS93
⤛GH Brook Farm Hotel** ☎Timberscombe
263 Closed Xmas Lic 6rm 5hc ✗ ♨ CTV
10P ⅏ S% B&b£4.35–£8.65 Bdi£7.44–
£11.64 W£46.52–£73.40 ⱡ (W only
24Jul–Aug) D10.30pm

LUDLOW Salop *Map 7 SO57*
⤛GH Cecil Private Hotel** Sheet Rd
☎2442 Lic 10hc CTV 10P S%
B&bfr£5.75 Bdifr£9 Wfr£54 ⱡ D5.30pm
⤛GH Croft** Dinham ☎2076 Lic 8hc
river B&b£5 Bdi£8.50 W£48 ⱡ Dnoon

LULWORTH Dorset *Map 3 SY88*
⤛GH Bishop's Cottage Hotel**
☎ West Lulworth 268 Mar–Oct Lic 11rm
(A 3rm) ♨ CTV 8P sea S% B&b£4.50–£6
Bdi£8–£9.50 W£50–£60 ⱡ D9.30pm
GH Gatton House Hotel ☎ West
Lulworth 252 Feb–Nov Lic 11hc ♨ CTV
12P 2🏠 ⅏ S% B&b£6.25 £7.50
Bdi£8–£9.50 W£52–£62
GH Lulworth Hotel Main Rd ☎ West
Lulworth 230 Mar–Oct rs Nov–Feb Lic
12hc ✗ nc5 CTV 12P
⤛GH Shirley Hotel** ☎ West Lulworth
358 Spring Bank Hol–mid Sep rs Mar,
Apr, May & Oct Lic 16hc 4⌂ CTV 20P
⅏ sea B&b£5.35–£6.45 Bdi£8–£9.60
W£52.50–£63 ⱡ D9pm

LUTON Beds *Map 4 TLO2*
GH Albany House Hotel 9 Marsh Rd
☎591033 Lic 10hc ✗ ♨ CTV 11P ⅏
S% ✱B&b£8.75–£10.50 D7pm

GH Arlington Hotel 137 New Bedford Rd
☎419614 Lic 14hc ✗ 14P ⅏ S% ✱B&bfr
£14.95 Bdifr£18.95 D6pm
GH Huberstone 618 Dunstable Rd
☎54399 10hc 2⌂ ✗ nc7 CTV 11P ⅏
S% B&b£6.90

LYDFORD Devon *Map 2 SX58*
GH *Moor View* Vale Down ☎220
Apr–Oct 7hc TV 6P 1🏠 D4pm
INN Castle ☎242 Lic 5hc nc5 12P ⅏
S% ✱B&b£7.50 sn L£3 alc D9.30pm£6
alc

LYME REGIS Dorset *Map 3 SY39*
⤛GH Coverdale** Woodmead Rd ☎2882
May–Sep rs Etr 9hc CTV 9P ⅏ sea S%
B&b£5.50–£6.50 Bdi£7.50–£8.50
W£47–£55 D4pm
GH Kent House Hotel Silver St ☎2020
Lic 10hc CTV 9P ⅏ lift S% ✱B&b£5.50–
£6.50 Bdi£8.50–£9.00 D7pm
GH Kersbrook Hotel Pound Rd ☎2596
Apr–Nov 10hc 2⌂ ♨ CTV 10P sea
B&b£7.20–£8.75 Bdi£9.95–£11.75
W£69–£79.50 ⱡ D6.30pm
⤛GH Old Monmouth Hotel** Church St
☎2456 Lic 7hc 1⌂ ✗ CTV sea
B&b£4.50–£6.00 Bdi£7.25–£8.75
W£44–£48 D8.30pm
⤛GH Rotherfield** View Rd ☎2811
Mar–Oct 7hc nc3 CTV 7P ⅏ sea S%
B&b£5–£6 Bdi£7–£8.25 W£48.50–
£53.50 D5pm
⤛GH White House** 47 Silver St ☎3420
Mar–Oct Lic 6hc 1⌂ nc3 CTV ⅏ S%
B&b£5.00–£5.50 Bdi£7.25–£7.85
W£49–£54.75 ⱡ (W only Jul & Aug)
D4pm

LYNDHURST Hants *Map 4 SU30*
⤛GH Bench View** Southampton Rd
☎2502 Closed Xmas 5hc CTV 5P ⅏
S% B&b£5–£6 Bdi£8–£9 W£50–£60
ⱡ D7pm
GH Forest Gardens Hotel Romsey Rd
☎2367 Closed Jan Lic 16hc 9⌂ CTV
28P ⅏ B&b£8.50–£9.75 Bdi£12.70–
£14.50 W£80–£92 ⱡ D10pm
GH Ormonde House Hotel Southampton
Rd ☎2806 Lic 17hc 4⌂ CTV 20P ⅏
S% B&b£6.50–£8.50 Bdi£10–£12
W£60–£72 ⱡ D7pm
GH Whitemoor House Hotel
Southampton Rd ☎2186 Lic 5hc ♨ CTV
8P ⅏ S% B&b£6–£7 W£62–£66 M
D6pm

1 Alford House *(see under Lynton)*
2 Bonnicott Hotel *(see under Lynmouth)*
3 Channel View *(see under Lynton)*
4 Conway Hotel *(see under Lynton)*
5 Longmead House *(see under Lynton)*
6 Countisbury Lodge *(see under Lynmouth)*
7 East Lyn *(see under Lynmouth)*
8 Lyncrest *(see under Lynton)*
9 Lynhurst *(see under Lynton)*
10 Mayfair Hotel *(see under Lynton)*
11 Neubia House *(see under Lynton)*
12 North Cliff Private Hotel *(see under Lynton)*

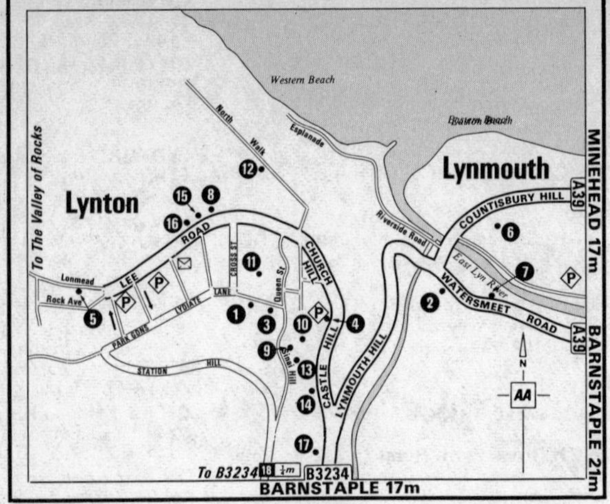

13 Pine Lodge *(see under Lynton)*
14 St Vincents *(see under Lynton)*
15 South View *(see under Lynton)*
16 Turret *(see under Lynton)*
17 Valley House Hotel *(see under Lynton)*
18 Woodlands Hotel *(see under Lynton)*

LYNMOUTH Devon *Map 3 SS74*
See Plan. See also Lynton
GH *Bonnicott Hotel* Watersmeet Rd
☎ Lynton 3346 Plan:**2** Mar–Oct Lic 11hc
CTV D5.30pm

GH Countisbury Lodge Countisbury Hill
☎ Lynton 2388 Plan:**6** Closed Nov Lic 8hc
2⇌🛁 nc8 CTV 10P 🍴 sea B&b£6.90–
£7.50 Bdi£10.35–£11.50 W£69–£77.05
D6pm

GH East Lyn Watersmeet Rd
☎ Lynton 2540 Plan:**7** Closed Dec & Jan
Lic 8hc 2⇌🛁 CTV 5P 3🏠 river S%
B&b£5–£7 Bdi£7.50–£9.75 D6.15pm

LYNTON Devon *Map 3 SS74* **See Plan.
See also Lynmouth**
GH Alford House ☎2359 Plan:**1**
29Mar–4Oct Lic 8hc 4⇌🛁 ⚅ nc5 CTV
🍴 sea S% Bdi£11.38–£12.19
W£69–£73.60 ⚿ D6.30pm

GH Channel View Alford Ter ☎3379
Plan:**3** Mar–Oct Lic 7hc ⚅ CTV sea S%
B&b£4.50–£6.00 Bdi£6.75–£8.25
W£40–£50 ⚿ D6.45pm

GH Conway Hotel Castle Hill ☎2291
Plan:**4** Mar–Oct Lic 10hc ⚅ CTV 🍴 S%
B&b£6.32–£7.48 Bdi£9.20–£10.35
W£57.50–£64.40 ⚿ D6pm

GH Longmead House 9 Longmead
☎2523 Plan:**5** Mar–Sep Lic 9hc ⚅ nc5
CTV 9P 🍴 S% B&b£5–£6.50 Bdi£8–£9.50
W£57–£65 ⚿ D4.30pm

GH *Lyncrest* Lee Rd ☎3269 Plan:**8**
Feb–Nov 6hc nc5 CTV 4P D4pm

GH Lynhurst Hotel Lynway ☎2241
Plan:**9** Mar–Oct Lic 7hc 7⇌🛁 CTV river
sea S% B&b£4.60–£6.60 Bdi£6–£7
W£42–£48 ⚿ D6pm

GH Mayfair Hotel Lynway ☎3227
Plan:**10** Mar–Oct Lic 13hc CTV 12P 🍴
sea B&b£4.95–£7.05 Bdi£6.55–£8.65
W£38.50–£52 ⚿

GH Neubia House Lydiate Ln ☎2309
Plan:**11** Lic 12hc 4⇌🛁 CTV 12P S%
B&b£5.50–£6.60 Bdi£8–£9.50
W£53–£64 ⚿ D7pm

GH North Cliff Private Hotel North Walk
☎2357 Plan:**12** Apr–Oct 24hc ⚅ CTV
17P sea B&b£7.75–£9 Bdi£10.50–£11.50
W£55.85–£58.75 ⚿ (W only mid Jul–Sep)
D6.30pm

GH Pine Lodge Lynway ☎3230 Plan:**13**
Etr–Sep 10hc nc4 TV 9P S% B&b£6.50–
£7 Bdi£8.50–£9 W£54–£58 ⚿

NORTH CLIFF
LYNTON, N. DEVON

Superb views, peaceful, sunny position overlooking Lynmouth Bay and Watersmeet Valley. Ideal centre for touring Exmoor. PARKING.
Adjacent Cliff Railway for Lynmouth and beach. Quiet restful lounge, bright attractive dining room. Games room, colour TV. Central heating in Public Room. Well appointed comfortable bedrooms some with shower-en-suite. Moderate terms, good food, full English breakfast. Children and pets welcomed.
Colour brochure, Res. Prop. Tel. Lynton 2357.

Conway Hotel

Lynton; Devon, EX35 6JA
Telephone Lynton (059 85) 2291

Built in the days of spacious living the Conway Hotel offers comfortable accommodation, good home cooking and service. All bedrooms are equipped with H&C, shaver points and tea making facilities. Electric radiators are provided for the off-peak visitor, and all public areas are centrally heated. Situated in the old Lynton village we are close to all local amenities. Write or phone for brochure and details.

THE MAYFAIR HOTEL
LYNTON, N. DEVON EX35 6AY

- Glorious sea and coastal views from all our bedrooms, each of which has interior sprung divans, H. & C. and razor sockets. ● Central heating in several rooms making "The Mayfair" ideal for early and late holidays. Open March 1st to October.
- Situated in its own grounds, the hotel has own free parking, also a garden entrance from the main public car park. ● A luxurious lounge overlooking Lynmouth Bay.
- Dining room with separate tables. ● Cocktail bar, well stocked wines and spirits, Colour t.v. ● We are highly recommended for good food and comfort. ● Tariff — Bed, Breakfast and Evening Meal from **£38.50**

Telephone: LYNTON 3227 Props: Janet & Phillip Annette. **SAE for colour brochure**

The Old Rectory — Martinhoe

A small personally run hotel, standing in three acres. Three miles from Lynton. Excellent food and wines. Every comfort and facility offered, including peace and quiet. Ideal centre for touring Exmoor and area.
For colour brochure. Stamp only.

Tony and Elizabeth Pring. The Old Rectory, Martinhoe, Parracombe, N. Devon.
Tel: (STD 059 83) 368

GH St Vincents Castle Hill ☎2244 Plan:**14** Feb–Nov & Xmas Lic 7hc ⊗ CTV 6P S% B&b£4.50–£6 Bdi£7–£8.50 W£45–£56 Ł D4pm

GH South View Lee Rd ☎2289 Plan:**15** Mar–Nov 8hc ⊗ nc5 TV 6P 🕾 S% B&b£5–£5.50 W£33–£36.50 M

GH Turret Lee Rd ☎3284 Plan:**16** Mar–Oct 6hc 2⇄🛭 ⊗ nc5 CTV 5🏠 S% B&b£3.95–£4.45 Bdi£6.45–£6.95 W£42–£45 Ł D5pm

GH Valley House Hotel Lynbridge Rd ☎2285 Plan:**17** Mar–Oct Lic 10hc ⊗ CTV 10P sea S% B&b£6.61–£7.47 Bdi£10.35–£11.21 W£72.50–£82.80 Ł W only mid Jul–mid Aug D6pm

GH *Woodlands Hotel* Lynbridge ☎2324 Plan:**18** rs Xmas Lic 10hc ⊗ CTV 11P 🕾 D6.30pm

LYTHAM ST ANNES Lancs *Map 7 SD32* **Telephone exchanges Lytham & St Annes**

GH Beaumont Private Hotel 11 All Saints Rd, St Annes ☎723958 Closed Xmas & New Year Lic 9hc ⊗ nc2 CTV S% ✳B&b£5.75 Bdi£6.90 W£48.30 Ł D6.15pm

GH *Gables Hotel* 35 Orchard Rd, St Annes ☎729851 Apr–Oct Lic 16hc ⊗ CTV 18P W only Jun–Aug D5.45pm

GH Harcourt Hotel 21 Richmond Rd, St Annes ☎722299 Closed Xmas & New Year Lic 10hc ⊗ CTV 6P 🕾 B&bfr£5.75 Bdifr£6.90 W£54.25 W only Jun–Sep D7pm

GH *Heath House Private Hotel* 4 Bromley Rd, St Annes ☎723109 Tem 6hc ⊗ CTV 4P

GH Westbourne Hotel 10–12 Lake Rd, Fairhaven, St Annes ☎734736 Closed Xmas & New Year 19rm 18hc 1⇄🛭 ⊗ CTV 6P 🕾 S% B&b£6.50–£8 Bdi£9–£10.50 W£60–£70 Ł D6.30pm

MAIDSTONE Kent *Map 5 TQ75* **GH Rock House Hotel** 102 Tonbridge Rd ☎51616 12hc ⊗ CTV 7P 🕾 S% B&b£8

MALDON Essex *Map 5 TL80* **INN Swan Hotel** Maldon High St ☎53170 Lic 8hc 3⇄🛭 ⊗ CTV 30P 4🏠 🕾 ⊛ S% B&b£8.63 Bdi£10.50 sn L75p–£3 D8.45pm75p–£3

MANCHESTER Gt Manchester *Map 7 SJ89* **GH Kempton House Hotel** 400 Wilbraham Rd, Chorlton-cum-Hardy ☎061-881 8766 Closed Xmas Lic 14hc ⊗ CTV 8P 🕾 S% B&b£5.50 Bdi£8 Dam

MAN, ISLE OF Details will be found between the England and Wales sections.

MARGATE Kent *Map 5 TR37* **GH Alice Springs Private Hotel** 6–8 Garfield Rd ☎ Thanet 23543 Lic 17hc 9⇄🛭 ⊗ nc6 CTV 🕾 S% B&b£4–£4.50 Bdi£5.50–£6.50 W£34–£42 D5.30pm

GH Burlington House 43 Norfolk Rd, Cliftonville ☎ Thanet 23712 5hc ⊗ CTV 🕾 S% B&b£5–£5.50 Bdi£6.50–£7 W£32.50–£36.50 Ł

GH Charnwood 20 Canterbury Rd ☎ Thanet 24158 Lic 12hc CTV S% B&b£5–£5.50 Bdi£7.50–£8.50 W£38–£42 D6pm

Sysonby Knoll Private Hotel

Asfordby Road, Melton Mowbray. Tel: Melton Mowbray 63563.

A small family hotel with outdoor swimming pool, set in two acres of ground. Our emphasis is on good food, pleasant and comfortably furnished bedrooms, with central heating, H&C. We have a residential licence and two lounges with colour TV. Facilities for children's cot, high chair. Dogs welcome.

GH Lancelot 39 Edgar Rd, Cliftonville ☎ Thanet 22944 Lic 8hc 1⇔📶 ✗ CTV 🍴 S% B&b£5 Bdi£7 D4.30pm

GH *Tyrella Private Hotel* 19 Canterbury Rd ☎ Thanet 22746 Lic 9hc ✗ nc5 CTV 🍴 D6.30pm

MARKET HARBOROUGH Leics *Map 4 SP78*
INN *Greyhound* 31 Kettering Rd ☎2324 Lic 4hc ✗ nc5 TV 20P sn D9.45pm

MARLOW Bucks *Map 4 SU88*
GH Glade Nook 75 Glade Rd ☎4677. 7hc 1⇔📶 nc5 CTV 6P 1🏠 🍴 S% B&b£8.50–£10.20

MARNHULL Dorset *Map 3 ST71*
INN Crown Hotel ☎820224 rs Xmas Lic 4hc ✗ 60P B&b£5.50–£7.50 sn Lfr£2.75 D9pm£6.05alc

MARSHBROOK Salop *Map 7 SO48*
INN Wayside ☎208 Lic 3hc ✗ CTV 40P 🍴 S% B&b£7–£10 Bdi£10.50– £13.50 W£70–£85 ⌇ Bar Lunch50p–£2

MARSHFIELD Avon *Map 3 ST77*
GH Beverley ☎248 6hc CTV 6P S% B&b£5–£5.25

MARTINHOE Devon *Map 3 SS64*
GH Old Rectory ☎ Parracombe 368 Apr–Oct Lic 11rm 4hc 7⇔📶 nc6 CTV 11P 🍴 B&b£5–£6 Bdi£9–£12 W£60–£78 ⌇ D7.30pm

MARYTAVY Devon *Map 2 SX57*
GH *Moorland Hall* ☎466 Mar–Nov Lic 9hc 🛁 CTV 20P D7.30pm

MASHAM N Yorks *Map 8 SE28*
GH Sutton Grange Country House Hotel Leyburn Rd ☎400 Lic 12hc nc3 CTV 20P 🍴 S% B&b£6–£8 Bdi£8–£10 W£50–£60 ⌇ D7pm

MATLOCK Derbys *Map 8 SK36*
GH Cavendish 26 Bank Rd ☎2443 14rm 11hc ✗ CTV S% B&b£5.75–£8 Bdi£8.25–£12 W£50–£80 ⌇ D10am

MAWGAN PORTH Cornwall *Map 2 SW86*
GH Pandora Tredragon Rd ☎ St Mawgan 412 Jun–Sep rs last wk Jul & 1st two wks Aug (B&b only) Lic 7rm 6hc ✗ CTV 10P sea S% B&b£5–£6.50 Bdi£6.75–£8.50 W£39.50–£51.50 ⌇ D4.30pm

GH Seavista Hotel ☎ St Mawgan 276 Lic 10hc ✗ CTV 7P sea S% ✳B&b£5.13– £6 Bdi £8.10 W£42–£54 D4.30pm

GH Surf Riders Hotel Tredragon Rd ☎ St Mawgan 383 Closed Xmas–Etr Lic 11hc ✗ CTV 15P 🍴 sea S% B&b£4.50–£5.50 Bdi£6–£7.50 W£38.50–£50 ⌇ (W only Jun–Aug)

GH *Thorncliff Hotel* Trenance ☎ St Mawgan 428 Lic 14hc CTV 18P sea D8pm

GH White Lodge Hotel ☎ St Mawgan 512 Apr–Sep Lic 20hc nc4 CTV 18P 🍴 sea S% ✳B&b£6.60–£7.60 Bdi£9.60– £10.60 W£63.50–£74.50 ⌇ D7pm

MAYFIELD Staffs *Map 7 SK14*
INN Queens Arms ☎ Ashbourne 2271 Lic 6rm 4hc TV 12P ⚓ S% B&b£5

MELBOURNE Derbys *Map 8 SK32*
INN Melbourne Hotel ☎2134 Lic 8hc CTV 50P 🍴 S% B&b£8.50 Bdi£13 sn L£2–£2.90 D10pm£5alc

MELKSHAM Wilts *Map 3 ST96*
GH Regency Hotel 10–12 Spa Rd ☎702971 12hc CTV 🍴 S% B&b£5.94 Bdi£9.18 Wfr£64.26 D6.30pm

GH York Church Walk ☎702063 10hc CTV 🍴 S% B&bfr£5.50 Bdifr£8.25

MELTON MOWBRAY Leics *Map 8 SK71*
GH Sysonby Knoll Hotel 225 Ashfordby Rd ☎63563 Closed Xmas Lic 16hc 3⇔📶 CTV 20P 🍴 S% B&b£5.50–£6 Bdi£8–£8.50

GH Westbourne House 11A Nottingham Rd ☎69456 17hc CTV 19P 🍴 S% B&b£5–£5.50 Bdi£7–£7.50 D7pm

MENHENIOT STATION Cornwall *Map 2 SX26*
INN Sportsman's Arms Station Rd ☎ Widegates 249 Lic 7hc 1⇔📶 CTV 75P 🍴 S% B&b£5–£6 Bdi£8–£9 sn L£2.75 alc D9.30pm£4.50alc

MERIDEN W Midlands *Map 4 SP28*
GH Meriden Hotel Main Rd ☎22005 8rm 6hc ✗ CTV 20P 🍴 S% B&b£7.50– £9.50 Bdi£11–£13 Dnoon

MEVAGISSEY Cornwall *Map 2 SX04*
GH *Headlands Hotel* Polkirt Hill ☎3453 Apr–Oct Lic 10hc ✗ nc5 CTV 8P 1🏠 sea D7.30pm

GH Polhaun Hotel Polkirt Hill ☎3222
Etr–Oct Lic 8hc ✋ nc10 TV 10P
⬚ sea S% B&b£6–£8 Bdi£8–£10
W£56–£70 ⓚ D6.30pm
GH Spa Private Hotel Polkirt Hill ☎2244
Etr–Oct Lic 6hc 3⇔🖾 ✋ nc4 TV 9P 1🏠
⬚ sea S% B&b£6.90–£9.20
Bdi£10.92–£13.23 W£68.42–£84.53
ⓚ Dprevious evening
GH Valley Park Tregoney Hill ☎2347
Closed Xmas–New Year Lic 8hc ✋ CTV
10P B&b£6.50 Bdi£10 W£65 ⓚ D4pm
INN Ship ☎3324 Closed Dec Lic 5hc
✋ CTV 🚗 S% B&b£6–£6.50 (W only
Jun–Sep)

MIDDLESBROUGH Cleveland
Map 8 NZ42
⋈**GH Chadwick Private Hotel**
27 Clairville Rd ☎245340 6hc ✋ CTV
⬚ S% B&b£5.75 Bdi£7.75
GH Longlands Hotel 295 Marton Rd
☎244900 Lic 7hc ✋ CTV 6P 4🏠 ⬚ S%
B&b£5.40–£6.48 Bdi£7.15–£8.32
W£45.36 ⓚ D4pm

MIDDLETON-ON-SEA W Sussex
Map 4 SU90
GH Ancton House Hotel Ancton Ln
☎2482 Lic 6hc 2⇔🖾 🅿 CTV 6P 5🏠 ⬚
S% B&b£7.50 Bdi£9.50 W£62–£65 ⓚ
(W only 15Jul–1Sep)
GH *Rendezvous Hotel* Elmer Sands
☎2896 rs Oct–Apr Lic 12hc nc3 🅿 CTV
10P ⬚ D7.30pm

MILFORD-ON-SEA Hants *Map 4 SZ29*
GH La Charmeuse 9 Hurst Rd ☎2646
rs Winter (B&B only) 5hc ✋ TV 8P ⬚
sea B&b£6.50–£7.25 Bdi£12–£13.50
GH Kingsland Hotel Westover Rd
☎2670 Lic 15hc nc3 CTV 1,2P ⬚ S%
✳B&b£6 Bdi£8.50 W£55 ⓚ D5pm
INN *Red Lion Hotel* 31 High St ☎2236
Lic ✋ TV

MILLOM Cumbria *Map 7 SD18*
INN *Peel Hotel* Bedford St ☎2245 Lic
8hc TV 7P

MILLPOOL Cornwall *Map 2 SW53*
⋈**GH Chyraise** ☎ Germoe 3485
Mar–Sep & Xmas Lic 9hc ✋ CTV 10P
S% B&b£5–£6 Bdi£8–£9 W£42.50–
£50.50 ⓚ W only Aug Dnoon

MINCHINHAMPTON Glos *Map 3 SO80*
GH Sherrards ☎ Brimscombe 2742
Closed Jan Lic 8rm 7hc 1⇔🖾 CTV 8P
⬚ S% B&bfr£6.75 Bdifr£10.25
Wfr£68.25 ⓚ

MINEHEAD Somerset *Map 3 SS94*
See Plan
GH Dorchester Hotel 38 The Avenue
☎2052 Plan:**1** Lic 13hc CTV 8P S%
B&b£6.25 Bdi£8.75 W£55.50 ⓚ D8pm
GH Gascony Hotel The Avenue ☎2817
Plan:**2** Closed Oct–Etr Lic 15hc 3⇔🖾
✋ CTV 10P ⬚ ⓚ S% B&b£8 Bdi£11
W£50–£65 D9pm
GH *Glen Rock Hotel* 23 The Avenue
☎2245 Plan:**3** Etr–mid Oct Lic 12hc
nc3 CTV 14P D7.30pm

1 Dorchester Hotel
2 Gascony Hotel
3 Glen Rock Hotel
4 Higher Woodcombe Hotel
6 Mayfair Hotel
7 Mentone Hotel
8 Red Lion Hotel *(Inn)*
9 Wyndcott Hotel

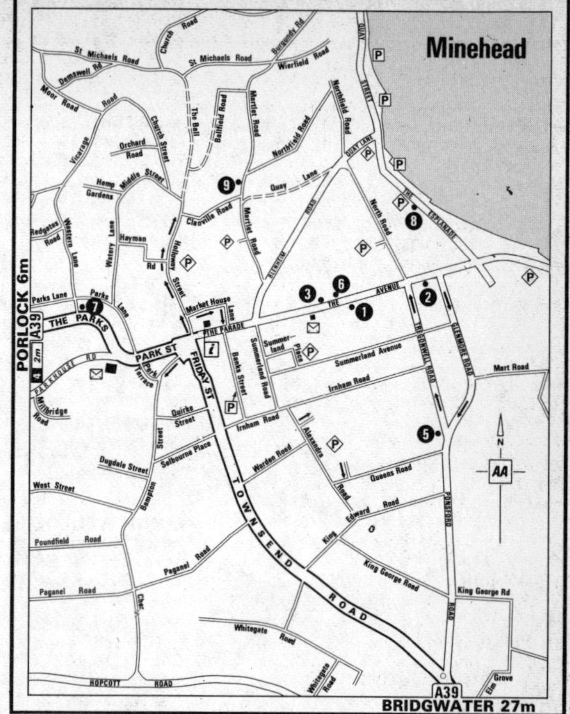

GH Higher Woodcombe Hotel
Bratton Ln ☎2789 Plan:**4** Apr–Oct Lic
9hc nc9 CTV 9P ⑴ S% B&b£8.50 £9.50
Bdi£10.50–£11.50 W£69–£75 ⚓
D6.30pm

GH Mayfair Hotel 25 The Avenue
☎2719 Plan:**6** mid Mar–mid Oct Lic
18hc CTV 14P ⑴ B&b£6–£7.50
Bdi£8.75–£9.75 W£50–£56 ⚓ D7pm

GH Mentone Hotel The Parks ☎2549
Plan:**7** Mar–Oct Lic 12hc 5⇨⑴ nc10
CTV 10P ⑴ lift S% B&b£6.75–£8.20
Bdi£11–£12.45 W£62.45–£71 ⚓ D5pm

GH Wyndcott Hotel Martlet Rd ☎4522
Plan:**9** Lic 13hc 4⇨⑴ CTV 13P ⑴ sea
S% ✱B&b£6–£8 Bdi£7.50–£9.50
W£57.50–£62.10 D7pm

INN *Red Lion Hotel* The Esplanade
☎2653 Plan:**8** Lic 7hc CTV 6P sea

MORECAMBE Lancs *Map 7 SD46*
GH Ashley Private Hotel 371 Marine
Road East ☎412034 rs Nov–mid Dec &
Jan–Etr B&b only Lic 14hc CTV 5P sea
S% ✱B&b£5.94 Bdi£7.83 W£51.84 ⚓
D6pm

GH *Beach Mount* 395 Marine Road East
☎420753 Mar–Oct Lic 20hc CTV sea
D5pm

GH *Channings Private Hotel* 455 Marine
Road East ☎417925 Lic 24hc TV sea

⋈**GH Ellesmere Private Hotel** 44
Westminster Rd ☎411881 Closed Xmas
6hc ⊘ CTV S% B&b£4.50–£6
Bdi£5–£6 W£36–£40 D5.30pm

GH *Elstead Private Hotel* 72 Regent Rd
☎412260 12hc ✎ D3pm

GH New Hazlemere Hotel 391 Marine
Rd, East Prom ☎417876 Etr–Oct Lic
19hc CTV 2P sea S% B&b£7
Bdi£9.50 W£57.50 ⱡ D5.30pm

⊷**GH Hotel Prospect** 363 Marine Rd,
East Prom ☎417819 Apr–Oct & Xmas
Lic 14hc 4⊸╗ CTV 6P ᵐ sea S%
B&b£4–£4.50 Bdi£6.50–£7 W£40–£44
ⱡ

GH *Rydal Mount Private Hotel* 361
Marine Road East ☎411858 Spring Bank
Hol–Oct rs Etr–Spring Bank Hol B&b only
Lic 14hc CTV 14P sea D4pm

GH *Hotel Warwick* 394 Marine Road
East ☎418151 Etr–Oct Lic 18hc CTV
ᵐ sea D5.30pm

GH Wimslow Private Hotel 374 Marine
Road East ☎417804 Etr–Nov & Xmas
Lic 15hc ✎ CTV 5P ᵐ sea S% Bdi£8.50–
£9.50 ⱡ D4pm

MORETONHAMPSTEAD Devon
Map 3 SX78
⊷**GH Cookshayes** 33Court St ☎374
Mar–Oct Lic 9hc 3⊸╗ nc8 CTV 15P ᵐ
B&b£5.50–£6.25 Bdi£8.75–£9.75
W£56–£66 ⱡ D6.30pm

⊷**GH Elmfield** Station Rd ☎327 Etr–Oct
Lic 6hc CTV 6P ᵐ S% B&b£5.50
Bdi£8.50 W£52 ⱡ D7.30pm

GH Moreton House Hotel 5 The Square
☎269 Lic 6hc CTV 4P ᵐ S% B&b£7
Bdi£9 W£42–£55 ⱡ D9pm

GH *Wray Barton Manor* ☎246 Closed
Xmas 7hc ✎ nc12 CTV P 2🏠 ᵐ river
D2.30pm

INN Ring of Bells North Bovey ☎375
Mar–Oct rs Nov–Feb (no accommodation)
Lic 4hc ✎ P 4🏠 🚲 B&b£8.75
Bdi£12.25 W£85.75 ⱡ Bar Lunch75p–£3
D9pm£4.50–£5

MORTEHOE Devon *Map 2 SS44*
GH Haven ☎ Woolacombe 426
Etr–Sep Lic 19hc 15⊸╗ CTV 20P ᵐ
S% B&b£6–£7 Bdi£10.30–£11.50
W£70–£80 ⱡ D7.30pm

GH *Sunnycliffe Hotel* ☎Woolacombe
597 8hc ✎ nc10 CTV 14P sea

MORVAL Cornwall *Map 2 SX25*
GH Snooty Fox Hotel & Restaurant
(2m N of Looe on A387 Torpoint Rd)
☎Widegates 233 Lic 11hc 10⊸╗ 60P
B&b£8–£11 Bdi£13.50–£16 W£87–£105
ⱡ D9.30pm

MOUSEHOLE Cornwall *Map 2 SW42*
GH Tavi's Vor ☎306 5hc CTV 8P sea
S% B&b£6–£7.50 Bdi £10–£11.50
W£70–£80.50 ⱡ D9pm

MUCH WENLOCK Salop *Map 7 SO69*
⊷**GH Wheatland Fox Hotel** ☎727292
Lic 4hc ✎ 15P B&b£5–£5.50 Bdi£7–
£7.50 W£35–£38.50 D9pm

MULLION Cornwall *Map 2 SW61*
⊷**GH Belle Vue** ☎240483 Etr–Oct
8hc ✎ CTV 10P S% B&b£4–£5
Bdi£6.50–£8.50 W£36–£50 ⱡ D4pm

GH Henscath House Mullion Cove
☎240537 Lic 6hc ✎ nc10 CTV 8P S%
Bdi£9 D7.30pm

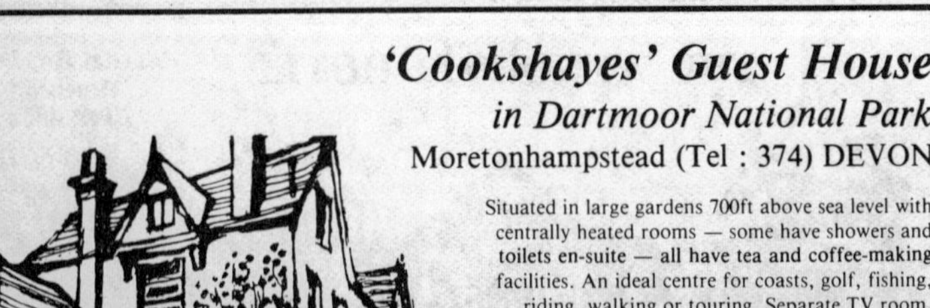

GH Trenowyth House Private Hotel
Mullion Cove ☎240486 Lic 5hc CTV
10P 🍽 sea S% ✳B&bf£7.56 Bdif£9.72
Wf£59.50 ⌁ D6.30pm

GH Trevelayan ☎240378 Etr–Oct
5hc (A 2rm 1hc 1⇆🁢) CTV 20P sea S%
✳B&bf£4.50–£5 Bdif£5.75–£6
Wf£40–£42 ⌁

INN *Old Inn* Church Town ☎240240
rs Xmas (no accommodation) Lic 6hc
(A 2hc) ⚘ nc15 CTV 9P alc

MUNDESLEY-ON-SEA Norfolk
Map 9 TG33
INN *Ingleside Hotel* Cromer Rd
☎720530 Lic 11hc TV 🍽 D9.30pm

MUNGRISDALE Cumbria *Map 11 NY33*
GH Mill Guest House ☎ Threlkeld 659
mid Mar–Oct Lic 9hc ⚘ 10P river S%
B&bfr£6.50 Bdifr£9.50 Wfr£60 ⌁ D5pm

▷◁INN Mill Inn ☎Threlkeld 632
Mar–Oct rs Nov–Feb (no accommodation)
Lic 8hc ⚘ 30P 🚗 river S% B&bf£5.50
Bar Lunch30p–£1.50 D9pm

MUSBURY Devon *Map 3 SY29*
▷◁GH Barley Close ☎ Colyton 52484
6hc ⚘ nc12 CTV 10P 🍽 S% B&bf£4–
£4.25 Bdif£6–£6.50 Wf£42–£45 ⌁ D3pm

MYLOR BRIDGE Cornwall *Map 2 SW83*
▷◁GH Penmere Rosehill ☎Penryn 74470
Etr–Oct 6hc ⚘ CTV 6P 🍽 river S% B&bf£5
Bdif£7.75–£8 Wf£44 ⌁ D5.30pm

NAILSWORTH Glos *Map 3 ST89*
GH Gables Private Hotel Tiltups End,
Bath Rd ☎2265 Lic 6rm 5hc CTV 10P
S% B&bf£6 Bdif£8.50 D9pm

NAYLAND Suffolk *Map 5 TL93*
INN White Hart Hotel ☎262382 Lic
5hc 15P 🍽 S% B&bf£6.70 Bar Lunch
fr£1 D9pmf£4.50 alc

NEAR SAWREY Cumbria *Map 7 SD39*
▷◁GH High Green Gate ☎ Hawkshead
296 Etr–Oct 7hc nc5 TV 7P 🍽 S%
B&bf£4.86 Bdif£7.56 Wf£48.60 ⌁
D4pm
GH Sawrey House Private Hotel
☎ Hawkshead 387 Apr–Nov Lic 11hc
1⇆🁢 CTV 20P 🍽 lake S% B&bf£5.94–
£6.48 Bdif£8.64–£9.72 Wf£59.40–£64.80
⌁ W only Spring Bank Hol–Aug D7pm

NEATISHEAD Norfolk *Map 9 TG32*
GH Barton Angler Hotel ☎ Horning
630740 Etr–Nov rs Dec (no
accommodation) Lic 8hc 1⇆🁢 nc5 CTV
12P river S% B&bf£7.50–£8.50 D8.30pm

NESSCLIFF Salop *Map 7 SJ31*
▷◁INN Nesscliff Hotel ☎253 Lic 5hc
TV 75P 2🛏 S% B&bf£5.70 Bdif£6.70–
£14.65 Wf£39.90 M sn Lf£1.70–£3.55&alc
D10pmf£1.70–£3.55&alc

NEWBURY Berks *Map 4 SU46*
▷◁GH The Guest House 133 Andover Rd
☎41359 11hc nc10 12P 🍽 S% B&bf£5
Wf£35 M

NEWCASTLE-UNDER-LYME Staffs
Map 7 SJ84
GH Grove Court Hotel 100 Lancaster Rd
☎614406 Lic 11rm 10hc ⚘ CTV P 🍽
✳B&bf£6–£7.50

NEWCASTLE UPON TYNE Tyne & Wear
Map 12 NZ26
GH Chirton House Hotel 46 Clifton Rd
☎730407 rs Xmas, New Year & Public
Hols Lic 12hc CTV 12P 🍴 B&b£7.56
Bdi£9.18–£11.34 D7.30pm

NEWHAVEN Derbys *Map 7 SK16*
INN Newhaven Hotel ☎ Hartington 217
Lic 11rm CTV 200P 🍴 B&b£7 sn
Lfr£2.50&alc D£2.50&alc

NEWLANDS (nr Keswick) Cumbria
Map 11 NY22
GH Stoneycroft Hotel ☎ Braithwaite 240
Apr–Oct Lic 10hc 1⇨🛏 nc5 CTV 15P 🍴
B&bfr£7.50 Bdifr£11.25 Wfr£70.50
⽕ D4pm

NEWQUAY Cornwall *Map 2 SW86*
See Plan
GH Arundell Hotel Mount Wise ☎2481
Plan:**1** May–Sep Lic 43hc 4⇨🛏 CTV 27P
sea S% B&b£6.50–£7.50 Bdi£7.50–
£8.50 W£44–£57 ⽕ D6.45pm

⋈**GH Castaways Hotel** 39 St Thomas Rd
☎5002 Plan:**2** Spring Bank Hol–Oct Lic
8hc ♨ CTV 8P S% B&b£4.50–£6
Bdi£5–£7.50 W only 23Jun–Aug D5pm

⋈**GH Cherington** 7 Pentire Av ☎3363
Plan:**3** Apr–Oct 22hc (A 6hc) CTV 16P
sea B&b£5.50–£6.50 Bdi£6.50–£8
W£40–£55 ⽕ W only Jul & Aug D6pm

GH Copper Beech Hotel 70 Edgcumbe
Av ☎3376 Plan:**4** Etr–Nov 16hc CTV
16P S% ✳B&b£5.75–£6.60
Bdi£6.90–£8.62 (W only late Jun–early
Sep) D6.45pm

⋈**GH Gluvian Park Hotel** 12 Edgcumbe
Gdns ☎3133 Plan:**5** Apr–Sep Lic 24hc
5⇨🛏 ⊗ nc3 CTV 10P S% B&b£5.50–
£7.50 Bdi£7.50–£10.50 W£51–£70
⽕ (W Jul & Aug) D7pm

GH Hepworth Hotel 27 Edgcumbe Av
☎3686 Plan:**6** Etr–Sep Lic 13hc 4⇨🛏 ⊗
CTV 10P 🍴 B&b£6.90 Bdi£8.62
W£51.75–£86.25 (W Jul & Aug) D6.30pm

⋈**GH Long Beach Hotel** 11 Trevose Av
☎4751 Plan:**7** Etr–Oct Lic 8hc CTV 7P
sea S% B&b£4.50–£5.50 Bdi£7–£8
W only Jul–Aug D6.15pm

GH Mellanvrane Hotel Trevemper Rd
☎2593 Plan:**8** Closed 2 wks Xmas Lic
25hc 6⇨🛏 CTV 50P 🍴 S% B&b£8 Bdi£9
W£66.70 ⽕ W Jun–Sep D6.30pm

⋈**GH Mount Wise Hotel** Mount Wise
☎3080 Plan:**9** Apr–Oct Lic 38hc 9⇨🛏
CTV 30P lift S% B&b£5.75–£9.20
Bdi£8.05–£12.65 W£46–£83.95 ⽕
D7.30pm

GH *Ocean Hill Lodge Private Hotel*
Trelawney Rd ☎4595 Plan:**10** May–Oct
Lic 16hc nc4 CTV 9P

GH Pine Lodge Hotel 91 Henver Rd
☎2549 Plan:**11** Closed Xmas Lic 11hc
3⇨🛏 ⊗ CTV 26P 🍴 S% B&b£6.95–
£11.75 Bdi£14 W£98 ⽕ W Jul & Aug
D7pm (summer) 8.30pm (winter)

GH *Quies Hotel* 84 Mount Wise ☎2924
Plan:**12** Etr–Oct Lic 10hc CTV 12P
W only 17Jun–16Sep

GH *Ranelagh Court Hotel* 101A Henver
Rd ☎49922 Plan:**13** Apr–Oct Lic 8hc
nc7 CTV 12P 🍴 S% Wfr£50 ⽕ D6.30pm

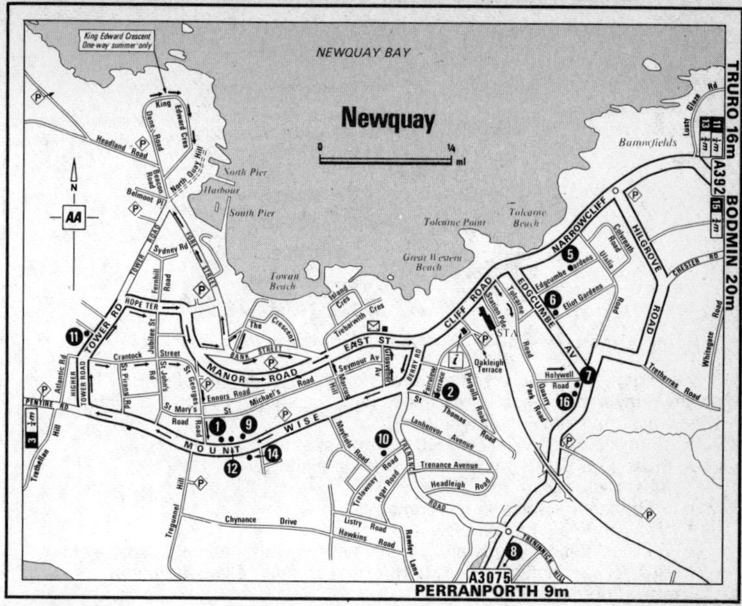

1 Arundell Hotel	**5** Gluvian Park Hotel	**10** Ocean Hill Lodge Private Hotel
2 Castaways Hotel	**6** Hepworth Hotel	**11** Pine Lodge
3 Cherington	**7** Long Beach Hotel	**12** Quies Hotel
4 Copper Beech Hotel	**8** Mellanvrane Hotel	**13** Ranelagh Court Hotel
	9 Mount Wise Hotel	**14** Trevone Hotel
		15 Viewpoint Hotel
		16 Wheal Treasure

GH *Trevone Hotel* Mount Wise ☎3039 Plan:**14** 28Apr–29Sep Lic 34hc ≪ CTV 28P sea D7pm

GH Viewpoint Hotel 89 Henver Rd ☎2170 Plan:**15** Lic 17hc 13⇌▥≪ nc3 CTV 14P ⬚ sea S% ✳B&b£6.48–£9 Bdi£9.67–£12.10 W£65–£81.70 ⚥ D summer 8pm winter 7.30pm

⊢⊣GH Wheal Treasure 72 Edgcumbe Av ☎4136 Plan:**16** Apr–Oct Lic 12hc ≪ nc4 CTV 12P ⬚ S% B&b£4.82–£5.40 Bdi£6.48–£8 W£41.58–£54 ⚥ W only Jul & Aug D5.30pm

NEWTON ABBOT Devon *Map 3 SS87* **⊢⊣GH Lamorna** Exeter Rd, Coombe Cross, Sandygate (3m N A380) ☎5627 Lic 7hc ≪ CTV 20P ⬚ S% B&b£5 Bdi£8 W£56 ⚥ D10pm

NITON Isle of Wight *Map 4 SZ57* **GH Windcliffe House Hotel** Sandrock Rd ☎730215 May–Oct & Etr Lic 12hc CTV 16P sea S% B&b£8.05–£9.77 Bdi£9.85–£11.92 W£69–£83.49 ⚥ D6pm

NORTHALLERTON N Yorks *Map 8 SE39* **GH Windsor** 56 South Pde ☎4100 6hc CTV ⬚ S% B&b£6–£8.50

INN Station Hotel 2 Boroughbridge Rd ☎2053 Lic 10hc CTV 50P ⬚ S% ✳B&b£8 Bdi£9.50 W£66.50 ⚥ Bar lunch 50p–£1.25 D6pm£1.50

NORTHAMPTON Northants *Map 4 SP76* **GH Langham** 4 Langham Pl, Barrack Rd ☎39917 Lic 16hc 9⇌▥≪ CTV 20P 2🏠 ⬚ S%✳B&b£5.40 Bdi£7.56 W£52.92 ⚥ D7pm

TREVONE HOTEL

NEWQUAY TR7 2BP

Tel: Management 3039
Visitors 3310

FRIENDLY AND INFORMAL WITH VERY GOOD FOOD. COCKTAIL BAR. TABLE TENNIS ROOM. LOUNGE WITH COLOUR TV. CENTRAL POSITION.

PROPRIETOR   PAMELA CHEGWIN

Henver Road, Newquay, Cornwall   Tel: Newquay 2170 (STD 063 73)

Viewpoint Hotel is charmingly situated within a few minutes of
Newquay's main beaches and easy reach of shops, theatres & cinemas
and has the following amenities:
★ 18 modern bedrooms all with central heating.
★ Most with bathroom en suite or private shower.
★ Most with colour TV.
★ Multi-channel radio in all rooms.
★ Many rooms with sea views.
★ Our cocktail bar offers a wide choice of liqueurs, aperitifs, spirits etc.
★ Our very attractive dining room offers a varied á la carte menu or
  table d'hôte.
★ Open all year.
★ Free car parking space.
Do write or phone for our colour brochure and tariff and sample
menus to:-
Resident Proprietors, John & Jacqueline Trotter.

GH Poplars Cross St, Moulton ☎43983
22hc 7⇥🛁 CTV 22P 🍽 B&b fr£6 Bdi fr£9
D5pm

NORTH HYKEHAM Lincs *Map 8 SK96*
GH Loudor 37 Newark Rd ☎ Lincoln
680333 Lic 9hc (A 3hc) CTV 14P 🍽
B&b£6.48–£6.80 Bdi£9.72–£10.05
D7.30pm

NORTH WALSHAM Norfolk *Map 9 TG23*
GH Beechwood Private Hotel
20 Cromer Rd ☎3231 Lic 11hc ⚓ CTV
11P 🍽 B&b£8.60 Bdi£12 W£70–£76 ⚡
W only 19Jul–30Aug D7pm

NORTHWOOD Salop *Map 7 SJ43*
⊢⊣**GH Woodlands Country House**
(1m S off B5063) ☎ Wem 33268
Closed Xmas Lic 8hc 3⇥🛁 ⚒ CTV 12P
🍽 B&b£5–£5.25 Bdi£7.50–£8.75
W£51–£60 ⚡ D6.30pm

NORWICH Norfolk *Map 5 TG20*
⊢⊣**GH Argyle House Hotel** 10 Stracey Rd
☎27493 11hc ⚒ nc5 CTV 🍽 S%
B&b£5.50 Bdi£8 W£56 ⚡ D5pm

GH Gables 240 Thorpe Rd ☎34841
12hc CTV 9P 🍽 S% B&b£6.50–£7.50

GH Grange Hotel 230 Thorpe Rd
☎34734 Lic 37hc 35⇥🛁 ⚒ CTV 36P 🍽
S% B&b£7.95–£14 Bdi£9.95–£16
D8pm

⊢⊣**GH Marlborough House Hotel**
22 Stracey Rd, Thorpe Rd ☎28005 Lic
11hc 3⇥🛁 CTV 5P 🏠 🍽 S%
B&b£5.75–£7 Bdi£8–£10

NOTTINGHAM Notts *Map 8 SK53*

GH Rufford Hotel Melton Rd,
West Bridgford (1m S on A52) ☎814202
Lic 22hc 10⇥🛁 CTV 40P 🍽 S%
✱B&b£8.64 Bdi£12.15 D7.30pm

⊢⊣**GH Waverley** 107 Portland Rd,
Waverley St ☎786707 Closed Xmas 17hc
CTV 1🏠 S% B&b fr£4.25 Bdi fr£6.50 D4pm

GH Windsor 4 Watcombe Circus
☎621317 9hc ⚒ CTV 6P 🍽 S% B&b£7
Bdi£10 W£63 ⚡ D6pm

GH Windsor Lodge Hotel 116 Radcliffe
Rd, West Bridgford (1m S on A52)
☎813773 Lic 40hc 7⇥🛁 ⚒ CTV 40P
4🏠 🍽 S% B&b£8.10 Bdi£11.10 D7.15pm

NUNEATON Warwicks *Map 4 SP39*
GH *Abbey Grange Hotel* 100 Manor
Court Rd ☎385535 Lic 9hc ⚒ TV 16P 🍽
D9pm

INN *Bull Hotel* Market Pl ☎386599 Lic
12hc CTV 18P 2🏠 🍽 D8pm

OAKS, THE, Charnwood Forest Leics
Map 8 SK31
INN Belfry Hotel Oaks Rd ☎ Shepshed
3247 Lic 10hc CTV 200P 🍽 ✱B&b£9.72
sn L£3.50alc D10pm£6alc

ODDINGTON Glos *Map 4 SP22*
INN *Fox* ☎ Stow-on-the-Wold 30446 Lic
4hc ⚒ TV 20P 🍽 sn D9pm

ODIHAM Hants *Map 4 TQ75*
INN *Kings Arms Hotel* High St ☎2559
Lic 4hc CTV 5P 3🏠 D9.30pm

OKEHAMPTON Devon *Map 2 SX59*
INN Fountain Fore St ☎2828 Etr–Sep
6hc ⚒ nc11 TV 6P 4🏠 🚗 S% B&b£6.50
Bar lunch fr£1 D7pm fr£4

The Poplars Hotel

**MOULTON, NORTHAMPTON
NN3 1RZ**
Tel: Northampton 43983

This is a small country hotel of character, situated in a quiet village only four miles from the centre of Northampton.
We welcome families, and children of all ages can be catered for.
There is a large car park and garden.
Personal attention is given to guests by the Proprietors — Peter and Rosemary Gillies.

BEECHWOOD HOTEL

NORTH WALSHAM, NORFOLK

Sandy beaches 5 miles. Broads 7 miles.
Highly recommended for:
Good food — licensed
Two lounges — colour TV
Central heating
Games room
Comfortable beds
Large attractive gardens
Children's playground
Free parking
Friendly personal service

Ring Ernest and Jenny Townsend   North Walsham 3231

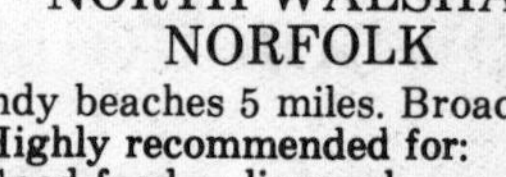

The GABLES

240 Thorpe Road, Norwich, NR1 1TW AA Listed

For reservations Tel: Norwich 34841 Residents Tel: Norwich 34475

The Gables is a delightful bed and breakfast hotel ideally situated on the Thorpe Road, (A47 Norwich to Gt. Yarmouth) placing it within easy reach of the city centre, Norfolk Broads and nearby coastal resorts. There is a frequent bus service into the city of Norwich — numbers 531, 532 and 533 all stop outside the hotel's front door.

Standing in picturesque gardens on an elevated site which overlooks the R. Yare valley, residents afford themselves a relaxing contained atmosphere with adjacent parking facilities. Accommodation consists of single, twin, large double and spacious family rooms all of which are tastefully furnished and decorated to a high standard. Each room is comfortably appointed with H & C water, mirrors and electric shaving points. The hotel is centrally heated throughout.

ORFORD Suffolk *Map 5 TM44*
INN King's Head Front St ☎271
rs Sun, Mon & Public Hols Lic 5hc ✖
100P 2🔒 🚲 B&bf9–£10 Bar lunch £1alc
D9pm£5alc

OSWESTRY Salop *Map 7 SJ22*
GH Ashfield Country House
Llwyn-y-Maen, Trefonen Rd ☎5200
Mar–Nov Lic 9hc 3⃫🚿🛏 ✖ 15P 🍴 S%
B&bf7–£9 Bdif10–£13 Wf75–£100
⅃ D8.30pm

OTHERY Somerset *Map 3 ST33*
GH Townsend Guest House & Restaurant ☎ Burrowbridge 382
Early Mar–Oct & Xmas Lic 9hc ✖ CTV
16P 🍴 S% B&bf5–£5.50 Bdif8.50–£9
Wf47–£55 ⅃ D9.30pm

OXFORD Oxford *Map 4 SP50*
GH Ascot 283 Iffley Rd ☎40259
6hc ✖ CTV 2P 🍴 S% B&bf4.50–£5
Wf28 M W only Nov–Apr

GH Brown's 281 Iffley Rd ☎46822
6hc 1⃫🚿🛏 CTV 3P 🍴 S% B&bf5–£5.50

GH Conifer 116 The Slade,
Headington ☎63055 8hc ✖ CTV 8P 🍴
S% B&bf5.50–£6.50

GH Earlmont 322–324 Cowley Rd
☎40236 5rm 4hc 2⃫🚿🛏 (A 5hc) ✖ CTV
11P 2🔒 🍴 S% B&bf4.50–£5

GH Falcon 88–90 Abingdon Rd
☎722995 10hc ✖ TV 7P 🍴 S%
B&bf5–£6 Wf35 £42 M

Brown's Guest House

281 Iffley Road, Oxford OX4 4AQ
Tel: Oxford 46822 (STD 0865)

Open twelve months a year.
There are 6 bedrooms all with hot and cold water and private shower.
A colour television is available for the use of guests.
Central heating throughout. Baby sitting/watching service and
special meals for children.
Fire certificate granted.
Please see the gazetteer entry for further details.

BOWOOD HOUSE, KIDLINGTON

Situated on the A423, 4½ miles north of Oxford city centre, Bowood
House offers accommodation of a high standard. All rooms have
intercom and hot and cold water, some with private bath or shower.
TV lounge is available for guests and there is ample parking space for the
number of guests catered for. Local amenities include swimming baths,
tennis and squash courts, and golf course.

Yours hosts: Mr and Mrs R Naylor

238 Oxford Road, Kidlington, Oxon. Tel: Kidlington 2839 (STD 08675)

GALAXIE PRIVATE HOTEL

180 Banbury Road, Oxford, OX2 7BT

Tel: Oxford 55688 (STD 0865)

Open throughout the year. There are 21 bedrooms all with hot
and cold water. Colour television available for the use of guests.
Car park for 25 cars. Television in all rooms. Some bedrooms with
scenic views. Fire certificate granted. Please see the gazetteer for
further details.

WILLOW REACHES

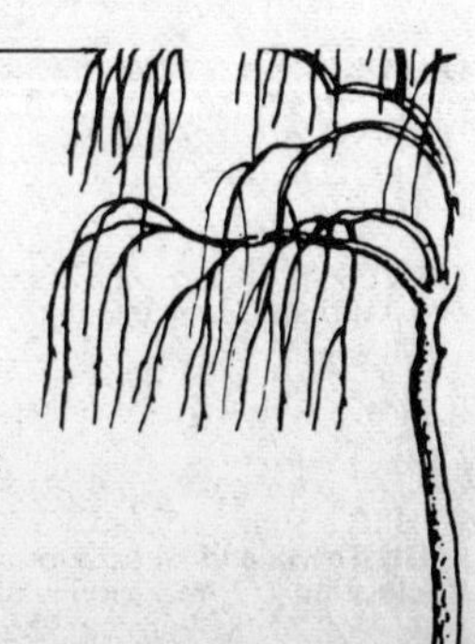

PRIVATE HOTEL
1 Wytham Street, Oxford
Tel: 721545

Residential licence
Comfortable accommodation with plenty of
character. 5 bedrooms with bathroom en suite. Hot
and cold water in all rooms. Colour TV lounge.
4 course evening meals. One mile only from city
centre in quiet position off main road. Garden
for use of guests. Five minute walk from lake,
parks and swimming pools. Garage accommodation.

GH Galaxie Private Hotel 180 Banbury Rd ☎55688 21hc 4⇌🗍 CTV 25P 🏢 S% B&bf7–£9.50

⤬**GH Melcombe House** 227 Iffley Rd ☎49520 6rm CTV 4P S% B&bf5–£6

⤬**GH Pine Castle** 290 Iffley Rd ☎41497 7hc ⊗ TV 4P 🏢 S% B&bf4–£5 Bdif6.50–£7 D9.30pm

GH St Giles Hotel 86 St Giles ☎54620 10hc ⊗ CTV S% B&bf8.56–£9.50

GH Victoria Hotel 180 Abingdon Rd ☎724536 Lic 12hc 2⇌🗍 CTV P 🏢 S% ✱B&bf7.50–£8.50 Bdif11.75–£12.75 Wfrf104.50

GH Westwood Country Hotel Hinksey Hill Top ☎735408 Closed Xmas & New Year Lic 12⇌🗍 ⊗ CTV 15P 1🏠 🏢 B&bf8–£12 D3pm

GH Willow Reaches Private Hotel 1 Wytham St ☎43767 Lic 9hc 4⇌🗍 CTV 4P 2🏠 🏢 S% B&bf7.50–£9 Bdif12–£13.50 D8.30pm

PADSTOW Cornwall *Map 2 SW97*
⤬**GH Cross House** Church St ☎532391 Mar–Oct 9hc ⊗ CTV 🏢 river B&bf5.75 Bdif8.05 Wf51.75 Ł D5pm

GH Duke House 48–50 Duke St ☎532372 10hc TV S% ✱B&bf4.50–£6.50 Wf30–£40 M

⤬**GH Nook** Fentonluna Ln ☎532317 Apr–20Oct Lic 10hc nc4 CTV 12P 🏢 S% B&bf5.75–£6.60 Bdif9–£10 Wf54–£60 Ł W only Jun, Jul & Aug D6.30pm

GH Tregea High St ☎532455 Etr–Sep 8hc ⊗ CTV 8P 🏢 S% B&bf7.50 Bdif10

PAIGNTON Devon *Map 3 SX86* **See Plan**
GH *Amaryllis Hotel* 14 Sands Rd ☎559552 Plan:**1** 10hc ⊗ CTV 10P W only Jul–Aug

⤬**GH Clennon Valley** 1 Clennon Rise ☎557736 Plan:**2** Closed Xmas rs Nov–Mar (B&b only) Lic 12hc CTV 10P 🏢 B&bf5.94–£6.48 Bdif8.10–£8.64 Wf51.30–£55.18 Ł D5pm

⤬**GH Cornerways Hotel** 16 Manor Rd ☎551207 Plan:**3** Etr–Oct Lic 22hc 13⇌🗍 🏠 CTV 25P 🏢 sea S% B&bf5.94–£6.78 Bdif9.18–£9.76 W only Jul & Aug D6pm

⤬**GH Nevada Private Hotel** 61 Dartmouth Rd ☎558317 Plan:**4** Closed Xmas Lic 12hc ⊗ CTV 12P 🏢 S% B&bf5.75–£6.90 Bdif7.47–£8.05 Wf52.90–£56.35 Ł D6pm

⤬**GH Orange Tubs Hotel** 14 Manor Rd, Preston ☎551541 Plan:**5** Apr–Oct Lic 11hc 2⇌🗍 ⊗ CTV 9P 🏢 sea S% B&bf5–£7 Bdif7–£8.50 Wf45–£60 D6.30pm

GH Redcliffe Lodge Hotel 1 Marine Dr ☎551394 Plan:**6** Mar–Oct Lic 16hc 4⇌🗍 CTV 24P ✱B&bf6.90–£8.05 Bdif9.77–£10.92 Wf52–£64 Ł D7pm

GH *Roseville Private Hotel* Marine Gdns ☎550530 Plan:**8** Lic 11hc CTV 12P

⤬**GH St Weonard Private Hotel** 12 Kernou Rd ☎558842 Plan:**9** Lic 9hc CTV S% B&bf5–£5.25 Bdif7–£7.50 Wf40–£45 Ł D4pm

⤬**GH San Remo** 35 Totnes Rd ☎557855 Plan:**10** Lic 18hc (A 4rm 3hc) ⊗ CTV 12P 1🏠 S% B&bf5.25–£8.50 Bdif7–£10 Wf40–£65 D6.30pm

West Wood Hotel
Hinksey Hill, Oxford

Mr and Mrs Parker wish to provide peaceful and comfortable accommodation for people who want to get away from the city, but still enjoy the amenities. Ideal for a quiet weekend and frequented by many honeymooners.

Westwood Country Hotel is situated in one of the most beautiful settings in Oxford and only a few minutes drive from the City centre. It is set in its own spacious grounds of around 3 acres of woodlands and gardens.

All 12 bedrooms have a private bathroom, along with radio-intercom and tea and coffee making facilities.

Good traditional English food is provided, along with a licensed bar. Amenities close at hand include golf, horse riding and boating. Brochure available on request with further details. Tel: Oxford (0865) 735408.

At second roundabout arriving from town centre take the second exit marked FARINGDON or WOOTON, then at top of hill bear left. Hotel is 100 yards on the right.

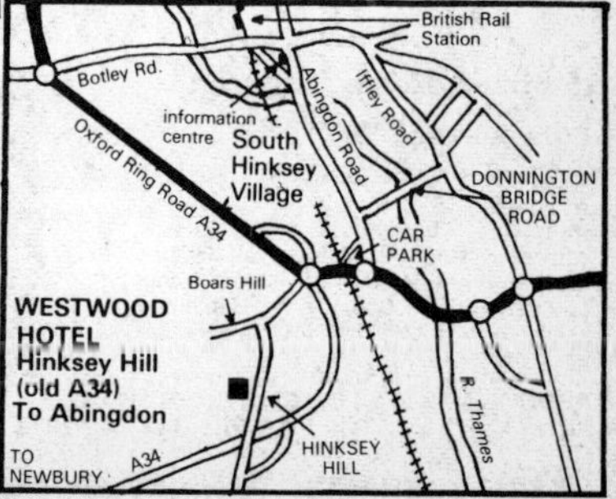

1 Amaryllis Hotel
2 Clennon Valley Hotel
3 Cornerways Hotel
4 Nevada Private Hotel
5 Orange Tubs
6 Redcliffe Lodge Hotel
8 Roseville Private Hotel
9 St Weonard Private Hotel
10 San Remo Hotel
12 Sea Verge Hotel
13 Shorton House
14 Stantor Private Hotel
15 Sunnybank Private Hotel

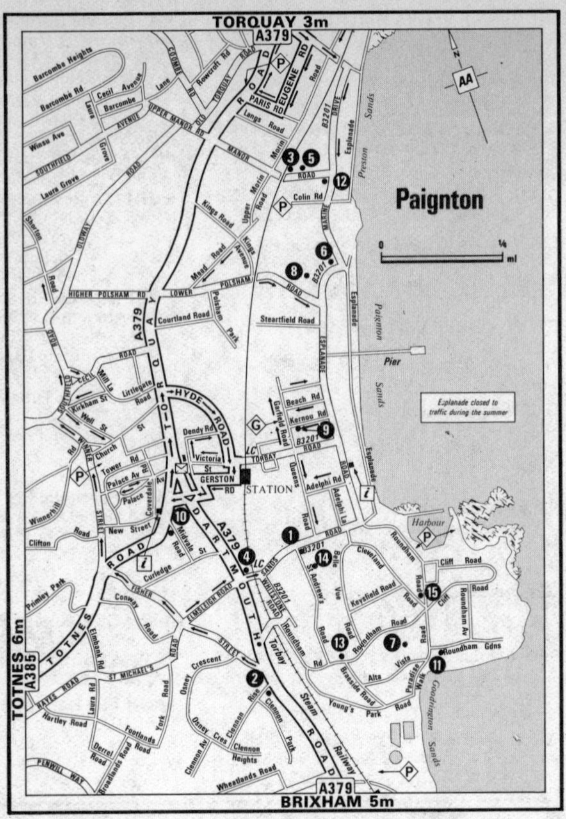

⊭GH Sea Verge Hotel Marine Dr, Preston ☎557795 Plan:**12** 12hc ⊗ CTV 20P sea S% B&b£5.80–£6.30 Bdi£9–£9.50 W£63–£66.50 Ł

GH Shorton House 17 Roundham Rd ☎557722 Plan:**13** Apr–Oct Lic 18rm ⊗ CTV 20P ♿ S% B&b£6–£8 Bdi£8–£10 D6pm

GH *Stantor Private Hotel* 7 St Andrews Rd ☎557156 Plan:**14** May–Oct 15hc CTV 16P D6pm

GH Sunnybank Private Hotel 2 Cleveland Rd ☎559153 Plan:**15** Mar–Oct Lic 12hc 2⇆⋒ ⊗ CTV 10P B&b£6.20–£6.80 Bdi£7.50–£9 W£49–£59 Ł D5pm

PAR Cornwall *Map 2 SX05*
⊭GH Par Farm ☎2756 Jan–Sep Lic 14hc 4⇆⋒ (A 2hc 1⇆⋒) CTV 100P S% B&b£5.50–£9.50 Bdi£7–£10 W£35–£60 W only Jul & Aug D6pm

PEACEHAVEN E Sussex *Map 5 TQ40*
INN Peacehaven Hotel South Coast Rd ☎4555 Lic 12hc 4⇆⋒ CTV 50P ⅢⅢ S% B&b£10–£14 Bdi£14–£20 sn L£7alc D9.45pm fr£3.95&alc

PEASMARSH E Sussex *Map 5 TQ82*
⊭GH Flackley Ash Hotel & Restaurant ☎381 10Jan–27Dec Lic 17rm 1hc 16⇆⋒ ⌂ CTV 40P 2⌂ ⅢⅢ B&b£5.50–£11 Bdi£10.50–£16 W£81–£92 Ł D10pm

PENRITH Cumbria *Map 12 NY53*
⊢⊣**GH Brandelhow** 1 Portland Pl
☎64470 6hc CTV S% B&b£4.50–£6
Bdi£7.50–£9 W£31.50–£42 M D8pm

⊢⊣**GH Kinsale** 24 Wordsworth St
☎63265 6hc ⍉ CTV S% B&b£4.50–£5.50
Bdi£7.50–£8.50 Wfr£52.50 ⌀ D7pm

⊢⊣**GH Pategill Villas** Carleton Rd
☎63153 Lic 12hc CTV 18P 🎱 S%
B&b£4–£5.50 Bdi£7–£10 D5.30pm

GH Waverley Hotel Crown Sq ☎63962
Lic 7hc 1⇌🔥 CTV 30P 2🏠 S%
✱B&b£7.25–£7.50 D8pm

⊢⊣**GH Woodland House Private Hotel**
Wordsworth St ☎64177 Lic 8hc CTV 12P
🎱 S% B&b£5.25 Bdi£8.25 W£57.75
⌀ D7pm

PENZANCE Cornwall *Map 2 SW43*
See Plan
⊢⊣**GH Alverton Court Hotel** Alverton Rd
☎2306 Plan:**1** Closed Oct Lic 15hc
2⇌🔥 ⍉ CTV 12P sea S% B&b£5.50–£8
Bdi£9.75–£12.25 D6pm

⊢⊣**GH Bella-Vista Private Hotel**
7 Alexandra Ter, Lariggan ☎2409 Plan:**2**
29Mar–17Oct 10hc ⍉ nc3 CTV 8P sea
S% B&b£5.75–£6.75 Bdi£8.50–£9.50
W£43–£57 ⌀ D5pm

⊢⊣**GH Camilla Hotel** Regent Ter ☎3771
Plan:**3** 10hc CTV 3P 🎱 sea S%
B&b£5–£5.50 Bdi£7–£7.50 W£49–
£52.50 ⌀ D6.30pm

GH Carlton Private Hotel ☎2081
Plan:**4** Mar–Oct Lic 12hc 3⇌🔥 nc12
CTV sea B&b£6.50–£10 Bdi£10–£13.50
W£60–£70 ⌀ D5pm

1 Alverton Court Hotel
2 Bella-Vista Private Hotel
3 Camilla Hotel
4 Carlton Private Hotel
5 Dunedin
6 Duporth Private Hotel
7 Essex
8 Estoril Private Hotel
9 Glencree Private Hotel
10 Hansord Private Hotel
11 Holbein Hotel
12 Hopedale
13 Kilindini Private Hotel
14 Kimberley House
15 Kirkstowe
16 The Longboat *(Inn)*
17 Mount Royal Hotel
18 Old Manor House Private Hotel
19 Penmorvah Hotel
20 Sea & Horses Hotel
21 Tarbert Hotel
22 Trenant Private Hotel
23 Trevelyan Hotel
24 Willows

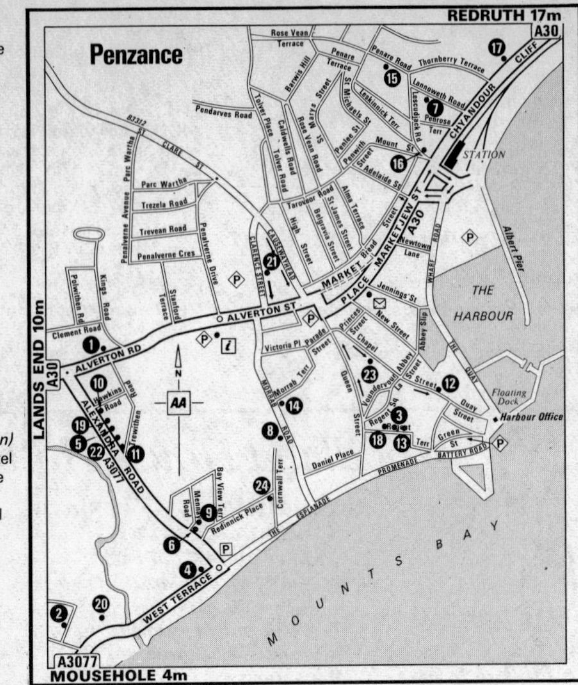

GH Dunedin Alexandra Rd ☎2652 Plan:**5** Feb–Nov Lic 9hc nc3 CTV ⦰ S% B&b£5–£6 Bdi£7.50–£8.75 W£47–£54 ⊬ D4pm

GH Duporth Private Hotel 1 Mennaye Rd ☎2689 Plan:**6** mid Mar–Oct 10hc CTV sea B&b£5.75–£6.50 Bdi£9–£10 W£50–£60 ⊬ D4pm

GH Essex 23 Lannoweth Rd ☎5129 Plan:**7** Apr–Oct Lic 1.1hc ⊗ nc10 CTV 5P sea S% B&b£5–£6 Bdi£7–£9 W£49–£63 ⊬ W only Jul & Aug D4pm

GH Estoril Private Hotel 46 Morrab Rd ☎2468 Plan:**8** Closed Xmas Lic 10⇆⌸ CTV 4P ⦰ S% B&b£8.05 Bdi£10.35–£11.50 W£72.45–£78.20 D7pm

GH *Glencree Private Hotel* 2 Mennaye Rd ☎2026 Plan:**9** Feb–mid Oct 9hc ⊗ CTV sea D7pm

GH Hansord Private Hotel Alexandra Rd ☎3311 Plan:**10** Mar–Oct rs Jan & Feb (No Dinner) 12hc nc3 CTV ⦰ S% B&b£6.20 Bdi£10 W£55.20 ⊬ D3pm

GH Holbein House Alexandra Rd ☎5008 Plan:**11** Lic 8hc 1⇆⌸ ⊗ nc3 CTV ⦰ S% ✻B&b£4.50–£6 Bdi£6.75–£8.50 W£42–£50 ⊬ D5.30pm

GH Hopedale 29 Chapel St ☎3277 Plan:**12** Lic 6hc ⊗ CTV sea S% B&bfr£5

GH Kilindini Private Hotel 13 Regent Ter ☎4744 Plan:**13** Feb–Nov 11hc ⊗ nc3 CTV 10P sea S% B&b£5–£6 Bdi£7–£8 W£43–£49 ⊬ D3pm

GH Kimberley House 10 Morrab Rd ☎2727 Plan:**14** Jan–Oct Lic 9hc ⊗ nc5 CTV 3P ⦰ S% B&b£6.50–£7.50 Bdi£10–£11 W£63–£70 ⊬ D6pm

GH Kirkstowe Penare Rd ☎3115 Plan:**15** Lic 9hc ⊗ nc9 CTV 5P ⦰ sea S% B&b£6 Bdi£8 D4pm

GH Mount Royal Hotel Chyandour Cliff ☎2233 Plan:**17** Mar–Oct 9hc 1⇆⌸ CTV 12P 4⌂ ⦰ sea S% B&b£5.50–£7 Bdi£9–£10.50 W£59.50–£70 ⊬ D7.30pm

GH Old Manor House Private Hotel Regent Ter ☎3742 Plan:**18** Lic 10hc ⊗ ⌂ CTV 10P sea S% ✻B&b£5–£7 Bdi£6–£7.75 W£40–£51 ⊬ D7pm

GH Penmorvah Hotel Alexandra Rd ☎3711 Plan:**19** Closed Nov Lic 10hc CTV 2P ⦰ S% B&b£6–£7 Bdi£8–£9 W£45–£54 ⊬ D6pm

GH Sea & Horses Hotel 6 Alexandra Ter ☎61961 Plan:**20** Apr–Oct Lic 11hc 1⌸ ⊗ CTV 9P 3⌂ ⦰ sea S% B&b£4.75–£7.75 Bdi£7.50–£10.50 W£50–£75 ⊬ D7.15pm

GH Tarbert Hotel 11 Clarence St ☎66326 Plan:**21** Lic 9hc ⊗ ⌂ CTV ⦰ S% B&b£5–£6 Bdi£7.50–£8.50 W£48–£55 ⊬ D9pm

GH Trenant Private Hotel Alexandra Rd ☎2005 Plan:**22** May–5th Oct 7hc nc9 TV S% B&b£4.80–£5.20 Bdi£7.30–£8 W£42.50–£50 ⊬ D5pm

GH Trevelyan Hotel 16 Chapel St ☎2494 Plan:**23** 7hc CTV 8P S% B&b£5–£6 Bdi£7.50–£8.50 W£52.50–£59.50 ⊬ D noon

GH Willows Cornwall Ter ☎3744 Plan:**24** 6hc nc5 CTV 8P ⦰ S% ✻B&b£4.95–£5.45 Bdi£7.15–£7.65 W£44–£49.60 ⊬ D5pm

INN Longboat Market Jew St ☎4137 Plan:**16** Lic 16hc 2⇆⌸ ⊗ CTV 2⌂ ⦰ sea S% B&b£5.50–£7 Bdi£7.50–£9.50 sn Bar lunch£1–£2.50&alc D9pm£2.50–£4.50&alc

---

Kirkstowe Guest House
PENARE ROAD, PENZANCE, CORNWALL

Tel: Penzance (0736) 3115   Table & Bar licence

*Private car Park
*Excellent cuisine
*Cornwall & Local Authority registered and approved.
*Close to sea and station

This is the guest house you will want to return to again. Remember prices are lower out of season September to May, but the weather in Penzance is still good.

*Open all the year.
Brochure on request.   Ron and Joan Mansfield

Bella Vista Private Hotel
7 Alexandra Terrace, Penzance, Cornwall TR18 4NX

Situated in a private garden terrace, overlooking the promenade, offering magnificent views across Mount's Bay. Overlooking the Bolitho gardens, bowling and putting greens, and tennis courts.
All bedrooms are fitted with hot and cold basins, spring interior mattresses, and bedside lamps; front rooms have sea views. Colour TV lounge. Separate tables. Car parking.
Bed, breakfast and evening dinner (optional). Colour brochure on request from resident proprietors Mr and Mrs M L Franklin.
Tel: Penzance (0736) 2409   Fire Certificate.

PENZANCE   # ESTORIL PRIVATE HOTEL

You will find this small comfortable hotel ideally situated between the promenade and the town centre. A warm welcome awaits guests at all times. Highly recommended.

Estoril Private Hotel, 46 Morrab Road, Penzance, Cornwall.
Tel 0736 2468

HANSFORD
PRIVATE HOTEL

Family Hotel: Good food and personal service: Comfortable accommodation, TV Lounge, 10 bedrooms. Centrally situated for sea front, towns and gardens. Brochure on request from proprietors: John and Hilary Rogers. Barclay cards and Access cards accepted.

Alexandra Road, Penzance, Cornwall. Tel: Penzance 3311.

KIMBERLEY HOUSE

Private Hotel

Doug & Jen Cooper's centrally situated, large, Victorian house, skillfully converted into a nine-bedroomed licensed hotel. It offers you a high standard of accommodation and cuisine to which you will want to return.

10 Morrab Road, Penzance, Cornwall. Tel: (0736) 2727

"LA CONNINGS" GUESTHOUSE

Licensed.   AA Listed.
Phone Germoe 2380

La Connings is open from Easter to October and offers a warm and friendly welcome to all its guests.

Situated in the country on the A394 between Penzance and Helston and within easy reach of many popular places of interest.

Reductions for early and late season. Good food, Children & pets welcome. Large car park.

SAE for colour brochure to B J Hosking or phone (STD 073 676) 2380

SEA & HORSES

AA   PRIVATE HOTEL

Alexandra Terrace, Penzance, Cornwall.
Tel: (0736) 61961

An exclusive private licensed hotel situated in a quiet garden terrace on the sea front, some 150 yards from the beach and commanding breathtaking views over Mounts Bay to the Lizard Peninsula.

Rates from:

£39.50 weekly   ●   £54.50 weekly - Dinner,
- Bed & Breakfast   Bed & Breakfast
(inclusive of VAT at 15%)

S.A.E. for colour brochure from the proprietors:-
Brenda and Peter Mackie

PERRANPORTH Cornwall *Map 2 SW75*
GH *Atlantic View Hotel* Ponsmere Rd
☎3171 Apr–Oct 13hc (A 6hc) CTV sea
D6pm
GH *Boscawen Private Hotel* ☎3472
Etr–5Oct Lic 15hc CTV 10P 1⋒
GH *Cellar Cove Hotel* Droskyn ☎2110
Etr–Sep Lic 14hc (A 2hc) ⊗ CTV 20P sea
D4pm
⋈**GH Gull Rock Private Hotel**
25 Tywarnhayle Rd ☎3289 Mar–Oct Lic
9hc CTV 3P 2⋒ sea S% B&b£4.32–£7.56
Bdi£6.32–£9.72 D8pm
⋈**GH Lake House Private Hotel**
Perrancombe ☎3202 late Mar–early Oct
Lic 10hc ⊗ CTV 7P 1⋒ B&b£5.40–£8.56
Bdi£6.48–£9.72 W£39.96–£57.24 ⱡ
D6pm
⋈**GH Lamorna Private Hotel**
Tywarnhayle Rd ☎3398 Closed Xmas

Lic 10hc CTV ⶈ B&b£5.94 Bdi£8.10
W£49.14–£52.92 ⱡ W only 26May–8Sep
D6.30pm
GH Lynton Cliff Rd ☎3457 8hc
1⊸⋒ ⊗ CTV 6P ⶈ sea S% *B&b£4–£5
Bdi£6–£7.50 W£35–£48 W only Jul–Aug
D5pm
⋈**GH Park View Private Hotel**
42 Tywarnhayle Rd ☎3009 Lic 10hc
CTV 10P S% B&b£5–£6.50 Bdi£7–£8.50
W£48–£56 ⱡ D6.30pm
GH *Sandy Beach Hotel* Ramoth Way
☎2263 Feb–Nov Lic 8hc (A 2hc) ⋒ CTV
15P ⶈ sea D8pm

PETERSFIELD Hants *Map 4 SU72*
GH Malva Hotel 3 Church Rd, Steep
(2m NW unclass) ☎2657 Lic 5hc ⊗
CTV 12P S% B&b£7 Bdi fr£13
W fr£115.50 D8.30pm

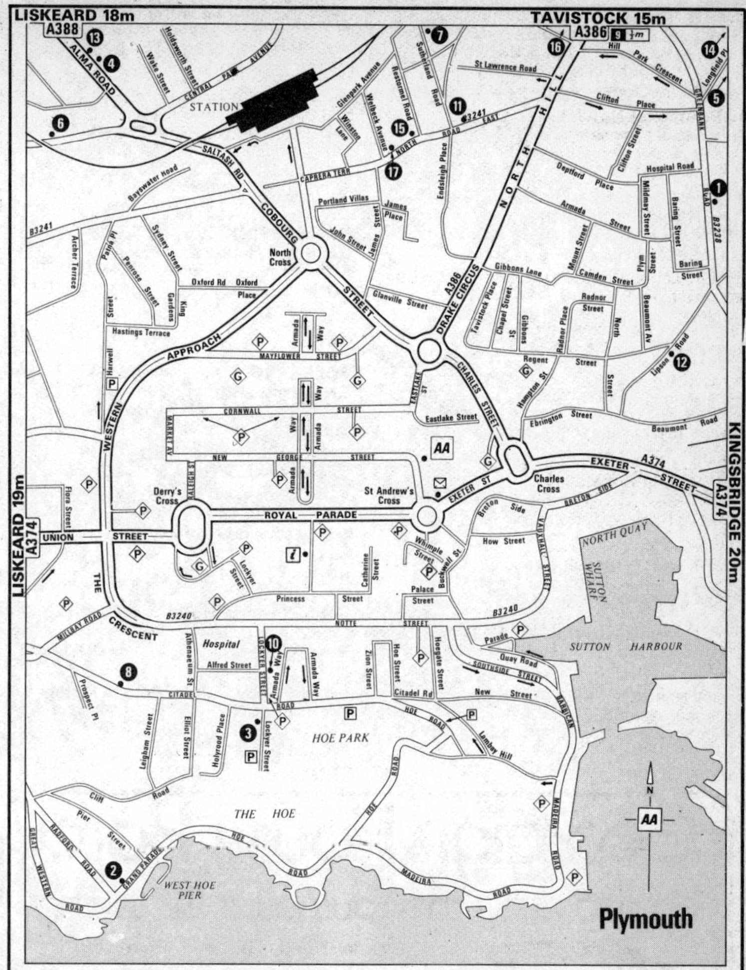

1 Akabo Hotel	**6** Chester	**10** Imperial Hotel	**14** Trenant House
2 Anchorage Hotel	**7** Dudley	**11** Kildare	**15** Welbeck House
3 Bowling Green Hotel	**8** Georgian House Hotel	**12** Lagos Hotel	**16** York
4 Burgoyne Villa	**9** Glendevon Hotel	**13** St Rita Private Hotel	**17** Yorkshireman Hotel
5 Cadleigh			

PILTON Somerset *Map 3 ST54*
⊶**GH Long House** ☎283 Lic 7hc
3⌂🍳 10P 2🏠 💷 S% B&b£4.95–£5.45
Bdi£8.20–£8.70 W£55–£59 ⒧
D5.30pm

PLYMOUTH Devon *Map 2 SX45* **See Plan**
⊶**GH Akabo Hotel** Greenbank Rd
☎63247 Plan:**1** Lic 10hc nc5 TV 8P S%
B&b£4.20 Bdi£6

⊶**GH Anchorage Hotel** Grand Pde
West Hoe ☎68645 Plan:**2** Closed Xmas
10hc nc3 CTV sea S% B&b£5.50 W£35
M

GH *Bowling Green Hotel* Lockyer St,
The Hoe ☎67485 Plan:**3** Tem 12hc CTV
P 4🏠 💷

⊶**GH Burgoyne Villa** 70 Alma Rd,
Mile House ☎62624 Plan:**4** 10hc nc6
CTV 8P B&b£4.50–£5 W only Sep–May

⊶**GH Cadleigh** 36 Queens Rd ☎65909
Plan:**5** 10rm 9hc CTV 💷 S% B&b£5.40–
£6.48 Bdi£8 64–£9.81 W£75.66 D3pm

⊶**GH Chester** 54 Stuart Rd,
Pennycomequick ☎63706 Plan:**6** 7hc
CTV 8P 💷 S% B&bfr£4.75 Bdi£7.75
D1pm

GH *Dudley* 42 Sutherland Rd, Mutley
☎68322 Plan:**7** 7hc CTV 2P 💷 D am

GH Georgian House Hotel 51 Citadel
Rd, The Hoe ☎63237 Plan:**8** Lic 10hc
CTV 💷 S% B&bf7 50–£8.50

GH Glendevon Hotel 20 Ford Park Rd,
Mutley ☎63655 Plan:**9** Closed 25 & 26
Dec Lic 8hc ✗ CTV ⴜ S% B&b£5.18–
£5.75 Bdi£8.05–£9.20 W£36.23–
£40.25 M D9pm

GH Imperial Hotel 3 Windsor Villas,
Lockyer St, The Hoe ☎27311 Plan:**10**
Closed 22Dec–1Jan Lic 24hc 7⇨ⴜ
CTV 20P 1⌂ ⴜ S% B&b£7.50–£10
Bdi£10.50–£13.50 W£64–£75 ⅃ D7pm

GH Kildare 82 North Rd East
☎29375 Plan:**11** 9hc ✗ CTV ⴜ S%
B&b£5–£6 W£32.50–£39.50 M

GH Lagos Private Hotel 46 Lipson Rd
☎69145 fr1980 669145 Plan:**12**
Closed Xmas Lic 8hc CTV S% B&b£4.70–
£5.50 Bdi£7.40–£8.20 W£50.40–£57.40
⅃ D4pm

GH Norway 70 Normandy Way,
St Budeaux ☎361979 Not on plan
6hc ✗ CTV river S% B&b£3.75–£4
Bdi£5.60–£5.85 W£36.60–£38.20 ⅃
D6pm

GH St Rita Private Hotel 76 Alma Rd
☎67024 Plan:**13** Lic 6hc ✗ ⌂ CTV 4P
4⌂ S% B&b£6.50 Bdi£9–£10
W£60–£62 ⅃ D am

GH *Trenant House* Queens Rd, Lipson
☎63879 Plan:**14** Closed Xmas wk Lic
23hc CTV 25P D10am

GH Welbeck Hotel North Rd East
☎61350 Plan:**15** Closed Xmas wk 7hc
1⇨ⴜ CTV S% B&b£4

GH York 23 Wilderness Rd,
Mannamead ☎266129 Plan:**16** 6hc
CTV S% B&b£4.50–£5.50 Bdi£6–£9.50
W£30–£33 ⅃ D4pm

GH Yorkshireman Hotel 64 North Rd East
☎68133 Plan:**17** Closed Xmas wk Lic
15hc ✗ CTV 7P S% ✳B&b£4.75–£5
Bdi£8 D am

POLBATHIC Cornwall *Map 2 SX35*
GH Tredis House Hotel ☎ St Germans
669 Lic 5hc ⌂ CTV 20P ⴜ S%
B&b£6–£7 Bdi£9.50–£10.50
W£42–£70 ⅃ D9pm

POLMASSICK Cornwall *Map 2 SW94*
GH Kilbol House ☎ Mevagissey 2481
Closed Xmas Lic 7hc 3⇨ⴜ ✗ CTV 12P
1⌂ ⴜ S% B&b£6–£6.60 Bdi£9.50–£9.90
W£63.75–£67.70 ⅃ W Jul & Aug
D9.30pm

POLPERRO Cornwall *Map 2 SX25*
GH Atlantis Hotel Polperro Rd ☎72243
Lic 12hc ✗ CTV 14P S% B&bfr£7.50
Bdifr£9.50 Wfr£55 ⅃

GH Kit Hill Talland Hill ☎72369
Closed Xmas & New Year Lic 6hc ✗ nc6
CTV 12P ⴜ sea S% B&b£6.50–£9
W£73.50–£91 ⅃ D4pm

GH Landaviddy Manor ☎72210
Mar–Oct Lic 8hc ✗ nc12 TV 12P ⴜ sea
B&b£6.61–£9.18 Bdi£10.93–£13.92
W£57.50–£64.98 ⅃ D7pm

GH Mill House Hotel Mill Hill ☎72362
Lic 12hc nc10 CTV 4P ⴜ S%
✳W£64.50–£70.85 ⅃ W only Oct–Mar
D noon

GH Sleepy Hollow Private Hotel
Brentfields ☎72288 7hc 2⇨ⴜ nc12
CTV 7P sea S% B&b£5–£7 Bdi£7.50–£9.50
W£52.50–£66.50 ⅃ D4pm

POLRUAN Cornwall *Map 2 SX15*
GH Florizel Fore St ☎208 Mar–Oct 12hc
2⇌🛏 nc8 CTV 4P 9🏠 sea S% B&bf6–£7
Bdif9–£10 Wf55–£60 ⱡ

POLZEATH Cornwall *Map 2 SW97*
⤚GH **White Lodge** Old Polzeath
☎Trebetherick 2370 Lic 6hc (A 4hc)
CTV 10P sea S% B&bf5–£6 Bdif8–£9
Wf49.50–£62 ⱡ D4pm

POOLE Dorset *Map 4 SZ09*
For locations and additional guesthouses
see **Bournemouth**
⤚GH **Avalon Private Hotel**
14 Pinewood Rd, Branksome Park
☎760917 Bournemouth district plan:**7**
Lic 14hc 2⇌🛏 nc6 CTV 14P 🍽 S%
B&bf5.50–£6 Bdif7.50–£8.50
Wf52–£55 ⱡ D6.30pm

⤚GH **Blue Shutters Hotel** 109 North Rd,
Lower Parkstone ☎748129
Bournemouth district plan:**11**
11hc ♨ TV 10P sea B&bf5.13–£5.67
Bdif7.29–£7.83 Wf48.60–£51.84 ⱡ
D10.30pm
GH Coniston 26 Sandringham Rd,
Parkstone ☎744409 Bournemouth district
plan:**26** Lic 10hc CTV 8P 🍽 S%
✳B&bf4.86–£5.40 Bdif6.50–£7.56
Wf45–£52.92 D4.30pm
GH Dene Hotel 16 Pinewood Rd,
Branksome Park ☎761143 Bournemouth
district plan:**29** Closed Nov & Feb Lic
15hc 4⇌🛏 ♨ CTV 18P 🍽 S%
B&bf6.90–£11.50 Bdif9.20–£15.53
Wf55.20–£86.25 ⱡ D5pm
⤚GH **Lewina** 225 Bournemouth Rd,
Parkstone ☎742295 Bournemouth district
plan:**50** 6hc ♨ TV 8P S% B&bf3.75–£4.25
Wfr£24 M

AVALON PRIVATE HOTEL

Member of Hotel Association

14 Pinewood Road, Branksome Park, Poole
Telephone: **Bournemouth 760917**

OPEN ALL THE YEAR • RESIDENTIAL LICENCE

Small Private Hotel set amongst the pines in the quiet residential area
of Branksome Park, yet only three minutes' walk from the beach.
Ample free parking in own grounds. Carefully prepared varied meals.
Full central heating. Every effort is made to ensure the comfort of our guests.
Electric blankets. Teasmade. Centrally situated for Yachting, Golf and Fishing.
Open for Christmas. Brochure and Terms on request. Fire Certificate.
Warm welcome and personal attention by the proprietors:.
Mr and Mrs M J Robinson and family.

Landaviddy Manor Polperro

FOR A HOLIDAY OF DISTINCT SATISFACTION
Private old English guest house, stands in its own grounds in a peaceful and attractive
setting. Commands beautiful views of Polperro Bay. Adjoins National Trust land —
near Cornish Moors and Dartmoor.
BTA commended. Centrally heated, cosy bar. Personal service — food at its very
best. H & C in all rooms. Free parking. Friendly and informal atmosphere.

Proprietors: Mr and Mrs A W Lester   **Tel: Polperro (0503) 72210**

Newton House Hotel

Sclerder Lane, Talland, Nr. Polperro, Cornwall PL13 2JD
Tel: Polperro 72413

A small Country Hotel with heated
swimming pool in the middle of farmland
with panoramic views over Talland
Bay. Our emphasis is on good food,
pleasant and comfortably furnished
bedrooms with hot and cold running
water. There is a licensed bar, residents'
lounge, colour TV, ample car parking
within hotel grounds and play centre
for children in hotel garden.

GH Ormonde House 18 Ormonde Rd,
Branksome Park ☎761093
Bournemouth district plan:**60** Mar–Oct
Lic 8hc ⊘ CTV 6P S% B&bf£5.60–£6.80
Bdif£8–£9.30 Wf£56–£65 ₭
W only Jul & Aug D6pm

GH Redcroft Private Hotel
20 Pinewood Rd, Branksome Park
☎763959 Bournemouth district plan:**66**
8hc ⊘ nc5 CTV 8P 🍴 S% B&bf£5–£7.50
Bdif£7.50–£10 Wf£52.50–£63 ₭
W only Jul & Aug D5.30pm

GH Sandbourne Hotel 1 Sandecotes
Rd ☎ Parkstone 747704 Bournemouth
district plan:**69** Closed Nov & Dec 7hc
CTV 9P 🍴 S% B&bf£5.50–£6 Bdif£7.50–£8
Wf£35–£49 D5pm

GH Sheldon Lodge 22 Forest Rd,
Branksome Park ☎761186 Bournemouth
district plan:**74** Etr–Oct Lic 15hc 4⊅🍴 ⊘
CTV 15P 3🏠 S% B&bf£6.50–£7.50
Bdif£8.50–£9.50 Wf£58–£65 ₭
W only Jul & Aug D6pm

GH Twin Cedars Hotel 2 Pinewood Rd,
Branksome Park ☎761339
Bournemouth district plan:**83** Mar–Oct
& Xmas wk Lic 12hc 6⊅🍴 CTV 15P 🍴 &
S% B&bf£4.86–£5.94 Bdif£7.56–£8.64
Wf£63.72–£70.74 D7pm

GH Westminster Cottage Hotel
3 Westminster Rd East, Branksome Park
☎765265 Bournemouth district plan:**90**
Lic 12hc 4⊅🍴 CTV 14P S% B&bf£6.32–
£8.85 Bdif£8.21–£10.12 Wf£53.12–
£66.40 ₭

PORLOCK Somerset Map 3 SS84
GH Cleeve Hawkcombe ☎862351
Mar–Nov 6hc 4⊅🍴 CTV 6P 🍴 S%
✱B&bf£5 Wf£32 M

Dene Hotel

**16 Pinewood Road,
Branksome Park, Poole.**

This family-owned, licensed hotel of
character is in a quiet residential
area, halfway between Bournemouth
and Poole town centres.
The sandy beaches of Bournemouth
bay are within three minutes' walk
through a wooded park.
Open all year. Excellent food with
choice of menu. A few bedrooms
with private shower/toilet. Ideal centre
for the many picturesque gardens,
historic houses of Wessex.

Open All The Year Round

Lewina Guest House

Proprietress: Mrs T Wright
225 Bournemouth Road, Parkstone, Poole,
Dorset BH14 9HU
Tel. Parkstone 742295
Member of Southern Tourist Board
Room & breakfast. Open all year. Central heating.
Ideally situated for country town & beaches. Ample
free parking. Tea-making facilities, H & C, razor
points, & electric fires in all bedrooms. TV lounge.
Mid week bookings taken. Access to rooms at all
times. Fire certificate.

Sandbourne Hotel

Winter or summer you'll enjoy staying at the Sandbourne Hotel,
midway between Poole and Bournemouth. Double glazing and
central heating, a well-furnished lounge with colour TV, and
good varied cuisine ensure your comfort.
Facilities include: Bed and breakfast and evening dinner, H & C
and shaving points in all bedrooms, ample car parking space,
centrally situated for golf, tennis, fishing.
Brochure and terms on request to:
Mrs Richards, Sandbourne Hotel,
Sandecotes Road, Parkstone, Poole, Dorset BH14 8NT
Tel: 0202 747704

GH *Gables* ☎862552 Etr–Oct 8hc ⊗ nc12 CTV ꟺ D4pm
GH *Lorna Doone Hotel* ☎862404 Mar–Dec Lic 11hc ⊗ CTV 8P D8pm
GH *Overstream* Parson St ☎862421 Etr–10Oct 7hc nc3 12P lift D7pm

PORTHCOTHAN BAY Cornwall
Map 2 SW87
GH Bay House ☎ St Merryn 520472 Etr–Sep Lic 17hc CTV 20P sea B&b£6–£7 Bdi£8–£9 W£55–£60 Ⱡ D noon

PORTHCURNO Cornwall *Map 2 SW32*
⋈**GH Corniche Trebehor Farm** ☎ Sennen 424 Mar–Nov Lic 6hc ⊗ nc7 CTV 8P ꟺ sea B&b£5.50–£6 Bdi£8.50–£9 W£60–£63 Ⱡ W only late Jul & Aug D6pm

PORTHLEVEN Cornwall *Map 2 SW62*
GH Torre Vean Manor House ☎ Helston 62412 Lic 8hc CTV 10P ꟺ S% B&b£6.95–£9.20 Bdi£11.50–£13.50 D7pm

PORT ISAAC Cornwall *Map 2 SW98*
⋈**GH Archer Farm** Trewetha (1m E B3267) ☎522 Apr–mid Nov 8rm 7hc 2⇋fl nc3 CTV 8P B&b£5.50–£6 Bdi£9–£9.50 W£62.50–£66 Ⱡ D7pm
⋈**GH Fairholme** 30 Trewetha Ln ☎323 Apr–mid Oct 7hc CTV 8P S% B&b£3.50–£4.50 Bdi£6–£7 W£42–£49 Ⱡ D6.30pm
GH Homer Park Farm 'otel ☎250 Apr–Oct Lic 20hc 4⇋fl ⌂ CTV 20P sea B&b£7–£10.50 Bdi£10–£14.75 W£71.50–£108 D9pm
GH Trethoway Hotel 98 Fore St ☎214 Lic 12hc ⌂ CTV 1⌂ sea S% B&b£6.25–£7.50 Bdi£7.45–£9.85 W£54.50–£64.50 Ⱡ D8pm

PORTSMOUTH & SOUTHSEA Hants
Map 4 SZ69
Telephone Exchange 'Portsmouth'
See Plan
GH *Averano* 65 Granada Rd, Southsea ☎20079 Plan:**1** 12hc CTV 8P 4⌂ sea D2.30pm
⋈**GH Birchwood** 44 Waverley Rd, Southsea ☎811337 Plan:**2** 6hc ⊗ nc3 TV S% B&b£5–£5.50 Bdi£7–£8 W£39–£42 D3pm
⋈**GH Elms** 48 Victoria Rd South, Southsea ☎23924 Plan:**3** Closed Xmas 7hc ⊗ nc6 CTV 2P S% B&b£4.50–£4.75 Bdi£6–£6.50 W£35–£38.50 Ⱡ D4pm
⋈**GH Embell Hotel** 31 Festing Rd, Southsea ☎25678 Plan:**4** Closed Xmas wk 8hc TV S% B&b£4.50 W£30 M
⋈**GH Grosvenor Court Hotel** 37 Granada Rd, Southsea ☎21653 Plan:**5** Closed Xmas rs Jan–Mar Lic 15hc nc4 CTV 11P S% B&b£4.50–£5.50 Bdi£6.50–£7.50 D3pm
GH Harwood Hotel 47/49 St Ronans Rd, Southsea ☎23104 Plan:**6** 13hc CTV ꟺ S% ✱B&b£4 Bdi£5.50
⋈**GH Homeleigh** 42–44 Festing Gv, Southsea ☎23706 Plan:**7** 10hc CTV S% B&b£4.60 Bdi£6.06 D6pm
GH *Jesamine* 57 Granada Rd, Southsea ☎734388 Plan:**8** 3Jan–23Dec 6hc ⊗ TV 6P ꟺ
⋈**GH Lyndhurst** 8 Festing Gv, Southsea ☎735239 Plan:**9** Closed Xmas 7hc CTV ꟺ S% B&b£5.25 Bdi£7 W£39.60 Ⱡ D4pm
GH Ryde View 9 Western Pde, Southsea ☎20865 Plan:**10** Closed Xmas Lic 15hc CTV ꟺ sea S% B&b£6–£7.50 Bdi£8.75–£10.50 D4pm

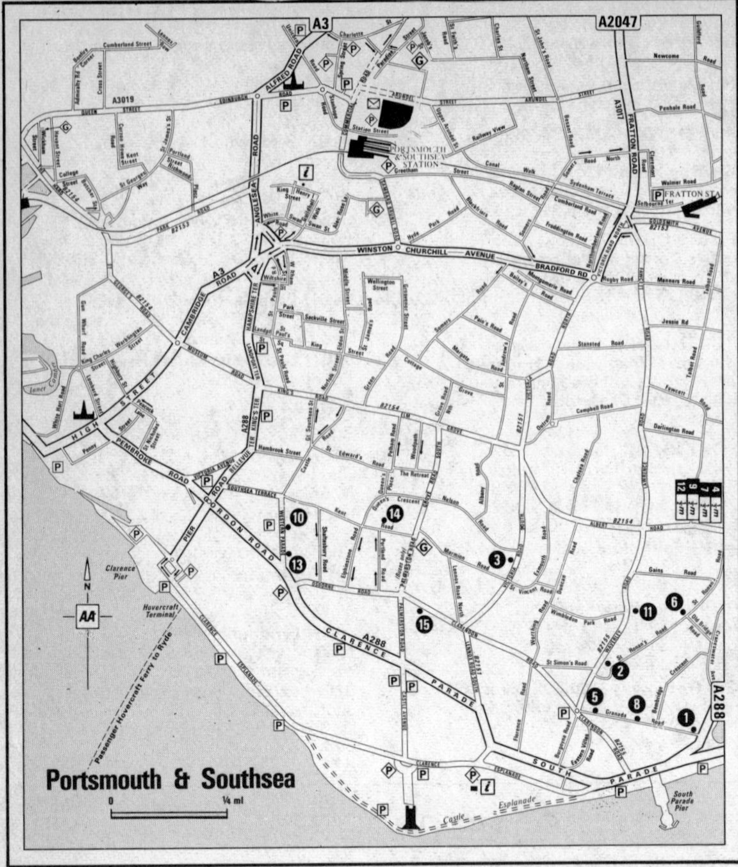

1	Averano	8	Jesamine
2	Birchwood	9	Lyndhurst
3	Elms	10	Ryde View
4	Embell Hotel	11	St Austell
5	Grosvenor Court Hotel	12	Salisbury Hotel
6	Harwood Hotel	13	Somerset Private Hotel
7	Homeleigh	14	Tudor Court Hotel
		15	Upper Mount House

⊢⊣GH St Austell 8 Herbert Rd, Southsea ☎29467 Plan:**11** Closed Dec 6hc ⊗ nc5 TV 2P S% B&b£4.50–£4.75 Bdi£5.80–£6.20 W£32.50–£36.50 ⱡ D4pm

GH *Salisbury Hotel* 57–59 Festing Rd, Southsea ☎23606 Plan:**12** Lic 23hc CTV 20P D6pm

GH Somerset Private Hotel 16 Western Pde, Southsea ☎22495 Plan:**13** Closed Xmas 16hc nc3 CTV ⊞ sea S% ✱B&b£5.95–£6.96 W£30.36–£48.70 M

GH Tudor Court Hotel 1 Queens Gv, Southsea ☎20174 Plan:**14** Lic 14hc 9⇆⋔ nc3 CTV 8P S% B&b£6 Bdi£9 W£36 M

GH Upper Mount House The Vale, Clarendon Rd, Southsea ☎20456 Plan:**15** Lic 12hc 4⇆⋔ ⊗ CTV 7P 1🏠 ⊞ S% B&b£7.50–£8.50 Bdi£11.25–£12.25 W£57.50–£64.50 ⱡ D8.30pm

POSTBRIDGE Devon *Map 3 SX67*
GH Lydgate House Hotel ☎88209 Closed Xmas Lic 9hc CTV 12P ⊞ river B&b£7–£8 Bdi£9.50–£11 W£68–£75 ⱡ D7.30pm

POTTER HEIGHAM Norfolk *Map 9 TG41*
⊢⊣GH Broadland House Bridge Rd ☎401 9hc CTV 30P S% B&b£5.50 Bdi£7.75 Wfr£40.50 ⱡ D5.30pm

POULTON-LE-FYLDE Lancs *Map 7 SD33*
For location see Blackpool Plan
GH *Breck Hotel* 28A Breck Rd ☎885702 Blackpool plan:**3** Lic 12hc ⊗ nc10 CTV 10P ⊞ D1pm

POUNDSGATE Devon *Map 3 SX77*
GH Leusdon Lodge ☎304 Etr–Oct rs Nov–Etr Lic 8hc TV 20P ⊞ B&b£6.75– £7.50 Bdi£9.75–£10.75 W£63.25–£69.75 ⱡ D9.30pm

PRAA SANDS Cornwall *Map 2 SW52*
⊢⊣GH La Connings ☎ Germoe 2380 Etr–Oct Lic 8hc 10P ⊞ lift sea S% B&b£5–£6.50 Bdi£6.50–£8 W£45–£56 ⱡ D7pm

PRESTON Lancs *Map 7 SD52*
GH *Beech Grove Hotel* 12 Beech Grove,
Ashton ☎729969 Lic 5hc ❤ CTV 8P ♨
D6pm

GH *Fulwood Park Hotel* 49 Watling
Street Rd ☎718067 rs Xmas Day Lic
21hc (A 4hc) CTV 30P 3🛏 D6.45pm

GH *Lauderdale Hotel* 29 Fishergate Hill
☎55460 Lic 18hc CTV 10P 6🛏 ♨ S%
✳B&b£6.90 Bdi£9.50 D6pm

GH *Withy Trees* 175 Garstang Rd,
Fullwood (2m N on A6) ☎717693 12hc
CTV 12P ♨

PULBOROUGH W Sussex *Map 4 TQ01*
INN *Arun Hotel* 87 Lower St ☎2162
Lic 9hc TV 4P 6🛏 river D9pm

QUEEN CAMEL Somerset *Map 3 ST52*
INN Mildmay Arms ☎Yeovil 850456
Lic 4hc CTV 30P S% B&b£6–£7 sn
L£1–£3 D9.30pm£1–£10&alc

QUORNDON Leics *Map 8 SK51*
INN Hurst Hotel 23 Loughborough Rd
☎ Quorn 42541 Lic 7hc 1🛏🍴 CTV P
♨ S% B&b£8 D7.30pm

RAMSGATE Kent *Map 5 TR36*
⊬GH **Abbeygail** 17 Penshurst Rd
☎ Thanet 54154 Closed Xmas 10hc ❤
nc4 CTV 1P S% B&b£4.50–£6
Bdi£6.50–£8.50 W£35–£45 ⌿ D2pm

GH Sylvan Hotel 160–162 High St
☎ Thanet 53026 Apr–Oct rs Xmas Lic
23hc ❤ CTV 12P ♨ S% ✳B&b£5.50
Bdi£8 W£45 ⌿ D6pm

GH Westcliff Hotel 9 Grange Rd
☎ Thanet 581222 Closed Nov Lic 10hc
nc5 CTV 13P 1🛏 ♨ S% B&b£7.50–£8.50

READING Berks *Map 4 SU77*
GH Aeron 191 Kentwood Hill,
Tilehurst (3m W off A329) ☎24119
Closed Xmas 8hc (A 10hc) CTV 12P ♨
S% B&b fr£7.50

GH Private House Hotel 98 Kendrick Rd
☎84142 Closed Xmas 7hc ❤ nc12 CTV
5P ♨ S% B&b£6.80 Bdi£10 D3pm

REDCAR Cleveland *Map 8 NZ62*
⊬GH **Claxton House Private Hotel**
196 High St ☎6745 Closed Xmas wk
14hc 5🛏🍴 ❤ CTV 6P ♨ S% B&b£5.50–
£6.50 Bdi£8–£9 D6.30pm

REDHILL Surrey *Map 4 TQ25*
GH Ashleigh House Hotel 39 Redstone
Hill ☎64763 9hc CTV 10P ♨ S%
B&b£8–£9.50

REDRUTH Cornwall *Map 2 SW64*
⊬GH **Foundry House** 21 Foundry Row,
Chapel St ☎215143 Closed Etr & Xmas
6hc nc3 CTV 5P S% B&b£4 Bdi£5 W£35
⌿ D4.30pm

⊬GH **Lyndhurst** 80 Agar Rd ☎215146
8hc CTV 8P S% B&b£4 Bdi£6 W£40–£42
⌿ D4pm

REIGATE Surrey *Map 4 TQ25*
GH Cranleigh Hotel 41 West St
☎40600 Lic 12hc 6🛏🍴 ❤ CTV 6P ♨
S% B&b£7.50–£9 Bdi£11.50–£13 D9pm

RICHMOND UPON THAMES
Gt London *Map 4 TQ17*
GH *Spa House Hotel* 52 Richmond Hill
☎01-940 4909 Mar–23Dec Lic 10hc
❀ nc1 TV 4P B&b£5.50–£6.25

RIPON N Yorks *Map 8 SE37*
⊶**GH Crescent Lodge** 42–42A North St
☎2331 Closed Xmas wk 12hc CTV 8P
S% B&b£5–£6 Bdi fr£7.50 W fr£50
D7.30pm

GH Nordale 2 North Pde ☎3557 12hc
CTV 12P S% ✱B&b fr£5.40 Bdi fr£8.64
W fr£51.84 Ł D5pm

⊶**GH Old Country** 1 The Crescent
☎2162 8rm 6hc ❀ CTV 8P 2🏠 ▥ S%
B&b£4.50–£5.50

ROBIN HOOD'S BAY N Yorks
Map 8 NZ90
⊶**GH Storra Lee** ☎ Whitby 880593
Mar–Nov 6hc ❀ P sea B&b£4–£5
Bdi£7–£8 D5pm

ROCHESTER Kent *Map 5 TQ76*
⊶**GH Greystones** 25 Watts Av
☎ Medway 47545 Closed Xmas 6hc
❀ CTV 5P 1🏠 ▥ S% B&b£5.75–£6.25

ROLLESBY Norfolk *Map 9 TG41*
⊶**GH Old Court House** Court Rd
☎ Fleggburgh 381 Lic 8hc CTV 16P ▥
S% B&b£5.40 Bdi£8.64 W£39.96–£55.08
Ł W only 26May–22Sep D6.30pm

ROMSEY Hants *Map 4 SU32*
⊶**GH Adelaide House** 45 Winchester Rd
☎512322 6hc ❀ TV 6P ▥ S%
B&b£5.50–£5.95 W£35 Ⓜ

⊶**GH Chalet** Botley Rd, Whitenap
☎514909 4hc ❀ CTV 6P ▥ S% B&b£5
Bdi fr£7 W fr£45 Ł

ROSS-ON-WYE Heref & Worcs
Map 3 SO52
⊶**GH Bridge House** Wilton ☎2655
11hc ❀ CTV 11P river S% B&b£5.50
Bdi£9 W£50 Ł D6pm

GH Orles Barn Hotel Wilton ☎2155
Lic 6hc CTV 12P ▥ S% ✱B&b fr£7

GH *Ryefield House* Gloucester Rd ☎3030
Lic 6hc ❀ CTV 10P ▥ D4pm

ROTHERFIELD E Sussex *Map 5 TQ52*
INN Kings Arms ☎2465 Lic 4hc ❀
nc14 CTV 50P ▥ ❀ S% B&b£7.50 sn
L£2 D9.30pm£4.50 alc

ROTHLEY Leics *Map 8 SK51*
GH Rothley 35 Mountsorrel Ln
☎ Leicester 302531 Lic 9🖴🕮 ❀ CTV
12P ▥ S% B&b fr£7.71 Bdi fr£12.13
D noon

ROTTINGDEAN E Sussex *Map 5 TQ30*
⊶**GH Braemar House** Steyning Rd
☎ Brighton 34263 15hc CTV S%
B&b£5.40–£5.67

GH Corner House Steyning Rd
☎ Brighton 34533 5hc ❀ CTV ▥ S%
B&b£6–£7 W£42–£49 Ⓜ

ROWLEY REGIS W Midlands
Map 7 SO98 **For location see
Birmingham Plan**
GH Highfield House Hotel Waterfall Ln
☎021-559 1066 Birmingham plan**2**
Lic 12hc ❀ nc14 CTV 10P ▥ S%
✱B&b£5.50 Bdi£8 D10am

RUGBY Warwicks *Map 4 SP57*
GH Grosvenor House Hotel 81 Clifton Rd
☎3437 Lic 9hc CTV 9P ▥ S%
B&b fr£8.13 Bdi fr£10.43 D7.30pm

GH Mound Hotel 17–19 Lawford Rd
☎3486 Closed Xmas Lic 17hc 1🖴🕮 ❀
CTV 14P ▥ S% B&b£6.75–£8.80
Bdi£10.50–£12.50 D3pm

RUISLIP Gt London *Map 4 TQ08*
GH 17th Century Barn Hotel West End
Rd ☎36057 Lic 50🖴🕮 TV 56P ▥
B&b fr£8.09 D8.20pm

RUMWELL Somerset *Map 3 ST12*
GH *Rumwell Hall Hotel* ☎ Bradford-on-
Tone 312 6rm 5hc TV 30P lift ▥

RUSTINGTON W Sussex *Map 4 TQ00*
⊶**GH Kenmore** Claigmar Rd ☎4634
5hc 1🖴🕮 6P ▥ S% B&b£4.50–£8.75
W£28–£56.50 Ⓜ

RYDAL Cumbria *Map 11 NY30*
GH Rydal Lodge Hotel ☎ Ambleside
3208 Apr–Oct Lic 8hc nc5 CTV 12P river
S% B&b£9 Bdi£13 W£85 Ł D2pm

RYDE Isle of Wight *Map 4 SZ59*
GH Dorset Hotel Dover St ☎64327
Apr–mid Oct rs mid Oct–Mar Lic 24hc
7🖴🕮 ❀ CTV 25P B&b£7.50–£8.50
Bdi£9.50–£10.50 W£45–£50 Ł
D6.30pm

⊶**GH Teneriffe** 36 The Strand ☎63841
Lic 16hc CTV 3P B&b£5 Bdi£7 W£45
Ł D3pm

The 17th Century **Barn Hotel** Ruislip

An original farmhouse listed as being of
historical interest. Restored in 1948.

54 rooms. Central heating. Private baths and
TV (B&B £7.50)

One of the most picturesque and photographed
hotels within 25 minutes of Central London.

Resident proprietors. Tel: Ruislip 36057

*2 acres of
landscaped gardens*

RYE E Sussex *Map 5 TQ92*
⊢⊣**GH Little Saltcote** 22 Military Rd
☎3210 6hc 1🛁🗒 ⊗ 3P 🍴 river S%
B&bf£5.50–£6.50

GH Mariner's Hotel High St ☎3480
Lic 16hc 8🛁🗒 ⚓ CTV 🍴 & S%
B&b£6.50–£8 Bdi£9.50–£11.50
W£57–£69 ⬡ D8.30pm

GH Monastery Hotel & Restaurant
6 High St ☎3272 Lic 7hc ⊗ nc7 CTV
🍴 S% B&b£9–£9.50

GH *Old Borough Arms* The Strand
☎2128 9hc TV 3🏠 🍴

GH Playden Oasts Hotel Playden ☎3502
Closed Mon eve & Sun lunch Lic 6🛁🗒
CTV 12P 4🏠 🍴 S% B&b£9–£10
Bdi£14–£16 W£90–£100 ⬡ D8pm

ST ALBANS Herts *Map 4 TL10*
GH Grange Hotel 276 London Rd
☎51232 Lic 15hc 1🛁🗒 ⊗ nc3 CTV 30P
🍴 B&b£9.20–£11.58

GH Melford 24 Woodstock Rd North
☎53642 Lic 12hc CTV 12P 🍴 S%
B&b£7.48–£10.35 W£48.30–£72.45
M W only Jan–Apr & Oct–Dec

ST AUSTELL Cornwall *Map 2 SX05*
⊢⊣**GH Alexandra Hotel** 52–54 Alexandra
Rd ☎4242 Lic 14hc 4🛁🗒 CTV 16P 🍴
sea S% B&b£4.86–£5.40 Bdi£7.56–
£8.64 W£45.36–£49.68 ⬡ D5pm

⊢⊣**GH Copper Beeches** Truro Rd,
Trevarrick ☎4024 Lic 8hc 1🛁🗒 CTV
8P 🍴 B&b£5.50–£6.25 Bdi£7.25–£8.50
W only Etr–Oct D6.30pm

⊢⊣**GH Cornerways** Penwinnick Rd
☎61579 Closed Xmas wk Lic 6hc ⊗
nc5 CTV 12P 🍴 S% B&b£5.75–£7 D am

⊢⊣**GH Lynton** 48 Bodmin Rd ☎3787
Lic 6hc ⊗ CTV 8P S% B&b£4.50–£5.50
Bdi£6.50–£7.50 W£40–£50 ⬡ D noon

GH Treskillon 26 Woodland Rd ☎2920
Lic 10hc ⊗ CTV 11P 🍴 ✳B&bfr£4.35
Bdi fr£6.85 Wfr£38 ⬡ D6.30pm

GH Wimereux Lodge 1 Trevanion Rd
☎2187 Lic 14hc 5🛁🗒 ⊗ nc2 CTV 14P
🍴 S% ✳B&b£5.13–£5.40 Bdi£7.56–
£8.10 W£49.68–£54 ⬡ D6pm

⊢⊣**INN Holmbush** 101 Holmbush Rd
☎3217 Lic 3hc 55P S% B&b£3.50–£4
sn Bar lunch50p–£1

ST BLAZEY Cornwall *Map 2 SX05*
⊢⊣**GH Moorshill House Hotel** Rosehill
☎ Par 2368 Lic 5hc ⊗ ⚓ CTV TV 6P 🍴
S% B&b£4.75–£5.25 Bdi£7.25
W£42.50–£48 ⬡ D8pm

ST ISSEY Cornwall *Map 2 SW97*
INN *Ring O'Bells* ☎ Rumford (Bodmin)
251 Lic 4hc CTV 40P D8pm

ST IVES Cambs *Map 4 TL37*
GH Firs 50 Needingworth Rd ☎63252
6rm 5hc ⊗ CTV 8P 🍴 S% B&b£7.50
Bdi£11 D noon

ST IVES Cornwall *Map 2 SW54* **See Plan**
During the currency of this publication
St Ives numbers are liable to change.
GH *Aquitaine* 4 Ocean View Ter ☎5049
Plan:**1** 5hc ⊗ nc5 CTV 4P sea D6pm
GH Boskerris Lodge Carbis Bay ☎7700
Not on plan Etr–Oct 7hc CTV 8P 🍴 sea
S% ✳B&b£4–£4.50 Bdi fr£6 W£40–£49
D6pm
GH Channings Private Hotel 3 Talland Rd
☎5681 Plan:**2** Mar–Oct Lic 11hc 3🛁🗒
⊗ ⚓ CTV 9P sea S% B&b£6–£8
Bdi£8–£10 D6pm

ST ALBANS

MELFORD GUEST HOUSE

24 Woodstock Road North, St Albans, Herts.
Tel: St Albans (0727) 53642

Situated in the best residential area in historical Roman town, easy walking distance station and town centre. 20 miles London. Very homely, personal attention, well appointed and run by experienced hoteliers of long standing who have managed large luxury hotels abroad. 11 bedrooms all hot and cold with shaver point. Full central heating, dining room, spacious residents' lounge, colour TV, car park, fire certificate, licensed, public call box. Bed and breakfast (full English breakfast). Open all year.

Proprietress: Mrs Vicki Mason
Chosen by the AA for the 'Seaside Hospitality — six of the best landladies in the country' feature in the 1977 edition of this guidebook.
'Better than a 5 star!'
— Mr & Mrs F H Lossing, Columbus, Ohio, USA.
'Thanks again Vicki for a lovely holiday. Good food, good digs, good landlady.'
— Jackie, Brian & Rachel Sorsby, 71 Trickett Rd., Sheffield.
Room & Breakfast.
If you want value for money send for a brochure now.

1 Aquitaine
2 Channings Private Hotel
3 Chy-An-Creet Private Hotel
4 Cortina
5 Hollies Hotel
6 Island View
7 Kandahar
8 Longships
9 Lyonesse Hotel
10 Pondarosa
11 Primrose Valley Hotel
12 Rosemorran Private Hotel
13 St Margarets
14 St Merryn Hotel
15 Shun Lee Private Hotel
16 Sunrise
17 Trelissick
18 Verbena
19 Woodside Hotel

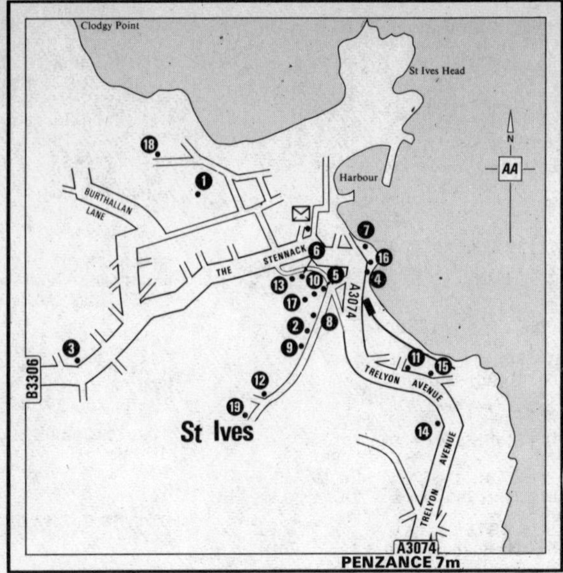

GH Chy-An-Creet Private Hotel Higher Stennack ☎6559 Plan:**3** Lic 12hc ☒ CTV 16P S% B&b£6–£7.50 Bdi£8.50–£9.50 W£54–£64 ⊬ D5.30pm

GH Cortina 26 The Warren ☎6183 Plan:**4** Etr & May–Oct 6hc CTV 6P B&b£5.50–£6.25

GH *Cottage Hotel* Carbis Bay ☎6351 Not on plan mid May–Sep Lic 52hc (A 10hc) ☒ CTV 100P lift 卿 sea D7pm

GH *Grey Tyles* Carbis Bay ☎6408 Not on plan Etr–Sep Lic 17hc CTV 14P sea D4pm

GH Hollies Hotel Talland Rd ☎6605 Plan:**5** Mar–Oct Lic 10hc 6⇨卿 ☒ ♨ CTV 12P B&b£5.40–£6.84 Bdi£8.10–£9.18 W£49.68–£66.96 D5.30pm

GH *Island View* 2 Park Av ☎5363 Plan:**6** Whit–Sep 9hc ☒ nc12 D6pm

GH Kandahar 11 The Warren ☎6183 Plan:**7** Closed Xmas 4rm CTV 6P 卿 B&b£5.50–£6.25

GH Longships 2 Talland Rd ☎6263 Plan:**8** Apr–Sep rs Xmas Lic 15hc 4⇨卿 CTV 10P sea S% B&b£5–£8 Bdi£7–£10 (W only Jul–Aug) D6pm

GH Lyonesse Hotel 5 Talland Rd ☎6315 Plan:**9** Apr–Oct Lic 15hc 5⇨卿 ☒ CTV 4P 卿 sea B&b£6–£10 Bdi£10–£13.50 W£50–£82 ⊬ D6pm

GH Pondarosa 10 Porthminster Ter ☎795875 Plan:**10** 10hc 1⇨卿 ☒ nc3 CTV 8P 卿 S% B&b£5–£7.50 Bdi£8–£10.50 W£47–£63 ⊬ D5pm

GH Primrose Valley Hotel Primrose Valley ☎5564 Plan:**11** Etr–Oct Lic 11hc 3⇨卿 ☒ ♨ CTV 11P sea ✱B&b£5.50–£6.50 Bdi£7–£9.14 W£45–£64 ⊬ D6pm

GH Rosemorran Private Hotel The Belyars ☎6359 Plan:**12** Mar–Oct Lic 11hc ♨ CTV 9P S% B&b£7–£8 Bdi£9.45–£10.60 W£66.15–£74 ⊬ D7pm

GH Hotel Rotorua Trencrom Ln, Carbis Bay ☎5419 Not on plan Lic 14hc 10⇨卿 ♨ CTV 14P S% B&b£6.16–£8.37 Bdi£8.37–£10.53 W£58.59–£73.71 ⊬ D7pm

GH *St Margarets* 3 Park Av ☎5785 Plan:**13** Closed Xmas Lic 8hc CTV sea

GH St Merryn Hotel Trelyon ☎5767 Plan:**14** Lic 12hc 2⇨卿 (A 3hc) ☒ CTV 18P 卿 S% B&b£5–£6.50 Bdi£7.50–£8.50

GH Shun Lee Private Hotel Trelyon Av
☎6284 Plan:**15** Mar–Oct Lic 11rm
1⊸🛏 ✍ nc6 CTV 12P 🍴 ✳B&b£5.94–
£7.02 Bdi£9.18–£10.26 W£60.48–
£65.88 ⸁ (W only May–Sep) D6.15pm

GH Sunrise 22 The Warren ☎5407
Plan:**16** 6hc (A 2hc) ✍ nc3 CTV 4P sea
S% B&b£4.20–£4.70 (W only Jun–Sep)

GH Trelissick Hotel Bishops Rd ☎5035
Plan:**17** 29Mar–Nov Lic 15hc 4⊸🛏 CTV
11P B&b£7–£10 Bdi£9–£12 W£50–£70
⸁ D6.45pm

◁**GH Verbena** Orange Ln ☎6396
Plan:**18** Etr–Oct Tem 7hc 2⊸🛏 ✍ nc6
CTV 8P sea S% B&b£4–£5 Bdi£6–£7
W£42–£49 ⸁ D3.30pm

GH Woodside Hotel The Belyars ☎6282
Plan:**19** Lic 11hc ♨ CTV 25P 🍴 S%
B&b£6.50–£7.50 Bdi£7.80–£9.28
W£55–£65 ⸁ (W only Jun–Aug) D6.30pm

ST IVES Dorset *Map 4 SU10*
GH Foxes Moon Hotel 40 Ringwood Rd
☎ Ringwood 4347 Jan–mid Nov Lic 6hc
CTV 9P 🍴 ✳B&b£4.75–£5.50
Bdi£6.95–£7.70 W£47.90–£52.40 ⸁
D7.15pm

ST JUST Cornwall *Map 2 SW33*
◁**GH Boscean Country Hotel** ☎788748
Etr–Oct Lic 9hc nc5 CTV 18P sea
B&b£5.07–£5.40 Bdi£8.32–£8.64
W£58.21–£60.48 ⸁ D11am

ST JUST-IN-ROSELAND Cornwall
Map 2 SW83
GH Rose-Da-Mar Hotel ☎ St Mawes 450
Etr–Oct Lic 9hc 5⊸🛏 nc7 CTV 10P 🍴
sea S% Bdi£12.90–£17

ST KEYNE Cornwall *Map 2 SX26*
GH Old Rectory Hotel ☎ Liskeard 42617
Apr–Oct Lic 10hc ✍ ♨ CTV 10P 🍴 S%
B&b£8.50–£10 Bdi£12.50–£15
W£72–£95 ⸁ W only–mid Jul–Aug D6pm

ST MARY'S Isles of Scilly *(No map)*
GH Evergreen Cottage ☎ Scillonia
22711 Mar–Oct 5hc ✍ nc6 TV 🍴 S%
✳B&b£5–£5.50 Bdi£8.50 D noon

GH Hanjague ☎ Scillonia 22531
May–Sep Lic 5hc ✍ nc10 🍴 Bdi£11.88–
£12.96 D6.15pm

GH Tremellyn Private Hotel ☎ Scillonia
22656 mid Mar–mid Oct Lic 7hc ✍ CTV
6P sea B&b£8.50 Bdi£11.75 W£82.25
⸁ W only May–7Oct D7pm

ST MARY CRAY Gt London *Map 5 TQ46*
GH *Sheepcote Farmhouse* Sheepcote Ln
☎ Orpington 70498 Apr–Oct 4hc ✍ CTV
P 🍴 D7.30pm

ST NEWLYN EAST Cornwall
Map 2 SW85
◁**GH Trewerry Mill** Trerice (2m W of
A3058 midway between Summercourt
& Quintrell Downs) ☎ Mitchell 345
Etr–Oct Lic 6hc ✍ CTV 20P S%
B&b£3.50–£6.80 Bdi£5.30–£8.60
W£37–£60 ⸁

SALCOMBE Devon *Map 3 SX73*
GH Bay View Hotel Bennett Rd ☎2238
Etr–Oct Lic 11hc 1⊸🛏 ✍ nc6 TV 8P
1🏠 🍴 sea B&b£7.50–£8.50 Bdi£11–
£12.50 W£70–£80 ⸁ W only mid Jul–Aug
D7.30pm

GH Charborough House Hotel Devon Rd
☎2260 Mid Mar–Nov Lic 10hc 2⊸🛏
✍ CTV 🍴 sea S% ✳B&b£6.40–£7.60
Bdi£9.80–£11 W£53–£70 ⸁ D5pm

Shun Lee Private Hotel

Trelyon Avenue, St Ives, Cornwall
Tel: (073 670) 6284

Residential licence. Central heating. Colour TV lounge. Quiet position off main road. Short walk to beaches and town. H & C in all rooms. Private car park. Four course evening dinner at 6.30pm. Fire certificate held.

Woodgrange Private Hotel

Devon Road, Salcombe, South Devon.

A small personally run hotel overlooking this beautiful estuary with its unspoilt coastal areas and numerous sandy bays. Ideal for bathing, sailing and walking. Mary and Peter Fleig offer you every comfort and excellent food, with a good selection of wines. Comfortable lounge and separate, well stocked cocktail lounge. Bedrooms with radio and colour television, half with private bathrooms. Central heating. Free car parking on premises.

Tel: Salcombe (054 884) 2439

GH Lyndhurst Hotel Bonaventure Rd
☎2481 Lic 8hc 2⇄🍳 ⊗ nc7 TV 8P 🍽
sea S% B&b£8–£10 Bdi£10–£12
W£55–£62.50 ⸔ D7pm
GH Melbury Hotel Devon Rd ☎2883
Spring Bank Hol–27Sep Lic 14hc
4⇄🍳 ⊗ nc5 CTV 18P sea B&b£8–£9
Bdi£9–£10.50 W£56.40–£69.60 ⸔
D7.30pm
GH *Stoneycroft Hotel* Devon Rd ☎2218
Etr–Sep Lic 10hc nc6 CTV 12P 🍽 sea
D4pm
GH Trennels Private Hotel Herbert Rd
☎2500 11hc ⊗ nc12 TV 8P 1🏠 🍽 sea
S% B&b£8–£9 Bdi£11–£12 W£55–£60
⸔ D am
GH Woodgrange Private Hotel Devon Rd
☎2439 Apr–Sep Lic 11hc 4⇄🍳 🏠 11P
🍽 sea S% B&b£6–£7 Bdi£10.50–£11.50
W£55–£65 ⸔ D7.30pm

SALISBURY Wilts *Map 4 SU12*
⊷**GH Byways House** 31 Fowlers Rd
☎28364 10hc CTV 3P 🍽 S%
B&b£5.50–£6.50
INN White Horse Hotel Castle St
☎27844 Lic 12hc CTV 4P 6🏠 ⇔ S%
B&b£8–£12 sn Lfr£2.50 D8.45pm
£3.60–£4.25&alc
SALTDEAN E Sussex *Map 5 TQ30*
⊷**GH Linbrook Lodge** 74 Lenham Av
☎ Brighton 33775 Lic 7hc 2⇄🍳 CTV
8P 🍽 sea B&b£5–£6.50 Bdi£7.50–£9
W£42–£49 ⸔ D2pm
SANDOWN Isle of Wight *Map 4 SZ58*
GH Chester Lodge Hotel Beachfield Rd
☎402773 Apr–Sep 18hc nc5 CTV 12P
B&b£5.94–£6.48 Bdi£8.10–£8.64
W£43.20–£51.84 (W only Jun–Aug)
D6.15pm
GH Cliff House Hotel Cliff Rd ☎403656

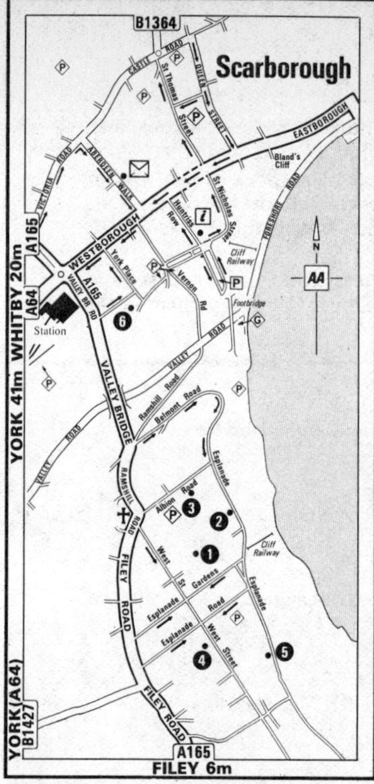

1 Bay Hotel	**4** Continental Lodge
2 Burghcliffe Hotel	**5** Green Park Hotel
3 Church Hills Private Hotel	**6** Ridbech Private Hotel

Mar–Nov Lic 16hc 8⇄🛏🕭 CTV 16P 🍴 sea B&bf9.20–£11.50 Bdi£12–£14.37 W£64.40–£69.57 Ł D6.30pm

⋈**GH Rostrevor Private Hotel** 96 Sandown Rd ☎402775 Mar–Oct Lic 17hc ✦ nc2 CTV 14P sea S% B&bf5.80–£7.75 Bdi£8–£9 W£46–£55.20 Ł D5pm

GH St Catherine's Hotel 1 Winchester Park Rd ☎402392 Closed Xmas Lic 18hc 7⇄🛏 ✦ nc5 CTV 8P 🍴 B&bf8.50–£10 Bdi£9.50–£12.50 W£66.50–£87.50 Ł D7pm

GH Trevallyn 32 Broadway ☎402373 Apr–Oct Lic 23hc (A 2hc) ✦ CTV 20P B&bf8.05 W£48.30–£54.70 Ⅿ D6.30pm

SANDPLACE Cornwall *Map 2 SX25*
GH Polraen Country House Hotel
☎ Looe 3956 Feb–Nov Lic 7hc 2⇄🛏 ✦ CTV 12P 1🏠 🍴 S% B&bf6.90–£9.78 Bdi£10.92–£13.80 W£71.30–£89.70 Ł D4pm

SANDWICH Kent *Map 5 TR35*
INN Fleur De Lis Delf St ☎3031 (from Sep '79–611131) Lic 5hc 2⇄🛏 CTV 3P 🚿 S% B&bf6–£8 Bdi£7–£9.50 sn Bar lunch 50p–£1.40 D8.30pm

SCARBOROUGH N Yorks *Map 8 TA08*
See Plan
GH Bay Hotel 67 Esplanade, South Cliff ☎73926 Plan:**1** Apr–Oct & rs Xmas Lic 20hc CTV 12P 🍴 sea S% B&bf7.50–£9.20 Bdi£10.75–£12.50 W£75.25–£87.50 Ł D6pm

GH Burghcliffe Hotel 28 Esplanade, South Cliff ☎61524 Plan:**2** Mar–Oct & Xmas Lic 15hc CTV sea S% B&bf7–£7.50 Bdi£8.50–£9 D5pm

GH Church Hills Private Hotel St Martins Av, South Cliff ☎63148 Plan:**3** Lic 16hc ✦ CTV 🍴 sea S% B&bf6.62–£7.77 Bdi£8.05–£9.78 W£64.40–£72.45 Ł D6pm

⋈**GH Continental Lodge** 37 West St, South Cliff ☎66976 Plan:**4** Closed 20Dec–3Jan Lic 7hc ✦ nc3 CTV 🍴 S% B&bf5.50–£6.50 Bdi£6.75–£7.75

GH Green Park Hotel 15 Prince of Wales Ter, South Cliff ☎65770 Plan:**5** Etr–Oct Lic 20hc 7⇄🛏 CTV lift S% ✳B&bf8–£10 Bdi£11–£12 W£72–£80 Ł D7.30pm

⋈**GH Ridbech Private Hotel** 8 The Crescent ☎61683 Plan:**6** Etr–Oct 25hc CTV sea S% B&bf5.75–£6.50 Bdi£7.50–£8.50 D5.45pm

SCILLY, ISLES OF *(No map)*
See St Mary's

SEAFORD E Sussex *Map 5 TV49*
GH Avondale Hotel Avondale Rd ☎890008 Jan–Oct 6hc CTV 🍴 ✳B&bf5.75–£6.75 Bdi£8.25–£9.25 W£50.50–£56.65 Ł D am

SEATON Devon *Map 3 SY29*
⋈**GH Eyre House** Queen St ☎21455 Etr–Oct Lic 8hc CTV 10P 🍴 S% B&bf5–£5.50

⋈**GH Glendare** Fore St ☎20542 Lic 6hc ✦ CTV 🍴 S% B&bf5.25–£5.50 Bdi£8.50–£9 W£35–£60 Ł D4.30pm

St Catherines Hotel

1 Winchester Park Road, Sandown, Isle of Wight Tel: 0983 402392
Resident Proprietors: Jim and Maureen Hitchcock

Relaxed, friendly atmosphere, comfortable furnishing, ample portions of quality food with full choice of varied menu are offered in this fully centrally heated, licensed hotel. Situated five minutes from the seafront and town centre. All bedrooms have radio/room call and free tea/coffee making facilities. Many have bath or shower and toilet en suite. Lounge with colour television.

Fleur de Lis Hotel

Delf Street, Sandwich, Kent. Tel: (03046) 611131

The hotel is situated in the centre of Sandwich, which is an old town and Cinque Port. Fully licensed with 3 bars. Good home-made food is provided, real ale served and there are coal fires in the winter. Part of the hotel is olde worlde with beams etc. in bedrooms. One bedroom, known as the Earl of Sandwich Bedchamber, has a half-tester bed.

Car parking facilities. Just 10 minutes from golf course and Ramsgate Hoverport. 30 minutes from Dover Car Ferry. 20 minutes from Canterbury.

⊢⊣**GH Mariners Homestead** Esplanade ☎20560 Feb–Nov Lic 11hc nc3 CTV 10P ᗰ sea ✱B&b£6.90–£7.50 Bdi£10.35–£10.80 W£66.10–£69 Ł D9am

GH Netherhayes Fore St ☎21646 Etr–Oct Lic 10hc ⊗ nc3 CTV 10P B&b£6–£6.50 Bdi£8.50–£9 W£55–£60 Ł D5.30pm

⊢⊣**GH St Margarets** 5 Seafield Rd ☎21134 Mar–Nov Lic 9hc CTV 7P ᗰ sea S% B&b£4.50–£5.50 Bdi£7.80–£8.80 D6pm

⊢⊣**GH Thornfield** 87 Scalwell Ln ☎20039 Etr–Oct rs Oct–mid Mar Lic 8hc (A 3hc) CTV 11P S% B&b£5–£7 Bdi£7–£8.50 W£45–£51 Ł D5pm

SELBY N Yorks *Map 8 SE63*
⊢⊣**GH Hazeldene** 34 Brook St ☎704809 8hc ⊗ CTV 6P S% B&b£4.50–£5

SELSEY W Sussex *Map 4 SZ89*
GH *Fairbrook* 71 Hillfield Rd ☎2914 Lic 6hc ⊗ nc7 TV 6P

GH *White Waves Private Hotel* Seal Rd ☎2379 Lic 4hc (A 2hc) CTV 6P D8pm

SEVENOAKS Kent *Map 5 TQ55*
GH Sevenoaks Park Hotel 4 Seal Hollow Rd ☎54245 Lic 15hc 4⇌⋒ (A 3hc 1⇌⋒) 25P 3⌂ ᗰ S% B&b£9.77–£19.55 Bdi£17.17–£26.95 W£110–£144 D9.30pm

GH Moorings Hotel 97 Hitchen Hatch Ln ☎52589 Closed Xmas wk Lic 9hc 1⇌⋒ (A 2hc 2⇌⋒) CTV 25P ᗰ S% ✱B&b£7.56–£12.96

SHANKLIN Isle of Wight *Map 4 SZ58*
See Plan
GH Afton Hotel Clarence Gdns ☎3075 Plan:**1** Apr–mid Oct Lic 9hc 3⇌⋒ ⊗ nc5 CTV 8P ᗰ S% Bdi£10.18–£11.88 W£61.12–£71.30 Ł D4.30pm

GH Aqua Hotel The Esplanade ☎3024 Plan:**2** Etr–mid Oct Lic 23hc 2⇌⋒ ⊗ CTV 6P sea B&b£8.05–£8.97 Bdi£10.93–£12.08 W£69–£78.20 Ł D7pm

GH Berry Brow Hotel Popham Rd ☎2825 Plan:**3** Etr–Oct Lic 21hc ⊗ CTV 16P S% B&b£8 Bdi£10 W£61.50 Ł D6.30pm

⊢⊣**GH Culham Private Hotel** 31 Landguard Manor Rd ☎2880 Plan:**4** 10hc 2⇌⋒ nc12 CTV 5P ᗰ S% B&b£5–£7 Bdi£6.50–£8.50 W£42–£56 Ł D4pm

GH *Cumberland Hotel* 26 Arthur's Hill ☎3000 Plan:**5** May–Sep Lic 17hc ⊗ nc5 CTV 12P D5.30pm

GH Fern Bank Highfield Rd ☎2790 Plan:**6** Closed Xmas Lic 17hc 4⇌⋒ nc3 CTV 15P ᗰ S% ✱B&b£5.60–£6.50 Bdi£8.35–£9.60 W£58.50–£67 Ł D6.30pm

⊢⊣**GH Langthorne Private Hotel** 3 Witbank Gdns ☎2980 Plan:**7** Apr–Sep 12hc 1⇌⋒ nc5 CTV 12P ᗰ S% B&b£4.15–£5.15 Bdi£5.25–£6.50 W£34.50–£43.70 Ł D8pm

⊢⊣**GH Meyrick Cliffs** Esplanade ☎2691 Plan:**8** 26May–7Sep Lic 20hc 1⇌⋒ ⊗ nc7 CTV 5P sea B&b£6–£7 Bdi£8–£10 W£50–£54 Ł D6.30pm

GH Ocean View Hotel 38 The Esplanade ☎2602 Plan:**9** Lic 37hc 9⇌⋒ ♨ CTV 25P ♿ sea B&b£9.20–£11.50 Bdi£11.50–£13.80 W£79.35–£95.45 Ł D8pm

GH *Overstrand Private Hotel* Howard Rd ☎2100 Plan:**10** rs 6Oct–6Apr (B&b only) Lic 14hc (A 1hc) ⊗ nc3 CTV 16P ᗰ sea D5pm

GH Sandringham Hotel Hope Rd ☎3189 Plan:**11** Etr–mid Oct Lic 28hc TV P sea

SHAP Cumbria *Map 12 NY51*
⊢⊣**GH Brookfield** ☎397 Closed Xmas, New Year & Jan Lic 5hc ⊗ CTV 30P 6⌂ ᗰ S% B&b£5.50–£6 Bdi£9.50–£10.50 D8.15pm

SHAW Wilts *Map 3 ST86*
GH Shaw Farm ☎ Melksham 702836 Lic 10hc 1⇌⋒ ⊗ CTV 12P ᗰ B&b£8–£9.50 Bdi£12–£14 W£78–£90 Ł D5pm

SHEERNESS Kent *Map 5 TQ97*
⊢⊣**GH Victoriana** 107 Alma Rd ☎2685 5hc ♨ CTV 5P 2⌂ ᗰ S% B&b£5.95–£8.58

SHEFFIELD S Yorks *Map 8 SK38*
GH *Millingtons* 70 Broomgrove Rd (off A625 Eccleshall Rd) ☎669549 7hc CTV 4P ᗰ

GH Sharrow View Hotel 13 Sharrow View ☎51542 Lic 15hc CTV 22P ᗰ S% B&b£8.50 Bdi£11.50 D6.30pm

SHEPTON MALLET Somerset *Map 3 ST64*
INN *Bell Hotel* 3 High St ☎2166 4hc TV 4⌂ D10pm

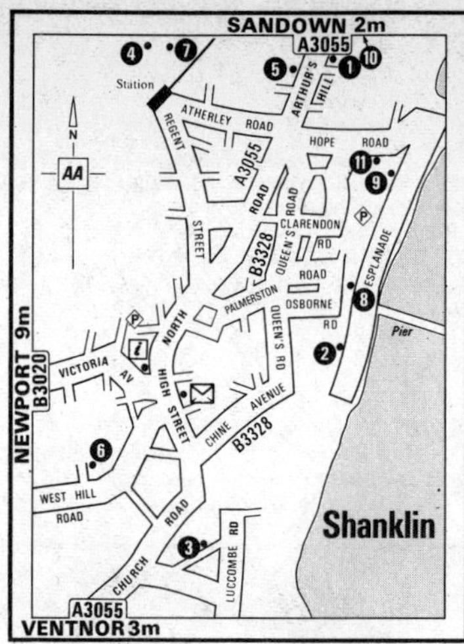

1 Afton Hotel	**7** Langthorne
2 Aqua Hotel	Private Hotel
3 Berry Brow Hotel	**8** Meyrick Cliffs
4 Culham Private	**9** Ocean View
Hotel	**10** Overstrand Hotel
5 Cumberland Hotel	**11** Sandringham
6 Fern Bank	Hotel

SHERFIELD ON LODDON Hants
Map 4 SU65
GH Wessex House Hotel ☎Turgis Green
243 Closed Xmas 8hc 8⇄🛁 CTV 14P
🍴 B&bfr£10

SHERINGHAM Norfolk *Map 9 TG14*
GH Beacon Hotel Nelson Rd ☎822019
Mar–Oct Lic 8hc ✗ nc5 CTV 10P 🍴 S%
B&b£7.50–£8 Bdi£11–£11.50
W£68–£73 ⊾ D6pm

⋈**GH Beeston Hills Lodge** 64 Cliff Rd
☎822615 May–Sep 6rm ✗ nc8 CTV
12P 🍴 sea S% B&bfr£5.60 Bdi fr£7.50
Wfr£48 ⊾

GH Camberley House Hotel 62 Cliff Rd
☎823101 May–Oct 9hc 🛁 CTV 12P 🍴
sea S% B&b£7–£8 Bdi£8.50–£10
W£50–£60 ⊾ (W only Jul–Aug) D7pm

GH *Crossways Hotel* 1 The Boulevard
☎823164 Apr–Oct Lic 21hc CTV 30P
D7pm

⋈**GH Melrose Hotel** 9 Holway Rd
☎823299 Mar–Oct rs Nov–Feb 10hc
nc8 TV 10P S% B&b£5.50–£6.50
Bdi£7–£7.50 W£46–£50 ⊾ D6pm

SHIPHAM Somerset *Map 3 ST45*
GH Penscot Farmhouse Hotel
☎ Winscombe 2659 Lic 10hc 2⇄🛁
(A 3hc) CTV 40P 🍴 sea B&b£6.90–£9.90
Bdi£9.90–£12.90 W£62–£83 ⊾ D9.30pm

SHIPSTON-ON-STOUR Warwicks
Map 4 SP24
INN Ye Olde White Bear Hotel High St
☎61558 Lic 9hc CTV 20P S% B&b£6–£7
W£42–£49 Ⓜ Bar lunch £2 alc
D9pm£5.50 alc

SHOREHAM-BY-SEA West Sussex
Map 4 TQ20
GH Pende-Shore Hotel 416 Upper
Shoreham Rd ☎2905 Lic 14hc 1⇄🛁 ✗
CTV 8P 🍴 B&b£7.70–£10 Bdi£11.70–
£14.00 W£81.90–£98 ⊾ D6pm

SHOTTENDEN Kent *Map 5 TR05*
GH Cona Goldups Ln ☎ Chilham 405
Lic 10hc 4⇄🛁 🛁 CTV 12P 🍴 B&b£6–
£8.50 Bdi£9.50–£11.50

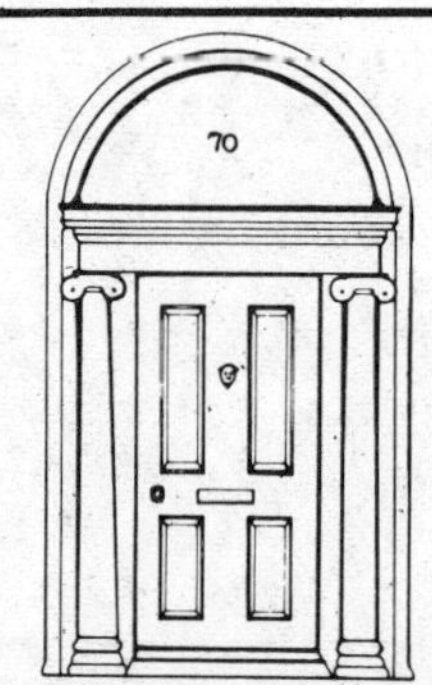

SHREWSBURY Salop *Map 7 SJ41*
GH Cannock House Private Hotel
182A Abbey Foregate ☎56043 7hc nc5
CTV 4P 🍴 S% B&b fr£4.50

GH Leagrove Hotel 29 Hereford Rd
☎52078 Lic 6hc CTV 8P 1🏠 S%
B&b£6.50 Bdi£9.80 D5.30pm

GH Shelton Hall Hotel ☎3982 Lic 15hc
6⇔🍴 CTV 50P 🍴 B&b fr£8.05 Bdi fr£12.08
W fr£104.65 ⅃ D9.30pm

SHUTE Devon *Map 3 SY29*
INN Shute Arms Hotel Seaton Junction
☎ Colyton 52276 Lic 5hc nc5 CTV 20P
S% B&b£6.25 Bar lunches 60p–£1.50

SIDMOUTH Devon *Map 3 SY18*
GH Canterbury Salcombe Rd ☎3373
Mar–Oct 6hc nc3 CTV 5P river S%
B&b£5.18–£6.33 Bdi£7.48–£9.78
W£48.30–£57.50 ⅃ D5.30pm

GH Mount Pleasant Hotel Salcombe Rd
☎4694 Etr–Sep Lic 13hc 7⇔🍴 CTV 20P
B&b£9 Bdi£11 W£77 ⅃ D6pm

GH Ryton House 52–54 Winslade Rd
☎3981 8hc CTV 8P 🍴 S% B&b£4–£4.50
Bdi fr£6.50 D6.30pm

GH Southernhay 3–4 Fortfield Ter
☎3189 18hc CTV sea S%
B&b£5.46–£6.24 Bdi£7.43–£8.61
W£51.68–£57.02 ⅃ D5pm

GH Westbourne Hotel Manor Rd ☎3774
Etr–2nd wk Oct Lic 13hc 7⇔🍴 (A 1hc)
CTV 14P B&b£6.60–£10.75
Bdi£10.50–£14 W£59.60–£82 ⅃
(W only Jun–Aug) D7pm

SKIPTON N Yorks *Map 7 SD95*
GH Highfield Hotel 58 Keighley Rd
☎3182 Closed Xmas & New Year Lic
10hc CTV S% B&b£7 Bdi£10.50 D7pm

- Comfortable accommodation with majestic Victorian decor.
- Specialists in wedding receptions, conferences and functions.
- Tourists welcome.
- Quietly situated near the sea-front and/shops.
- Bed & Breakfast, central heating and Colour TV. Open all year round, 7 days a week. Home cooking and friendly service. Morning Coffee and Cream Teas.

107 ALMA ROAD, SHEERNESS, KENT.
TEL: **SHEERNESS 2685**

Sharrow View Hotel

Sharrow View, Sheffield, S7 1ND

Warm, friendly atmosphere, excellent food and cosy cocktail bar — in a quiet district, 1½ miles from the City Centre. Bus service nearby.
20 rooms, all H & C. Lounge with colour TV. Central heating throughout. Large car park. Moderate terms.

Margaret Hargreaves, MHCIMA
Reservations : Sheffield (0742) 51542

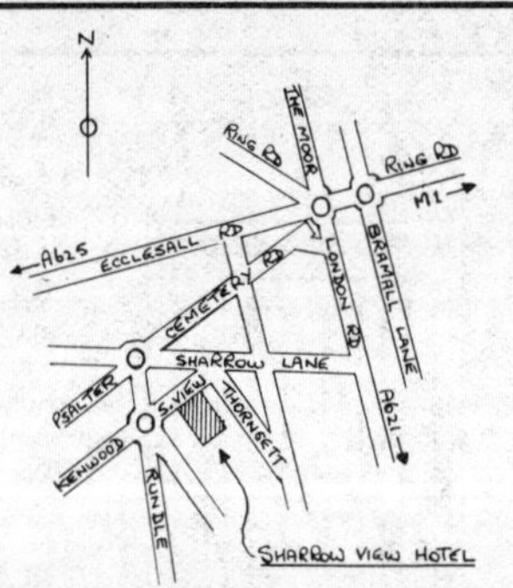

Camberley House Hotel
Sheringham

Telephone: 823101

A family hotel on the Norfolk Coast in an ideal, peaceful position with no passing traffic.
Situated in own grounds overlooking sea and putting green, opposite slipway to beach. Car parking space.
Babies and children heartily welcomed. Cots, high-chairs, washing facilities, babysitter evenings. Playground.
FIRE CERTIFICATE
Write or phone for tariff. *Proprietors:* **Graham and Andrea Simmons**
BB or BB & ED
Special rates family rooms. Reduced charges early and late season.
Bonus offer: one child free up to 5 yrs in September.

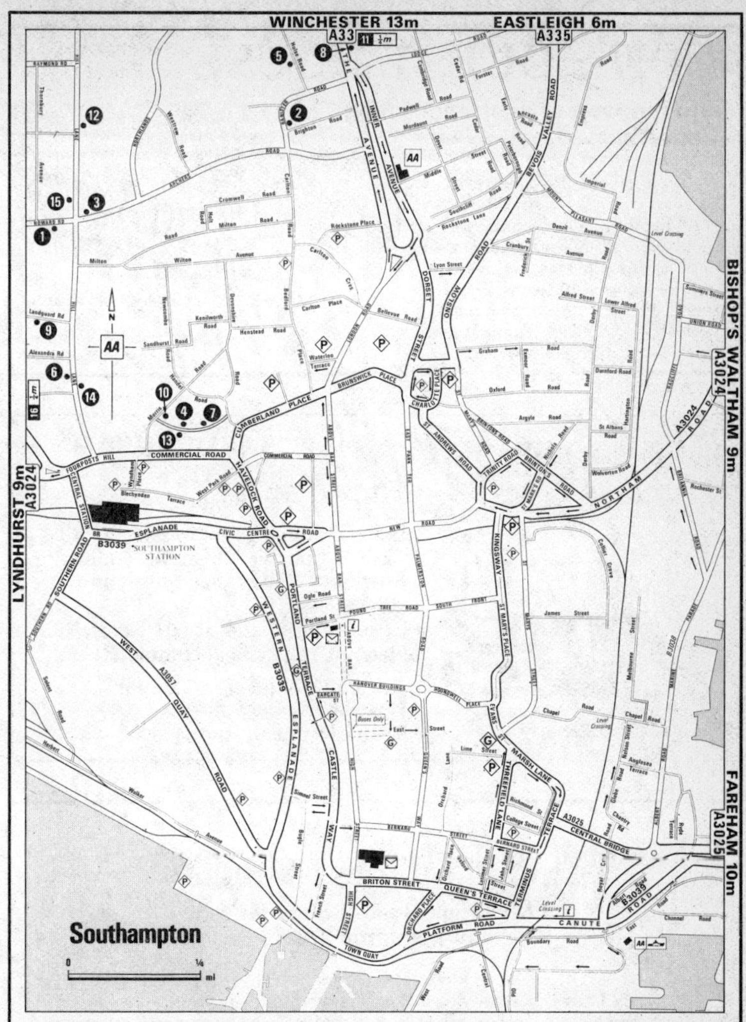

1 Amberley	**6** Eaton Court Hotel	**9** Hunters Lodge Hotel	**13** Polygon
2 Banister	**7** Eden Court	**10** Linden	**14** Rosida Hotel
3 Beacon	**8** Elizabeth House Hotel	**11** Lodge	**15** St Andrews
4 Claremont		**12** Madison House	**16** La Valle
5 County Hotel			

SNAPE Suffolk *Map 5 TM35*
INN *Crown* ☎324 Lic 4hc nc12 TV 50P ⊞ D8.45pm

SOUTHAMPTON Hants *Map 4 SU41*
See Plan
⊢⊣**GH Amberley** 1 Howard Rd ☎23789 Plan:**1** 8hc nc6 CTV 8P ⊞ S% B&b£4.50–£5.50 Bdi£7.50–£8.50 W£52.50–£59.50 D am
GH Banister 11 Brighton Rd ☎21279 Plan:**2** Lic 20hc CTV 14P ⊞ S% B&b£6.50 D7.30pm
⊢⊣**GH Beacon** 49 Archers Rd ☎25910 Plan:**3** Tem 6hc CTV 4P S% B&b£4–£4.25 Bdi£7–£7.25 W£47 D1pm
⊢⊣**GH Claremont** 33 The Polygon ☎23112 Plan:**4** 11hc TV 7P ⊞ S% B&b£4.50–£5 W£31.50 M
GH Country Hotel Hulse Rd ☎24236 Plan:**5** 15hc CTV 10P S% B&b£6.40–£7.46

GH Eaton Court Hotel 32 Hill Ln ☎23081 Plan:**6** Lic 17hc 4⇋🚿 CTV 14P ⊞ S% B&b£7.50–£8.50 Bdi£11–£12 D7pm
GH *Eden Court* 29–31 The Polygon ☎20540 Plan:**7** 19hc ✻ CTV 14P ⊞
GH Elizabeth House Hotel 43–44 The Avenue ☎24327 Plan:**8** Lic 17hc CTV 22P ⊞ S% B&b£7.40 Bdi£10 W£44.39 M D9pm
GH Hunters Lodge Hotel 25 Landguard Rd, Shirley ☎27919 Plan:**9** Lic 16hc ✻ CTV 14P 4🏠 ⊞ S% B&b£7.50 Bdi£11 W£70 Ŀ D6pm
⊢⊣**GH Linden** 51 The Polygon ☎25653 Plan:**10** Closed Xmas wk 10hc ✻ CTV 6P ⊞ S% B&b£4.25 £5.25
GH Lodge 1 Winn Rd, The Avenue ☎557537 Plan:**11** Closed Xmas wk 10hc CTV 8P ⊞ S% B&b£6–£7 Bdi£8.50 £9.50 D noon

⋈**GH Madison House** 137 Hill Ln
☎22374 Plan:**12** 9hc TV 15P 1🏠 S%
B&b£4.50–£5.50

GH Polygon 40 The Polygon ☎28162
Plan:**13** 17hc ⊗ nc5 TV 6P 🍴 S%
✳B&b£4.50–£5

GH *Rosida* 25–27 Hill Ln ☎28501
Plan:**14** Closed Xmas wk Lic 36hc CTV
26P 🍴 D7.30pm

⋈**GH St Andrews** 128 Hill Ln ☎21140
Plan:**15** Lic 11hc ⊗ nc8 TV 7P 🍴 S%
B&b£4.50 Bdi£9 D8pm

⋈**GH La Valle** 111 Millbrook Rd ☎27821
Plan:**16** Closed Xmas 6hc CTV 6P 🍴
S% B&b£3.75

SOUTHEND-ON-SEA Essex *Map 5 TQ88*
GH Cobham Lodge Private Hotel
2 Cobham Rd, Westcliff-on-Sea ☎46438
Lic 15hc ♨ CTV 🍴 sea S%
B&b£6.50–£7.50 Bdi£9.50–£10.50
W£61–£70 D10pm

GH Ferndown Hotel 136 York Rd
☎68614 Lic 14hc CTV 12P 🍴 S%
B&b£6 Bdi£9 D3pm

⋈**GH Gladstone** 40 Hartington Rd
☎62776 Closed Xmas 7hc ⊗ nc3 CTV
🍴 S% B&b£5.50–£6.50 Bdi£7.50–£9
W£36.50–£43.50 M D am

GH Haven Private Hotel 32–34 Burgess
Rd, Thorpe Bay ☎585085 Lic 17hc ♨
CTV 10P 🍴 S% B&b£8.25 Bdi£10.25
D7pm

GH Maple Leaf Private Hotel
9–11 Trinity Av, Westcliff-on-Sea ☎46904
Lic 16hc CTV 🍴 S% B&b£7.50–£8
Bdi£10.20–£11.10 W£62.20–£66.50
⌁·D6pm

⋈**GH Marine View** 4 Trinity Av,
Westcliff-on-Sea ☎44104 6hc ⊗ CTV 🍴
S% B&b£5.50–£6 Bdi£7.50–£8.20
W£45–£50 ⌁ D4.30pm

⋈**GH Mayfair** 52 Crowstone Av,
Westcliff-on-Sea ☎40693 Closed Xmas
6hc ⊗ nc5 CTV 4P 🍴 S% B&b£4.75–£5.25
Bdi£6.50–£7 W£34–£37.50 ⌁ D3pm

GH Miramare Hotel 84 Station Rd,
Westcliff-on-Sea ☎44022 Closed Xmas Day
Lic 8hc 2⊷🚿 ♨ CTV 3P 🍴 river S%
✳B&b£6 Bdi£9 W£58 ⌁ D7.45pm

GH Pavillion 1 Trinity Av,
Westcliff-on-Sea ☎41007 Closed Xmas
8hc CTV 🍴 B&b£6.50 Bdi£9.65 W£57.50
⌁ D4pm

⋈**GH Terrace Hotel** 8 Royal Ter ☎48143
Closed Xmas Lic 9hc ⊗ CTV sea S%
B&b£5.50 W£38.50 M

GH West Park Private Hotel 11 Park Rd,
Westcliff-on-Sea ☎330729 Lic 11hc
6⊷🚿 ♨ CTV 16P 🍴 B&b£9.50 Bdi£12.50
D4pm

SOUTH LUFFENHAM Leics *Map 4 SK90*
INN *Boot & Shoe* ☎ Stamford 720177
Lic 4rm 3hc ⊗ TV 20P 🍴 sn D9.30pm

SOUTHPORT Merseyside *Map 7 SD31*
See Plan
⋈**GH Abbey Hotel** 6 Lathom Rd ☎38430
Plan:**1** 11hc ⊗ CTV 10P 🍴 lake sea S%
B&b£4.55–£5.56 Bdi£6.70–£7.71
W£46–£53 ⌁ D4pm

⋈**GH Cumberland Hotel** 43 Promenade
☎30970 Plan:**2** Lic 11hc 3⊷🚿 CTV 10P
lake S% B&b£5.94–£6.43
Bdi£8.10–£9.67 W£54–£64.80 ⌁
(W only Jul & Aug) D4pm

**Maple Leaf
Private. Hotel**

9/11 Trinity Avenue, Westcliff On Sea,
Essex SSO 7PU

Tel: Southend (0702) 46904
   – Guests 40282
On bus routes from Westcliff and
Southend Stations. Near Cliff Gardens,
Pavilion and Bandstage. Frequent train
service to London. Comfort, excellent
food and service. English Breakfast.
Full Central Heating. Street Parking.
Open throughout the year.

Fully licensed. Open to non-residents.

Members of the Southend and Essex Hotel
and Catering Association.

Resident Proprietors: Mr & Mrs F J Goodhew

The Boot and Shoe Inn 10 The Street, South Luffenham, Rutland LE15 8NX

This charming 18th-century Inn is situated in a
picturesque village surrounded by rolling countryside. Four miles from Rutland Water (trout fishing
and sailing) and within easy distance of golf course,
tennis courts, country walks and horse riding
stables. The Inn has public bar, lounge bar and
attractive restaurant with an inglenook fireplace.
Accommodation is very pleasant in country style.
In summer you may drink in the beer garden or
patio. In the bars, the owners are proud to be able to
serve real, traditional English Ale at very reasonable prices. (Residential guests will receive a free
pint on arrival).

Coming from Leicester, on the A47, turn left at Morcott to South Luffenham and turn left at the
sign to the Inn. Approaching from the south (on the A1) go through Stamford and proceed
through Ketton until you approach South Luffenham and then turn right at the sign.
Accommodation available: 2 twin, one double and one single. 2 bathrooms, both with toilet.
Telephone: Stamford (0780) 720177.

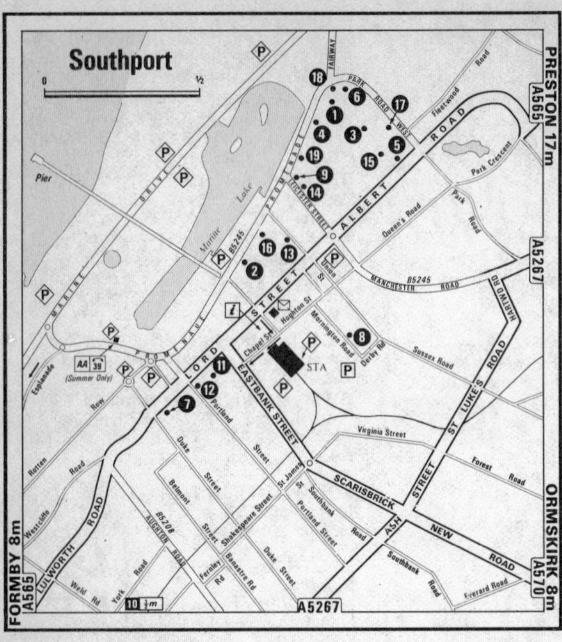

GH *Fairway Private Hotel* 106 Leyland Rd ☎42069 Plan:**3** Mar–Oct Lic 9hc CTV 20P 泗 W only Jul & Aug D6.30pm

GH Fernley Private Hotel 69 The Promenade ☎35610 Plan:**4** Lic 22hc 1⇔🍽 CTV 12P lake sea B&bf6.90 Bdif9.20 Wf54.05 ⊬ D6pm

⊢⊣GH Fulwood Private Hotel 82 Leyland Rd ☎30993 Plan:**5** Lic 12hc CTV 7P 泗 S% B&bf4.60 Bdif7.47 Wf63.25 D4pm

GH *Garden Hotel* 19 Lathom Rd ☎30244 Plan:**6** Lic 10hc CTV 2P 1🏠 泗 D6pm

⊢⊣GH Glenwood Private Hotel 98–102 King St ☎35068 Plan:**7** Lic 14hc CTV 8P 泗 B&bf4.86 Bdif7.02 Wf43.20 ⊬ (W only Jul–Aug) D2pm

⊢⊣GH Hollies Private Hotel 7 Mornington Rd ☎30054 Plan:**8** 17hc 4⇔🍽 ⊗ CTV 17P 泗 S% B&bf5.75–f6.70 Bdif8.30–f9.55 Wf54–f62 ⊬ D1pm

⊢⊣GH Knowsley Private Hotel Promenade, 2 Knowsley Rd ☎30190 Plan:**9** Closed Oct Lic 14hc TV 14P 泗 S% B&bf4.86 Bdif7.56 Wf52.92 ⊬ D6pm

GH *Lockerbie House Hotel* 11 Trafalgar Rd, Birkdale ☎66692 Plan:**10** Lic 10hc ⊗ nc12 CTV 9P 1🏠

⊢⊣GH Newnholme 51 King St ☎30425 Plan:**11** 6hc nc3 CTV 2P 泗 S% B&bf5–f6 Bdif6.50–f8 Wf45.50–f56 ⊬ D5.30pm

GH Oakwood Private Hotel 7 Portland St ☎31858 Plan:**12** Etr–Sep 8hc ⊗ nc5 CTV 6P 泗 S% B&bf6 Bdif8.50

⊢⊣GH Ocean Bank 16 Bank Sq, Central Prom ☎30637 Plan:**13** 7hc ⊗ CTV 3P 泗 S% B&bf3.50 Bdif5 Wf33 ⊬ D3pm

GH *Savoia Hotel* 37 Leicester St ☎30559 Plan:**14** Lic 14hc CTV 10P 泗 lake sea D2pm

GH Sunningdale Hotel 85 Leyland Rd ☎30042 Plan:**15** Closed Xmas & New Year Lic 14rm 13hc 4⇔🍽 ⊗ CTV 10P 泗 S% B&bf6.62–f7.77 Bdif10.06–f11.22 Wf66.42–f74.47 ⊬ D5pm

⊢⊣GH Westhaven 22 Bank Sq ☎30219 Plan:**16** Closed 2wks Oct Lic 7rm ⊗ nc5 ⚘ CTV 2P S% B&bf3.25–f3.75 Bdif4.50–f5.25 Wf31.50–f36.75 ⊬ D4.30pm

GH Whitworth Falls Hotel 16 Lathom Rd
☎30074 Plan:**18** Lic 14hc CTV 10P S%
✱B&bf£6.62 Bdi£9.20 W£55.20 ⌁ D6pm

GH Windsor Lodge Hotel 37 Saunders St
☎30070 Plan:**19** Closed 2wks late Nov
Lic 12hc 1⇱🛏 ⊗ CTV 9P S%
B&bf£6.50–£7.50 Bdi£9.50–£10.50
W£55–£60 ⌁ D6pm

SOUTHREPPS Norfolk *Map 9 TG23*
GH Forge Upper St ☎267 5rm 4hc ⊗
nc8 CTV 1P 3🕾 🍴 S% ✱B&bfr£4.75
Bdifr£6.75 Wfr£43.75 ⌁ D6.30pm

SOUTHSEA Hants see **PORTSMOUTH
& SOUTHSEA**

SOUTH TAWTON Devon *Map 3 SX69*
⋈**INN Seven Stars** ☎ Stickle Path 292
Lic 4hc CTV 4P 🍴 S% B&bf£5.50–£6
W£42.35 Ⓜ D10.15pm

SOUTHWOLD Suffolk *Map 5 TM57*
GH Craighurst Hotel ☎723115
Closed Jan–Feb Lic 18hc CTV 6P
B&bf£8–£11 Bdi£10–£14 W£65–£75
⌁ D5pm

⋈**GH Mount** North Parade ☎722292
Closed Xmas 7hc ⊗ TV 🍴 sea
B&bf£5.95–£6.90 W£34.92–£43.70 Ⓜ

SOUTH ZEAL Devon *Map 3 SX69*
GH Poltimore ☎ Sticklepath 209 Lic 7hc
nc7 CTV 12P 🍴 B&bf£6.50–£7
Bdi£10.50–£11 W£63–£67 ⌁
W only Jun–15Sep D2pm

SPREYTON Devon *Map 3 SX79*
INN Tom Cobley Tavern ☎ Whiddon
Down 314 Apr–Sep Lic 4hc CTV 20P 🍴
S% B&bf£3.50–£4 W£24–£28 Ⓜ
Bar lunch 20–50p

STAFFORD Staffs *Map 7 SJ92*
⋈**GH *Leonards Croft Hotel*** 80 Lichfield
Rd ☎3676 12hc (A 6hc) CTV 16P 🍴
INN Royal Oak Rising Brook ☎58402
Lic 12hc CTV 250P 🍴 ✱B&bf£7 sn
L£2.65–£5&alc D10pm£2.65–£5&alc

STAINTON Cumbria *Map 12 NY42*
⋈**GH Limes Country Hotel** Redhills
☎ Penrith 63343 8hc ⊗ CTV 12P 🍴
B&bfr£5.18 Bdifr£7.77 Wfr£52.32 ⌁
D6pm

STAMFORD Lincs *Map 4 TF00*
GH St Martin's ☎3359 Closed Xmas Day

& New Year Lic 10hc CTV 3P 7🕾 🍴
B&bfr£7

STANFORD LE HOPE Essex *Map 5 TQ68*
⋈**GH Homesteads** 216 Southend Rd
☎2372 Closed 2wks Xmas Lic 11hc ⊗
CTV 8P 2🕾 🍴 S% B&bf£5–£6 Bdif£7–£8
W£49 ⌁ D5.30pm

STICKLEPATH Devon *Map 2 SX69*
INN *Taw River* ☎377 Lic 6hc CTV 25P
3🕾 sn D9.30pm

STITHIANS Cornwall *Map 2 SW73*
GH Crellow Country House Hotel
☎860523 Etr–Oct Lic 9hc CTV 15P S%
B&bf£6.20–£7 Bdi£9.50–£10.30
W£61.60–£64.90 ⌁ D8.30pm

STOCKBRIDGE Hants *Map 4 SU33*
GH Carbery Salisbury Hill ☎771
Closed 2wks Jan Lic 11hc ⊗ CTV 12P 🍴
river S% B&bf£6.50 Bdi£9.50 Wfr£65 ⌁
D6pm

STOKEINTEIGNHEAD Devon
Map 3 SX97
⋈**GH Bailey's Farm** ☎ Shaldon 3361
Apr–Sep 10hc TV 8P S% B&bf£4–£5
Bdi£6.50–£7.50 W£44.50–£50 ⌁
W only Jul & Aug D7pm
⋈**GH Santa Rosa** ☎ Shaldon 2607
6hc CTV 6P 🍴 S% B&bf£4–£5 Bdi£7–£8
W£42–£49 ⌁ D6pm

STONE Glos *Map 3 ST69*
GH Elms ☎ Falfield 279 (260279 from
Jan 1980) Lic 8hc CTV 12P 2🕾 🍴 S%
✱B&bf£6.50 Bdi£9 D4pm

STOURBRIDGE W Midlands *Map 7 SO98*
GH Limes 260 Hagley Rd, Pedmore
☎ Hagley 882689 10hc ⊗ CTV 12P 🍴
S% B&bf£8

STOURPORT-ON-SEVERN Heref &
Worcs *Map 7 SO87*
⋈**INN Angel Hotel** Severnside ☎2661
Lic 5hc CTV 40P 🍴 river S% B&bf£5 Bdif£8
sn L£1–£4&alc D9pm£3–£5.50

STOW-ON-THE-WOLD Glos *Map 4 SP12*
GH Parkdene Hotel Sheep St ☎30344
Closed Xmas & Jan Lic 11hc 2⇱🛏 CTV 🍴
S% B&bfr£7.51 Bdifr£11 Wfr£77 ⌁
D9.30pm

GH Old Farmhouse Hotel Lower Swell
(1m W A436) ☎30232 Closed Xmas
Eve–mid Jan Lic 5hc 2⇱🛏 ⊗ TV 15P 🍴
S% B&bfr£9.90 Bdifr£16.40 Wfr£114.75
⌁ D8.45pm

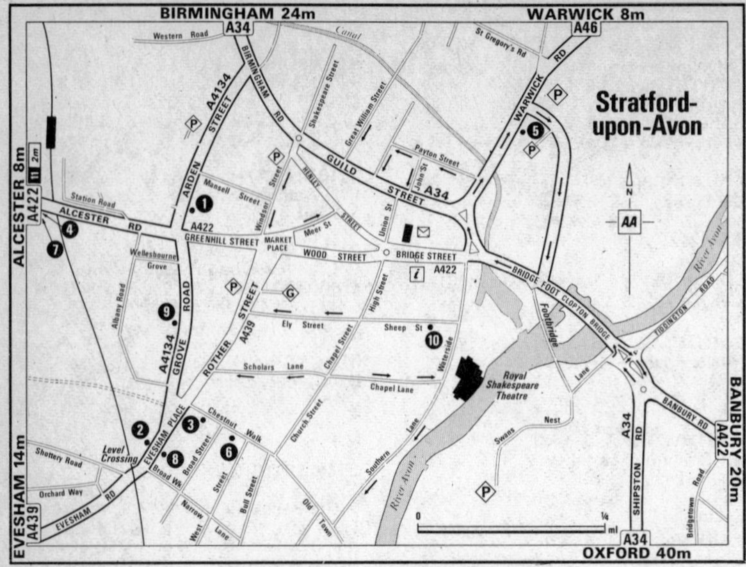

1 Argos Hotel	**4** Hunter's Moon	**7** Moonraker House	**10** Stratford House Hotel
2 Avon House	**5** Hylands Hotel	**8** Penshurst	
3 Glenavon Private Hotel	**6** Marlyn	**9** Salamander	**11** Wildmoor

STRATFORD-UPON-AVON Warwicks
Map 4 SP25 **See Plan**
⊫◄**GH Argos Hotel** 5 Arden St ☎4321
Plan:**1** Closed Xmas 9hc ⊗ nc10 TV 📺
S% B&b£5.50–£6

⊫◄**GH Avon House** 8 Evesham Pl
☎293328 Plan:**2** 8hc CTV 1🏠 📺
B&b£4.50–£5.25

⊫◄**GH Glenavon Private Hotel**
Chestnut Walk ☎292588 Plan:**3** 11hc TV
6P 📺 S% B&b£5–£6.50

⊫◄**GH Hunters Moon** 150 Alcester Rd
☎292888 Plan:**4** 6hc CTV 6P 📺 S%
B&b£4.50–£5.50

GH Hylands Hotel Warwick Rd ☎297962
Plan:**5** Lic 12hc 10🛏📶 ⊗ CTV 20P 📺 S%
B&b£8.80–£10.17 Bdi£13.20–£14.27
D6pm

⊫◄**GH Marlyn** 3 Chestnut Walk ☎293752
Plan:**6** Closed Xmas 8hc ⊗ TV 📺 S%
B&b£4.60–£7.30

⊫◄**GH Moonraker House** 40 Alcester Rd
☎67115 Plan:**7** 7hc 4🛏📶 CTV 8P 📺
S% B&b£4–£5.50 Bdi£7–£8 D previous day

⊫◄**GH Penshurst** 34 Eversham Pl ☎5259
Plan:**8** 8hc CTV P 📺 S% B&b£4.50–£5.25

⊫◄**GH Salamander** 40 Grove Rd ☎5728
Plan:**9** 6hc TV 📺 S% B&b£4.75–£5.50

GH Stratford House Hotel Sheep St
☎68288 Plan:**10** Lic 10hc 8🛏📶 CTV 📺
S% B&b£10–£12.50

INN Wildmoor Alcester Rd ☎67063
Plan:**11** Lic 7hc 1🛏📶 CTV 50P S%
B&b£7.50–£11 sn L£5alc D10pm£5alc

STREET Somerset *Map 3 ST43*
GH *Houndswood Villa Hotel*
13 Farm Rd ☎42983 Lic 6hc (A 6hc) CTV
4P 📺 D4pm

STRETE Devon *Map 3 SX84*
⊫◄**GH Highcliff** ☎ Stoke Fleming 307
Etr–Oct Lic 10hc 1🛏📶 CTV 10P S%
B&b fr£4.70 Bdi fr£7 Wfr£49 ⌁ D6pm

GH *Tallis Rock Private Hotel* ☎ Stoke
Fleming 370 May–Sep 9hc CTV 6P 1🏠 sea

STRETTON Leics *Map 8 SK91*
INN Olde Greetham Hotel ☎ Castle

Broad Marston Manor
Broad Marston, Nr Stratford-upon-Avon, Warwickshire

12th-century, Cotswold stone Manor House
and out-buildings of historic interest, set in
its own 5 acres of delightful grounds and
gardens in a quiet, peaceful hamlet midway
between Stratford-upon-Avon and the
beautiful Cotswold Country. Retains its
12th-century character within and without,
unspoilt but with its beamed interior offers
complete relaxation and comfort.
SAE to Mrs E V Rochfort.
**Tel: Stratford-upon-Avon
(STD 0789) 720252.**
Moderate terms: bed and breakfast.

Bytham 365 Lic 5hc 40P 🍴 S%
✳B&bfr£6.52 sn L£1.95–£3&alc
D9pm£3.50alc

STROUD Glos *Map 3 SO80*
GH Downfield Private Hotel Caincross Rd
☎4496 Lic 17hc 3⊐🛉 CTV 20P 🍴 S%
B&b£6.32 Bdifr£8.80 W£50 ⚡ D8pm

STUKELEY, GREAT Cambs *Map 4 TL27*
GH Stukeley ☎ Huntingdon 56927
8hc CTV 10P 🍴 S% B&b£6.25 Bdi£10.25
D9pm

SUDBURY Suffolk *Map 5 TL84*
INN *White Horse Hotel* North St ☎72340
Lic 5hc ⊗ CTV 20P sn D10.30pm

SUNDERLAND Tyne & Wear
Map 12 NZ35

GH St Annes Private Hotel 1 Northcliff,
Roker Ter ☎72649 rs Xmas & New Year
Lic 12hc CTV 12P 🍴 sea B&b£6.48–£7.50
D9pm

SURBITON Gt London *Map 4 TQ16*
GH *Dalton Private Hotel* 317 Ewell Rd,
Tolworth ☎01-399 8663 15hc CTV 8P 🍴

GH Holmdene 23 Cranes Dr
☎01-399 9992 Closed 1wk Xmas
6hc nc5 CTV 🍴 S% B&bfr£6

GH *Villiers Lodge* 1 Cranes Pk
☎01-399 6000 6hc ⊗ CTV 6P

GH *Warwick* 321 Ewell Rd
☎01-399 5837 9hc CTV 4P 1🏠 🍴

SUTTON Gt London *Map 4 TQ26*
GH Dene Private Hotel 39 Cheam Rd
☎01-642 3170 17rm 14hc 2⊐🛉 ⊗ nc5
TV 8P 🍴 S% B&b£8.05–£17.25

Moonraker House

**40 Alcester Road,
Stratford-upon-Avon,
Warwickshire Tel: 67115**
Moonraker Guesthouse is 5 minutes' walk
from the perfect centre for exploring
Warwick and Kenilworth Castles, Coventry
Cathedral and all the attractions of the
Shakespeare countryside.
All rooms have central heating, H & C and
coffee/tea making facilities. Some have
showers and TV. There is a comfortable
lounge/dining room with colour TV
for residents.

PENSHURST GUEST HOUSE

34 Evesham Place, Stratford-upon-Avon
Tel: Stratford-upon-Avon 5259

Ideally situated for the Theatre and for touring the Cotswolds.
Penshurst offers friendly and comfortable accommodation with a first
class, full English breakfast.
Also included are colour TV lounge; dining room with separate tables;
bath and showers and private parking.
Full central heating. H & C all rooms.

"Salamander"
Guest House

**40 Grove Road, Stratford-upon-Avon, Warwickshire
Tel: Stratford-upon-Avon 5728**

Bed and breakfast. Hot and cold all rooms. Full Central
heating. TV lounge. Shower room.

Few minutes from theatre and historic buildings.

Proprietress: Mrs J Copestick.

GH Eaton Court Hotel 49 Eaton Rd
☎01-642 4580 Closed Xmas Lic 12hc
nc2 CTV 8P ⅏ S% ✱B&b£6.50 W£45.50
Ⓜ

GH Thatched House Hotel 135 Cheam
Rd ☎01-642 3131 Lic 18hc 6⇄🖩 CTV
12P ⅏ S% B&b£10 Bdi£14 W£70
D6.30pm

SUTTON COLDFIELD W Midlands
Map 7 SP19
For location see Birmingham Plan
GH Cloverley Hotel 17 Anchorage Rd
☎021-354 5181 Not on plan Lic 18🖩
14P ⅏ B&b£9–£16 Bdi£12–£19 D8pm
GH Standbridge Hotel 138 Birmingham
Rd ☎021-354 3007 Birmingham plan:**5**
Closed 1wk Xmas Lic 8hc (A 1hc) CTV 11P
⅏ S% B&b£8.25 Bdi£10.85 W£75.95
Ł D noon

SWANAGE Dorset *Map 4 SZ07*
GH Boyne Hotel Cliff Av ☎2939
Mar–Oct Lic 15hc 1⇄🖩 nc3 CTV 7P sea
B&b£6.50–£7.02 Bdi£7–£8.10
W£43.20–£53.46 Ł (W only Jul & Aug)
D5.30pm
⊨GH Byways** 5 Ulwell Rd ☎2322
mid May–mid Sep 11hc nc6 CTV 4P S%
B&b£5.50–£6 Bdi£7.70–£8.50
W£46–£49 (W only Jun, Jul & Aug)
D6.30pm
⊨GH Castleton Private Hotel** Highcliff
Rd ☎3972 Feb–Oct Lic 12hc nc3 CTV 8P
⅏ sea S% B&b£4.86–£6.48
Bdi£6.48–£8.64 W£45.36–£54 Ł D5pm
GH Eversden Private Hotel Victoria Rd
☎3276 Lic 10hc 3⇄🖩 ⊗ nc3 CTV 10P ⅏
S% ✱B&b£5.17–£6.33 Bdi£7.48–£8.63
W£51.75 D4pm
⊨GH Golden Sands Private Hotel**
10 Ulwell Rd ☎2093 5Jan–12Dec Lic
11hc 6⇄🖩 ⊗ CTV 14P ⅏ sea
B&b£4.50–£6 Bdi£6.50–£7.50
W£42–£58 Ł (W only Jun & Aug)
D6.30pm
GH Havenhurst Hotel 3 Cranbourne Rd
☎4224 Mar–Oct Lic 16hc 1⇄🖩 CTV 16P
⅏ B&b£6.75–£7.75 Bdi£10–£11
W£62.50–£68.50 Ł D6.30pm
GH Horseshoe House Hotel Cliff Av
☎2194 Lic 9hc nc10 CTV 5P ⅏ S%
B&b£6–£7 Bdi£8.50–£10 W£52.50–£60
Ł D9.30pm
⊨GH Ingleston Private Hotel** 2 Victoria
Rd ☎2391 Apr–Oct Lic 8hc ⊗ CTV 10P
S% B&b£5.50–£6.50 Bdi£8–£9.50
W£47.42–£52.92 Ł D5pm

GH Oxford Hotel 3–5 Park Rd ☎2247
Closed Nov & Xmas 14hc ⊗ nc2 CTV S%
B&b£6 Bdi£8.50 W£54.30 Ł D6.30pm
⊨GH Tower Lodge Private Hotel**
17 Ulwell Rd ☎2887 Mar–Nov Lic 11hc
2⇄🖩 ⊗ CTV 9P S% B&b£5.72–£6.71
Bdi£7.92–£8.91 W£47.52–£53.46 Ł
D5pm
GH Westbury Hotel 6 Rempstone Rd
☎2345 Etr–Oct Lic 20hc CTV 12P sea
B&b£6.20–£7.30 Bdi£8.50–£9.80
W£50–£63 Ł D7.15pm

SWYNNERTON Staffs *Map 7 SJ83*
INN Fitzherbert Arms ☎241 Lic 5hc
(A 9hc 5⇄🖩) CTV 100P 7🏠 ⅏ S%
B&b£6.50–£8 D9.30pm

SYMONDS YAT, EAST Heref & Worcs
Map 3 SO51
GH Garth Cottage Hotel ☎890364
Etr–Oct Lic 7hc 2⇄🖩 CTV 7P ⅏ river S%
B&b£6.90–£8 Bdi£10.65–£12.25
W£70.30–£82 Ł D6pm

SYMONDS YAT, WEST nr Ross-on-Wye
Heref & Worcs *Map 3 SO51*
GH Woodlea ☎890206 10rm 9hc 1⇄🖩
CTV 9P ⅏ river S% ✱B&b£4.50–£6.50
Bdi£7.50–£9.50 D7pm

TADCASTER N Yorks *Map 8 SE44*
GH Shann House 47 Kirkgate ☎833931
8⇄🖩 CTV 8P ⅏ lift B&b£10 W£70 Ⓜ

TALLAND BAY Cornwall *Map 2 SX25*
GH Newton House Hotel Sclerder Ln
☎Polperro 413 Lic 8hc ⊗ ♨ CTV 12P sea
D7.30pm

TARPORLEY Cheshire *Map 7 SJ56*
GH Perth Hotel High St ☎2514 Lic 9hc
2⇄🖩 CTV 12P ⅏ B&b£9 Bdi£12–£13.60
D9pm

TAUNTON Somerset *Map 3 ST22*
GH Brookfield House 16 Wellington Rd
☎2786 Closed 24Dec–2Jan 7hc CTV 7P ⅏
GH Meryan House Hotel Bishops Hull
☎87445 Lic 8hc ♨ 20P ⅏ S%
B&b£6–£7 Bdi£9–£10.50 D7pm
⊨GH White Lodge** 81 Bridgwater Rd
☎3287 10hc ⊗ CTV 15P ⅏ S% B&b£10
Bdi£14 W£90 Ł D7.30pm

TAVISTOCK Devon *Map 2 SX47*
⊨GH Cherrytrees** 40 Plymouth Rd
☎3070 5hc ⊗ TV 1P 4🏠 S%
B&b£5.50–£6.50

TEIGNMOUTH Devon *Map 3 SX97*
GH Bay Cottage Hotel 7 Marine Pde,
Shaldon ☎2394 Mar–Oct Lic 8hc ⌖
CTV 4P ⸙ river sea B&b£6.50–£7
Bdi£9–£9.50 W£60–£63 ⸗ D5pm

GH Bay Hotel Sea Front ☎4123
Closed Nov, Jan & Feb Lic 20hc CTV 14P
sea S% B&b£6.50–£7.50 Bdi£9–£10
W£48.60–£58.50 ⸗ D7pm

⊶**GH Glen Devon** 3 Carlton Pl ☎2895
8hc ⌖ CTV 8P ⸙ S% B&b£5–£6
Bdi£6–£7.50 W£38–£50 ⸗ D5pm

GH Hillsley Upper Hermonsa Rd ☎3878
May–Sep Lic 7hc nc3 CTV 10P river sea
S% B&b£6.50–£7 Bdi£9.50–£10
W£39–£43 ⸗ D6pm

⊶**GH Leafield** 61 Dawlish Rd ☎2986
May–Oct 6hc nc5 CTV 6P ⸙ river sea S%
B&b£4–£5 W£26–£32.50

GH *New Strathearn Hotel* Bitton Park Rd
☎2796 Closed Xmas Lic 11hc ⌖ CTV 10P
sea S% D6.30pm

⊶**GH Ocean View Hotel** Sea Front
☎2953 10hc CTV ⸙ sea B&b£5–£6.70
Bdi£7.40–£9.10 W£45.50–£55.50 ⸗
D2pm

⊶**GH Overstowey Hotel** Dawlish Rd
☎4251 rs Oct–Apr (B&b only) Lic 10hc ⌖
CTV 10P ⸙ S% B&b£5.92–£6.33
Bdi£7.08–£7.48 W£49.50–£52.33 ⸗
W only May–Oct D6pm

⊶**GH Thornhill Hotel** Sea Front ☎3460
Etr–mid Oct Lic 12hc CTV 3P sea
B&b£5.50–£7.50 Bdi£7–£9 W£36–£44
⸗ D6.30pm

GH Westlands Hotel Reed Vale ☎3007
Lic 16hc 5⇱🛆 CTV 16P river S%
✻B&b£4–£5 Bdi£5.40–£6.50
W£33–£41.50 ⸗ D7pm

TEWKESBURY Glos *Map 3 SO83*
GH South End House 67 Church St
☎294097 8hc CTV 3P ⸙ S% B&bfr£7

THORNTHWAITE *(Nr Keswick)* Cumbria
Map 11 NY22
GH Ladstock Country House Hotel
☎ Braithwaite 210 Mar–Nov Lic 18hc
1⇱🛆 ⌖ CTV 20P ⸙ S% B&bfr£8 Bdifr£12
Wfr£74 ⸗ D6pm

THORNTON CLEVELEYS Lancs
Map 7 SD34
GH *Lyndhope* 2 Stockdove Way, Cleveleys
☎ Cleveleys 852531 6hc ⌖ nc3 CTV 8P
⸙ D3pm

THORNTON HEATH Gt London
Map 4 TQ36

⊶**GH Clock House Hotel** 47 Brigstock
Rd ☎01-684 8480 12hc CTV 7P ⸙
S% B&b£5.40

THORPE BAY Essex see **SOUTHEND-
ON-SEA**

THORVERTON Devon *Map 3 SS90*
GH Berribridge ☎ Silverton 259
Lic 6hc 1⇱🛆 CTV 5P 1🏠 ⸙
B&b£7–£9.25 D9pm

THURLESTONE SANDS Devon
Map 3 SX64
GH La Mer ☎ Galmpton 207 Etr–15Sep
Lic 10hc nc5 CTV 10P sea S%
B&b£7.50–£8.50 Bdi£11–£13
W£74–£80 ⸗ D7pm

TICEHURST E Sussex *Map 5 TQ63*
INN Bell Hotel The Square ☎200234
Lic 3hc ⌖ nc3 30P ⸙ ⇒ B&b£6.50
L£3.50alc D9.30pm£3.50alc

TICKENHAM Avon *Map 3 ST47*
INN Star ☎ Nailsea 2071 Lic 4hc ⌖
nc14 CTV 60P S% B&b£6 Bdi£8 W£56

TIDEFORD Cornwall *Map 2 SX35*
⊶**GH Kilna House** ☎ Landrake .236
Closed Xmas Lic 6hc CTV 8P S%
B&b£5–£5.50 Bdi£8–£9 W£35–£56 ⸗

TINTAGEL Cornwall *Map 2 SX08*
GH Halgabron House ☎667 Etr–Oct Lic
5hc ♨ CTV 6P sea S% B&b£6 Bdi£9.50
W£49–£56 ⸗ W only Jul & Aug D3pm

GH Penallick Hotel Treknow ☎296
Lic 10hc 1⇱🛆 CTV 14P ⸙ sea S%
B&b£6–£8 Bdi£8–£9.50 W£49–£59 ⸗
W only Jul & Aug D6.30pm

GH Trebrea Lodge Trenale ☎410
Apr–mid Oct Lic 8hc 1⇱🛆 CTV 10P ⸙
sea S% ✻B&b£5 Bdi£8 W£45–£50 ⸗
D6.30pm

TIVERTON Devon *Map 3 SS91*
GH *Bridge* 23 Angel Hill ☎2804
5Jan–12Oct Lic 10hc CTV ⸙ river D5pm

TIVETSHALL ST MARGARET Norfolk
Map 5 TM18
⊶**GH Glenhaven** ☎238 4hc TV 8P ⸙
S% B&bfr£5 Bdi£7

TORBAY Devon See under Brixham,
Paignton and Torquay.

TORCROSS Devon *Map 3 SX84*
During the currency of this publication
Torcross numbers are liable to change.

GH Cove House ☎580448 Mar–Nov Lic
12hc 4⇆🛏 ⊗ nc10 12P sea S%
B&bf6.75–£7.50 Bdif10–£11 Wf75 ⱡ

⋈**GH Shingle** ☎782 Closed Xmas Lic
6hc 1⇆🛏 ⊗ nc5 5P lake sea S%
B&bf5.50–£6.25 Bdif8.80–£9.80
Wf57–£64 ⱡ D7pm

TORMARTON Avon *Map 3 ST77*
INN Compass ☎ Badminton 242 Lic 6hc
2⇆🛏 TV 100P 🍴 🚗 B&bf9.90–£11.90
Bar lunch £2.20–£4 D10.10pm

TORPOINT Cornwall *Map 2 SX45*
⋈**GH Elms** 16 St James Rd
☎ Plymouth 812612 6hc ⊗ CTV 6P 🍴
S% B&bf5 Bdif7.50 Wf45 ⱡ D3pm

TORQUAY Devon *Map 3 SX96* **See
Central & District plan**
GH Albaston House Hotel 27 St
Marychurch Rd ☎26758 Central plan:**1**
mid Jan–mid Dec Lic 13hc 6⇆🛏 CTV
12P sea S%✱B&bfrf5.25 Bdifrf9.25
Wfrf57.50 W only Jul & Aug D8pm

GH Bowden Close Hotel Teignmouth Rd,
Maidencombe Cross ☎38029
District plan:**39** Mar–Nov & Xmas Lic
20hc 3⇆🛏 ⊗ CTV 50P 🍴 sea
✱B&bf5.50–£7 Bdif9–£10.50
Wf50–£60 ⱡ D7pm

⋈**GH Braddon Hall Hotel** Braddons Hill
Road East ☎23908 Central plan:**2**
Lic 13hc 1⇆🛏 ⊗ CTV 8P 🍴 sea S%
B&bf5–£7 Bdif7.50–£9.50 Wf48–£65
ⱡ D7.30pm

⋈**GH Brookesby Hall Hotel** Hesketh Rd
☎22194 Central plan:**3** 12hc CTV 12P
🍴 sea S% B&bf5.65–£7.50
Bdif9.07–£10.85 Wf61.92–£72.50
ⱡ D5.30pm

GH Burley Court Hotel Wheatridge Ln,
Livermead ☎67879 District plan:**40**
Apr–Sep Lic 22hc 10⇆🛏 ⊗ CTV 30P
sea S% ✱B&bf4.50–£7.50 Bdif7–£10
Wf42.50–£69 ⱡ W only Jul & Aug
D6.30pm

⋈**GH Carn Brea** 21 Avenue Rd
☎22002 Central plan:**4** Lic 17hc 2⇆🛏
CTV 12P S% B&bf5.50–£8.50
Bdif8.25–£12.50 Wf47–£70 ⱡ D6.30pm

GH Casey's Court Motel 127 Newton Rd
☎63909 District plan:**41** 6hc ⊗ nc2
6P 1🏠 🍴 S% ✱B&bf3.75–£4.75

⋈**GH Castle Mount Hotel** 7 Castle Rd
☎22130 Central plan:**5** Closed Xmas
9hc nc5 CTV 6P S% B&bfrf4.55
Bdifrf7.55 Wfrf46 ⱡ D6.30pm

GH Castleton Private Hotel Castle Rd
☎24976 Central plan:**6** 17Mar–Dec Lic
13hc ⊗ nc3 CTV 7P 🍴 sea D5pm

⋈**GH Chelston House Hotel** Chelston
Rd ☎65200 Central plan:**7** Etr–mid Oct
Lic 18hc ⊗ CTV 18P 🍴 S%
B&bf5.75–£8.50 Bdif7.75–£11
Wf54–£73 ⱡ D5pm

GH Chelston Tower Hotel Rawlyn Rd
☎67351 Central plan:**8** Lic 24hc
9⇆🛏 CTV 50P sea S% ✱B&bf5.70–£7.45
Bdif8.85–£11.25 Wf57–£69.75 ⱡ
D6.30pm

GH Clevedon Private Hotel Meadfoot
Sea Rd ☎24260 District plan:**42**
Apr–Oct 16hc nc5 CTV 10P
B&bf7–£7.50 Bdif9.50–£10
Wf66.50–£70 ⱡ D7pm

GH *Hotel Concorde* 26 Newton Rd
☎22330 Central plan:**9** Jan–30Oct Lic
17hc ⊗ nc2 CTV 16P

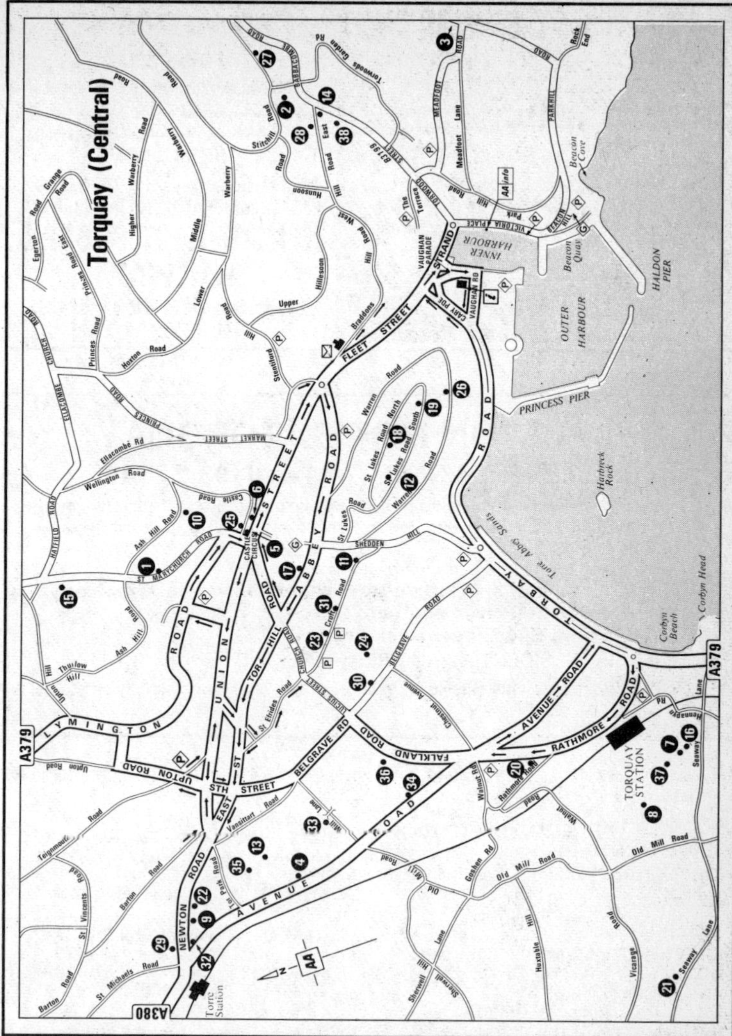

1	Albaston House Hotel	10 Craig Court Hotel	20 Normanhurst Hotel	30 Southbank Hotel

1 Albaston House Hotel
2 Braddon Hall Hotel
3 Brookesby Hall
4 Carn Brea
5 Castle Mount
6 Castleton Private Hotel
7 Chelston House Hotel
8 Chelston Tower Hotel
9 Hotel Concorde
10 Craig Court Hotel
11 Devon Court Hotel
12 Fretherne Hotel
13 Glenorleigh Hotel
14 Gresham Court Hotel
15 Hatherleigh Hotel
16 Ingoldsby Hotel
17 Lindum Hotel
18 Mapleton Hotel
19 Mount Nessing Hotel
20 Normanhurst Hotel
21 Rawlyn House Hotel
22 Richwood Hotel
23 Riva Lodge
24 Rothesay Hotel
25 St Bernard's Private Hotel
26 Seacliff Hotel
27 Sea Point Hotel
28 Shirley Hotel
29 Silverlands Hotel
30 Southbank Hotel
31 Torcroft Hotel
32 Tormohun Hotel
33 Trafalgar House Hotel
34 Tregantle Hotel
35 Tregenna Hotel
36 Westgate Hotel
37 Westowe Hotel
38 Four Seasons Hotel *(Inn)*

GH *Craig Court Hotel* 10 Ash Hill Rd Castle Circus ☎24400 Central plan:**10** Mar–Oct Lic 10hc (A 2hc) nc5 CTV 10P ⚻ D6pm

GH *Devon Court Hotel* Croft Rd ☎23603 Central plan:**11** Etr–Oct Lic 15hc 2⇨🚿 ⚻ nc5 CTV 14P ⚻ S% B&b£7–£9 Bdi£9–£12 W£55–£85 ⱡ W only Jun–Aug D6.30pm

GH Exmouth View Hotel Bedford Rd, Babbacombe Downs ☎37307 District plan:**43** Etr–Oct Lic 18hc 4⇨🚿 CTV 14P ⚻ sea B&b£5–£6.50 Bdi£8–£9 W£58–£65 ⱡ D6.30pm

GH Fairmount House Herbert Rd, Chelston ☎65446 District plan:**44** 8hc CTV 9P 1🏠 ⚻ S% B&b£5–£6.50 Bdi£7–£8.50 W£46–£58 ⱡ W only Jul & Aug D7pm

GH Forest Hotel Haldon Rd ☎24842 District plan:**45** Etr & mid May–mid Oct Lic 34rm 24hc 10⇄ nc2 CTV 20P sea B&b£9.20–£13.80 Bdi£10.35–£17.25 W£50–£90 ⱡ D7pm

⊢⊣**GH Fretherne Hotel** St Lukes Road South ☎22594 Central plan:**12** May–Oct Lic 24hc CTV 24P S% B&bfr£5.40 Bdifr£7.56 D4pm

⊢⊣**GH Glenorleigh Hotel** 26 Cleveland Rd ☎22135 Central plan:**13** Apr–Oct & Xmas Lic 15hc CTV 15P S% B&b£5.50–£7 Bdi£6–£8 D8pm

GH Gresham Court Hotel Babbacombe Rd ☎23007 Central plan:**14** 2May–mid Oct Lic 34hc 8⇄🍽 ⊗ CTV 4P lift B&b£6.50–£8 Bdi£9.75–£11.25 W£65–£77 D7.45pm

GH Hatherleigh Hotel 56 St Marychurch Rd ☎25762 Central plan:**15** Apr–Sep Lic 18hc CTV 18P ₺ S% B&b£6.60–£8 W£52–£65 D10am

GH Holly House Hotel York Rd ☎311333 District plan:**47** May–Sep Lic 14hc 1⇄🍽 ⊗ ⚓ CTV 14P 2🏠 ⵗ S% ✳B&b£6.33–£8 Bdi£8.53–£10 W£58.23–£69.88 W only 14Jul–18Aug D6.30pm

GH *Ilsham Valley* Ilsham Marine Dr ☎22075 District plan:**48** Mar–Oct rs Feb Lic 19hc (A 3hc) CTV 20P 3🏠 ⵗ D6pm

GH Ingoldsby Hotel 1 Chelston Rd ☎67497 Central plan:**16** Mar–Oct Lic 16hc CTV 18P sea S% ✳B&b£6–£8 Bdi£7.50–£10 W£50–£68 ⱡ D4pm

GH Lindum Hotel Abbey Rd ☎22795 Central plan:**17** 29Mar–Oct 21hc 4⇄🍽 nc3 CTV 17P S% B&b£6.50–£7.15 Bdi£8.26–£9.80 W£55.20–£69.80 ⱡ D6pm

⊢⊣**GH Mapleton Hotel** St Lukes Road North ☎22389 Central plan:**18** mid Mar–Oct Lic 9hc ⊗ CTV 8P S% B&b£5.50–£7.50 Bdi£7.50–£9.50 W£46–£62 ⱡ W only mid May–mid Sep D5pm

⊢⊣**GH Mount Nessing Hotel** St Lukes Road North ☎22970 Central plan:**19** end Mar–Oct Lic 12hc ⊗ nc2 CTV 12P sea S% B&b£5.90–£7.90 Bdi£8.50–£11 W£50.50–£66 ⱡ D4pm

⊢⊣**GH Normanhurst Hotel** Rathmore Rd ☎22420 Central plan:**20** 4Apr–4Oct Lic 14hc CTV 10P S% B&b£4.50–£6.75 Bdi£6.70–£8.75 W£46.44–£61.56 ⱡ W only Jul–Sep D5pm

GH Overdale Hotel Great Hill, Barton ☎311280 District plan:**49** Lic 11hc ⊗ ⚓ CTV 20P 1🏠 S% B&b£7–£8.90 Bdi£10.85–£13.85 W£65–£90 ⱡ D7pm

GH *Pembroke Hotel* Meadfoot Sea Rd ☎22837 District plan:**50** Lic 19hc ⊗ CTV 13P W only Jul & Aug D9.30pm

GH Pines Hotel St Marychurch Rd ☎38384 District plan:**51** Apr–mid Oct Lic 22hc CTV 25P S% ✳B&b£4.32–£6.48 Bdi£6.48–£8.64 W£40–£54 D6.30pm

GH Rawlyn House Hotel Rawlyn Rd, Chelston ☎65208 Central plan:**21** Lic 12hc (A 4hc) ⊗ CTV 10P S% B&b£6.75–£7.50 Bdi£8.75–£9.75 W£55–£65 ⱡ D6.30pm

GH Richwood Hotel 20 Newton Rd ☎23729 Central plan:**22** Apr–Oct Lic 24hc CTV 12P S% B&b£6–£9

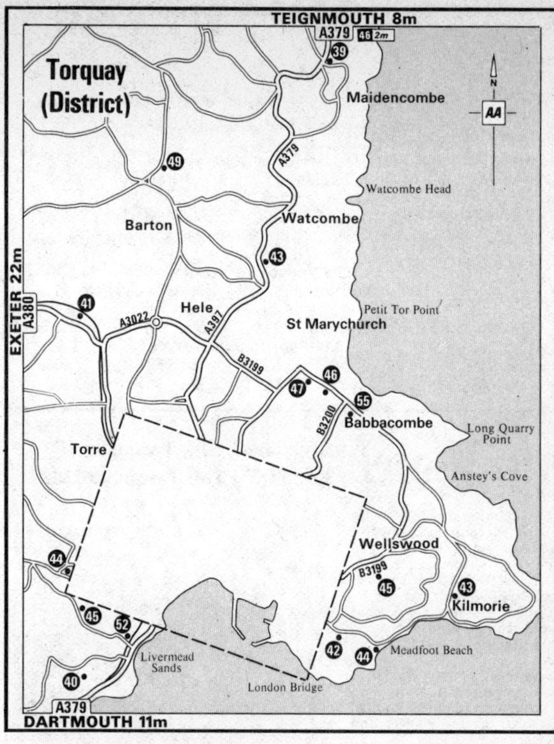

39 Bowden Close Hotel
40 Burley Court Hotel
41 Casey's Court
42 Clevedon Private Hotel
43 Exmouth View Hotel
44 Fairmount
45 Forest Hotel
46 Higher Commons
47 Holly House Hotel
48 Ilsham Valley
49 Overdale Hotel
50 Pembroke Hotel
51 Pines Hotel
52 Sunleigh Hotel
53 Villa Marina Hotel
54 Watcombe View Hotel
55 Rose Grange Hotel *(Inn)*

Bdi£8–£11 W£55–£75 W only Jul & Aug

GH *Riva Lodge* Croft Rd ☎22614 Central plan:**23** Apr–Oct Lic 19hc ⊗ nc8 TV 16P

GH Rothesay Hotel Scarborough Rd ☎23161 Central plan:**24** Apr–Oct Lic 18hc ⊗ CTV 12P sea B&b£4.40–£7.42 Bdi£7.54–£10.44 W£50.11–£70.16 ⌧ W only last wk Jul–1st wk Aug D3pm

GH St Bernard's Private Hotel Castle Rd ☎22508 Central plan:**25** Lic 12hc ⊗ CTV 9P ⑩ sea S% B&b£5–£6.50 Bdi£7–£8.50 W£50–£56 ⌧ D6pm

GH Seacliff Hotel Warren Rd ☎24975 Central plan:**26** 17May–3Oct 20hc CTV B&b£6–£8 Bdi£8–£9.50 W£56–£66.50 ⌧ W only 28Jun–26Jul D6.30pm

GH Sea Point Hotel 5 Clifton Gv ☎28012 Central plan:**27** Lic 8hc ⊗ CTV 3P ⑩ S% B&b£4.32 Bdi£6.48–£8 W£41.58–£54 ⌧ D2pm

GH Shirley Hotel Braddons Hill Road East ☎23016 Central plan:**28** 5Apr–11Oct Lic 14hc nc3 CTV 6P S% B&b£4.75–£7.50 Bdi£7.25–£10 W£45–£58 ⌧ D6.45pm

GH *Silverlands Hotel* 27 Newton Rd ☎22013 Central plan:**29** Closed Xmas 12hc CTV 12P ⑩

GH Southbank Hotel 15 & 17 Belgrave Rd ☎26701 Central plan:**30** Lic 20hc ⊗ CTV 14P S% B&b£6–£8 Bdi£8–£11 W£53–£74 ⌧ W only mid Jun–mid Sep D5.30pm

GH Sunleigh Hotel Livermead Hill ☎67137 District plan:**52** Etr–last wk Sep Lic 19hc 8⇨🍴 CTV 16P sea S% B&b£6.20–£6.72 Bdi£8.40–£9.60 W£42.75–£63.84 ⌧ W only Jul & Aug D6pm

GH Torcroft Hotel Croft Rd ☎28292 Central plan:**31** Etr–Sep & Xmas Lic

20hc 6⇄🛏 CTV 20P sea B&b£5–£7.50
Bdi£7–£11 W£49–£69 ⌧ D6.45pm

⋈GH **Tormohun Hotel** 28 Newton Rd
☎23681 Central plan:**32** Lic 20hc
6⇄🛏 ⌕ CTV 30P 🍽 S% B&b£5.18–£7.48
Bdi£8.53–£9.78 W£51.75–£73.60 ⌧
D7pm

⋈GH **Trafalgar House Hotel** Bridge Rd
☎22486 Central plan:**33** Apr–Oct Lic
11hc ⌕ CTV 6P S% B&b£5–£6.50
Bdi£7–£8.50 W£49–£59.50 ⌧ D6pm

GH **Tregantle Hotel** 64 Bampfylde Rd
☎27494 Central plan:**34** Apr–Oct 11hc
⊗ nc5 CTV 11P 🍽 S% ✳B&b£4–£5.50
Bdi£5.50–£7 W£35–£48 ⌧ D6pm

GH **Tregenna Hotel** 20 Cleveland Rd
☎23578 Central plan:**35** Closed Xmas
Lic 12hc ⌕ CTV 10P S% B&bfr£7
Bdifr£8 Wfr£50 ⌧ W only Jul–Aug D noon

GH **Villa Marina Hotel** Cockington Ln,
Livermead ☎65440 District plan:**53**
Apr–Oct 26hc 19⇄🛏 CTV 23P 🍽 S%
B&b£6–£8 Bdi£7–£10 D7.15pm

GH *Watcombe View Hotel* St Albans Rd,
Babbacombe ☎39967 District plan:**54**
Etr–Oct Lic 18hc ⊗ nc3 CTV 16P 🍽
D6.30pm

⋈GH **Westgate Hotel** Falkland Rd
☎25350 Central plan:**36** Etr–mid Oct
Lic 14hc ⌕ CTV 12P S% B&b£5–£7
Bdi£7.50–£9.50 W£52–£70 ⌧
W only last 2 wks Jul & 1st wk Aug
D6.30pm

GH **Westowe Hotel** Chelston Rd ☎65207
Central plan:**37** Mar–Oct Lic 13hc ⊗
nc5 CTV 6P 🍽 sea S% B&b£6.10–£6.80
Bdi£8.10–£8.90 W only Jul–Aug D6.30pm

INN *Four Seasons Hotel*
547 Babbacombe Rd ☎25292 Central
plan:**38** Lic 34hc ⊗ TV 10P

𝔖unleigh 𝔥otel

**Livermead Hill, Torquay,
TA2 6QY   Tel: Torquay 67137**

SUNLEIGH — The family Hotel, standing in its own grounds, facing south overlooking beautiful Torbay. Well situated only approximately 150 yards from the sea front and Livermead Beach, where you may swim or water-ski. The hotel is licensed, with an attractive comfortable bar.
There is ample free parking space and a colourful garden with lawn for sunbathing. You may come and go as you please, no restrictions, and late keys provided.
All the hotel bedrooms are comfortably furnished with spring interior mattresses, H&C water and razor points. There are large family rooms, double, twins and singles, some with private shower and toilet, some with sea views.

HERMITAGE HOTEL
CLIFF ROAD, TOTLAND BAY

A small Hotel in secluded grounds bordering the sea and superbly situated for the beach, Tennyson Downs, Needles and Alum Bay.
Excellent English cooking to be enjoyed in a relaxed informal atmosphere. Licensed. Rooms with showers. Midweek bookings. Swimming pool. Children and pets welcomed. Log fires and heating in the Spring and Autumn.
Write or telephone for Brochure:
Freshwater 2518

𝔒akwood 𝔥ouse 𝔥otel

Tel: 0553 810256

Tottenhill, King's Lynn,
Norfolk PE33 0RG

Situation
on the A10 trunk road, 4 miles south of King's Lynn. Ideal touring centre. Sandringham 15 minutes by road.

Premises
of Tudor origin, the house was refaced in 1774 and now has a typical Georgian facade.

Gardens
over 2½ acres of gardens and paddock with badminton court.

Menus
Home-cooked and carefully chosen à la carte menus. Supervised by proprietors.

Amenities
9 bedrooms, all with H & C, razor points and thermostatically-controlled radiators. Some with shower attached to rooms. Large lounge with colour TV. Period dining room and well-stocked bar. Restaurant and residential licence.

INN *Rose Grange Hotel* Babbacombe Rd
☎37074 District plan:**55** Lic 19hc TV
20P 6🏠 sn D10pm

TORRINGTON, GREAT Devon
Map 2 SS41
⊨GH Smytham ☎2110 May–Oct Lic
12hc CTV 12P S% B&b£5.50 Bdi£8.50
Wfr£59.50 ⌀ D9.30am

⊨INN Globe Hotel ☎2220 Lic 9hc
CTV 6P 6🏠 🚲 B&b£5.75–£6.28
Bdi£6.90–£7.48 sn D6.30pm£2.30–£2.88

TOTLAND BAY Isle of Wight *Map 4 SZ38*
GH Garrow Hotel Church Hill
☎ Freshwater 3174 May–Sep Lic 18hc
2⇃🔥 nc3 CTV 18P 🍺 sea B&b£6.90
Bdi£8.05–£8.25 W£54.05–£55.50 ⌀
D7pm

GH Hermitage Hotel Cliff Rd
☎ Freshwater 2518 Apr–Oct Lic 13hc ♨
CTV 12P S% B&b£7–£9.50
Bdi£11–£14.50 W£70–£94.50 ⌀ D7pm

⊨GH Lismore Private Hotel
23 The Avenue ☎ Freshwater 2025
Jan–Oct 8hc 🚲 nc4 CTV 8P S%
B&b£5–£6 Bdi£7.50–£8.50 W£42–£49
⌀ D6pm

GH Randolph Private Hotel Granville Rd
☎ Freshwater 2411 Closed Oct & Xmas
8hc CTV 6P 🍺 S% B&b£6 Bdi£9 W£53
⌀ D6.30pm

⊨GH Sandy Lane Colwell Common Rd,
Colwell Bay ☎ Freshwater 3330 Lic 9hc
CTV 5P S% B&b£4.90–£5.25
Bdi£6.65–£7 W£41.40–£43.70 ⌀ D7pm

TOTTENHILL Norfolk *Map 9 TF61*

GH Oakwood House Private Hotel
☎ King's Lynn 810256 Closed Xmas &
New Year Lic 9hc 2⇃🔥 🚲 CTV 10P 3🏠 🍺
S% B&b£7.50–£8.75 Bdi£10–£13
W£63–£81.90 D7.30pm

TOWCESTER Northants *Map 4 SP64*
INN Brave Old Oak Watling St ☎50533
Lic 12hc 1⇃🔥 CTV 8P 🍺 ✳B&b£7.70–£12
Bdi£14–£18 Bar lunch £1.50–£2.80
D10.45pm£6alc

TREGONY *(Nr Truro)* Cornwall
Map 2 SW94
GH Tregony House 15 Fore St ☎671
Mar–Oct Lic 7hc 🚲 nc7 CTV 6P S%
✳B&b£5.50–£6 Bdi£8.50–£9 W£56–£59
⌀ D6pm

TRESILLIAN Cornwall *Map 2 SW84*
⊨GH Manor Cottage ☎212 Closed Nov
Lic 7hc CTV 8P 🍺 river S%
B&b£5.50–£6.50 W£38.50–£45.50 M

TREVONE Cornwall *Map 2 SW87*
⊨GH Bowen House Hotel
☎ St Merryn 520389 Etr–mid Oct Lic
15hc nc4 16P sea B&b£5.75–£6.90
Bdi£6.90–£8.05 W£43.70–£51.75 ⌀
D6.30pm

⊨GH Coimbatore Hotel ☎ St Merryn
520390 May–Sep rs Oct (wknds only)
Lic 11hc 🚲 CTV 6P 10🏠 🍺 sea S%
B&b£5.50–£6.20 Bdi£7.60–£8.25
W£46–£57 W only Jul & Aug D8pm

⊨GH Green Waves Private Hotel
☎ St Merryn 520114 Mar–Sep 14hc
(A 7hc) CTV 15P 5🏠 ⌃ S% B&b£4–£5
Bdi£7–£8 W£45–£50 D7pm

GH Newlands Hotel ☎ St Merryn
520469 May–Sep Lic 12hc nc4 CTV 15P
W£47.50–£61.50 (W only) ⌀ D6.30pm

The Manor Cottage Guest House

**Tresillian, Near Truro, Cornwall
Tel: Tresillian 212**

6 bedrooms, 17th-Century charm,
modern comfort and a warm
welcome from Margery and Graham
Neville. Open all year, an ideal
touring base, three miles east of
Truro (A390), residential licence,
colour TV, central heating, double
glazing, ample parking. Fire
Certificate held.
Bed and breakfast terms according
to room and season, £5 to £6.50
inclusive per person nightly.

The Farley Hotel

Falmouth Road, Truro, Cornwall Tel: Truro 3680 (STD 0872)

Comfortable, family and commercial
private hotel. Open all year except at
Christmas. Excellent food and
friendly service. 23 Bedrooms. Radio,
electric blankets in rooms. Some
double rooms with showers. AMPLE
CAR PARKING. Ideal centre for
touring. Brochure on request.

GH Sea Spray Hotel Trevone Bay
☎ St Merryn 520491 Mar–Oct & Xmas
Lic 6🖪 nc3 CTV 8P sea S%
✳Bdi£9.75–£10.50 W£60–£70
W only Jun–Sep ⱡ D7.30pm
GH Trevistas ☎ St Merryn 520510
17May–27Sep 14hc nc4 CTV 14P sea S%
✳B&b£6–£7.50 Bdi£8–£9 W£50–£58
ⱡ W only 19Jul–30Aug D4.30pm

TREWARMETT Cornwall *Map 2 SX08*
GH Trevervan Hotel ☎ Tintagel 486
Lic 6hc ⚘ CTV 8P sea S%
B&b£6.50–£7.50 Bdi£8.50–£9.50
W£55–£62 D7.30pm

TRURO Cornwall *Map 2 SW84*
◄GH Colthrop Tregolls Rd ☎2920
7rm 6hc 6🖪 nc7 CTV 8P 🍴 S%
B&b£4.50–£5 Bdi£7.50–£8 W£50–£54
ⱡ D7pm

GH Farley Hotel Falmouth Rd ☎3680
Closed Xmas 23hc CTV 23P S% D6pm
GH *Pencowel* 12 Ferris Town ☎74946
Closed Xmas Lic 15hc CTV 9🏠 🍴
◄INN Globe Hotel Frances St ☎3869
Lic 4hc ⊘ nc8 CTV 4P S% B&b£5.50–£6
Bdi£7.50–£8 W£47 ⱡ Bar lunch 25–75p
D2.30pm£2–£2.50
TUNBRIDGE WELLS (ROYAL) Kent
Map 5 TQ53
GH The Guest House 89 Frant Rd
☎25596 Closed Jan 6hc 2⇄🖪 CTV 10P
🍴 S% B&b fr£9

GH Marlborough Hotel 57 Mount
Ephraim ☎21328 Lic 23hc 2⇄🖪 CTV 12P
🍴 S% ✳B&b£9.50 Bdi£13.50–£15.50
W£58–£80 D8pm

TWO BRIDGES Devon *Map 2 SX67*
GH Cherrybrook Hotel ☎ Tavistock 88260

Venn Ottery Barton

Venn Ottery, Near Ottery St Mary, Devon EX11 1RZ

Five miles from Sidmouth beach, in its own garden amid unspoilt farmlands. Family run, full central heating and every comfort, with charm of 16th century beams. Bar, lounge with colour TV, large games room, ample parking, private trout fishing. Dinner (at 7.30pm), bed and breakfast from mid-March to October. Bargain weekends until May.

Tel: Ottery St Mary 2733 (040-481)

Cross Keys Inn

Wansford, Peterborough, Cambs PE8 6LJ
Tel: Stamford 782266 (STD 782)

Open throughout the year. There are 6 bedrooms all with hot and cold water. Colour television available for the use of guests. Car Park. Fire certificate granted.

Please see the gazetteer for further details.

THE ROCK INN

**WATERROW
TAUNTON, SOMERSET
Tel: Wiveliscombe 23293
(STD code 0984)**

Situated on the A361, 14 miles west of Taunton in the Brendon foothills making places like Exmoor, Clatworthy Reservoir and the north and south coasts very accessible. Fully central heated, all bedrooms have private bath & wc. Luncheon & dinner are served in addition to food at the bar, all year round.

Closed Xmas Lic 8hc 15P 📺 S% B&b£7
Bdi£10.25 D7.30pm

ULVERSTON Cumbria *Map 7 SD27*
GH Sefton House Hotel Queen St
☎52190 Lic 8hc ⊗ CTV 3P 2🏠 📺
B&b£6.60–£7.30 Bdi£9.15–£9.95
W£61.95–£65.65 ⌖ D8.30pm

VENN OTTERY Devon *Map 3 SY09*
GH Venn Ottery Barton
☎ Ottery St Mary 2733 15Mar–Oct Lic
11hc 2🛏 CTV 14P 📺 B&b£7.15–£8.80
Bdi£8.53–£10.18 W£54.73–£64.45 ⌖
D7.30pm

VENTNOR Isle of Wight *Map 4 SZ57*
GH Channel View Hotel Hambrough Rd
☎852230 Etr–Sep Lic 14hc CTV sea S%
B&b£7–£8.50 Bdi£11–£12.50
W£55–£60 ⌖ D6pm

⋈**GH Delamere** Bellevue Rd ☎852322
Apr–Oct 7hc CTV 6P sea S%
B&b£5.50–£6.50 Bdi£6.50–£7.50
W£37.50–£51 ⌖ D4pm

GH *Kings Bay Hotel* Kings Bay Rd
☎852815 Etr–Oct Lic 6hc ⊗ nc2 CTV
10P 📺 sea

GH Macrocarpa Mitchell Av ☎852428
Etr–Oct & Xmas Lic 20hc 11🛏 (A 3hc)
CTV 20P sea B&b£7.50–£8.50
Bdi£10.50–£11.75 W£55–£95 ⌖
D7.30pm

GH Picardie Hotel Esplanade
☎852647 Apr–Oct Lic 15hc CTV sea S%
✳B&b£6–£7.50 Bdi£7–£9 W£46–£52
⌖ D7pm

GH Richmond Private Hotel
Esplanade ☎852496 Mar–Oct Lic
12hc 2🛏 CTV 8P sea S% ✳B&b£5.50
Bdi£7.25 W£46–£50 ⌖ W only Jun–Aug
D7pm

GH St Maur Hotel Castle Rd ☎852570
Lic 10hc ⊗ nc3 CTV 12P 📺 sea S%
B&b£6.25–£7 Bdi£8.50–£9 W£48–£54
⌖ D6.30pm

GH Under Rock Hotel Shore Rd,
Bonchurch (1m E) ☎852714 Mar–Oct
Lic 9hc ⊗ nc8 12P 📺 sea S% B&b£9.20
Bdi£10.35 W£96.60 D6.30pm

WALBERSWICK Suffolk *Map 5 TM47*
INN Bell Hotel ☎ Southwold 723109
Lic 4hc 1🛏 ⊗ nc12 TV ⇔ S%
B&b£8–£10 W£48–£54 W only Jul & Aug
sn L£2.50–£5&alc D9pm

WALLASEY Merseyside *Map 7 SJ29*
⋈**GH Divonne Private Hotel**

71 Wellington Rd, New Brighton
☎051-639 4727 Lic 15hc 5🛏 CTV 8P
📺 S% B&b£5.50–£6.50 Bdi£8.50–£9.50
D6pm

⋈**GH Sandpiper Private Hotel**
22 Dudley Rd, New Brighton
☎051-639 7870 7hc ⊛ CTV 7P 📺 S%
B&b£5.50 Bdi£7.75 W£47.50 ⌖ D4pm

WALL HEATH W Midlands *Map 7 SO88*
INN *Prince Albert Hotel* High St
☎ Kingswinford 3905 Lic 5hc ⊗ TV 200P
📺 sn

WALTON-ON-THE-NAZE Essex
Map 5 TM22
GH Blenheim House Hotel 39 Kirby Rd
☎ Frinton-on-Sea 5548 Lic 11hc 1🛏 ⊗
TV 16P B&b£8–£9 Bdi£11–£12
W£70–£77 ⌖ D5pm

WANSFORD Cambs *Map 3 TL09*
INN Cross Keys ☎ Stamford 782266
Lic 2hc (A 3hc) CTV P 📺 ⇔ S%
✳B&b£6.50–£7 Bar lunch £2alc
D10pm£6.50alc

GH Golden Acre Hotel ☎ Bindon Abbey
462563 Apr–Sep Lic 6hc CTV 12P 📺
S% ✳B&b£6.50–£7.75 Bdi£10–£11.50
W£68–£80 ⌖ D8.30pm

WARWICK Warwicks *Map 4 SP26*
⋈**GH Avon** 7 Emscote Rd ☎41367
7hc ⊗ TV 6P 1🏠 📺 S% B&b£4.50–£5

⋈**GH Cambridge Villa** 20A Emscote Rd
☎41169 10hc ⊗ CTV 10P 📺 S% B&b£4

INN Wheatsheaf Hotel 54 West St
☎42817 Lic 5hc ⊗ CTV 15P 📺 S%
B&b£7

WASHFORD Somerset *Map 3 ST04*
GH *Washford House* ☎484 Etr–Oct 6rm
5hc ⊗ CTV 10P 📺

WATERBEACH Cambs *Map 5 TL46*
INN Bridge Hotel Clayhythe ☎ Cambridge
(Cambs) 860252 Lic 30hc 14🛏 CTV
80P 📺 river S% B&b fr£7.50 Bar lunch
75p–£1.95 D8.45pm£3.50–£5.50

WATERLOOVILLE Hants *Map 4 SU60*
GH Far End Private Hotel 31 Queens Rd
☎3242 2Jan–24Dec rs 25Dec–1Jan
Lic 9hc 1🛏 CTV 20P 5🏠 📺 S%
B&b£10 Bdi£13 W£72 ⌖ D4pm

WATERMILLOCK Cumbria
Map 12 NY42

GH Knotts Mill Country House
☎ Pooley Bridge 328 Etr–Oct Lic 5hc
⊗ TV 5P ▥ B&b£6.35–£6.90 D7pm

WATERROW Somerset *Map 3 ST02*
INN The Rock ☎ Wiveliscombe 23293
rs Xmas day (no dinner) Lic 6hc 6⇔▥
CTV 15P ▥ ⇔ B&b£8.64–£9.72 W£75
Ł sn L£4 alc D9pm£5 alc

WATFORD Herts *Map 4 TQ19*
GH White House Hotel 26–29 Upton Rd
☎37316 Lic 65hc 42⇔▥ CTV 36P ▥
S% B&b£8–£15 Bdi£12.50–£19.50
W£79.50–£121.50 Ł D8.30

WEDMORE Somerset *Map 3 ST44*
⊷**GH Hall Farm** Sand Rd ☎712517
Etr–Oct Lic 6rm 5hc TV 6P 1⌂ ▥ S%
B&b£5 Bdi£8 W£50 Ł D9am

WELLINGBOROUGH Northants
Map 4 SP86
GH High View Hotel 156 Midland Rd
☎226060 Lic 17hc CTV 8P ▥ S%
B&b£7.56 Bdi£10.80 D7.15pm

WELLINGTON Somerset *Map 3 ST12*
GH Blue Mantle House Hotel 2 Mantle
St ☎2000 Lic 8hc CTV 3P ▥
B&b£7–£8 Bdi£10–£12 W£50–£55
Ł D8.30pm

WELLS Somerset *Map 3 ST54*
⊷**GH Tor** 20 Tor St ☎72322
rs Nov–Feb 8hc CTV 12P S%
B&b£5.75–£6.35 Bdi£8.70–£9.60
W£57.85–£63.85 Ł D4pm

WELLS-NEXT-THE-SEA Norfolk

Map 9 TF94
⊷**GH Arch House** 50 Mill Rd
☎ Fakenham 710696 Closed Dec Lic
5hc ⊗ TV 5P ▥ B&b£5–£8
Bdi£8.50–£11.50 W£57–£76.50 Ł
D noon

WEST ANSTEY Devon *Map 3 SS82*
INN Jubilee ☎ Anstey Mills 200
3hc CTV 100P 3⌂ S% B&b£6 Bdi£8.50
W£56 Ł Bar lunch £1–£3.25
D10.45pm£2–£4.50

WEST CHARLETON Devon *Map 3 SX74*
INN Ashburton Arms ☎ Frogmore 242
Closed Xmas wk Lic 5hc ⊗ nc7 TV 20P
▥ ⇔ S% B&b£7.20 W£48.40 M
W only Jul & Aug Bar lunch 40p–£2.50

WESTCLIFF-ON-SEA Essex see
SOUTHEND-ON-SEA

WESTGATE-ON-SEA Kent *Map 5 TR36*
GH Beach House Hotel 3 Beach Rise,
St Mildreds Bay ☎ Thanet 33846 Lic
12hc ⌂ CTV P sea ✳Bdi£7.50–£8.50
W£35–£40 Ł D7.30pm

WEST HUNTSPILL Somerset
Map 3 ST34
⊷**GH Huntspill Villa** 82 Main Rd
☎ Burnham-on-Sea 782291 rs Mon Lic
6hc ⊗ nc12 CTV 20P S% B&b£5–£6
Bdi£8–£9 W£48–£50 Ł D9.30pm

WEST LULWORTH Dorset see
LULWORTH

WESTON-SUPER-MARE Avon
Map 3 ST36 **See Plan**
GH Beachlands Hotel 17 Uphills Road
North ☎21401 Plan:**1** Closed Xmas Lic
22hc CTV 16P 2⌂ ▥ ✳B&b£6.90–£7.47

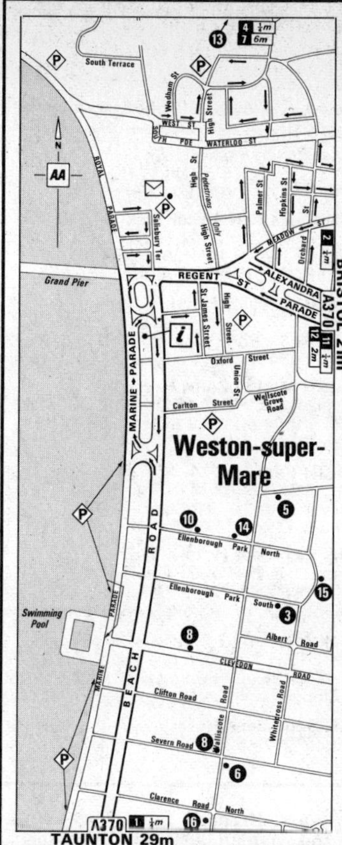

1	Beachlands Hotel	**10**	Scottsdale Hotel
2	Fourways	**11**	Shire Elms
3	Glenelg	**12**	Southmead
4	Inwood Hotel	**13**	Stanton Lodge Hotel
5	Kew Dee		
6	Oaklands Hotel	**14**	Tower House Hotel
7	Owl's Nest Hotel	**15**	Westgate Private Hotel
8	Russell Hotel		
9	St Anne's Hotel	**16**	Willow

Bdi£10.06–£10.95 W£56.92–£59.80 ⊬ D7pm

GH Fourways 2 Ashcombe Rd ☎23827 Plan:**2** Apr–Oct rs Nov–Mar (closed Sat & Sun) 6hc (A 3hc) ⊗ nc8 TV 6P S% B&b£3.50–£4.75 Bdi£5.25–£7.25 W£34–£38 ⊬ W only Apr–Oct D5.30pm

GH Glenelg 24 Ellenborough Park South ☎20521 Plan:**3** Etr–Oct Lic 15hc CTV 14P ⊞ S% B&b fr£5.50 Bdi fr£7.50 W fr£47 ⊬ D5.30pm

GH Inwood Hotel 59 South Rd ☎29756 Plan:**4** May–Sep Lic 15hc 2⇔🛁 (A 2hc 2⇔🛁) CTV 15P sea S% B&b£6.50–£7.50 Bdi£8.50–£9.50 W fr£55 ⊬ W only Jul & Aug D6pm

GH Kew Dee 6 Neva Rd ☎29041 Plan:**5** 6hc CTV 5P ⊞ S% ✳B&b£3.50–£4 Bdi£4.50–£5.50 W£30–£36 ⊬

GH Oaklands 26 Severn Rd ☎25253 Plan:**6** Etr–Oct Lic 10hc ⊗ nc10 CTV 6P S% B&b£4.25–£5.25 Bdi£6.25–£7.75 W£41–£52 ⊬ D4.30pm

GH Owl's Nest Hotel Kewstoke ☎417672 Plan:**7** rs Nov Lic 6hc ⊗ nc10 CTV 8P S% B&b£6–£7 Bdi£8–£9 W£56–£63 ⊬ D7pm

GH Russell Hotel 15–17 Clevedon Rd ☎20195 Plan:**8** Closed Xmas wk rs Nov–Mar Lic 18hc 4⇔🛁 ⊗ nc5 CTV 10P ⊞ S% B&b£9.20 Bdi£10.93–£11.50 W£74.75–£80.50 ⊬ D6.30pm

GH St Annes Hotel 35 Severn Rd ☎20487 Plan:**9** Mar–Nov rs Nov–Mar (B&b only) Lic 13hc ⊗ nc9 CTV 8P S% B&b£5.40–£7.02 Bdi£7.56–£9.18 W£43.20–£51.84 ⊬ D4.30pm

GH Scottsdale Hotel 3 Ellenborough Park North ☎26489 Plan:**10** Mar–Oct rs Nov & Feb 13hc ⊗ nc14 CTV 13P ⊞ S% B&b£6–£6.50 Bdi£7.50–£8 W£49–£54 ⊬ D5.30pm

GH Shire Elms 71 Locking Rd ☎28605 Plan:**11** Closed Dec Lic 11hc 1⇔🛁 ⊗ CTV 12P ⊞ S% B&b fr£4.95 Bdi fr£7.50 W fr£32 M D5pm

GH Southmead 435 Locking Road East ☎29351 Plan:**12** 6hc CTV 6P ⊞ S% B&b£3.50–£5 Bdi£6–£7.50 W£35–£48 ⊬

GH Stanton Lodge Hotel Kew Rd ☎22261 Plan:**13** Mar–Sep Lic 14hc ⊗ nc8 CTV 14P ⊞ S% B&b£5 Bdi£7 W£40–£50 ⊬ W only Jul & Aug

GH Tower House Hotel Ellenborough Park North ☎21393 Plan:**14** Apr–Oct rs Feb, Mar & Nov (B&b only)

14rm 13hc ✏ CTV 12P 3🛏 🍽 S%
B&b£6.32–£7.50 Bdi£8.62–£9.75
W£55–£63 ⅃ D4pm

GH Westgate Private Hotel
5 Ellenborough Cres ☎21952 Plan:**15**
Apr–Oct rs Apr Lic 8hc nc8 CTV
B&b£7.50–£8.80 Bdi£9–£10.50
W£57–£61 ⅃ D5.30pm

GH Willow 3 Clarence Road East
☎413736 Plan:**16** Etr–Sep 9hc ✏ CTV
9P 🍽 S% ✻B&b£4–£5 Bdi£5–£6.50
W£30–£38 ⅃

WEST PENNARD Somerset *Map 3 ST53*
⊷INN Red Lion ☎ Glastonbury 32941
Lic 7hc 100P 4🛏 🍽 B&b£5.25–£5.75
Bdi£9–£10 W£60 ⅃ sn L£2.75–£3.50&alc
D9.30pm£4.50 alc

WESTWARD HO! Devon *Map 2 SS42*
GH *Culverkeys* Buckleigh Rd ☎ Bideford
4218 Mar–30Oct Lic 7hc ✏ CTV 8P 🍽
D3pm

WETHERBY W Yorks *Map 8 SE44*
GH Prospect House 8 Caxton St ☎62428
6hc TV 6P 🍽 S% B&b£6–£6.50

GH *Swan* 38 North St ☎62381 Closed
24Apr–10May & 15–31Oct & Xmas 7hc
TV 5P

WEYMOUTH Dorset *Map 3 SY67*
GH Dorincourt Hotel 183 Dorchester Rd
☎786460 Lic 11hc 2⊷🔥 ✏ CTV 16P
🍽 S% ✻B&b£5.50–£6 Bdi£7.50–£8
D6pm

⊷**GH Ellendale Private Hotel** 88
Rodwell Av ☎786650 Lic 11hc ✏ CTV
5P 3🛏 🍽 S% B&b£4.75–£5.50

Bdi£6.50–£7.50 W£39.50–£60
W only Jul & Aug D7pm

GH Greenhill Hotel 8 Greenhill
☎786026 Mar–Oct Lic 18hc 1⊷🛏🔥 ✏
nc3 CTV sea S% B&b£6–£7.56
Bdi£8–£10 W£49.68–£54 ⅃ D5.30pm

⊷**GH Kenora** 5 Stavordale Rd ☎71215
Etr & Spring Bank Hol–Sep Lic 18hc ✏
CTV 12P B&b£5.50 Bdi£7.50 W£45–£50
⅃ W only Jul & Aug D11.59am

GH Kings Acre Hotel 140 The
Esplanade ☎782534 Feb–Nov Lic 14hc
CTV 9P 🍽 sea S% B&b£6.25–£8
Bdi£8.25–£10 W£40–£60 ⅃ D6pm

⊷**GH Kingsley Hotel** 10 Kirtleton Av
☎785676 Closed Xmas Lic 12hc ✏ CTV
16P 🍽 S% B&b£4.25–£5.50 Bdi£6–£7.25
W£36–£49.50 ⅃ W only Jul & Aug D4pm

⊷**GH Marina Court Hotel** 142 The
Esplanade ☎782146 Lic 14hc CTV 10P
S% B&b£4.50–£8 Bdi£5.50–£8
Wfr£35 ⅃ D6pm

⊷**GH Redlands** 14–16 Carlton Road
South ☎786204 May–Sep Lic 14hc nc2
CTV 10P 🍽 S% B&b£5.50–£6.50
Bdi£8–£9 W£49–£55 ⅃ D6pm

GH Richmoor Hotel 146 The
Esplanade ☎785087 Lic 22hc ✏ CTV
10P 🍽 S% B&b£6–£10 Bdi£9–£13
W£60–£80 W only Jul & Aug D5pm

GH Rosedene 1 Carlton Road North
☎784021 May–Sep 6hc ✏ nc3 CTV
8P S% ✻B&b£4.50 Bdi£6.25 W£42.50
⅃ D6pm

GH Southdene Hotel 24 Carlton Road
South ☎784621 Lic 18hc ✏ nc3 CTV

14P lake sea B&bf£6.50–£9
Bdif£8.50–£11 Wf£46.20–£53.90 ⚓
D6.15pm
GH Sunningdale Private Hotel 52
Preston Rd, Overcombe ☎ Preston (Dorset)
832179 Mar–Nov Lic 20hc 8⇔ CTV
20P 2🚗 S% B&bf£7.47–£8.92
Bdif£10.06–£11.50 Wf£63.25–£72.45 ⚓
D7.15pm

WHIMPLE Devon *Map 3 SY09*
GH Woodhayes ☎822237 Lic 6rm 5hc
1⇔ CTV 8P 2🚗 🐾 S% B&bf£6–£7.50
Bdif£9–£10.50 Wf£60–£70 ⚓ D8.30pm

WHITBY N Yorks *Map 8 NZ81*
GH *Europa Private Hotel* 20 Hudson St
☎2251 Closed 20Dec–6Jan 8hc 🐾 nc5
CTV D4pm
GH Prospect of Whitby 12 Esplanade
☎3026 Mar–Oct rs Nov–Feb (B&b only)
Lic 16hc CTV S% B&bf£6–£6.50
Bdif£8.90–£9.50 Wf£59.50–£64.50 ⚓
D4.30pm
GH Seacliffe Hotel North Prom, West
Cliff ☎3139 Etr–Dec Lic 18hc 🐾 nc2
CTV 8P sea S% B&bf£6.50–£7.25
Bdif£9.50–£10.50 Wf£63–£70 ⚓ D5pm

WHITCHURCH Heref & Worcs
Map 3 SO51
GH Portland ☎ Symonds Yat 890757
Closed Nov & Jan 8hc CTV 10P 🐾
✱B&bf£7–£8 Wf£44.10–£50.40 M

WHITESTONE Devon *Map 3 SX89*
INN Travellers Rest Okehampton Rd
(Old A30) ☎ Longdown 217 Lic 4hc
CTV 40P 🐾 S% B&bfr£6.50 Wf£80 sn
L55p–£3&alc D9.50pmf£3&alc

WHITFORD Devon *Map 3 SY29*
GH Chantry House ☎ Colyton 52359
Etr–Oct 7hc 🐾 TV 12P ✱B&bf£3.50–£4
Bdif£5.75–£6.25 Wf£38–£42 ⚓ D7pm

WHITLEY BAY Tyne & Wear
Map 12 NZ37
GH Croglin Hotel 35–41 South Pde
☎523317 25Dec–1Jan Lic 40hc 12⇔
CTV 16P 🍺 S% B&bf£6–£7 Bdif£9–£10
Wf£55–£65 ⚓ W only May–Aug D9.20pm

WHITNEY-ON-WYE Heref & Worcs
Map 3 SO24
INN Rhydspence ☎ Clifford 262
rs Oct–Apr Lic 3hc 1⇔ 🐾 nc10 60P 🍺
♿ S% B&bf£7.50–£9.50 Bdif£10.50–
£12.50 Wf£66.50–£80.50 ⚓
Bar lunch £2.20 alc D9.45pmf£2.20 alc

WICKFORD Essex *Map 5 TQ79*
GH Wickford Lodge 26 Ethelred Gdns
☎62663 6hc nc2 CTV 6P 🍺 S%
B&bf£7.50–£8 Wf£49–£52.50 M

WICKHAM Berks *Map 4 SU47*
INN Five Bells ☎ Boxford 242
rs Xmas Lic 4hc 70P 🍺 B&bf£7.50 sn
Lunch £1.25–£3 D9.45pmf£6.50 alc

WIDEGATES Cornwall *Map 2 SX25*
⋈**GH Coombe Farm** ☎223 8hc 🐾 ⚘
CTV 10P 🍺 B&bf£5–£6 Bdif£8–£9
Wf£70–£77 D9.30pm

WIDEMOUTH BAY Cornwall *Map 2 SS20*
GH *Beach House Hotel* ☎256 May–Sep
Lic 8hc 🐾 CTV 20P sea D7pm

WIGAN Gt Manchester *Map 7 SD50*
GH *Bel-Air Private Hotel* St Aubyns Rd
☎41410 Lic Tem 15hc CTV 3🏠

WILLITON Somerset *Map 3 ST04*
GH Fairfield House 51 Long St
☎32636 Lic 6hc CTV 8P 🍴 S% B&b£6
Bdi£9 D9pm

GH Old Rectory Nettlecombe (2m SW on
B3188, 1m E of junc with B3190)
☎ Washford 444 Mar–Oct 6hc ⊗ nc10
CTV 8P 1🏠 🍴 S% B&b£7.25–£7.75
Bdi£11.25–£12 W£77–£82 ⌁ D4pm

WILMINGTON E Sussex *Map 5 TQ50*
GH Crossways Hotel ☎ Polegate 2455
Lic 10hc 2⇥🛁 nc2 CTV P 6🏠 🍴 S%
B&b£6–£7

WILSHAMSTEAD (WILSTEAD) Beds
Map 4 TL04

GH Old Manor House Hotel Cotton
End Rd ☎ Bedford 740262 rs Sun
(no dinner) Lic 9hc CTV 10P 🍴 S%
B&b£8.05 D7pm

WINCHESTER Hants *Map 4 SU42*
GH Clownstown Sleepers Hill ☎63990
Closed Xmas 6 hc 1⇥🛁 ⊗ nc10 CTV 8P
🍴 S% ✳B&b£6 Bdi£10 W£64 ⌁

WINDERMERE Cumbria *Map 7 SD49*
See Plan
GH *Bickenhill Hotel* Lake Rd, Bowness-
on-Windermere ☎3624 Plan:**1** Lic 7hc
CTV 8P 🍴 lake D9.30pm

GH Clifton House Ellerthwaite Rd
☎4968 Plan:**2** Lic 6hc nc12 CTV 5P
1🏠 🍴 S% Bdi£7.90–£9.50
W£47.50–£58.50 ⌁ D7.30pm

GH *Craig Foot Hotel* Lake Rd ☎3902
Plan:**3** Etr–Nov Lic 10hc (A1) ⊗ nc12
CTV 20P 🍴 lake

GH Elim Bank Hotel Lake Rd, Bowness-
on-Windermere ☎4810 Plan:**4**
Mar–Nov Lic 8hc ⊗ CTV 7P 🍴 S%
✳B&b£7.50 Bdi£11.80 W£82.60 ⌁
D5.30pm

Craig Foot Country House Hotel
Lake Road, Windermere. Tel: 3902

Craig Foot was built in 1846, for SIR THOMAS PAISLEY, a retired Admiral.
It is an original Lakeland country house situated in its own grounds, with beautiful views of Windermere Lake, rolling meadows, forests and surrounding mountains. The hotel is elegantly furnished. Most bedrooms overlook the lake. Cosy cocktail bar. Car Park. Resident proprietors Mr and Mrs T A Thwaites.

Elim Bank Hotel

Telephone: Windermere 4810

Lake Road, Bowness-on-Windermere, Cumbria LA23 2JJ

For the discerning patron requiring quality and refinement

Spacious bedrooms equipped with basins and shaver points.
Central heating thoughout. Residential licence and bar. Latest fire precautions and alarm system. Colour televison. Car park. Written recommendations of excellence are normal.

HAISTHORPE

Holly Road, Windermere, LA 23 2AF
Telephone Windermere 3445

Small select Guest House situated in quiet residential area but very close to shops and all main services. Centrally heated throughout. Large lounge with colour television. Dining room with separate tables. Dogs by arrangement. Fire certificate. Bed and breakfast — dinner optional. Under the personal supervision of the resident proprietors José and Peter Millar. SAE please for brochure.

MAY WE HELP YOU TO ENJOY YOUR HOLIDAY?

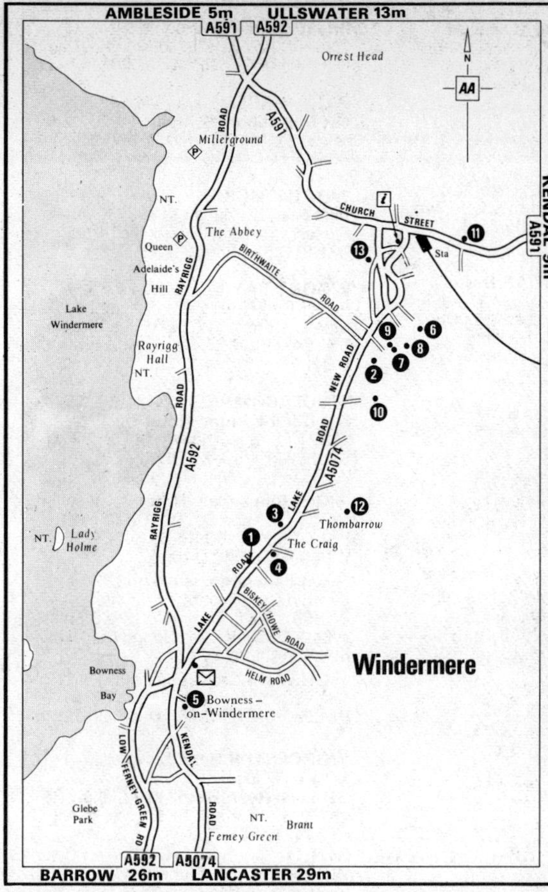

GH Fairfield Country House Hotel
Brantfell Rd ☎3772 Plan:**5** Closed Jan
Lic 8hc 5⇊🛏🚿 nc4 10P 🍴 S%
B&b£7.50–£10.50 Bdi£12.50–£15
D5pm

⨝GH Green Riggs 8 Upper Oak St
☎2265 Plan:**6** Mar–Oct 6hc CTV 4P
🍴 S% B&b£4.50 Bdi£8 W£54 ⦗ D5.30pm

⨝GH Haisthorpe Holly Rd ☎3445
Plan:**7** Etr–Oct rs Jul & Aug (B&b only)
7hc nc4 CTV 🍴 B&b fr£4.75 Bdi fr£7.50
W fr£50 ⦗ D4pm

⨝GH Hollythwaite Holly Rd ☎2219
Plan:**8** 7hc CTV S% B&b£4.50–£5.50
Bdi£7.25–£7.75 W£50–£55 ⦗

⨝GH Kenilworth Holly Rd ☎4004
Plan:**9** Mar–Oct 7hc 🚿 CTV 🍴 S%
B&b fr£4.75 Bdi fr£7.50 W fr£50 ⦗
D2.30pm

⨝GH Mylne Bridge Brookside ☎3314
Plan:**10** Mar–Oct Lic 7hc 🚿 nc9 CTV
7P 🍴 S% B&b£5.50–£6.50 Bdi£9–£10
W£58–£65 ⦗ D4.30pm

GH Orrest Head House Kendal Rd
☎4315 Plan:**11** mid Mar–Oct Lic 9hc
⚘ nc5 CTV 10P S% B&bf6.30–£7
Bdif10–£11 Wf65–£72.50 ⸗

⊷**GH Thornleigh** Thornbarrow Rd
☎4203 Plan:**12** Etr–Nov Lic 6hc ⚘
CTV 6P 🍴 S% B&bf4.75–£5.50
Bdif7.75–£8.50

⊷**GH Waverley Hotel** College Rd
☎3546 Plan:**13** Closed Xmas Lic 11hc
⚘ CTV 8P S% B&bf5.75 Bdif8.63
Wf60.38 ⸗ D9pm

WINTERBOURNE ABBAS Dorset
Map 3 SY69
GH Whitefriars ☎ Martinstown 206
Mar–Oct Lic 7hc ♨ CTV 18P 🍴 S%
✳B&bf6–£9 Bdif9–£12 Wf60–£80
⸗ D9.30pm

WINTHORPE Notts *Map 8 SK85*
INN *Lord Nelson* The Green ☎ Newark
3578 Lic 3hc nc14 20P 🍴 sn

WISBECH Cambs *Map 5 TF40*
GH Glendon Sutton Rd ☎4812
Mar–Oct Lic 18hc 1⇄🛁 CTV 60P S%
B&bf8–£9

WITHYPOOL Somerset *Map 3 SS83*
INN Royal Oak ☎ Exford 236 Lic 9hc
2⇄🛁 CTV 24P 3🏠 🍴 ⇜ river
B&bf8.50 Bdif13.50 Wf85
Bar lunch 50p–£1.50 D8.30pmf5.50&alc

WITNEY Oxon *Map 4 SP30*
INN Red Lion Corn St ☎3149 Lic
6hc CTV 2P 1🏠 S% B&bf7 Bdif8.50
sn Lf1.40&alc D9pmfr£2&alc

WIVELISCOMBE Somerset *Map 3 STO2*
⊷**INN Bear** 10 North St ☎23537 Lic
5rm 4hc CTV 6P ⇜ S% B&bf5.50–£6.50
Bdif8–£10 Wf55 ⸗ sn Lf2 alc
D9.30pmf2 alc

WOLVERHAMPTON W Midlands
Map 7 SO99
GH *Clarence Hotel* Queens St ☎24017
16hc CTV D6.15pm

WOMENSWOLD Kent *Map 5 TR25*
GH Woodpeckers Country Hotel
☎ Barham 319 Closed 24Dec–2Jan Lic
14hc (A 4hc 2⇄🛁) ♨ CTV 30P 2🏠 🍴
S% B&bf7.50–£8.50 Bdif10.50–£11.50
Wf63–£70 ⸗ D8.30pm

WOODFORD GREEN Essex *Map 5 TQ49*
GH Torry-Glen (London Motorists')

Private Hotel 17 Broomhill Rd
☎01-504 5742 Closed Xmas–15Jan
Lic 10hc ⚘ CTV 9P 🍴 S% ✳B&bf5–£10

WOODGREEN Hants *Map 4 SU21*
GH Millersholt ☎ Breamore 220 6hc
⚘ nc12 CTV 8P 🍴 S% B&bf6.50–£7
Bdif9.50–£10.50 D noon

WOODSTOCK Oxon *Map 4 SP41*
INN Star 22 Market Pl ☎811209
Closed Xmas Day Lic 3hc nc14 S%
B&bfrf8 Bar lunch 70p–£1.60

WOODY BAY Devon *Map 3 SS64*
⊷**GH Red House** ☎ Parracombe 255
Mar–Oct 6hc nc4 CTV 6P sea S%
B&bf4–£6 Bdif7.40–£9.40 Wf50–£60
⸗ D2pm

WOOLACOMBE Devon *Map 2 SS44*
GH Combe Ridge Hotel The Esplanade
☎321 Etr–Sep 8hc ⚘ nc3 CTV 8P ⇐
S% ✳B&bf4.50–£6 Bdif7–£9
Wf41–£54 ⸗ (W only Jun, Jul & Aug)

⊷**GH Holmesdale Hotel** Bay View Rd
☎335 Lic 15hc ♨ CTV 10P 🍴 sea S%
B&bf4.50–£5.50 Bdif6.50–£7.50
Wf40.50–£58 ⸗ D4pm

⊷**GH Seawards** Beach Rd ☎249
Etr–mid Oct 6hc nc2 TV 6P sea
B&bf5.25–£6.25 Bdif7.75–£8.75
Wf44–£50 ⸗ W only Spring Bank Hol–
mid Sep D4.30

⊷**GH Wave Crest** Sunnyside Rd ☎334
May–Sep 6hc nc3 TV 6P sea S%
B&bf4.50–£5 Bdif6.50–£7 D6.30pm

WORCESTER Heref & Worcs
Map 3 SO85
GH Loch Ryan Hotel 119 Sidbury Rd
☎351143 13hc (A 5hc 1⇄🛁) ⚘ nc6
CTV 🍴 S% B&bf8.05

WORKINGTON Cumbria *Map 11 NYO2*
⊷**GH Morven** Siddick ☎2118 Lic 4rm
CTV 8P 🍴 sea S% B&bf5–£5.50
Bdif7–£7.50 Wfrf48 ⸗ D4pm

WORTHING W Sussex *Map 4 TQ10*
⊷**GH Belmont Private Hotel**
211 Brighton Rd ☎202678 Lic 6hc CTV
3P 6🏠 🍴 sea S% B&bf5–£5.50
Bdif7–£7.50 Wf36–£46 D6.30pm

⊷**GH Burcott** 6 Windsor Rd ☎35163
5hc ⚘ CTV 4P 🍴 S% B&bf4–£5.50
Bdif6–£8 Wf39–£50 ⸗ D6pm

⊷**GH Camelot House** 20 Gannon Rd
☎204334 Closed 25 & 26Dec 7hc ⚘

nc5 3P 🕮 S% B&b£4–£5.50
Bdi£6.10–£7.70 W£38.20–£50.50 ⌇
D5pm
⋈GH **Eleanor Lodge** 9–11 Alexandra Rd
☎33788 Closed Xmas 11hc CTV 🕮 S%
B&b£5.17–£6.32 Bdi£7.47–£8.62
W£46–£54.62 ⌇ D3pm
⋈GH **Meldrum House** 8 Windsor Rd
☎33808 Apr–Oct 6hc ⊗ CTV 🕮 sea
S% B&b£5–£6.50 Bdi£7.50–£8.50
D5pm
GH **Pleasington** 2 Wyke Av ☎30834
Closed Xmas 8hc ⊗ nc8 CTV 1P 🕮 S%
B&b£6–£8 Bdi£8–£10 W£48–£54 ⌇
D1.30pm
GH **St Georges Lodge Hotel** Chesswood
Rd ☎32621 Lic 9hc 2⇥🛏 ⊗ 12P 2🏠 🕮
S% B&b fr£6.75 Bdi fr£8.50 W£55–£69
⌇ D7pm
⋈GH **Southdene** 41 Warwick Gdns
☎32909 Lic 6hc ⊗ nc10 CTV 🕮 S%
B&b£5–£5.50 Bdi£7.50–£8 W£50–£52
⌇ D4pm
GH **Wansfell Hotel** 49 Chesswood Rd
☎30612 11hc 1⇥🛏 ⊗ 8P 🕮
B&b£6.50–£7.50 Bdi£9.50–£10.50
W£66–£73 D7pm
⋈GH **Williton** 10 Windsor Rd ☎37974
6hc TV 2P 🕮 S% B&b£5–£7 W£30–£42
M
⋈GH **Windsor House** 16–18 Windsor Rd
☎39655 12hc 1⇥🛏 CTV 12P 🕮 S%
B&b£5–£7.50 Bdi£7–£10 W£45–£63
⌇ D6pm
GH **Windsor Lodge** 3 Windsor Rd
☎200056 7hc TV 4P ✳B&b£5–£6
Bdi£7–£8
GH **Wolsey Hotel** 179–181 Brighton Rd
☎36149 Lic 14hc CTV 🕮 sea S%

B&b£7.15 Bdi£10.50 W£72.50 ⌇
D6.30pm

WROTHAM Kent *Map 5 TQ65*
INN **Moat Hotel** London Rd ☎ Borough
Green 882263 Lic 8hc 1⇥🛏 300P 🕮
S% B&b£9 sn L£2.95–£3.45&alc
D10.30pm£4.50&alc

WYCHBOLD Heref & Worcs *Map 3 SO96*
INN *Crown Hotel* Droitwich Spa ☎413
rs Xmas Day & New Years Eve Lic 7hc
CTV 🕮 sn D9.30pm

YARMOUTH, GT Norfolk *Map 5 TG50*
⋈GH **Frandor** 120 Lowestoft Rd,
Gorleston-on-Sea (2m S A12) ☎62112
Closed Xmas & New Year Lic 8hc CTV
10P S% B&b£4.32–£5.40 Bdi£6.48–£7.56
W£35.64–£45.90 ⌇ D4.30pm
GH **Georgian House Private Hotel**
16 & 17 North Dr ☎2623 rs winter
(B&b only) Lic 22hc 6⇥🛏 ⊗ CTV 10P
🕮 sea S% B&b£6–£14 W£40–£75 M
GH **Palm Court Hotel** 10 North Dr
☎4568 Etr–Nov Lic 48hc 18⇥🛏 CTV
40P 🕮 lift sea S% B&b£9–£14
Bdi£12–£17 W£60–£95 ⌇ D8pm
GH **Porthole** 52 Avondale Rd,
Gorleston-on-Sea (2m S A12) ☎61451
Apr–Sep & Xmas rs Dec & Jan 6hc CTV
🕮 S% B&b£6–£7 Bdi£8–£9 W£45–£48
⌇ W only last 2 wks Jun–end Aug D4pm

YATTON Avon *Map 3 ST46*
INN **Prince of Orange** High St ☎832193
Lic 8hc 5⇥🛏 CTV 40P B&b£9–£11
Bdi£12–£14 W£90 ⌇ Bar lunch 70p alc
D9.30pm£4 alc

YEOVIL Somerset *Map 3 ST51*
GH *Pickett Witch House Hotel* 100
Ilchester Rd ☎4317 Closed Xmas 11hc
(A 6hc) CTV 20P 2🏠 ⴄ

⋈**GH Wyndam** 142 Sherbourne Rd
☎21468 Closed 22–29Dec Lic 6hc CTV
6P S% B&b£4 Bdi£6.50 D4pm

YORK N Yorks *Map 8 SE65*
GH *Acomb Road* 128 Acomb Rd
☎792321 Feb–Oct 11hc CTV 14P

GH Alhambra Court Hotel 31 St Marys
☎28474 Lic 29hc 7⇌🛁🚿 CTV 18P ⴄ
S% B&b£6.50–£7 Bdi£9.50–£10
W£65.50–£70 ⱡ D11pm

⋈**GH Avenue** 6 The Avenue, Clifton
☎20575 6hc CTV S% B&b£5.50–£6
Bdi£8–£8.50 W£53–£56 ⱡ D4pm

GH Bootham Bar Hotel 4 High
Petergate ☎58516 Closed Xmas 8hc
🚿 nc12 CTV ⴄ lift S% B&b£6.48

GH Clifton Bridge Hotel Water End
☎53609 Closed Xmas wk Lic 10hc CTV
12P ⴄ S% B&b£8.50 D7.30pm

GH Coach House Hotel Marygate
☎52780 Lic 12hc CTV 10P ⴄ S%
B&b£8.60–£10.90 D10.30pm

GH Hobbits Hotel 9 St Peters Gv
☎24538 Lic 13hc 1⇌🛁🚿 CTV 6P ⴄ S%
✱B&bfr£6.21 Bdifr£9.35 Wfr£65.45
ⱡ D10am

GH Inglewood 7 Clifton Gn ☎53523
Closed Dec 6hc CTV ⴄ S%
B&b£6–£6.50

GH Jorvik Hotel 52 Marygate, Bootham
☎53511 Closed Xmas Lic 16hc 7⇌🛁
CTV 20P ⴄ S% ✱B&b£7–£8.50
Bdi£10.50–£12 D4.30pm

⋈**GH Linden Lodge** Nunthorpe Av,
Scarcroft Rd ☎20107 Closed Xmas 5hc
🚿 nc5 CTV ⴄ S% B&b£5–£5.50
Bdi£8–£8.50 D noon

GH *Moat Hotel* Nunnery Ln ☎52926
9hc 🚿 CTV 10P

GH Old Vic 2 Wenlock Ter, Fulford Rd
☎37888 Lic 6hc 🚿 CTV 4P ⴄ S%
B&b£6–£7 D5pm

GH Orchard Court Hotel 4 St Peter's Gv
☎53964 Lic 10hc 🚿 CTV 8P S%
B&b£8.50–£9.50 D8.30pm

GH Priory Hotel 126 Fulford Rd ☎25280
Closed Xmas 17hc 3⇌🛁 🚿 CTV 18P
ⴄ S% B&b£6.35–£8.05

⋈**GH St Raphael** 44 Queen Ann's Rd,
Bootham ☎54187 7hc CTV ⴄ S%
B&b£5.50–£6

GH Sycamore Hotel 19 Sycamore Pl
☎24712 6hc 🚿 nc5 CTV 3P ⴄ S%
✱B&b£5–£6 Bdi£7–£8 W£47.25–£54.25
ⱡ D6pm

PRIORY HOTEL

**126 Fulford Road, York YO1 4BE
Tel: Reception 25280 Guests 34809
STD code 0904**

The Priory offers comfortable accommodation
and English breakfast and is situated on the
A19 south of the City with adjacent riverside
walk to the City centre.
Some of the 17 bedrooms have shower and
toilet facilities and all have H & C and razor
points. Large private car park.
Full central heating.

𝕾𝖙 𝕽𝖆𝖕𝖍𝖆𝖊𝖑 𝕲𝖚𝖊𝖘𝖙𝖍𝖔𝖚𝖘𝖊

44 Queen Anne's Road, Bootham, York YO3 7AF
Telephone: York 54187

St Raphael Guesthouse is situated in a quiet cul-de-sac in close
proximity to The Minster, Theatre Royal, City Centre and our
famous mediaeval street, The Shambles.
All rooms have H & C water, shaving points and full central
heating. A large lounge with colour TV is available any time
of day. Parking facilities available.
This is a family run concern under the personal supervision of
the proprietress.   Fire certificate.

ABBERTON Essex *Map 5 TM01*
Oxley Hill *(TM002194)* Layer Rd
☎ Colchester 66422
*Modern bungalow farmhouse with its own
private nature reserve. Beautiful
countryside views.*
6hc ⌘ nc5 CTV 12P 3🏠 💷 55acres mixed
S% B&b£6–£8 D8pm

ABBOTS BICKINGTON Devon
Map 2 SS31
Court Barton *(SS385133)* ☎ Milton
Damerel 214
*Stone-built farmhouse in an area of great
natural beauty. Panoramic views from
most windows. Rough shooting, fishing
and riding available.*
May–Oct 6rm 5hc TV 10P 600acres
mixed D5pm

ABBOTS BROMLEY Staffs *Map 7 SK02*
Marsh *(SK069261)* ☎ Burton on Trent
840323
*Large two-storey, cement-rendered
farmhouse.*
2rm TV 8P 45acres dairy S%
B&b£4–£5.25 Bdi£5.25–£6.75 D6.30pm

ALDWARK Derbys *Map 8 SK25*
Lydgate *(SK228577)* ☎ Carsington 250
*Stone-built traditional farmhouse, about
300 years old, in quiet rural setting.*
3rm ⌘ CTV 3P 1🏠 💷 250acres dairy
S% B&b£5–£6 Bdi£7–£8 D10am

ALFRISTON E Sussex *Map 5 TQ50*
Pleasant Rise *(TQ516027)* ☎870545
*Attractive farm set in typical Sussex
downland. Adjacent to B2108 Seaford rd.*
3hc TV 5P 20acres non-working S%
B&b£5.25–£5.50

ALLENSMOOR Heref & Worcs
Map 3 SO43
Mawfield *(SO453366)* ☎ Belmont
(Hereford) 266
*Large farmhouse set in narrow lane off
the beaten track, but close enough for
Hereford's amenities.*
Apr–Oct 3rm 2hc ⌘ nc12 CTV P
176acres arable & mixed S%
B&b£4–£4.25 Bdi fr£7

ALVERDISCOTT Devon *Map 2 SS52*
Garnacott *(SS516240)* ☎ Newton
Tracey 282
*Farmhouse standing in small garden
surrounded by open fields. Traditional
farmhouse furnishings. Facilities nearby
include fishing, golf and bathing.*
Etr–Oct 3rm 1hc ⌘ TV 3P 85acres mixed
S% B&b£3–£3.50 Bdi£6–£6.50 W£40
⌇ D6.30pm

APPLEBY Cumbria *Map 12 NY62*
Gale House *(NY695206)* ☎51380
*Comfortable, quiet farmhouse with
friendly atmosphere. Situated in delightful
position.*
Apr–Sep 2rm ⌘ nc5 3P 167acres dairy
S% B&b£4.50 Bdi£7

ASHBURTON Devon *Map 3 SX77*
Bembridge *(SX785701)* ☎52426
*Clean and brightly decorated farmhouse,
parts of which date back to early 16th
century.*
3rm 2hc ⌘ ♨ CTV 3P 💷 8acres mixed
S% Bdi£6–£8.50 W£40–£45
Parkfield *(SX764882)* ☎52318
Comfortable farmhouse in beautiful

*countryside on south east edge of
Dartmoor, also within easy reach of
South Devon.*
Apr–Sep 2rm 1hc ⌘ ♨ CTV 6P 💷
400acres arable S% B&b£5.75–£6.80
W£39–£43 Ⓜ

ASH MILL Devon *Map 3 SS72*
West Ford *(SS789229)* ☎ Bishop's
Nympton 231
*Georgian farmhouse of architectural
interest within easy reach of Exmoor and
Dartmoor. Market town of South Molton
5 miles.*
Closed Nov 3hc ⌘ TV 6P 💷 32acres
dairy S% B&b£6.50 Bdi£10 W£60 ⌇
D7.30pm

ASPATRIA Cumbria *Map 11 NY14*
Scales Demesne *(NY183461)* ☎20847
*Comfortably furnished accommodation.
Two separate staircases and front doors
offer independence. Within easy reach of
sea and Lake District.*
Jun–Aug 3rm ⌘ nc3 CTV P 231acres
dairy S% B&b£5 Bdi£7 D5pm

ATCHAM Salop *Map 7 SJ50*
Chilton Grove *(SJ526090)* ☎ Cross
Houses 215
*Large Georgian mansion with Tudor
wing. Elizabethan dovecote in grounds.
Linked with National Trust. Secluded and
quiet with 10 mile views.*
3rm 1 ⌘ 6P 2🏠 💷 34acres beef S%
B&b£5–£6 W£32–£40 Ⓜ

AUSTWICK N Yorks *Map 7 SD76*
Rawlinshaw *(SD781673)* ☎ Settle 3214
*200-year-old farmhouse with attractive
views to the front of the house.*
Etr–end Sep 3hc ⌘ CTV 6P 206acres
dairy, mixed & sheep

AVONWICK Devon *Map 3 SX75*
Supers Horsebrook *(SX711587)*
☎ South Brent 3235
Old farmhouse situated in quiet valley.
May–Sep 2hc ⌘ CTV 2P 100acres mixed
S% B&b£3.75–£4.25 Bdi£6–£7
W£40–£45 ⌇ W only Aug D5pm

AXBRIDGE Somerset *Map 3 ST45*
Manor *(ST420549)* Cross (on A38)
☎732577
*400-year-old farmhouse formerly a
coaching inn. Farm offers horse riding
facilities. On A38.*
9rm 3hc nc5 TV P 250acres mixed D5pm

AXMINSTER Devon *Map 3 SY39*
Annings *(SY299966)* Wyke ☎33294
*Large secluded farmhouse with modern
furnishings. Situated in elevated position
with fine views. Coast nearby. S of town
on unclass rd between A35 & A358.*
Etr–Sep 4rm 3hc ⌘ CTV 4P 54acres
dairy S% B&b£4–£4.50 Bdi£6.50–£7
W£45–£49 ⌇ D5pm

AYLESBEARE Devon *Map 3 SY09*
Rosamondford *(SY027918)*
☎ Woodbury 32448
*Pleasant farmhouse conveniently placed
for Exeter, the airport and East Devon.*
Etr–Oct 2hc ⌘ CTV 10P 125acres dairy
S% B&b fr£4 Bdi fr£6 D noon

BAMPTON Devon *Map 3 SS92*
Holwell *(SS966233)* ☎452
*14th-century farmhouse with thatched
roof, studded oak front door and many*

oak beams inside. Attractive gardens.
4⇄🛏🅿 ⊗ nc CTV 6P 1🏠 🍴 25acres mixed
S% B&b£5–£6 Bdi£7.50–£8.30
W£50–£55 ⚡ D4.30pm
Hukeley *(SS972237)* ☎267
*16th-century farmhouse, on the edge of
Exmoor. Fine old beams. Rooms are
comfortable and well decorated.*
Mar–Oct 2hc ⊗ TV 6P river 200acres
arable, beef, mixed & sheep

BARNSTAPLE Devon *Map 2 SS53*
Home *(SS555360)* Lower Blakewell,
Muddiford ☎2955
*Farmhouse situated in peaceful North
Devon countryside.*
Mar–Oct 4hc ⚘ TV 4P 42acres mixed
S% B&b£4–£8 Bdi£7–£10 W£40–£60
⚡ D8pm

BASSENTHWAITE Cumbria
Map 11 NY23
Bassenthwaite Hall *(NY231322)*
☎ Bassenthwaite Lake 393
*Fully modernised 17th-century farmhouse
in picturesque village close to quiet
stream.*
Etr–Oct rs Feb 3hc TV 3P 200acres
mixed S% B&b£4.25–£5 W£28–£35 M

BECKINGTON Somerset *Map 3 ST85*
Clifford *(ST799521)* Bath Rd ☎427
*17th-century stone-built farmhouse on
private track off A36.*
Mar–Oct 4hc ⊗ nc5 4P 🍴 river 7acres
non-working S% B&bfr£5.50

BICKINGTON *(Nr Ashburton)* Devon
Map 3 SX77
West Downe *(SX794705)* ☎258
Modernised, 16th-century farmhouse.

Etr–Sep 3rm 2hc CTV 6P 64acres mixed
D4pm

BIDDISHAM Somerset *Map 3 ST35*
Green *(ST382538)* ☎ Edingworth 258
*In secluded cul-de-sac with attractive
surroundings.*
Etr–Oct 4rm 3hc TV 4P 2🏠 209acres
mixed

BIRCHER Heref & Worcs *Map 7 SO46*
Leys *(SO471673)* Leys Ln
☎ Yarpole 367
*17th-century farmhouse in rural setting
with pleasant grounds. Close to Croft
Castle and Bircher Common with its
magnificent views.*
4rm 2hc TV 4P 120acres dairy sheep
S% B&b£4 Bdi£6 W£42 ⚡

BISSOE Cornwall *Map 2 SW74*
Holly Tree *(SW763416)* Fernsplatt
☎ Devoran 862126
*Isolated farmhouse in beautiful countryside.
Large garden with putting, pets' corner
and pony rides.*
May–Oct 5hc CTV 10P 10acres mixed

BLACK CROSS Cornwall *Map 2 SW96*
Homestake *(SW910606)*
☎ Fraddon 860423
*Pleasant house with garden on main
village road. In central position for touring
Cornwall.*
Etr–Nov 8hc ⊗ CTV 11P 82acres dairy
S% B&bfr£4.50 Bdifr£6 W£36–£39 ⚡
W only Spring Bank Hol–mid Sep
D6.30pm

BLEADON Avon *Map 3 ST35*
Purn House *(ST334571)* ☎812324

Pleasantly situated amid open fields with views of the Mendip and Quantock Hills and Brent Knoll.
Mar–Dec 6rm 5hc ✿ nc3 CTV 5P 330acres mixed S% B&b£4–£5 Bdi£6–£7 W£40–£48 ⅃ (W only Aug) D previous day

BLEATHWOOD Heref & Worcs *Map 7 SO57*
Bleathwood Manor *(SO560696)*
☎ Tenbury Wells 810446
Imposing manor house dating back over 600 years. Mixture of architectural designs. Large lounge with open fireplace. Country views.
5hc ✿ TV 10P 114acres mixed D7pm

BLORE Staffs *Map 7 SK14*
Coldwall *(SK144494)* Okeover
☎ Thorpe Cloud 249
Stone-built farmhouse approximately 200 years old. Good views of the surrounding hills. 4 miles NW of Ashbourne.
Etr–Oct 2hc ✿ TV 8P 200acres dairy sheep S% B&b£4–£5 Bdi£6–£7.50 D7.30pm

BLUNTS Cornwall *Map 2 SX36*
Trebrown *(SX335636)* ☎ Landrake 246
Farmhouse surrounded by pastureland. 7 miles from Liskeard and Saltash.
Etr–Oct 3hc ✿ CTV P ½acre non-working

BOTALLACK Cornwall *Map 2 SW33*
Manor *(SW368331)* ☎ St Just 788525
Previously known as 'Nanparra', home of Ross Poldark from the television series filmed here. Area steeped in history.
Mar–Nov 3hc (A 3hc) ✿ nc CTV P 📟 150acres mixed S% B&b fr£5 Bdi fr£8

BOVEY TRACEY Devon *Map 3 SX87*
Willmead *(SX795812)* ☎ Lustleigh 214
Farmhouse dating from 1327 situated on the edge of Dartmoor National Park in a delightful valley.
3hc nc12 CTV 10P 31acres beef sheep S% B&b£7.50 Bdi£12.50 D8pm

BRADNINCH Devon *Map 3 SS90*
White Heathfield *(ST012029)*
☎ Hele 300
Farmhouse in typical East Devon scenery. On E side of A38.
Apr–Sep 3rm TV 3P 127acres mixed S% ✱B&b£4–£4.50 Bdi£5.50–£6 W£38.50–£40 ⅃ D6pm

BRADWORTHY Devon *Map 2 SS31*
Dinworthy *(SS311156)* ☎297

Farmhouse set in secluded locality. Fishing and rough shooting available.
Apr–Sep 3hc ✿ TV 3P 105acres beef, dairy & mixed D noon

Lew *(SS326140)* ☎404
Stone-built farmhouse on the outskirts of the village.
Jun–Sep 3rm 2hc ✿ nc5 CTV 2P 60acres mixed B&b£4 Bdi£6 W£42 ⅃ D4pm

BRANSCOMBE Devon *Map 3 SY28*
Higher Bulstone *(SY176898)* ☎391
Fully modernised farmhouse dating from 1450. Situated about 2 miles from Branscombe Beach.
Etr–Sep 6hc ✿ CTV 10P 100acres dairy & mixed D5pm

BRAUNTON Devon *Map 2 SS43*
Denham Farm Holidays *(SS480404)*
North Buckland ☎ Croyde 890297
Large farmhouse, parts of which are 18th century, set in lovely countryside. 2 miles from Croyde and within easy reach of Barnstaple and Ilfracombe.
Closed 10–29Dec 8hc ✿ CTV 1P 7🏠 160acres mixed B&b£4.50–£5 Bdi£6.90–£8.10 W£48.50–£56 ⅃ W only 24Jun–Aug D4pm

Middle Spreacombe *(SS479421)*
☎ Woolacombe 370
Well-decorated, comfortable farmhouse 3m N of A361. Good location for country walks, fishing and bathing.
May–Oct 3hc ✿ CTV 3P 162acres mixed S% ✱Wfr£38 ⅃ D6.30pm

Park *(SS499363)* ☎812079
Farmhouse well-furnished with traditional simplicity. On the outskirts of Braunton, there are some good walks in the area.
4hc TV 6P 150acres arable dairy S% B&b£3.50–£4

BREAGE Cornwall *Map 2 SW62*
Sethnow *(SW614286)* ☎ Helston 3603
Long, low, 17th-century granite farmhouse with oak panelling. Fully modernised. Picturesque setting.
Apr–Oct 3hc TV 4P 110acres mixed S% ✱B&b£3.50–£4

BRENDON Devon *Map 3 SS74*
Farley Water *(SS744464)* ☎272
Comfortable farmhouse adjoining the moors. Good home cooking and freedom for children.
May–Nov 5rm 4hc TV P 223acres beef & sheep S% B&b fr£3.45 Bdi fr£5.75 Wfr£40.25 D7pm

Homestake Farm Guest House

Blackcross, Newquay, Cornwall TR8 4LU

A warm welcome awaits you at Homestake Farm. Sea 6 miles. Ideal for children and touring. Accommodation comprises 4 family and 4 double bedrooms, all with wash basins. Spacious colour TV lounge. Suitable for disabled guests. Sorry no pets. Reductions for children sharing and for O.A.Ps out of season. Open Easter to November. Sae for brochure please.
Telephone: Fraddon 860423 (STD 0726).

BRENT ELEIGH Suffolk *Map 5 TL94*
Street *(TL945476)* ☎ Lavenham 247271
*A most beautiful period house, tastefully
furnished to a high standard.*
Apr–Oct 2hc ⊗ nc TV 2P ₪ 140acres
arable S% B&b fr£6

BRIDESTOWE Devon *Map 2 SX58*
Ebsleigh *(SX510903)* ☎225
*Beautifully situated in 24 acres of ground
overlooking Dartmoor.*
5rm 4hc nc14 CTV 20P 24acres mixed
Little Bidlake *(SX494887)* ☎233
*Neat, clean and efficient farmhouse
adjacent to A30 between Bridestowe and
Launceston.*
Spring Bank Hol–Oct 2hc ⊗ CTV P 2🏠 ₪
170acres beef dairy
Town *(SX504905)* ☎226
*Tile-hung farmhouse with a pleasant,
homely atmosphere.*
Etr–Sep 3hc CTV 4P 150acres dairy S%
B&b£4.50–£5.50 Bdi£6.50–£7 Wfr£45
Ł D7pm
Week *(SX519913)* ☎221
*Farm is situated east of Bridestowe and
signposted from A30.*
6hc CTV 6P ₪ 160acres mixed S%
B&b£4–£4.50 Bdi£5.75–£6.50
W£40–£43 Ł D7pm

BRIDGERULE Devon *Map 2 SS20*
Buttsbeer Cross *(SS266043)* ☎210
*Modernised farmhouse dating from 15th
century. Within easy reach of Bude and
North Cornish coast.*
Etr–Oct 3rm 2hc ⊗ nc11 CTV 3P 143acres
mixed S% ✳B&b fr£4 Bdi fr£6 D5.30pm

BROUGH Cumbria *Map 12 NY71*
Augill House *(NY814148)* ☎305
*Stone-built Victorian farmhouse 1 mile
from village. Quiet, clean and comfortable.*
Closed Xmas & New Year 3hc CTV 5P ₪
40acres dairy

BRUTON Somerset *Map 3 ST63*
Gilcombe *(ST696364)* ☎3378
*Small, well furnished farmhouse
surrounded by countryside, one mile
from Bruton.*
Apr–Oct 2hc ⊗ nc3 TV 4P 2🏠 400acres
dairy S% B&b£4.50–£5

BUCKLAND BREWER Devon
Map 2 SS42
Holwell *(SS424159)* ☎ Langtree 288
*16th-century farmhouse with a friendly
and homely atmosphere.*
5rm 4hc CTV P 310acres mixed

BUDLEIGH SALTERTON Devon
Map 3 SY08
Tidwell House *(SY060834)* ☎2444
*Georgian farmhouse built in 1725,
standing in own grounds. Near coast,
on B3178, and convenient for touring
the moors.*
Closed Xmas 9hc ⚓ CTV 10P 2🏠 6acres
non-working S% B&b£6.50–£8
Bdi£8.50–£10 W£52–£64 Ł W only mid
Jun–mid Sep D5pm

BUDOCK Cornwall *Map 2 SW73*
Menehay *(SW787322)* Bilckland Rd
☎ Penryn 72550
*Pleasant farmhouse with good standard
of furnishings and decoration, convenient
for beach.*
Apr–Oct 3hc CTV P 69acres mixed

BULKWORTHY Devon *Map 2 SS31*
Blakes *(SS395143)* ☎ Milton Damerel 249
*Pleasant, comfortable and well-decorated
house in peaceful setting close to the
River Torridge.*
Apr–Oct 2hc ⊗ nc13 CTV 4P 155acres
mixed S% B&b£4–£4.50

BURNISTON N Yorks *Map 8 TA09*
Beaconsfield House *(NZ014928)*
South End ☎ Scarborough 870439
*Well furnished and decorated farmhouse
in village.*
Spring Bank Hol–Sep 3rm ⊗ nc3 TV 4P
1🏠 45acres dairy S% ✳B&b£4

BURRINGTON Avon *Map 3 ST45*
Bourne *(ST485599)* ☎ Blagdon 62255
*Attractive stone-built house with
surrounding farmland countryside.
Near village.*
Etr–Sep 3rm 2hc ⊗ nc5 CTV P ₪
300acres arable, beef, dairy & mixed

BUTTERLEIGH Devon *Map 3 SS90*
Sunnyside *(ST975088)* ☎ Bickleigh 322
*Farmhouse, built about 1700, is situated
in heart of the Devonshire countryside
3 miles west of Cullompton.*
5hc CTV 5P 110acres mixed
B&b£3.50–£5 Bdi fr£6 Wfr£40 Ł
D6.30pm

BUXTON Derbys *Map 7 SK07*
Priory Lea Guest House *(SK059719)*
50 White Knowle Rd ☎3737
*Situated in quiet cul-de-sac surrounded
by wooded countryside. Fine views across
open fields to Grin Low Tower.*
Etr–Nov 10hc ⚓ CTV 11P 100acres
beef S% B&b£5–£6 Bdi£8–£9 W£49–£52
Ł D5pm

CABUS Lancs *Map 7 SD44*
Wildings *(SO489479)* ☎ Garstang 3321
*Modernised Victorian farmhouse on A6.
Clean and pleasant with plenty of home
produce used in cooking.*
Etr–Oct 2hc ⊗ nc12 TV 8P 60acres dairy
S% B&b fr£4

CADELEIGH Devon *Map 3 SS90*
West Ridge *(SS904093)* ☎ Bickleigh 295
*Part 16th-century farmhouse set in a
secluded, wooded valley. Farmhouse fare
is home produced.*
Apr–Sep 3rm 1hc ⊗ nc5 TV 3P 109acres
dairy S% ✳B&b£3.50 Bdi£5.50 W£35
Ł D7pm

CADNAM Hants *Map 4 SU21*
Copythorne Lodge *(SU308148)* ☎2127
*Two-storey Victorian house set back from
the main road in wooded and rural
surroundings.*
4rm 1🏠🛋 TV 6P ₪ 30acres dairy S%
B&b fr£4

CALDBECK Cumbria *Map 11 NY33*
Friar Hall *(NY324399)* ☎633
*Modernised two-storey stone-built
farmhouse. Well-decorated and contains
good quality furniture.*
Apr–Sep 2hc ⊗ CTV 2P river 140acres
mixed S% B&b£4.25–£4.50 Bdi£6.75–£7

CAMELFORD Cornwall *Map 2 SX18*
Melorne *(SX099856)* Camelford Station
☎3200
*Situated approximately 1m N of village
near site of old railway station. Fishing*

and rough shooting available to guests.
Etr–Oct 7rm 6hc CTV 10P 100acres dairy
S% B&b fr£4.32 Bdi fr£6.90 Wfr£48.30 ⌊

CARKEEL Cornwall *Map 2 SX46*
Eales *(SX414605)* ☎ Saltash 2865
Clean and well decorated farmhouse.
Saltash 2 miles.
4rm TV 6P 11acres dairy

CASTLE CARROCK Cumbria
Map 12 NY55
Gelt Hall *(NY542554)* ☎ Hayton 260
Two-storey, stone-built farmhouse dating
from 1818. Situated in village centre.
Closed Xmas 3rm 3P 65acres dairy

CATLOWDY Cumbria *Map 12 NY47*
Bessiestown *(NY457768)*
☎ Nicholforest 219
Neat farmhouse, tastefully furnished and
comfortable. Visitors welcome to stroll
around farm buildings.
5rm 4hc CTV 6P 🍴 53acres mixed S%
B&b fr£4.50 Bdi£7–£7.50 W£45–£50
⌊ D4pm

CERNE ABBAS Dorset *Map 3 ST60*
Giants Head *(ST675029)*
Old Sherborne Rd ☎242
A modernised, detached farmhouse in
elevated position at the head of the
famous Cerne Giant. Open rural views.
Etr–Sep 5rm 3hc ⊗ nc10 TV 10P
4acres sheep S% B&b fr£4.75 Bdi fr£7.50
Wfr£42 ⌊ D7pm

CHAPMANSLADE Wilts *Map 3 ST84*
Spinney *(ST839480)* ☎412
Two-storey stone-built farmhouse

surrounded by fields and woodland
with farm buildings at rear.
Closed 22Dec–5Jan 3hc 1⇩🍴 TV 10P 🍴
4acres sheep & goats S% B&b£5–£6
W£28–£32 M

CHAWLEIGH Devon *Map 3 SS71*
Toatley *(SS710108)* ☎ Lapford 206
15th-century farmhouse in mid Devon
within easy reach of the north and south
coasts.
5rm 4hc CTV 20P 160acres mixed S%
Bdi fr£7 Wfr£40 ⌊ D7pm

CHELVEY Avon *Map 3 ST46*
Midgell *(ST461680)* ☎ Flax Bourton 2213
A pleasant old farmhouse in a peaceful,
rural setting. Garden with lawns.
Etr–Sep 3rm 2hc ⊗ TV P 🍴 160acres
arable & beef D7.30pm

CHERITON FITZPAINE Devon
Map 3 SS80
Brindiwell *(SS896079)* ☎357
Farmhouse situated on the side of a valley
with views of Exe Valley and Dartmoor.
Apr–Oct 3rm 1⇩🍴 ⊗ 🐾 CTV 4P 120acres
mixed S% B&b£4–£5 Bdi£6.50–£7
W£38–£40 ⌊ D7.30pm

CHILSWORTHY Devon *Map 2 SS30*
East Youldon *(SS322087)*
☎ Bradworthy 322
Farm located midway between Bradworthy
and Holsworthy.
mid May–Sep 3hc ⊗ CTV 135acres dairy

CHURCHILL Avon *Map 3 ST45*
Churchill Green *(ST432603)* ☎852438
Creeper-clad 16th-century farmhouse

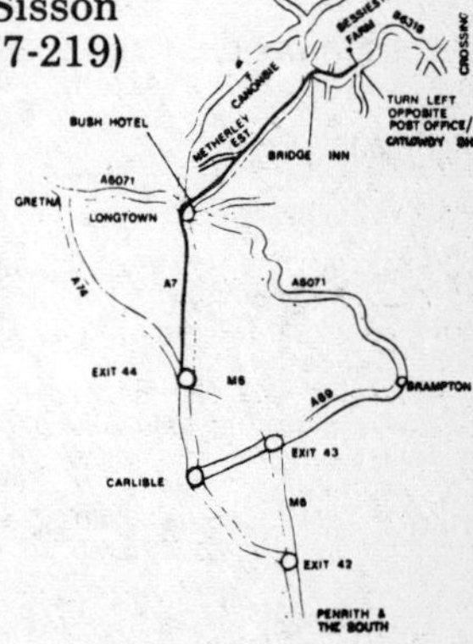

Bed, breakfast and evening meals are available in the
delightful and spacious farmhouse. The house is
central heated, has guests' dining room and lounge
with colour TV, five, modern comfortable, bedrooms —
four double and one twin-bedded — each with wash
hand basins. Excellent accommodation, friendly
atmosphere and good food.
BESSIESTOWN FARM is a small beef/sheep rearing farm situated in a quiet rural area
approximately 17 miles north of Carlisle and only 3 miles from the Scottish Border,
making it an ideal base for a family/touring holiday or for breaking your journey to and
from Scotland. There is a childrens' play area and games room (pool, table tennis and
darts) and many farm animals (cattle, sheep, a pony, donkey, cats, a dog and chickens)
to interest the children and adults alike. For the tourist it is convenient for the Lake
District, Roman Wall, Galloway and Solway Coast or pleasant country walks, riding,
fishing and golf within a 15 mile radius. There are also three self catering cottages with
evening meals in the farm house if desired.

which has been modernised but retains old world character. Comfortable lounge with log fires. Large pleasant garden and heated outdoor pool.
7hc ✷ TV 50P ⬤ 25acres mixed
Bdi fr£9.78 W£46–£57.50 ⊾ D6pm

Primrose *(ST456609)* ☎852358
Attractive, two-storey, stone-built farmhouse with a pretty, landscape garden.
6rm nc5 CTV 6P ⬤ 12acres non-working
S% B&b fr£6 Bdi fr£9 Wfr£63 ⊾ D6.30pm

CHURCHINFORD Somerset
Map 3 ST21
Hunter Lodge *(ST212144)*
☎ Church Stanton 253
Detached, two-storey farmhouse with slate roof and large garden.
3rm nc5 TV 4P 31acres mixed S%
B&b£4–£6 Bdi£6–£8 W£28–£42 M

CLAVERHAM Avon *Map 3 ST46*
Green *(ST454662)* ☎ Yatton 833180
Long, low farm cottage located in a 'picture postcard' setting.
Jan–Nov 3hc CTV P 2🏠 4acres
non-working

CLOVELLY Devon *Map 2 SS32*
Burnstone *(SS325233)* Higher Clovelly
☎219
Large, comfortably furnished farmhouse with open fire in spacious lounge. Good farmhouse fare.
Etr–Sep 4hc ✷ nc8 CTV 4P ⬤ 240acres
arable & dairy

CLUN Salop *Map 7 SO38*
Llanhedric *(SO283841)* ☎203
Large and well furnished farmhouse with oak beams and antique furniture.
May–Oct 2rm 1hc ✷ ♨ CTV 2P 400acres
dairy & mixed

CLUNTON Salop *Map 7 SO38*
Hurst Mill *(SO318811)* ☎ Clun 224
Small stone-built farmhouse in picturesque setting, surrounded by tree-clad hills. Friendly atmosphere.
4rm ♨ TV 4P river 100acres mixed S%
B&b£5.50–£6.50 Bdi£7–£8 D7.30pm

CLYST ST MARY Devon *Map 3 SX99*
Ivington *(SX985912)* ☎ Topsham 3290
Large brick-built farmhouse surrounded by lawns and gardens.
3rm 2hc CTV 6P 200acres dairy S%
B&b£4 W£24.50 M

CODSALL *(Nr Wolverhampton)* Staffs
Map 7 SJ80
Moors *(SJ868043)* Mill Ln ☎2330
Modernised early 19th century farmhouse with quality furniture and decor and beamed ceilings. Beautiful views of surrounding area which is of historical interest.
4hc nc4 TV 10P 60acres mixed S%
B&b£7–£7.50 Bdi£11–£12 W£55–£58
⊾ D4pm

COLEFORD Devon *Map 3 SS70*
Butsford Barton *(SS764004)*
☎ Copplestone 353
New brick-built farmhouse with fine pastoral views over Devonshire countryside.
Etr–Sep 3rm 2hc ✷ CTV P 156acres
arable dairy S% B&b£4.25 Bdi£7.25
W£45 ⊾ D5pm

COMBE MARTIN Devon *Map 2 SS54*
Longlands *(SS614451)* ☎3522

Farmhouse amid unspoilt woods and valleys with fine views.
mid Mar–Oct 6hc TV 12P ⬤ 25acres
beef sheep ✱B&b£3.50–£4 Bdi£5.50–£6
W£36–£40 ⊾ D6.30pm

COOKLEY Suffolk *Map 5 TM37*
Green *(TM337772)* ☎ Linstead 209
17th-century farmhouse with exposed timbers in an area of rural peace and quiet. Friendly atmosphere.
Mar–Nov 3hc ✷ nc8 TV 4P 45acres mixed
S% B&b fr£4.50 Bdi fr£7 Wfr£46.50 ⊾
D3.30pm

COOMBE Cornwall *Map 2 SW95*
Treway *(SW945505)*
☎ Grampound Road 882236
Pleasant, comfortable farmhouse in isolated rural setting about 8 miles from St Austell.
3rm 2hc ♨ CTV 4P 1🏠 ⬤ 160acres dairy
S% B&b£4–£4.25 Wfr£28 M

COTLEIGH Devon *Map 3 ST20*
Barn Park *(ST218050)* ☎ Upottery 297
Comfortably furnished farmhouse offering tasty country fare.
Mar–Sep 2rm ✷ CTV 3P 82acres dairy S%
B&b fr£3.75 Bdi fr£6 Wfr£37 ⊾ D6pm

CREDITON Devon *Map 3 SS80*
Wellparks *(SS845996)* ☎2727
19th-century, brick-built farmhouse overlooking fields and woodlands. Useful overnight stop for tourists.
12rm ♨ CTV 50P 4🏠 112acres ⊾

CROMHALL Avon *Map 3 ST69*
Varley *(ST699905)* Talbot End
☎ Wickwar 292
Spacious, two storey, stone-built farmhouse with garden. Well maintained and neatly decorated throughout.
Etr–Sep 4hc ✷ CTV 6P ⬤ 70acres dairy
B&b£4.50–£5 Bdi£7.50–£8
W£49.50–£53 ⊾ (W only Jul & Aug) D1pm

CROOK Cumbria *Map 7 SD49*
Greenbank *(SD462953)*
☎ Kendal 821216
Attractive farmhouse near village centre. Pleasant gardens. Mainly dairy plus small mushroom farm.
18Mar–Nov 5hc nc10 TV 6P ⬤ 14½acres
mixed S% B&b£4.50 Bdi£6.50 W£45
⊾ D noon
Warriner Yeat *(SD438950)*
☎ Windermere 3828
Large, attractive house in small garden. Pleasant setting with fine views.
Apr–Oct 3hc ✷ nc4 6P 75acres mixed
B&b£3–£3.50

CRUCKTON Salop *Map 7 SJ41*
Woodfield *(SJ432108)* ☎ Hanwood 249
Large, modern, detached farmhouse with neat gardens.
3rm ✷ nc7 CTV 3P 83acres ✱B&b fr£5

CUBERT Cornwall *Map 2 SW75*
Treworgans *(SW787589)*
☎ Crantock 200
Detached bungalow, situated approximately 1m from the village of Cubert.
Closed Xmas 5hc CTV 6P 72acres mixed
S% ✱B&b£4 Bdi£5 W£35 D4pm

CULLOMPTON Devon *Map 3 ST00*
Five Bridges *(ST026095)* ☎3453
Well-maintained, brick-built farmhouse. Clean and well-decorated.

Closed Xmas 5hc ⚘ TV 6P 1🏠 22acres
non-working S% B&bf3.75 Bdif6 Wf38
⚿ D noon

CURRY RIVEL Somerset *Map 3 ST32*
Hillards *(ST385249)* ☎ Langport 251737
*Well-furnished farmhouse. Private tennis
court and sometimes horse-riding available.*
4hc ⊗ nc3 TV 12P 8acres mixed S%
B&bf5 Wf35 M

CURY Cornwall *Map 2 SW62*
Nanplough *(SW687215)*
☎ Mullion 240232
*Attractive, comfortable farmhouse. Access
via ½-mile gravel lane.*
Etr–Oct 4hc ⊗ nc5 CTV 3P 50acres arable
beef sheep S% B&bf4.50 Bdif8 Wf30
M D6.30pm

CURY CROSS LANES Cornwall
Map 2 SW62
Polglase *(SW286213)* ☎ Mullion 240469
5 miles from Helston.
Etr–Sep 4rm 3hc ⊗ CTV 4P 70acres
mixed D6.30pm

DALWOOD *(Nr Axminster)* Devon
Map 3 ST20
Elford *(ST258004)* ☎ Axminster 32415
*17th-century farmhouse in country setting.
Panoramic, pastoral views.*
Feb–Oct Lic 5rm 4hc 2⇄🏠 ⊗ TV 8P
50acres beef dairy sheep S%
B&bfrf4.75 Bdifrf7 Wf47.50 ⚿ D5pm

DENTON Norfolk *Map 5 TM28*
Upland *(TM273887)* ☎ Homersfield 235
*Simple but cosy farmhouse set in remote
area.*
4rm 2hc ⊗ ⚘ TV P 16acres non-working
S% B&bf4–f4.50 Bdif6–f6.50 Wf39
⚿ D6.30pm

DOCKLOW Heref & Worcs *Map 3 SO55*
West End *(SO559578)* ☎ Steens
Bridge 256
*Large, three-storey 17th-century farmhouse.
Solid oak floors and huge doors. A listed
building with large garden and coarse
fishing pool.*
May–Oct 4rm ⊗ TV 6P 91acres beef sheep
S% B&bf3.50 Bdif5.50 Wfrf35 ⚿
D5pm

DRIMPTON Dorset *Map 3 ST40*
Axe *(ST415061)* ☎ Crewkerne 72422
*Stone-built, detached, double-fronted
farmhouse standing in isolated rural
position.*
3hc ⊗ TV 6P 🍺 160acres arable dairy
S% B&bf5.50–f6.50 Wf35–f45 M

DULFORD Devon *Map 3 ST00*
Nap *(ST069065))* ☎ Kentisbeare 287
*Well appointed farmhouse set in the
hamlet of Dulford on main road to
Cullompton.*
Closed Xmas 5hc TV 4P 🍺 36acres
mixed B&bf3.50–f3.75 Bdif5–f5.50
Wf33–f35 D noon

DULVERTON Somerset *Map 3 SS92*
Warmor *(SS944259)* ☎23479
*Very old farmhouse with a lot of character.
Parts are 400 years old.*
May–Sep 3hc ⊗ CTV 4🏠 70acres mixed
S% B&bf4.50 Bdif8 Wf56 ⚿ D5pm

EAST TAPHOUSE Cornwall *Map 2 SX16*
Pendower *(SX184635)* ☎ Dobwalls
20332

*Double-fronted, stone-built farmhouse on
main A390. Main farm buildings 2 miles
away. Ideal centre for touring.*
6hc CTV 8P 🍺 5acres non-working
B&bf4.50–f5 Bdif6–f6.50 Wf40–f45
⚿ D6pm

EDINGWORTH Avon *Map 3 ST35*
Rookery *(ST359532)* ☎200
*Stone-built manor house-style farm with
extensive outbuildings. Set in Sedgemoor.*
6rm 5hc ⊗ ⚘ CTV 6P 1🏠 🍺 200acres
mixed W only last wk Jul & 1st wk Aug
D7pm

EDLINGHAM Northumb *Map 12 NU10*
Lumby Law *(NU115096)*
☎ Whittingham 277
*Modernised stone built farmhouse in rural
surroundings.*
May–Sep 3hc ⚘ CTV 3P 3🏠 🍺
900acres mixed B&bf5–f6
Bdif7.50–f9 Wf50–f61 ⚿ (W Jul–Aug)
D6pm

EGLINGHAM Northumb *Map 12 NU11*
West Ditchburn *(NU131207)*
☎ Powburn 337
*Comfortable farmhouse with garden
available to guests. Overlooking unspoilt
countryside.*
2hc CTV 6P 🍺 beef sheep S%
B&bf5–f5.50 Bdif7.50–f8 D7.30pm

EGLOSHAYLE Cornwall *Map 2 SX07*
Croanford *(SX034715)* Ford
☎ St Mabyn 349
*Small, compact farmhouse in pleasant
countryside. Stream in side garden.
Wadebridge 2½ miles.*
May–Sep 3rm ⊗ nc5 CTV 2P 1🏠 113acres
mixed S% B&bf4.50–f5 Bdif6.50
Wf45 ⚿ D5pm

ELLESMERE Salop *Map 7 SJ33*
Mereside *(SJ408343)* ☎2404
*Three-storey farmhouse 17th-century in
parts. Close to local beauty spot, The Mere.
Bird sanctuary and abundant wild life.*
5hc TV 🏠 55acres dairy

ELSDON Northumb *Map 12 NY99*
Dunns *(NY937969)* ☎ Hepple 40219
*Old farmhouse in quiet position amongst
the Cheviot Hills and Coquet Valley.*
3rm 2hc CTV P 1000acres mixed
✳B&bf5

Raylees *(NY926915)*
☎ Otterburn 20287
Comfortable, well furnished farmhouse.
3rm 2hc ⊗ CTV 3P 🍺 700acres mixed
S% B&bfrf5

ETTINGTON Warwicks *Map 4 SP24*
Whitfield *(SP265506)* Warwick Rd
☎ Stratford-on-Avon 740260
*Pleasant house set in active farm with a
wide variety of animals for interest.*
Apr–Aug 3hc ⊗ CTV 3P 220acres mixed
S% B&bf3.50–f3.75

EXETER Devon *Map 3 SX99*
Hill Barton *(SX956932)* 133 Hill Barton
Rd ☎67630
*Attractive, well built farmhouse with small,
trim garden and lawn. Situated on Exeter
bypass (A30).*
Closed Xmas 7hc TV 15P 80acres mixed
S% B&bf4.50

EXMOUTH Devon *Map 3 SY08*
Maer *(SY018803)* Maer Lane ☎3651
*In large garden which has views of sea and
Haldon Hills. Approximately 5 min walk
to beach and 20 min walk to town.*
May–Sep 2rm ⌘ TV 4P ♨ sea 300acres
mixed S% B&b£5 W£35 M
Quentance *(SY037812)* Salterton Rd
☎ Budleigh Salterton 2733
*Superior style farmhouse. Bedrooms
overlook South East Devon coastline.*
Apr–Sep 3hc ⌘ nc4 CTV 4P sea 260acres
mixed D7pm

FALFIELD Avon *Map 3 ST69*
Green *(ST687943)* ☎319 (260319
fr Jan '80)
*A two-storey, colour-washed, stone-built
farmhouse. Lawns, hard tennis court and
swimming pool in the grounds.*
Jan–22Dec (No dinner Sep–May) 6hc
CTV 10P 100acres dairy S%
B&b£4.50–£6 Bdi£8–£9.50 W£50–£60
Ł D2pm

FARRINGTON GURNEY Avon
Map 3 ST65
Hayboro *(ST628555)* ☎ Temple
Cloud 52342
*Small farmhouse adjacent to the
Farrington Inn. Garden adjoining the
farm and fields.*
15Jan–Nov 3rm 5P 78acres dairy S%
B&b£5–£5.50 Bdi£7.50–£8 W£34–£37
M D10am

FELMINGHAM Norfolk *Map 9 TG22*
Felmingham Hall *(TG245275)*
☎ Swanton Abbott 228
*Large, interesting old manor house.
Remote but near North Walsham. Big
rooms comfortably appointed.*
11hc 5→♨ ⌘ nc15 CTV 100P 2🏠 ♨
60acres sheep S% B&b£9.20–£12.36
Bdi£14.66–£16.96 D6pm

FLASH (Buxton, Derbys) Staffs
Map 7 SK06
Far Brook *(SK017670)* Quarnford
☎ Buxton 3085
*Old stone-built farmhouse situated in
picturesque and peaceful surroundings
in upper reaches of Dane Valley.*
Etr & Jun–Oct 3rm 2hc nc5 2P 1🏠
65acres beef S% B&b£4.50–£5.50

FOWEY Cornwall *Map 2 SX15*
Trezare *(SX112538)* ☎3485
*Farmhouse conveniently situated 1 mile
from Fowey. Pleasant atmosphere and good
farmhouse fare.*
Jun–Sep 3rm 2hc ⌘ CTV 4P 2🏠
230acres arable, beef & sheep

FRESSINGFIELD Suffolk *Map 5 TM27*
Priory House *(TM256770)* Priory Rd
☎254
*Attractive 400-year-old brick-built
farmhouse with beamed interior. Quality
furniture. Secluded garden. Ideal touring
centre.*
Closed Xmas 4rm 3hc ⌘ nc9 TV 7P ♨
2acres pigs S% B&b£6.25 Bdi£8.50–£9
Wfr£55.50 Ł (W only Jul & Aug) D7pm

GATE HELMSLEY N Yorks *Map 8 SE65*
Lime Field *(SE693534)* Scoreby
☎ York 489224
*Comfortably furnished farmhouse with big
garden, set in the largely agricultural
Yorkshire Wolds.*
Mar–Oct 4rm 2hc ⌘ nc3 CTV 4P 125acres
arable S% B&b£5–£5.50

GEDNEY HILL Lincs *Map 8 TF31*
Sycamore *(TF336108)* ☎ Whaplode
Drove 445
*Brick farmhouse built about 1850. Near
small village of Gedney Hill in quiet rural
surroundings.*
Closed Xmas 3rm CTV 6P ♨ 100acres
mixed S% B&bfr£5.50 Bdifr£8
Wfr£56 Ł D5pm

GIGGLESWICK N Yorks *Map 7 SD86*
Close House *(SD801634)*
☎ Settle 3540
*17th-century farmhouse with tree-lined
private drive. Well kept gardens. River
bathing and fishing nearby.*
May–Sep 3hc ⌘ nc 5P 230acres dairy
B&b£9.18 Bdi£16.20 W£102.06 Ł

GLASTONBURY Somerset *Map 3 ST53*
Cradlebridge *(ST477385)* ☎31827
*Large, renovated farmhouse with vegetable
and fruit gardens.*
Closed Xmas 3hc TV 6P ♨ 170acres
dairy S% B&b£5–£5.50 Bdi£9–£10
W£54–£60 Ł D noon

GRAMPOUND Cornwall *Map 2 SW94*
Ventonwyn *(SW957501)*
☎ Grampound Rd 882349
*Well preserved, 13th-century farmhouse.
¾ mile from the main St Austell to Truro
road, A390.*
Etr–Oct 6rm TV 10P 177acres mixed

GULVAL Cornwall *Map 2 SW43*
Kenegie Home *(SW481327)*
☎ Penzance 2515
*15th-century, 'olde-worlde' farmhouse.
1 mile from Penzance. Accent on good
farmhouse food.*

Close House

Giggleswick, N. Yorkshire
Tel: Settle 3540

BTA Commendation 'Taste of England'
Table licence
Lovely 17th century farmhouse standing in 230 acres
of farmland in the Yorkshire Dales. Situated in a
private drive between Settle and Giggleswick station.
Tastefully furnished — antiques etc. Excellent
breakfasts and dinners. The ideal place for a quiet
relaxing holiday in beautiful surroundings. No
children under eight or dogs. One of seven
establishments chosen for the 1976 Spotlight feature.
Mr and Mrs H R S Hargreaves.

Apr–Sep 3hc ✻ CTV 4P 300acres arable
dairy S% B&b£5.50–£7 W£38–£45 **M**

GUNNISLAKE Cornwall *Map 2 SX47*
Whimple *(SX428708)* ☎832526
*Attractive 17th-century farmhouse. Oak
beams and panelling in lounge. On banks
of River Tamar.*
Closed Xmas 3hc ✻ TV 6P river 50acres
dairy S% B&b£6.50 Bdi£8.50 W£52
Ł D5pm

GWEEK Cornwall *Map 2 SW72*
Tregoon *(SW699271)* ☎ Mawgan
(Helston) 286
*Recently built bungalow in a convenient
location about 1 mile west of the village.*
Apr–Sep 4rm 3hc ✻ CTV 6P river 54acres
arable & beef D5pm

GWINEAR Cornwall *Map 2 SW53*
Chycoose *(SW608367)* 33 Wall Rd
☎ Leedstown 357
*Modern farmhouse situated in old Cornish
village. Small front garden. Home produced
farmhouse meals.*
Mar–Oct 3rm 2hc ✻ nc TV 4P 🍺 46acres
mixed S% B&bfr£4 Bdi fr£5.50
Wfr£40 Ł

HABBERLEY Salop *Map 7 SJ40*
Hall *(SJ397036)* ☎ Pontesbury 689
*Farmhouse reputed to be 16th-century.
Large comfortable rooms with antique
furniture.*
3rm 1hc ✻ 200acres mixed

HADLEY HEATH Heref & Worcs
Map 3 SO86
The Farmhouse *(SO858622)*
☎ Worcester 620837
*Recently converted farmhouse, fully
modernised. Set in a quiet area.*
34rm 1hc TV 20P 🍺 D9pm

HAILSHAM E Sussex *Map 5 TQ50*
Chicheley *(TQ576103)* Hempstead Ln
☎841253
*Large house divided in two; set in typical
Sussex countryside.*
3hc ✻ nc3 TV 6P 5½acres poultry S%
B&b£5

HALFWAY HOUSE Salop *Map 7 SJ31*
Willows *(SJ342115)* ☎233
*Small farm cottage well situated for those
travelling to Wales. Cottage surrounded
by Long Mountain and Middlebar Hills.*
Mar–Oct 2rm 1hc ✻ nc5 CTV 10P 35acres
mixed S% ✳B&b£3.75–£4.25 Bdi£5–£6
W£35–£45 Ł D4pm

HALSTOCK Dorset *Map 3 ST50*
New Inn *(ST532036)* ☎ Corscombe 256
*Detached, cottage-style farmhouse in quiet
situation.*
Apr–Oct 2rm ✻ TV 3P 55acres arable
beef sheep S% B&b£4–£5 W£26–£32 **M**

HALTWHISTLE Northumb *Map 12 NY76*
White Craig *(NY713649)* Shield Mill
☎20565
*Stone-built Georgian style bungalow in an
elevated position, providing excellent
views. Within walking distance of
Hadrian's Wall.*
3hc nc11 CTV 3P 🍺 17acres mixed S%
B&b£4.50–£6 W£30–£40.50 **M**

HARBERTON Devon *Map 3 SX75*
Preston *(SX777587)* ☎ Totnes 862235
*Old farmhouse on outskirts of quaint and
attractive village. Totnes about 2½ miles.*
Apr–Sep 3hc ✻ nc3 CTV 2P 1🏠
200acres dairy B&b£5 Bdi£7.50
W£47.50 Ł

Tristford *(SX780594)* ☎ Totnes 862418
*Charming house with 'olde worlde'
atmosphere. Good centre for touring the
coast between Plymouth and Tor Bay.*
3hc ✻ nc CTV 5🏠 🍺 147acres mixed
sheep S% B&b£4 Bdi£7

HARMER HILL Salop *Map 7 SJ52*
Hill *(SJ487232)* Newton-on-the-Hill
☎ Clive 273
*Two-storey, red brick house in quiet rural
situation.*
Etr–Oct 3rm 1hc ✻ nc10 TV 4P 76acres
mixed D6.30pm

HARROP FOLD Lancs *Map 7 SD74*
Harrop Fold *(SD746492)* ☎ Bolton-by-
Bowland 600
*Lancashire longhouse built around 17th
century. Nestling in pleasant quiet valley.
Excellent accommodation, interesting
meals.*
Closed Xmas 3hc (A 2hc) ✻ 🐕 4P 🍺
280acres beef & sheep D10am

HARTLAND Devon *Map 2 SS22*
Edistone *(SS249219)* ☎212
*Isolated farmhouse offering wholesome
country fare.*
mid May–mid Sep 3rm ✻ CTV 3P
80acres mixed

Holloford *(SS289236)* ☎275
*Two storey, stone-built Devonshire
farmhouse in rather isolated countryside.
Oak beams in bedrooms. Near Hartland
Point.*
Spring Bank Hol–mid Sep 3hc CTV P
200acres arable & dairy

Mettaford *(SS284245)* ☎249
*Attractive Georgian farmhouse, 2 miles
from the village of Hartland. In woodland
setting with panoramic views of
coastline and Lundy Isle.*
5rm ♨ CTV 10P 17acres mixed S%
B&b£6.48 Bdi£8.64 W£54 Ł D8.30pm

HATHERSAGE Derbys *Map 8 SK28*
Highlow Hall *(SK219802)*
☎ Hope Valley 50393
*16th-century house of character. Well
furnished interior containing several
antiques. Isolated position south of
Hathersage.*
Etr–Nov 6hc ⊗ CTV 12P 900acres mixed
D6pm

HEASLEY MILL Devon *Map 3 SS73*
Crangs Heasleigh *(SS735325)* ☎ North
Molton 268
*Old farmhouse in North Devonshire
scenery, convenient for touring Exmoor.
Tasty farmhouse fare.*
Closed Xmas 6rm 5hc CTV 10P 185acres
mixed

HENLADE Somerset *Map 3 ST22*
Musgrave *(ST269236)* ☎442346
*Small farmhouse with side garden and
orchard. 400yds from main road.*
Closed Xmas 2rm ⊗ nc7 CTV 3P 107acres
dairy S% B&b£4–£4.50 Bdi£5.25–£5.70
Wfr£35 Ł

HENSTRIDGE Somerset *Map 3 ST71*
Manor *(ST692206)* Bowden
☎ Templecombe 213
*16th-century, stone-built farmhouse with
lattice windows. Surrounded by grassland
and wooded areas.*
May–Sep 2rm ⊗ CTV P 2🏠 🍴 250acres
arable dairy S% B&b£5.50 W£30 M

HENTON Somerset *Map 3 ST44*
Church *(ST493455)*
☎ Wells (Somerset) 72469
*Two storey, 150-year-old farmhouse in
very good condition. Furnished in traditional
style. Surrounded by gardens.*
May–Sep 4hc (A 2rm) nc14 TV 6P 3acres
non-working

HERRINGFLEET Suffolk *Map 5 TM49*
Pond *(TM475978)* ☎ Fritton 253
*Very pleasant, rather isolated farmhouse.
Fishing nearby.*
Etr–mid Oct 3rm 1hc ⊗ 4P 140acres
mixed

HETHERSETT Norfolk *Map 5 TG10*
Park *(TG148037)* ☎ Norwich 810264
*Modernised Georgian farmhouse.
Interestingly furnished; part modern,
part antique. Well situated for excursions
to Norfolk Broads.*
5hc 3🍴 (A 12hc 6🍴) ⊗ ♨ CTV 12P
12🏠 🍴 200acres mixed B&b£6–£7
Bdi£10–£11.50 W£55–£60
W only Jul & Aug D6pm

HITCHAM Suffolk *Map 5 TL95*
Chiltern End Fruit Farm *(TL986511)*
Fen Ln ☎ Bildeston 740608
*Modern bungalow on four-acre fruit farm.
Very rural setting. Reasonably central for
West Suffolk.*
Etr–Sep 5hc nc12 CTV 20P 2🏠 🍴 4acres
D noon

HOLBETON Devon *Map 2 SX65*
Keaton *(SX595480)* ☎255
*Large, stone built and well maintained
farmhouse. Some walls 18in thick. Isolated
rural position. Yachting at Newton Ferrers
3 miles away.*
Apr–Oct 2rm ⊗ nc5 TV 2P sea 117acres
mixed S% B&b£4–£5.50

HOLNE Devon *Map 3 SX76*
Wellpritton *(SX716704)*
☎ Poundsgate 273
*Tastefully modernised farmhouse in
Dartmoor National Park. There are
panoramic views and the farm has its own
swimming pool.*
Mar–Nov 3rm 2hc nc7 CTV 3P 1🏠 🍴
15acres mixed ✳B&b£4.50–£5.50
Bdi£7–£7.50 W£45–£49 Ł

HOLSWORTHY Devon *Map 2 SS30*
Leworthy *(SS323012)* ☎253488
*Low, black and white farmhouse with
attractive garden facing open country.
Pleasantly situated.*
Closed Xmas 10rm 8hc 2🛏🍴 ⊗ nc4
CTV 20P 2🏠 240acres mixed
S% B&b£7–£9 Bdi£9–£11.50
W£55–£70 Ł D6pm

HONITON Devon *Map 3 ST10*
Roebuck *(ST147001)* Weston ☎2225
*Modern farm on western end of Honiton
bypass, 8 miles from the coast.*
4rm 3hc CTV P 🍴 180acres dairy S%
B&b£4.50 Bdi£6.50

HORNS CROSS Devon *Map 2 SS32*
Steart *(SS389237)* ☎ Clovelly 239
*Old style house with low-ceilinged rooms.
Pleasant atmosphere. Good farmhouse
fare.*
Whit–Sep 2hc ⊗ 2P 40acres mixed S%
B&b£4

Swanton *(SS355227)* ☎ Clovelly 241
*Modern, dormer-style bungalow
pleasantly situated overlooking Bristol
Channel.*
Mar–Oct 3rm 2hc ⊗ TV P sea 50acres
dairy S% B&b£3.75 Bdi£5.25 W£32.50
Ł D noon

HULME END Derbys *Map 7 SK15*
Lower Hurst *(SK118592)* ☎ Hartington
278
*Older-style farmhouse offering simple
accommodation. Rather isolated position.*
Etr–Oct 3rm ⊗ nc TV 150acres dairy

ILAM Staffs *Map 7 SK15*
Beechenhill *(SK129525)*
☎ Alstonfiield 274
*Two-storey, stone-built farmhouse with
exposed beams. Built about 1720.
Unspoilt rural area with panoramic views.*
Jun–Sep 2rm ⊗ nc5 TV 2P 92acres dairy

IPSTONES Staffs *Map 7 SK04*
Glenwood House *(SK006488)* ☎294
*Large house about 100 years old built of
dressed sandstone blocks in very
picturesque and peaceful rural
surroundings.*
2rm TV 2P 🍴 58acres dairy S%
B&b£4.20–£5 Bdi£6.70–£8.50
W£46.90–£59.50 Ł D5pm

IRTHINGTON Cumbria *Map 12 NY46*
Seat Hill *(NY483634)* ☎ Kirklinton 226
*Sandstone building dating from 1726.
Interior fully modernised. Attractive*

flower garden and lawn. On A6071.
Mar–Oct 4rm 1hc CTV P 2🏠 217acres
mixed

IVYBRIDGE Devon *Map 2 SX65*
White Oaks *(SX654562)* Filham ☎2207
*Large bungalow with well kept gardens
and lawns. 1m E on B3213.*
4hc 🕸🐾 CTV 10P 💷 4acres dairy S%
B&bfr£5.40 Bdifr£8.10 D8.30pm

JACOBSTOWE Devon *Map 2 SS50*
Higher Cadham *(SS585026)*
☎ Exbourne 647
*Well decorated and comfortably
furnished farmhouse.*
Etr–Oct 4rm 1hc 🕸 nc3 CTV 6P
139acres mixed B&b£3.50 Bdi£5.50
W£35 ⌧ D5pm

KEA Cornwall *Map 2 SW84*
Higher Lanner *(SW831414)*
☎ Truro 3037
*Farmhouse 3 miles west of Truro on
unclassified road. Overlooks River Fal.*
Etr–Sep 3hc TV 6P river 150acres dairy
S% B&b£3.75–£4 Bdi£5.50–£6
W£38–£42 ⌧ D2pm

KENDAL Cumbria *Map 7 SD59*
Bank Head *(SD496926)* Underbarrow Rd
☎21785
Etr–Oct 4rm 3hc 🕸 TV 6P 💷 240acres
dairy sheep S% ✳B&b£4
Garnett House *(SD500959)* Burnside
☎24542
*A 15th-century stone-built farmhouse
standing in an elevated position
overlooking Howgill Fells. Close to
both Windermere and Kendal.*
Closed Xmas 4hc 🕸 nc CTV 6P 270acres
mixed S% ✳B&b£4.50 Bdi£6 D7pm
Natland Mill Beck *(SD520907)* ☎21122
*17th-century, local stone farmhouse with
original beams, doors and cupboards.
Large, well furnished rooms. Attractive
garden.*
Closed Nov–Feb 2rm 1hc 🕸 CTV 4P
100acres dairy S% B&b£4–£4.50

KENNFORD Devon *Map 3 SX98*
Holloway Barton *(SX893855)* ☎832302
*Two storey, stone-built cottage set amid
farm buildings. Good views of surrounding
countryside.*
4hc 🕸 nc5 CTV 4P 2🏠 💷 360acres
mixed S% B&bfr£4.50 Bdifr£7
Lynwood *(SX892859)* ☎832517
*Well furnished farmhouse, about 5 miles
from Exeter. Rough shooting in grounds.*
3hc CTV 3P river 350acres mixed S%
B&bfr£4.80 Bdifr£7 D6.30pm

KESWICK Cumbria *Map 11 NY22*
Low Nest *(NY291226)* ☎72378
*Comfortable farmhouse with beamed
ceiling in dining room. Clean and tidy
decor.*
May–Oct 5rm 4hc nc4 6P 120acres
mixed S% ✳B&b£4.60–£5
Bdi£8–£8.50 W£52–£56 ⌧ D4pm

KIMBOLTON Heref & Worcs *Map 3 SO56*
Menalls *(SO528611)* ☎ Leominster 2605
*Delightful farmhouse set in herefordshire
valley scenery.*
Apr–Oct 2hc 🕸 nc5 CTV 4P 40acres
mixed

KINGSCOTT Devon *Map 2 SS51*

Flavills *(SS538182)* St Giles
☎ Torrington 3250
*Well maintained, large Elizabethan
farmhouse, situated in the village of
Kingscott. Torrington 3½ miles.*
May–Oct 4rm TV 10P 125acres mixed
D4pm

KINGSLAND Heref & Worcs *Map 3 SO46*
Tremayne *(SO447613)* ☎233
*Deceptively large, two storey building
on one of main routes to Leominster.*
Apr–Oct 3rm 1hc CTV 4P 💷 42acres
mixed sheep S% B&b£4
Westfield *(SO436622)* ☎348
*Two-storey, 17th-century farmhouse with
original oak beams and brasses. Trout
fishing in River Pinsey which runs
through farm.*
Etr–Oct 2rm 🕸 nc TV 2P 1🏠 60acres
mixed

KINGSWEAR Devon *Map 3 SX95*
Boohay *(SX899520)* ☎284
*Large, comfortable farmhouse, well
situated for touring the beaches of South
Devon.*
3hc (A 2rm) 🕸 CTV 6P 560acres mixed
D6pm

KINGTON Heref & Worcs *Map 3 SO25*
School *(SO266550)* Up Hergest
☎230453
*Large farmhouse dating back to c1625
perched high on Hergest Ridge,
overlooking valley of the River Arrow
2m SW of town.*
4hc 🕸 CTV 6P 290acres mixed S%
B&b£5–£5.50 Bdi£7–£7.50
W£49–£52 D6pm

KIRK IRETON Derbys *Map 8 SK25*
Sitch *(SK260515)* ☎ Wirksworth 2454
*Large sandstone farmhouse with extensive
outbuildings standing in a fairly remote
but picturesque area.*
4rm 2hc CTV 3P 3🏠 💷 327acres arable,
beef & sheep S%

KNAPTOFT Leics *Map 4 SP68*
Knaptoft House *(SP619894)*
Bruntingthorpe Rd ☎ Peatling Magna 388
*Modern building on site of Georgian
farmhouse. Medieval fishponds being
restored. Off Shearsby–Bruntingthorpe rd,
1m E from its junc with A50. Or leave
M1 at junc 20 then via Kimcote and
Watton.*
3hc CTV 6P 145acres mixed sheep S%
✳B&bfr£4.25 Bdifr£6.25 W£45–£52
⌧ D2pm

KNOWSTONE Devon *Map 3 SS82*
Eastacott *(SS837231)* ☎ Anstey Mills 215
*Isolated farmhouse in the heart of north
Devon. Large sun lounge at entrance.*
Feb–Nov 3rm 1hc TV 3P 1🏠 💷
110acres arable dairy S% B&b£4.75
Bdi£7 W£42–£45 ⌧ W only Jul & Aug
D5.30pm

LADOCK Cornwall *Map 2 SW85*
Tregear *(SW870506)* ☎ Mitchell 214
*Attractive farmhouse set slightly back from
unclassified road. Lawn at front.*
Etr–Oct 3rm 🕸 nc5 TV P 250acres mixed
B&bfr£4 Wfr£28
Treveale *(SW874518)* ☎ Mitchell 326
*Farm is 1½ miles from village off A39 in
open country. Extensive views.*
Etr–Oct 3rm 2hc 🕸 CTV 3P 230acres
mixed

LAITY Cornwall *Map 2 SW63*
Crowgey *(SW698308)*
☎ Constantine 436
*Pleasantly situated farmhouse. Quiet but
not isolated. Off Falmouth rd A3594 3m
NE towards Helston.*
Etr–Sep 3hc ⚡ CTV 3P 40acres mixed

LANGPORT Somerset *Map 3 ST42*
Woodstock *(ST442264)* Pibsbury
☎250394
*Small, well furnished and decorated
farmhouse with a pleasant garden.*
Apr–Sep 4hc nc8 CTV 8P 1🏠 river
60acres dairy D4pm

LANLIVERY Cornwall *Map 2 SX05*
Treganoon *(SX065589)* ☎ Lostwithiel
872205
*Farmhouse with small garden in fairly
isolated position amid beautiful
countryside.*
Closed Nov–Apr 7rm 6hc ⚡ CTV 8P
107acres beef S% B&b£5–£7 Bdi£7–£8
W£38–£45 W only Jul & Aug D7pm

LAUNCELLS Cornwall *Map 2 SS20*
Moreton Mill *(SS283085)*
☎ Kilkhampton 306
*Pleasant, 15th-century, cottage-style
farmhouse with oak beams. Small
attractive garden.*
Etr–Oct 5rm 3hc ⚡ TV 8P 52½acres
mixed S% B&b£3.80–£4 Bdi£6–£6.50
W£42–£45.50 ⚡ W only Jul & Aug

LEEK Staffs *Map 7 SJ95*
Holly Dale *(SK019556)* Bradnop
☎383022
Two-storey stone-built farmhouse typical

*of the area. 2m SE on an unclassified
road off A523.*
Etr–Sep 2rm ⚡ 3P 72acres dairy S%
✱B&b£4 Bdi£6.50 W£45 ⚡ D7pm

LEOMINSTER Heref & Worcs
Map 3 SO45
Stagbatch *(SO465584)* ☎2673
*14th-century, half-timbered farmhouse
which is a listed building. Peaceful setting.
2m W off A4112.*
Feb–Dec 3⮡🍽 ⚡ nc10 CTV 8P 🚽
67acres mixed S% B&b£5–£6.50
W£35–£40 M

Wharton Bank *(SO508556)* ☎2575
*Extensively modernised farmhouse.
Comfortable, pleasant atmosphere.*
Mar–Nov 3hc ⚡ nc8 TV 6P 2🏠 🚽
212acres dairy & mixed

LEW Oxon *Map 4 SP30*
University *(SP322059)*
☎ Bampton Castle 850297
*17th-century farmhouse, modernised
without losing traditional character. House
set back from road in secluded position
behind farm buildings.*
Mar–Oct rs Nov, Jan & Feb (B&b only)
4rm 2hc 2⮡🍽 ⚡ nc8 CTV 6P 🚽
216acres mixed S% B&b£6.50–£7.60
D4pm

LEWDOWN Devon *Map 2 SX48*
Venn Mill *(SX484885)* ☎ Bridestowe 288
*Large modern bungalow set in attractive
countryside. Guests welcome to watch
farm activities.*
Etr–Oct 4rm 3hc ⚡ CTV 4P 2🏠
160acres dairy mixed S% B&b£4–£4.25
Bdi£6–£6.50 W£42–£45 ⚡ D5pm

Hillards Farm
CURRY RIVEL, LANGPORT, SOMERSET

A beautiful 17th century farmhouse with
many historical listed features and
buildings set in lovely grounds with a
tennis court.

Bedrooms of luxury standard with H/C in
every room. Oak panelled sitting room and
dining room. Real farmhouse. English
breakfast.

Antiques for sale in historical thatched
barn.

Horse riding, fishing and golf nearby.

Tel. Langport 251737 Proprietor M. Ribbons

𝕾𝖙𝖆𝖌𝖇𝖆𝖙𝖈𝖍 𝕱𝖆𝖗𝖒

LEOMINSTER

A 14th Century, half-timbered
farmhouse which is a listed
building. Situated ½ mile from
road in peaceful countryside.
All bedrooms have private bathroom and fitted carpets. Central
heating. Heated swimming pool
available ½ day. Evening meal
served, except Sundays. Stagbach
is a mixed farm, with a horse stud.
Fishing available. Colour TV.
Own lounge.

LIFTON Devon *Map 2 SX38*
Markstone *(SX429825)* ☎289
Pleasant, well decorated house with small attractive garden.
Etr–Sep 3rm 2hc TV 3P 48acres dairy

LISKEARD Cornwall *Map 2 SX26*
Tencreek *(SX265637)* ☎43379
A clean, well decorated farmhouse set in beautiful countryside. Liskeard 1 mile.
2hc ⊗ P 250acres mixed ✳B&b£4

LITTLE EVERSDEN Cambs *Map 5 TL35*
Five Gables *(TL371535)* Bucks Ln
☎ Comberton 2236
Historic farmhouse of 15th and 17th centuries. Oak beams and inglenook fireplace. Listed as being worthy of preservation.
May–Sep 3rm 2hc ⊗ nc12 6P 240acres arable S% B&b£4.75

LITTLEHEMPSTON Devon *Map 3 SX86*
Buckyette *(SX812638)* ☎ Staverton 638
19th century, stone farmhouse. Set in a spacious garden, its position provides excellent views of surrounding Devon countryside.
Spring Hol–Sep 7rm 6hc ⊗ TV 7P 51acres S% ✳B&b£5.13 Bdi£7.02 W£43.20–£45.36 ⌁

LITTLE TORRINGTON Devon
Map 2 SS41
Lower Hollam *(SS501161)*
☎ Torrington 3253
Historic house in an unusually peaceful position. Good play facilities for children.
May–Sep 4hc ⊗ CTV 4P 160acres

mixed S% B&b£3–£4.50 Bdi£4.75–£5.50 W£35 ⌁ D5pm

LITTLE WALDEN Essex *Map 5 TL54*
Sadlers *(TL558416)* ☎ Saffron Walden 23280
Small farmhouse, attractive interior with exposed beams. Peacefully situated in Essex countryside.
3rm ⊗ nc2 CTV 6P ⊞ 10acres non-working S% B&b£6

LLANFAIR WATERDINE Salop
Map 7 SJ27
Selley Hall *(SO264766)* Waterdine
☎ Knighton 528429
Old, stone-built three storey house dating back to 1780. Situated in rather remote but very picturesque area. Offa's Dyke runs within 200yds of farm. 5m NW of Knighton; take A488 then unclass on N side of River Teme.
May–Sep 3rm 1hc ⊗ TV 3P 500acres mixed S% B&b£4–£5 Bdi£6–£7 W£42–£49 ⌁ D4pm

LODDISWELL Devon *Map 3 SX74*
Reads *(SX727489)* ☎317
Two storey, stone-built farmhouse in isolated position. Fine countryside views. Full working farm using own produce.
Jun–Sep 2rm 1hc 3P 100acres mixed S% B&b£4.25–£5

LODDON Norfolk *Map 5 TM39*
Stubbs House *(TM358977)* ☎20231
Fine old house with excellent kitchen producing delicious, professional meals.
9hc ⊗ nc10 TV 20P ⊞ 300acres arable S% B&bfr£6.50 Bdifr£10.50
(W only last 2 wks Sep–Jun except Bank Hols)

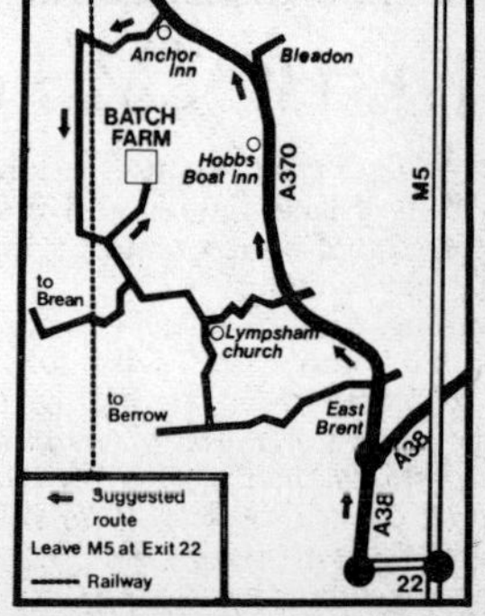

Licensed lounge bar.
150 acre working beef farm.
Farmhouse completely modernised but still retains old-world charm. 5 miles Weston. 3 miles sea and sandy beaches. Centrally situated for Cheddar, Bath and Longleat. Dining room — separate tables, Lounge — colour TV. Large games room with table tennis, darts etc. Central heating and fitted carpets throughout. Now open from Easter to end of October. Fishing on the river that runs through the farm. Bed and breakfast OR Dinner, bed and breakfast. Mrs J Brown.

LOIS WEEDON Northants *Map 4 SP64*
Croft *(SP600465)* Milthorpe
☎ Blakesley 475
New detached house in rural surroundings.
Mar–Oct 2rm ✵ CTV 2P ᗑ 24acres
mixed S% ✳Bdi£7.80 W£54.50 ₭
D7.30pm

LONGDOWN Devon *Map 3 SX89*
Steep Acres *(SX885912)* Bakers Hill
☎291
*Modern, bungalow-style farmhouse
situated in an elevated position, with
views of the moors. Off B3212.*
Apr–Oct 4hc 6P 10acres mixed S%
B&b£4

LONGDOWNS Cornwall *Map 2 SW73*
Calamankey *(SW746343)*
☎ Stithians 860314
*Small farmhouse of Cornish granite; down
a short lane off A394.*
Mar–Oct 3rm ✵ nc6 TV P 55acres
dairy S% B&b£3.50–£4.50

LOOE Cornwall *Map 2 SX25*
Tregoad *(SX272560)* St Martins ☎2718
*Large, well built, stone farmhouse on
high ground with sea view over Looe.*
Etr–Sep 6hc CTV 10P sea 60acres dairy

LOSTWITHIEL Cornwall *Map 2 SX15*
Pelyn Barn *(SX091588)* Pelyn Cross
☎872451
*Large farmhouse, formerly an old toll
house, with a well kept lawn enclosure
at rear.*
4hc ✵ CTV 6P 367acres mixed S%
B&bfr£6.50 Wfr£42.50 M

LYDBURY NORTH Salop *Map 7 SO38*
Brunslow *(SO366849)* ☎244
*Old brick-built Georgian farmhouse in rural
setting.*
Closed Xmas 4rm 3hc CTV 4P 150acres
dairy & sheep D5pm

LYDFORD Devon *Map 2 SX58*
Kirtonia *(SX524862)* Vale Down ☎331
*Detached farmhouse adjacent to main
A386. Bedrooms overlook scenic views
of Dartmoor and surrounding countryside.*
Etr–mid Sep 5hc ✵ ♨ CTV 6P 6acres
mixed S% B&b£5.17 Bdi£6.33 W£39.10
₭ D7.15pm

LYDHAM Salop *Map 7 SO39*
Pultheley *(SO324945)* ☎ Linley 214
*Pleasant farmhouse set amid picturesque
countryside. 2¾m N A488.*
Apr–Oct 2rm ✵ 3P 264acres mixed S%
B&b£4 Bdi£6 W£26.50 M D7pm

LYME REGIS Dorset *Map 3 SY39*
Middle Mill *(SY335930)* ☎2722
*Whitewashed, detached farmhouse in quiet
location, yet within walking distance of sea
front and shops.*
Jun–Sep 3rm 1hc ✵ nc5 CTV 3P river
38acres mixed S% B&bfr£4.25
Bdifr£6.50 Wfr£45.50 ₭ D3pm

LYMPSHAM Somerset *Map 3 ST35*
Batch *(ST330555)* Batch Ln
☎ Edingworth 371
*Large, attractive and well equipped
farmhouse. Pleasant gardens and lawns.
Fishing available in River Axe on farm
land.*
Etr–Oct 10hc ✵ nc4 CTV 20P 4🏠 ᗑ
150acres beef sheep S% B&b£5.50–£6.50
Bdi£8–£9 W£54–£58 ₭ D6.30pm

Lower *(ST339534)* South Rd
☎ Edingworth 206
*Large, two storey farmhouse with tile roof.
Extensive views of surrounding countryside.*
13rm 12hc TV 12P mixed D6.30pm

Mendip View *(ST334540)* South Rd
☎ Edingworth 296
*Small farmhouse with garden. On
secluded moorland near attractive and
ancient village.*
Etr–Sep 3rm 2hc ✵ nc5 CTV 2P 60acres
beef S% B&b£3.50–£4 Bdi£6–£6.50
D5.30pm

LYONSHALL Heref & Worcs *Map 3 SO35*
Holme *(SO339553)* ☎216
*Fully modernised farmhouse standing
on outskirts of village.*
Mar–Oct 4hc ✵ nc9 TV 6P ᗑ 270acres
dairy S% B&b£4.50–£5 Bdi£7 W£50
D8pm

Park Gate *(SO332575)* ☎243
*Two-storey, stone-built farmhouse with
land overlooking Wales. Offa's Dyke runs
through part of farm.*
Closed Xmas 2hc ✵ ♨ CTV P ᗑ
230acres beef sheep S% B&b£4.50
Bdi£7.50 W£49 ₭ D6pm

MABE Cornwall *Map 2 SW73*
Higher Halvosso *(SW740335)*
☎ Stithians 860430
Small farmhouse 3 miles from Penryn.
May–Oct 2rm ♨ 2P 44acres mixed S%
B&b£3–£3.50 W£20–£22 M

MALPAS Cheshire *Map 7 SJ44*
Kidnal Grange *(SJ473493)* ☎344
*Clean and comfortable farmhouse.
Attractive rural surroundings. Duck pond.
Much home produce used in cooking.*

THE HOLME Lyonshall

Part Tudor/Georgian farmhouse
which is a listed building. Tastefully
adapted to offer accommodation of a
very high standard.
Panoramic views of completely
unspoilt countryside. Ideal base for
touring or relaxing among the many
castles, historic houses or antique and
curio shops, in the area. Speciality,
Dinner & bed/breakfast from £7.50 or
bed/breakfast from £4.50.
Send for colour brochure.

Etr–Sep 5rm TV 10P 120acres mixed
S% B&b£6–£6.50

MALVERN WELLS Heref & Worcs
Map 3 SO74
Brick Barns *(SO783420)* Hanley Pl
☎ Malvern 61775
*Imposing old farmhouse standing in its
own grounds.*
Etr–Oct rs Oct–Etr 3rm TV P ﾞﾞ 200acres
mixed

MANATON Devon *Map 3 SX78*
Langstone *(SY747823)* ☎266
*Long, low granite farmhouse in traditional
Dartmoor style. Lawn with children's
swings. On edge of the moor. Fine views.*
Mar–Nov 3hc ✿ nc5 TV 2P 130acres
beef S% B&b£4.50–£5 Bdi£7.50–£8

MARDEN Heref & Worcs *Map 3 SO54*
Woodbine *(SO520477)* ☎ Sutton St
Nicholas 291
*Two-storey, red brick, Georgian-style
farmhouse. Large lawns at front.
Situated on edge of small village.*
Closed Xmas 3rm 2hc ✿ TV 4P ﾞﾞ 49acres
beef D5.30pm

MARK CAUSEWAY Somerset
Map 3 ST34
Croft *(ST355475)* ☎ Markmoor 206
*Comfortable and well decorated farmhouse
with traditional furnishings throughout.*
4rm ✿ nc CTV 3P 2🏠 130acres mixed
S% B&bfr£5.50 Bdifr£6 Wfr£33 ⌁
(W only Jun–Sep) D6pm

MARSHFIELD Avon *Map 3 ST77*
Motcombe *(ST784718)* ☎201
*Modernised, Cotswold-stone farmhouse.
In pastureland and woodland. Views across
valley to Salisbury Plain and Mendip Hills.*
Apr–20Oct 4hc ✿ nc6 20P ﾞﾞ 40acres
beef S% B&b£8.20–£9.50
Bdi£14–£15.30 D4pm

MARSHGATE Cornwall *Map 2 SX19*
Carleton *(SX153918)*
☎ Otterham Station 252
*Farmhouse is situated adjacent to the
Boscastle road in Marshgate. Views over
the surrounding farmlands.*
Map–Sep 3rm TV 4P 150acres mixed
D8pm

MARTOCK Somerset *Map 3 ST41*
Vicarage *(ST454205)* Coat ☎2591
*Large farmhouse set in a compact, walled
garden. Small working farm 1 mile from
village.*
Etr–Sep 4hc ✿ nc5 CTV 9acres mixed

MATHON Heref & Worcs *Map 3 SO74*
Moorend Court *(SO726454)*
☎ Ridgeway Cross 205
*Beautiful 15th-century farmhouse in
secluded position with panoramic views
towards Malvern. Trout fishing on farm.*
Closed Xmas 3hc P ﾞﾞ 100acres mixed
S% B&b£3–£4.50 Bdi£5–£6.50 D am

MATLOCK Derbys *Map 8 SK36*
Packhorse *(SK323617* Matlock Moor
☎2781
*Former inn on much travelled Chesterfield
to Manchester packhorse route.
Tastefully furnished. Lawns and putting
greens.*
Mar–Oct 4hc nc2 CTV 6P ﾞﾞ 60acres
dairy S% B&b£4

Wayside *(SK324630)* Matlock Moor
☎2967
*Pleasant, modernised, stone-built
farmhouse adjacent to A632 Matlock–
Chesterfield road.*
Closed Xmas & New Year 3hc nc3 TV
6P ﾞﾞ 60acres dairy S%

MATTISHALL Norfolk *Map 9 TG01*
Moat *(TG049111)* ☎ Dereham 850288
*Period farmhouse standing back from road.
Being modernised. Good friendly
atmosphere.*
May–Oct 2rm ✿ nc4 TV 2P 50acres
mixed S% B&bfr£4.50 Bdifr£7 W£42
⌁ D noon

MAWNAN SMITH Cornwall *Map 2 SW72*
Penwarne Barton *(SW773301)*
☎250331
*Interesting farm with many animals and
much equipment. In very good position
within sight of the sea.*
Etr–Nov 3rm TV 3P sea 118acres mixed
S% B&b£4–£4.50

MENDHAM Suffolk *Map 5 TM28*
Weston House *(TM292828)*
☎ St Cross 206
*Fine old house about 300 years old.
Fishing nearby.*
Mar–Oct 3hc nc6 CTV 6P ﾞﾞ 150acres
mixed S% B&b£4 Bdi£6 W£40

MENHENIOT Cornwall *Map 2 SX26*
Tregondale *(SX294643)*
☎ Liskeard 42407
*Farm situated 1½ miles north of A38 east
of Liskeard.*
Closed Xmas 3rm ✿ 🐎 CTV 3P 330acres
mixed S% B&b£3.75–£4.50 Bdi£5.50–£6
D5pm

MERRYMEET Cornwall *Map 2 SX26*
Merrymeet *(SX279660)* ☎ Liskeard
43231
*A small two-storey, tile-hung farmhouse
with small front garden. Yard and
buildings at rear.*
Spring Bank Hol–Sep 3rm ✿ TV 2P
40acres mixed S% ✳B&b£4 Bdi£5.50
W£35 ⌁

MIDDLETON ON THE HILL Heref &
Worcs *Map 3 SO56*
Moor Abbey *(SO545633)*
☎ Leysters 226
*Former monastery about 400 years old.
Original oak staircase and upper floors.
Dining room in refectory with open log
fire. Access from A4112 1m W of
Leysters.*
Apr–Oct 3hc ✿ nc 6P 225acres mixed

MILBORNE PORT Somerset *Map 3 ST61*
Venn *(ST684183)* ☎250208
*Modern, purpose-built farmhouse in
mellow stone. Situated amid rural
scenery on outskirts of village.*
Mar–Nov 3rm 2hc ✿ 🐎 CTV P ﾞﾞ
300acres mixed S% B&b£4.75
(W only Mar–30Oct)

MOLLAND Devon *Map 3 SS82*
Yeo *(SS785266)* ☎ Bishops Nympton 312
*Well maintained farmhouse with good
furnishings and decor. Set in large garden.*
Apr–7Nov 3hc CTV P 200acres mixed
S% B&b£4.50–£5 Bdi£7.50–£8.50
W£50–£55 ⌁ (W only Apr–Nov)

MONKTON Devon *Map 3 ST10*
Pugh's *(ST186029)* ☎ Honiton 2860
Well situated farmhouse on the A30 at
Monkton. Honiton about 1½ miles.
Feb–Oct 3rm 2hc nc3 CTV 6P 🍴 8acres
mixed S% B&b£4.50–£5 Bdi£7–£7.50
W£45–£49 ⃝ D5pm

MORNINGTHORPE Norfolk
Map 5 TM29
Hollies *(TM212939)* ☎ Long Stratton
30540
Large Georgian property standing in own
grounds, in quiet rural area. ¾m E of A140.
Good atmosphere plenty of amenities.
Apr–Sep 9hc 2⇆🛏🍴 ⊘ CTV 7P 🍴
350acres arable B&b£5–£5.50
Bdi£7–£7.50 W£52.50 ⃝ (W only Jul–Aug)
D6.30pm

MORVAH Cornwall *Map 2 SW33*
Merthyr *(SW403355)* ☎ Penzance
788464
Well appointed farmhouse on B3306
north west of Penzance.
May–Oct rs Nov–Apr Closed Xmas 6hc
⊘ CTV 6P 100acres mixed S%
B&b£4.50–£5.50 Bdi£6.50–£7.50
W£31.50–£38.50 M (W only end Jul–1 wk
Sep)

MOSEDALE Cumbria *Map 11 NY33*
Mosedale House *(NY358317)*
Mungrisdale
Stone-built farmhouse in peaceful rural
setting. Good views of surrounding hills
and fells.
Etr–Sep 4rm 2hc 4P 52½acres mixed

MOUNT Cornwall *Map 2 SX16*
Mount Pleasant *(SX152680)*
☎ Cardinham 342
Farm 6 miles east of Bodmin in open
country on the edge of Bodmin Moor. Own
transport essential.
Mar–Oct 5hc CTV 12P 🍴 50acres arable
S% B&b£4.50–£5 Bdi£7–£7.50
W£44–£51 ⃝

MUSBURY Devon *Map 3 SY29*
Higher Bruckland *(SY284933)*
☎ Colyton 52371
Farmhouse completely surrounded by
farmland. Seaton 4 miles.
Feb–Nov 3hc TV P 236acres mixed
D4.30pm

NETHER COMPTON Dorset *Map 3 ST51*
Halfway House *(ST603163)*
☎ Sherborne (Dorset) 2781

Mellow, stone-built house in elevated
position. Well kept gardens. Interesting
display of horseriding awards. On A30.
Mar–Oct 3hc CTV 6P 🍴 110acres beef
S% B&b£5

NEWBOLD ON STOUR Warwicks
Map 4 SP24
Berryfield *(SP216483)* ☎ Ilmington 248
A deceptively large farmhouse in
secluded position.
Etr–Oct 3hc ⊘ nc6 P 100acres mixed
S% B&b fr£4.50 W fr£30 M
(W only Etr–Oct)

NEWCASTLE Salop *Map 7 SO28*
Lower Spoad *(SO257821)* ☎ Clun 246
Interesting farmhouse. Exposed beams
and carved chimney beam reputed to be
13th-century. Antique furniture and
fittings.
Apr–Oct rs Mar & Nov 5hc nc12 30P 🍴
50acres mixed D6pm
Newcastle Hall *(SO246824)* ☎ Clun 350
Large stone-built Georgian farmhouse
in peaceful setting surrounded by tree
clad hills.
Etr–Oct 4rm 3hc TV P 275acres mixed
S% B&b£5.50 Bdi£8.50 D4.30pm

NEWQUAY Cornwall *Map 2 SW86*
Legonna *(SW834594)* ☎2272
Granite farmhouse in beautiful wooded
valley. Swimming pool, tennis court,
private fishing lake, children's play area
and pony riding. 2½m SE of Newquay.
May–Sep 10hc TV 10P 140acres
mixed S% W£46–£48 ⃝ D6pm

Manuels *(SW839601)* Lane ☎3577
Closed Xmas 4rm ♨ CTV 4P 30acres
mixed S% B&b£5–£7 Bdi£6–£8.50
W£42–£59.50 ⃝ (W only May–Sep) D5pm

NEWTON (Nr Vowchurch) Heref & Worcs
Map 3 SO33
Little Green *(SO335337)*
☎ Michaelchurch 205
Modernised farmhouse which used to be
an inn; friendly atmosphere.
3hc ⊘ CTV 3P 50acres mixed S%
B&b£4–£4.50 Bdi£6–£7 W£40–£45 ⃝

NEWTON ARLOSH Cumbria
Map 11 NY15
Oak Tree *(NY199553)* ☎ Kirkbride 418
Clean, unpretentious farmhouse in rural
surroundings ¾ mile from sea.
May–Oct 1rm ⊘ CTV 150acres arable &
dairy D8.30pm

NEWTON-IN-CARTMEL Cumbria
Map 7 SD38
Yew Tree *(SD405823)*
☎ Newby Bridge 278
*Early 18th-century, stone-built farmhouse
in ½ acre of lawn and flower gardens.
Grange seaside resort 3 miles.*
Apr–Oct 5hc ♨ TV 4P 50acres
non-working S% ✳B&bfr£5 Bdifr£7.50
Wfr£52 ⚓ D7pm

NOMANSLAND *(nr Tiverton)* Devon
Map 3 SS81
Moor Barton *(SS844134)*
☎ Witheridge 325
*Farmhouse is well placed for touring
North Devon and Exmoor. In peaceful
surroundings. Friendly atmosphere.*
9hc ♨ CTV 10P 🍴 175acres mixed S%
B&bfr£5.45 Bdifr£7.75 Wfr£46 ⚓
(W only Jul–Aug) D5pm

NORMANBY N Yorks *Map 8 NZ90*
Heather View *(NZ928062)*
☎ Whitby 880451
*Attractive, modern farmhouse. Well
appointed and comfortable. Conveniently
situated for coastal visits.*
Apr–Sep 5hc ✄ nc5 CTV 6P 🍴
40acres mixed S% B&bf£4–£4.50
Bdi£6–£6.50 D5.30pm

NORTH CADBURY Somerset
Map 3 ST62
Ferngrove *(ST637274)* Woolston
☎40329
*In a pleasant secluded locality. Lawn and
produce garden adjoining house.*
Mar–Sep 4rm ✄ TV P 🍴 130acres
mixed S% B&b£4.50

Hill *(ST634279)* ☎40257
*Two-storey, red brick, double-fronted
farmhouse with front garden and
extensive outbuildings.*
Etr–Sep 3rm 1hc ✄ TV P 90acres S%
B&bfr£4.50 Wfr£30 M

NORTH WOOTTON Somerset
Map 3 ST54
Barrow *(ST553416)* ☎ Pilton 245
*Stone-built farmhouse with beams. Garden
and concreted yard. ¼ mile from village.*
Mar–Oct 3hc ✄ CTV 3P 145acres dairy
S% B&b£5 Bdi£7 W£50 ⚓ D10am

NORTON Heref & Worcs *Map 3 SO85*
Grange *(SO878508)*☎ Worcester 820456
*Large, late Victorian brick building in
isolated location.*
3rm 2hc ✄ TV 4P 40acres mixed

NORTON Notts *Map 8 SK57*
Norton Grange *(SK572733)* ☎ Warsop
2666
*A 200-year-old stone-built farmhouse
fronted by tidy gardens at edge of village.*
Etr–Sep 3rm 1hc CTV 6P 🍴 175acres
beef & mixed

NOTTER Cornwall *Map 2 SX36*
Notter *(SX390609)* ☎ Saltash 3593
*Quietly situated farmhouse a few yards
off the A38 overlooking the valley.*
3rm 2hc ✄ TV 6P 200acres mixed S%
B&b£4.25–£5 W£27–£32 M

ODDINGLEY Heref & Worcs *Map 3 SO95*
Pear Tree's *(SO909589)* ☎ Droitwich
8489
*Large modern farmhouse in quiet
country lane close to M5 motorway.*
Closed Dec rs Nov & Jan–Etr (B&b only)
4rm 2hc ✄ nc5 CTV P 🍴 17acres mixed
S% B&b£5.50–£6 Bdi£7.50–£8

OKEHAMPTON Devon *Map 2 SX59*
Agiestment *(SX603979)* ☎2359
*Well appointed farmhouse with extensive
moor and forest views.*
Apr–Sep 2rm ✄ nc12 CTV 4P 150acres
mixed S% B&b£5–£6 Bdi£7.50–£8.50
W£46–£47.50 ⚓

Hill Barton *(SX594984)* ☎2454
*Good working farm in peaceful setting in
the heart of beautiful, well-wooded
countryside.*
Mar–Nov 3rm 2hc ✄ nc5 TV P
280acres mixed B&bfr£5.50 Bdifr£9.50

Hughslade *(SX561932)* ☎2883
*Pleasant farmhouse on the edge of town.
Ideal base for exploring Dartmoor and
north and south coasts.*
Closed Xmas 4hc CTV 6P 500acres
mixed S% B&b£6–£9 Bdi£9–£10
Wfr£50 ⚓ D5.30pm

OKEOVER Staffs *Map 7 SK14*
Little Park *(SK160490)*
☎ Thorpe Cloud 341
*Red brick and stone farmhouse. Interior
abounds with oaken beams.*
May–Aug 3rm 2hc nc3 CTV 3P
123acres dairy S% B&b£4 Bdi£6 W£40
⚓ D6.30pm

OLD DALBY Leics *Map 8 SK62*
Home *(SK673236)* Church Ln
☎ Melton Mowbray 822622
*19th-Century farmhouse, parts dating from
1730. Former bailiff's house when property
was part of estate.*

Hughslade Farm Okehampton, Devon

The farm is ideally situated for touring Devon,
Cornwall, Dartmoor and Exmoor. Hughslade is a
large working farm with plenty of animals around.
The farmhouse is comfortably furnished. Lounge
with colour TV and central heating on the ground
floor. Meals served in the dining room, are mainly
made from home-produced vegetables and meat.
Bed, breakfast and evening meal or bed and
breakfast daily. Okehampton is just 2 miles from
the farm and has a superb golf course, tennis courts
and covered swimming pool. Horse riding
available at the farm. Happy holiday assured. SAE
please for terms to Mrs. K. C. Heard, Hughslade
Farm, Okehampton, Devon. Tel: Okehampton
2883.

Closed Dec 3hc TV 3P 🕮 3acres
non-working S% ✱B&b£4.50 Bdi£8

OTTERBURN Northumb *Map 12 NY89*
Monkbridge *(NY913917)* ☎20639
*Well cared for, comfortable farmhouse in
the attractive environment of the
Northumberland Moors.*
Closed Dec–Jan 2rm ⌘ CTV 3P 1,400acres
mixed S% B&b£6 Bdi£8.50 W£59 ⎱ D3pm

OUNDLE Northants *Map 4 TL08*
Biggin Grange *(TL024886)* ☎3563
*Fine, spacious, stone-faced three-storey
house overlooking a golf course.*
Mar–Oct 3rm TV 4P 🕮 river 600acres
mixed

OXENHOPE W Yorks *Map 7 SE03*
Lily Hall *(SE023362)* Uppermarsh Ln
☎ Haworth 43999
*Pleasant farmhouse in 9 acre smallholding
rearing turkeys and hens. Overlooking
valley. Horse riding, golf, tennis and
bathing 4 miles.*
2hc ⌘ ♨ CTV 12P 2🏠 🕮 9acres
non-working S% B&b£4–£5 W£25–£30 Ⓜ

PANCRASWEEK Devon *Map 2 SS20*
Higher Kingford *(SS285061)*
☎ Bridgerule 281
Small working farm 6 miles from Bude.
5rm 2hc ⌘ CTV 6P 80acres mixed

PEBWORTH Heref & Worcs *Map 4 SP14*
Pebworth Fields *(SP134459)*
☎ Stratford-on-Avon 720318
*Unusual, colonial-style farmhouse. Trim
grounds. Fairly remote and ideal for local
tourist areas.*
May–Sep 3rm 1hc ⌘ TV P 100acres
mixed S% B&b£5.25–£5.75 W£35–£38.50
Ⓜ

PELYNT Cornwall *Map 2 SX25*
Trenderway *(SX214533)* ☎ Polperro 214
*Comfortable and well maintained farmhouse
about 3 miles from Looe.*
3rm 2hc ⌘ P 400acres mixed

PENRUDDOCK Cumbria *Map 12 NY42*
Highgate *(NY444275)* ☎ Greystoke 339
*250-year-old, stone-built farmhouse with
beamed ceilings; tastefully modernised.
Good base for touring and recreational
facilities. Children's playground.
2m E on A66.*
Mar–Oct 3rm 2hc ⌘ nc10 CTV 3P
400acres beef, mixed & sheep D6pm

PILSDON Dorset *Map 3 SY49*
Monkwood *(SY429986)*
☎ Broadwindsor 723 2rm 3P 130acres
mixed✱B&b£4–£5 Bdi£6–£7 W£40–£42
⎱

PLAYING PLACE Cornwall *Map 2 SW84*
Halvarras *(SW814415)*
☎ Devoran 862305
*Typical stone-built farmhouse about
1½ miles from A39.*
Apr–Sep 6hc ⌘ 6P 115acres arable & beef

PLYMOUTH Devon *Map 2 SX45*
Ford *(SX582554)* Plympton ☎336863
*Clean and well decorated farmhouse.
Ideal base for riding, golf, tennis. Near
local beaches. 4m E off A38.*
Closed Xmas 3rm 2hc ⌘ CTV 6P 2🏠
110acres dairy S% B&b£4–£5

POCKLINGTON Humberside *Map 8 SE84*
Mill *(SE817513)* Ousethorpe ☎2366
Simple, plain and comfortable farmhouse

*off the beaten track, on the edge of the
Yorkshire Wolds. 2m NE off the Millington
rd.*
2rm CTV 4P 42acres mixed S% B&b£4.50
Bdi£6 D noon

PONSWORTHY Devon *Map 3 SX77*
Old Walls *(SX697745)*
☎ Poundsgate 222
*Farmhouse standing in its own small
estate. Isolated location near Dartmoor.
Pleasant atmosphere.*
Closed Xmas Day 3rm CTV 6P 🕮 36acres
beef S% B&b£5.22

POOLEY BRIDGE Cumbria *Map 12 NY42*
Barton Hall *(NY478251)* ☎275
*Attractive farmhouse, well furnished and
decorated. Large garden with lawn and
summer house. Boating, fishing and golf
nearby.*
Mar–Oct 3rm 2hc ⌘ nc8 P 🕮 65acres
mixed S% B&b£4.50

POUNDSGATE Devon *Map 3 SX77*
Lowertown *(SX712729)* ☎282
*Pleasantly situated farmhouse with
wooden beams in entrance hall.*
Closed Xmas 3rm 3P 🕮 120acres beef
sheep S% B&b£4–£4.50

REDMILE Leics *Map 8 SK73*
Olde Mill House *(SK789358)*
☎ Bottesford 42460
*A beautiful house approximately 250 years
old, which has been considerably
modernised; set in peaceful Belvoir Valley.*
4hc nc12 CTV 4P 2🏠 🕮 5½acres non
working S% B&b£6–£7 Bdi£10–£11
W£66.50–£73.50 ⎱ D1pm
Peacock *(SK791359)* ☎ Bottesford 42475
*Modernised 250-year-old farmhouse.
Hunter stud farm with paddocks. Horse
riding available. In rural vale of Belvoir
close to Castle.*
Closed Xmas & Pub Hols Lic 4rm ♨ CTV
12P 🕮 5acres S% B&b£5.50–£7.50 Bdi£9
W£63 ⎱ D7.30pm

ROBOROUGH Devon *Map 2 SS51*
Rapson Court *(SS573179)*
☎ High Bickington 246
*Typical small Devonshire farmhouse dating
from 17th century. Thatched roof, oak
beams, horse brasses. Good views of
surrounding countryside.*
Etr–mid Sep 2hc ⌘ nc5 TV 2P 125acres
mixed S% B&b£5

ROSTON Derbys *Map 7 SK14*
Roston Hall *(SK133409)* ☎ Ellastone 287
*Former Manor House, part Elizabethan,
part Georgian in centre of quiet village.
Ideal centre for touring Peak District.*
May–Sep 2rm 1hc ⌘ nc13 3P 100acres
arable beef S% D10am

RUSHTON SPENCER Staffs *Map 7 SJ96*
Barnswood *(SJ945606)* ☎261
*Large stone-built farmhouse. Grounds
stretch to edge of Rudyard Lake. Splendid
views across lake to distant hills.*
Etr–24Dec 3rm 2hc ⌘ TV 5P lake 100acres
dairy D noon

RUYTON-XI-TOWNS Salop *Map 7 SJ32*
Lower *(SJ362261)* Shotatton
☎ Knockin 461
*Smallholding with well furnished
accommodation. Well placed for touring.
Two acres of private ground. Fishing and
golf 3 miles.*
3hc 1⎘ CTV 6P 🕮 2acres mixed S%
B&b£5–£7 Bdi£7–£9 W£45–£60 ⎱
D10pm

RYDE Isle of Wight *Map 4 SZ59*
Aldermoor *(SZ582906) Upton Rd*
☎64743 Closed Nov 3hc CTV 6P
50acres dairy S% B&b£3.75 Bdi£5.50
D6.30pm

ST AGNES Cornwall *Map 2 SW75*
Mount Pleasant *(SW722508)* Rosemundy
☎2387
*Spacious bungalow set in the farm
meadows. Stands in its own large garden
with beautiful views.*
Etr–Sep 11hc TV 20P 40acres dairy

ST ALLEN Cornwall *Map 2 SW85*
Honeycombe *(SW827527)* ☎ Zelah 411
*Detached house on smallholding. Lawned
garden at front. Fine views over unspoilt
countryside.*
May–mid Sep 3hc ⚘ nc12 TV 4P 13½acres
beef

ST BURYAN Cornwall *Map 2 SW42*
Boskenna Home *(SW423237)* ☎250
*Farmhouse situated in a convenient
position. Beaches a few miles away.
Pleasant spacious rooms with traditional
furniture.*
Etr–Sep 3rm 2hc ⚘ ♨ CTV P 75acres dairy
B&b£4 Bdi£5.75–£6 W£40–£42 ⚖ D6pm

Burnew Hall *(SW407236)* ☎200
*Fair sized farmhouse with lawns back and
front. Extensive farm buildings.*
Mid May–mid Oct rs Wed 3hc ⚘ CTV 4P
sea 150acres mixed D4pm

ST COLUMB MAJOR Cornwall
Map 2 SW96
Polita *(SW914626)* Station Rd
☎ St Columb 533
*Small but comfortable farmhouse. Quiet at
night.*
May–Sep 3rm 2hc ⚘ nc10 4P 30acres
mixed D6pm

ST ERME Cornwall *Map 2 SW85*
Pengelly *(SW856513)* Trispen
☎ Mitchell 245
*Attractive, well built farmhouse. Good
central base for touring Cornwall.*
Mar–Oct 4hc ⚘ nc10 CTV 4P 230acres
mixed B&b£3.50–£4.50

Trevispian Vean *(SW850502)* Trispen
☎ Mitchell 217
*Extensively modernised farmhouse.
Clean and well maintained. Large sun
lounge at the front.*
Etr, mid May–mid Sep 7rm 6hc ⚘ CTV P
400acres arable beef sheep S% B&b£6
Bdi£7.50 W£40–£41 ⚖ D6pm

ST EWE Cornwall *Map 2 SW94*
Lanewa *(SW983457)* ☎ Mevagissey 3283
*Comfortable farmhouse situated in the
small village of St Ewe. St Austell about
6 miles.*
3hc ⚘ CTV 3P 60acres mixed S% B&b fr£4
Bdi fr£6 D6.30pm

ST JOHN'S IN THE VALE Cumbria
Map 11 NY32
Shundraw *(NY308236)* ☎ Threlkeld 227
*Large, well maintained, stone-built
farmhouse, parts dating from 1712.
In elevated position with views across
valley.*
Etr–Oct 3rm ⚘ TV 3P 52acres sheep
S% B&b fr£3.75

ST JUST-IN-ROSELAND Cornwall
Map 3 SW83
Commerrans *(SW842375)*
☎ Portscatho 270
Pleasant modernised farmhouse,

*attractively decorated throughout. Large
garden. Wonderful scenery in the area.*
Etr–Oct 5rm 4hc ⚘ nc2 CTV 6P 61acres
beef sheep ✳B&b£5 Bdi£6.50 W£42 ⚖
D am

ST KEW HIGHWAY Cornwall *Map 2 SX07*
Kelly Green *(SX047758)*
☎ Bodmin 850275
*Old, two-storey farmhouse with lawn at
the front.*
Closed Xmas 5rm 4hc ⚘ ♨ CTV 5P
300acres mixed S% B&b£4–£4.50
Bdi£6–£6.50 W£42–£45.50 ⚖

ST KEYNE Cornwall *Map 2 SX26*
Killigorrick *(SX228614)*
☎ Dobwalls 20559
*Farmhouse, lies 3½ miles from Liskeard,
1m W off Dulce–Dobwalls road.*
4hc ⚘ nc5 TV 4P 1🏠 21acres mixed
S% B&b£4.75–£5.50

ST MARGARET, SOUTH ELMHAM
Suffolk *Map 5 TM38*
Elm House *(TM310840)* ☎ St Cross 228
*Delightful period farmhouse in extremely
quiet location; friendly atmosphere.*
Apr–Oct rs Nov–Mar 3hc ⚘ nc10 TV 6P
🎱 240acres arable sheep S% B&b fr£4
Bdi fr£6 Wfr£60 ⚖ D5pm

SALCOMBE REGIS Devon *Map 3 SY18*
King's Down Tail *(SY173907)*
☎ Branscombe 313
*Modern, two storey brick and plaster-faced
farmhouse. Guests are invited to participate
in the farm activities.*
Etr–Oct 2hc CTV 2P 22acres mixed S%
B&b£4–£5.50

SAMPFORD PEVERELL Devon
Map 3 ST01
Higher Shutehanger *(ST030133)*
☎820569
*Secluded farmhouse adjacent to the Grand
Western Canal. Well situated for touring
Devon and the Dartmoor and Exmoor
National Parks.*
Etr–Oct 3hc ⚘ CTV 3P 3🏠 🎱 15acres
mixed S% B&b£5 W£32 M

SANDFORD Devon *Map 3 SS70*
Woolsgrove *(SS793028)*
☎ Copplestone 246
*Part 14th century farmhouse overlooking
acres of grassland.*
Mar–Oct 3rm 2hc ⚘ TV 3P 160acres
mixed S% B&b£4.50 Bdi£7 D8pm

SAXELBY Leics *Map 8 SK62*
Manor House *(SK701208)*
☎ Melton Mowbray 812269
*Part 12th, part 15th-century farmhouse
in high Leicestershire village. Feature is
15th century staircase.*
Etr–Oct 2hc ⚘ ♨ TV 6P 🎱 125acres dairy
S% B&b£6–£7 Bdi£10–£11 Wfr£65 ⚖

SEABOROUGH Dorset *Map 3 ST40*
West Swillets *(ST428056)*
☎ Broadwindsor 264
*Stone, detached, long-fronted farmhouse.
Lawns at front, with kitchen at side.
Located in valley.*
Mar–Sep 4hc TV 4P 200acres arable &
beef

SEBERGHAM Cumbria *Map 11 NY34*
Bustabeck *(NY373419)*
☎ Raughton Head 339
*Stone built farmhouse dating from 1684.
Extensively modernised.*
May–Aug 3rm ⚘ nc6 CTV 3P 72acres
mixed

SHAP Cumbria *Map 12 NY51*
Green *(NY551121)* ☎619
Large farmhouse dating from 1705.
Countryside suitable for walking holidays.
Etr–Sep 3rm 2hc ✵ TV P 167acres mixed
S% ✱B&b£4
Southfield *(NY561184)* ☎282
Farmhouse set in pleasant area. Guests
welcome to interest themselves in farm
work.
Etr–Sep 2rm 1hc ✵ nc10 TV 3P 110acres
beef dairy sheep S% B&b£4.50–£6

SHAWBURY Salop *Map 7 SJ52*
Braggs Country Suppers *(SJ602228)*
Longley Farm, Stanton Heath
☎ Shawbury 289
Originally dating back to 1710, this
attractive brick and tile cottage was
named after Paul C Bragg the world
authority on Natural Farming. $2\frac{1}{4}$m NE
off A53.
Lic 3rm 1hc 8P 2🏠 ⱜ 23acres mixed
D8.30

SHILLINGFORD Devon *Map 3 SS92*
Zeal *(SS998226)* ☎ Clayhanger 231
Old farmhouse with low ceilings and oak
beamed rooms.
Etr–Nov 3rm 2hc ✵ 3P 283acres arable
beef sheep S% B&b£3–£3.50 Bdi£4.50–£5
W£30–£35 ⱜ D5pm

SIMONSBATH Somerset *Map 3 SS73*
Gallon House *(SS810394)* ☎ Exford 283
Small, detached farmhouse, formerly an
inn. Surrounded by grassland. Horse riding
facilities are available.
Apr–Oct 4rm 2hc nc13 CTV 4P ⱜ
50acres beef

SITHNEY Cornwall *Map 2 SW63*
Tregoose *(SW647298)* ☎ Helston 2612
Etr–Oct 5rm 4hc ✵ nc10 TV 4P non-
working

SKELSMERGH Cumbria *Map 7 SD59*
Hollin Root *(SD526976)* Garth Row
☎ Selside 638
Clean and comfortable farmhouse situated
in attractive valley.
Etr–Oct 4hc ✵ nc10 TV 4P 60acres mixed
B&bfr£4.50

SLAGGYFORD Northumb *Map 12 NY65*
Crainlarich *(NY680523)* ☎ Alston 329
Attractive, modern farmhouse built of
local stone. Situated in rolling hill land.
Etr–Sep 7rm 6hc ✵ nc3 CTV 6P 1,900acres
S% ✱B&b£4 Bdifr£5.50 Wfrf£38 ⱜ D6pm

SLAIDBURN Lancs *Map 7 SD75*
Parrock Head Farm Guest House
(SD697527) Woodhouse Ln ☎614
Modernised farmhouse dating back to
1677, set in the Bowland Fells.
Mar–18Nov 3hc (A 1hc) nc8 CTV 6P ⱜ
200acres beef mixed & sheep D9pm

SOUTH BRENT Devon *Map 3 SX66*
Great Aish *(SX689603)* ☎2238
Situated near Dartmoor National Park.
Extensive views of countryside from
farmhouse.
Closed Dec 5rm 4hc ✵ CTV 6P 60acres
mixed S% B&b£4–£4.50 Bdi£5.50–£6
D5pm

SOUTH MOLTON Devon *Map 3 SS72*
Hacche Barton *(SS713278)* ☎2112
Modern, brick-built farmhouse of stylish
design.
Etr–Sep 2hc 6P 212acres dairy S%
B&b£4–£6

SPARROWPIT Derbys *Map 7 SK08*
Whitelee *(SK099814)*
☎ Chapel-en-le-Frith 2928
Modernised farmhouse, parts built in 1600.
In pleasant hillside setting. Good centre for
hill walking or touring.
Etr–Oct 3rm 1hc nc3 TV 3P ⱜ 42acres
dairy S% B&b£4.25–£4.50 Bdi£6.75–£7
W£47.25–£49 ⱜ D5pm

SPAXTON Somerset *Map 3 ST23*
Parish Land *(ST214353)* Higher
Merridge ☎391
Small, pleasing farmhouse situated in
attractive countryside. Spaxton $1\frac{1}{2}$ *miles.*
Mar–Oct 2rm ✵ CTV 2P 4acres sheep S%
B&b£5 Bdif£8 Wfr£52 ⱜ D2.30pm

STALBRIDGE Dorset *Map 3 ST71*
Thornhill *(ST741149)* ☎62751
Exposed, mellow-stoned, modernised
farmhouse. Gabled out-buildings.
Elevated position offering open views
across Dorset.
May–Sep 2rm ✵ nc8 CTV P 240acres
dairy sheep S% B&b£4 Bdi£6 W£42
ⱜ D4pm

STANTON Staffs *Map 7 SK14*
Shrewsbury *(SK127462)*
☎ Ellastone 310
Stone built farmhouse in centre of village.
Apr–Sep 2hc (A 2rm 1hc) CTV 4P ⱜ
100acres beef dairy S% B&b£4 Bdi£6.50
D10am

STAPLE FITZPAINE Somerset
Map 3 ST21
Rutters Leigh *(ST261164)*
☎ Buckland St Mary 392
Small very pleasant farmhouse off A303.
3rm ✵ CTV 2P 70acres dairy S% D noon

STAWELL Somerset *Map 3 ST33*
Fruit & Honey *(ST376382)*
☎ Chilton Polden 722459
Renovated, single-storey farmhouse set in
an orchard.
5rm 1hc nc7 CTV 10P ⱜ 10acres mixed
& sheep W only Jun–Aug D3pm

STOCKLEIGH POMEROY Devon
Map 3 SS80
Westwood *(SS869029)*
☎ Cheriton Fitzpaine 202
Large, well equipped farmhouse 3 miles
from Crediton.
4rm TV P 117acres

STOKE HOLY CROSS Norfolk
Map 5 TG20
Salamanca *(TG235022)*
☎ Framingham Earl 2322
Old house with large garden on City
outskirts. Simple but comfortable.
Mar–Sep 3hc (A 1hc) ✵ nc6 TV 6P
170acres arable & dairy D6.30pm

STOKEINTEIGNHEAD Devon
Map 3 SX97
Lower Rocombe *(SX910701)*
☎ Shaldon 3367
Large farmhouse situated in secluded
valley.
Lic 12hc ✵ TV 16P 235acres mixed
D6.30pm

STOKE PRIOR Heref & Worcs
Map 3 SO55
Norman's *(SX524555)*
☎ Steensbridge 221
Secluded farm approached by rough

track; entrance of which is near the village Post Office.
Etr–Oct 3rm 1hc ⚡ TV 2P 50acres mixed
S% B&bf£4–£4.50 Bdi£5.50–£6
W£36–£40 ⚱ D4.30pm
Wheelbarrow Castle *(SO516573)*
☎ Leominster 2219
Large, imposing, brick-built manor house overlooking River Luss. Four-poster bed available. Numerous antiques.
3rm ⚡ ♨ TV 6P 2🏠 ⚱

STON EASTON Somerset *Map 3 ST65*
Manor *(ST626533)*
☎ Chewton Mendip 266
Well kept and furnished farmhouse. Lawn at the front and a produce garden. Situated in quiet minor road.
Closed Dec 2hc ⚡ CTV ⚱ 250acres
beef dairy

STOWFORD Devon *Map 2 SX48*
Stowford Barton *(SX434870)*
☎ Lewdown 272
Signposted from main road north of the A30.
Mar–Sep 3rm ⚡ CTV 3P 53acres dairy
S% B&bf£3.50–£4.50 Bdi£5–£6
W£40–£45 ⚱ D5pm

STRATFORD-UPON-AVON Warwicks
Map 4 SP25
Monk's Barn *(SP206516)* Shipston Rd
☎293714
Well appointed farm offering clean and tidy accommodation. Adjacent to A34 Stratford–Oxford rd.
Closed Xmas 4hc ⚡ CTV 4P ⚱ 75acres
arable beef sheep S% B&bf£3.75–£4

STREET Somerset *Map 3 ST43*
Marshalls Elm *(ST485348)* ☎42878
Old well preserved farmhouse with back and front gardens. Set in country surroundings. Street 1½ miles.
10Jan–10Dec 3rm ⚡ TV 2P 200acres
mixed S% B&bfr£4 Bdifr£7 Wfr£42 ⚱
(W only Feb–Nov) D4.30pm

SUMMERCOURT Cornwall *Map 2 SW85*
Trenithon *(SW895553)*
☎ Fraddon 860253
Modern farmhouse situated in quiet location in open countryside a few miles from the coast.
Closed Dec 4hc CTV 6P ⚱ 148acres
mixed S% B&bf£4.30–£4.50
Bdi£5.40–£5.60 W£37.50–£39 ⚱ D3pm

SWINSCOE Staffs *Map 7 SK14*
Calton Moor House *(SK115487)*
☎ Waterhouses 221

Large, Georgian-style farmhouse.
Etr–Oct 3rm 2hc 1⚿🌀 ⚡ nc5 CTV 4P ⚱
200acres dairy S% ✳B&bf4 Bdif£5.50
W£37 ⚱ D noon

TACOLNESTON Norfolk *Map 5 TM19*
White House *(TM142940)*
24 Bentley Rd ☎ Bunwell 220
Small, well kept property fairly close to Norwich. Large rooms, comfortably appointed.
Etr–Oct 4rm nc3 4P 2🏠 ⚱ 1000acres
mixed S% B&bf£4.95–£6.50
Bdif£7.30–£9.25 W£34.65–£45.50 M
D3pm

TALATON Devon *Map 3 SY09*
Harris *(SY068997)*
☎ Whimple 822327
16th century stone-built farmhouse set in quiet village. Large concrete yard. Lawns and gardens.
3rm 2hc ⚡ CTV 10P 123acres dairy S%
B&bfr£4.50 Wfr£30 M

TAVISTOCK Devon *Map 2 SX47*
Bungalow *(SX464731)* Parswell ☎2789
Well situated building on the Callington road, commanding good views of surrounding countryside.
Etr–Nov 2rm ⚡ TV 2P 106acres beef
sheep S% ✳B&bfr£4

TAWSTOCK Devon *Map 2 SS52*
Charlacott *(SS532280)*
☎ Newton Tracey 321
Farm set in a peacefully remote countryside position.
20May–14Sep 5hc ⚡ ♨ CTV 6P 192acres
mixed

TEIGNMOUTH Devon *Map 3 SY97*
Ringmore *(SX925719)* Shaldon
☎ Shaldon 3228
400-year-old thatched farmhouse near Shaldon and Teignmouth. Attractive and conveniently placed for holidaymakers.
Spring–Sep 5rm 4P 150acres mixed S%
Wfr£45 ⚱

TEMPLECOMBE Somerset *Map 3 ST72*
Manor House *(ST709221)* ☎560
3rm 2hc 6P

TEMPLE SOWERBY Cumbria
Map 12 NY62
Skygarth *(NY612262)*
☎ Kirkby Thore 300
Attractive farmhouse with high standard of facilities and furnishings. Large airy rooms. Overlooks River Eden.
May–Oct 3rm ⚡ CTV 6P river 220acres
mixed S% B&bf£4.25 W£29 M

THORNCOMBE Dorset *Map 3 ST30*
Higher *(ST376034)* ☎ Winsham 340
Detached, two storey, brick and stone
farmhouse. Milking parlour and farmland
adjacent. Large lawn.
Closed Xmas 3hc nc1 CTV 3P 50acres
dairy B&bf£4.50–£5.50 Bdi£6.50–£7.50
Wfr£45 ⊬ (W only mid Jul–Aug)

THROWLEIGH Devon *Map 3 SX69*
East Ash Manor *(SX680911)*
☎ Whiddon Down 244
17th century, oak beamed farmhouse
situated in beautiful countryside. 1m E
on Whiddon Down road.
3hc ⊗ ⚓ TV 4P ⬛ 160acres dairy S%
B&bf£5.50–£6.50 Bdi£8.50–£9.50 D8pm

TIDEFORD Cornwall *Map 2 SX35*
Trenance *(SX340600)* ☎ Landrake 319
Large, stone-built farmhouse situated
north of the A38 west of Saltash.
Etr–Sep 3hc ⊗ TV P 87acres dairy

TIVERTON Devon *Map 3 SS91*
Lower Collipriest *(SS953117)* ☎2321
Modernised, scheduled building on the
banks of River Exe.
Apr–Oct 4hc 2⊣🔥 ⊗ nc10 CTV 6P 3⚓ ⬛
river 230acres beef dairy S% ✳Bdifr£7.50
Wfr£50 ⊬ D5pm

TODMORDEN W Yorks *Map 7 SD92*
Todmorden Edge South *(SD924246)*
Parkin Ln, Sourhall ☎3459
Converted 17th-century farmhouse on
rural hillside. Clean, comfortable rooms.
Cosy residents' lounge. Ample
entertainments nearby.
3hc ⊗ nc8 CTV 10P ⬛ 1acre non-working
S% B&bf£5.25–£7 Bdi£9–£12 D8pm

TOTNES Devon *Map 3 SX86*
Broomborough House *(SX793601)*
☎863134
Spacious, country manor-style house in
hilly parkland. Games room. Views of
Dartmoor and surrounding countryside.
Local game fishing.
Mar–Oct 3hc 2⊣🔥 ⊗ ⚓ CTV P ⬛
590acres mixed S% ✳B&bf£5.70 Bdi£9.70
Wfr£29 ⊬ D10am

TRENEAR Cornwall *Map 2 SW63*
Longstone *(SW664318)* ☎ Helston 2483
Well appointed farmhouse set in beautiful
countryside. Facilities include a playroom
and sun lounge. Off B3297 N of Wendron.
Closed Xmas & New Year 5hc CTV 5P
62acres dairy S% B&bf£5.18–£6.33
Bdi£6.90–£8.05 Wf£43.70–£49.45 ⊬
D6.30pm

TRESPARRETT Cornwall *Map 2 SX19*
Tresparrett House *(SX146919)*
☎ Otterham Station 272
Situated in quiet surroundings in village.
Good approach road and parking area.
2hc CTV 5P ⬛ 30acres dairy S%
B&bf£4.50 Bdi£7 Wf£49 ⊬ D4pm

TRESPARRETT POSTS Cornwall
Map 2 SX19
Wilslea *(SX153934)* ☎ St Gennys 231
Typical Cornish farmhouse set in
downland. Adjacent to A39.
May–Oct 3rm 1hc TV 10P 183acres
dairy mixed & sheep S% B&bfr£3.50

TREVALGA Cornwall *Map 2 SX08*
Reddivallen *(SX099887)* ☎ Boscastle 361
Comfortable house with garden in isolated

position off the B3266.
Jun–Sep 2rm ⊗ CTV 2P 320acres arable,
dairy & sheep

TREVEIGHAN Cornwall *Map 2 SX07*
Treveighan *(SX075795)*
☎ Bodmin 850286
Two-storey, stone built farmhouse with
farm buildings attached. Situated in
isolated village. Views over valley.
Mar–Oct 3rm ⊗ TV 4P 100acres beef &
dairy S% B&bf£4.50 Bdi£6.50 Wf£45
D7pm

TREVENEN BAL Cornwall *Map 2 SW62*
Roselidden House *(SW676297)*
☎ Helston 2118 Etr–Sep 3hc ⊗ nc5
CTV 6P sea 17½acres beef S% Bdi£8.50
Wf£55 ⊬ W only mid Jun–early Sep D7pm

TROON Cornwall *Map 2 SW63*
Sea View *(SW671370)* ☎ Praze 260
Farmhouse has been modernised, yet still
retains atmosphere of family run farm.
Tastefully furnished with extensive pine
wood décor.
Mar–Oct 11rm 10hc CTV 10P 5⚓ ⬛ sea
8acres mixed S% B&bf£3.65 Bdi£5.85
Wfr£44 ⊬ W only Jul & Aug D6pm

TROUTBECK *(Nr Penrith)* Cumbria
Map 11 NY32
Askew Rigg *(NY371280)*
☎ Threlkeld 638
17th century stone built farmhouse.
Attractively modernised to retain original
character. Entrance to drive is situated
only a few yards from the A66.
Mar–Oct 3rm 1hc ⚓ CTV 5P ⬛ 200acres
mixed S% B&bf£3.75–£4 Bdi£5.50–£6
D6pm
Riverside *(NY382253)* ☎ Greystoke 220
Stone-built house and buildings in quiet
rural setting. Fine views of surrounding
hills.
Etr–Oct 3rm ⊗ nc4 CTV 4P 87acres
mixed S% B&bf£4 Bdi£5.50 D2pm

TYWARDREATH Cornwall *Map 2 SX05*
Great Pelean *(SX085563)* ☎ Par 2106
Situated near Pempillick with walled
garden to front entrance. Par beach 2
miles. ½m N towards A390.
May–8Sep 6rm 5hc ⊗ TV P 140acres
mixed

UFFCULME Devon *Map 3 ST01*
Houndaller *(ST058138)*
☎ Craddock 40246
Very old, attractive farmhouse standing in
beautiful garden.
Apr–Oct 2hc ⊗ CTV 4P 1⚓ 176acres
dairy & mixed S% B&bf£4.50 Bdi£6.50
Wfr£48 ⊬ D5.30pm

Woodrow *(ST054107)* ☎ Craddock 40362
Farmhouse set in pleasant lawns and
gardens with meadow land stretching to
River Culm. Trout fishing available.
3hc (A 2rm) ⊗ CTV 10P 200acres mixed
S% ✳B&bf£4.50 Bdi£7 Wf£49 ⊬ D9pm

ULEY Glos *Map 3 ST79*
Newbrook *(ST775980)* ☎251
Stone-built farmhouse with lawn, garden
and orchard. In attractive village below
western escarpment of Cotswolds.
3rm 2hc ⊗ nc5 CTV P ⬛ 120acres mixed
S%

UPOTTERY Devon *Map 3 ST20*
Hoemoor *(ST218104)*
☎ Churchstanton 265

Well.kept, small, modern farmhouse. Rather isolated but with beautiful views. Etr–Oct 4rm 1hc nc12 2P 3🏠 50acres mixed S% B&bfr£5 Bdifr£7 Wfr£48 ⌗ D7pm

Yarde *(ST193045)* ☎318
Old farmhouse with interesting oak panelling. Near Monkton on the A30. Mar–Oct 3rm 2hc ⊗ CTV 3P 68acres dairy S% B&b£4–£4.50 W£35–£37.50 ⌗ D5pm

UPPER ELKSTONE Staffs *Map 7 SK05*
Mount Pleasant *(SK056588)*
☎ Blackshaw 380
Stone built in 1869 in elevated position with excellent views of surrounding countryside. Off B5053. Mar–Nov 3hc nc6 CTV 6P 🍴 2acres non-working S% B&bfr£5.50 Bdifr£9.75 Wfr£68.25 ⌗ W only Jun, Jul & Aug D6.30pm

UPTON PYNE Devon *Map 3 SX99*
Cox's Hill *(SX914978)*
☎ Stoke Canon 552
16th century, thatched farmhouse with walled garden. Situated on the outskirts of Exeter. 2rm ⊗ TV 3P 200acres mixed S% B&b£4.50–£5.50 Bdif£7–£8 D3.30pm

Pierce's *(SX910977)*
☎ Stoke Canon 252
Large farmhouse about 1 mile north of A377 Exeter to Barnstaple road. Etr–Sep 2hc ⊗ CTV 6P 🍴 300acres mixed S% B&bfr£4.50 Wfr£29 M

UTTOXETER Staffs *Map 7 SK03*
Moorhouse *(SK102327)* Wood Ln ☎2384
Stone-rendered farmhouse about 200 years old. Extensively renovated and modernised. Antiques. Rural setting close to racecourse. 4hc 1🛁🍴 🕭 CTV P 180acres dairy B&bfr£6 Bdifr£10

WALL Cornwall *Map 2 SW63*
Reawla *(SW605363)* ☎ Leedstown 320
Pleasant, well situated farmhouse close to beaches. Small, well kept garden. Etr–Sep 3hc CTV P 50acres beef

WARCOP Cumbria *Map 12 NY71*
Highwood Holme *(NY760150)* Flitholme
☎ Brough 304
Modern bungalow of local stone adjacent to original farmhouse. Well decorated and comfortable. Apr–Sep 2rm CTV 2P 🍴 S% B&b£3.50

WAREHAM Dorset *Map 3 ST98*
Redcliffe *(SY932866)* ☎2225
Modern farmhouse in quiet, rural surroundings. Pleasant location adjacent to River Frome and overlooking hills and fields. ½ mile from Wareham. 4rm 3hc ⊗ CTV 4P 🍴 river 250acres arable beef & mixed

WATERMILLOCK Cumbria
Map 12 NY42
Longthwaite *(NY439228)* Ullswater
☎ Pooley Bridge 297
Farmhouse built from local stone, parts dating from 1695. Situated in elevated position overlooking Lake Ullswater. Etr–Oct 4hc ⊗ nc10 5P lake 50acres mixed

WATERROW Somerset *Map 3 ST02*
Hurstone *(ST056252)*
☎ Wiveliscombe 23441
Set on the edge of Brendon Hills overlooking the valley of the River Tone.

Moor House Farm

Wood Lane, Uttoxeter (Mrs P. J. Tunnicliffe, UTT 2384)
The olde world farm is situated within easy distance of Chatsworth, Blithfield, Kedleston and Sudbury Halls, National Peak District and is adjacent to Uttoxeter Race Course. Guests and children welcome all year round. Accommodation comprises family, single, twin and double-bedded rooms with wash basins in rooms. 2 dining rooms, TV lounge, shower etc. Cot, high chair and baby sitting arranged. Cuisine superb, variety a speciality. Unlimited car parking. Terms on application.

HURSTONE FARM
Waterrow, Wiveliscombe,
Somerset

Hurstone is a 65 acre mixed farm on the edge of the Brendon Hills 600ft above sea level. The bedrooms face south and are comfortably furnished and fitted with handbasins. We provide good home produced farmhouse food and keep a small selection of quality wine as well as our own cider.
John and Alison Bone, Hurstone Farm, Waterrow, Wiveliscombe, Somerset, TA4 2AT. Tel: Wiv. 23441 (0984).

Comfortably furnished with log fires during winter months and chilly evenings.
5hc TV 8P river 65acres mixed S% B&bf6–£8 Bdif8–£12 Wf50–£75 ⚹
W only Jul & Aug D7.30pm

WEETON Lancs *Map 7 SD33*
High Moor *(SD388365)* ☎273
Compact, homely farmhouse. Clean and tidy. Much farm produce used in cooking.
Closed Xmas 2rm ⚹ CTV 10P 7acres mixed S% B&bf4.50–£5

WEST TAPHOUSE Cornwall *Map 2 SX16*
Penadlake *(SX144636)* The Waters Foot
☎ Lostwithiel 872271
Old farmhouse, modernised, overlooking woodland. Large garden.
Mar–Oct 2rm TV 3P 250acres mixed S% ⚹B&bf4–£5

WETTON Staffs *Map 7 SK15*
Yew Tree *(SK111553)* ☎ Alstonefield 202
Natural stone house with pleasant lawns and rose gardens. In village in renowned Manifold Valley, part of Peak District National Park.
4rm 2hc 4P 178acres mixed S% B&bfr£4

WHATSTANDWELL Derbys *Map 8 SK35*
Watergate *(SK328545)*
☎ Wirksworth 2135
Stone house built in 1779. Set in quiet surroundings.
Mar–Nov 2rm 1hc TV 3P ⚏ 112acres non-working S% B&bf6 Bdif9 Wf55 ⚹ D8.30pm

WHEDDON CROSS Somerset
Map 3 SS93
Triscombe *(SS921377)* ☎ Winsford 227
Large, modernised, 17th century farmhouse on elevated site. Secluded from main road. 1 mile from village.
Etr–Oct 5hc CTV 16P ⚏ 30acres mixed ⚹B&bf5.75–£6.25 Bdif8.60–£9.20 Wf57–£59.20 ⚹ D7pm

WHIDDON DOWN Devon *Map 3 SX69*
South Nethercott *(SX688947)* ☎276
Brick-built farmhouse in mature gardens 1½ miles from Whiddon Down.
3rm 1⇆🖼 ⚹ nc8 CTV P 170acres arable & dairy S% B&bf7–£8 Bdif10–£13.50

WHIMPLE Devon *Map 3 SY09*
Down House *(SY056968)* ☎822475
Spacious farmhouse with large garden of lawns, attractive flower beds and shrubs. Pleasant and homely atmosphere.
6hc nc5 TV 8P 5acres mixed S% B&bfr£4.50 Bdifr£7 Wfr£45 D7.30pm
Lower Southbrook *(SY024964)* ☎822534
Farmhouse in secluded position with extensive views over open countryside.
Apr–Oct 3rm 2hc ⚹ ⚱ CTV P ⚏ 100acres beef S% B&bf4–£4.50

WHITCHURCH CANONICORUM
Dorset *Map 3 SY49*
Taphouse *(SY395975)* ☎ Chideock 375
Small, modernised, brick-built farmhouse in an isolated position. 2¾m N of village.
Etr–Oct 2rm ⚹ nc3 2P 310acres mixed

WHITE CROSS Cornwall *Map 2 SW97*
Torview *(SW966722)* ☎ Wadebridge 2261
Modern farmhouse on main A39. Wadebridge 1½ miles.
4hc CTV 6P 22acres mixed S% B&bf4 Bdif6 Wf42 ⚹ D6pm

WHITESTONE Devon *Map 3 SX89*
Rowhorne House *(SX880948)*
☎ Exeter 74675
Farmhouse set in attractive gardens and lawns. Exeter 6 miles.
3hc ⚹ CTV 6P 90acres dairy D5pm

WIDECOMBE IN THE MOOR Devon
Map 3 SX77
Scobitor *(SX725750)* ☎254
Well appointed, moorland farmhouse set in the heart of Dartmoor National Park.
Closed Xmas 6rm 5hc 3⇆🖼 ⚱ CTV 6P ⚏ 50acres beef S% Bdif18 D8pm

WILLAND Devon *Map 3 ST01*
Doctors *(ST015117)* Halberton Rd
☎ Sampford Peverell 820525
Farmhouse situated in garden and farmland. Tiverton and Cullompton 4 miles.
Mar–Oct 3rm ⚹ CTV P 90acres dairy S% B&bfr£4.25 Bdifr£6 Wfr£38 ⚹
W only mid Jul–1Sep D noon

WILLITON Somerset *Map 3 ST04*
Rowdon *(ST082381)* ☎ Stogumber 280
Solidly built stone farmhouse with attractive beamed rooms.
4hc ⚹ CTV 4P ⚏ 150acres mixed S% B&bf5–£6
Yarde *(ST059392)* Yarde
☎ Washford 8848
Once a coaching inn, this Grade III listed farmhouse is surrounded by agricultural land and situated in Exmoor National Park. 2½m S off B3188.
Etr–Oct 3hc ⚹ nc12 CTV 3P ⚏ 6acres sheep B&bf5–£5.50 Bdif8–£8.50 Wf45–£50 ⚹ D7pm

WINFRITH Dorset *Map 3 SY88*
Home *(SY828860)* Dorchester Rd (A352)
☎ Warmwell 852847
Modern, red brick farmhouse in rural surroundings ¾ mile from village of Wool. Surrounded by rolling countryside.
Apr–Sep 3hc ⚹ nc6 TV 3P 17acres non-working

WITHERIDGE Devon *Map 3 SS81*
Cannington House *(SS805144)* ☎440
Farmhouse is situated in the village of Witheridge.
Apr–Oct 3hc ⚹ nc5 CTV 1P 2🏠 ⚏ 120acres mixed D5pm

WITHIEL Cornwall *Map 2 SW96*
Tregawne *(SX002662)* ☎ Lanivet 303
Charming, carefully modernised farmhouse furnished with antiques. Stands in Ruthern Valley away from the farm. Heated outdoor pool.
Closed Xmas 4rm 1hc 1⇆🖼 6P ⚏ 160acres dairy B&bf6.90–£8.05 Bdif8.51–£10.24 Wf55.20–£67.28 ⚹ D8pm

WITHLEIGH Devon *Map 3 SS91*
Jurishayes *(SS913121)* ☎ Tiverton 2984
Warm and comfortable farmhouse with pleasant atmosphere. Well positioned for touring North and mid Devon.
5rm 2hc ⚹ TV 100P 134acres mixed D6pm

WIVELISCOMBE Somerset *Map 3 ST02*
Deepleigh *(ST079294)* Langley Marsh
☎23379
16th century farmhouse, converted into small hotel. Comfortable lounge with original beams, panelling and log fire.

1m N unclass rd.
6hc 1⇌🛊 ♨ CTV 6P 🍴 15acres mixed
S% B&b£8.25 Bdi£11.75 W£75 ⅙
(W only Jul & Aug) D5.30pm
Hillacre *(ST104275)* ☎23355
Traditional farmhouse set back about
200yds to the north of A361.
3rm 2hc CTV P 1🏠 700acres mixed

WOODBURY SALTERTON Devon
Map 3 SY08
Stallcombe House *(SY039891)*
Sanctuary Ln ☎32373
Early 17th century cottages converted
into fine farmhouse with oak beams. 3½
miles E of Clyst St Mary.
Closed Xmas 3rm 2hc ♨ CTV 4P 🍴
55acres dairy S% B&bfr£4.50
Bdi fr£6.50 Wfr£45 ⅙

WOOKEY Somerset *Map 3 ST54*
Honeycroft *(ST509453)* Worth
☎ Wells (Somerset) 78971
Large whitewashed cottage with lawns
and orchard. On B3139.
Feb–Dec 3rm 2hc ♨ nc3 CTV 6P
21acres beef & pigs S% B&b£4.25

WOOLFARDISWORTHY Devon
Map 2 SS32
South View *(SS335213)*
☎ Clovelly 397
Farmhouse set in very quiet and peaceful
surroundings.
Etr–Sep 3rm 1hc ♨ CTV 3P 45acres dairy
Stroxworthy *(SS341198)* ☎ Clovelly 333
10rm 9hc ♨ CTV 25P 90acres dairy S%
B&b£3.85 Bdi£7.70 W£53.90 ⅙
W only Jul–14Sep D8pm
Westvilla *(SS329215)* ☎ Clovelly 309
Well decorated accommodation. Good
farmhouse meals served.
Etr–Oct 3hc ♨ CTV P 22acres beef &
sheep S% B&b£5–£6 Bdi£7.50–£8
Wfr£40 D6.30pm

WOOLLEY Cornwall *Map 2 SS21*
East Woolley *(SS254167)*
☎ Morwenstowe 274
Farm set in undulating pasture land, close
to A39. Homely atmosphere.
Etr–Oct 3rm ♨ CTV TV 6P 190acres
mixed S% B&b£3.75–£4 Bdi£6.50–£7
W£38–£40 D6pm

WOOTTON COURTENAY Somerset
Map 3 SS94
Ford *(SS929426)* ☎ Timberscombe 211

A genuine working farm.
5rm 4hc ♨ TV 5P 150acres dairy D6.30pm
Ranscombe *(SS947433)*
☎ Timberscombe 237
Dark redstone house with gardens at front
and a duck pond to the side. Easy access
via M5.
Etr–Oct 4hc 10P 130acres mixed S%

WORMBRIDGE Heref & Worcs
Map 3 SO43
Wormbridge Court *(SO429309)* ☎239
A 400-year-old manor house standing
adjacent to A465 Hereford–
Abergavenny road.
Etr–Oct 5rm 4hc ♨ ♨ CTV 6P 2🏠
250acres arable & beef S% B&b£5
Bdi£9 D6.30pm

YARCOMBE Devon *Map 3 ST20*
Broadley *(ST239069)* ☎ Upottery 274
Traditional style farmhouse in remote East
Devon countryside. Good home cooking.
May–Sep 2rm ♨ nc5 TV P 136acres
dairy sheep & pigs S% B&b£3.50–£3.75
Crawley *(ST259079)* ☎ Chard 2259
Attractive stone building with a thatched
roof.
Apr–Oct 3rm 2hc ♨ CTV 1P 1🏠
200acres mixed

YEALMPTON Devon *Map 2 SX55*
Broadmoor *(SX574498)*
☎ Plymouth 880407
Stone built farmhouse and outbuildings.
3hc ♨ nc7 CTV P 207acres mixed S%
B&bfr£5

YEOVIL Somerset *Map 3 ST51*
Carents *(ST546188)* Yeovil Marsh ☎6622
Clean, pleasant traditional style
farmhouse on the outskirts of Yeovil.
2m N of A37.
Closed Xmas 3rm 1hc ♨ CTV P
350acres mixed S% B&b£4.50–£5
Bdi£6.50–£7.50 W£49 ⅙

ZENNOR Cornwall *Map 2 SW43*
Osborne's *(SW455385)* Boswednack
☎ St Ives (Cornwall) 6944
Farmhouse offering own dairy produce
and vegetables. Wholesome country food.
Lands End about 5 miles. Bathing in nearby
coves.
Etr–Oct 2hc ♨ nc10 CTV 3P 70acres
beef S% B&b£4.50–£5

CHANNEL ISLANDS

GUERNSEY (No map)

CÂTEL
GH Lilyvale Private Hotel Hougue du
Pommier ☎ Guernsey 56868 May–Oct
Lic 13hc 5⇌🛊 ♨ nc2 CTV 10P sea S%
B&b£7.50–£10 D6.30pm

ST MARTIN
GH Santi Villa La rue Maze
☎ Guernsey 37332 11hc ♨ CTV 12P
S% Bdi£6.50–£7.75 W£45.50–£54.25
⅙ D6.30pm

⊨GH Triton Les Hubits ☎ Guernsey
38017 mid May–mid Sep 14hc 5⇌🛊 ♨
nc4 CTV 12P 🍴 S% B&b£5–£6
Bdi£7.50–£8.50 D6.30pm

ST PETER PORT
⊨GH Changi Lodge Private Hotel
Les Baissieres ☎ Guernsey 56446
May–Oct Lic 13hc CTV 14P 🍴 S%
B&b£5–£6 Bdi£7.75–£8.50
W£54.25–£59.50 ⅙ D4pm

GH Maison Du Guet Private Hotel
Amhurst ☎ Guernsey 22007 Feb–Nov
Lic 18hc 3⇌🛊 ♨ CTV 10P 🍴 S%
B&b£6.25–£8.50 Bdi£7.25–£9.50
W£50.75–£66.50 D7pm

JERSEY (No map)

BEAUMONT
GH Seawold Private Hotel St Aubin's Rd
☎ Jersey 20807 22hc 22⇌🛊 ♨ CTV
5P 🍴 sea S% Bdi£7.50–£9
W£45–£63 ⅙ (W only May–Sep)
D6.45pm

GOREY
GH Lavender Villa Hotel Grouville
☎ Jersey 54937 Mar–19Dec Lic 17hc
10⇋🛁 ⊗ nc7 10P 🍴 S%
B&b£9.50–£10.50 D6.30pm

LA HAULE
⊶GH **Au Caprice Private Hotel** Route
de La Haule ☎ Jersey 20334 Mar–Nov
Lic 14hc ⊗ nc3 CTV sea S%
B&b£5–£6 Bdi£7.50–£8.75
W£52.50–£61.25 ⚓ (W only Jun–Sep)
D6.30pm

ROZEL BAY
⊶GH **Chateau la Chaire**
☎ Jersey 63354 Mar–Oct Lic 17hc
9⇋🛁 20P 🍴 B&b£5–£10 Bdi£8–£13
W£56–£98 ⚓ D7.30pm

ST AUBIN
⊶GH **Panorama Private Hotel** High St
☎ Jersey 42429 17hc 1⇋🛁 ⊗ nc5 CTV
sea S% B&b£4.50–£10.50
W£31.50–£73.50 Ⓜ

ST BRELADE
⊶GH **Arnewood Lodge** Route Des
Genets ☎ Jersey 41516 Apr–Oct rs Nov–
Mar Lic 14rm 6hc 8⇋🛁 ⊗ nc3 CTV S%
B&b£4–£5.50 Bdi£7–£9.50
(W only Jun–Sep) D9.30am

ST CLEMENTS
GH Linden Jambart Ln, Pontac
☎ Jersey 51115 Closed Dec 6hc (A 2hc)
🛁 CTV 8P D6.30pm

ST HELIER
GH Ainsdale Private Hotel 82 Rouge
Bouillon ☎ Jersey 31612 Mar–mid Oct
Lic 17hc ⊗ nc CTV 3P D6.15pm

GH Almorah Hotel La Pouquelaye
☎ Jersey 21648 Apr–Oct Lic 17hc
5⇋🛁 ⊗ nc4 TV 10P 🍴 S%
B&b£6–£8.50 Bdi£7–£10 D6.30pm

⊶GH **Merton** 48 Roseville St
☎ Jersey 20044 Mar–Nov 45hc 23⇋🛁 ⊗
CTV S% B&b£5–£8.50 Bdi£7–£10.50
W£50–£77 D6.30pm

ST MARTIN
GH St Martin's House ☎ Jersey 53271
Closed Xmas Lic 11hc 4⇋🛁 ⊗ CTV 10P
🍴 S% ✳B&b£5.25–£7 Bdi£7.25–£9.25
D7.15pm

ST PETER'S VALLEY
⊶GH **Midvale Private Hotel**
☎ Jersey 42498 Etr–Oct Lic 21hc
11⇋🛁 🛁 CTV 20P B&b£5.50
Bdi£6.50–£8.25 (W only Jun–Aug)
D6.30pm

ST SAVIOUR
GH Redwood Private Hotel Five Oaks
☎ Jersey 26370 2Jan–29Oct Lic 22hc
10⇋🛁 ⊗ CTV 20P B&b£6
Bdi£7–£9.75 W£49–£68.25 ⚓ D9pm

TRINITY
GH Highfield Country Hotel Route du
Ebenezer ☎ Jersey 62194 Apr–Oct Lic
26hc ⊗ CTV 24P D7.30pm

ISLE OF MAN

DOUGLAS *Map 6 SC37*
GH Ainsdale 2 Empire Ter, Central
Prom ☎6695 Mar–Oct 19hc 🛁 CTV
D4.30pm

⊶GH **Rosslyn Private Hotel** 3 Empire
Ter, Central Prom ☎ Douglas 6056 19hc
⊗ CTV sea S% B&b£5.46–£5.75
Bdi£6.04–£6.61 W£42.26–£46.29 ⚓
D previous day

GH Rutland Hotel Queens Prom
☎21218 Etr–Oct Lic 93hc 13⇋🛁 ⊗
CTV lift B&b£7.49–£8.28
Bdi£8.88–£9.66 D noon

PORT ERIN *Map 6 SC26*
GH Golf Links Hotel ☎832270
May–29Sep Lic 64hc ⊗ 🛁 CTV 35P sea
D8pm

⊶GH **Regent Hotel** ☎833454 May–Sep
13hc CTV sea S% B&b£4.20–£5
Bdi£4.60–£5.25

GH Snaefell The Promenade ☎832273
May–Sep Lic 54hc 🛁 CTV 40P sea D7pm

PORT ST MARY *Map 6 SC26*
GH Mallmore Private Hotel The
Promenade ☎833179 Etr–1st wk Oct
47hc CTV P sea D8pm

GUESTHOUSES

ABERDARE Mid Glam *Map 3 SO00*
GH *Cae-Coed* Craig St ☎871190 Lic
5hc TV 5P 🕮 D7pm

ABERDOVEY Gwynedd *Map 6 SN69*
⊷**GH Cartref** ☎273 6hc ⊗ CTV 6P S%
B&bf4–£4.50 Bdif6–£7 Wf42–£49
Ł D7pm

GH Maybank Private Hotel ☎500
Apr–Oct Lic 7hc 2⇌🛏 nc4 CTV 🕮 river
S% B&bf8–£10 Bdif11–£13 Wf73–£80
Ł D9pm

ABERGAVENNY Gwent *Map 3 SO21*
⊷**GH Park** 36 Hereford Rd ☎3715 Lic
7hc CTV 8P 🕮 S% B&bf5 Bdif8 Wf53
Ł D5.30pm

INN Great George Hotel Cross St
☎4230 Lic 4hc CTV 11🏠 🕮 S%
B&bf7–£7.50 sn Lf1.20 alc
D9.30pmf4 alc

ABERGELE Clwyd *Map 6 SH97*
⊷**GH Coed Mor** Groes Lwyd ☎822261
7hc 2⇌🛏 TV 4P 🕮 S% B&bf3.75
Bdif4.75 D5pm

INN Bull Hotel Chapel St ☎822115
Lic 6hc ⊗ CTV 15P S% B&bfrf6

Bdifrf9 Wfrf70 sn Lf2–£4&alc
D8.30pmf3.20–£6.50

ABERSOCH Gwynedd *Map 6 SH32*
⊷**GH Llysfor** ☎2248 Etr–Oct Lic 9hc
CTV 12P river sea S% B&bf5.50
Bdif8.50 D6.30pm

GH *Wylfa* Golf Rd ☎2333 Closed Xmas
wk Lic 6rm 5hc (A 2hc) CTV 5P sea
D7.30pm

ABERYSTWYTH Dyfed *Map 6 SN58*
See Plan
GH Four Seasons Hotel 50–54 Portland
St ☎612120 Plan:**1** Lic 17hc 5⇌🛏 ⊗
nc5 CTV 14P 🕮 B&bfrf7.48 Bdifrf11.50
Wfrf69 Ł D7.30

GH Glan-Aber Hotel Union St ☎617610
Plan:**2** Closed last 2 wks Dec Lic 14hc
(A 3rm 2hc) CTV S% B&bf6.80–£7.90
Bdif10.25–£11.30 Wf54–£60 Ł
D6.45pm

⊷**GH Glyn-Garth** South Rd ☎615050
Plan:**3** Closed 2 wks Xmas rs Nov–Apr
(No evening meals) Lic 12hc 2⇌🛏 ⊗
nc7 CTV 🕮 sea S% B&bf4.50–£5
Bdif6.75–£8 Wf42–£47 Ł D4pm

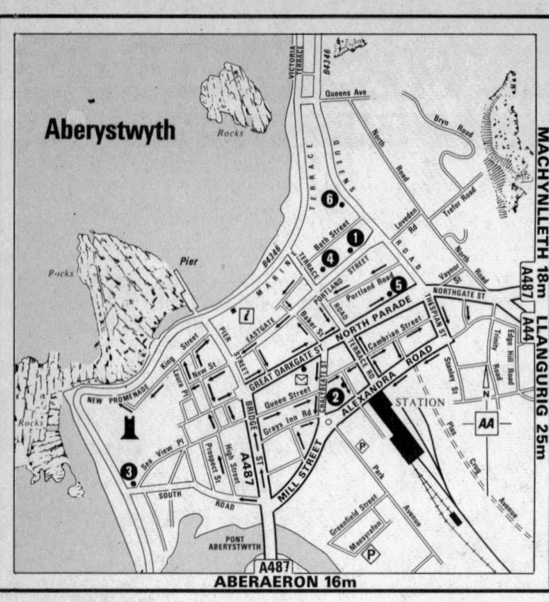

➤◄GH **Shangrila** 36 Portland St
☎617659 Plan:**4** 6hc CTV P 🏠 ▥ S%
B&bf4.50–£5 Bdif7–£7.50 Wf49 ⌖
D4pm

GH **Swn-y-Don** 40–42 North Pde
☎615059 Plan:**5** Lic 25hc CTV 10P
▥ B&bf6.90 Bdif9.27 D8.30pm

➤◄GH **Windsor Private Hotel** 41 Queens
Rd ☎612134 Plan:**6** 10hc ⊗ CTV 7P
S% B&bf5.35–£5.75 Bdif8.50–£9.70
Wf56.50–£64 ⌖ D5pm

AMROTH Dyfed *Map 2 SN10*
GH **Sunnyridge** ☎ Saundersfoot 812335
May–Sep 8hc nc3 CTV 7P S% B&bf6.50
Bdif7.75–£8.50 D5pm

BALA Gwynedd *Map 6 SH93*
GH **Frondderw** ☎520301 Feb–Nov
Lic 7hc 2⇱▥ ⊗ 🛁 CTV 10P S% B&bf6
Bdif10.50 Wf70 ⌖ D6pm

GH **Plas Teg** Tegid St ☎520268
Closed Xmas Lic 8hc CTV 8P lake S%
B&bfrf6 Bdifrf9 Wfrf60 ⌖ D7pm

BANGOR Gwynedd *Map 6 SH57*
➤◄GH **Dilfan** Garth Rd ☎53030 8hc
CTV 6P ▥ S% B&bf4.50 Bdif7
Wf45.50 ⌖ D6pm

GH **Glen Aethy Hotel** Holyhead Rd
☎52543 Closed Xmas Lic 9hc 4⇱▥ ⊗
CTV 14P ▥ ✳B&bf9.35–£12.25
Bdif13.85–£16.75 D8.30pm

BARMOUTH Gwynedd *Map 6 SH61*
➤◄GH **Belgrave Hotel** Marine Pde
☎280369 Lic 12hc CTV 6P 1🏠 sea S%
B&bf5.50 Bdif8.25 Wf52 ⌖ D6pm

GH **Lawrenny Lodge** ☎280466
Etr–Oct Lic 10hc TV 10P S%
✳B&bf7.75–£8.05 Bdif11.50
Wf79.35–£81.35 ⌖ D6.30pm

GH **Morwendon** Llanaber (1m N A496)
☎280566 Mar–Oct & Xmas Lic 7hc ⊗
nc7 CTV 8P sea S% B&bf6.35 Bdif8.30
Wfrf57.50 ⌖ D5.30pm

BEAUMARIS Gwynedd *Map 6 SH67*
➤◄GH **Sea View** West End ☎810384
6hc nc10 CTV 5P ▥ sea S% B&bf4.50
Bdif7 Wf49 ⌖

BEDDGELERT Gwynedd *Map 6 SH54*
GH **Sygyn Fawr** ☎258 Lic 7hc CTV 25P
B&bf7.50–£8 Bdif12.75–£14 Wfrf75
⌖ D7.30pm

SWY-Y-DON Guest House

RESIDENTIAL GUEST HOUSE
40-42 North Parade, Aberystwyth SY23 2NF. Tel: 615059

A Fire Certificate has been granted.

Near shopping centre, sea front and railway station.
Full board — dinner — bed and breakfast. Open all
year — Commercials welcome. Licence bar. Private
parties, wedding receptions and special dinners catered
for. Colour TV in lounge. Hot and cold, shaving
points in all bedrooms. Gas central heating in all
rooms. Overnight parking on premises. Terms on
request (SAE for reply). Every convenience for a
comfortable and happy holiday. Under the personal
supervision of the Proprietors Mrs. A. M. Owen
Evans who wishes to thank all her regular clients for
their continued support and extends a warm welcome
to all new clients.

BENLLECH BAY Gwynedd *Map 6 SH58*
GH Rhostrefor ☎ Tyn-y-Gongl 2347
Etr–Oct Lic 4hc (A 6hc) 10P S% B&b£8
Bdi£10 Wfr£80 W only Jul & Aug

BERRIEW Powys *Map 7 SJ10*
⋈**INN Talbot Hotel** ☎260 Lic 8hc
1⇨🛁 CTV 40P B&b£4.50–£5.50 Bdi£8.50
Wfr£56 ⚷ sn L70P–£3.50&alc
D9.30pm£3.50&alc

BETWS-Y-COED Gwynedd *Map 6 SH75*
⋈**GH Bod Hyfryd** Holyhead Rd ☎220
6hc 2⇨🛁 TV 6P river S% B&b£4.50
Bdi£6.50 Wfr£45.50 ⚷ D6.30pm

⋈**GH Fairy Glen Hotel** Dolwyddelan Rd
☎269 Lic 10hc 1⇨🛁 12P 1🏠 river
S% B&b£5.50–£6.75 Bdi£8.50–£9.75
Wfr£76 D7pm

GH *Gwynant* ☎372 5hc TV 5P

⋈**GH Hafan** ☎233 Closed Xmas & Jan

Lic 7hc 1⇨🛁 CTV 10P 🍺 S%
B&b£4.50–£5.50

⋈**GH Henllys (Old Court) Private Hotel**
☎534 Feb–Nov and Xmas rs Dec Lic
10hc 4⇨🛁 nc6 CTV 14P B&b£5.50–£8
Bdi£9–£11.50 Wf58–£77 ⚷ D6pm

GH Mount Garmon Hotel ☎335 Mar–Oct
Lic 6hc ⊗ nc5 TV 6P 🍺 S% B&bfr£6.32
Bdifr£10.35 D5pm

BODEDERN Gwynedd *Map 6 SS38*
⋈**INN Crown Hotel** ☎ Valley 740734
Lic 5hc ⊗ 100P 🍺 S% B&b£4.50
Bdi£6.50 Wf45 ⚷ Bar lunch 90p–£1.10
D7pm

BONTDDU Gwynedd *Map 6 SH61*
INN Halfway House Hotel ☎635 Etr–
Dec Lic 5hc (A 1⇨🛁) ⊗ CTV 12P 3🏠 🏕
✳B&b£6.50–£8.50 Bdi£11.50–£13.50
Wf80.50 ⚷ Bar lunch £1.75
D9pm£5&alc

Sunnyridge

AMROTH, DYFED.
(Pembrokeshire)
Tel: Saundersfoot 812335

Stands in an ideal position in own grounds in the seaside village of Amroth.
120 yards to fine stretch of sandy beach with safe bathing. Excellent
centre for touring Pembrokeshire. Most bedrooms have sea views.
Panoramic views of Camarthen Bay from Dining room and lounge.
Secluded lawn for your relaxation. Excellent cuisine, Farm and garden
produce used. All mod. cons. Parking space. Brochure on request.
(stamp please).
Prop: Mr and Mrs C Evans.

Plas Teg Guest House

Plas Teg Guest House is pleasantly situated
on the outskirts of the charming little
town of Bala and overlooks the lake. It
has ample parking facilities and is within
walking distance of the excellent and
varied shops in the main street, yet is
quiet and secluded itself.

If you are looking for a pleasant, peaceful
holiday with excellent food and service
and within easy reach of fine Welsh
scenery with golf, sailing and fishing on
your doorstep, this is the place.
Please see the gazetteer entry for details
of the tariff.

Lawrenny Lodge

Homely Guest House
Barmouth, Merioneth, North Wales
Tel: 0341-280466
Pleasant, sunny position overlooking the
estuary and harbour.
Residential and restaurant licence VAT will be
added to all accounts. No added service charge.
Parking facilities.
All fire precautions completed.
Resident proprietors: Mr and Mrs J Townshend

TALBOT HOTEL

BERRIEW, Nr WELSHPOOL, POWYS Tel: Berriew 260

Set in a beautiful village which has won top awards as the Best Kept Village in Wales and only 5 miles from Welshpool. This is a place to relax in. With a restaurant, which is alongside the river, and with 8 bedrooms and an attractive Lounge Bar. Discos on certain days of the week in a separate room, also alongside the river. For residents there are 2 miles of river, on both banks, for good trout and grayling fishing. Golf, shooting and pony trekking can be arranged.

Visit for a week or so, for a few days or a weekend.

Give us a ring or drop us a line.

Henllys (Old Court) Private Hotel

Betws-y-Coed. Telephone: 534 (06902)

The old court house is now a small private hotel with residential licence. Situated on the banks of River Conwy. Off main A5 Road. Nicely furnished throughout. Heating in all bedrooms. Some bedrooms with king and queen size beds. Unique split-level dining room where magistrates once presided. Good food. Warm, friendly, relaxing atmosphere. Adjacent to Golf course. Free Golf. Large car park.

Resident Proprietors:
Joan and Pete Smart

Mount Garmon Hotel

Small, licensed hotel situated on the A5. Ideal touring centre for North Wales. Comfortable TV lounge and lounge bar. Separate tables in dining room. Central heating. H&C, razor points, spring interior mattresses, electric heaters in all bedrooms. Table d'hôte dinner, bar lunches, full English breakfast, all home cooking. Private car park. Personal service by proprietors, Mr and Mrs W Major.

Mount Garmon Hotel, Betws-y-Coed, Gwynedd LL24 0AN. Tel: Betws-y-Coed 335 (code 06902)

The Halfway House Hotel

BONTDDU, DOLGELLAU, NORTH WALES
Tel: Bontddu 635. (STD 034 149)

Picturesque village. Coaching Inn set in spectacular mountain scenery.

Completely modernised bedroom accommodation. Intimate, candle-lit dining room specialising in Welsh lamb, local salmon and seafood.

Resident proprietors:
Maggie and Bill Hutchinson

BONTNEWYDD Gwynedd *Map 6 SH46*
⊷**GH Dwynfa** ☎ Llanwnda 830414
Mar–Oct 12hc ⚹ nc10 CTV 15P river
B&bf£5.50–£6.50

BRIDGEND Mid Glam *Map 3 SS97*
INN Wyndham Dunraven Pl ☎2080
Closed 25–26Dec Lic 22hc 1⇦🍴 CTV
S% B&b fr£7.50 Bdi fr£10.50 Wfr£70
sn L£2.50–£3.50&alc D9pm£3.75–£5&alc

BROAD HAVEN *(Nr Haverfordwest)*
Dyfed *Map 2 SM81*
⊷**GH Broad Haven Hotel** ☎366 Lic
42hc 13⇦🍴 ♨ CTV 90P B&bf£4.50–£6.50
Bdif£7.50–£9.50 Wf£59.50–£79.50 ⎩
W only Jul & Aug D7pm

BUILTH WELLS Powys *Map 3 SO05*
INN Lion Hotel ☎3670 Lic 18hc TV
16P 4🏠

CAERNARFON Gwynedd *Map 6 SH46*
⊷**GH Bryn-Menai** Llanbellig Rd ☎2120
Etr–mid Dec 7hc ♨ CTV P sea S%
B&bf£4.50–£5 Bdif£8–£8.50 D6.30pm
⊷**GH Caer Menai** 15 Church St ☎2612
7hc TV sea S% B&bf£4.50–£5.50
INN Black Boy Northgate St ☎3604
Lic 16hc 6⇦🍴 CTV 9P B&bf£6–£8
Bdif£10–£12 sn L£3 D9pm£4

CAPEL ISAAC Dyfed *Map 2 SN52*
GH Maesteilo Mansion ☎ Dryslwyn 510
Mar–Oct rs Jan, Feb, Nov–15Dec Lic
7⇦🍴 ⚹ nc14 CTV 20P 4🏠 🍴 S%
B&bf£7.50–£13.50 Bdif£13.50–£18.50
Wf£70–£120 ⎩ D7pm

CARDIFF S Glam *Map 3 ST17*
GH Alva Hotel 132 Cathedral Rd ☎23413
33hc TV 12P 2🏠
GH Ambassador 4 Oakfield St ☎33288
Closed Xmas Lic 16hc ⚹ CTV 🍴
B&bf£6.33 Bdif£9.78 D3pm
GH Balkan Hotel 144 Newport Rd
☎491790 10rm 9hc 1⇦🍴 ⚹ CTV 15P
🍴 ✳B&bf£6.48–£7 Bdif£10.50
Wf£73.50 D7pm
⊷**GH Domus** 201 Newport Rd ☎495785
Closed Xmas Lic 10hc ⚹ CTV 10P 🍴 S%
B&bf£5 Bdif£8 D noon
GH Dorville Hotel 3 Ryder St ☎30951
13hc ⚹ CTV P 1🏠 🍴 S% B&bf£6–£6.75
GH Princes Princes St, Roath ☎491732
7hc ⚹ CTV 3P 🍴 S% ✳B&bf£4.50
Bdif£7 Wfr£40 ⎩ D noon
⊷**GH St Winnow's Hotel** Tygwyn Rd,
Penylan ☎45577 9hc 1⇦🍴 (A 2hc) CTV
11P 🍴 S% B&bf£4–£6 Bdif£6.75–£8.75
D noon

CHEPSTOW Gwent *Map 3 ST59*
GH Castle View Hotel 16 Bridge St
☎3565 Lic 9hc ♨ CTV 🍴 S%
B&bf£7.70–£9.70

CILIAU AERON Dyfed *Map 2 SN55*
GH Ty Lôn ☎ Aeron 726 Apr–Oct Lic 5hc
nc5 TV 8P 🍴 D5.30pm

COLWYN BAY Clwyd *Map 6 SH87*
See Plan
⊷**GH Ashmount Hotel** College Av,
Rhos-on-Sea ☎44582 Plan:**1** Lic 12hc
CTV 10P 🍴 S% B&bf£5.94
Bdif£7.45–£7.78 D7pm

GH Brompton Lodge Hotel Rhos Rd,
Rhos-on-Sea ☎44784 Plan:**2**
mid May–Sep 15hc nc2 CTV 13P
B&bf6.50–£7.50 Bdif9–£10.50
Wf60–£70 D6.30pm
GH Cabin Hill Private Hotel College Av,
Rhos-on-Sea ☎44568 Plan:**3** Mar–Oct
Lic 10hc 3⇔🍴 ⊗ nc3 CTV 4P 🍴 S%
B&bf6–£7 Bdif7.50–£-.50 D4pm
GH Clevedon Private Hotel Hawarden Rd
☎2368 Plan:**4** Lic 13hc CTV 6P 🍴 S%
B&bf6–£6.60 Bdif8.75–£9.50
Wf56.34–£62 ⥙ D7pm
GH _Green Lawns_ 14 Bay View Rd
☎2207 Plan:**5** Closed Nov Lic 16hc
(A 2hc) nc4 CTV 10P D6pm
GH Grosvenor Hotel 106–108 Abergele
Rd ☎30798 Plan:**6** Jan–Nov Lic 18hc
⊗ CTV 12P S% B&bf6.61–£8.05
Bdif9.48–£11.22 Wf55.20–£63.25 ⥙
D2pm
GH Northwood Hotel Rhos Rd,
Rhos-on-Sea ☎49931 Plan:**7**
May–Oct rs Nov–Apr Lic 14hc 4⇔🍴 nc3
CTV 12P 🍴 S% B&bf8–£9 Bdif12–£13
Wf84–£91 ⥙ D7pm
⊨◁GH _Southlea_ 4 Upper Prom ☎2004
Plan:**8** Lic 11hc CTV S% B&bf5.13
Bdif7.02 Wf45.36 ⥙ D6.30pm
GH _Sunny Downs Private Hotel_ 66
Abbey Rd, Rhos-on-Sea ☎44256 Plan:**9**
Mar–Oct rs Nov–Feb Lic 10hc ⊗ nc6
TV 6P 🍴 D4pm
GH _West Mains Private Hotel_ Trillo Av,
Rhos-on-Sea ☎44664 Plan:**10** May–Sep
Lic 10hc CTV 15P sea D6.30pm
GH West Point Hotel Conway Rd
☎30331 Plan:**11** Closed 2 wks mid Oct
Lic 12hc CTV 12P 🍴 B&bf7.75–£8
Bdif10.25–£10.50 Wf68–£73 ⥙
D6.45pm

⊨◁GH Whitehall Hotel Cayley Prom,
Rhos-on-Sea ☎47296 Plan:**12**
Etr–Oct Lic 14hc ⊗ nc3 CTV 6P sea S%
B&bf6.50–£7.50 Bdif8.50–£10.50
Wf60–£70 ⥙ D6.30p

CONWY Gwynedd _Map 6 SH77_
GH Cyfnant Private Hotel Henryd Rd
☎2442 Apr–Sep Lic 6hc 4⇔🍴 ⊗ CTV
6P 🍴 S% B&bf6–£6.50 Bdif9–£9.50
D4.50pm
⊨◁GH Sunnybanks Woodlands,
Llanrwst Rd ☎3845 Etr–Sep 7hc TV
6P 🍴 S% B&bfr£4.50 Bdifr£7
Wfr£38 ⥙ D7.30pm
CORWEN Clwyd _Map 21 SJ04_
GH _Central Hotel_ ☎2462 10hc TV P
2🏠 🍴 D9pm
GH _Hafryn_ ☎2318 Etr–Sep 5rm 4hc ⊗
CTV 6P river
CRICCIETH Gwynedd _Map 6 SH53_
⊨◁GH Min-y-Gaer Private Hotel
Portmadoc Rd ☎2151 Etr–Oct 10hc
CTV 12P S% B&bf4.50–£5.50
Bdif6.50–£8 Wf49–£56 ⥙ D8pm
⊨◁GH Môr Heli Private Hotel
Marine Ter ☎2878 Apr–Sep rs Oct–Mar
Lic 14hc CTV 20P sea S%
B&bfr£5.50 Bdifr£7 Wfr£45 D6.30pm
⊨◁GH Neptune Private Hotel Marine Ter
☎2794 Apr–Sep rs Oct–Mar Lic 14hc
CTV 20P sea S% B&bfr£5.50 Bdifr£7
Wfr£45 ⥙ D6.30pm
CRICKHOWELL Powys _Map 3 SO21_
**GH Dragon Country House Private
Hotel** High St ☎810362 Lic 9hc ♠
CTV 6P 3🏠 🍴 S% ✳B&bf5.50–£6.50
Wfr£55 ⥙ D8pm

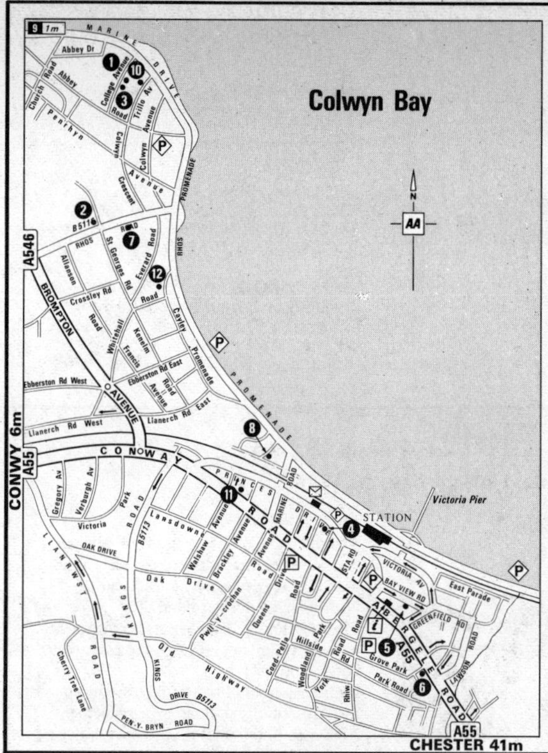

CLEVEDON PRIVATE HOTEL

Hawarden Road, Colwyn Bay, North Wales Tel: 0492 2368

Although not a large hotel, the Clevedon will offer visitors a warm welcome and the personal attention of the proprietors. This can add to your enjoyment in many ways, for instance the liberal and varied menus served in a delightful dining room.

We offer Bargain Mini Breaks (some with entertainment provided) and a Christmas programme.

The hotel is centrally-heated , has a colour TV in the lounge, cocktail bar, own private car park and we are pleased to baby-sit while Mum and Dad enjoy a night out. Resident proprietors: Mr and Mrs N Tomkinson.

Neptune & Môr Heli Hotels

Min-y-Môr, Criccieth, Gwynedd LL52 0EF
Telephone: 2794/2878 — STD 076671

Two, well-established, family-run hotels situated on sea-front, noted for good food and friendly atmosphere. Comfortably furnished throughout with an attractive licensed bar for guests and diners.
For brochure and terms contact resident proprietors:- WJ J & E Williams.
Fire certificate granted
Licensed
Car park

INN Beaufort Arms Hotel ☎810402
Jun–Sep rs Oct–May (B&b only) Lic
6hc 🖭 S% B&b£6.90 Bdi£10.64 sn
L£1.25–£3 D9pmf£3.25

CROSS GATES Powys *Map 3 SO06*
GH *Guidfa* ☎ Pen-y-bont 241 May–Sep
Lic 6hc TV 6P D7.30pm

DINAS MAWDDWY Gwynedd
Map 6 SH81
INN Buckley Arms Hotel ☎261
Mar–Dec Lic 14hc 2⇨🛊 TV 60P 🖭 river
S% B&b£7.20 Bdi£11.20 W£68 ⫧
D8.45pm

DINORWIC Gwynedd *Map 6 SH50*
⊱◄GH **Hafodty** ☎ Llanberis 548
Etr–Sep Lic 5rm 4hc 5P S%
B&b£5.75–£6.25 Bdi£9.50–£10
W£56–£60 ⫧ D6pm

DOLWYDDELAN Gwynedd *Map 6 SH75*
INN *Gwydyr* ☎209 Lic 2hc ⌘ nc14
12P sn D9.30pm

FAIRBOURNE Gwynedd *Map 6 SH61*
GH Brackenhurst Hotel ☎250226
Closed Nov Lic 12hc (A 1hc 1⇨🛊) ⌘
CTV 11P 🖭 B&b£7 Bdi£10.50 W£62
⫧ D8.30pm

⊱◄**GH Liety Heulog** 2–4 Alyn Rd
☎250228 Mar–Oct rs Nov–Feb
(bookings only) Lic 12hc CTV 12P sea
S% B&bfr£5 Bdifr£8 Wfr£46 ⫧ D8.30pm

FFESTINIOG Gwynedd *Map 6 SH64*
⊱◄**GH Newborough House Hotel**
Church Sq ☎2682 Lic 8rm 7hc ⌂ CTV
7P 1🏠 🖭 S% B&b£5.40–£7
Bdi£8.64–£10.80 W£56–£65 ⫧ D6pm

Southlea Hotel Tel: (0492) 2004
4 Upper Promenade, Colwyn Bay, N. Wales

Prop. Val and Mike Andrews
A small, family hotel close to the beach
and all amenities. Ideal to use as a base
with all the spectacular attractions of
North Wales close at hand.
Licensed lounge bar. Separate comfortable
lounge. Intimate period dining room with
good food.
Radio, intercom in all rooms. Reduced
rates for children. Dogs by arrangement.
Access to hotel at all times. Open all year.

SUNNY DOWNS
PRIVATE HOTEL
**66 Abbey Road, Rhos-on-Sea, Colwyn Bay, North Wales
Tel: 0492 44256**

The Hotel is just 3 minutes from the sea, there is free parking, central heating,
H & C in all rooms. We offer reduced terms for children sharing their parents'
room. Keys are provided for free access to rooms at all times.
RHOS-ON-SEA is regarded as one of Nature's unspoilt beauty spots, having
as a background a range of beautifully wooded hills, which help to form its
most temperate climate, making it an ideal resort for both early and late
holidays.

West Mains Private Hotel

**Trillo Avenue, Rhos-on-Sea, Colwyn Bay, Clwyd
Tel: 44664**

Open from May to September. Licensed. 10 bedrooms all with hot and
cold water. Colour television available for the use of guests. Car park
for 15 cars.

Please see the gazetteer for further details.

GAERWEN Gwynedd *Map 6 SH47*
INN *Holland Arms* ☎651 Lic 6hc CTV
70P D9.30pm

GOVILON Gwent *Map 3 SO21*
GH Llanwenarth House
☎ Gilwern 830289 Lic 3hc 3⇥🛏 CTV
P 🍴 B&b£11.50–£19.50
Bdi£23–£25.50 Wfr£136 ₺

GWBERT-ON-SEA Dyfed
Map 2 SN15
GH Anchor Hotel ☎ Cardigan 2638
Mar–Oct Lic 13hc CTV 12P 1🏠 🍴
B&b£6–£6.75 Bdi£9–£10 W£50–£58
D6pm

HARLECH Gwynedd *Map 6 SH53*
⋈**GH Cemlyn** ☎425 Mar–Oct Lic 6hc
CTV 🍴 S% B&b£4.75 D9.30pm

INN Rum Hole Hotel ☎477 Lic 10hc
3⇥🛏 CTV 20P 🍴 sea B&b£8–£9
Bdi£10.50–£11.50 W£54 Ⓜ sn
L£2–£3 D10.30pm£2–£3

HAVERFORDWEST Dyfed *Map 2 SM91*
⋈**GH Elliots Hill Hotel** Camrose Rd
☎2383 Lic 22hc 1⇥🛏 ⊗ 🐕 CTV 20P
2🏠 🍴 B&b£5–£6.50 Bdi£9–£12
Wfr£50 ₺ D6.30pm

HAY-ON-WYE Powys *Map 3 SO24*
INN Old Black Lion Lion St ☎820841
Lic 6hc 4⇥🛏 CTV 20P 🍴 ⇶
B&b£7.71–£9.25 W£48.30–£67.28 Ⓜ
✳L£5.29 alc D9pm£5.29 alc

HOLYHEAD Gwynedd *Map 6 SH28*
⋈**GH Fensaler Private Hotel** Marine Sq
☎3512 Lic 12hc ⊗ nc3 TV 16P 🍴 sea
S% B&b£5 Bdi£8 W£70 D7pm

HUNDLETON Dyfed *Map 2 SM90*
INN Corston Guest House Axton Hill
☎ Castlemartin 242 Lic 12hc ⚙ TV 30P
🍽 ⇔ S% ✳B&b£4.86 Bdi£7.02 W£40
ⱡ D6pm

LANGLAND BAY W Glam *Map 2 SS68*
⋈**GH Wittemberg Hotel** 2 Rotherslade
Rd ☎ Swansea 69696 Closed Xmas Lic
12hc ⚙ nc3 CTV 12P 🍽 S%
B&b£5.50–£6 Bdi£8.50–£9 W£50–£55
ⱡ D6.30pm

LITTLE HAVEN Dyfed *Map 2 SM81*
⋈**GH Pendyffryn Private Hotel** ☎ Broad
Haven 337 Etr–Oct Lic 7hc ⚙ nc4 CTV
6P 🍽 sea B&b£5 Bdi£8.50 Wfr£55 ⱡ
W only Jul & Aug D6.45pm

LLANARTHNEY Dyfed *Map 2 SN52*
INN Golden Grove Arms Hotel
☎ Dryslwyn 551 Lic 5hc 70P 🍽
B&b£7.47 W£47.06 Ⓜ Bar lunch £1.20–
£3.50&alc D10pm£3.50–£5&alc

LLANBEDROG Gwynned *Map 6 SH33*
⋈**GH Glyn Garth Hotel** ☎268
Etr–Oct rs Nov–Mar Lic 10hc 3⇆🛁 ⚙
CTV 20P B&b£5.50–£7
Bdi£9.50–£11 W£50–£65 D9.30pm

LLANBERIS Gwynedd *Map 6 SH56*
⋈**GH Lake View** Tan-y-Pant (1m W on
A4086) ☎422 Lic 6hc TV 7P 🍽 lake
S% B&b£5.50–£6.50 D8.30pm

LLANDDERFEL Gwynedd *Map 6 SH93*
GH Berwyn View ☎270 Lic 11rm 7hc
TV 20P 🍽

INN Bryntirion Hotel ☎205 Lic
4hc ⚙ nc8 CTV 50P 🍽 river
B&b£7–£9 W£42–£54 Ⓜ sn L£2.50
alc D10pm£3.75 alc

LLANDOGO Gwent *Map 3 SO50*
GH *Craiglas* ☎ St Briavels 348 Mar–Oct
7hc TV 15P 🍽 river D4pm
⋈**GH Eddis Tea Gardens & Restaurant**
☎ St Briavels 262 Closed Dec & Jan Lic
8hc (A 2hc) 40P S% B&bfr£5.80
Bdi fr£9 D10pm

LLANDOVERY Dyfed *Map 3 SN73*
GH Dyfri Hotel Market Sq ☎20297
15hc 1⇆🛁 TV 10P S% B&b£6
⋈**GH Llwyncelyn** ☎20566 Closed Xmas
6hc ⚙ CTV 12P 🍽 river S%
B&b£5.50–£6.30 Bdi£9.30–£10.10
W£61.25–£66.25 ⱡ D7.30pm

LLANDUDNO Gweynedd *Map 6 SH78*
See Plan
⋈**GH Albatross Hotel** 9 North Pde
☎75991 Plan:**1** May–mid Oct Lic 18hc
CTV 6P sea S% B&b£5.50–£6 Bdi£7.50
D6pm
GH *Bella Vista Private Hotel* 72 Church
Walks ☎76855 Plan:**2** Closed Xmas Lic
12hc CTV 2P 🍽 sea D5.30pm
⋈**GH Braemar Hotel** 5 St David's Rd
☎76257 Plan:**3** Closed Xmas & New Year
6hc CTV S% B&b£4.75 Bdi£6.25 Wfr£42
ⱡ D4pm
GH Brannock Private Hotel 36 St David's
Rd ☎77483 Plan:**4** Closed Jan Lic 8hc ⚙
nc3 CTV 5P 🍽 S% B&b£6–£6.50
Bdi£8–£8.50 W£59.50 ⱡ D6.30pm
GH Brigstock Private Hotel 1 St David's
Pl ☎76416 Plan:**5** Closed Nov & Dec Lic
10hc CTV 7P S% B&b£6–£6.75
Bdi£8.25–£9 W£52–£60 ⱡ D6pm
GH Buile Hill Private Hotel St Mary's Rd
☎76972 Plan:**6** Etr–Oct Lic 15hc 4⇆🛁 ⚙
CTV 6P 🍽 S% B&b£6–£7 Bdi£7.90–£8.90
W£51.80–£58.80 D6.30pm

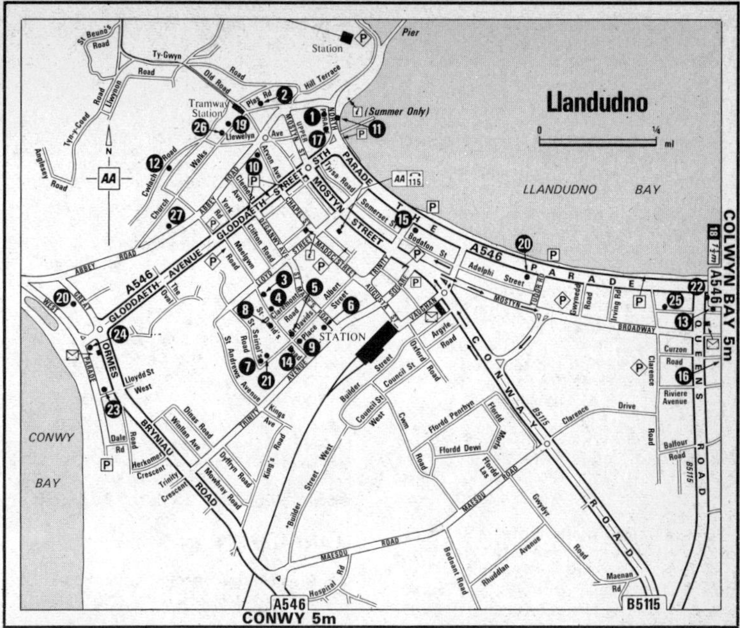

1 Albatross Hotel	8 Cliffbury Private Hotel	14 Heatherdale	21 Rosaire Private Hotel
2 Bella Vista Private Hotel	9 Cornerways Private Hotel	15 Lynwood Private Hotel	22 St Hilary Hotel
3 Braemar Hotel	10 Craig Ard Private Hotel	16 Minion Private Hotel	23 Sandilands Private Hotel
4 Brannock Private Hotel	11 Cumberland Private Hotel	17 Montclare Hotel	24 Sandringham Hotel
5 Brigstock Private Hotel	12 Cwlach Private Hotel	18 Orotava Private Hotel	25 Victoria House
6 Buile Hill Private Hotel	13 Grafton Hotel	19 Plas Madoc Private Hotel	26 Warwick Hotel
7 Cleave Court Private Hotel		20 Puffin Lodge Hotel	27 Westdale Private Hotel

GH Cleave Court Private Hotel
1 St Seirol's Rd ☎77849 Plan:**7** May–Sep
9hc TV 8P S% B&bf6–£7 Bdif7–£8
Wf45–£52 ⱡ D6pm

⤬**GH Cliffbury Private Hotel** 34 St
David's Rd ☎77224 Plan:**8** Etr–Oct 6hc ⚹
nc6 CTV 4P S% B&bf4.75–£5
Bdif5.50–£6 Wf40–£43 ⱡ D4.30pm

⤬**GH Cornerways Private Hotel**
2 St David's Pl ☎77334 Plan:**9** Mar–Oct
11hc nc5 CTV 6P 🕭 S% B&bf4–£5
Bdif5.50–£6.50 Wf37.50–£45.50 ⱡ
D4pm

GH *Craig Ard Private Hotel* Arvon Av
☎77318 Plan:**10** Mar–Oct Lic 18hc CTV
11P D6pm

GH Cumberland Hotel North Pde
☎76379 Plan:**11** Mar–Oct Lic 19hc ⚹
CTV 3P 🕭 sea B&bf7.50–£8 Bdif9–£10
Wf63–£70 ⱡ D6pm

GH *Cwlach Private Hotel* Cwlach Rd
☎75587 Plan:**12** Spring Bank Hol–Sep
Lic 12rm 11hc ⚹ nc5 TV D5pm

⤬**GH Grafton Hotel** 13 Craig-y-Don Pde
☎76814 Plan:**13** Etr–Nov Lic 21hc ⚹
CTV 12P sea S% B&bf5.25–£8
Bdif8–£10 Wf66–£80 D5pm

⤬**GH Heatherdale** 30 St David's Rd
☎77362 Plan:**14** Mar–Oct 6hc CTV S%
B&bf3.50–£4.50 Bdif5–£6 D6pm

Cumberland Hotel
North Promenade, Llandudno
Telephone (0492) 76379
Residential/Licence

* Ideally situated overlooking Llandudno's beautiful bay
* Full fire Certificate
* Central heating throughout
* Colour TV Lounge
* Reduced terms for children sharing parents' bedroom
* Coach and private parties catered for at reduced terms during early & late season
* Ideal for all conference delegates

Send SAE for brochure & terms to:
Resident Proprietors David & Yvonne Kavanagh.

GH Lynwood Private Hotel Clonmel St
☎76613 Plan:**15** Lic 12hc ⊗ CTV sea S%
B&b£6.50–£8.50 Bdi£7.50–£10
D5.45pm

⋈**GH Minion Private Hotel**
21–23 Carmen Sylva Rd, Craig-y-Don
☎77740 Plan:**16** Etr & 20May–5Oct Lic
14hc CTV 8P S% B&b£4.50
Bdi£5.75–£6.90 W£40.25–£48.30
ᴸ D5pm

⋈**GH Montclare Hotel** North Pde
☎77061 Plan:**17** Mar–Nov Lic 18hc
CTV 4P 🍴 B&b£5.25–£6 Bdi£7.25–£8
W£54 ᴸ D6pm

⋈**GH Orotava Private Hotel**
105 Glan-y-Mor Rd, Penrhyn Bay ☎49780
Plan:**18** Etr–Oct 6hc ⊗ CTV 6P sea S%
B&b£5.75–£6 Bdi£8.75–£9 D6.30pm

⋈**GH Plas Madoc Private Hotel**
60 Church Walks ☎76514 Plan:**19**
Lic 6hc nc4 CTV 6P 🍴 river sea S%
B&b£4.50–£5 Bdi£6.50–£7
W£45.50–£49 ᴸ D6.30pm

⋈**GH Puffin Lodge Hotel** ☎77713
Plan:**20** Mar–Oct rs Feb & Nov Lic 15hc
⊗ CTV 15P sea S% B&b£5–£6 Bdi£7–£8
W£49–£56 ᴸ D4.30pm

⋈**GH Rosaire Private Hotel** 2 St Seiriols
Rd ☎77677 Plan:**21** Etr–Oct 12hc nc6
CTV 7P 4🏠 S% B&b£4.54–£5.60
Bdi£7–£7.56 W£44.82–£48.60 ᴸ D6pm

⋈**GH St Hilary Hotel** Promenade,
Craig-y-Don ☎75551 Plan:**22** Mar–Nov
11hc CTV sea S% B&b£4.50–£4.75
W£31.50–£33.25 M

GH Sandilands Private Hotel Dale Rd,
West Shore ☎75555 Plan:**23** Jun–Sep
rs Oct–May Lic 11hc CTV 11P 🍴 S%
B&b£6 Bdi£8 W£53.20 ᴸ
(W only Jul & Aug) D4pm

⋈**GH Sandringham Hotel** West Pde
☎76513 Plan:**24** Etr–Oct Lic 18hc CTV
8P 🍴 sea B&b£5.50–£6 Bdi£8.50–£9
W£54–£56 ᴸ D7.30pm

⋈**GH Victoria House** 4–5 Victoria St
☎79920 Plan:**25** 9hc ⊗ CTV S%
B&b£4.10–£5 Bdi£5.10–£6 W£36–£40 ᴸ

⋈**GH Warwick Hotel** 56 Church Walk
☎76823 Plan:**26** Apr–Oct Lic 16hc ⚭
CTV sea B&b£5.25–£6 Bdi£7–£7.75
W£45–£50 ᴸ (W only Jul & Aug) D7pm

GH Westdale Private Hotel 37 Abbey Rd
☎77996 Plan:**27** Etr–Oct Lic 12hc nc5
CTV 7P S% B&b£6–£6.25 Bdi£7.75–£8
W£54–£55 D6pm

LLANDYBIE Dyfed *Map 2 SN61*
GH Mill Glyn Hir ☎850672 Lic 5⊐🍴
nc11 10P 🍴 river S% B&b£12
Bdi£18.60 W£86–£112 ᴸ D8.30pm

LLANELLI Dyfed *Map 2 SN50*
GH Croft 89 Queen Victoria Rd ☎4539
Lic 17hc ⊗ nc3 CTV 20P 🍴 S%
✳B&b£5.25 Bdi£8.25 Wfr£57.75 ᴸ D6pm

LLANFAIRFECHAN Gwynedd
Map 6 SH67
GH Plas Menai Hotel Penmaenmawr Rd
☎680346 Mar–Oct 29hc 5⊐🍴 TV 20P
sea ✳Bdi£6.90–£8.63 W£40.25–£59.80
ᴸ D7pm

⋈**GH Queens House** ☎680509
11rm 9hc 2⊐🍴 ⚭ CTV 30P S%
B&b£4.25–£4.75

GH Rhiwiau Riding Centre Gorddinog
☎680094 Lic 4hc ⊗ CTV 15P sea S%
B&b£6.50 Bdi£8.75 Wfr£65 D6pm

Buile Hill Hotel
St Mary's Road, Llandudno
Tel: (0492) 76972

Well situated, detached and in own grounds.
Only minutes' walk from two shores, rail
and coach stations. First class service and
every modern comfort. Lounge with colour
TV, large dining room with separate tables.
Good, wholesome food and varied menus.
All bedrooms have every modern
convenience. Hotel is open throughout the
day with access to all rooms. Car park. We
cater for bed, breakfast and dinner or just
bed and breakfast.
A complete fire alarm system is fitted.
Brochure on request — Joan and Tony Flint.

ROSAIRE PRIVATE HOTEL
2 St Seiriols Road, Llandudno, Gwynedd LL30 2YY
Tel: (0492) 77677 Proprietors: Mr and Mrs Bryant

* Excellent cuisine served in a pleasant dining room
* Separate tables * Spacious lounge for your relaxation.
Colour/B & W TV * Many single rooms available
* Access to bedrooms and lounge at all times * Wall-
to-wall carpeting throughout the hotel * Free private
car park in own grounds * All bedrooms have H & C
water, shaver sockets and lights, spring interior
mattresses, infra-red fires * Full fire certificate * Modern
decor and utmost cleanliness.

Situated in Llandudno's loveliest, select garden areas, yet convenient for both shores,
entertainments and shops.
SAE for further details.

Featured in the AA 1977 Guide to
Guesthouses, Farmhouses and Inns.

LLANGATTOCK Powys *Map 2 SO21*
⊮**GH Park Place** The Legar
☎ Crickhowell 810562 7hc ⊗ TV 8P ▦
S% B&b fr£5.50 W fr£32.50 Ⓜ

LLANSANTFFRAID YM MECHAIN
Powys *Map 7 SJ22*
GH Bryn Tanat Hall Hotel
☎ Llansantffraid 259 mid May–Sep Lic
12hc ⊗ CTV 12P 2🏠 river S%
✱B&b£6.40 Bdi£9.50 W£58.50 D7pm

LLANYSTUMDWY Gwynedd
Map 6 SH43
⊮**GH Gwyndy** ☎ Criccieth 2591 Etr–Oct
Lic 6hc nc3 TV 20P ▦ river B&b£5.50–£6
Bdi£8.75–£9.25 W£38.50–£42 D8.50pm

LLWYNGWRIL Gwynedd *Map 6 SH50*
⊮**GH Gwelfor** ☎ Fairbourne 343

Etr–Sep Lic 7hc ⊗ nc3 CTV 8P ▦ sea S%
B&b£5 Bdi£8 W£50 ⓛ D6pm

MORFA NEFYN Gwynedd *Map 6 SH23*
GH Erw Goch ☎ Nefyn 539 (720539
fr Jan '80) Etr–mid Sep Lic 15rm 14hc
CTV 15P ▦ ✱Bdi£8.33 W£50.88 ⓛ D5pm

MUMBLES W Glam *Map 2 SS68*
GH Carlton Hotel 654–656 Mumbles Rd,
Southend ☎ Swansea 60450 Closed Xmas
Lic 19hc 2⊣🖼 CTV ▦ sea B&b fr£7.50
Bdi fr£10.50 W fr£60 ⓛ D7pm

GH Harbour Winds Private Hotel
Overland Rd, Langland ☎ Swansea 69298
Closed Jan 8hc 1⊣🖼 ⌂ CTV 20P ▦ S%
B&b£6.50–£7.70 Bdi£9.80–£10.80
W£54–£60 ⓛ D5.30pm

GWELFOR GUEST HOUSE

Ideal for rail enthusiasts. Ample walks in the area. We supply our own eggs, also fruit and vegetables in season. Local fresh meat. Home cooking.

All rooms have H&C + radiators. All double rooms face the sea.

Two miles from Fairbourne Beach. Local beach quiet but stony.

Gwelfor Guest House, Llwyngwril, Gwynedd, LL37 2JQ   Tel: Fairbourne 343.

---

plas menaí

A warm welcome awaits you at Plas Menai. This hotel, renowned for its Christian Fellowship, is a place where Christians from many parts of the British Isles meet and enjoy each others company and where life-long friendships are often formed. There is a well appointed dining room where meals are served which would tempt and satisfy the most fastidious. The comfortable lounge overlooks the Menai Straits.
There are recreational facilities at the hotel and tennis, golf, pony trekking and fishing are close at hand.

**Plas Menai Christian Hotel
Llanfairfechan, North Wales.
Tel: (0248) 680347**

**NORTH WALES BORDER
ASHFIELD COUNTRY
HOUSE**

**Llwyn y Maen, Trefonen,
Oswestry SY10 9DD**

Telephone: Oswestry 5200

Peacefully situated in the Candy valley surrounded by beautiful countryside, a few miles from the world famous town of Llangollen, an ideal centre for touring the wealth of beauty to be seen in North Wales. Accommodation quietly luxurious with 10 spacious bedrooms some with private suites, oak lounge and dining room with Welsh slate features. Licence. Menu à la Carte.
1 Week accommodation for 2 persons with private suite from £100.00 to £120.00.
S.A.E. Brochure to Welsh proprietors Mr & Mrs W M Lewis. Gazetteer entry under Oswestry, England.

GH *Southend Hotel* 724 Mumbles Rd
☎ Swansea 66329 Lic 11hc CTV 20P
sea D9.30pm

NARBERTH Dyfed *Map 2 SN11*
GH Blaenmarlais ☎860326
Spring Bank Hol–mid Sep Lic 11hc
1⇔⌷ ⊗ CTV 30P 8🏠 Bdi£8 W£38–£42 ⫩
(W only mid Jul–Aug) D6.30pm
GH Parc Glas Country House Hotel
☎860947 Etr–Oct Lic 8hc 2⇔⌷ ⊗ ♨ CTV
10P S% B&b£6.48–£7.56 Bdi£8.64–£9.72
W£55–£60 ⫩ D8pm

NEWPORT Dyfed *Map 2 SN03*
GH Gellifawr Pontfaen (4m S unclass rd)
☎820343 May–Oct Lic 10rm 9hc ⊗
CTV P S% B&b£6 Bdi£9 W£60 ⫩

INN Golden Lion Hotel East St ☎820321
Lic 8⇔⌷ ⊗ CTV 10P 💷 S% B&b£7
Bar lunch £1alc D10pm£5alc

NEWPORT Gwent *Map 3 ST38*
⊷⊶**GH Caerleon House Hotel** Caerau Rd
☎64869 8hc CTV 8P 💷 S%
B&b£5.50–£6.50

NEW QUAY Dyfed *Map 2 SN35*
INN *Queens Hotel* Church St ☎560678
Mar–Oct Lic 8hc CTV 8P 💷 sea sn
D9.30pm

OXWICH W Glam *Map 2 SS58*
GH Oxwich Bay Hotel Gower
☎ Gower 329 Etr–mid Sep Lic 19hc ⊗
♨ CTV 40P 💷 ✳B&b£5.53–£6.45
Bdi£8.53–£9.45 W£52.69–£59.32 ⫩
(W only 15Jul–Aug) D6.30pm

Carlton Hotel

The Carlton Hotel is situated on the sea
front near the yachting anchorage on
picturesque Swansea Bay, 5 miles from the
City centre and within easy reach of Gower
beaches and moorlands.
It is comfortably furnished and tastefully
decorated and has a friendly atmosphere.
Licensed.
654 Mumbles Road, Mumbles,
Swansea SA3 4EA.
Tel: 0792-60450, 0793-60820.

Harbour Winds Hotel

**Overland Road. Langland,
Mumbles, Swansea,
West Glamorgan SA3 4LP
Telephone: Swansea 69298**

Open all year   AA recommended

Compact mansion hotel in own grounds set at the
entrance to Gower with its many secluded beaches
and within 5 minutes walk of Rotherslade Bay and
Langland Bay, both ideal bathing beaches. The
hotel has spacious bedrooms all with wash basins
and razor points, tea making facilities in all
bedrooms, central heating throughout, lounge,
colour television and ample free car parking.

Write to the resident proprietors Pat and John
Mallett for brochure and tariff.

Southend Hotel & Restaurant

**724 Mumbles Road Mumbles
Tel: Swansea 66329/68651
Member WTB**

The hotel is on the sea front, separated from sea
only by the road. Panoramic views of the bay and
sporting activities from the lounge, restaurant and
raised patio where drinks can be enjoyed.
Licensed restaurant open until late evening offers
first class menu at reasonable prices. Darts etc:
Separate bar. Personal supervision by owner Mr. &
Mrs. Soper.

Access & Barclay cards accepted.

PEMBROKE Dyfed *Map 2 SM90*
GH Camrose House 106 St Michaels Sq
☎5383 6hc 2⇌🕭 CTV 🛏 S%
✳B&b£4.50–£6 Bdi£6.50–£8 Wfr£40
Ŀ D6.30pm

INN Coach House St Michaels Sq
☎2149 Lic 13⇌🕭 ⊗ 8P 🛏 🚲 S%
B&bfr£12.50 Bdifr£15.50 Wfr£125 Ŀ
sn Lfr£3&alc D10pmfr£3&alc

PENARTH S Glam *Map 3 ST17*
⋈**GH Alanleigh Hotel** 14 Victoria Rd
☎ Cardiff 701242 9hc CTV 8P 🛏
B&b£5.40–£6 Bdi£9.20 W£54 D4pm

GH *Westbourne Hotel* 8 Victoria Rd
☎707268 Lic 11hc CTV 5P 🛏 D7pm

PENDINE Dyfed *Map 2 SN20*
INN New ☎250 Lic 4hc TV 30P S%
B&b£6–£7.50 Bdi£9–£10.50

W£58–£70 Ŀ sn L£2.50–£4&alc
D10.30pm£3–£4&alc

PONTLYFNI Gwynedd *Map 6 SH45*
GH Bron Dirion Hotel ☎ Clynnogfawr 346
Mar–Oct Lic 9hc CTV 10P 🛏 S%
✳B&b£6–£6.50 Bdi£7.50–£8
W£45.50–£49.50 Ŀ D6.30pm

PORTHCAWL Mid Glam *Map 3 SS87*
GH *Collingwood Hotel* 40 Mary St
☎2899 6hc ⊗ CTV P 🛏 D6.30pm

GH *Craig-y-Don Private Hotel*
30 The Esplanade ☎3259 10hc CTV 🛏
sea D7.30pm

⋈**GH Gwalia Private Hotel** 40 Esplanade
Av ☎2751 7hc ⊗ TV 🛏 S% B&b£4.50–£5
GH Seaways Hotel 28 Mary St ☎3510
Lic 12hc ⊗ CTV 🛏 S% B&b£8.50–£13
Bdi£12.50–£17.50 W£62–£69
W only Jul–Sep D9pm

PARC GLAS COUNTRY HOUSE HOTEL

Narberth, Dyfed. Tel: Narberth 860947

'PARC GLAS' is a small friendly hotel
peacefully situated in grounds of 7 acres.
Some bedrooms have private shower-room
or bathroom. There is a cosy bar with
dart-board.
The cuisine is excellent and a good selection
of wines available.
All public rooms and most bedrooms have
central heating radiators.
All sporting facilities within reasonable
distance.

The Coach House Inn
Pembroke, Dyfed Tel: Pembroke 2149

Businessman and holidaymaker alike are
equally welcome at the Coach House Inn.
While providing every modern amenity it
still retains its old-world charm. The
spacious dining room and two lounges offer
complete relaxation and comfort.
The bedrooms are attractively furnished, with
H & C and razor points. Free launderette
facilities are available.
Pembroke is an ideal holiday centre. The
Coach House stands in the main street,
conveniently placed for the shops and close to
the picturesque Pond Walk which leads to
Pembroke's ancient castle.

WESTBOURNE HOTEL

Tel: Penarth 707268 (STD 0222)

The Westbourne Hotel is a small quiet family hotel with twelve rooms,
incorporating single, double and twins. The manager is constantly in
residence to supervise and control our very popular Fisherman's Bistro
and our exclusive dining room 'la Chambre Privée'.
Both restaurants have first-class grills with a superb bistro flavour which
incorporates the taste of Normandy and Brittany, and which fills the air
and atmosphere of the restaurants with the smell of garlic, herbs, and
calvados.

PORTHMADOG Gwynedd *Map 6 SH53*
GH Oakleys The Harbour ☎2482
Mar–Oct Lic 7hc ⊗ CTV 12P S%
B&b£6.50–£7.50 Bdi£8.50–£9.50
W£50–£60 Ⱡ D5pm

GH *Owen's Hotel* High St ☎2098
Closed Xmas Lic 12hc CTV 3P 6🏠 🍴
D7pm

GH Tan-Yr-Onnen Hotel Penamser Rd
☎2443 Closed Dec Lic 10hc 1🛏🍴 ⊗
CTV 10P 🍴 B&bfr£6 Bdi fr£9.50 W£70
Ⱡ D9.30pm

PRESTATYN Clwyd *Map 6 SJ08*
GH Bryn Gwalia Hotel 17 Gronant Rd
☎2442 Lic 9hc ⊗ TV 10P S%
B&b£6.60–£7.50 Bdi£9.35–£10.50
W£61.60–£70 Ⱡ D8pm

PWLLHELI Gwynedd *Map 6 SH33*
GH Seahaven Hotel West End Pde
☎2572 Etr–Sep Lic 10hc CTV sea S%
B&b£6–£8 Bdi£8–£10 W£48–£60 Ⱡ
D7pm

RAGLAN Gwent *Map 3 SO40*
GH Grange Abergavenny Rd ☎690260
Lic 5hc 1🛏🍴 CTV 10P 🍴 S% B&b fr£12.50
Bdi fr£18 Wfr£150.50 D9pm

RHES-Y-CAE Clwyd *Map 7 SJ17*
INN Miners Arms ☎ Halkyn 780567
Lic 8hc 150P 3🏠 🍴 S% ✳B&b£6 Bdi£11
W£70 sn L£3.50&alc D10pm£4–£5.50&alc

RHOS-ON-SEA Clwyd *Map 6 SH88*
See Colwyn Bay

The Grange

Mrs M Butler

Raglan, Gwent NP5 2YA
Tel: Raglan 690260 (STD code 0291)

Elegant Victorian country-house
surrounded by 1½ acres of lawns and
trees. Ideally situated for Wye Valley,
Forest of Dean, Black Mountains,
Brecon Beacons. Within easy reach of
Abergavenny, Monmouth and
St Pierre golf courses.
Licensed. Open all the year. All meals
served; home-grown vegetables and
home-baked bread. Spacious,
comfortable bedrooms. Log fires and
central heating.
Small private and wedding parties arranged.
Collections of local artists' paintings on display.

The New Inn Pendine West Wales

NEW INN PENDINE, DYFED SA33 4PD
TEL: PENDINE (STD 09945) 250

New Inn, an old Welsh Farmhouse overlooking Pendine Sands and
Carmarthen Bay.
Pendine has a 7 miles stretch of beach made famous in the 1920s by Sir
Malcolm Campbell and Parry Thomas when they broke the world land
speed records.
The beach is ideal for children.
Fishing, pony riding and sailing etc., all within easy reach.
A warm welcome awaits you all year round from John and Bette
McMillan Logan.

BRON DIRION HOTEL

Pontllyfni, Caernarvon, Gwynedd.
Tel: Clynnog Fawr 346

9 bedroomed charming 19th Century family
owned hotel. Set in 8 acres of secluded
grounds overlooking Caernarvon Bay. The
hotel has a licensed bar, television lounge
and excellent cuisine in the restaurant.
Ideally situated for family touring, angling
and golfing holidays, with Snowdonia,
Caernarvon, Pwllheli, Porthmadog and
Anglesey all within easy reach. Many
beautiful beaches locally.

RHUALLT Clwyd *Map 6 SJ07*
INN White House ☎ St Asaph 582155
Lic 5hc CTV 100P S% B&b£6 sn
L£2.50&alc D10.30pm£2–£4&alc

RHYL Clwyd *Map 6 SJ08*
GH *Anchorage* 25 Seabank Rd ☎50698
7hc ⌖ CTV D3pm
⊢⊣**GH Ashurst Private Hotel** 7 Seabank
Rd ☎50417 Jun–Aug Lic 7hc ⌖ nc6 TV
P S% B&b£4.50 Bdi£5.50 W£35 ⌊ D6pm
GH *Ingledene Hotel* 6 Bath St ☎4872
Jan–Nov Lic 11hc TV
GH Pier Hotel 23 East Pde ☎50280
Closed Dec Lic 12hc 3⇔╫ CTV 2P ⊞
✳B&b£4.60–£5.60 Bdi£6.67–£7.20
W£42–£47.15

⊢⊣**GH Toomargoed Private Hotel**
31–33 John St ☎4103 Mar–Oct Lic 15hc
⌖ CTV S% B&b£5–£6 Bdi£6.50–£8
W£45–£50 ⌊
GH *Walcott Private Hotel* 77 Dyserth Rd
☎50843 Etr–Oct 11hc ⌖ nc2 CTV 12P
sea D4pm

ROEWEN Gwynedd *Map 6 SH77*
GH Tir-y-Coed Country House
☎ Tyn-y-Groes 219 Etr, May–Sep Lic
8⇔╫ ⌖ nc3 CTV 10P ⊞ ✳B&b£7.50
Bdi£10 W£60 ⌊ D6.30pm

ROSSETT Clwyd *Map 7 SJ35*
INN Golden Lion ☎ Chester 570316
Lic 4hc ⌖ CTV 50P ⊞ S%
✳B&b£6.50–£7.50 sn L£2alc
D9.15pm£4alc

The Glanteifi

St Dogmael's, Nr Cardigan, Dyfed

Family-run guesthouse in a superb position overlooking the
estuary, with river frontage and moorings. Licensed. Home
cooking and choice of menu. Two lounges, one with colour
TV. 12 rooms with hot and cold, some with private bath.
Central heating. Children's playroom with colour TV. Near
sandy beaches, safe bathing, lovely walks in the National
Park. Ideal for a quiet holiday. Also available from the
premises: riding and trekking (licensed premises), dinghy
sailing and instruction, coastal cruising, canoeing and fishing.
Golf nearby. Write for brochure or telephone Cardigan
(0239) 2353.

THE OAKLEYS GUEST HOUSE

The Harbour, Porthmadog Telephone: Porthmadog 2482 (STD 0766)

Proprietors: Mr & Mrs A H Biddle.
H & C in bedrooms, electric shaver points.
Licensed. Spacious free car park. No undue
restrictions. Informal atmosphere. Personal
attention.
Comfortable lounge. Interior sprung beds.
Teas and snacks obtainable during the day.
Excellent facilities for salmon and trout
fishing. Also some excellent sea fishing.
Comparatively close to an excellent golf
course.

Owen's Commercial and Residential Hotel

Porthmadog, Gwynedd (Caerns.)

Telephone Porthmadog (STD 0766) 2098   *AA Listed*

A small private hotel with restaurant licence situated in the centre of
Porthmadog and under the personal supervision of the resident props.
Mr & Mrs Edwin Owen.
Garage. Colour TV, H & C in all rooms, central heating throughout.
The popular yachting harbour and Festiniog Narrow Gauge Railway
terminal only five minutes' walk from hotel. Within easy reach of many
lovely beaches and the Snowdonia mountain range.

RUTHIN Clwyd *Map 6 SJ15*
INN Wynnstay Arms Hotel Well St
☎3147 Lic 8hc 2⇋🛏 ⊗ CTV 10P 🕮 S%
B&bf6–£7.50 Bdif8–£10 D9pm

ST DAVIDS Dyfed *Map 2 SM72*
⊷GH **Pen-Y-Daith** 12 Millard Park
☎720 Lic 8hc ⊗ CTV 🕮 B&bf5
Bdi fr£8.50 D7pm

⊷GH **Y Glennydd** 51 Nun St ☎576
Feb–Nov Lic 8hc ⊗ CTV 🕮 S%
B&bf5.30–£6.25 Bdif8.80–£9.75
Wf50—63 ⚓

ST DOGMAELS Dyfed *Map 2 SN14*
GH **Glenteifi** ☎ Cardigan 2353 Etr–Oct
Lic 11hc 4⇋🛏 CTV 20P 🕮 S%
B&bf6..03–£8.62 Bdif9.77–£13.80
Wf72.57–£90.56 ⚓ D5..30pm

ST FLORENCE Dyfed *Map 2 SN00*
⊷GH **Flemish Court** ☎ Manorbier 413
Mar–Oct 5hc CTV 5P 🕮 S% B&bf4.70
Bdif7 Wf45–£47.50 ⚓
(W only 22Jul–1Sep) D4.30pm

GH *Parsonage Farm* ☎ Manorbier 436
Mar–Oct, Xmas & New Year Lic 11hc
CTV 25P 🕮 D9pm

GH *Ponterosa* Eastern Ln
☎ Manorbier 378 Apr–Sep Lic 8hc ⊗ ♨
CTV

SALEM Dyfed *Map 2 SN62*
INN Angel ☎ Llandeilo 3394
Lic 3⇋🛏 CTV 50P 🕮 S% ✱B&bf5–£7.50
Bdif10–£12.50 Wf82 ⚓
Bar lunch 85p–£3.20 D10pmf5&alc

SAUNDERSFOOT Dyfed *Map 2 SN10*
⊷GH **Harbour Lights Private Hotel**
2 High St ☎813496 Lic 12hc ⊗ CTV 8P
S% B&bf5.75 Bdif8.50 Wf58 ⚓ D4pm

GH **Jalna Hotel** Stammers Rd ☎812282
Etr–Oct Lic 14hc 6⇋🛏 ♨ CTV 16P 🕮 S%

B&bf7.50–£8.50 Bdif10–£11
Wf62–£74 ⚓ D6.30pm

GH *Malin House* St Bride's Hill ☎812344
Etr–mid Oct Lic 14hc ⊗ CTV 14P 2🏠
D7.30pm

GH *Rhodewood House* St Bride's Hill
☎812200 25hc CTV 25P D6pm

STEPASIDE Dyfed *Map 2 SN10*
GH *Bay View* Pleasant Valley
☎ Saundersfoot 813417 Lic 12hc ⊗ ♨
CTV 20P 🕮 W only Spring Bank Hol–Sep
D6.30pm

SWANSEA W Glam *Map 3 SS69*
⊷GH **Casa Del Sol** 1 Bonvil Ter, Uplands
☎59046 9hc 8⇋🛏 CTV 4P 2🏠 🕮
B&bf5–£6.50 Bdif7.50–£9
Wf45–£54 D8pm

⊷GH **St Anne's Hotel** 6 Gore Ter
☎50914 9hc CTV S% B&bf4.50

⊷GH **Tregare Hotel** 9 Sketty Rd, Uplands
☎56608 Lic 11hc 3⇋🛏 CTV 5P 🕮 S%
B&b fr£5 Bdi fr£7.75 Wf46.50 D4pm

⊷GH **Westlands** 34 Bryn Rd, Brynmill
☎466654 6hc CTV 🕮S% B&bf4–£4.50
Bdif6–£6.50 Wf42–£45 ⚓ D9am

TAL-Y-LLYN Gwynedd *Map 6 SH70*
GH **Minffordd Hotel** (2m E on A487)
☎ Corris 665 Apr–Oct rs Nov–Mar
(wknds only) Lic 7hc ⊗ nc5 12P 🕮 S%
B&bf10.90 Bdif16.90 Wf104.30 ⚓
D8.30pm

TENBY Dyfed *Map 2 SN10*
GH **Belvedere Private Hotel**
Serpentine Rd ☎2549 Etr–Oct Lic 16hc
1⇋🛏 ⊗ CTV 20P S% B&bf6–£7.50
Bdif7.50–£9.50 Wf50–£55 ⚓ D6pm

Parsonage Farm Country Hotel

St Florence Tenby Dyfed
Tel: Manorbier 436

The award-winning hotel is situated in the centre of the floral village of Wales, some 2½ miles from Tenby. Surrounded by beautiful country, magnificent beaches and historic castles.

The 300-year-old Parsonage has been completely modernised, yet still retains its original character. Well-equipped bedrooms, comfortable lounges, TV lounge, superb bars and a first-class dining room. Children have their own play area and may enjoy the facilities of the ponies and donkeys.

Swimming, sailing, golf, fishing, water-skiing, tennis, sub-aqua, horse-riding are all at hand.

There are also four self-contained flats fully furnished. Available for self-catering or with bed, breakfast and evening meal.

Excellent parking facilities, good food, relaxed atmosphere.

Send a large, stamped addressed envelope to the Resident proprietors. *Mr & Mrs F P White.*

JALNA HOTEL

Stammers Road, Saundersfoot, Dyfed.
Tel: Saundersfoot 812282

Resident Proprietors:
Mr. & Mrs. Frank Williams

Purpose built and situated on the flat just two minutes walk from sea front and harbour.
Overlooking bowling green and tennis courts.
Food of the best quality. Bar and TV lounge.
Ample car parking. Laundry room.
Small dogs by arrangement.
Double, twin-bedded and family rooms, some with private bathrooms.
TV and tea making facilities in all bedrooms.

The Angel Inn

Salem, N Llandeilo, Dyfed.
Tel: Llandeilo 3394

A small "away from it all" with a big reputation for the warmth of its welcome, superb food and high standards of comfort.
An ideal base from which to sample the beautiful scenery, fishing and riding in the region. In the restaurant relax and enjoy our delicious home-made bread, soups, patés, sweets, Continental and British dishes. All rooms with bath and WC en suite. Restaurant reservations advisable.

MALIN HOUSE HOTEL

St. Brides Hill, Saundersfoot

Telephone Saundersfoot 812344

Malin is a house of character, Situated in peaceful surroundings 400 yards from the beach and shopping centre with ample car parking. Residentially licensed with a high standard of accommodation, food and wine. Some rooms with private shower or bath, H and C in all rooms. Malin, now under the same management as the Merlewood Hotel next door; who aim to maintain their high standard of service. Guests may make full use of all the facilities at Merlewood:— Heated swimming pool etc.
Send stamp to Dennis, Irene and Janet Williams for brochure and tariff.

Rhodewood House Hotel

LICENSED
Open all year round

St Brides, Saundersfoot,
Dyfed   Tel: 812200

Rhodewood House is situated in 1½ acres of woodlands and gardens, overlooking Carmarthen Bay and only two minutes from Glen Beach. This hotel of charm and character offers a warm welcome to all ages. There is a friendly atmosphere and excellent food, together with all the amenities that ensure the visitor of a most enjoyable holiday. The hotel is within easy reach of golf course, swimming, sailing, water ski-ing, fishing, riding and pony trekking and lovely woodland walks.

GH Buckingham Hotel Esplanade
☎2622 Dec & Jan Lic 25hc 8⇌🛏 nc5
CTV ✳B&bf6.50–£7 Bdif7.50–£9
D7.30pm

GH Hotel Doneva The Norton ☎2460
Lic 14hc 4⇌🛏 nc4 CTV 20P S%
B&bf6.50–£7.50 Bdif8.50–£9.50
Wf61 W Jul & Aug D6.30pm

GH Harbour Heights Hotel 11 The Croft
☎2264 May–Oct Lic 11hc 2⇌🛏 ≉ nc2
CTV S% ✳B&bf7–£8.10
Bdif10.50–£11.50 Wf59.50–£74
Ɫ D7.30pm

GH Heywood Lodge Heywood Ln
☎2684 Etr–Nov Lic 14hc 4⇌🛏 ⚊ CTV
15P ᵐ S% ✳B&bf6–£6.50
Bdif7.75–£8.50 Wf54–£56 Ɫ D7.30pm

GH Sea Breezes Hotel 18 The Norton
☎2753 Apr–Sep Lic 17hc 3⇌🛏 ≉ nc3
CTV 3P 1🏠 ᵐ sea S% B&bf6.32–£8.62

Bdif9.20–£11.50 Wf51.75–£66.70
Ɫ D6pm

TRETOWER Powys *Map 3 SO12*
INN Tretower Court ☎ Bwlch 730204
Lic 6hc 2⇌🛏 ≉ CTV 90P ᵐ B&bf5.92
Bar lunch 70p–£1.50alc D10pmf5

TYWYN Gwynedd *Map 6 SH50*
GH *Greenfield Private Hotel* High St
☎710354 Etr–Dec Lic 9hc TV D7pm

⋈**GH Min-y-Mon** Marine Pde ☎710139
Lic 8hc 3⇌🛏 ≉ CTV 3P S% B&bf5.50–£7
Bdif8–£10 Wf56–£70 Ɫ D5pm

WELSHPOOL Powys *Map 7 SJ20*
GH Garth Derwen Buttington
(2½m NE A458) ☎ Trewern 238
Closed mid Dec–mid Jan Lic 8hc ⚊ CTV
20P S% B&bf6–£7 Bdif9.75–£10.75
Wf63–£70 Ɫ D7.30pm

ABBEY CWMHIR Powys *Map 6 SO07*
Home *(SO091724)* ☎ Penybont 66
Smart, stone-built house in the village.
Small trout stream passes through the
farm.
2hc ⊗ TV 4P 1🏠 450acres mixed

ABEREDW Powys *Map 3 SO04*
Danycoed *(SO079476)* ☎ Erwood 298
Stone-built, two-storey farmhouse.
Pleasant situation on edge of River Wye.
Etr–Oct 4rm 2hc P 235acres mixed S%
B&b£5.50–£6.50 Bdi£7.50–£8.25
W£45.50 ⅙ D3pm

ABERGAVENNY Gwent *Map 3 SO21*
Newcourt *(SO317165)* Mardy ☎3734
16th-century, stone-built farmhouse with
views of Sugar Loaf Mountain.
3hc ⊗ nc6 P 🏠 85acres dairy

BABELL Clwyd *Map 7 SJ17*
Bryn Glas *(SJ155737)* ☎ Caerwys 493
May–Sep rs Mar, Apr, Oct & Nov 2rm
CTV 3P 🍽 40acres mixed S% B&b£4–£5
Bdi£6.50–£7 W£45 ⅙ D6.30pm

BALA Gwynedd *Map 6 SH93*
Tytandderwen *(SH944345)* ☎520273
Two storey manor house-style farmhouse
in open country. Stone built and modernised
in parts. Borders on River Dee.
Closed Xmas & New Year 6rm 3hc TV 6P
40acres 🍽 mixed S% B&b fr£6 W fr£55 ⅙

BERRIEW Powys *Map 7 SJ10*
Upper Pandy *(SJ149995)* ☎338
Isolated, black and white-timbered
farmhouse. Berriew 1½ miles.
Etr–Oct 3rm 2hc TV P 140acres mixed
S% B&b£5 Bdi£6.50 W£42 ⅙

BETHESDA Gwynedd *Map 6 SH66*
Pentre *(SH639615)* Nant Ffrancon Pass
☎600407
Stone-built farmhouse in isolated position.
Some distance from main road in the heart
of Snowdonia.
3rm ⊗ CTV 6P river 1,500acres sheep
D7pm

BRYNGWYN Powys *Map 3 SO14*
Newhouse *(SO191497)* ☎ Paincastle 671
200-year-old, two-storey, stone-built
farmhouse set in 150 acres of mixed
farmland.
2hc ⊗ nc8 CTV 3P 🍽 150acres mixed
B&b fr£5.18 Bdi fr£8.05 W fr£56.35 ⅙
D4.30pm

CAPEL BANGOR Dyfed *Map 6 SN68*
Fron *(SN663804)* ☎221
Elevated, stone-built farmhouse with
splendid views of the Rheidol Valley.
4hc 5P 100acres mixed B&b£4–£4.50

CAPEL GARMON Gwynedd *Map 6 SH85*
Maes y Garnedd *(SH816548)*
☎ Betws-y-Coed 428
Isolated farmhouse in elevated position.
2rm ⊗ nc TV P 150acres mixed

CAPEL SEION Dyfed *Map 6 SN67*
Rhoslawdden *(SN628794)* Moriah
☎ Aberystwyth 612585
Comfortable farmhouse overlooking fields.
Apr–Oct 3rm 1hc CTV 4P 112acres dairy
S% B&b£4.50–£5.50 Bdi£6.50–£7.50
W£44–£46

CARNO Powys *Map 6 SN99*
Y Grofftydd *(SN981965)* ☎274
Farmhouse is situated off A470 overlooking
typical mid-Wales scenery. Ideal centre for
walking. Sporting clay-pigeon shoot on
premises.
4hc ⊗ CTV 4P 180acres sheep S%
B&b£5 Bdi£7 W£63 D8.30pm

CEMMAES Powys *Map 6 SH80*
Rhydygwiel *(SH826056)*
☎ Cemmaes Road 205
Remote, detached, stone-built farmhouse
on north side of Dovey Valley. Attractive
gardens at back of house.
4rm 1hc CTV P 200acres mixed S%
B&b fr£4

CLAWDDNEWYDD Clwyd *Map 6 SJ05*
Maestyddyw Isa *(SJ054535)* ☎289
Old farmhouse filled with antiques.
Positioned in rural setting on the
outskirts of Cleanog Forest.
Closed Dec–Feb 3hc ⊗ CTV 🍽 365acres
mixed ✻Bdi£7.50 W fr£50

CLYRO Powys *Map 3 SO24*
Crossway *(SO216459)*
☎ Hay-on-Wye 820567
Small farm situated in the hills. Quiet
and peaceful surroundings. Clyro village
1¾ miles.
Mar–Oct 2rm ⊗ nc5 TV P 50acres mixed
S% B&b£3.50 Bdi£5.50 W£36 ⅙ D noon

CROESGOCH Dyfed *Map 2 SM83*
Torbant *(SM845307)* ☎276
Well kept farmhouse, tastefully furnished.
Situated in pleasant spot overlooking open
country.
Etr–Sep 11rm 12hc (A2) ⊗ CTV 30P
158acres arable, beef & sheep D8pm

CYNWYD Clwyd *Map 6 SJO4*
Ceamawr *(SJO48419)* ☎ Corwen 2421
Pleasant, two-storey, stone-built farmhouse in an elevated position.
Jan–Nov 4hc ❄ TV P ⅏ 60acres arable & dairy

DERWEN Clwyd *Map 6 SJO5*
Aberclwyd *(SJO68509)*
☎ Clawdd Newydd 639 Closed Xmas & New Year 3rm 1hc ❄ ♨ TV 6P ⅏ 4acres sheep S% B&b£3.50–£4.50
Bdi£4.50–£5.50 W£24.50–£31.50 M D9pm

DOLFOR Powys *Map 6 SO18*
Penhempen *(SO106887)* Upper Dolfor Rd
☎ Newton (Powys) 26216
Farm lies in sylvan surroundings encircled by hills. South of market town of Newtown. Ideally situated for touring mid and north Wales.
4hc 1⇌⒨ nc5 4P 3🏠 ⅏ 4acres non-working S% B&b£5–£5.50
Bdi£8–£8.50 W£56–£59.50 ⱡ D6pm

DOLGELLAU Gwynedd *Map 6 SH71*
Glyn *(SH704178)* ☎422286
Stone-built farmhouse of historical interest with oak beams, floors and doors. Well situated for coastal resorts.
Mar–Aug rs Sep–Nov 5rm 4hc TV 5P river 150acres mixed S% B&b£4–£4.50
Bdi£6–£7 W£35–£40 ⱡ D previous day

GARTHMYL Powys *Map 7 SO19*
Trwstllewelyn *(SO189984)* ☎ Berriew 295
Spacious 17th-century farmhouse, traditionally furnished with some antiques

and open fires in the recently discovered and restored inglenook fireplace.
Etr–Sep 3rm 1hc 1⇌⒨ ❄ ♨ TV 3P 300acres mixed S% B&bfr£4.50
Bdifr£7.50 Wfr£50 ⱡ D6.30pm

GLAN CONWY Gwynedd *Map 6 SH87*
Plas Ucha *(SH818752)* ☎276
Elizabethan farmhouse of historical interest with oak beams, floors and doors. Well situated for coastal resorts.
Jul–Aug 4rm ❄ 8P 240acres beef & sheep

GLAN-YR-AFON Gwynedd *Map 6 SJO4*
Llawr-Bettws *(SJO16424)* Bala Rd
☎ Maerdy (Clwyd) 224
Rambling, stone-built farmhouse with pleasant, homely atmosphere. At Druid traffic lights on A5 follow A494 Bala rd for 2m.
5rm 3hc ❄ CTV 6P ⅏ 72acres beef sheep S% B&b£4–£5 Bdi£6–£7 D9.30pm

GWYDDELWERN Clwyd *Map 6 SJO4*
Bryngwenallt *(SJO67473)*
☎ Corwen 2312
Situated in a rural setting with excellent views of countryside.
Jun–Oct 3rm ❄ CTV 3P 110acres mixed S% B&b£3.75–£4

GWYSTRE Powys *Map 3 SO06*
Gwystre *(SO070656)* ☎ Penybont 316
Typical Welsh hill farm near to Elan Valley reservoir.
Mar–Oct 2rm TV P 160acres mixed S% B&b£4.25–£4.50 Bdi£6–£7 D5.30pm

HAVERFORDWEST Dyfed *Map 2 SM91*
Cuckoo Grove *(SM928162)* ☎2429
*Comfortable accommodation, for
non-smokers only, in recently refurbished
farmhouse. Swimming pool in grounds
and views of the distant Prescelly
Mountains.*
Apr–Oct 5hc ⊗ TV P ▥ 206acres dairy
& mixed S% B&b£4.50–£5 W£30–£33 Ⓜ

HOLT Clwyd *Map 7 SJ35*
New Farm *(SJ394538)* Commonwood
☎ Farndon 270358
Small, comfortable and cosy farm.
Apr–Oct 1rm ⊗ TV 4P 84acres dairy S%
✻B&b£4–£4.75 Bdi£5.50–£6.50
W£37–£44 ⅃ D9.30am

HOLYWELL Clwyd *Map 7 SJ17*
Garneddwen Fawr *(SJ173707)* Lixwm
☎ Halkyn 780298
*16th-century, stone-built farmhouse with
oak beams.*
Apr–Oct 2hc 1⇔▥ ⊗ nc7 CTV 4P 1🏠
66½acres non-working S% B&b£4–£5
W£28–£30.50 Ⓜ

HOWEY Powys *Map 3 SO05*
Three Wells *(SO062586)*
☎ Llandrindod Wells 2484
7rm 6hc ♣ CTV 20P ▥ 51acres mixed
S% B&b fr£5.50 Bdi fr£7.50 D6.30pm

HUNDRED HOUSE Powys *Map 3 SO15*
Box *(SO129531)* ☎240
*Two-storey, 17th-century stone farmhouse.
In elevated position with good views of the
Edw Valley.*
Mar–Oct 3rm nc TV P mixed B&b£4

IDOLE Dyfed *Map 2 SN41*
Pantgwyn *(SN419157)*
☎ Carmarthen 5859
*Spacious, rebuilt farmhouse. 3 miles south
of Carmarthen.*
Apr–Oct 3rm ⊗ CTV 4P 35acres dairy
✻B&b£4–£4.50

KERRY Powys *Map 6 SO19*
Goitre *(SO176918)* ☎248
*Modernised farmhouse with comfortable
traditional furnishings in peaceful rural area.*
4rm 1 hc ⊗ CTV P 2🏠 ▥ 190acres
mixed S% B&b£4.50–£5 Bdi£6.50–£7
W£45–£49 ⅃

KNIGHTON Powys *Map 7 SO27*
Heartsease *(SO343725)* ☎ Bucknell 220
*Large, mellow-stoned residence over 300
years old. Country house atmosphere.
Large garden.*
3rm 2hc 1⇔▥ ♣ CTV 3P 2🏠 ▥
600acres mixed S% B&b£5–£5.50
Bdi£7.50–£8 W fr£52 D8pm

LLANARTH Gwent *Map 3 SO31*
Llwynderi *(SO382130)* ☎ Llantillio 226
*Secluded, stone-built farmhouse with
many period features, including a classical
oak staircase. Rooms larger than average.*
Mar–Oct 5hc CTV 8P 120acres arable
dairy S% B&b fr£5.50 Bdi fr£9 W fr£60
⅃

LLANARTHNEY Dyfed *Map 2 SN52*
Glantowy *(SN534206)* ☎ Dryslwyn 275
*Spacious, well-maintained farmhouse
near River Tywi.*
2hc ⊗ TV 4P ▥ 140acres dairy S%
B&b£4 W£28 Ⓜ

LLANDEGLA Clwyd *Map 7 SJ15*
Dol Ddu *(SJ188503)* ☎219
Modern, two-storey farmhouse.
2rm ⊗ nc10 CTV 4P 95acres mixed S%
B&b fr£4

Graig *(SJ202506)* ☎272
*Recently built (1974) farmhouse in
elevated position. 1m S of junc
A525/A5104.*
Mar–Nov 2hc ⊗ TV 120acres mixed D7pm

Pentre Isa *(SJ195498)* ☎220
*Pleasant, stone-built, two-storey
farmhouse in elevated position.*
Etr–Oct 1rm ⊗ TV P 128acres mixed
S% B&b fr£4.50 Bdi fr£6.50 W fr£43 ⅃
D previous day

LLANDINAM Powys *Map 6 SO08*
Llandinam Hall *(SO028903)*
☎ Caersws 234
*Two-storey, half-timbered farmhouse
probably late 17th-century, backing onto
River Severn. Fine views of the Cambrian
Mountains.*
Etr–Oct 6rm 5hc nc4 CTV P 450acres
mixed S% ✻B&b£5–£6

LLANDOVERY Dyfed *Map 3 SN73*
Glangwydderig *(SN789347)* ☎20381
*Small farmhouse on the outskirts of
Llandovery alongside the Brecon Beacons
National Park. Fishing available in farm
grounds.*
May–mid Oct 2rm 3P 75acres sheep

LLANDRINDOD WELLS Powys
Map 3 SO06
Highbury *(SO044623)* Llanyre ☎2573
*Typical Welsh beef and sheep farm.
Situated 2m W of Llandrindod Wells, ½m
off A4081.*
Etr–Sep 4rm TV 4P 184acres beef sheep
S% B&b fr£4 Bdi fr£6.75 D noon

LLANDYSSIL Powys *Map 7 SO19*
Gwern-yr-Uchain *(SO193960)*
☎ Montgomery 298
May–Sep 2rm ⊗ CTV 2P B&b£4.50
Bdi£7 W£45 ⅃

LLANEGRYN Gwynedd *Map 6 SH60*
Argoed *(SH604057)* ☎ Tywyn 710361
*Homely, comfortable farmhouse with tasty
country food.*
Etr–Oct 3hc ⊗ nc10 TV P 10acres beef
sheep

LLANELIDAN Clwyd *Map 6 SJ15*
Trewyn *(SJ138515)* Rhydymeudwy
☎ Clawdd Newydd 676
*Homely farmhouse in valley of fields and
trees. Ruthin about 5 miles. 2m E of
B5429.*
Mar–Oct 3rm ⊗ TV 6P ▥ 80acres mixed
S% B&b£3.50–£4 Bdi£4.50–£5
W£28–£30 ⅃ D5.30pm

LLANFACHRETH Gwynedd *Map 6 SH72*
Rhedyncochion *(SH762222)*
☎ Rhydymain 600
*100-year-old, stone-built farmhouse with
extensive views of surrounding
countryside and mountains.*
2rm 1hc ⊗ ♣ TV P ▥ 120acres mixed
S% Bdi£4.03–£4.60 D6.30pm

LLANFAIR DYFFRYN CLWYD Clwyd
Map 6 SJ15
Llanbenwch *(SJ137533)* ☎ Ruthin 2340
*Modernised farmhouse with oak beams
situated on the A525, Wrexham to Ruthin
road.*
Feb–Nov 3hc ⊗ TV P ⅏ 40acres mixed
S% B&b£4 Bdi£5.50 W£35 D7pm

LLANFAIR TALHAIARN Clwyd
Map 6 SH96
Bodrochchwyn *(SH938731)*
☎ Abergele 823525
*Large, brick-built, L-shaped farmhouse of
distinction.*
Etr–Oct 3rm 1hc TV 174acres

LLANGERNYW Clwyd *Map 6 SH86*
Tan-y-Craig *(SH875669)* ☎249
*Large farmhouse on hillside. Situated 1
mile north of village.*
Etr–Oct 3hc ⊗ nc3 TV 4P 100acres mixed
D8pm

LLANGOLLEN Clwyd *Map 7 SJ24*
Rhydonnen Ucha Rhewl *(SJ174429)*
☎860153
*Large, stone-built, three storey farmhouse,
pleasantly situated. Shooting on farm.
Trout fishing in River Dee (permit).*
Etr–Nov 4rm 3hc TV 5P river 115acres
dairy S% B&b£4.25–£4.75 Bdi£7
Wfr£44 ⅃ D5pm

LLANRHAEADR Clwyd *Map 6 SJ06*
Pen-y-Waen *(SJ074615)* ☎ Llanynys 234
*Positioned between sloping hills with views
of valleys.*
Etr–Oct 2rm ⊗ CTV 2P ⅏ 100acres
mixed S% B&b fr£4 Bdi fr£6.50 Wfr£42
⅃ D5pm

LLANRWST Gwynedd *Map 6 SH86*
Bodrach *(SH852629)* Gwytherin
☎640326
*Farm situated in remote position about
3½m E off unclass road between B5113
and Gwytherin.*
Mar–Nov 2rm ⊗ TV 6P ⅏ 184acres
mixed S% ✳B&b fr£4 Bdi fr£6 Wfr£42
⅃ D8pm
Tyn-y-Fford *(SH796607)* Carmel
☎640343
*Recently built farmhouse. Simple and
modern. Tastefully decorated. Isolated
position for those seeking a quiet holiday.*
Apr–Oct 3rm ⊗ TV 4P 77acres mixed

LLANSANNAN Clwyd *Map 6 SH96*
Fferwd *(SH933658)* ☎230
*Remote, brick-built farmhouse on the
main Denbigh to Llansannan road.
Denbigh about 7 miles.*
Apr–Oct 3rm 1hc ⊗ nc14 CTV ⌂
200acres mixed

LLANSANTFFRAID-YM-MECHAIN
Powys *Map 7 SJ22*
Glanvyrnwy *(SJ229202)* ☎258
*Two-storey, stone-built, detached
farmhouse set back from road behind
pleasant lawns and orchard.*
Mar–Oct 3hc ⊗ CTV 6P 42acres dairy
S% B&b£5–£6 Bdi£8.50–£9.50
Wfr£65 ⅃ D6pm
Greenacres *(SJ206172)* (Rhosddu Farm)
☎392
*Pleasant farmhouse in rural surroundings.
River Vyrnwy runs through farm. Salmon
and trout fishing. Slides and swings for
children.*
Apr–Aug 3rm ⊗ ⌕ 6P 2⌂ 116acres
mixed D5pm

LLANUWCHLLYN Gwynedd *Map 6 SH83*
Bryncaled *(SH866314)* ☎270
*Farmhouse with beamed ceiling.
Overlooking Aran Mountains and has
fishing river running through grounds.*
Closed Xmas day 3rm 2hc TV P ⅏
500acres beef sheep S% B&b£4.50
Bdi£7.50
Bryn Gwyn *(SH862309)* ☎272
*80-year-old, stone-built farmhouse with
fine view of the Aran Mountains and Lake
Bala.*
Etr–Oct 2hc ⊗ ⌕ TV 3P river 400acres
mixed

LLECHWEDD Gwynedd *Map 6 SH77*
Henllys *(SH779466)* ☎ Conwy 3269
*Large, stone-built farmhouse, signposted
from the main road.*
Apr–Oct 2rm TV 4P 30acres mixed S%
B&b£4–£5 Bdi£6–£7 D6pm
Llechan Ucha *(SH755757)*
☎ Conwy 2451
*Modern farmhouse in isolated position.
High on mountainside with good views
of the surrounding area.*
Etr–Oct 3rm CTV 3P ⅏ river 102acres
mixed S% B&b£4.60–£5.75
Bdi£6.90–£8.05 W£43.70–£52.90 ⅃
D3pm

MIDDLETOWN Powys *Map 7 SJ21*
Bank *(SJ325137)* ☎ Trewern 260
Traditional farmhouse with rear garden
and an attractive outlook.
Etr–Oct 2hc CTV P 🗰 30acres mixed
S% ✱B&bfr£4

MONTGOMERY Powys *Map 7 SO29*
East Penyllan *(SO244941)* ☎246
Farmhouse is in England, 2m SE of
Montgomery on B4385.
3rm CTV 4P S% B&b£4 Bdi£5.75 W£38
ᵏ D7.30pm

MOYLGROVE Dyfed *Map 2 SN14*
Penrallt Ceibwr *(SN116454)* ☎217
A very pleasant farm off A487. ½m from
Ceibwr beach.
7hc ⚘ CTV P 🗰 254acres arable & dairy
D7pm

PADOG Gwynedd *Map 6 SH85*
Dylasau Isa *(SH832157)*
☎ Betws-y-Coed 265
Stone-built farmhouse ½ mile from A5,
east of town.
Mar–Oct 3rm ❦ TV 3P 300acres mixed
B&b£3.75–£4 W£25–£27 Ⓜ
Ty-Uchaf *(SH830503)*
☎ Pentrefoelas 280
Stone-built farmhouse on hill farm.
Closed Xmas 4hc ⚘ CTV 12P 160acres
mixed sheep S% B&b£5–£5.50
Bdi£7–£7.50 W£44–£49 ᵏ D7pm

PANDY TUDUR Clwyd *Map 6 SH86*
Llywn Llydan *(SH851647)*
☎ Llangernyw 243
Modernised farmhouse in an elevated
situation. Magnificent views.
2rm 1hc ❦ nc8 4P river 85acres mixed

PANTYGELLI *(Nr Abergavenny)* Gwent
Map 3 SO31
Lower House *(SO314159)* Old Hereford
Rd ☎ Abergavenny 3432
Isolated, stone-built farmhouse. Well
situated 3 miles from Abergavenny.
Etr–Oct 3hc TV 6P 209acres beef mixed
sheep S% B&b£4.50–£5

PENEGOES Powys *Map 6 SH70*
Abergwydol *(SH794031)*
☎ Cemmaes Road 270
Large, stone-built, half-timbered
farmhouse. Typical old farm kitchen with
stone floor. Lots of character.
Whit–Sep 2rm ❦ TV 2P river 350acres
mixed D7pm,

PENMACHNO Gwynedd *Map 6 SH75*
Tyddyn Gethin *(SH799514)* ☎392
Farm situated high on mountainside with
panoramic views of surrounding country.
3hc ❦ TV P 60acres beef, mixed & sheep

PENTREFOELAS Clwyd *Map 6 SH85*
Tai Hirion *(SH839525)* ☎202
Two-storey, stone-built house. Adjacent
to A5 Corwen to Betws-y-Coed road.
3hc ❦ TV P 204acres mixed
B&b£4–£4.50 Bdi£6–£6.50 D6pm

PENYBONT Powys *Map 3 SO16*
Bryhunllef *(SO107664)* ☎045
Situated in quiet rural area overlooking
River Ithon.
Apr–Oct 2rm TV P 55acres dairy S%
B&b£4.50 Bdi£7 W£47 ᵏ D5pm

Neuadd *(SO092618)* Cefnllys
☎ Llandrindod Wells 2571
Two-storey, isolated farmhouse situated
in elevated position. Fine views.
May–Oct 5rm 3hc CTV 8P 🗰 330acres
mixed S% B&b£6 Bdi£8.50 W fr£57.50
ᵏ D5.30pm

PONTARDULAIS W Glam *Map 2 SN50*
The Croft *(SN612015)* Heol-y-Barna
☎883654
Farmhouse has open aspect to the Gower
Peninsula and the Laughor Estuary.
Closed Xmas 3rm 1hc 1⇥🅟 ❦ nc5 TV
4P 1🏠 🗰 5acres beef S% B&b£6 Bdi£8
W£53 ᵏ D4pm

PWLLGLAS Clwyd *Map 6 SJ15*
Llanerchgron Isa *(SJ112532)*
☎ Clawdd Newydd 260
Intensive dairy farm situated on main
A494.
Etr–Oct 3hc ❦ TV 3P 🗰 40acres dairy
sheep S% ✱B&b£4 Bdi£6 W£35 ᵏ D2pm

PWLLHELI Gwynedd *Map 6 SH33*
Bryn Crin *(SH379358)* ☎2494
Large, stone-built farmhouse in an
elevated position overlooking Cardigan
Bay and Snowdonia. Within easy reach of
sandy beaches.
May–Oct 3rm 2hc ❦ 3P sea 80acres
beef sheep S% B&b£4–£4.25

RHANDIRMWYN Dyfed *Map 3 SN74*
Galltybere *(SN772460)* ☎218
Isolated farmhouse 9 miles north of
Llandovery amid splendid scenery. Ideal
for bird watching and hikers.
May–Oct 1rm (Ă 2hc) ❦ nc10 CTV 5P
320acres mixed sheep ✱B&b fr£5
Bdi fr£7.50 W fr£49 D6.30pm

RUTHIN Clwyd *Map 6 SJ15*
Pen-y-Coed *(SJ107538)* Pwllglas
☎ Clawdd Newydd 251.
Isolated farmhouse on high ground with
extensive views. Stone-built with timbered
ceilings.
3hc TV P 🗰 160acres mixed S%
✱B&b fr£3.75 Bdi fr£5.25 W fr£35 ᵏ
D6.30pm
Plas-y-Ward *(SJ118604)* Rhewl ☎3822
Period farmhouse, dating back to 14th
century. 2m N A525.
20May–Sep rs Oct & Nov 2rm nc3 TV
10P 2.16acres mixed S% B&b£5.50
W fr£30 Ⓜ

ST DOGMAELS Dyfed *Map 2 SN14*
Granant Isaf *(SN126473)* Cipyn
☎ Moylegrove 241
The Pembrokeshire Coastal Path runs
along the boundary of this farm which
enjoys spectacular views of the sea and
cliffs.
Apr–Oct rs Nov–Mar 2rm ⚘ CTV 2P 2🏠
🗰 sea 400acres dairy S% B&b£3.25–£3.75
Bdi£6–£6.50 W£38.50–£42 ᵏ
D6.30pm

TREFEGLWYS Powys *Map 6 SN99*
Cefn-Gwyn *(SO993923)* ☎648
Clean and homely farmhouse.
2rm ❦ ⚘ CTV 12P 2🏠 🗰 mixed S%
B&b£3.75 Bdi£5.50 W fr£38 ᵏ D7.30pm

TREFRIW Gwynedd *Map 6 SH76*
Cae-Coch *(SH779646)*
☎ Llanrwst 640380.
Pleasant farmhouse in elevated position.
Etr–Oct 3rm ✗ nc2 TV 4P 2🏠 river
50acres mixed S% ✳B&b£4.50 W£28 M

TREGARON Dyfed *Map 3 SN65*
Aberdwr *(SN672597)* Abergwesyn Rd
☎255
*Farm overlooks the River Brennig. Meadows
to the front lead to woodland.*
Mar–Oct 8hc ✗ TV 12P river 12acres
non-working

TYWYN Gwynedd *Map 6 SH50*
Dolgoch *(SH648049)*
☎ Abergynolwyn 229
*Two-storey, brick farmhouse with 200
acres of pasture and mountain land.*
May–Oct·3hc ✗ 4P 356acres mixed S%
✳B&b£4–£4.25 Bdi£6.50–£7
W£45–£48.50 ⫽

Dyffryngwyn *(SH632984)* Happy Valley
☎710305
*Modern clean bungalow. Follow A493
south for 1¾m then unclass road east
(SP Happy Valley) for 2½m; farmhouse
on right.*
May–Oct 3rm 3P 600acres beef sheep
S% B&b£4.25–£5 Bdi£7.50–£8
W£50–£55 ⫽ D3pm

WELSHPOOL Powys *Map 7 SJ20*
Gungrog House *(SJ235089)* Rhallt
☎3381
300-year-old farmhouse in quiet
*situation high on hillside, commanding
superb views of the Severn Valley. 1m
NE off A458.*
Apr–Oct 2rm ✗ ♨ CTV 4P 🍴 15acres
beef S% B&b£4 Bdi£6.25 W£43.75 ⫽

Tynllwyn *(SJ215085)* ☎3175
*Large brick-built farmhouse, dating from
1861, in peaceful surroundings with lovely
views. One mile from Welshpool.*
6rm 4hc CTV 6P 150acres arable dairy
mixed S% B&bfr£4.50 Bdifr£7.25
Wf.£45 ⫽ D6.30pm

WHITE MILL Dyfed *Map 2 SN42*
Pencnwc *(SN464232)* ☎ Nantgaredig 325
*Two-storey, stone-built Victorian residence.
Large lawned and wooded garden
adjacent. 1 mile from village.*
Etr–Oct 4rm 3hc ✗ CTV 6P 82acres mixed
S% ✳B&bfr£3.50 Bdifr£5.25 D4pm

WHITLAND Dyfed *Map 2 SN21*
Cilpost *(SN191184)* ☎280
*Two-storey, 300-year-old farmhouse in an
elevated position. 1½ miles north of the
village amid extensive gardens.*
Apr–Sep 9hc 5⫽🍴 15P 🍴 160acres
dairy B&b£6–£7 Bdi£7–£10 W£52–£64
⫽ W only Jul & Aug D4pm

YSBYTY IFAN Gwynedd *Map 6 SH84*
Ochr Cefn Isa *(SH845495)*
☎ Pentrefoelas 602
*Farm set in elevated position with good
views high above A5.*
Mar–Oct 3rm 2hc ✗ TV 3P 124acres
mixed S% B&b£4.50 Wfr£30.50 M

GUESTHOUSES

Details for islands off the mainland of Scotland are shown under the individual placename. A useful first point of reference is to consult the location maps which show where guesthouses or inns are located.

ABERDEEN Grampian *Aberdeens*
Map 15 NJ90 **See Plan**
⊷**GH Ashgrove** 9 Forest Av ☎36226
Plan:**1** 6hc ✷ nc12 CTV S%
B&bf£4.75–£5 Wf£31–£32 M

GH Broomfield Private Hotel 15
Balmoral Pl ☎28758 Plan:**2** 8hc CTV
20P ⁙ S% B&bfr£6 Bdifr£9 D5pm

GH *Carden Hotel* 44 Carden Pl ☎26813
Plan:**3** 7hc nc5 CTV 6P ⁙

GH Crown Private Hotel 10 Springbank
Ter ☎26842 Plan:**4** 9hc nc4 CTV S%
B&bf£6.25 Bdif£9 D5pm

GH Dunromin 75 Constitution St
☎56995 Plan:**5** 5hc CTV S%
✳B&bf£4–£5

⊷**GH Klibreck** 410 Great Western Rd
☎36115 Plan:**6** 7hc ✷ CTV 3P ⁙
B&bfr£5 Bdifr£7.75 Wfr£58 ⱢD3pm

GH Mannofield Hotel 447 Great
Western Rd ☎35888 Plan:**7** Lic 10hc
✷ nc10 CTV 14P ⁙ S% B&bf£11.50–
£12.65 Bdif£16.10–£17.25
Wf£112.70–£120.75 Ⱡ D5pm

GH Russell Private Hotel 50 St Swithin
St ☎323555 Plan:**8** Closed 15Dec–6Jan
Lic 9hc ✷ nc6 CTV 9P ⁙ S% B&bf£10.98
Wf£76.80 M

GH *Shieldaig House Hotel* 21 Albert St
☎28067 Plan:**9** Closed Apr & Oct rs
Nov–Mar 10hc ✷ nc10 CTV 6P D5pm

⊷**GH Urray House** 429 Great Western Rd
☎35204 Plan:**10** 6hc nc5 CTV 5P 1🏠 ⁙
S% B&bf£5–£6 Bdif£7.50–£8.50 D3pm

GH Western 193 Great Western Rd
☎56919 Plan:**11** 6hc ✷ CTV 10P ⁙
S% ✳B&bf£6

ABERFELDY Tayside *Perths*
Map 14 NN84
⊷**GH Balnearn Private Hotel** Crieff Rd
☎431 Apr–Oct 13hc (A 2hc) CTV 15P
2🏠 B&bf£5.75–£7.45 Bdif£9.20–£10.95
Wf£64.40 Ⱡ D7pm

GH Nessbank Private Hotel Crieff Rd
☎214 21Mar–Oct rs Nov–20Mar
Bookings only Lic 7hc CTV 7P S%
B&bfr£7 Bdifr£11 Wfr£70 Ⱡ D7pm

⊷**GH Tirinie** (4m W B846)
☎ Kenmore 362 5hc 1🛏🏠 10P ⁙ S%
B&bfr£5 Bdifr£8.50 D6pm

ANNAN Dumfries & Galloway
Dumfriesshire Map 11 NY16
⊷**GH Ravenswood** St Johns Rd ☎2158
Lic 11hc CTV 2P 1🏠 S% B&bf£5
Bdif£7.50 Wfr£52 Ⱡ D5.30pm

ARBROATH Tayside *Angus*
Map 12 NO64
GH *Davanna-Kingsley* 29 Market Gate
☎72417 CTV 2P

GH *Gladsheil* 38 Ogilvy Pl ☎73470
Closed Oct rs Nov–Apr (B&b only) 6hc
CTV 7P

ARDGOUR Highland *Inverness-shire*
Map 14 NN06
⊷**GH Ardvulin** ☎224 Mar–Oct Lic 10hc
TV 15P 4🏠 sea B&bf£5.50 Bdif£9.50
Wf£65 Ⱡ D8pm

ARDROSSAN Strathclyde *Ayrs*
Map 10 NS24
⊷**GH Ellwood House** 6 Arran Pl
☎61130 7hc CTV sea B&bfr£4
Wfr£28 M

AVIEMORE Highland *Inverness-shire*
Map 14 NH81
GH Aviemore Chalets Motel Aviemore
Centre ☎810618 80hc CTV 300P
⁙ S% B&bf£6.80–£8 Bdif£11.50–£13.20
D10pm

1 Ashgrove	4 Crown Private Hotel	7 Mannofield	9 Shiedaig House Hotel
2 Broomfield Private Hotel	5 Dunromin	8 Russell Private Hotel	10 Urray House
3 Carden Hotel	6 Klibreck		11 Western

GH Corrour House Inverdruie ☎810220
Closed Nov Lic 10rm 8hc CTV 12P 🍳
S% B&b£6.75–£8.10 Bdi£11.07–£15.12
W£81.34–£98.28 ₭ D6.30pm

GH Craiglea Grampian Rd ☎810210
12rm 10hc 1⇨🍲 CTV 12P S%
✻B&b£4.50–£5

GH Ravenscraig ☎810278 4hc nc3 CTV
12P 🍳 S% B&b£6–£7

AYR Strathclyde *Ayrs Map 10 NS32*
⊫**GH Clifton Hotel** 19 Miller Rd ☎64521
Lic 11hc ✺ nc5 CTV 16P B&b£5.35–
£6.75 Bdi£9.10–£10.75 W£54.50–£60
D5.30pm

GH *Daviot House* 12 Queens Ter
☎63672 Dec–Sep 6hc ✺ CTV D5.30pm

⊫**GH Inverlea** 42 Carrick Rd ☎61538
Jan–mid Oct 9hc CTV 6P B&b£5–£5.50

BALLATER Grampian *Aberdeens*
Map 15 NO39
GH Moorside Braemar Rd ☎492
Apr–Oct Lic 7hc 1⇨🍲 CTV 10P 🍳 S%
B&b£7 Bdi£9.75 W£63 ₭ D7pm

BALLOCH Strathclyde *Dunbartons*
Map 10 NS48
INN *Lomond Park Hotel* Balloch Rd
☎ Alexandria 52494 Lic 7hc ✺ CTV 30P
🍳 D7.45pm

BALMAHA Central *Stirlings Map 10 NS49*
⊫**GH Arrochoile** ☎231 Etr–Oct 6hc ✺
CTV 12P 🍳 lake S% B&b£4 Bdi£6 D3pm

BANFF Grampian *Banffs Map 15 NJ66*
⊫**GH Carmelite House Private Hotel**
Low St ☎2152 Lic 8hc ⚓ CTV 8P 🍳 S%
B&b£4.25–£4.75 Bdi£6–£6.75
W£40–£45 ₭ D7pm

⊫**GH Ellerslie** 45 Low St ☎5888
6hc CTV sea S% B&b£4 Bdi£5.50
W£38 ₭ D4.30pm

BEAULY Highland *Inverness-shire*
Map 14 NH54
⊫**GH Chrialdon** Station Rd ☎2336
Apr–Oct Lic 14hc CTV 16P B&b£4.50–£5
Bdi£7.50–£8 D7.45pm

BLACKWATERFOOT Isle of Arran
Strathclyde *Bute Map 10 NR92*
INN *Greannan Hotel* ☎ Shiskine 200
Lic 12rm 11hc ⚓ CTV 14P 🍳 sea D10pm

BLAIR ATHOLL Tayside *Perths*
Map 14 NN86
GH Invergarry The Terrace ☎255
Apr–Oct 7rm 6hc ✺ nc10 12P 🍳 S%
B&b fr£6 Bdi fr£8.25 Wfr£55.50 ₭ D6pm

BLAIRGOWRIE Tayside *Perths*
Map 11 NO14
⊫**GH Kintrae House Hotel** Balmoral Rd

☎2106 Lic 8hc nc11 TV 16P 🍴 S%
B&b£5.50–£6.50 Bdi£8.50–£9 W£56
⌇ D8pm

BONAR BRIDGE Highland *Sutherland*
Map 14 NH69
⊷**GH Glengate** ☎ Ardgay 318 Mar–Sep
4hc CTV 4P S% B&b£4.50

BRAEMAR Grampian *Aberdeens*
Map 15 NO19
GH *Braemar Lodge* ☎617 Lic 8hc (A 4hc)
TV 20P 🍴 D6pm

GH Callater Lodge ☎275 26Dec–mid Oct
Lic 9hc 42P 🍴 S% B&b£7.35 Bdi£12.35
W£76.47 ⌇ D8pm

BROADFORD Isle of Skye, Highland
Inverness-shire Map 13 NG62
GH *Hilton* ☎322 Apr–Oct 10rm 9hc TV
10P 🍴

BURNT ISLAND Fife *Map 11 NT28*
⊷**GH Forthaven** 4 South View,
Lammerlaws ☎872600 4hc TV 4P S%
B&b£4 W£25 Ⓜ

CALLANDER Central *Perths*
Map 11 NN60
⊷**GH Abbotsford Lodge** Stirling Rd
☎30066 Lic 18hc CTV 20P 🍴 S%
B&b£5.50 Bdi£9.75 W£63.25 ⌇ D6.45pm
⊷**GH Annfield** 18 North Church St
☎30204 Etr–Oct 8hc ⊗ nc7 TV 8P S%
B&bfr£4.50

GH Ashlea House Hotel Bracklinn Rd
☎30325 Mar–mid Oct rs Jan & Feb 20hc
2🛏🖿 ⊗ CTV 17P 🍴 B&b£8.10 Bdi£12.45
W£44–£75 ⌇ D6.30pm

GH *East Mains House* Bridgend ☎30080
Lic 8hc CTV 12P D6.30pm

𝕶innell 𝕳ouse

24 Main Street, Callander, Perthshire

Kinnel is an attractive Victorian Town House which
backs onto the scenic beauty of the River Teith. It
is convenient for the shops, bus service and other
amenities. The house has a reputation for good food
and comfortable accommodation. Facilities include
a private car park, wash hand basins in all rooms, a
colour TV in the lounge and electric blankets on all
beds. Callander is set in the beautiful Trossachs
area and is the ideal centre for those interested in
sport, scenic beauty and history. Write, or
telephone Callander (0877) 30181, for brochure.

KINTRAE
HOUSE HOTEL
GUEST HOUSE

Balmoral Road, Blairgowrie.
Proprietors: J & C McClymont
tel **Blairgowrie 2106**

Situated in half an acre of ground on Royal
Route to Balmoral, opposite pine woods
which slope down to the River Ericht. High
standards of comfort, cleanliness and cuisine.
Bed, breakfast and evening dinner, or bed and
breakfast only. Open all year. Emphasis on
Scottish fare — salmon, rainbow trout and
Angus steak, fresh fruit and vegetables from
our policies, complemented by extensive wine
cellar. Central heating. Ample parking. Each
bedroom has hot and cold water with facilities
for coffee/tea making.
Grand touring centre — Scone Palace, St
Andrews, Carnoustie, and Gleneagles. Fishing
and Pony trekking arranged.
SAE please for terms (which are reduced for
children).

BRAEMAR LODGE
HOTEL

Braemar, Aberdeenshire   Tel. 033 83 617

The Braemar Lodge Hotel, which was once a
hunting lodge, is situated in the finest position
in Braemar and stands in its own 2 acres of
wooded grounds. The tourist may relax in the
magnificent highland scenery and peaceful
atmosphere.

Proprietor: Mr R S McKay

GH Edina 11 Main St ☎30004 8hc CTV 8P S% ✻B&b£4.05 Bdi£6.75 Wfr£43.20 ⅃ D6.30pm

⊶**GH Kinnell** 24 Main St ☎30181 Mar–Nov 8hc ⌀ nc6 CTV 8P ⍟ river S% B&b£4.50–£5 Bdi£8–£8.50 W£52.50–£55 ⅃ D7.30pm

GH Lubnaig Leny Feus ☎30376 Mar–14Oct Lic 10hc 10⊷⌓ ⌀ nc7 CTV 14P ⍟ S% B&b£8.63 Bdi£14.23 W£86.25 ⅃ (W only mid May–mid Sep) D8pm

⊶**GH Rock Villa** 1 Bracklinn Rd ☎30331 Etr–mid Oct 6hc ⌀ 6P ⍟ S% B&b£4.25–£4.50

GH Tighnaldon Private Hotel 156 Main St ☎30703 Lic 6hc TV ✻B&b£4–£4.50 Bdi£7–£8 W£45–£50 ⅃ D6pm

CAMPBELTOWN Strathclyde *Argyll Map 10 NR72*
⊶**GH Westbank** Dell Rd ☎2452 Feb–Nov 7hc CTV S% B&b fr£4 Wfr£28

CANONBIE Dumfries & Galloway *Dumfriesshire Map 11 NY37*
INN Riverside ☎295 Closed last 2wks Jan Lic 7hc ⌀ CTV 25P ⊞ S% B&b£7.45 Bar lunch 85p–£3.55 D8.30pm£5–£5.75&alc

CARISHADER Isle of Lewis, Western Isles *Ross & Crom Map 13 NB13*
GH *No 10 Carishader* ☎ Timsgarry 337 3rm 2hc nc8 TV 6P ⍟ D7.30pm

CARRADALE Strathclyde *Argyll Map 10 NR83*
GH *Drumfearne* ☎232 Etr–Oct 5rm 4hc ⌀ TV P sea D6pm

GH *Duncrannag* ☎224 Apr–Sep Tem 11hc 8P

⊶**GH Dunvalanree** Portrigh ☎226 Etr–Sep 12hc ⌀ TV 9P sea S% B&b£4.50–£5 Bdi£6.50–£7 W£45.50–£49 ⅃ D5pm

CARRBRIDGE Highland *Inverness-shire Map 14 NH92*
GH Ard-na-Coille Station Rd ☎239 Lic 6hc TV 7P S% ✻B&b£4.50–£5.50 Bdi£7.50–£8.50 W£45–£51 ⅃ D4.30pm

⊶**GH Dalrachney Lodge Private Hotel** ☎252 6hc ⌀ nc8 CTV 10P ⍟ B&b£5–£5.50 Bdi£9.50–£10.50 D6.30pm

GH Old Manse Private Hotel Duthil (2m E A938) ☎278 Closed Nov 9hc CTV 10P ⍟ B&b£6–£8 Bdi£8.20–£10.50 W£53.20–£68 ⅃ D noon

CASTLE DOUGLAS Dumfries & Galloway *Kirkcudbrights Map 11 NX76*
⊶**GH Almar** 21 Ernespie Rd ☎2771 Etr–Oct rs Feb–Etr (advance bookings only) 5hc ⌀ nc7 5P S% B&b£4.50–£5 Bdi£7.50–£8 W£49–£52.50 ⅃

CHAPELHALL Strathclyde *Lanarks Map 11 NS76*
GH Laurel House Hotel 101 Main St ☎ Airdrie 63230 Lic 6rm 5hc ⌀ CTV 6P ⍟ S% B&b£6 Bdi£8 D8pm

CLACHAN-SEIL Strathclyde *Argyll Map 10 NM71*
⊶**GH Old Clachan Farmhouse** ☎ Balvicar 281 Closed Xmas 3hc ⌀ 6P ⍟ S% B&b£4.50–£5.50

COMRIE Tayside *Perths Map 11 NN72*
GH Mossgiel ☎567 Closed Nov 6hc nc6 CTV 6P ⍟ S% ✻B&b£4.50 Bdi£7 W£28–£49 ⅃ D5pm

CORRIE Isle of Arran, Strathclyde *Bute Map 10 NS04*
⊶**GH Blackrock House** ☎282 Mar–Oct 8rm 5hc TV 7P ⍟ sea S% B&b£4.50 Bdi£6.50 W£49 ⅃ D5pm

CRAIL Fife *Map 12 NO60*
⊶**GH Caiplie House** 51–53 High St ☎564 Apr–Sep 7hc CTV 15P sea S% B&b£4.50–£5

CREETOWN Dumfries & Galloway *Kirkcudbrights Map 6 NX45*
⊶**GH Creetown Arms** ☎282 Lic 6hc CTV 15P S% B&b£5.50 Bdi£9.50 D9.30pm

GH *Mayburn* ☎317 Etr–Sep 5hc TV 6P D8pm

CRIANLARICH Central *Perths Map 10 NN32*
⊶**GH Mountgreenan** ☎286 Closed Xmas & New Year's Day 5hc ⌀ CTV P S% B&b fr£4.50 D5.30pm

CRIEFF Tayside *Perths Map 11 NN82*
GH Comely Bank 32 Burrell St ☎3834 Closed 2wks Xmas & 2wks Oct rs Oct–Etr 6hc CTV S% ✻B&b£4 Bdi£6 Wfr£38 ⅃ D7pm

⊶**GH Heatherville** 31 Burrell St ☎2825 Mar–Oct 5hc ⌀ CTV 6P S% B&b£4.50 Bdi£7.50 W£52.50 ⅃ D7pm

GH *Keppoch House* Perth Rd ☎2839 mid May–Sep 6hc ⌀ nc3 TV 6P

GH Lockes Acre Hotel Comrie Rd
☎2526 Lic 7hc CTV 5P 🍴 S% B&b£6.48
Bdi£10.74 D7pm

CULLEN Grampian *Banffs Map 15 NJ56*
⊢⊣**GH Wakes** Seafield Pl ☎40251
Apr–Oct Lic 22hc CTV 26P S%
B&b£5–£5.50 Bdi£8–£8.50 W£43–£45

CUMMERTREES Dumfries & Galloway
Dumfriesshire Map 11 NY16
⊢⊣**GH Richmond Private Hotel** ☎255
Lic 6hc TV 6P S% B&b£4 Bdi£6 D7pm

CUPAR Fife *Map 11 NO31*
GH Edenhouse Hotel East Rd
☎2510 (Due to change to 52510)
Closed New Year Lic 10hc CTV 20P S%
B&b£6.50–£7.50 Bdi£10.50–£11.50
W£73.50–£80.50 Ƚ D8pm

DIRLETON Lothian *E Lothian*
Map 12 NT58
INN Castle ☎221 Apr–Oct rs Nov–Mar
(B&b only) Lic 5hc (A 4hc) CTV 12P 🍴
B&b£7.50–£8 Bdi£11.50–£12.50 W£70
Ƚ Bar lunch 75p–£2 D9pm£4–£4.50

DRUMNADROCHIT Highland *Inverness-shire Map 14 NH53*
INN Lewiston Arms Hotel Lewiston
☎225 Lic 4rm 3hc (A 4hc) TV 40P 🚗 S%
B&b£7–£7.50 Bdi£12–£12.50 W£84
Ƚ Bar lunch £1.50alc D8pm£5–£6

DUMFRIES Dumfries & Galloway
Dumfriesshire Map 11 NX97
GH Dalston Hotel 5 Laurieknowe
☎4422 9hc 🕸 🦢 CTV 10P 🍴 S% B&b£6
Bdi£9 W£60 Ƚ D7pm

⊢⊣**GH Fullwood Private Hotel** 30 Lovers
Walk ☎2262 5hc TV 3P S% B&b£4
Wfr£25 M

⊢⊣**GH Huntington Hotel** 32 Lovers Walk
☎4001 Lic 6rm 4hc CTV 4P S%
B&b£4–£5 (W only Oct–May)

GH *Newall House* 22 Newall Ter ☎2676
Lic 7hc (A 4hc) 🦢 CTV 6P 🍴 S% D7pm

DUNBAR Lothian *E Lothian Map 12 NT67*
⊢⊣**GH Cruachan** East Links Rd ☎63595
Closed Dec–Mar & 2wks late Sep 6hc 🕸
CTV 🍴 sea S% B&b£4.75–£5.50
Bdi£7–£7.75 W£47–£50 Ƚ D6pm

⊢⊣**GH Fiddlers Yard** Woodbush Brae
☎63293 8hc CTV 9P 🍴 S%
B&b£4.50–£5 Bdi£6.50–£7

⊢⊣**GH Marine** 7 Marine Rd ☎63315
10hc CTV 🍴 S% B&b£4–£4.50
Bdi£5.75–£6.50 W£35–£40 Ƚ D5pm

⊢⊣**GH St Laurence** North Rd ☎62527
6hc 🕸 3P sea S% B&bfr£5.25 Bdifr£7.25
Wfr£48 D5.30pm

GH Springfield House Edinburgh Rd
☎62502 Apr–Oct 6hc 🕸 CTV 8P 🍴 S%
B&b£6.50 Bdi£9.50 W£63 Ƚ D5pm

DUNBLANE Tayside *Perthshire*
Map 11 NN70
GH Altair Neuk Hotel Doune Rd
☎822562 Closed Xmas & New Year Lic
8hc CTV 10P 🍴 S% B&b£7.50–£8.50
Bdi£11.50–£13.50 W£70–£80 Ƚ D8pm

DUNOON Strathclyde *Argyll*
Map 10 NS17
GH Cedars Private Hotel Alexandra Pde
☎2425 Closed Dec Lic 14hc 2🛏🍴 CTV
🍴 sea S% B&b£6.21–£7.29
Bdi£9.45–£10.53 W£62.64–£70.20
Ƚ D7.30pm

EDINBURGH Lothian *Midlothian*
Map 11 NT27 **See Plan**
GH Adam Hotel 19 Lansdowne Cres
☎031-337 1148 Plan:**1** Lic 9hc CTV S%
B&bf7–£8.50 Bdif9.50–£11.50
Wf60–£78 ʎ D6pm

GH *Albany Hotel* 39 Albany St
☎031-556 0397 Not on plan Lic 10hc
CTV 🌀

►◄**GH Ben Doran Hotel** 11 Mayfield Gdns
☎031-667 8488 Plan:**2** 9hc TV 6P S%
B&bf5.17–£6.32 Wfrf32.20 M
(W only Nov–Mar)

►◄**GH Boisdale Hotel** 9 Coates Gdns
☎031-337 4392 Plan:**3** 11hc 11↔🛋
CTV P 🌀 S% B&bf5–£9 Bdif7.50–£12.50
D8.30pm

GH *Clans Hotel* 4 Magdala Cres
☎031-337 6301 Plan:**4** Lic 8hc ⊗ CTV 🌀

GH Cumberland Hotel 1 West Coates
☎031-337 1198 Plan:**5** 7hc ⊗ CTV 9P 🌀
S% B&bf6.85–£7.85

GH Dorstan Private Hotel 7 Priestfield Rd
☎031-667 6721 Plan:**6** Closed Xmas,
New Year & 1wk Oct 14hc 3↔🛋 CTV 9P
🌀 S% ✱B&bf5.94–£7.02
Bdif9.72–£10.80 Wf66.42–£73.98
ʎ D am
GH *Eden* 12 Osbourne Ter
☎031-337 4185 Plan:**7** 6hc TV 8P 🌀
►◄**GH Elmington House Private Hotel**
45 Leamington Ter ☎031-229 1164
Plan:**8** Lic 7hc 7↔🛋 ⊗ nc3 CTV S%
B&bf4.75–£6 Bdif7.75–£9.50
Wf54–£62 ʎ D6.30pm
►◄**GH Glendale House Hotel** 5 Lady Rd
☎031-667 6588 Plan:**9** 8rm 7hc ⊗ nc3
CTV 8P 🌀 S% B&bf5.50–£8
GH Glenisla Hotel 12 Lygon Rd
☎031-667 4098 Plan:**10** Closed 2wks
Xmas & New Year 9hc CTV 5P 🌀 S%
B&bf8.50 Bdif12 D2.30pm
GH Golf View Hotel 2 Marchall Rd,
(off Dalkeith Rd) ☎031-667 4812 Plan:**11**
Mar–Oct Lic 11hc 8↔🛋 CTV 12P 🌀 S%
B&bf6.90–£10.35

DORSTAN PRIVATE HOTEL

7 Priestfield Road, Edinburgh
EH16 5HJ Tel: 031-667 6721

Private car park. Off Dalkeith Road. Near
Commonwealth Pool.
Modernised to a high standard.
Fitted wardrobes, H & C, razor points in all
bedrooms.
2 bathrooms, TV lounge. Full central heating.
Reduced terms for children. Babysitting.
Evening meals available.

Fire precautions carried out.

Member of the Scottish Tourist Board, and
Edinburgh Guest House & Private Hotel
Association. Under the personal supervision of
the Proprietors: Mr. & Mrs. W. S. Bradford.
Send SAE for brochure.

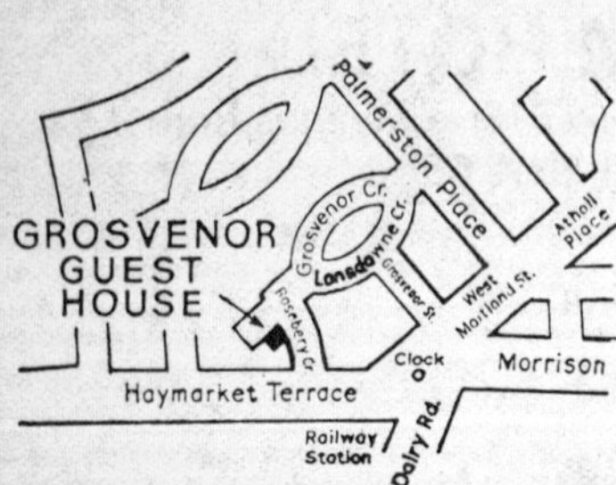

Grosvenor
Guest House

Quiet cul-de-sac. Spacious rooms. All
bedrooms with H&C, electric blankets,
shaving points and television. Near City
centre.

Bed and breakfast £5.00 to £6.00 inclusive.
Special off-season rates on weekly basis.
Resident proprietor: John G. Gray.

1 Grosvenor Gardens, Haymarket, Edinburgh EH12 5JU. Tel: 031 337 4143

EDINBURGH

Hillview Guest House

We do care for our guests. That is why we
claim to provide comfort, good food and
that rare commodity, personal service for
no extra charge. Route A68 — within one
mile of City centre — parking bays. Bed
and Breakfast from £4.40 plus VAT.
Dinners 6.30pm.

**Hillview House, 92 Dalkeith Road, Edinburgh.
EH16 5AF Tel: 031 667 1523**

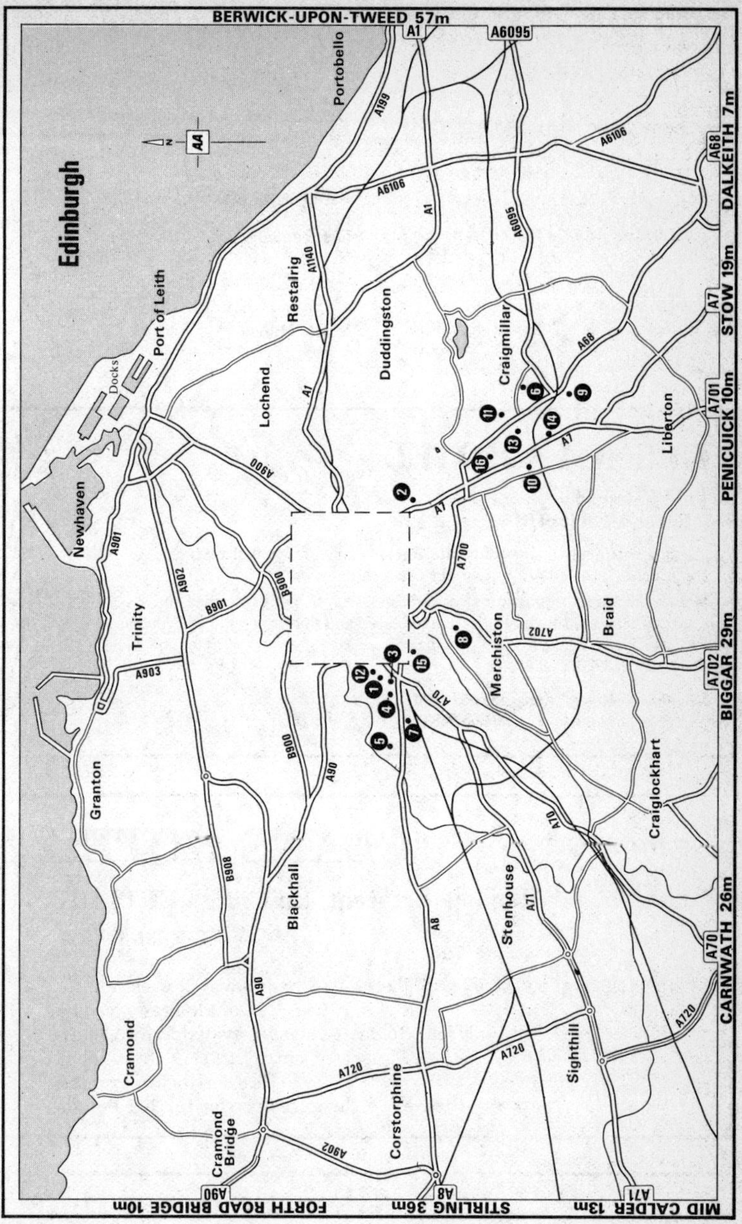

1 Adam Hotel
2 Ben Doran Hotel
3 Boisdale Hotel
4 Clans Hotel
5 Cumberland Hotel
6 Dorstan Private Hotel
7 Eden
8 Elmington House Private Hotel
9 Glendale
10 Glenisla Hotel
11 Golf View Hotel
12 Grosvenor
13 Hillview
14 Kildonan Lodge
15 Quinton Lodge
16 Thrums Private Hotel

GH Greenside Hotel 9 Royal Ter ☎031-557 0022 Not on plan Closed Xmas & New Year 13hc nc5 CTV ♛ S% B&b£7.56–£9

GH Grosvenor 1 Grosvenor Gdns, Haymarket ☎031-337 4143 Plan:**12** 7hc 1⇌fl ⊗except guide dogs ♛ S% B&b£6.50–£7.50

⊨**GH Halcyon Hotel** 8 Royal Ter ☎031-556 1033 Not on plan 16hc ⊗ CTV ♛ S% B&b£5.94–£6.48 W£37.45–£40.81 M

⊨**GH Hillview** 92 Dalkeith Rd ☎031-667 1523 Plan:**13** 8hc nc3 CTV 5P ♛ S% B&b£4.75–£5.40 Bdi£8.10–£8.65 W£56–£60 ⱡ D noon

GH Kildonan Lodge Hotel 27 Craigmillar Pk ☎031-667 2793 Plan:**14** 12hc CTV 18P ⋓ S% B&b£7

⊷**GH Northesk Hotel** 23 Pibig St ☎031-554 4205 Not on plan 12hc TV 2🏠 ⋓ S% B&b£5.75–£6.90 Bdi£9.20–£11.50 Wfr£76.50 ⊾ D am

⊷**GH Quinton Lodge** 24 Polwarth Ter ☎031-229 4100 Plan:**15** Closed Xmas & New Year 6hc ⊗ ♨ CTV 8P ⋓ S% B&bfr£5 Bdifr£7.50 D6.30pm

⊷**GH Thrums Private Hotel** 14 Minto St, Newington ☎031-667 5545 Plan:**16** Lic 6hc 1⇥🍴 CTV S% B&b£5–£6 Bdi£8–£9

ELIE Fife *Map 12 NO40*
GH Elms Park Place ☎330404 Lic 6hc 2⇥🍴 ⊗ CTV 8P ⋓ S% ✽B&b£5.50–£6 Bdi£8.50–£9 Wf£57 ⊾ D6pm

FORRES Grampian *Moray Map 14 NJ05*
⊷**GH Regency** 66 High St ☎72558 7hc CTV S% B&b£4–£4.50

FORTROSE Highland *Ross & Crom Map 14 NH75*
GH Strathallan 17 Deans Rd ☎20481 Apr–Oct Lic 4hc ⊗ nc CTV 10P ⋓ sea S% B&b£7–£7.50 Bdi£10.50–£11 Wf£70–£75 ⊾ D5pm

FORT WILLIAM Highland *Inverness-shire Map 14 NN17*
GH Benview Beford Rd ☎2966 Mar–Dec 15hc ⊗ TV 16P ⋓ D6pm
⊷**GH Guisachan** Alma Rd ☎3797 9hc TV 10P ⋓ lake S% B&b£5–£6.50 Bdi£8–£9.50 Wf£56–£66.50 ⊾ D6pm
⊷**GH Hillview** Achintore Rd ☎4349 Closed Winter 9hc CTV 9P ⋓ lake S% B&bfr£4.25 Bdifr£7.25

GLENISLA HOTEL

**12 Lygon Road
Edinburgh EH16 5QB**

A small, personally-managed private hotel in a quiet residential area, conveniently situated for buses to the City centre.

Recommended for good, home-cooked food. Comfortably furnished and centrally heated throughout. Wash hand basin and shaver point in all bedrooms. Pleasant TV lounge.   Private parking. Dinner served 6.30pm.

**Telephone: Reservations   031 667 4098
           Guests   031 667 4877**

CLANS HOTEL

4 Magdala Crescent, Edinburgh EH12 5BE

Tel: 031 337 6301

Open throughout the year. There are 8 bedrooms all with hot and cold water. Children of all ages welcome. Special meals for children. Colour television available for the use of guests. Central heating throughout. Fire certificate granted. Please see the gazetteer for further details.

Glendale House Hotel

Mrs K Philip, Proprietrix

5 Lady Road, Edinburgh

EH16 5PA
Tel: 031-667 6588

Glendale House where comfort and cleanliness are our first priority. A warm welcome is extended to everyone by friendly hostess. Enjoy your breakfast in the wood-panelled dining room. Adjacent to bus route, 10 minutes' from town centre, buses direct every few minutes. Leave your car in the large private car park. Full central heating. TV in most bedrooms.

⊢⊣**GH Loch View** (Off Argyll Ter) ☎3149 Etr–Sep 7hc 1⇌⋒ CTV 8P ▥ lake S% B&b£4–£5

⊢⊣**GH Rhu Mhor** Alma Rd ☎2213 Mar–Oct 7hc ⊗ 9P lake B&b£5.50–£6.50 Bdi£8.50–£9 D7pm

FOYERS Highland *Inverness-shire*
Map 14 NH42

⊢⊣**GH Foyers Bay House** ☎ Gorthleck 631 Apr–Oct rs Nov–Feb (no dinner) 6hc ⊗ CTV 5P ▥ lake S% B&b£5.50–£6 Bdi£10–£11 D5pm

GAIRLOCH Highland *Ross & Crom*
Map 14 NG87

⊢⊣**GH Horisdale House** Strath-Gairloch ☎2151 May–Sep 9hc ⊗ TV 20P ▥ S% B&bfr£5

GARTMORE Central *Perths*
Map 11 NS59

⊢⊣**GH Baad Springs Farm** ☎ Aberfoyle 207 2hc (A 3⇌⋒) CTV 10P ▥ S% B&b£5–£6 Bdi£8–£10 W£70–£84 D9pm

GARTOCHARN Strathclyde *Dunbartons*
Map 10 NS48

INN *Gartocharn Hotel* ☎204 Lic 5hc CTV 35P ▥ D8.25pm

GIFFORD Lothian *E Lothian*
Map 12 NT56

GH Cornerways ☎238 4hc 4P S% B&bfr£6.50

GIRVAN Strathclyde *Ayrs Map 10 NX19*

GH Barbara 16 Louisa Dr, Sea Front ☎2398 Etr–Sep Lic 6hc ⊗ nc8 CTV sea D6pm

GH Westcliffe Hotel Louisa Dr ☎2128 Etr–Oct Lic 14hc ⊗ CTV ▥ S% B&bfr£6 Bdifr£8.30 Wfr£50 Ł (W only Jun–Aug) D6pm

GLASGOW Strathclyde *Lanarks*
Map 11 NS56 **See Plan**

⊢⊣**GH Auld's** 8 Belgrave Ter, Hillhead ☎041-339 8668 Plan:**1** 4hc ⌂ TV 4P S% B&b£4.50–£5

GH Burnbank Hotel 67–85 West Prince's St ☎041-332 4400 Not on plan rs Xmas Day 36hc 6⇌⋒ ⌂ CTV ▥ S% B&b£7 Bdi£10 D6.30pm

⊢⊣**GH Chez Nous** 33 Hillhead St, Hillhead ☎041-334 2977 Plan:**2** 17rm 16hc TV 9P ▥ S% B&b£5–£6 W only Nov–Mar

GH Dalmeny Hotel 62 St Andrews Dr, Nithsdale Cross ☎041-427 1106 Plan:**3** Closed New Year Lic 10hc 4⇌⋒ CTV 20P ▥ S% B&bfr£8

GH Devonshire Hotel 5 Devonshire Gdns, Great Western Rd, Kelvinside ☎041-334 1308 Plan:**4** 15hc 2⇌⋒ CTV P S% B&b£6.48 Bdi£9.48 D7pm

⊢⊣**GH Kelvin Private Hotel** 15 Buckingham Ter, Hillhead ☎041-339 7143 Plan:**5** 16hc CTV B&b£5.40–£6.48

GH Linwood House 356 Albert Dr, Pollokshields ☎041-427 1642 Plan:**6** Lic 16hc CTV 8P lift *B&b£6–£6.50

GH Marie Stuart Hotel 46–48 Queen Mary Av, Cathcart ☎041-423 6363 Plan:**7** Closed Xmas Lic 24hc 1⇌⋒ CTV 50P ▥ S% *B&b£7.59–£13.92 Bdi£10.42–£16.75 D6.30pm

GH Smith's Hotel 963 Sauchiehall St ☎041-339 7674 Plan:**8** 26hc ⊗ CTV ▥ S% B&b£6.32–£7.47 W£44.24–£52.29 M

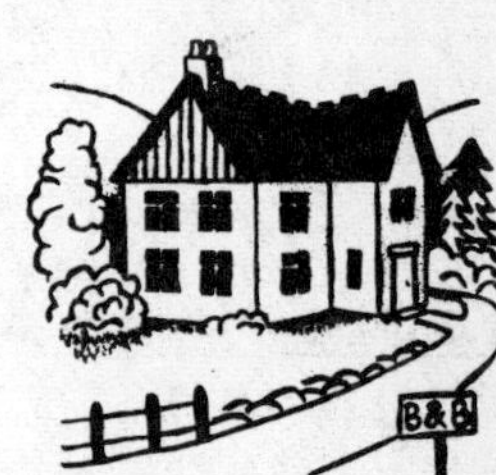

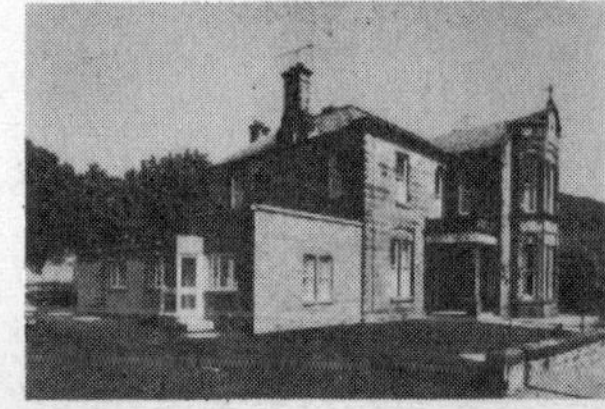

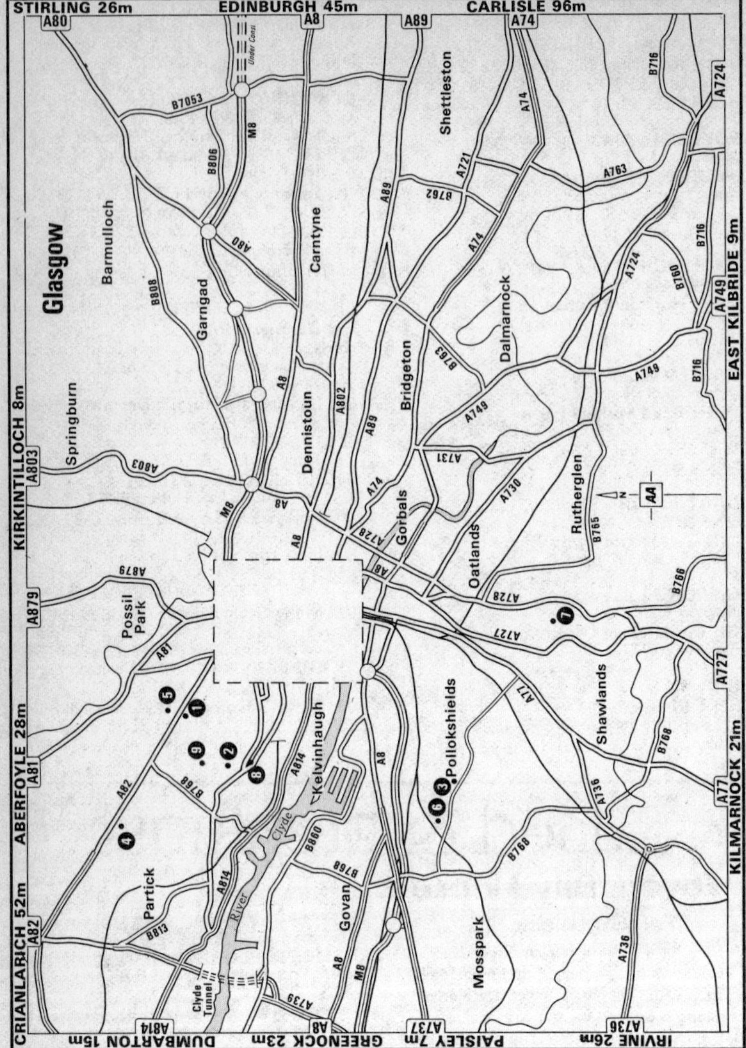

1 Aulds	**4** Devonshire Hotel	**6** Linwood House	**9** Wilkies
2 Chez Nous	**5** Kelvin Private	**7** Marie Stuart Hotel	
3 Dalmeny Hotel	Hotel	**8** Smith's Hotel	

GH *Wilkies* 14–16 Hillhead St, Hillhead
☎041-339 6898 Plan:**9** Closed Xmas
Day 14hc CTV 4P

GLASGOW AIRPORT Strathclyde
Renfrews Map 11 NS46
GH Ardgowan 92 Renfrew Rd, Paisley
☎041-889 4763 Closed Xmas & New
Year 6hc 6P 🎮 S% B&b£7

GH Broadstones Private Hotel
17 High Calside, Paisley, ☎041-889 4055
8hc CTV 12P 🎮 S% B&b£7–£8

GLENCOE Highland *Argyll Map 14 NN15*
⊶GH Dunire ☎ Ballachulish 318 6hc
3⊶🛏 TV 10P 🎮 S% B&b£4–£4.50
Bdi£6.50–£7 D6pm

GH Scorrybreac ☎ Ballachulish 354
Closed Nov & Dec 6hc ⚸ CTV 10P 🎮
lake S% ✸B&b£4–£4.50 Bdi£7–£7.50
W£47–£50 ⅼ D6pm

GOUROCK Strathclyde *Renfrews
Map 10 NS27*
⊶GH Claremont 34 Victoria Rd ☎31687
6hc CTV 🎮 lake sea S% B&b£5–£6

GRANTOWN-ON-SPEY Highland
Moray Map 14 NJ02
GH Dar-il-Hena ☎2929 7hc CTV 10P
🎮 S% B&b£6.21–£7.25 Bdi£9.18–£10.55
W£60.48–£70.20 ⅼ D6pm

⊶**GH Dunachton** off Grant Rd ☎2098
7hc 1⊶🛏 TV 9P 🎮 B&b£5.40–£5.90
Bdi£8.40–£8.90 W£55.50–£59.80 D7pm

KELVIN HOTEL

Tel: 041 339 7143

15 Buckingham Terrace, Glasgow G12

Comfortable, family hotel. B & B only. TV lounge and dining room. Situated in the West End of Glasgow, off the Great Western Road and on route A82 to Loch Lomond. Ten minutes from the city centre and near to the University, Botanic Gardens and the B.B.C.

SMITH'S HOTEL

(Est. 1928)

963 Sauchiehall Street, Glasgow G3
Telephone 041-339 6363 and 7674

Resident Proprietors:
Mr & Mrs S Ireland

Enjoy a comfortable stay in this old established Private Hotel situated adjacent to Kelvingrove Park and within short walking distance of Glasgow University, Kelvin Hall, and City Art Museum.

Being 5 minutes' from the City Centre, the Hotel is most convenient for all shopping precincts and Bus, Rail and Airport Terminals.

- Convenient Parking
- Central Heating
- Colour TV Lounge
- Telephone intercom all rooms
- Conforms to' Higher Standard' of S.T.B.

Terms: Full Breakfast inclusive — from Single Room £5.94   Double or Twin £11.88
Family £15.00   **Tax inclusive. No service charge**

NEAR CITY CENTRE (5 minutes)
BUT RESIDENTIAL AREA

EASY ACCESS FROM KINGSTON
(M8) BRIDGE

EN-ROUTE TO/FROM AIRPORT (M8)

BUS No. 59 (FROM CENTRAL STATION)
STOPS AT HOTEL

VERY LARGE CAR PARK

LICENSED

SCOTTISH TOURIST BOARD HIGHER
STANDARD QUALIFICATION

ENJOY THE COMFORT AND COMPANY
OF YOUR ALTERNATIVE HOME

DALMENY HOTEL

62 ST. ANDREW'S DRIVE,
NIGHSDALE X, GLASGOW
G41 5EZ 041-427 1106
AND 041-427 6288

'It is unwise to pay too much — but it is unwise to pay too little.
When you pay too much you lose a little money, that is all.
When you pay too little, you sometimes lose everything because the thing
you bought was incapable of doing the thing you bought it to do.
The common law of business balance prohibits paying a little and getting a lot
it can't be done.
If you deal with the lowest bidder, it is well to add something for
the risk you run.
And if you do that, you will have enough to pay for something better'.

John Ruskin
(1819 - 1900)

GH Kinross House Woodside Av
☎2042 Closed Xmas 6hc 6P 🍴 S%
B&b£6.78–£8.10 Bdi£10.58–£11.90
W£70.61–£79.86 ⚓ D4pm

GH Pines Woodside Av ☎2092
Apr–Sep 10hc CTV 4P ✳B&b£6.90
Bdi£9.49 W£58.38 ⚓ D7pm

⋈**GH Riversdale** Grant Rd ☎2648
7hc ♨ CTV 8P 🍴 S% B&b£5.50–£6
Bdi£8.50–£9 W£56–£59.50 ⚓ D6pm

GH Umaria Woodlands Ter ☎2104
8hc TV 10P S% B&b£6 Bdi£9 W£60
D5pm

GRETNA Dumfries & Galloway
Dumfriesshire Map 11 NY36
GH Surrone House Annan Rd ☎341
Lic 7⇄🍴 ✖ P 🍴 B&b£7.25–£8.25
Bdi£10.25–£11.25 W£64.57–£70.87
⚓ D7.30pm

GRETNA GREEN Dumfries & Galloway
Dumfriesshire Map 11 NY36
⋈**GH Greenlaw** ☎361 Mar–Nov 8hc
CTV 8P S% B&b£4.50–£5

GUILDTOWN Tayside *Perthshire*
Map 11 NO13
INN Angler's Rest Main Rd
☎ Balbeggie 329 Lic 5hc ✖ CTV 40P 🚗
S% ✳B&b£8 sn L£2.50alc
D9.45pm£3.75alc

HELENSBURGH Strathclyde *Dunbartons*
Map 10 NS28
⋈**GH Aveland** 91 East Princes St ☎3040
6hc nc3 CTV 8P S% B&b£4.50–£5.50
Bdi£6.50–£7.50 W£40–£50 ⚓ D6.30pm

HOWMORE South Uist, Western Isles
Inverness-shire Map 13 NF73
GH *Ben Mor* ☎ Grogarry 283 8hc (2A)
9P D7pm

HUNA Highland *Caithness Map 15 NO37*
GH *Haven Gore* ☎ John O'Groats 314
5hc ♨ CTV 8P 🍴 sea D7pm

INVERGARRY Highland *Inverness-shire
Map 14 NH30*
GH Craigard Private Hotel ☎258
Etr–mid Oct Lic 7hc ✖ nc5 CTV 7P
✳B&b£5.15 Bdi£7.80 W£47 ⚓ D7pm

⋈**GH Lundie View** Aberchalder
(3m NE A82) ☎291 6hc CTV 6P 🍴 ♿ S%
B&b£4.50–£5 Bdi£7–£8 W£47–£54
D8pm

INVERMORISTON Highland *Inverness-
shire Map 14 NH41*
GH Tigh Na Bruach
☎ Glenmoriston 51208 Apr–mid Oct
7rm 5hc ✖ nc5 12P lake B&bfr£7.50
Bdifr£11.50 W£62 ⚓ D7pm

INVERNESS Highland *Inverness-shire
Map 14 NH64*
⋈**GH Ardnacoille House** 1A Annfield Rd
☎33451 May–mid Oct 5hc ✖ nc10 CTV
6P 🍴 S% B&b£5–£6 Bdi£8.50–£9.50
W£55–£63 ⚓ D3pm

⋈**GH Arran** 42 Union St ☎32115
7hc TV S% B&b£4.50–£5

GH Craigside 4 Gordon Ter ☎31576
Mar–Nov 6hc ✖ nc9 3P 🍴 S% B&b£6–£7
W£68–£73 ⚓ D7pm

⋈**GH Four Winds** 42 Old Edinburgh Rd
☎30397 Closed Xmas Day & New Years
Day 6hc CTV 15P 🍴 S% B&b£4.50–£5

THE ANGLER'S REST INN,
GUILDTOWN, PERTHSHIRE

This old and comfortably appointed coaching inn, idylically set in
the historic centre of Scotland and close to Scone where Scottish
kings were crowned, offers a relaxing sojourn for the tourist. Located
5¼ miles north of Perth on the A93 Royal Deeside route, the inn is
an ideal stopover before touring the Highlands or West Coast. Noted
for good food, the restaurant serves snacks and meals between 12.00–
2.15 pm and 5.00–9.45 pm.

Open throughout the year under the personal supervision of the
resident proprietor, Charles Webster.

Fishing and golf facilities available locally. Car park for 30 cars.

Telephone: Balbeggie 329

⊶◄**GH Glencairn** 19 Ardross St ☎32965
Closed Dec 10hc CTV 🍴 S%
B&bf4.50–£5.50

⊶◄**GH Lyndale** 2 Ballifeary Rd ☎31529
Mar–Oct 5hc TV 6P S% B&bf4.50–£5.50

GH Moray Park Hotel Island Bank Rd
☎33528 7hc CTV 10P 🍴 river S%
B&bfr£6.20 Bdifr£10.95 W£70.20 ⫧
D7pm

⊶◄**GH Riverside Hotel** 8 Ness Bank
☎31052 9hc ✗ CTV river S% B&bfr£5.50

GH Tigh a' Mhuillinn 2 Kingsmill Gdns
☎38257 6hc CTV 8P S% ✱B&bf5.90
Bdif7.90 W£49 ⫧ D2pm

JEDBURGH Borders *Roxburghs.
Map 12 NT62*
GH Kenmore Bank Oxnam Rd ☎2369
6hc TV 5P 1🏠 🍴 S% ✱B&bfr£5 Bdifr£8
D7.30pm

KELSO Borders *Roxburghs Map 12 NT73*
⊶◄**GH Bellevue** Bowmont St ☎2588
8hc ✗ TV 6P S% B&bf4.50 Bdif7.50

KENSALEYRE Isle of Skye, Highland
Inverness-shire Map 13 NG45
GH *Corriemar House Hotel*
☎ Skeabost Bridge 210 Apr–Sep 9hc TV
20P sea D8pm

KILLIECRANKIE Tayside *Perths
Map 14 NN96*
⊶◄**GH Dalnasgadh House** ☎237
Apr–Oct 6hc ✗ CTV 10P 🍴 S% B&bfr£5.25

KILMARTIN Strathclyde *Argyll
Map 10 NR89*
⊶◄**INN Kilmartin Hotel** ☎250
Lic 5hc CTV 10P 🚻 B&bf5.50–£6

Bdif9.50–£10 W£80 Lf1.60alc
D9pmf4–£5.50

KIRKBEAN Dumfries & Galloway
Dumfriesshire Map 11 NX95
GH Cavens House ☎234
Closed 15Dec–15Jan Lic 6hc 6⇨🛁🍴 ⛺ CTV
500P S% ✱B&bf6 Bdif10 D previous day

KYLE OF LOCHALSH Highland
Ross & Crom Map 13 NG72
⊶◄**GH Retreat** ☎4308 Etr–Oct 14hc TV
13P 2🏠 S% B&bf5–£6

LAIRG Highland *Sutherland Map 14 NC50*
⊶◄**GH Carnbren** ☎2259 Apr–Oct 3hc
TV 4P 🍴 S% B&bf4.50

LAMLASH Isle of Arran, Strathclyde
Bute Map 10 NS03
⊶◄**GH Glenisle Hotel** ☎258
Mid Mar–mid Oct 14hc 3⇨🛁 (A 8hc)
nc3 CTV 18P sea S% B&bf5.25–£5.75
Bdif8.85–£9.75 W£52.50–£57.75 ⫧
D4pm
⊶◄**GH Marine House Hotel** ☎298
Apr–Oct 20rm 19hc 6⇨🛁 CTV 15P 🍴
sea S% B&bf5.67 Bdif7.56 W£54
D6pm

LARGS Strathclyde *Ayrs Map 10 NS25*
See Plan
⊶◄**GH Aubery** 22 Aubery Cres ☎672330
Plan:**1** Apr–Sep 6hc nc3 TV 5P S%
B&bf4.80 Bdif6 W£42 ⫧ D6pm
⊶◄**GH Douglas House** 42 Douglas St
☎672257 Plan:**2** Closed Oct–Apr Lic
14hc ✗ CTV 12P S% B&bf5.50 Bdif7.50
W£52.50 ⫧

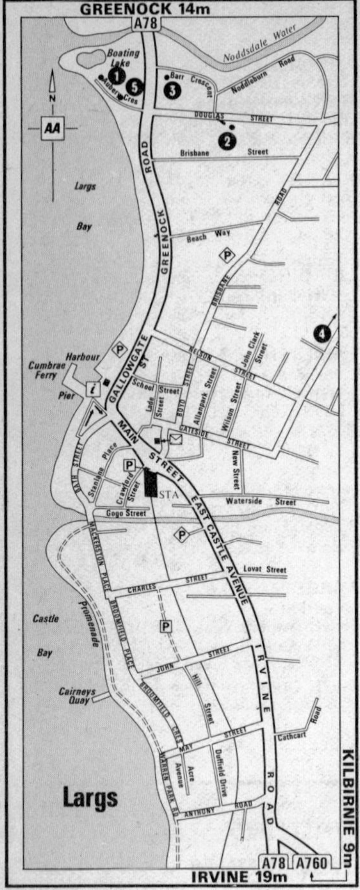

1 Aubery   4 Holmesdale
2 Douglas House   5 Sunbury
3 Gleneldon Hotel

GH Gleneldon Hotel 2 Barr Cres
☎673381 Plan:**3** Mar–Jan Lic 11hc ⚘
CTV 10P 🍴 S% B&bfr£7.50 Bdifr£12

GH Holmesdale 74 Moorburn Rd
☎674793 Plan:**4** Closed Oct 8hc ⚘ nc1
CTV 6P 🍴 S% B&b£4.75 Bdi£7 W£49
£ D9am

GH Sunbury 12 Aubery Cres ☎673086
Plan:**5** May–Oct 6hc ⚘ CTV 8P 🍴 sea S%
B&b£5.50–£6.50 Bdi£8–£8.50
W£56–£60 D6.30pm

LERWICK Shetland *Map 16 HU44*
GH Carradale 36 King Harald St
☎2890 Closed 18Dec–12Jan 4hc CTV
6P sea S% ✽B&b£6 Bdi£9.50 D7pm

GH Glen Orchy Lee Knab Rd ☎2031
6hc ⚘ CTV sea S% B&b£7–£10

GH Solheim ☎3613 4hc CTV sea
B&bfr£5 Bdifr£8 D7pm

LESLIE Fife *Map 11 NO20*
GH Rescobie ☎ Glenrothes 742143
Lic 8hc 3⇆🛏 10P 🍴 ✽B&b£7.50–£9.50
Bdi£11.50–£13.50 D7.30pm

LEYSMILL Tayside *Angus Map 15 NO64*
GH Spynie ☎ Friockheim 328
Closed Oct Lic 5hc TV 7P 🍴 lift S%
B&bfr£5.50 Bdifr£7.50 Wfr£50 £ D10pm

LOCHINVER Highland *Sutherland
Map 14 NCO2*
GH Ardglas ☎257 8hc CTV 15P 🍴
S% B&b£4.25–£4.50

GH Park House Hotel Main St ☎259
Lic 4hc CTV 10P 🍴 river S% B&b£7
W£70 £ D8pm

LOCHRANZA Isle of Arran, Strathclyde
Bute Map 10 NR95
GH Kincardine Lodge ☎267 8hc 6P
lake S% B&b£6.04 Bdi£9.20 W£60.38
£ D4pm

LOCKERBIE Dumfries & Galloway
Dumfriesshire Map 11 NY18
GH Rosehill Carlisle Rd ☎2378
5hc CTV 4P S% B&b£4.25

LUNDIN LINKS Fife *Map 12 NO40*
GH *Elmwood Hotel* Links Rd ☎320397
Mar–Oct Lic 12hc CTV 8P 🍴 sea D7.15pm

MOFFAT Dumfries & Galloway
Dumfriesshire Map 11 NT00
GH Allanton House 22 High St
☎20343 Lic 7hc CTV 5P 🍴 S%
B&b£5–£6.25 Bdi£9 W£80 D8pm

GH Arden House High St ☎20220
Jan–Oct 7hc 4⇆🛏 CTV 9P 🍴 S%
B&b£4.25–£5 Bdi£6.85–£7.25 D6pm

GH Buchan House 13 Beech Gv
☎20378 6hc 2⇆🛏 TV 6P 🍴 S%
B&b£3.75–£4 Bdi£6.25–£6.50
W£43–£48 £ D7pm

GH Craigieburn 14 Selkirk Rd
(2m E on A708) ☎20229
mid Mar–mid Oct Lic 7hc ⚘ TV 10P 🍴
S% B&b£6.50 Bdi£10.50 W£66.50 £
D8.30pm

GH Hartfell House Hartfell Cres
☎20153 Closed Jan & Feb 9hc TV 10P
🍴 S% B&b£4.85–£5.23 Bdi£8.15–£8.80
W£55–£59.40 £ D7pm

GH Rock Hill 14 Beech Gv ☎20283
Mar–Oct 10rm 9hc CTV 🍴 S%
B&b£4–£4.50 Bdi£6.50–£7 W£42–£46
£ D6.30pm

GH St Olaf Eastgate, off Dickson St
☎20001 Etr–Sep 7hc ✽B&b£3.75
Bdi£6.50 D6pm

MONTROSE Tayside *Angus
Map 15 NO75*
GH Linksgate 11 Dorward Rd ☎2273
6hc CTV 6P S% B&bfr£5 Bdifr£6.50
Wfr£45 D6pm

MOODIESBURN Strathclyde *Lanarks
Map 11 NS67*
GH El Ranchero Western
6 Cumbernauld Rd (On A80)
☎ Glenboig 874769 5hc ⚘ CTV 30P
S% B&b£5.25 Bdi£7.50 W£53–£55
D7pm

MOY Highland *Inverness-shire
Map 14 NH73*
GH Invermoy House ☎ Tomatin 271
8rm 7hc ⚘ ⚘ CTV 10P 🍴 lake S%
B&b£4.50–£5 Bdi£7–£7.50
W£45.50–£49 £ D8pm

MUSSELBURGH Lothian *Midlothian*
Map 11 NT37
GH Parsonage 15 High St
☎031-665 4289 7hc 1⇨📶 CTV 10P 🍴
S% B&b£6–£7

NAIRN Highland *Nairns Map 14 NH85*
GH Dun-Craig Glebe Rd, off Marine Rd
☎53345 May–Sep 10hc CTV 12P
B&b£6.25 Bdi£8.50 D7pm
GH *Glen Lyon Lodge* Waverley Rd
☎52780 Etr–Oct Tem 5hc ⊗ nc10 5P 🍴
⋈**GH Greenlawns** 13 Seafield St
☎52738 Etr–Sep 6hc 2⇨📶 CTV 6P S%
B&b£4.50–£5 Bdi£6.50–£7 W£40–£45
Ⱶ D6pm
GH *Lothian House Private Hotel*
10 Crescent Rd ☎53555 Lic 9hc CTV 10P
sea D7pm

GH *Ramleh* ☎53551 Mar–Nov 9hc CTV
10P D noon

NEWTONMORE Highland *Inverness-shire*
Map 14 NN79
⋈**GH Alder Lodge** ☎376 Lic 7rm 6hc
CTV 10P 🍴 S% B&b£5.50 Bdi£8 W£52
Ⱶ D9.30pm
⋈**GH Alvey House Hotel** Golf House Rd
☎260 7hc nc1 TV 10P river S% B&b£5.50
Bdi£8.50 W£56 Ⱶ D7pm
GH Ard-na-Coille Hotel ☎214 Etr–Oct
Lic 13hc 4⇨📶 CTV 20P 🍴 S% B&b£9.40
Bdi£13.35 D7.15pm
⋈**GH Cairn Dearg** Station Rd ☎398
6hc ⚙ CTV 8P S% B&b£5.50–£6
Bdi£8.80–£9.50 W£60–£63 Ⱶ D8pm

GH Coig na Shee Fort William Rd ☎216
Closed Dec 6hc ♨ TV 8P 🍴 S% B&bfr£6
Bdifr£10 Wfr£63 ⚹ D7pm

NEWTON STEWART Dumfries &
Galloway *Wigtowns Map 10 NX46*
⊷**GH Duncree Hotel** Girvan Rd ☎2001
Lic 6hc CTV 30P S% B&b£5–£6
Bdi£7.50–£9 W£52–£63 ⚹ D4.30pm

NORTH BERWICK Lothian *E Lothian*
Map 12 NT58
GH Belhaven Private Hotel Westgate
☎2573 Apr–Sep 6hc sea S% ✳B&bfr£6
Bdifr£10 Wfr£50 ⚹ D6pm

⊷**GH Cragside Private Hotel**
16 Marine Pde ☎2879 Apr–6Oct 6hc
CTV 🍴 sea B&b£5.25 Bdi£8.40 W£52.50
⚹ D6.30pm

OBAN Strathclyde *Argyll Map 10 NM83*
See Plan
⊷**GH Ardblair** Dalriach Rd ☎2668
Plan:**1** May–29Sep 15hc (A 7hc) ✿ CTV
11P B&bfr£4.54 Bdifr£7.78 D6.30pm

⊷**GH Barriemore Private Hotel**
Esplanade ☎2197 Plan:**2** Etr–mid Oct
14hc nc7 CTV 15P S% B&b£5.50–£6.50
Bdi£8–£9.50 D6.45pm

GH Corriemar Hotel Corran Esp ☎2476
Plan:**3** Mar–Sep Lic 18hc CTV 10P sea
S% B&b£6.75–£9.05 Bdi£13.48–£14.77
W£78.48–£92.77 ⚹ D7pm

⊷**GH Crathie** Duncraggen Rd ☎2619
Plan:**4** May–Oct 9hc nc3 CTV 12P sea
B&bfr£5 Bdifr£7 Wfr£46 ⚹ D6.30pm

GH Glenburnie Private Hotel
The Esplanade ☎2089 Plan:**5** May–Oct
15hc ✿ nc8 TV 12P 1🏠
✳B&b£6.33–£8.05

⊷**GH Heatherfield Private Hotel**
Albert Rd ☎2681 Plan:**6** Apr–Oct 10hc
nc5 TV 10P B&b£4.50–£5.50
Bdi£9–£10.10 W£64–£69 ⚹ D7pm

⊷**GH Kenmore** Soraba Rd ☎3592
Plan:**7** 6hc ✿ CTV 20P 1🏠 S% B&b£5

⊷**GH Roseneath** Dalriach Rd ☎2929
Plan:**8** Mar–Oct rs Nov–Feb (B&b only)
Closed Xmas & New Year 10hc CTV 8P 🍴
sea B&b£4.59–£5 Bdi£7–£8.02
W£42–£51 ⚹ W only Jun–Aug D6.30pm

ONICH Highland *Inverness-shire*
Map 14 NN06
⊷**GH Tigh-a-Righ** ☎255
Closed 21Dec–6Jan Lic 5hc CTV 20P 🍴
S% B&b£4.03–£4.60 Bdi£7.25–£8.05
D8pm

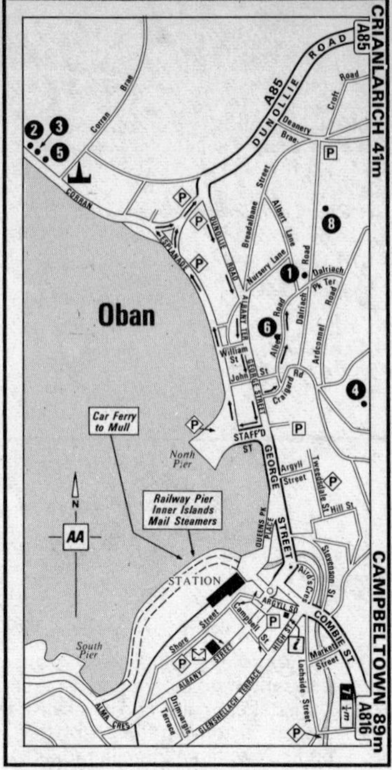

1 Ardblair
2 Barriemore Private
   Hotel
3 Corriemar Hotel
4 Crathie
5 Glenburnie Private
   Hotel
6 Heatherfield
   Private Hotel
7 Kenmore
8 Roseneath

PAISLEY Strathclyde *Renfrews*
Map 11 NS46 For accommodation details
see under Glasgow Airport

PEEBLES Borders *Peebles Map 11 NT24*
⊷**GH Lindores** Old Town ☎20441 5hc
TV 3P 🍴 S% B&b£4.50–£4.75
W£31.50–£33.25 M

PERTH Tayside *Perths Map 11 NO12*
⊷**GH The Darroch** 9 Pitcullen Cres
☎22083 7hc TV 12P 🍴 S% B&bfr£4.50
Bdifr£6.50 Wfr£45.50 ⚹ (W only Oct–May)
D10am

1. Acarsaid Hotel
2. Adderley Private Hotel
3. Balrobin Private Hotel
4. Craig Urrard Hotel
6. Fasganeoin Hotel
7. Poplars Private Hotel
8. Well House Private Hotel

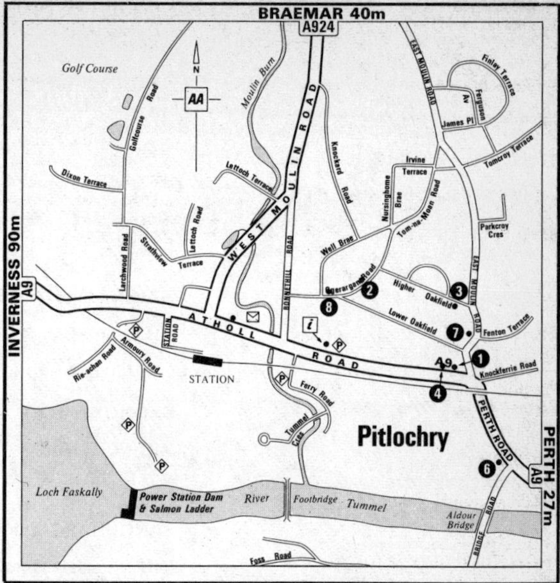

ⵀⵀ**GH Garth** Dundee Rd ☎22368 6hc CTV 8P ▥ S% B&bf4–£5

ⵀⵀ**GH Pitcullen** 17 Pitcullen Cres ☎26506 8hc CTV 10P ▥ B&bfr£4 Bdfr£7 D5pm

PITLOCHRY Tayside *Perths Map 14 NN95* **See Plan**
GH *Acarsaid Hotel* 8 Atholl Rd ☎2389 Plan:**1** Lic 21hc ⚹ TV 20P D7.15pm

GH Adderley Private Hotel 23 Toberargan Rd ☎2433 Plan:**2** Etr–mid Oct 10hc ⚹ nc11 CTV 9P Bdif£9.48–£10.46 Wf£61.32–£70.95 ⵎ D6.30pm

GH Balrobin Private Hotel Higher Oakfield ☎2901 Plan:**3** Jun–Sep 7hc 2⭗🝙 8P S% B&bf£6–£7 Bdif£9–£12 Wf£60–£75 ⵎ D6.45pm

GH Craig Urrard Hotel 10 Atholl Rd ☎2346 Plan:**4** Mar–Nov 12hc 2⭗🝙 (A 2hc) ⚹ nc3 TV 16P S% B&bf£7.02–£9.43 Bdif£10.60–£13.13 Wf£71.30–£87.40 ⵎ D6.45pm

GH Fasganeoin Hotel Perth Rd ☎2387 Plan:**6** May–Sep Lic 9hc TV 20P ▥ S% B&bf7–£7.80 Bdif£10.80–£11.50 D8pm

GH Poplars Private Hotel Lower Oakfield ☎2129 Plan:**7** Mar–Oct Tem 8hc 3⭗🝙 CTV 10P ▥ S% B&bf£6.90–£7.47 Bdif£10.35–£11.50 Wf£71.30–£74.75 D6pm

GH Well House Private Hotel Toberargan Rd ☎2239 Plan:**8** Etr–Oct Lic 8hc ⚹ nc10 CTV 10P S% B&bf£6.50–£6.90

PLOCKTON Highland *Ross & Crom Map 14 NG83*
GH Haven ☎223 15Jan–15Dec 15hc 1⭗🝙 TV 9P ▥ S% B&bfr£6.50 Bdifr£10 Wfr£66.50 ⵎ D8pm

PORT ELLEN Isle of Islay, Strathclyde *Argyll Map 10 NR34*
GH Tighcargaman ☎2345 Lic 3hc 1⭗🝙 (A 6rm 4hc 1⭗🝙) 10P ▥ sea S% B&bf8.50–£11.60 Bdif£14.25–£17.60 Wf£92.25–£109.25 ⵎ D8pm

PORTPATRICK Dumfries & Galloway *Wigtowns Map 10 NX05*
ⵀⵀ**GH Blinkbonnie** School Brae ☎282 Closed Xmas, New Year & Mar 6hc nc4 CTV 10P ▥ B&bf4.40–£4.80 Bdif7–£7.80 Wf£49–£51.20 ⵎ D6pm

⋈**GH Carlton** 21 South Cres ☎253
Mar–Oct 8hc ✻ nc TV 🍽 sea S%
B&bf£5.50–£6 Bdif£7.75–£8.75
W£51.25–£58.25 ⌖ D6pm

⋈**GH Melvin Lodge** Dunskey St ☎238
Etr–Sep 13hc CTV 8P B&bf£5.50–£5.75
Bdif£7.50–£8 W£49–£52 ⌖ D7pm

PORTREE Isle of Skye, Highland
Inverness-shire Map 13 NG44
⋈**GH Bosville** Bosville Ter ☎2846
May–Sep 13hc CTV 8P sea S%
B&bfr£5 Bdi fr£8 D7.45pm

GH *Craiglockhart* Beaumont Cres ☎2233
Mar–Oct 4hc (A 4hc) TV 4P 🍽 ⓗ S%
D7pm

PRESTWICK Strathclyde *Ayrs*
Map 10 NS32
⋈**GH Kincraig Private Hotel** 39 Ayr Rd
☎79480 Lic 7hc ✻ CTV 8P 🍽 S%
B&bf£4.50–£5 Bdif£7.50–£8 Wfr£52
⌖ D6pm

ROSKHILL Isle of Skye, Highland
Inverness-shire Map 13 NG24
⋈**GH Argyll House** Kensalrog
☎ Dunvegan 230 Apr–Oct 6rm 5hc CTV
5P S% B&bf£4.25 Bdif£6.50 D7pm

⋈**GH Roskhill** ☎ Dunvegan 317
Mar–Dec 5hc TV 6P 🍽 river S%
B&bf£4.75–£5 Bdif£8–£8.25 D6pm

ROTHESAY Isle of Bute, Strathclyde
Bute Map 10 NS06
⋈**GH Alva House Private Hotel** 24
Mountstuart Rd ☎2328 May–Oct 7hc
CTV sea S% B&bf£4.50 Bdif£5.50 W£40
⌖ D4pm

GH *Battery Lodge Private Hotel* 25
Battery Pl ☎2169 Closed Oct Lic 9hc
nc18 TV 4P 🍽 sea D6pm

⋈**GH Morningside** Mount Pleasant Rd
☎3526 Apr–mid Oct 9hc CTV 3P S%
B&bf£4.50–£5 Bdif£6.50–£7 W£44–£47
⌖ D6.15pm

⋈**GH St Fillans** 36 Mountstuart Rd
☎2784 Apr–Oct 6hc ✻ nc3 CTV 5P 🍽
sea S% B&bf£4.50–£5 Bdif£6–£6.50
W£40–£44 ⌖ D6pm

ST ANDREWS Fife *Map 12 NO51*
⋈**GH Argyle Hotel** 127 North St
☎73387 Apr–Oct Lic 18hc CTV 🍽 S%
B&bf£5.50–£7 Bdif£8.50–£10
W£55–£70 ⌖ D6pm

⋈**GH Beachway House** 4–6 Murray Pk
☎73319 Closed Dec 11hc CTV 🍽 S%
B&bf£4.25–£6 Bdif£7–£9 W£45–£59
⌖ W only Jul & Aug D1pm

GH Cleveden House 3 Murray Pl
☎74212 6hc ✻ CTV 2OP S%
✳B&bf£4.50–£5.50

⋈**GH Craigmore** 3 Murray Pk ☎72142
Apr–mid Dec rs Jan–Mar 12hc CTV 🍽
B&bf£5.75 Bdif£9 W£58.50 ⌖ D6.15pm

⋈**GH Hazelbank Private Hotel** The
Scores ☎72466 Mar–Nov 10hc ✻ CTV
🍽 sea B&bf£4.60–£7.50 Bdif£7–£9
W£45–£58 ⌖ D6pm

⋈**GH Lorimer House** 19 Murray Pk
☎76599 Apr–Oct 4hc nc2 CTV 🍽
B&bf£4.50–£5.50 Bdif£7–£8 W£47–£54
⌖ D3.30pm

⋈**GH Nithsdale Hotel** The Scores
☎75977 Mar–Nov Lic 9hc CTV 🍽 sea
B&bf£5–£8 Bdif£8–£10 W£50–£65 ⌖
D6.30pm

GH Yorkston Hotel 68–70 Argyle St
☎72019 Lic 12hc CTV 🍽 B&bf£6–£9
Bdif£10–£14 W£70–£90 ⌖ D7.30pm

ST CATHERINE'S Strathclyde *Argyll*
Map 10 NN00
GH Thistle House ☎209 Etr–Oct 6hc
nc8 10P 🍽 ✳B&bfr£6.32

ST OLA Orkney *Map 16 HY40*
GH Foveran ☎ Kirkwall 2389
Closed Oct Lic 10hc CTV 12P 🍽 S%
B&bf£9–£10 Bdi £13–£14 W£85–£95
⌖ D9pm

SALEN Isle of Mull, Strathclyde
Argyll Map 10 NM54
GH Craig Hotel ☎ Aros 347 Lic
7hc 7P 🍽 sea S% B&bf£8.75–£10.75
Bdif£12.50–£14 D6pm

SANNOX Isle of Arran, Strathclyde *Bute*
Map 10 NS04
⋈**GH Cliffdene** ☎ Corrie 224 Closed Nov
5hc ✻ TV 6P sea S% B&bf£4.54
Bdif£6.70 W£46.87 ⌖

SANQUHAR Dumfries & Galloway
Dumfriesshire Map 11 NS71
INN Nithsdale Hotel High St ☎506
Lic 6hc CTV 🍽 S% B&bf£6.50 Bdif£10
W£63 ⌖ sn L£2.20–£5 D8.30pm
£3.50–£6

SEAMILL Strathclyde *Ayrs Map 10 NS24*
INN Galleon Ardrossan Rd
☎ West Kilbride 822121 Closed New
Year's Day Lic 7hc ✻ CTV 24P 🍽 sea
B&bf£8–£9 Bdif£12–£12.50 sn L£3.50–
£5&alc D8.30pm£5&alc

SOUTH ERRADALE Highland *Ross &*
Crom Map 13 NG77
GH Glendale ☎ Badachro 256 Lic 9hc
5⇄🍽 CTV 15P 🍽 S% B&bf£6.50–£7.25
Bdif£10–£12.50 W£65–£75 ⌖ D9pm

SOUTH LAGGAN Highland *Inverness-*
shire Map 14 NN29
GH *Forest Lodge* ☎ Invergarry 219
Apr–Oct 6hc ✻ nc3 CTV 8P 🍽 lake
D7.30pm

SPEAN BRIDGE Highland
Inverness-shire Map 14 NN28
⋈**GH Coire Glas** ☎272 Mar–Oct 15hc
TV 2OP 🍽 S% B&bf£4–£4.29
Bdif£6.75–£7.15 W£47.25–£50.05 ⌖
D7pm

⋈**GH Lesanne** ☎231 Feb–Nov 5hc ✻
nc2 TV 8P S% B&bf£4.50–£5.25
Bdif£6.75–£8 D6.30pm

STORNOWAY Isle of Lewis, Western Isles
Ross & Crom Map 13 NB43
⋈**GH Ardlonan** 29 Francis St ☎3482
5rm 3hc ✻ TV 🍽 S% B&bfr£5

GH *Hebridean* 61 Bayhead ☎2268 6hc
TV D2pm (Sun only)

⋈**GH Park** 30 James St ☎2485 7rm
5hc (A 2hc) CTV 🍽 S% B&bfr£5

STRANRAER Dumfries & Galloway
Wigtowns Map 10 NX05
⋈**GH Lochview** 52 Agnew Cres ☎3837
6hc CTV 6P S% B&bf£4.50–£5
Bdif£6.50–£7.50 D noon

STRATHAVEN Strathclyde *Lanarks*
Map 11 NS74
GH *Springvale Hotel* 18 Letham Rd ☎21131 Lic 5hc (A 6hc) CTV 6P ⚲ D7.30pm

STRATHPEFFER Highland *Ross & Crom*
Map 14 NH45
⟼**GH Kilvannie Manor** Fodderty ☎389 Apr–Aug Lic 8hc ⊘ ♨ CTV 12P S% B&b£4.50–£5.50 Bdi£8–£9.50 W£56–£66.50 D7pm

⟼**GH Rosslyn Lodge Private Hotel** ☎281 Feb–Nov Tem 15rm 14hc ♨ CTV 20P ⚲ B&b fr£4.80 Bdi fr£9 Wfr£58 ʟ D6.30pm

STRATHYRE Central *Perths Map 11 NN51*
INN Strathyre ☎224 Lic 6hc 6🛁 30P 2🏠 ⚲ ⊘ ✻B&b£9.18 Bdi£14.04 W£60.48 M sn L£1.67–£4.65&alc D10.30pm £1.67–£4.65&alc

STROMNESS Orkney *Map 16 HY20*
GH Oakleigh Private Hotel Victoria St ☎850447 Lic 3hc ⊘ CTV sea ✻B&b£5.94–£6.48 Bdi£7.56–£8.64 W£64.80–£70.20 ʟ D5pm

SWINTON Borders *Berwicks*
Map 12 NT84
INN *Wheatsheaf Hotel* Main St ☎257 Lic 4hc CTV 15P D9.30pm

TARBET Strathclyde *Dunbartons*
Map 10 NN30
GH Edendarroch ☎ Arrochar 223 Mar–Oct 7hc CTV 20P ⚲ S% Bdi£11.50–£12.65 W£80.50–£88.55 ʟ D8.30pm

TOBERMORY Isle of Mull, Strathclyde
Argyll Map 13 NM55
GH Suidhe Hotel 59 Mains St ☎2209 Mar–Oct Lic 9hc 1🛁 ⊘ CTV 9P ⚲ sea ✻B&b£8–£9 Bdi£11.50–£12.50 W£77–£84 ʟ D7pm

GH Tobermory 53 Main St ☎2091 Closed Xmas 11hc CTV S% ✻B&b£7.35 Bdi£10.92 W£69 ʟ D7.30pm

TROON Strathclyde *Ayrs Map 10 NS33*
GH *Glenside* Bentinck Dr ☎313677 Closed Oct 6hc CTV 6P ⊘

GH Troon 5 Bentinck Dr ☎311177 9hc 1🛁 CTV 12P ⚲ B&b£6.50–£8 W£39–£56 M

WAMPHRAY Dumfries & Galloway
Dumfriesshire Map 11 NY19
⟼**GH Manse Country** ☎ Johnstone Bridge 367 May–Oct 5hc ⊘ TV 20P ⚲ river B&b£5–£5.50 Bdi£9–£10 W£63–£68.50 D7pm

WATERLOO Isle of Skye, Highland
Inverness-shire Map 13 NG62
⟼**GH Ceol-na-Mara** ☎ Broadford 323 Etr–Sep 5hc TV 6P sea S% B&b£5–£5.60 Bdi£9.50–£10.50 W£56–£60 ʟ D8pm

WEST LINTON Borders *Peebleshire*
Map 11 NT15
⟼**GH Rutherford Coaching House** ☎231 6hc CTV 12P ⚲ S% B&b£5–£6.50 Bdi£7.75–£9.50 W£53–£64 ʟ D8.30pm

WHITING BAY Isle of Arran, Strathclyde
Bute Map 10 NS02
⟼**GH Trareoch Hotel** Largie Beg ☎226 Mar–Oct Lic 12hc ♨ CTV 20P S% B&b£6.32 Bdi£8.62

Details for islands off the mainland of Scotland are shown under the individual placename. A useful first point of reference is to consult the location maps which show where farmhouses are located.

ABERFELDY Tayside *Perths*
Map 14 NN84
Tom of Cluny *(NN875515)* ☎477
Small hillside farmhouse reached by long steep tarmac/rough drive. Magnificent views southward across the River Tay and Aberfeldy.
3rm CTV P 120acres mixed S% B&b£4.50 Bdi£6.50 D6pm

ABINGTON Strathclyde *Lanarks*
Map 11 NS92
Craighead *(NS914236)* ☎256 (from 1980 Crawford 356)
Large farm building in courtyard design. Set amid rolling hills on the banks of the River Duneaton. Main building dates from 1780. Off unclass Crawfordjohn rd, 1m N of A74/A73 junc.
May–Sep 3rm ♨ CTV 6P 2🏠 ⚲ river 814acres mixed S% B&b£4 Bdi£6 W£40 ʟ D6pm

Crawfordjohn Mill *(NS897242)* Crawfordjohn ☎ Crawfordjohn 248
Two storey, brown brick farmhouse. Set in its own land. 4m W off A74.
May–mid Oct 3rm TV 4P ⚲ 180acres dairy S% B&b£4 Bdi£6 W£40 ʟ D7pm

ACHARACLE Highland *Argyll*
Map 13 NM66
Dalilea House *(NM735693)* ☎ Salen 253
A splendid turretted house with surrounding grounds giving excellent views over farmland, hills and Loch Shiel. A blend of the ancient and modern.
Apr–Oct 6hc P lake 1300acres beef sheep S% B&b fr£7.47 Bdi fr£11.50 Wfr£72.45 ʟ D7pm

ANNAN Dumfries & Galloway
Dumfriesshire Map 11 NY16
Beechgrove *(NY213652)* ☎2220
Attractive redstone house with attractive garden, surrounded by pastureland. Views of Solway Firth.
3hc TV 12P sea 78acres beef D7pm

ARDBRECKNISH Strathclyde *Argyll*
Map 10 NN02
Rockhill *(NN072219)* ☎ Kilchrenan 218
Loch shore farm. Trout and perch fishing (free) and on the farms private loch by arrangement.
Etr–Sep 6hc nc6 8P ⚲ lake 200acres sheep horses S% B&b£6.50–£7.50 Bdi£9–£10 W£55–£65 ʟ D7pm

ARDEN Strathclyde *Dunbartons*
Map 10 NS38
Mid Ross *(NS359859)* ☎655
Farmhouse pleasantly located 6 miles from Helensburgh. E off A82.
May–mid Oct 3hc CTV P ⚲ lake 32acres mixed S% B&b£4–£5

ARDERSIER Highland *Inverness-shire*
Map 14 NH75
Milton of Gollanfield *(NH809534)* ☎2207
Stone farmhouse set on north side of A96 5 miles west of Nairn.
Apr–Oct 3rm 2hc ⊘ CTV P 365acres mixed S% B&b£4.50–£8

ARDFERN Strathclyde *Argyll*
Map 10 NM80
Corranbeg *(NM801045)* ☎ Barbreck 207
Large rambling farmhouse in quiet spot
surrounded by beautiful scenery.
Etr–Oct 3rm ⚹ P lake 208acres mixed
S% B&b fr£3.75 Bdi fr£8.62 W fr£60.38
(W only Aug)
Traighmhor *(NM800039)* ☎ Barbreck 228
Etr–Oct 3rm ⚹ nc5 CTV 3P S%
✳B&b£4.50 Bdi£8 D8.30pm

AUCHENCAIRN Dumfries & Galloway
Kirkcudbrights Map 11 NX75
Bluehill *(NX786515)* ☎228
Farm offers panoramic views overlooking
the Solway Firth and the English
lakeland hills.
Etr–Sep 4hc ⚹ nc5 CTV 6P ▥ sea
120acres dairy S% B&b£5–£5.25
Bdi£8 D6pm

AYR Strathclyde *Ayrs Map 10 NS32*
Trees *(NS386186)* ☎ Joppa 270
Comfortable accommodation in a quiet
location. 4m E on unclass rd, between
A70 and A713.
May–Sep 3rm ⚹ CTV P ▥ 125acres
mixed S% B&b£4 Bdi£7 W£49 ⚹
D4pm

BALFRON STATION Central *Stirlings*
Map 11 NS58
Clachanry *(NS512888)* ☎ Balfron 335
Pleasant little hillside farmhouse with
reasonable access from the main road.
Apr–Sep 3rm ⚹ TV 3P ▥ 135acres mixed

BALNAGUARD Tayside *Perthshire*
Map 14 NN95
Balmacneil *(NN979507)* ☎ Ballinluig 213
Modern bungalow on hillside of west
bank of River Tay. Good views of South
Down & Tay Valley.
Mar–Nov 2hc CTV 2P 1🏠 ▥ river
2,600acres arable, beef, mixed & sheep
D6pm

BANAVIE Highland *Inverness-shire*
Map 14 NN17
Burnside *(NN138805)* Muirshearlich
☎ Corpach 275
Small, stone-built farmhouse with open
views over Caledonian Canal, loch and Ben
Nevis. 3m NE off B8004.
Apr–Sep 3hc CTV 3P 69acres mixed S%
B&b£4–£4.50 Bdi£6–£6.50 W£40–£43
⚹ D7pm

BARBRECK Strathclyde *Argyll*
Map 10 NM80
Glenview *(NM841079)* Turnalt Farm
☎277
Apr–Oct 4rm ⚹ CTV 4P 3,500acres
sheep S% ✳B&b fr£4.50 Bdi fr£8
W fr£56 ⚹ D6pm

BEESWING Dumfries & Galloway
Kirkcudbrights Map 11 NX86
Garloff *(NX912702)* ☎ Lochfoot 225
Pleasant farmhouse set at end of farm road
on south east side of A711 6m west of
Dumfries.
6hc TV 12P ▥ 220acres dairy D5pm

BOGHEAD Strathclyde *Lanarks*
Map 11 NS74
Dykehead *(NS772417)*
☎ Lesmahagow 892226
Roughcast, two-storey farmhouse just
fifty yards from Strathaven/Lesmahagow
road.
Mar–Oct 2rm CTV P ▥ 200acres dairy
sheep S% ✳B&b£4

BORVE Isle of Barra, Western Isles
Inverness-shire Map 13 NF60
Ocean View *(NF655014)* ☎ Castlebay 397
Detached bungalow standing in natural
farmland facing west over Atlantic Ocean.
3rm ⚹ P sea 2¾acres D6pm

BRECHIN Tayside *Angus Map 15 NO56*
Blibberhill *(NO553568)* ☎ Aberlemno 225
Well maintained, two storey farmhouse
with attractive gardens.
3hc ⚹ CTV P 300acres arable beef S%
B&b fr£4 Bdi fr£6

Wood of Auldbar *(NO554556)* Aberlemno
☎ Aberlemno 218
Fairly large farmhouse well back from road
amid farmland and woods. 5m SW on
unclass rd, between B9134 and A932.
3rm TV P ▥ 187acres arable S%
B&b£4–£4.50 Bdi£6–£6.50

BROADFORD Isle of Skye, Highland
Inverness-shire Map 13 NG62
Alltan *(NG655230)* 10 Harrapool ☎324
Small farmhouse with sea views.
3rm 2hc P sea 12acres mixed

BUCHLYVIE Central *Stirlings*
Map 11 NS59
Balwill *(NS548927)* ☎239
White-painted farmhouse and buildings
set off main road in the upper Forth Valley
Etr–Oct 4rm 1hc ⚹ TV 4P 200acres beef &
sheep D6pm

Rockhill Farm Guesthouse

Ardbrecknish, By Dalmally,
Argyll PA33 1BH
Tel: 086 63 218

Rockhill is situated on the south-east shore of
Lochawl, and commands panoramic views of
Cruachan Mountain. Breeding Hanovarian horses
and sheep. Attractively modernised farmhouse.
Peaceful holidays, beautiful surroundings, first
class home cooking. Guests keep returning.
Facilities include Loch fishing, and guests may
bring their own boat, hill walking and pony
trekking in the area. Fire certificate granted. SAE
please for comprehensive brochure.

BUCKIE Grampian *Banffs Map 15 NJ46*
Mill of Rathven *(NJ446657)* ☎31132
*Farmhouse with attractive garden. On edge
of village of Rathven and surrounded by
arable land and several outbuildings.*
3rm CTV 2🏠 200acres arable S%
B&b£6.50–£7.50 Bdi£9–£10

BURNHOUSE Strathclyde *Ayrs
Map 10 NS35*
Burnhouse Manor *(NS383503)*
☎ Dunlop 406
*Large farmhouse in own grounds. Visible
and well signposted from main Paisley/
Irvine road. Off B706.*
Closed Sun, Mon (Oct–Feb) & Mon
(Mar–Sep) 7hc CTV 40P 🍴 160acres
beef B&b£5.75 Bdi£9.75 W£37.50 M
D8.30pm

CARRONBRIDGE Central *Stirlings
Map 11 NS78*
Lochend *(NS759856)* ☎ Denny 822778
*Modernised, 18th century hill farm.
Pleasant farmyard with rose garden in
centre set in quiet, isolated position.*
Closed Oct–Jun 2rm 1hc ⊗ nc5 TV P 🍴
380acres beef sheep S% B&b£4.75

CARRUTHERSTOWN Dumfries &
Galloway *Dumfriesshire Map 11 NY17*
Domaru *(NY093716)* ☎260
*Modern, detached, two storey farmhouse
built at side of farm road. About 300 yards
from farm buildings. Carrutherstown ½ mile.*
3rm nc10 TV 3P 🍴 sea 140acres dairy S%
B&bfr£4 Bdifr£6 W£42 ⽊ D8pm

CAWDOR Highland *Nairns Map 14 NH85*
Little Budgate *(NH834503)* ☎267
*Small, cottage style farmhouse set amid
fields. Cawdor 1 mile.*
May–Sep 2rm (A 2hc) ⊗ P 50acres arable
S% B&b£3.50

CHAPELTOWN Strathclyde *Lanarks
Map 11 NS64*
East Drumloch *(NS678521)* ☎236
*Large stone built farmhouse with a
modern, well furnished interior.*
3rm 1hc CTV 20P 🍴 260acres beef S%
B&b£4–£4.25 D9pm
Millwell *(NS653496)*
☎ East Kilbride 43248
*Small, 18th century farm set in
tree-studded land.*
4rm CTV 93acres dairy

CLACHAN Isle of Sky, Highland
Inverness-shire Map 13 NG46
Windyridge *(NG492666)* ☎ Staffin 222
*Small, white painted croft with blue tiled
roof. At north end of island in a very
pleasant situation.*
May–Oct 3rm ⊗ nc5 TV 12P 🍴 10acres
sheep S% B&b£3.50–£4 Bdi£5.75–£6
D7pm

CLARENCEFIELD Dumfries & Galloway
Dumfriesshire Map 11 NY06
Kirkbeck *(NY083705)* ☎284
*Attractive farmhouse with a high standard
of decor. Near to Solway coast. Fishing
and golf. N on A724.*
Etr–Oct 2hc ⊗ CTV 2P 🍴 107acres
arable pigs S% B&b£4 Bdi£6.50 W£42
⽊ D8pm

COLPY Grampian *Aberdeens
Map 15 NJ63*
Old Inn *(NJ644313)* ☎213
*Attractive roadside farmhouse with several
outbuildings. On main Aberdeen/Huntly
road.*
4rm 🐕 TV 6P lake 130acres arable beef
& sheep D6.30pm

COMRIE Tayside *Perths Map 11 NN72*
West Ballindalloch *(NN744262)* ☎282
*Cosy, small farmhouse with neat garden
set amid hills in secluded glen. Comrie
4 miles.*
4Apr–10Oct 2rm ⊗ CTV 3P 1500acres
sheep S% B&b£3.75

CROIK Highland *Ross & Crom
Map 14 NH49*
Forest *(NH454914)* ☎ The Craigs 322
*Two-into-one 1870 farmhouse. Beautiful
location but very isolated. 10 miles of
single track road from Ardgay.*
May–Oct 3rm ⊗ 🐕 TV 4P river 900acres
mixed S% B&b£3.50 Bdi£6.50 D9.30pm

CULLODEN MOOR Highland *Inverness-
shire Map 14 NH74*
Culdoich *(NH755435)* ☎268
*18th century, two storey farmhouse in
isolated position near Culloden Battlefield
and Clava standing stones.*
Etr–Oct 2rm ⊗ TV P 200acres mixed S%
B&b£4–£4.50 Bdi£6–£6.50 W£40–£42
⽊ D7.30pm

CUSHNIE Grampian *Aberdeens
Map 15 NJ51*
Brae Smithy Croft *(NJ520108)*
☎ Muir of Fowlis 215
*Approach from A980 (3m) W or B9119
(3m) N.*
Apr–Sep 3rm CTV P 🍴 20acres arable
S% B&b£3 Bdi£5

DALGUISE Tayside *Perths
Map 14 NN94*
Easter Dalguise *(NN994470)*
☎ Dunkeld 206
*18th century farmhouse set on hillside
overlooking valley of the Tay and hills
beyond.*
May–Sep 2rm ⊗ nc3 4P 🍴 river 130acres
mixed S% B&b£4 Bdi£7 W£45 ⽊ D6pm

DAVIOT Highland *Inverness-shire
Map 14 NN74*
Craggiemore *(NH735396)* ☎225
*Modern farmhouse situated 1m from
main road.*
May–Oct 3hc TV 3P 🍴 120acres mixed
S% B&b£4

DORNIE Highland *Ross & Crom
Map 14 NG82*
Bungalow *(NG871272)* Ardelve ☎231
Farmhouse situated on main A87.
Apr–Sep 3hc ⊗ nc7 3P mixed S%
B&b£4.50–£5.50

DOUNBY Orkney *Map 16 HY22*
Chinyan *(HY307200)* ☎ Harray 372
*Small farm cottage overlooking Loch
Harray. Free loch fishing.*
2rm ⊗ 🐕 TV P lake 342acres arable beef
S% B&b£4 Bdi£7 W£50 ⽊ D2pm

DUNLOP Strathclyde *Ayrs Map 10 NS44*
Old Struther *(NS412496)* ☎346
Large farmhouse in its own gardens.
On edge of Dunlop village.
6hc TV 6P 50acres non-working S%
✳B&b£5.50–£6.50 Bdi£8.50–£9.50
W£56–£63 ⌀

DUNSYRE Strathclyde *Lanarks*
Map 11 NT04
Dunsyre Mains *(NT074482)* ☎251
3rm 2hc ⊗ ⚘ CTV P 400acres arable
beef sheep S% B&b£4.25 Bdi£7 Wfr£47
⌀ D5pm

DUNVEGAN Isle of Skye, Highland
Inverness-shire Map 13 NG24
Feorlig House *(NG297422)* ☎232
Two storey, white painted farmhouse
dating from 1820. Situated off main road
looking onto Loch Caroy.
May–Sep 3rm TV 4P sea 1112acres beef
sheep S% B&b£4.50–£5 Bdi£7.50–£8
W£49–£55 ⌀ D8pm

DURNESS Highland *Sutherland*
Map 14 NC46
Ceol-Na-Mara *(NC421667)* Lerin ☎240
Small white painted farmhouse standing
in rocky hill country. Overlooks sea and
mouth of Loch Erriboll.
May–Sep 5rm 2hc (A 2rm) ⊗ nc8 8P sea
21acres sheep S% B&b£5

EAGLESFIELD Dumfries & Galloway
Dumfriesshire Map 11 NY27
Newlands *(NY240741)* ☎ Kirtlebridge 269
Attractive white faced farmhouse in
secluded position. At end of ½ mile drive.
May–Oct 2hc TV 2P ▥ 150acres beef
sheep S% B&b fr£4.50 Bdi fr£7

EAST MEY Highland *Caithness*
Map 15 ND37
Glenearn *(ND307739)* ☎ Barrock 608
Small croft situated on the main coast
road. Thurso 15 miles.
Etr–Oct 4rm 2hc 2⇆▥ CTV 4P ▥ sea
7½acres mixed S% B&b£4–£4.50
Bdi£6–£7 W£40–£46 ⌀ D4pm

EDINBURGH Lothian *Midlothian*
Map 11 NT27
Tower Mains *(NT267693)*
Liberton Brae ☎031-664 1765
Farmhouse in its own grounds on
residential area, but backed by farmland.
Overlooks golf course, city centre at
Arthur's seat.
5hc CTV 15P ▥ 200acres arable S%
B&b£4.60–£5 Bdi£7.20 W£48 ⌀ D7pm

ETTRICK Borders *Selkirks Map 11 NT21*
Thirlestane Hope *(NT285167)*
☎ Ettrick Valley 229
Quaint, white painted farm in border hill
country. Small burn flows through farmland.
Good access by ¾ mile track.
Closed Dec–Mar 2rm TV P 900acres sheep
S% B&b fr£4.50 Bdi fr£7 D6.30pm

FINTRY Central *Stirlings Map 11 NS68*
Nether Glinns *(NS606883)* ☎207
Well maintained farmhouse situated among
rolling hills. Access via signposted ½ mile
gravel drive.
May–Sep 3rm CTV P 2🏠 150acres arable
dairy S% B&b£4

FOCHABERS Grampian *Moray*
Map 15 NJ35
Castle Hill *(NJ310605)* ☎820351
Small farmhouse 200 yards off A96,
3 miles from Fochabers.
Mar–Oct 2rm ⊗ TV P 100acres mixed

FYVIE Grampian *Aberdeens*
Map 15 NJ73
Macterry *(NJ786424)* ☎555
Two storey farmhouse with adjoining
farm buildings in rural setting.
May–Oct 2rm ⊗ nc3 TV 2P 105acres
mixed S% B&b fr£4 Bdi fr£7 Wfr£49
⌀ D10am

GLENMAVIS Strathclyde *Lanarks*
Map 11 NS76
Braidenhill *(NS742673)*
☎ Glenboig 872319
300 year old farmhouse on the outskirts
of Coatbridge. About ½ mile from town
boundary. N off B803.
3hc CTV 3P ▥ 50acres arable S%
B&b£4.50–£5

HAUGH OF URR Dumfries & Galloway
Kirkcudbrights Map 11 NX86
Markfast *(NX817682)* ☎220
Pleasant farmhouse with attractive
appearance.
3rm ⊗ TV 3P 140acres beef S% B&b£4
Bdi£6.50 W£45.50 ⌀

HELENSBURGH Strathclyde *Dunbartons*
Map 10 NS28
Duirland *(NS299872)* Glen Fruin ☎3370
A comfortably-sized farmhouse situated
away from main road.
Jun–15Sep 3hc ⊗ nc5 CTV 5P 2🏠
775acres mixed S% B&b£4

HOLLYBUSH Strathclyde *Ayrs*
Map 10 NS31
Borland *(NS400139)* ☎ Patna 228
Two-storey building with roughcast
exterior. West off A713 south of village.
Jun–Sep 2rm ⊗ TV P ▥ 105acres dairy
S% B&b£4.50–£5

HUNTLY Grampian *Aberdeens*
Map 15 NJ53
Burnend *(NJ518383)* ☎2956
Old, attractive farmhouse with modern
extensions. Well tended flower and
vegetable gardens. Huntly 1½ miles.
May–Oct 3rm 1hc ⊗ 6P 3acres
non-working S% B&b£5–£6

INVERGARRY Highland *Inverness-shire*
Map 14 NH30
Ardgarry *(NH286015)* Faichem ☎226
Farmhouse with converted outbuildings
in a quiet position off A87.
2rm 1hc (A 3hc) CTV 8P 10acres mixed
S% B&b fr£4.50 Bdi fr£8 Wfr£56 ⱠK
D6.30pm

INVERURIE Grampian *Aberdeens*
Map 15 NJ72
Auchencleith *(NJ760264)*
☎ Wartle 232
Small, pleasant farmhouse with several
outbuildings. 4 miles north of Inverurie
off B9001.
Apr–Oct 2rm 1hc TV 3P 250acres S%
B&b£3.50–£4.50 Bdi£5–£6 D6pm

KEITH Grampian *Banffs Map 15 NJ45*
Haughs *(NJ416515)* ☎2238
Attractively decorated farmhouse. 1 mile
from Keith off A96.
15May–5Oct 4hc ⊗ CTV 6P 2⌂ 220acres
mixed S% B&b£4.25–£4.50 W£28–£29
M

Mains of Tarrycroys *(NJ404537)*
Aultmore ☎2586
Attractive stone farmhouse with large
farmyard and several outbuildings
surrounded by arable land.
4rm 2hc ⊗ nc5 TV 5P 43acres arable
dairy S% B&b£4.25 Bdi£6 W£36 D5pm

Montgrew *(NJ453517)* ☎2852
Farmhouse with several outbuildings and
pleasant views. 2m E off A95.
4rm 1hc CTV 4P 211acres arable beef
S% B&b fr£3.50 Bdi fr£5 Wfr£35 ⱠK
D6.30pm

Tarnash House *(NJ442490)* ☎2728
Two storey, stone farmhouse with well
maintained garden to the front. Surrounded
by farmland. 1m S off A96.
May–Oct 4hc CTV 12P 1⌂ ▥ 100acres
arable S% B&b£4.50 W£29.50 M

KILBIRNIE Strathclyde *Ayrs*
Map 10 NS35
Place *(NS303543)* Largs Rd ☎3287
Attractive farmhouse with modern extension
set in pleasant countryside. Kilbirnie ½ mile.
Etr–Oct 3hc ⊗ TV 8P 220acres beef

KILMACOLM Strathclyde *Renfrews*
Map 10 NS36
Pennytersal *(NS338714)* ☎2349
Well maintained building and courtyard
set in rolling farmland. Kilmacolm 2 miles.
Etr–Sep 3rm 2hc ⊗ TV P 125acres mixed
S% B&b£4.25

KILTARLITY Highland *Inverness-shire*
Map 14 NH54
Glebe *(NH513415)* ☎252
A comfortable, well furnished farmhouse
½ mile off A833.
May–Sep 2rm ⊗ nc10 CTV P 63acres
arable mixed S% B&b fr£3.75

KINCARDINE-ON-FORTH Fife
Map 11 NS98
Kennels *(NS944880)* Tulliallan ☎30277
One-level cottage in attractive gardens, set
amid woodlands. Small loch behind the
house. Numerous forest walks.
2rm CTV 6P ▥ 1¼acres non-working D noon

KING EDWARD Grampian *Aberdeens*
Map 15 NJ75
Blackton *(NJ726583)* ☎205
A well run working farm catering for
family holidays. Banff 6 miles.
May–Oct 5hc ⌂ CTV 6P 113acres arable
beef S% B&b£4 Bdi£6.50 W£45.50 ⱠK
(W only Jul–Aug) D6pm

KINGSWELLS Grampian *Aberdeens*
Map 15 NJ80
Kingshill *(NJ868055)*
☎ Aberdeen 740618
Modernised and extended farm cottage
on quiet road and set amid farmlands.
Centre of Aberdeen about 4 miles.
3hc ⌂ CTV 3P ▥ 200acres arable dairy
S% B&b£4–£5 Bdi fr£7 D6pm

KIPPEN Central *Stirlings Map 11 NS69*
Powblack *(NS670970)* ☎260
Pleasant farmhouse near the River Forth
on the Kippen to Doune road.
May–Sep 2hc CTV 3P ▥ 300acres mixed
S% B&b£4.50–£5

KIRKCONNEL Dumfries & Galloway
Dumfriesshire Map 11 NS71
Niviston *(NS691135)* ☎346
Pleasant, well maintained farm delightfully
set in elevated position overlooking
Nethsdale.
May–Sep 2rm CTV P 1⌂ river 345acres
beef sheep S% B&b£3.50 Bdi£6 W£40
ⱠK D noon

KIRKHILL Highland *Inverness-shire*
Map 14 NH54
Cononbank *(NH542447)*
☎ Drumchardine 216
Well decorated farmhouse, 2½ miles South
of Beauly on A9.
May–Sep 4rm 2hc 6P ▥ 1,500acres dairy

Wester Moniack *(NH551438)*
☎ Drumchardine 237
Small, modern, two storey house with a
relaxing tranquil atmosphere.
Apr–Oct 2hc CTV P ▥ 1000acres dairy
mixed S% B&b£3.75–£4 Bdi£5.75–£6
W£40–£42 ⱠK D5pm

KIRKTON OF DURRIS Grampian
Kincardines Map 15 NO79
Wester Durris Cottage *(NO769962)*
☎ Crathes 638 May–mid Oct 2rm 4P
300acres arable S% B&b£3.75–£4

KIRKWALL Orkney *Map 16 HY41*
Heathfield *(HY413108)* St Ola ☎2378
Two-storey, stone farmhouse on a gently
sloping hill. There are distant views over
Scapa Flow.
Feb–Oct 4hc ⊗ TV 8P ▥ 500acres dairy
& sheep

LAIRG Highland *Sutherland*
Map 14 NC50
Alt-Na-Sorag *(NC547123)*
14 Achnairn ☎2058
Attractive farmhouse with good views of
Loch Shin. Lairg 5 miles.
May–Sep 2rm CTV 3P lake 50acres mixed
S% B&b£4

No 5 Tirryside *(NC570110)* ☎2332
May–Sep 3rm CTV 3P 50acres mixed
S% ✱B&b£4.20

Woodside *(NC533147)* West Shinness
☎2072
Homely house surrounded by fields and
overlooking Loch Shin. Lairg about 7 miles.
May–Sep 3rm ⌘ CTV 4P 360acres mixed
S% B&b£4

LATHERON Highland *Caithness*
Map 15 ND13
Upper Latheron *(ND195352)* ☎224
Two storey house in elevated position
with fine views out across North Sea.
Farm also incorporates a pony stud.
May–Sep 4rm 1⇦🏠⌘ CTV 4P sea
200acres arable beef sheep S%
B&b£3.50–£4.50

LAWERS Tayside *Perths Map 11 NN63*
Croftintygan *(NN676389)* ☎234
Secluded stone farmhouse standing on
hillside with dramatic views over Loch Tay.
Between A827 and Lochside.
May–Sep 6rm 4hc TV lake 3,000acres
mixed

LINLITHGOW Lothian *W Lothian*
Map 11 NS97
Woodcockdale *(NS973760)* Lanark Rd
☎2088
Modern two storey house lying about
50 yards from farmyard and outbuildings.
3rm CTV 8P 🍴 300acres dairy S% B&b£5
Bdi£6.50 W£42 ⌁ D4pm

LOCHGOILHEAD Strathclyde *Argyll*
Map 10 NN10
Pole *(NN192044)* ☎221
Pleasant, well kept farmhouse.
Lochgoilhead 2 miles.
Etr–Sep 3rm 1⇦🏠 3P 🍴 2,750acres sheep
S% B&b£5–£6 Bdi£7–£8 W£48–£50
D7.30pm

LOCHWINNOCH Strathclyde *Renfrews*
Map 10 NS35
High Belltrees *(NS377584)* ☎842376
5rm 3hc CTV 6P 🍴 160acres dairy S%
B&b£4–£5 Bdi£6–£7 W£37.50–£42
⌁ D6.30pm

LONGMORN Grampian *Moray*
Map 15 NJ25
Cockmuir *(NJ232571)* ☎227
Clean, pleasant farmhouse in attractive
position. Farm is set off main road down
farm track.
May–Oct 4rm TV 4P 50acres arable &
mixed D6.30pm

LUSS Strathclyde *Dunbartons*
Map 10 NS39
Duchlage *(NS350872)*
Pleasant, homely house. Luss 4 miles, S
off B832.
Etr–Sep 3rm ⌘ nc12 TV 2P 1🏠 135acres
mixed

MILNGAVIE Strathclyde *Dunbartons*
Map 11 NS57
High Craigton *(NS525766)*
☎041-956 1384
Two storey, stone built farmhouse with
numerous outbuildings. Good access road.
2hc ⌘ CTV P 🍴 1200acres sheep S%
B&b£4

MONEYDIE Tayside *Perths Map 11 NO02*
Moneydie Roger *(NO054290)*
☎ Almondbank 239
A substantial, two storey farmhouse
standing amid good arable land. Perth
7 miles.
Apr–Sep 2rm ⌘ 2P 143acres arable
mixed S% B&b£4.25

NEWBRIDGE Lothian *Midlothian*
Map 11 NT17
Easter Norton *(NT157721)*
☎031-333 1279
Small attractive farmhouse. Excellent
position for motorway and Edinburgh
Airport.
Apr–Sep 3rm 3P 🍴 7acres poultry S%
B&b£4

NEWBURGH Fife *Map 11 NO21*
Glen Duckie *(NO283188)* ☎352
A large farm set amid rolling hills with
main farmhouse dating from 16th century.
May–Sep 2rm ⌘ TV 4P 358acres mixed

NEW CUMNOCK Strathclyde *Ayrs*
Map 11 NS61
Pollshill *(NS652132)* ☎301
Pleasant, well kept old mill house parts
of which date back 300 years.
Jun–Oct 2rm ⌘ nc TV 3P 230acres mixed
S% B&b fr£3.50

ONICH Highland *Inverness-shire*
Map 14 NN06
Cuilcheanna House *(NN019617)* ☎226
Large Victorian house with gardens set in
sloping fields leading to Loch Linnhe.
Excellent views over lochs and mountains.
Secluded.
Etr–Sep 9rm 8hc ♨ 8P 🍴 120acres
arable beef B&b£4.50–£5.50
Bdi£8–£9.50 D7pm

ORPHIR Orkney *Map 16 HY30*
Orakirk *(HY302047)* ☎328
Pleasant farmhouse reached by a typical
farm road almost ½ mile long.
2rm ⌘ nc10 CTV 2P 114acres arable
beef S% B&b£5–£5.50 Bdi£8–£9
W£45–£60 D7.30pm

PITLOCHRY Tayside *Perths*
Map 14 NN95
Faskally House *(NN918601)* ☎2007
Pleasant 'U' shaped farm with popular
caravan site attached. Set on west side of
A9 on northern outskirts of Pitlochry.
Sheltered Loch Faskally by trees.
Apr–Oct 7rm 6hc 10P 100acres arable
✱B&b£3.70–£4

PORT OF MENTEITH Central *Perths*
Map 11 NN50
Collymoon *(NN593966)*
☎ Buchlyvie 268
Attractive white painted farmhouse near
lake. Situated just off B8034.
Apr–Oct 3rm 1hc ⌘ CTV 3P 🍴 160acres
arable dairy sheep B&b£5 Bdi£8 W£56
⌁ D6pm

Newton *(NN614014)* ☎249
Small, stone farmhouse about 150 years old. Located just off the A81. Home produced milk and butter.
2hc ⊗ TV P 100acres mixed

PORTREE Isle of Skye, Highland *Inverness-shire Map 13 NG44*
No 1 Uigishadder *(NG430463)*
☎ Skeabost Bridge 279
Small crofting farm situated high on moor in isolated position facing north west. Portree about 4 miles.
Apr–Sep 3rm ⊗ 6P 6acres arable

Upper Ollach *(NG518362)* Braes
☎ Sligachan 225
Grey, stone, crofting farm in 7 acres of hilly farmland with gardens and trees screening the house. Close to coastline. 6½m SE on B883.
Apr–Oct 3rm ⊗ TV 4P sea 8acres mixed S% B&b fr£4 Bdi fr£7

RENDALL Orkney *Map 16 HY32*
Lower Ellibister *(HY386213)* ☎ Evie 224
Farmhouse set amid beautiful countryside with extensive views across the bay to Kirkwall.
Jun–Sep 3rm ⊗ CTV 3P sea 344acres arable beef sheep S% B&b£3.50–£5 Bdi£6.50–£8 D previous day

ROGART Highland *Sutherland Map 14 NC70*
Rovie *(NC716023)* ☎209
Farmhouse situated in the Strathfleet valley, 4 miles from sea. Rabbit shooting on farm and fishing locally in River Fleet. S off A839.
Mar–Oct 3hc ⊗ CTV 3P 2120acres arable beef sheep S% Bdi£8 W£70 D6.30pm

ROTHESAY Isle of Bute, Strathclyde *Bute Map 10 NS06*
Birgidale Crieff *(NS073591)*
☎ Kilchattan Bay 236
Well cared for, attractively furnished farmhouse on south end of island. Well maintained garden. 3m S off A845.
Apr–Oct 2rm nc4 TV 3P ⊞ sea 300acres arable dairy S% B&b£4–£4.25

RUSKIE Central *Perths Map 11 NN60*
Lower Tarr *(NN624008)*
☎ Thornhill (Stirling) 202
Large, well maintained farm over 200 years old, with partly modernised interior. Good views over rolling hill land.
May–Oct 2rm 1hc CTV P 161acres arable beef sheep S% B&b£3.75–£4 Bdi£6–£7 D5pm

SCANIPORT Highland *Inverness-shire Map 14 NH63*
Antfield *(NH616371)* ☎219
Large, two storey building ½ mile off B862.
May–Oct 2rm ⊗ nc CTV 10P 354acres mixed S% B&b fr£4

SCARISTA Isle of Harris, Western Isles *Inverness-shire Map 13 NG09*
Croft *(NG002926)* Scarista Vore ☎201
Small, well maintained croft which doubles as local Post Office. Good position facing west overlooking golden sands and ocean.
2rm 2P sea 19acres mixed S% B&b£4.50–£5 Bdi£8.50–£9

SHAWHEAD Dumfries & Galloway *Dumfriesshire Map 11 NX87*
Henderland *(NX872746)*
☎ Lochfoot 270
Small farmhouse about 5 miles from Dumfries. Golf, fishing and tennis are available.
May–Oct 4rm CTV 3P 210acres dairy S% B&b£3.50–£4

STEWARTON Strathclyde *Ayrs Map 10 NS44*
Low Gallowberry *(NS434494)*
☎ Dunlop 279
Two storey, stone farmhouse, comfortably furnished. Secluded setting. 3m NE off unclass rd.
May–Sep 4rm TV 6P river 134acres beef D8pm

STIRLING Central *Stirlings Map 11 NS79*
King's Park *(NS787936)* Dunbarton Rd
☎4142
Large, modernised farmhouse situated on the outskirts of the town and offering splendid views of Stirling Castle.
Etr–Sep 3rm CTV 5P ⊞ 230acres mixed

Powis Mains *(NS819959)*
Causewayhead ☎3820
Well sited, stone farmhouse dating from 1840. Stands in Forth Valley overlooked by Wallace Monument and Ochill Hills. 3m NE A91.
Jun–Sep 2rm ⊗ CTV 6P 250acres mixed

STRAITON Lothian *Midlothian Map 11 NT26*
Straiton *(NJ273667)* Straiton Rd
☎031-440 0298
Georgian farmhouse with garden on southern outskirts of Edinburgh.
Mar–Nov 4hc ⌂ CTV 10P 200acres arable mixed S% B&b£5.50

STRATHAVEN Strathclyde *Lanarks*
Map 11 NS74
Laigh Bent *(NS701413)* ☎20103
Attractive, stone built farmhouse with
outbuildings surrounding the courtyard.
Jun–Sep 2rm 2⇋🛏 ⚤ nc8 TV P 1🏠 🍲
100acres beef S% B&b£4 W£25 M

Tower of Udstonhead *(NS704469)*
Hamilton Rd ☎20907 2rm ⚤ CTV 6P
🍲 5¾acres poultry S% B&b£5.50
Bdi£8.50 D am

STRICHEN Grampian *Aberdeens*
Map 15 NJ95
Bransbog *(NJ949559)* ☎240
Farmhouse standing on hillside above
Strichen. Only short distance from White
Horse at Mormand Hill.
May–Sep 3rm ⚤ nc5 TV 4P 🍲 94acres
arable, beef & mixed D8pm

SYMINGTON Strathclyde *Ayrs*
Map 11 NS93
Eastfield *(NS968334)* Eastfield of Wiston
☎ Lamington 270
Stone built farmhouse about ¾ mile from
A73. Good views of surrounding hills.
2m SW off A73.
3rm TV 3P 3🏠

THORNHILL Dumfries & Galloway
Dumfriesshire Map 11 NX89
Waterside Mains *(NS870971)* ☎30405
Farmhouse set on banks of River Nith.
Fishing parties catered for.
Etr–Oct 3hc TV 3P river 145acres arable
dairy S% B&b£4.50 Bdi£6.50

TOMDOUN Highland *Inverness-shire*
Map 14 NH10
No 3 Greenfield *(NH201006)* ☎221
Small modern bungalow set in isolated
position in rugged, hilly countryside.
3m E, on S side of Loch Garry.
15May–Sep 3rm ⚤ TV 6P 172acres
mixed S% B&b£4 Bdi£7 Wfr£44 ⑁

UIG Isle of Skye, Highland
Inverness-shire Map 13 NG36
No 11 Earlish *(NG388614)* ☎319
Mar–Oct 3rm TV 8P sea 36acres mixed
sheep S% B&b£3.50–£4

WIGTOWN Dumfries & Galloway
Wigtowns Map 10 NX45
Moorhead of Glenturk *(NX414569)*
☎3293
Isolated, homely farm, with attractive views
over Solway Firth and surrounding
countryside.
May–Oct rs Nov–Apr (1dbl rm open all yr
(book 1wk advance)) 2rm CTV 2P
62acres mixed S% B&b£5 Bdi£8 D4pm

Display of Hotel Prices

All hotels, motels, inns and guest houses in Britain,
with four bed-rooms or more (including self-
catering accommodation) and offering accommodation to guests, are required to display notices
showing minimum and maximum overnight
charges. The notice must be displayed in a
prominent position in the reception area, or at
the entrance.

The prices shown must include any service charge,
and may include Value Added Tax, and it must be
made clear whether or not these items are included
If VAT is not included then it must be shown
separately. If meals are provided with the
accommodation, this must be made clear too. If
prices are not standard for all rooms, then only
the lowest and highest prices need be given.

REPORT FORM

cut along here

To:
The Automobile Association,
Hotel and Information Services Department,
5th Floor,
Fanum House,
Basingstoke,
Hampshire
RG21 2EA

Name of establishment

Town	County

Date of visit

Did you find:

	above expectation	satisfactory	below expectation
Service			
Accommodation			
Meals			

Do you agree with the classification or recommendation

YES	NO

May we quote your name when taking up any complaint with the hotel/restaurant?

YES	NO

Did you take up your complaint with the manager at the time of your visit?

YES	NO

Name

Address

Date	Membership no.

Signature

Further copies of this form can be obtained from any AA office

Additional remarks:

For office use:

Head office action	Regional office action
Acknowledged	Inspected by
Recorded	Date
Action	
File	
Inspect	